Theodor W. Adorno

THEODOR W. ADORNO

One Last Genius

DETLEV CLAUSSEN

Translated by Rodney Livingstone

The Belknap Press of
Harvard University Press
Cambridge, Massachusetts
London, England
2008

For my mother-in-law, Erna Leszczyńska, and my mother, Carla Claussen, both of whom have helped me to understand the twentieth century through *experience.*

Originally published as *Theodor W. Adorno: Ein letztes Genie,* © S. Fischer Verlag GmbH, Frankfurt am Main, 2003.

Library of Congress Cataloging-in-Publication Data

Claussen, Detlev.
    [Theodor W. Adorno. English]
    Theodor W. Adorno : one last genius / Detlev Claussen ; translated by Rodney Livingstone.
        p.   cm.
    Includes bibliographical references and index.
    ISBN-13: 978-0-674-02618-6 (hardcover : alk. paper)
    1. Adorno, Theodor W., 1903–1969. 2. Philosophers—Germany—Biography.
3. Philosophy, Modern—20th century. I. Title.

    B3199.A34C5813 2008
    193—dc22   2007039108

Contents

Illustrations

How to Read This Book

The aim of this book is to help Adorno's texts speak for themselves and emerge in their original form from behind the secondary literature that has proliferated endlessly. Each chapter is designed so that it can also be read on its own. Adorno's works are interpreted as a palimpsest, works full of overlapping ideas. References to all sources cited in the text can be found by those who wish to inspect them critically, or extend their reading, in the endnotes or at the end of the book under the heading "Sources."

Like most so-called child prodigies, I am a very late developer and I still feel today that whatever I truly exist for still lies before me.

THEODOR W. ADORNO TO ERNST BLOCH, 26 JULY 1962

I feel very strongly that in my case work is a drug that helps me to overcome what would otherwise be an almost unbearable melancholy and loneliness. I fear that this is the secret of my so-called productivity.

31 MARCH 1960, NOTEBOOK F

. . . and conceive the better state as one in which people could be different without fear.

MINIMA MORALIA, 1945

1. | Instead of an Overture: *No Heirs*

The news of his death came suddenly and quite unexpectedly. People had just started to breathe freely again in Frankfurt after a turbulent summer semester. In mid-July 1969 Theodor Adorno and his wife, Gretel, had escaped from the usual sultry Frankfurt summer heat and, as he had done for the previous two decades, withdrawn to the Swiss mountains "like old mountain cattle changing their pasture."[1] Even at this distance he was able to deal with essential administrative matters and correspondence. On Wednesday, 6 August, a letter to Herbert Marcuse was being typed up in the office of the Institute for Social Research. The secretarial staff were waiting for alterations and a final approval from Zermatt. After a phone call to the Hotel Bristol, Adorno's secretary in Frankfurt, Hertha Georg, was told that "Herr Professor" had "gone to the hospital." It sounded to her as if this was nothing more than an excursion to the Magic Mountain. But toward noon, definitive word arrived in Frankfurt from Gretel Adorno. By Saturday a death notice signed by her appeared in the *Frankfurter Rundschau,* stating simply, "Theodor W. Adorno, born on 11 September 1903, died quietly in his sleep on 6 August 1969."

The German public was quite unprepared for the news of Adorno's death in Switzerland. The obituaries lying in the file drawers of newspaper editors had not been updated. Most of the people who might have been entrusted with the task of writing a fresh one were on vacation. Unusually, no one rushed to the fore to make a public comment. The stormy political quarrels with his students that Adorno had endured in 1969 seemed obscure and had never been clarified. The public, which was not particularly well informed, appeared to expect disturbances during the funeral. Although it was the middle of the summer holiday season, almost two thousand mourners turned out for the funeral in the Frankfurt Central Cemetery. Famous faces could be seen following the coffin, accompanying Gretel Adorno. Not just Max Horkheimer, the man who had given a name to the Critical Theory that Adorno had made world-famous. Other old acquaintances were present, too: Ernst Bloch, aged but still very alert, and also Alfred Sohn-Rethel. Adorno had been exchanging ideas with them since the 1920s. The radical students, whom some people regarded as being responsible for Adorno's early death, quietly mourned their teacher. Herbert Marcuse was the first to find the right words: "There is no one who can represent Adorno and speak for him."[2]

Adorno's death left a vacuum. Something had disappeared irrevocably. But people were at a loss for words to describe this feeling. Was it because they were so close to this departed genius that they found themselves unable to speak? Adorno himself had skewered the clichés of conventional biography in his writings. He had described the professional gravediggers of the "Culture Industry" so precisely that hardly any space remained for spontaneous statements. His older friend Horkheimer, who had nevertheless outlived him, had no doubt in this moment of loss that the term "genius" was appropriate as a description of Adorno.[3] Knowing as we do how close the two men were during their exile in America, it is inconceivable that he could have been unaware of Adorno's reservations about the traditional concept of genius: "If anything is to be salvaged of this concept it must be stripped away from its crude equation with the creative subject, who through vain exuberance bewitches the work of art into a document of its maker and thus diminishes it."[4] A history of Adorno's life and work that simply ignores his cutting criticism of the biographies of geniuses cannot be written in good faith. One way of diminishing Adorno's work, one that has only become popular since his death, has been to revere him as an artist while spurning him as a scholar. During his lifetime, his critics mostly took the opposite course: they represented him as a failed artist, leaving him to preside over theory in all its grayness.

Readers who take a look at Adorno's last great work, his *Aesthetic Theory*—the work from which this quotation comes—will not need to search far before coming across the name of Goethe. Goethe's name is intimately connected not only with the bourgeois concept of genius but also with the model of a successful life capable of being captured in a biography. For the generation that, like Adorno, was born in the long bourgeois century between 1815 and 1914, Goethe stands at the beginning of this bourgeois epoch, to which even someone born in 1903 could feel he belonged. By the end of this period, of course, Goethe's works had long since been buried beneath the Goethe cult dedicated to the worship of the artistic genius. "This suits crude bourgeois consciousness as much because it implies a work ethic that glorifies pure human creativity regardless of its aim as because the viewer is relieved of taking any trouble with the object itself.

The viewer is supposed to be satisfied with the personality of the artist—essentially a kitsch biography. Those who produce important works of art are not demigods but fallible, often neurotic and damaged, individuals."[5] Adorno's fierce criticism of the bourgeois world and its religion of art does not end up as an ill-tempered rejection of a superannuated form of life. "The element of truth in the concept of genius is to be sought in the object, in what is open, not confined by repetition."[6] It is not only a Goethe who can be measured against the yardstick of such a concept of genius; Horkheimer's reference to his deceased younger friend as a genius in "an age of transition" likewise appears entirely appropriate.[7]

Goethe recurs constantly in Horkheimer's writings, too, as the epitome of the successful individual. In 1961 he wrote in the "Afterword" to his portraits from German Jewish intellectual history: "Origins shine through the thoughts and feelings of the adult human being. Even Goethe was recognizably a citizen of Frankfurt."[8] Reverence for Goethe, which at that time was still accompanied by a knowledge of his works, continued to play an important role among the educated German middle classes throughout the nineteenth century. The Jews in Germany, however, who took a positive view of assimilation and who experienced their social ascent into the middle classes at this time, saw in Goethe's life a promise of human community made real. The young Felix Mendelssohn, whom Goethe loved, set the latter's poems to music. Germanness on the road to humanity: even in Goethe's lifetime this utopia was sustained by Rahel Varnhagen and Felix's aunt Dorothea Veit, who later became Dorothea Schlegel, and who had lived for over ten years next door to the house in which Adorno was born, in Schöne Aussicht. Schopenhauer, too, who was highly thought of by Horkheimer though judged more coolly by Adorno, maintained sporadic contact with Goethe and lived in a house redolent of upper-middle-class affluence on the same street. The image of Goethe must have been a constant presence in Adorno's youth in Frankfurt.

A familiarity with Goethe's *Poetry and Truth* belonged to the canon of bourgeois knowledge. Its title had acquired common currency as an index of the questionable nature of the relationship between autobiography and truth. Many biographers of Goethe have sought to legitimate their own dealings with the life of that genius by drawing upon the vulgar bourgeois idea of a commerce with truth as distorted by self-interest. Goethe himself talked about the impossibility of biography in the preface to his book:

For the chief goal of biography appears to be this: to present the subject in his temporal circumstances, to show how these both hinder and help him, how he uses them to construct his view of man and the world, and how he, providing he is an artist, poet or author, mirrors them again for others. But something nearly impossible is required for this, namely, that the individual know himself and his century—himself, as a constant entity in the midst of all the circumstances, and the century, as a force pulling him along willy-nilly, directing and developing him to such an extent that one may well say he would have been a different person if born ten years before or after, as far as his own cultural development and his effect on others are concerned.[9]

"To know himself and his century": this scarcely attainable ideal of the bourgeois individual was not regarded as a hurdle to the production of large-scale biographies by successful writers of the Weimar Republic such as Emil Ludwig and Stefan Zweig. In an article in the *Frankfurter Zeitung* in 1930, Siegfried Kracauer, Adorno's mentor during his early years in Frankfurt, referred to biography as the "modern bourgeois art form," as distinct from the old biographies from the "period before the war" which he thought of as "rare works of scholarly learning."[10] A sense that the old bourgeois society had now become a thing of the past was widely shared. It became standard for the new generation of intellectuals to criticize biographies as the mere product of fashion. Toward the end of the Weimar Republic, conscious of the growing sense of crisis, Kracauer began to talk about biography as an escapist phenomenon surrounded by an "aura of departure." Kracauer himself tried his hand at biography at a time of crisis, when he was fleeing from the Nazis. He wrote *Orpheus in Paris: Offenbach and the Paris of His Time*, a book which Adorno did not much admire. On 1 October 1950 Kracauer reported to Adorno that he had brought back chests full of manuscripts and old letters from his period of exile in Paris—including texts by Adorno. "But the main point is that this rummaging around in the past, with heaps of letters on top, aroused in me an irresistible desire to write my memoirs—in truly grand style, I mean. But that would be a luxury that I shall perhaps never be able to afford."[11] Unfortunately, he was right about this. A book that aims to depict Adorno's life and work will be forced to dispense with such a document from Kracauer's hand. Moreover, it is a matter of regret that even today, permission has still not been granted to quote from important letters written by Adorno to Kracauer.

Writers such as Kracauer and Adorno noticed early on that the emergence of psychoanalysis in the twentieth century both inspired biography and raised questions about it. Sigmund Freud felt distrustful of his admirer Stefan Zweig; he strongly advised the latter's namesake, Arnold Zweig, to avoid writing biographies of Nietzsche and even Freud himself. In a letter from Vienna on 31 May 1936 he wrote: "Whoever becomes a biographer commits himself to lies, dissimulation, hypocrisy, whitewashing, and even to concealing his own lack of understanding, for biographical truth is not to be had, and if it were, it would not be usable."[12] Yet he was unable to refuse the request of his disciple Marie Bonaparte that he write a preface for her great biography of Poe: "Such enterprises should not explain the poet's genius, but should show what motives stimulated it and what subject matter fate presented him with."[13] Perhaps the most successful psychoanalytical biography of an artist has come from the pen of Kurt R. Eissler, who emigrated to the United States from Vienna in 1938 and who published a two-volume study of Goethe in 1963. This book confirms the presence of "the loving reverence for Goethe . . . in the milieu of assimilated Jewry in Vienna" so familiar to Adorno. The well-documented life of Goethe seems to provide the ideal material for an artist's biography, and one that was familiar to more than just a literary elite. In Eissler's unique analysis, Goethe appears as the exemplary genius—a category of human being "with the ability to recreate the human cosmos or a part of it in a significant manner and one with which earlier attempts at re-creation cannot be compared."[14] This statement really applies to Adorno as well, and it is for this reason that the present study aims to let his texts speak for themselves instead of using biographical information to explain Adorno's works.

Even in American exile the Frankfurt sociologists continued to be fiercely critical of the mass production of biographies as a key to understanding social conditions that were relatively advanced in comparison to those in Europe. Leo Löwenthal, who was the only native Frankfurter besides Adorno in the circle of the Institute for Social Research, produced a study, "Biographies in Popular Magazines," in the early 1940s that stimulated Adorno to write a lengthy letter to him dated 25 November 1942:

> At bottom, the concept of life as a meaningful unity unfolding from within itself has ceased to possess any reality, much like the individual himself, and the ideological function of biographies consists in demonstrating to people with reference to various models that something like life still exists, with all the em-

phatic qualities of life. And the task of biography is to prove this in particular empirical contexts which those people who no longer have any life can easily claim as their own. Life itself, in a highly abstract form, has become ideology, and the very abstractness that distinguishes it from older, fuller conceptions of life is what makes it practicable (the vitalist and existentialist concepts of life are stages on this path).[15]

The routine production of biographies exerted an idiosyncratic charm that opened Adorno's eyes to the possibility of exploiting autobiographical elements in his own writings. His collection of aphorisms titled *Minima Moralia,* which dates back to 1944, bears the programmatic subtitle *Reflections from Damaged Life.*

Minima Moralia is an Adorno text that bears repeated rereading, and like the most famous book by Horkheimer and Adorno, *Dialectic of Enlightenment,* it encapsulates experience at a moment in history that calls all traditional experience of the world into question. The reason why it is no longer possible to experience world-historical events in the Goethean sense is formulated "out of the firing-line" in *Minima Moralia* in acknowledgment of Karl Kraus's efforts to comprehend the "destruction of mankind" in the First World War. Every sentence in these books by Adorno and Horkheimer acquires its argumentative force from their consciousness of a world-historical catastrophe that will leave nothing unchanged: "Despair has the accent of irrevocability not because things cannot improve, but because it draws the past too into its vortex."[16] The appalling death of his friend Walter Benjamin during his flight from the National Socialists reverberates in these lines. In his reflections on Kafka, in whom Benjamin, as a connoisseur of Goethe, detected the historical shift, Adorno attempted to think through the implications of what his deceased friend had anticipated with his own suicide: "As in Kafka's twisted narratives, what perished there was that which had provided the criterion of experience—life lived out to its end. Gracchus is the consummate refutation of the possibility banished from the world: to die after a long and fulfilled life."[17] Adorno dated his "Notes on Kafka" to the years 1942–1953, as if he wished to document his contemporaneity precisely. The essays he collected in *Prisms* and published in 1955 speak with a clarity that made him many enemies in post–National Socialist Germany. The historical context in which this interpretation of Kafka is to be read is made quite clear: "In the concentration camps, the boundary between life and death was eradicated. A middle ground was created, inhabited by living skeletons and putrefying bodies, victims unable to take their own lives, Satan's laughter at the hope of abolishing death."[18]

Adorno's most famous saying, "To write poetry after Auschwitz is barbaric," is rooted in this context, one that reappears in his last great publication, his "fat child,"[19] that is, *Negative Dialectics*, under the heading "After Auschwitz." If we have to ask the question "whether after Auschwitz you can go on living,"[20] then the question of the story of an individual life, of a biography, seems utterly obsolete. The experience of the loss of experience is one of the oldest motifs of Critical Theory, one also articulated as early as the 1920s by outsiders such as Kracauer and Benjamin, beyond the circle around Max Horkheimer. Adorno turned this motif into a touchstone of the philosophy of history of Critical Theory. To know oneself and one's century, Goethe's yardstick for biography, holds good for literature as well as for theory. If we ignore the devaluation of experience, it will prove impossible to tell the story either of individuals or of the century as a whole. Like Kracauer, Benjamin regarded the First World War as the crucial turning point in the experience of a generation: "A generation that had gone to school in horse-drawn streetcars now stood under the open sky in a landscape where nothing remained unchanged but the clouds and, beneath those clouds, in a force field of destructive torrents and explosions, the tiny, fragile human being."[21] Adorno's childhood in Frankfurt around 1910 echoes Benjamin's childhood in Berlin around 1900.

Adorno was one of the younger actors to share in his generation's experience of this transition, even though he was too young to take an active part in the war itself. The key aphorism in *Minima Moralia*, the fragment "Out of the Firing-Line," which he wrote in California in 1944, develops Benjamin's ideas of 1928 about the loss of experience in and after the First World War, the inflation, and the crisis in the global economy:

> But the Second War is as totally divorced from experience as is the functioning of a machine from the movement of the body, which only begins to resemble it in pathological states. Just as the war lacks continuity, history, an "epic" element, but seems rather to start anew from the beginning in each phase, so it will leave behind no permanent, unconsciously preserved image in the memory. Everywhere, with each explosion, it has breached the barrier against stimuli beneath which experience, the lag between a healing forgetting and a healing recollection, forms. Life has changed into a timeless succession of shocks, interspaced with empty, paralyzed intervals. But nothing, perhaps, is more ominous for the future than the fact that, quite literally, these things will soon be

past thinking on, for each trauma of the returning combatants, each shock not inwardly absorbed, is a ferment of future destruction.[22]

Adorno's life, reflected in his writings and his friendships, cannot be narrated without the history of the twentieth century. The historian Eric Hobsbawm has coined the memorable expression "the short century" in contrast with the long bourgeois era from 1815 to 1914. Adorno's childhood falls within what had been up to then the longest period of peace in modern European history, but there can be no doubt that what we think of as his century must be the more recent age of contradictions for which it is hard to find an appropriate description. Hobsbawm speaks of the "Age of Extremes." Extremes are indeed prominent: an age of mass misery and unimaginable excess, an age of totalitarian dictatorships and permissive societies, a period of the most terrible wars and a long, sustained peace.[23] The period that included Adorno's death is vividly described by Hobsbawm as the "Golden Age" of the century, a period characterized by sustained economic growth and the worldwide expansion of a consumer lifestyle. The Critical Theorists attempted to grasp the unity of the age in this simultaneous manifestation of living experience and social change. According to their diagnosis, the century has done irreparable damage to the individual. In the present book I attempt to take account of the limitations on individual experience by emphasizing the biographical aspects contained in the testimony of Adorno's contemporaries. In retrospect we can see that we are dealing with the last generation to write letters and to leave behind documents of human relationships. Adorno's life and works can also be revealed through the history of his friendships.

The Critical Theorists, Adorno among them, were extremely distrustful of autobiographical statements. At first glance their writings appear to contain none. Nevertheless, the bourgeois tradition of the public appreciation of friends—in birthday tributes, reviews, and obituaries—can be regarded as legitimate sources of autobiographical information. An obituary for Kracauer in 1967 provides information about Adorno's youth; a congratulatory notice on Horkheimer's seventieth birthday sheds light on Adorno's years as a student. Adorno cryptically formulates the differences he perceived between himself and his older friend Horkheimer, the founder of Critical Theory, in an "Open Letter" he published in 1965 in *Die Zeit*, which at the time was the weekly paper favored by the educated West German middle class:

But our experiences did not run in parallel. . . . Your primary experience was your indignation about injustice. To transform this into a knowledge of social antagonisms, and in particular your reflections on a practice that was explicitly intended to coincide with theory, forced you in the direction of philosophy as the unremitting rejection of ideology. In contrast, I was an artist, a musician, by both origin and early training, but I was inspired by a desire to give an account of art and its possibilities today that should include objective factors, a sense of the inadequacy of a naïvely aesthetic stance in the face of social tendencies.[24]

In the same way, even public documents need to be decoded if we are to grasp their autobiographical implications. Their meaning is not self-evident. The exiles commonly employed a "slave language" to express, indirectly or in a coded form, thoughts that in earlier days had been uttered openly. Its purpose was to enable them to speak to one another in a foreign land without attracting the attention of the police. It was a language that Adorno never fully abandoned in later years.

In emigration, letter writing had perforce to replace face-to-face discussions. This gives posterity the opportunity to gain an insight into the ideas and feelings of the correspondents that would have been irretrievably lost in the absence of such letters. Of course, these documents need to be handled sensitively: many letters have gone missing, and some have not been released for publication. Moreover, even though those that have survived are communications between friends, they are sometimes couched in diplomatic terms. The self-conscious community of friends, a supra-individual "we," has been an integral part of the history of utopian ideas ever since the Enlightenment. Goethe's *Wilhelm Meister* characterizes the image of the good society as a community of fraternal émigrés preparing to depart for America. There is a remarkable statement in the decisive letter of 27 November 1937 in which Adorno writes to Walter Benjamin, who was in Paris, that he was proposing to leave Europe for good so as to work with Horkheimer in New York: "The fact that we have no 'heirs' rather fits in with the general catastrophic situation."[25] The utopia of artists and émigrés that Goethe had conceived at the beginning of the bourgeois era is now transformed by the blows inflicted by the actual course of history into a picture of catastrophe, a premonition of annihilation. The same sentiment reappears in a sociologically more precise form in Adorno's *Notes on Kafka,* a companion piece to Benjamin's great essay on Kafka, where he writes, "The horror, however, consists in the fact that the bourgeois was unable to find a successor."[26]

The emotionally charged relations between Adorno and his students will be incomprehensible to anyone who is unfamiliar with this background. He experienced teacher-pupil relationships for the first time after his return from exile, since he did no teaching in either England or the United States. On 3 January 1949 Adorno wrote to Leo Löwenthal from Frankfurt: "My seminar is like a Talmud school—I wrote to Los Angeles that it was as if the ghosts of the murdered Jewish intellectuals had entered the German students. Slightly uncanny. But for that very reason it was also homely, in the genuine Freudian meaning of the word."[27] Adorno thought of his return to Germany as part of a common project, one that he calls to mind once again in the "Open Letter" of 1965:

> Once we had finished the *Dialectic of Enlightenment,* a book that has continued to be our philosophical benchmark, you turned your energies as an academic and organizer to the task of teaching students how to grasp the incomprehensible fact that became known to us in its full implications only toward the end of the war. You started from the insight that if a repetition of the horror is to be prevented, an understanding of the mechanisms at work will be of greater benefit than remaining silent or freezing in impotent indignation. The same motives persuaded you to return to Germany and rebuild the Institute for Social Research, whose director you had been before the Hitler dictatorship.[28]

Horkheimer and Adorno attracted generations of students who longed to discover credible authorities in the landscape of a restored West German society. The ranks of Adorno's listeners undoubtedly produced many of the political activists who were involved in the large-scale conflicts that arose during the student unrest in the second half of the 1960s. Herbert Marcuse was right to remind Adorno of this on 5 April 1969: "We are in a poor position to deny that these students have been influenced by us (and by you perhaps most of all)."[29] Adorno's last letter to Marcuse, dated 6 August, a letter he never had time to sign, contains the statement: "I am the last person to underestimate the merits of the student movement; it has disrupted the smooth transition to the totally administered world. But it contains a grain of insanity in which a future totalitarianism is implicit."[30]

In an interview with *Der Spiegel* on 11 August, Horkheimer, considering the question from a distance, gave a more positive gloss to the relations between Adorno and his students: "The students resisted him at various points, and they also protested against him. But at the same time, not a few of them knew very well what he stood for, and they retained a certain affection for him notwithstanding all their protests. Needless to say, he was deeply hurt by their demonstrations. On the other hand, when he talked with them individually, they often said things to him that gave him great pleasure."[31] The dramatic mood that overcame Adorno in the summer of 1969 was intensified by the conflict with students whom he greatly respected for the most part and of whom he felt proud when they declared that they were his pupils. He was upset by the quarrel with Herbert Marcuse, which threatened to cast a shadow over his memories of the community of exiles, particularly since Marcuse had himself reacted with annoyance to some disparaging remarks Horkheimer had made to journalists. Adorno's friendship with Horkheimer remained for him the last utopian relationship, apart from family ties: "From you I have learned solidarity, a concept that has seeped from politics into private life. . . . We are utterly free, you and I, from the illusion that the private person might achieve in isolation what has failed in the public realm."[32] Even earlier, following the traumas of the Second World War, Adorno had thought of the childless marriage as the degenerate form of the bourgeois family. As late as 1955 he had drawn attention to the utopia of the free family from Goethe's *Wilhelm Meister,* to "the confirmed idea of permanence," "a form of the intimate and happy community of individuals that protects them from barbarism without doing violence to the nature that is preserved within it. Such a family, however, can no more be imagined than any other social utopia."[33]

Individuality was regarded as the possibility and the promise of the bourgeois world. The motif of childhood that seemed to promise everything, and that can be found in Goethe's *Poetry and Truth,* recurs in Benjamin and also in the late Adorno—but the experience of the century belies it. The negativity that became the keynote of Adorno's post-1945 writings can be perceived as the hallmark of the terror of the century. The disappearance of individuality converts the self-determined autobiography into an unsustainable fiction. Chance decides more than life and death. As early as *Minima Moralia,* we find an idea that is by no means peculiar to Adorno: "Freedom has contracted to pure negativity, and what in the days of *art nouveau* was known as a beautiful death has shrunk to the wish to curtail the infinite abasement of living and the infinite torment of dying, in a world where there are far worse things to fear than death."[34] This idea, dating from 1944, reflects a dream about living on beyond the end of the world, a dream that became a lived reality for Adorno. In an essay of 1955,

"Wird Spengler recht behalten?" (Will Spengler Turn Out to Be Right?), Adorno once again notes in connection with this dream that what seems to be absolutely personal is in fact universal: "We only have any chance at all of withstanding the experiences of recent decades if we do not forget for a moment the paradox that despite everything, we are still alive."[35]

Unlike Goethe, Adorno formulates something that is "scarcely attainable," namely, the ever-present experience of the century that birth, marriage, and death have now been abolished as the cornerstones that give meaning to a bourgeois biography. The awareness that "a zone in which it is impossible to die is also the no-man's-land between man and thing"[36] had become reality in the concentration camps; it also sheds light on the history that had preceded it and is seemingly unconnected with it. The notion that the past can be modified by the present belongs to the inventory of ideas contained in Benjamin's posthumous *On the Concept of History,* without which the self-image of the group around Horkheimer after 1941 cannot be understood. All the more shocking is the concluding sentence of a reflection that Adorno dates to the period 1946–1947: "But he who dies in despair has lived his whole life in vain."[37] Gretel Adorno, who was more than just superficially familiar with her husband's philosophical thinking, must have been aware of the contrast when she wrote in the notice announcing Adorno's death, "Theodor W. Adorno, born on 11 September 1903, passed away peacefully on 6 August 1969."

2. | The House in Schöne Aussicht: A Frankfurt Childhood around 1900

The magical power to manipulate childhood is the strength of the weak.

One glance at the street known as Schöne Aussicht is enough to see that it has changed. This change is not simply due to the bombing of Frankfurt Old Town during the Second World War, as one is seduced into believing by what one has seen and heard. Admittedly, what has survived includes all sorts of things that lie beneath the earth's surface. The section of the river Main embankment in Frankfurt where Adorno's great-grandfather established his wine merchant's business under the name Bernhard Wiesengrund in 1864 had been built up in 1792 and is still furrowed by deep cellar vaults which provided outstanding storage facilities for wine at the time. A local proverb testifies to this tradition: "In Frankfurt there is more wine in the cellars than water in the wells." The old blue files of the Frankfurt city council contain a petition to the senate in 1867 in which Bernhard Wiesengrund applied for permission to transfer his business to Frankfurt am Main from Dettelbach in Lower Franconia, where it had been established in 1822. The "Register of Old Frankfurt Companies" of 1926 recorded the centenary celebrations of the export-import business of Bernhard Wiesengrund on 25 July 1922. The firm's address, Schöne Aussicht 7, had remained unchanged since 1864. A file card in the Frankfurt tax office notes that the last owner of the business was Adorno's father, Oscar Alexander Wiesengrund, who had been born in 1870. It bears a stamp with the laconic inscription, "Business ceased on 31.12.38—deregistered on 11.4.39."

If we look back from the middle of the twentieth century, the picture of Schöne Aussicht clouds over. As early as the onset of the Nazi period, Adorno's friend Walter Benjamin attempted to capture the "decline of the bourgeoisie" in two projects that Adorno greeted enthusiastically: the volume of letters titled *Deutsche Menschen* (German Men and Women) and the autobiographical sketch *Berliner Kindheit um 1900* (Berlin Childhood around 1900). On 7 November 1936 Adorno wrote from Oxford to Benjamin, who was in Paris:

> Your book on "Germans" has indeed been a great delight to me. I read it immediately after it arrived, from the first sentence to the last throughout the night. The expression of grief which the book exudes seems remarkably close to that of the Berlin Childhood, the composition of which may indeed have coincided in time with making the selection of the letters and writing the introduction to them. If the earlier piece reproduced images of a life which a certain class forbade itself to see without revealing any other life, so the perspective you cast on these letters, reproduces, as it were, the very same process of concealment in objective form, where the *Childhood* had testified to its subjective form.[1]

What could have induced Benjamin, who was proud of "never using the word 'I'" in his published works,[2] to write a memoir of childhood—and what could have led Adorno, who often appears in their correspondence as Benjamin's implacable literary conscience, to put aside all scruples about autobiography? To both, looking back from exile, childhood appeared a utopia—an age-old utopian motif "that appears to everyone in their childhood and where no one ever was: home."[3] This was the way it was expressed by a third person, one with whom the two often engaged in discussions: Ernst Bloch, in *The Principle of Hope*.

When asked by the German postal workers' magazine in 1962 "Why have you returned?" Adorno had no qualms about replying:

> I simply wanted to return to where I spent my childhood, and ultimately I acted from my own feeling that what we realize in life is little more than the attempt to recover one's childhood in a different form. I did not underestimate the risk and the difficulty of my decision, but I have not rued it to this day. Precisely because my work in Germany is essentially critical in character, and because I believe that I make so few concessions to the dominant spirit here, I may perhaps be allowed to express these ideas without exposing myself to accusations of pusillanimity or sentimentality.[4]

Adorno's reply to this deceptively straightforward question is linked to a second question that he responded to in a broadcast on German radio that same year: "What is German?" The text—which he thought well enough of to include in his last collection of essays in June 1969, the volume titled *Catchwords*—contains the same, perhaps even more highly polished formulations that he had used in the postal workers' magazine to describe the childhood "in which what is specific to me is imparted down to its innermost essence."[5] There is an attempt at clarification in the notes he wrote after his return from exile and which were only published posthumously in 2003. These notes, which were conceived as a continuation of *Minima Moralia,* contain a statement from April 1960 in Notebook F in which he says: "It is a wholly irreparable disaster that in Germany everything connected in any way at all with a nearby happiness, with home, has been taken over by the reactionary camp: by philistinism, by cliquishness, by the self-righteousness of the narrow-minded, by the heart-warmingly sentimental, by nationalism and, ultimately, fascism. One cannot enjoy so much as an old nook or cranny without feeling shame or a sense of guilt. This means the loss of something that should have been preserved for the progressive cause."[6]

What is specific to Adorno, however, cannot be identified simply by attributing to him certain characteristics such as "German" or "Jewish" or "bourgeois," terms that mainly trigger stereotyped associations. A Frankfurt childhood around 1900 was as much influenced by the long bourgeois century as by the structural changes in the city, the secular bourgeoisification of the Jews in Germany, or indeed the transformation of the German bourgeoisie itself, a topic explored by Thomas Mann in his novel *Buddenbrooks,* which appeared in 1901. Can we perhaps speak of Frankfurt as a spiritual form of life, as Mann spoke of Lübeck? Certainly, like Lübeck, Frankfurt has its own marzipan in the shape of the Bethmännchen, which, like its wine, raises sensuous pleasure to the level of a basic right. If we are mindful of Goethe's saying about the difference it makes to be born ten years later, we shall have to ask why Adorno's childhood is so different from that of his considerably older friend and mentor Siegfried Kracauer. Kracauer, who had been born in Frankfurt in 1889, produced a novel, *Ginster: Von ihm selbst geschrieben* (Ginster: Written by Himself), which contains an unmistakable picture of Frankfurt:

> Ginster came from F., a large town with a long history on a river, set against a low range of hills. Like other towns, it made use of its past to stimulate tourism. Imperial coronations, international congresses, and a Federal Shooting Festival took place within its walls, which have long since been replaced by public parks. A monument has been erected to the garden designer. There are Christian and Jewish families that can trace their roots back to their ancestors. Even families of humble origin have produced banking firms with connections in Paris, London, or New York. Centers of worship are separated only geographically from the stock exchange. The climate is temperate; people who, unlike Ginster, do

not live in Westend are of no importance. Since he had grown up in F., he knew even less about the town than about towns he had never been to.[7]

Kracauer deliberately chose a tone free of the sentimentality that threatens to accompany every mention of a hometown. An additional factor was that in the mid-1920s a novelist's style was supposed to demonstrate a clean break with that of the nineteenth century, which had attempted, as it drew to a close, to invent a tradition for itself. In the 1920s, after the first Great War, the need was felt to tart up Frankfurt's past with its stone witnesses, and especially its decaying Old Town. The appearance of relative timelessness that determines the tone of the opening of Kracauer's novel underscores the provinciality of Frankfurt in a way that even then amounted to a provocation to the local patriotism of the townsfolk. The long shadow of tradition favored a cultural climate that turned the town into a breeding ground for nostalgia. The predominance of a tradition that had ceased to have any validity and that threatened to subside into the eternal recurrence of mediocrity had with a time lapse of twenty years summoned the forces of modernity to sweep away the cobwebs of an idealized past. For the fact was that the nineteenth century had brought continuous progress to Frankfurt as part of the general industrialization of Germany. Until the 1870s the patriarchal authorities of the town produced a dogged resistance to the process of industrialization and strove to perpetuate and even expand the role of the ancient imperial city as a center of trade and luxury.

Old prints of Schöne Aussicht provide evidence of an elegant ambience, a grand bourgeois environment of a preindustrial kind, one suitable for a demanding man of private means like Arthur Schopenhauer, who moved there before the 1848 revolution and lived there until his death in 1860. The row of white neoclassical buildings with an expansive view on the edge of the medieval town is praised in the accounts of knowledgeable travelers during the first half of the nineteenth century and is contrasted with the more forbidding Rhineland fortress towns of Mainz and Koblenz. The development of Frankfurt, however, was hampered by the political restorations that followed the Congress of Vienna in 1815 and the failure of the revolution in 1848. The old Frankfurt Fair had long since lost its significance; in the mid-1830s the Frankfurt wine trade, traditionally one of the most successful businesses in town, collapsed. Both before and after the 1848 revolution, the general mood in the Free City tended more toward pessimism than toward the feeling of a progressive nineteenth-century metropolis. The status of a Free City proved to be more of a hurdle to bourgeois progress than the city walls, which had been razed in 1806. The Frankfurt upper class did not find it easy to come to terms with change. After Bismarck's unification of Germany by force from above, Frankfurt am Main was unable to preserve its autonomy as an independent city-state. The Austro-Prussian dualism that had also been a determining factor in public opinion in Frankfurt was resolved by force of arms in favor of Prussia in 1866. A few Frankfurt patricians, but also some long-established Jews, resolutely refused to become Prussians. A coincidental but spectacular event was widely interpreted as the visible end of Old Frankfurt as the center of the German Empire: during the night before the visit of the king of Prussia on 15 August 1867, Frankfurt Cathedral was destroyed by fire. The town resolved to rebuild it in neo-Gothic style, a monument to the fashion for historicist architecture.

The unification of Germany, belated as it was in comparison to the western European nations, brought new economic prospects after 1866. When Bernhard Wiesengrund, Theodor W. Adorno's forebear, moved his wine and spirits business down the river Main to Frankfurt from the Franconian town of Dettelbach, he was looking for a place with a future, for his firm and his family, a commercial center with fine prospects on the burgeoning national and international markets. In 1867, as can be seen from the records of the Frankfurt senate, the freedom of domicile that had recently been introduced and had also been extended to Jews, enabled him to acquire the narrow house at Schöne Aussicht 7, together with its cellars. At around the same time, other Wiesengrunds from Dettelbach came to settle in Frankfurt. The time seemed favorable, since the Frankfurt of tradition was in crisis and the road seemed open for the town to develop into an important German metropolis. Thus the Wiesengrunds did not belong to the established Frankfurt Jewish community, who, like the Rothschilds, could trace their origins to houses in the ghetto, the legendary Judengasse. The French Revolution had put an abrupt end to the ghetto existence of the Frankfurt Jews in 1796, when the Judengasse was demolished by the cannon of General Kléber. But the restoration following the Congress of Vienna had encouraged the Frankfurt senate to reverse in part the progressive legislation with regard to the Jews that had been introduced by Prince Primate Karl von Dalberg in 1806 with backing from Napoleon. Ludwig Börne, who, after the founder of the Rothschild dynasty, was undoubtedly the best-known product of the Frankfurt ghetto, never concealed his pride at being a "juif de Frankfort," or his contempt for the antidemocratic senti-ments of the Frankfurt patricians.

The Wiesengrunds' move to Frankfurt was part of the secularizing pro-cess that might well be called the golden age of Jewish bourgeoisification in Germany. The history of the Wiesengrund firm fits in with the general trend of economic and social development among south German Jews. The founding of the firm in 1822 coincided with the growth in trade fol-lowing the end of the Napoleonic Wars. The wine trade calls for a combi-nation of local knowledge and a broader, national vision. With the opening up of international markets after the ending of the Continental Blockade, Jewish businessmen, who had often enough started out as peddlers, be-gan to open shops and to engage in new branches of trade, such as grocer-ies. Looked at from Lower Franconia, the nearest larger market towns were, first, Würzburg and then Frankfurt, which from around 1830, feeling constricted by the new Prussian-German customs union surrounding it, began to extend feelers beyond the German frontiers in search of new commercial links. The Jews who lived in Lower Franconia were Bavarian subjects who found themselves subjected to periodic pressures after 1815 in the small towns and villages where they had traditionally lived. With the end of the so-called Wars of Liberation, the governments in the Ger-man Confederation made efforts to reverse the emancipation of the Jews, which, where it had taken place at all, was very imperfect and was subject to a great number of local variations. Furthermore, there were numerous populist outbreaks of violence, particularly against Jewish merchants. The so-called Hep-Hep Riots, which first occurred in Würzburg and the sur-rounding area, were an ugly introduction to the period of restoration in 1819. In the succeeding decades, Lower Franconia remained the focus of anti-Jewish agitation. In 1866 in particular, violent anti-Semitic outbursts were reported in this region. What could have seemed more natural for Bernhard Wiesengrund than to distance himself as much as possible from these inhospitable places and to seek out the anonymity of a larger com-mercial center, without, however, moving too far away from the wine-producing region he knew so well?

In 1867 there was a revival in modified form of a coalition of would-be emancipated Jews and democratic citizens. They included Leopold Sonne-mann, the founder of the *Frankfurter Zeitung*, and Friedrich Stoltze, a democrat with a revolutionary past in the pre-1848 period. With the end of Frankfurt's status as a free city, they thought the town had a real opportunity to become a major democratic force in Prussia. The process of modernization which changed the face of Frankfurt over the next fifty years established its best-known landmarks in the Eiserne Steg (Iron Bridge) and the Opera House, the university and the Palmengarten. The town shifted its center of gravity to the west, increased its size by swallowing up nearby villages, and in 1888, with its newly built Central Station, became a major railway junction in the new German Empire. There was something of a time lag, however, before Frankfurt responded to the stimuli of industry, although from 1890 on its mayor, Franz Adickes, promoted industrialization in an almost systematic way. Between 1872 and 1884 the houses in the Judengasse were gradually torn down, since, after the abolition of the ghetto in 1811, it had become a sad focus of social deprivation. The year 1895 might be regarded as a turning point. Frankfurt had now become a modern big city, the eighth largest in Germany. This process continued with undiminished force until well into the First World War. Large-scale projects such as the founding of the university and the expansion of the eastern harbor, the Osthafen, were not completed until the outbreak of war.

If we look back at the epoch in which the Wiesengrunds settled in Frankfurt, we can define it as the decisive phase of the transformation from a traditional agrarian world into a modern industrial society. The change from the old commercial center on the river Main to a modern German metropolis gave rise to a particular synthesis of old and new that resulted in the concrete image of the city in which Adorno was born on 11 September 1903. The reform period after 1866 gave birth to the great plans to alter the appearance of the town, but they were the work of a mayor still under the influence of the Old Frankfurt senatorial tradition. This was Daniel Heinrich Mumm von Schwarzenstein. He was an adherent of the idea of the "beautiful town" that was to be an attraction to affluent outsiders. The Eiserne Steg and the Palmengarten, both privately financed, were soon built. The Frankfurt Opera House was the scene of a spectacular struggle in which the new forces in society demanded a say in the project that would not be confined to questions of location and cost. A decisive role was played by Leopold Sonnemann, who set out to speak for both democratic aspirations and a new social distinctiveness. The rivalry between the modern middle class and the patrician tradition was visible in the personalities involved. The public debates about the Opera House appear confusing to us because the class differences seem to have become blurred. The unresolved nature of this paradoxical modernity in Wilhelminian form is reflected in its architecture. The Opera House is a bombastic revival of the High Renaissance. In the same way, the neo-Gothic and neo-baroque compete with each other to provide the exteriors of both old and new buildings of the period.

We can imagine the sights that must have greeted Adorno in 1951 when he responded to the New Year's survey of the *Neue Zeitung,* which had wanted to know "When would you have most liked to live?" His "almost too earnest" reply turned into a lengthy meditation. In his response Adorno defends the idea of wishing but offers a different defense of the nineteenth century from the customary one: "The nineteenth century—which incidentally no longer figures in the replies with the malicious contempt that was customary when people's parents were still around to be feared, and justifiably so—this same nineteenth century had openly displayed the desire to escape from itself. But what is more characteristic of it than the knightly castles and Renaissance palaces that it bequeathed to its children?"[8] The childlike heart of utopia seems to be within one's grasp. The following sentence sounds almost as if it could have come from the pen of Ernst Bloch: "But the man who casts his wish into the remote distance is the defeatist of the happiness that lies to hand. One feels ashamed of utopia because there no longer needs to be one."[9] This reflection would have been feeble without the veiled allusion to his own parents. The conflict with one's own bourgeois nature animates the hidden topic of the parental utopia. Gershom Scholem, Walter Benjamin's friend from their time together in their youth in Berlin, describes this in a way that is representative for his entire generation. His narrative has greater conviction because of his early decision to become a Zionist and thus to dismiss as an illusion the assimilation into the German bourgeoisie to which the parental generation had aspired. Scholem wrote in 1978: "Looking back, I am even more convinced than I could be in my youth, when I was filled with the passions of protest, that for many people illusion and utopia were hopelessly mixed up together and that this state of mind anticipated the feeling of happiness at being at home. There was something genuine in this, namely, the genuine quality that we must admit is contained in utopia."[10]

The Wiesengrunds arrived in Frankfurt from Dettelbach at a time of profound demographic change. During the period 1866–1910 the town's population increased fivefold while its area merely doubled in size. We can only guess at the social fault lines lying behind the bare figures. In 1913, 87 percent of the population of Frankfurt was held to have become less well off. Just behind Schöne Aussicht lay the decaying Frankfurt Old Town, where social deprivation had begun to concentrate during the last third of the nineteenth century. If the Wiesengrunds had been pioneer immigrants from the agrarian south of Germany, there was now a flood of non-Jewish newcomers from the countryside. The lead of the early migrants soon expressed itself in economic terms. As homeowners who could also muster the five thousand guilders that were needed to obtain citizenship, the Wiesengrunds belonged to the narrow band of the growing middle class, but they were far from qualifying for inclusion in the ranks of the wealthy according to the census of 1913, namely, the 224 millionaires and the 160 multimillionaires who built their villas in the truly upper-middle-class Westend and later on in the western part of Sachsenhausen. With the growth of industry on the edge of the town and the extension of the Eastern Docks, the area around Schöne Aussicht became increasingly undesirable as a residential quarter. It seems only logical, then, for Adorno's father to have moved in 1914 to a house at 19 Seeheimerstrasse, in the suburb of Oberrad, which had become part of Frankfurt in 1900. The family had now become well placed in social terms but stayed quite close to the business, which could be reached quickly just by crossing the bridge. Mühlberg, which was also quite close by, was fast becoming a center of the beverage industry but remained distinct from the new residential district in Oberrad, where the Frankfurt colors of red and white dominated on the façades of the houses.

Paul Arnsberg, who wrote a continuation to the history of Frankfurt's Jews that had been written by Siegfried Kracauer's uncle Isidor Kracauer, notes that in 1875 the number of Jews in Frankfurt had reached a record 11.54 percent of the population.[11] By comparison, the average across the whole empire was 1.25 percent, and the proportion in Berlin was 4.7 percent. The Wiesengrunds were among the first of a great wave of immigrants in the 1890s of whom the Jews formed a minuscule fraction, scarcely visible in the general trend toward urbanization. It was at this time that the much commented on division of the Jews into Ostend and Westend started to become visible, even though the distinction remained superficial. More than a few Jews succeeded in moving to prestigious Westend only by overstretching their resources. Toward the end of the century, the movement of inner-city Jews, whether through trade or education, tended to lead not so much from east to west as into Nordend or newly incorporated areas like Bockenheim. The trend among Jews to achieve middle-class status overlapped with the tendency toward secularization, a process that affected not just Jews but society as a whole. This secularizing tendency had serious consequences for Jews, however, because the gradual loosening of religious ties transformed their entire network of relationships. Traditionally, abandoning one's Jewish faith was accompanied by the obnoxious taint of betrayal, of apostasy. This was a hangover from the nonsecularized world, in which to abandon the solidarity of the persecuted meant joining the ranks of the persecutors of the Jewish people. In the Middle Ages and the early modern age, apostates frequently allowed themselves to be used as crown witnesses against the allegedly sinister customs of the Jews. This changed after the secularization process set in after 1815 with the European wars of liberation. That led to paradoxical results during the Biedermeier period of the 1820s and 1830s. Nonreligious Jews quickly found themselves falling between all available stools. Heine's famous dictum about baptism as the "entry ticket to European culture" has rarely been correctly understood. His own decision both to undergo baptism in order to circumvent reactionary anti-Jewish legislation in the so-called *Vormärz,* the period before 1848, and also to make no attempt to disguise his Jewish origins dismayed both Jews and Christians. The same may be said of Ludwig Börne, who later became the object of Heine's invective. After his disappointments in Frankfurt at the time of the war of liberation, Börne adopted the Protestant faith without ever renouncing his right to take up the cudgels on behalf of the Jews.

The granting of equal rights to Jews did not become a reality until the belated unification of the German Empire in 1871. Once the Judengasse had disappeared physically from the map of Frankfurt in the 1870s, the streets and squares in the neighborhood were renamed. In 1885 the Frankfurt town council resolved to rename the former Judengasse "Börnestrasse," while the Judenmarkt was transformed into "Börneplatz." These changes were in tune with the advances made by the Jewish middle classes in the second half of the nineteenth century. Monuments were erected posthumously to men whose ideas had been bitterly contested during their lifetime. Yet it was not until 13 December 1913, in Friedberger Park in Frankfurt, that Mayor Georg Voigt was able to unveil the first monument in Germany to Heinrich Heine. In 1956 Adorno gave a talk, "Heine the Wound," on West German Radio. It was only through the historical experience of mass murder and expulsion, he suggested, that Heine's "vision of victimhood" had been given its edge. Adorno locates that vision in one of Heine's poems in the cycle "The Return Home" *(Die Heimkehr)*, adding that it had lost its contours in the Heine cult of the turn of the twentieth century. "Heine the wound" sounds highly ambiguous and is meant to do so. The elegant formulations of the final version of the essay obscure the origins of this wound; they appear more openly in an English-language text of 1945 in which Adorno observes that "something disquieting and unsolved remains in the phenomenon Heine."[12] He talks of the ambivalent reaction provoked by Heine's name. According to Adorno, at the height of his popularity in nineteenth-century Germany, Heine was influential among both artists and intellectuals and also among middle-class consumers. And he follows up this observation with a comment about artistic laymen who had found inspiration in Heine: "It is hardly an exaggeration to say that there was no German businessman with cultural ambitions who would not, when he felt compelled to write a birthday poem for his wife or mother, imitate some established model of Heine's.[13]

Adorno exaggerated here, no doubt, but his exaggeration tells us something of the cultural aspirations of middle-class households in Germany around 1910. But "Heine the Wound" reveals something specific that the attribute "Jewish" points to but does not capture precisely. We can in fact speak of a general Heine cult in Germany at the turn of the century which enraged the anti-Semitic pseudo-rebels, but against which they fulminated without success at the time. Their attempts to prevent the erection of the Heine monument in Frankfurt speak volumes. Toward the end of the century Heine had become such a controversial figure that the growth of the nationalist and anti-Semitic parties made it impossible to put up monuments to him anywhere in Germany. In 1913 a committee in Frankfurt succeeded in gaining approval to establish the first monument to him in any town in Germany; but even this could not be erected in the center, near the Goethe monument, but only in the eastern part of the city, in Friedberger Park. Twenty years later, after having been daubed frequently with swastikas during the Weimar era, it was pulled down by the Nazis, then rescued by local patriots who kept it hidden in the Städel Art Gallery. Finally, in 1947, it was reinstated, this time somewhat shamefacedly, in Taunus Park, which separated the banking quarter from the red-light district for forty years. It stands there to this day, unnoticed. Among the upwardly mobile Jewish middle-class families of the nineteenth century, Heine did not just stand for a literary fashion; he also represented a social metaphor. He was perceived as a successful Jew who achieved in the sphere of culture what was expected from Jews only in economic terms. For the aspiring Jewish middle classes, he embodied their utopia made real; he was the living example of an enlightened way of life that had gained success and recognition. Heine's long exile in France was taken as proof that such a way of life had been prevented by the reactionaries in Germany, especially in Prussia. The success of Jewish emancipation, by which was meant complete equality for Jews, became the core program of almost all Jewish organizations of every shade of opinion. This meant, however, that unlike a large part of the German middle class, the Jews realized that there was no room for them on the political right. The unfulfilled promises of revolution and democracy going back to the *Vormärz,* the promising time before the failed revolutions of 1848, were carried forward with the names of Heine and Börne on their banners. Their feeling that they might legitimately claim to belong to an avant-garde was confirmed by the idiosyncratic reactions of those who were hostile to Jews, many of whom were, like Treitschke, to be found in the Hohenzollern establishment of the empire.[14]

Germans and Jews are inextricably intertwined in Heine's life and works. Even the National Socialists were forced to acknowledge this fact: the songbooks of the Nazi period were unable to dispense with "The Lorelei." Beneath the text they printed the lie "author unknown." At around the same time, the mainly German Jewish emigrants to the United States came together under the name of Heinrich Heine. These events provided Adorno and also Horkheimer with pretexts to comment on Heine's own experience. The basic elements of their joint magnum opus, *Dialectic of Enlightenment,* are already thematized in Heine's own works and implicit in his ambivalent reception in Germany, in particular the idea of the inexorable advance of a modern, enlightened culture that liberates self-destructive forces. In the English-language essay he wrote in 1949, Adorno refused to explain Heine's achievement in terms of his Jewishness. It is not Heine's Jewishness that explains the unmistakable color and texture of his work; such a classification is superficial. Rarely do we find a passage in Adorno that comes as close to an understanding of himself as this one. It sounds like a reminiscence of the paternal ideal of a secularized Jewishness that succeeds in giving expression to universal tendencies. It is easy for us to imagine how in his youth he may well have opposed his father's proudly held though perhaps near-sentimental belief in his own utopia with an even greater conviction, albeit one tinged with melancholy. In every text dealing with Heine, Adorno always invokes those antipodes Karl Kraus and Stefan George as the household gods of artistic contempt for the journalese and the cheap effects in Heine's writing. Nevertheless, the self-assurance of their nonconformist judgments is dissipated by Adorno's own experience of emigration. Adorno now reads Heine with different eyes. The experience of emigration was one that Kraus was spared. Heine anticipated the universal condition of *homelessness.* Adorno's note of 1963 in Notebook O reads like a late summation of his maxims and reflections: "Whoever belongs among the persecuted has ceased to possess any unbroken form of identification. The concepts of native land [*Heimat*], country, are all shattered. Only one native land remains from which no one is excluded: mankind."[15]

In 1949, over and above any criticism, Adorno credits Heine with having been the first to articulate certain historical experiences of the century. He does not shy away from ascribing to Heine the authoritative ideal for a writer that had been formulated by Karl Kraus, Heine's archenemy. This was "to hearken to the sounds of the day as if they were the chords of eternity."[16] In *Minima Moralia,* Adorno had attempted to do precisely that. The aphoristic form cultivated by both Heine and Kraus seemed to be ideal for such a project. *Minima Moralia,* which Adorno dedicated to Max Horkheimer, opens with a reflection on parents. His tone seems to be unusually personal: "Once we rebelled against their [i.e., our parents'] insistence on the reality principle, the sobriety forever prone to become wrath against those less ready to renounce. But today we are faced with a generation purporting to be young, yet in all its reactions insufferably more grown-up than its parents ever were."[17] Put so generally, this might be said of almost every generation that feels itself to be sandwiched between the young and the old. But the mass murder of the European Jews by the Nazis forced him to depart from the usual line of thought: "One of the Nazis' symbolic outrages is the killing of the very old. Such a climate fosters a late, lucid understanding with our parents, as between the condemned, marred only by the fear that we, powerless ourselves, might now be unable to care for them as well as they cared for us when they possessed something."[18] There is no mention of the word "Jewish" in these early pages of *Minima Moralia.* Only the very first aphorism, "For Marcel Proust," alludes to a specific generational experience that can be seen as a veiled comment on Adorno himself as well as his two older friends, Horkheimer and Benjamin: "the son of well-to-do parents who, whether from talent or weakness, engages in a so-called intellectual profession, as an artist or scholar."[19] This reflection would lose its specific flavor if the word "Jewish" had been added here. We have to read on for a few pages to become aware of the subterranean displacement of the relations between the generations: "Proust's observation that in photographs, the grandfather of a duke or of a middle-class Jew are so alike that we forget their difference of social rank, has a much wider application: the unity of an epoch objectively abolishes all the distinctions that constitute the happiness, even the moral substance, of individual existence."[20]

The attribute "Jewish" would not explain the experience of the grand-parents' generation but only describe it superficially. What Adorno empha-sizes about Heine is that Heine was a genuine child of the emancipation of the Jews who arrived in Germany in the wake of the Napoleonic Wars. This emancipation was accompanied by the process of secularization that was feared by Jewish traditionalists as a threat to the Jewish way of life that had been handed down. The abolition of restrictions, the opening of society to new careers, and hence ultimately the rise of an ostracized minority to the point where it could become an integral part of western European society cannot be understood without the stimulus of the French Revolution.

The material destruction of the power of the churches and monasteries opened doors in southern Germany to the Jews, enabling them to acquire property and gain entry into towns that had hitherto been closed to them. The founding of the firm of Bernhard Wiesengrund at the beginning of the Biedermeier period comes at a time of epochal conflict which Heine was the first to articulate. Adorno perceives in Heine's lyrics the "full con-sciousness of the dialectics of progress"—both political and aesthetic.[21] This dialectic can also be discovered in the history of the Wiesengrunds in the nineteenth century. The firm's founder must have been open-minded in his attitude toward progress; his awareness of future economic possibili-ties, and the early transfer of the firm down the river Main, suggest that this was the case. The process of secularization is reflected in the family names: explicitly Jewish given names do not recur. The Wiesengrund who inherited the firm, and who was born in 1838, was called David Theodor. He was Adorno's grandfather. Adorno's father, who was born in 1870, was called Oscar Alexander. He evidently had to join his father's firm because his older brother, Paul Friedrich, had died earlier, in 1886, at the age of sev-enteen. According to the register of the Jewish community in Frankfurt, the members of the family living at Schöne Aussicht 7 in 1880 included, under the name of Wiesengrund, Adorno's great-grandmother Caroline, who had been born in 1812, and his grandfather David Theodor. His grand-father's brother, who was also active in the wine trade, was recorded as living at Königswarterstrasse 15 in the east end of Frankfurt. His place of work is given as Schöne Aussicht 13. The tradition of the extended Jewish family was still maintained by Adorno's grandfather David Theodor, after whom Adorno was named. Oscar Wiesengrund was the first member of the family to marry a Catholic—without, however, abandoning his Jewish religion. Why he should have left the community, which incidentally he did at the same time as Leo Löwenthal's father, remains a mystery.

The Frankfurt registry of residents has recorded the history of the family of Oscar Wiesengrund down to the graduation of his only son, Theodor Ludwig. An entry on 21 October 1900 announces the birth of a stillborn child. It is possible that Teddie's mother, Maria Barbara, née Calvelli-Adorno, kept this to herself. The official in charge of the registry seems to have been so confused by the religious affiliations that he made the additions "Israelite" and "Catholic": a genuine mixed marriage. Maria did not give birth to her son Theodor Ludwig until a relatively advanced age, shortly before her thirty-eighth birthday. The Wiesengrunds did not possess Frankfurt "ancestors" of the kind ascribed to the established Jewish families in Kracauer's novel *Ginster*. Fantasies about their origins, cultivated by Adorno among others, were all associated with his mother's hyphenated name: Calvelli-Adorno. Her father, a retired army officer of Corsican origin, is rumored to have earned his living in Frankfurt as a fencing master. His wife, Elisabeth Henning, earned a living as an artiste. Calvelli was forced to marry her in secular London because he could not afford the costs of citizenship in Christian, patriarchal Frankfurt. Since French citizenship did not apply to children born and brought up abroad, Maria Calvelli-Adorno remained stateless until her marriage to Oscar Wiesengrund. This also explains why the wedding took place in London in 1898, for if the different religious allegiances had been the sole problematic factor, there would have been no impediment in Frankfurt according to the Civil Law of 1850. Adorno's fantasies about his ancestors focused on his mother's name. According to a report of Peter von Haselberg which needs to be taken with some caution, Adorno himself linked her name with that of the aristocratic Genoan family Adorno della Piana. This might easily be dismissed as a character quirk. Adorno himself pointed out that Thomas Mann found such a foible for the nobility amusing in the case of Rudolf Borchardt and Hugo von Hofmannsthal.

Adorno made use of Hofmannsthal's strategy "that he would rather give a good explanation for a weakness that he had been reproached with than deny it" in defending Marcel Proust against the accusation of snobbery.[22] The fantasy of exalted origins ignited by an aristocratic name rescues the imagined person from the trammels of bourgeois competition. Selmar Spier, who spent his childhood in Frankfurt before 1914 although he belonged to a Jewish family that arrived in the town later than the Wiesengrunds, points to the deep satisfaction felt in his judgment by "most German Jews" when Commercial Councillor Friedländer-Fuld was granted permission around 1900 to put a "von" before his name. The social advancement which in the case of Jews was generally the reward for economic achievement did not just mean integration into the middle classes but could even include entry into the nobility. This paradox characterizes the idea of incontrovertibly high rank that does not need to be acquired through achievement, such as is to be found in both Hofmannsthal and Proust. "Like every love, snobbery wants to escape from the entanglement of bourgeois relationships into a world that no longer uses the greatest good of the greatest number to gloss over the fact that it satisfies human needs only by accident. Proust's regression is utopian."[23] In the fin de siècle the principle of bourgeois society that what counts is merit, not origins, is exposed as untrue. In Germany the incomplete nature of bourgeois emancipation during the Second Empire became inescapable. "German society, recruited from the rural gentry and the big industrialists, was less closely bound to the artistic and philosophical tradition than Western European society. After 1870 the leisure class was in general nervous and unsure of itself in its relations to culture; the intellectuals it saw were nervous and unsure of themselves, unable to forget how ready their patrons were to throw out anyone who became troublesome."[24]

The fact that Adorno's mother, Maria Calvelli-Adorno, had enjoyed some success in Vienna as a court singer allowed Adorno to speak of Vienna as his "second home."[25] From this perspective, origins are no longer a fate but a choice. Even Adorno's insistence in 1949 that Heine's Jewish origins were merely an accidental feature of his work is a response to the anti-Semitic reproach that Heine's works were "Jewish." The fiction of origins that Hofmannsthal did not weary of entertaining and whose parameters are defined by Proust is an attempt to escape from this dilemma. Adorno's interest in origins and names as a specific phenomenon independent of the mechanics of competition can be seen not just in the "Short Commentaries on Proust" but also in the 1942 essay on the correspondence between George and Hofmannsthal that he dedicated to Walter Benjamin. As early as 1922, Benjamin, who was distantly related to Hofmannsthal, had written an essay on Goethe's *Wahlverwandtschaften* (Elective Affinities) in which he explored the theme of contingency and freedom as something that entered into the most intimate relationships. The hopeless situation of a society that closes itself off to the Other was a source of painful experience to the generation of both Benjamin and Adorno, whose parents aspired to combine bourgeois culture with the ideal of the gentleman. "The impossibility of love that Proust depicts in his socialites . . . has since then spread like a deadly chill over all of society, where a functionalized totality stifles love wherever it still stirs. In this respect Proust was prophetic, a quality he once attributed to the Jews."[26] It is through reflection on works of art that the unconscious history of the epoch is rendered visible.

Personal secrets, the source of pleasure and suffering, are encoded as social riddles. The persistence with which Adorno keeps returning to Proust and Thomas Mann, George and Hofmannsthal, seems closely related to the "childlike obstinacy" that he praises in Proust. Adorno is on the track of the process of concealment characteristic of bourgeois society, but he does not content himself with the artists' self-idealizations, which he sees through as the "masks of genius."[27] In the literary essays of the 1940s, 1950s, and 1960s, something of Adorno the child shines through, "that aura of disguise, of miming, which attracts the child to the theater, not because the child wants to see a work of art, but because it wants to have its own pleasure in dissimulation confirmed."[28] The theater public, all dressed up for the occasion, provides a model of society in which even the individual is ready to don masks and draperies which, through the very act of cloaking him, reveal his social status. In Proust's novel *The Guermantes Way*, Adorno praises "the description of the theater as a prehistoric Mediterranean landscape,"[29] and this elicits from him the comment that "Proust, born in 1871, already saw the world with the eyes of someone thirty or fifty years younger; hence . . . at a new stage in the novel form he also represents a new mode of experience."[30] Adorno's sense of his closeness to Proust's novel, whose chronology he reckoned coincided with his own childhood, makes this passage especially illuminating. Society as an unresolved part of "history's bondage to nature" appears as "the mythical landscape into whose allegorical image what is unattainable and unapproachable congeals."[31]

Reading these sentences enables us to imagine a visit to the Frankfurt Opera House around 1910, an age in which the private sponsors of the costly neo-Renaissance building still had their own private boxes. Selmar Spier recalls in his memoirs *Vor 1914* how "in front of the Opera House after the evening performance, a commissionaire in livery called out the names of the families to the waiting carriages that belonged to them: 'Bethmann, Passavant, Koch, etc.'"[32] These opera-goers can be thought of as the symbol of continental European society before 1914; this can be contrasted with America, which, as an immigrant, Adorno thought of as a "radically bourgeois country."[33] Adorno's Frankfurt childhood is marked by the experience of liberalism as a mixed social form in which the vestiges of feudalism overlap with the forces of industrialism. The specific German variant of continental European society in the last third of the nineteenth century is something Adorno described as "semi-civilized."[34] The conflict between belonging and being excluded is the signature of bourgeois literature. Goethe himself had treated this subject in exemplary fashion in *Wilhelm Meister*. In the nineteenth century the artist novel became a literary genre in Germany; it runs like a thread through Thomas Mann's entire oeuvre. The lack of clarity about the role of the bourgeois in German society caused Hofmannsthal to make his escape into high society, with its greater urbanity, whereas Stefan George toyed with the role of the pariah who suddenly stands revealed as a gentleman. "Overwhelming anxiety fosters the image of the gentleman as the historical model for the timeless George—the phantasma of the *fin de siècle*."[35] Similarly, Adorno's father, Oscar Wiesengrund, cultivated close business ties with England and oriented himself toward the ideal of the English gentleman in a way that was not uncommon for Jewish businessmen in Frankfurt at the time.

Conflicts with one's bourgeois father form part of the staple diet of the experience of entire generations. The theme of patricide in the literature of Expressionism thrives on this. The reflection titled "For Marcel Proust" in *Minima Moralia*, which promises to deliver fragments of a "doctrine of the good life,"[36] is followed by an aphorism titled "Grassy Seat." Considered from the vantage point of 1944, Adorno's picture of his bourgeois parents looks different: "One realizes with horror that earlier, opposing one's parents because they represented the world, one was often secretly the mouthpiece, against a bad world, of one even worse."[37] In bourgeois families the conflict between earning a living and pursuing one's cultural interests was an immediate experience. As the second son who was compelled to follow in the economic footsteps of the eldest son who had died prematurely, Adorno's father must have felt the force of circumstances directly. He was evidently attracted to the stage; the singer Maria Calvelli-Adorno had turned his head. As far as social standing was concerned, a marriage between the two was completely unsatisfactory, both in religious terms and by bourgeois criteria. Maria's mother, Elisabeth Henning, the only daughter of a master tailor in Bockenheim, had met and then married the lodger Jean Calvelli. She had already had the advantage of training in singing. There is a photograph of Adorno's grandmother with her three children, Maria, Agathe, and Louis, in the Frankfurt "Saalbau" in 1879. Louis too had to abandon music for a more practical profession, although, admittedly, he had success in it, ending up as a bank director. Maria's sister Agathe was saved from this fate by the unconventional conduct of Teddie's father. Following his marriage to Maria, who had enjoyed her greatest success at the Vienna Hofoperntheater in 1885, both she and her sister joined his household.

In this unusual family circle Teddie must have felt the "urge to resolve a conflict,"[38] against which, as the artistically gifted son, he must have rebelled. The Wiesengrund-Adorno household, which still inhabited the ground floor of the house in Schöne Aussicht as late as 1914, cannot be imagined as the typical middle-class household of the period. Nor can it be maintained, as we find suggested in the legends that have grown up around Adorno, that his non-Jewish relatives belonged to the cultivated upper bourgeoisie. The Calvelli-Adornos were really outsiders and a bit of a motley crew, something that Teddie may well have found attractive. He enjoyed clambering down into the cellar to play with boys from the pub milieu of Sachsenhausen, or making a surprise appearance in the street dressed up as a Spanish nobleman. At any rate, Adorno provided Andreas Count Razumovsky with a story along these lines so as to enable the latter to publish a well-informed article in the *Frankfurter Allgemeine Zeitung* for Adorno's sixty-fifth birthday. The article is notable for the absence of such Adorno legends as the claim that Agathe was a famous concert pianist on the grounds that she was said to have once accompanied the world-famous singer Adelina Patti. The reality was that both sisters and even their mother, Elisabeth, had once accompanied Patti to New York on her triumphal tour celebrating her Silver Jubilee on the stage; they did not accompany her on the piano, however, but only on board the *City of Berlin*. Maria made an appearance in Boston and then returned to Frankfurt. At home there was not only constant music but also amateur dramatics and performances with highly elaborate costumes that went back to his earliest childhood. These were not things that Teddie had to learn outside the home; they were things with which he was already familiar. His mother performed in public even after he was born, and according to her, Teddie is supposed on one occasion to have made his way onto the stage uninvited and to have recited some poems by heart. Even then, appearing before an audience had already become second nature to him.[39]

"Music that we are accustomed to calling 'classical' is something I came to know as a child through playing duets on the piano,"[40] he observes in a piece he wrote for the *Vossische Zeitung* in 1933, a piece that spurred Walter Benjamin to pursue his studies on his own childhood in Berlin.[41] "This music, more than any other, was suited to playing at home. It was produced on the piano, which was simply a piece of furniture, and those who set about it without fear of stumbling or playing false notes all belonged to the family."[42] In these words we can hear the echo of the descriptions of the ideal nineteenth-century middle-class family for whom Goethe's maxims were still an integral part of daily life. Adorno was thinking of Felix Mendelssohn's *Songs without Words* when he wrote his *Words without Songs* in 1931, a piece that leads directly back to his own childhood.[43] "Playing duets was a gift I received at birth at the start of the twentieth century at the hands of the genii of the bourgeois nineteenth century. Music for duets was the kind of music that you could get on with and live with before musical constraints ordained solitude and secret craftsmanship."[44] As early as 1930 the long bourgeois nineteenth century had already ceased being any more than a memory, but it could still be retained as a significant social experience: "That every individual could find himself to a greater or lesser degree in the symphony is demonstrated by the fact that he could respond to it with his family in his own home, without its losing any of its authority, just as he could hang classical pictures on the walls. But playing duets was even better than [Böcklin's] 'The Isle of the Dead' over the sideboard; one had constantly to earn the symphony if one was to possess it, by playing it."[45] Within the family at the turn of the century, Adorno could still experience the nineteenth-century bourgeoisie as a living reality in which the individual might be oppressed, but by which he was also strengthened, if not indeed produced.

In his brief text "Piano Duets, Once Again" (*Vierhändig, noch einmal*), Adorno pays a literary tribute to his family by singling out "its sheltering, protective quality that was uniquely capable of nurturing a talent in isolation."[46] Adorno did not suggest that this middle-class educational tradition was without flaws. As early as the fin de siècle, this kind of music making in the family home seemed old-fashioned:

> In the age of a strict division of labor, the middle class defended their ultimate music in the fortress of the piano, which they occupied in force; ruthlessly, indifferent to the way it must have sounded to others, the alienated. Even the mistakes which they inevitably made preserved an active link with the works that those who listened enthralled to concert performances had long since ceased to possess as their own. The price for this had of course to be paid by the duet players, with their old-fashioned domestic approach and their untrained dilettantism. But this dilettantism is nothing but the echo and the degenerate product of the true music-making tradition. It remains to be asked for whom the last artist will meaningfully play once the last dilettante who still dreams of being an artist has died out.[47]

This criticism can be seen in its true light only when we know that as an adult, Adorno used to play duets even with friends who were not professional musicians. In "Piano Duets, Once Again," we can see Adorno as a child turning the pages of a score, following "only his ear and his memory" long before he could read the notes.[48] It was not just his mother who sat next to him at the piano but also her sister, Agathe, a highly accomplished pianist, whom Adorno sometimes called "Dädd" [i.e., Dad]. Agathe, whom Horkheimer affectionately referred to as Adorno's second mother, must also have assumed some paternal characteristics.[49] In the family and also among Adorno's friends, Agathe was regarded as an impressive figure to be treated with respect. She insisted on the highest musical standards and was known for her apodictic judgments, but she also followed the intellectual fashions of the 1920s, ranging from Kierkegaard to the cinema. In a letter in which his distress is evident, Adorno reported her death on 26 June 1935 to Ernst Křenek, writing from Nazi Germany, where he had gone to visit his family despite the great anxiety of his friends. Having retreated to the familiar old holiday resort, the Bären Hotel in Hornberg in the Black Forest, Adorno wrote some of his most moving letters to his composer friend from Vienna and to Walter Benjamin in Paris. He also wrote after some delay "for the well-known reasons"—the Nazi censors in the post office were opening the letters—to Horkheimer and to Gabriele Oppenheim, who was likewise already in exile.[50] "I cannot express what losing her really means to me; it is not so much the death of a relative as above all that of the person closest to me of all, my most faithful friend, a piece of nature that has always enabled me to regenerate myself. I am utterly at a loss and am only gradually coming to visualize the possibility that, and how, I am to go on living."[51] As if he suspected that the disinterested reader might well just shake his head in bewilderment on reading these lines and find this account of the loss of an aunt on the part of a man of thirty-two somewhat overstated, Adorno added, "This sounds highly excessive, but you can believe me that it does not contain an atom of exaggeration and sentimentality."[52]

Adorno's image of "a life lived rightly" and his critique of the "wrong life"[53] seems to be bound up with this unusual household, in which his father renounced his own artistic leanings in order to pursue them in his private life. "The end of the family paralyses the forces of opposition. The rising collectivist order is a mockery of a classless one: together with the bourgeois it liquidates the Utopia that once drew sustenance from motherly love."[54] "The dream of being an artist" is hard to resist in an atmosphere of this kind. Adorno could see that Thomas Mann was motivated by something that he too felt: "a longing for applause." Anyone who ever saw Adorno take a bow at the end of a lecture can understand his appreciation of Mann's coyness: "There is something in the gracefulness of the form of even an intellectual work of art that is related to the grace with which the actor takes his bow. Mann wanted to charm and to please."[55] This theatrical element was linked to memories of his own childhood performances. Adorno has drawn attention to Hugo von Hofmannsthal's preference for blank verse, which is "designed to serve the needs of the actor inherent in the theatrical form. . . . It is also, however, the verse bequeathed to the child by a theatre which, since Hofmannsthal's youth, had reserved *Hamlet* and Schiller for school." Hofmannsthal himself had "traced his efforts at intellectual disguise back to his childhood."[56] His fantasy of noble birth, one he shared with Adorno, corresponds to this liking for fancy dress. Adorno produced an elegant description to define Hofmannsthal's love of the theater: "The magical power to manipulate childhood is the strength of the weak."[57] His observations impressed Benjamin, who not only knew Hofmannsthal well but also produced a literary exploration of memories of a secularized Jewish childhood during the final phase of the German Empire which has no equal.

Although children from good families such as Adorno and Benjamin enjoyed excellent prospects for improving their social position in the first decade of the twentieth century, this does not mean that they were spared sorrow and trauma during their childhood. In 1950 Adorno commented on Benjamin's *Berlin Childhood around 1900:* "For the images that it evokes in disconcerting immediacy are not idyllic, nor are they contemplative. Over them lies the shadow of the Hitlerian Reich. As in a dream they marry the anticipatory horror of that Reich with processes that lie deep in the past. With a sense of panic the bourgeois mind becomes conscious of the disintegrating aura of its own biographical past, and indeed of itself: it appears as illusion."[58] As a social theorist. Adorno was attempting to define in sociological terms what Benjamin had tried to encapsulate as a specific experience:

> The family is presented with the bill not just for the brutal oppression that was experienced right up to the threshold of the modern age by the weaker sex and especially by children at the hands of the head of the family, but also for economic injustice, the exploitation of domestic labor in a society that otherwise works in obedience to the laws of the market, as well as the renunciation of instincts exacted by family discipline from its members without their feeling certain that this discipline was always justified and without their truly believing that they would receive proper compensation, in the form of, say, secure property to be handed on, as had appeared to be the case at the height of the liberal era.[59]

This comment was written in 1955, in other words, after the fact. It could also be read as a warning not to idealize the bourgeois family of the age of liberalism.

The deceptive nature of the bourgeois family follows a historical tendency that is traced back to early experiences. In his *Berlin Chronicle,* the studies for his memoirs which echoed Adorno's "Piano Duets, Once Again" and which remained unpublished during his lifetime, Benjamin speaks of the economic basis "on which the finances of my parents rested" as of something that was shrouded "in deepest secrecy," a secrecy that long outlasted his childhood and youth.[60] It is easy to understand the attractions of a Marxist critique of political economy for many children from bourgeois families in which the father earned his living as a merchant in the realm of the circulation of capital, for that theory promised to resolve the mystery. The threats which seemed to hang over the security of the parental household were connected with the veiling of its economic dependency. With the family's move from Schöne Aussicht to Seeheimerstrasse in 1914, the separation of the family from its economic basis became a lived fact. The culture that was enjoyed in the bourgeois household now came to contain an element of illusion: "Like all forms of mediation between individual biological creatures, the nuclear individual, and an integrated society, the family finds its substance sucked from it by that society, as does the economic sphere of circulation or the category of culture which is so intimately bound up with the family."[61] The classic novelist of the German bourgeoisie, Thomas Mann, played with this veiling of reality by presenting himself as the somewhat stiff and chilly son of a Hanseatic magnate. Adorno referred to disguises like this as "masks of genius" which were designed to oppose the nineteenth-century cult of genius, with its "Rembrandtian head, the velvet and the artist's beret."[62] One could go further and argue that behind the bourgeois façade of the artist lay concealed the feeling of shame "that from the standpoint of the individual and his fate, . . . it is a matter of chance whether a person turns out to be a genius or not."[63]

The individual is mediated by his family down to his innermost core. It is for this reason that Adorno starts out in *Minima Moralia* with reflections on origins and professions. This collection of aphorisms is not merely dedicated to his older friend Max Horkheimer: it fits him like a glove. Comparisons with like and unlike are initiated with the very first aphorism, the one titled "For Marcel Proust," to which the preceding "Dedication" leads up: it represents "the attempt to present aspects of our shared philosophy from the standpoint of subjective experience."[64] This process of identifying with a self-chosen elder brother is part of a pattern that recurs in a number of Adorno's friendships: those with Kracauer, with Benjamin, and with Horkheimer himself. All four men come from similar though by no means identical backgrounds. The spectrum extends from the lower middle class right through to the upper. In his last letter to Adorno, on 7 May 1940, shortly before his abortive flight to Spain, Benjamin wrote about Adorno's essay on the correspondence between George and Hofmannsthal. He praises Adorno's insight into the "child in Hofmannsthal," but, as a notorious loner, he also refers to something that is only hinted at by Adorno:

You are quite right to bring up Proust. I have been thinking about his work a great deal recently. And once again, my thoughts seem to correspond closely with your own here. You speak felicitously about the experience of "that's not what I meant at all"—that experience when time turns into something we have lost. And it seems to me that Proust was able to find a deeply hidden (but not, therefore, necessarily an unconscious) model for this fundamental experience, namely the experience of "that's not it" with regard to the assimilation of French Jews. You will remember the famous passage in *Sodom et Gomorrhe* in which the complicity of sexual inverts is compared with the constellation governing the way the Jews behave amongst one another. The very fact that Proust was only half Jewish allowed him insight into the highly precarious structure of assimilation: an insight which was then externally confirmed by the Dreyfus Affair.[65]

Gershom Scholem, Benjamin's friend from childhood who also formed a friendship later on with Adorno (though not with Horkheimer), never tired of pointing to this "that's not it at all" as a mark of the assimilation of the German Jews. The daily experience of Jews who had risen into the middle classes flatly contradicted the ideology of the enlightened, liberal bourgeoisie to which they thought they belonged. "One day, it suddenly struck me that the friends who came to visit us at home were all Jews. The exceptions were all restricted to formal occasions when people came to offer congratulations. They included my father's colleagues from the printing trade—we were a family of printworkers—from the health insurance company where he held an honorary position on the board, or from some other association he belonged to."[66] This was the position in what was on the whole the lower-middle-class environment in which the Scholems moved in the mid-1890s in Berlin. Here too baptism was looked at askance, while the situation with mixed marriages was quite different:

Their attitude toward mixed marriages was very divided and frequently quite irrational. My father, who was a vocal advocate of assimilation, refused to accept mixed marriages among his own family and friends. In accordance with his theory, he should have welcomed them. But when my brother married a non-Jewess, he never exchanged another word with her again after a single brief encounter. My mother, on the other hand, who came from a family dominated by a traditional Jewish piety and who regarded her Judaism, when she thought about it at all, as a matter of feeling rather than a biological fact, was untroubled by mixed marriages. She had not the slightest difficulty with the marriages of either my brother or her own sister, who was one of the first women to be allowed to qualify as a doctor in Berlin.[67]

Similar reactions were no doubt to be expected in Frankfurt on the marriage of Oscar Alexander Wiesengrund and Maria Calvelli-Adorno, whose wedding took place in London in July 1898. Everything about the family history of the Wiesengrunds bears the marks of the process by which Jews who sought integration into civil society were affected by the specifically German problems of citizenship arising from the principle of descent (the *ius sanguinis*, according to which citizenship could be granted only to people of German parentage). Toward the end of the century, Berlin and Frankfurt am Main became centers of German Jewry. At the time of Adorno's birth, 20 percent of all Jews in the German Empire lived in one or the other of these two cities. Throughout the entire century, Jews had been in the vanguard of the trend toward urbanization, while the Christian population followed in their wake. But by the end of the century, the social structure of the Jewish population did exhibit one special feature: 56 percent of active Jewish adults were employed in trade.[68] Their children, however, tended to move away from industry and turned instead to the independent or academic professions. A particular domestic climate came to prevail in secularized Jewish households which made it difficult to maintain Jewish traditions. Heine's tongue-in-cheek quip about baptism as "the entry ticket to European culture" had referred to an entirely different social situation, one in which reactionary laws explicitly blocked access to the independent and academic professions for the children of Jewish tradesmen. Toward the end of the nineteenth century, baptism had become anathema to aspiring middle-class Jews. Since the different faiths had been granted formal equality, baptism had ceased to be necessary. What distinguished Jewish families from the average German family was the emphasis they placed on education and culture. What merged was not ethnic designations such as "German" and "Jew" but Enlightenment and classicism, humanism and progress. While traditional and neo-Orthodox Jews tended politically toward conservatism, the advocates of progress among the Frankfurt Jews identified with the left-liberalism of Leopold Sonnemann's *Frankfurter Zeitung*.

Leo Löwenthal's father, Victor, who was born in 1864, formed a friendship with Oscar Alexander Wiesengrund, who was six years his junior. One of nine siblings, he succeeded in qualifying as a doctor. Leo Löwenthal reported later that all his father's siblings stayed loyal to Orthodox Judaism and the traditional Jewish way of life: "My father wanted to be a lawyer. But my grandfather—according to my father, at least—refused to grant him permission because he thought this would mean that my father would have to work and write on the Sabbath. Consequently, he prevailed on my father to study medicine, which my father did, though his heart wasn't in it at all. But then he took his revenge—either consciously or unconsciously—when he later became totally 'free': not just irreligious, but decidedly anti-religious."[69] Löwenthal's paternal grandfather was a teacher in the neo-Orthodox Samson Raphael Hirsch School. According to Selmar Spier, this was the most "'pious' school that a German Jew could conceivably imagine."[70] It was highly conservative but fostered a synthesis of Jewish orthodoxy and classical German humanism in a way that would be barely comprehensible today. Not even such products of the Christian musical tradition as the *Saint Matthew Passion* were felt to be in conflict with neo-Orthodox Judaism. In the case of the Spier family, the choice of a Jewish school was still the prerogative of his grandfather. A possible alternative in Frankfurt would have been the celebrated Philanthropinum, where Siegfried Kracauer's uncle Isidor worked as a teacher. But what decided the choice of school was of course its distance from the family home. The Jewish secondary school was simply closer to the Spiers' home at Eschenheimer Anlage 2. For his father, this may simply have represented a pragmatic compromise between family tradition and everyday practicality; for his son, the Hebrew classes were sheer torture.

The existential compromise of Selmar Spier's father consisted not just in his accepting his father-in-law's dominance within the family, which meant that it was his father-in-law who decided what school his son should attend. In addition, Selmar's father, Simon, experienced the maxim governing the Haskalah, the Jewish Enlightenment, as a complete contradiction. According to this maxim, one should live as a human being in society while remaining a Jew at home: "My father used to put on tefillin, but he also went to work on the Sabbath."[71] The pressure of competition toward the end of the nineteenth century must have been especially intense: people simply could not afford to observe the traditional festivals. We should not allow ourselves to paint too rosy a picture of economic prospects during the last third of the nineteenth century. The extended depression reinforced the views of those who thought that the future lay in more education rather than in business. The education of children was often left in the hands of their mothers, since the fathers were absorbed in their activities away from home. This too was a feature characteristic of Jewish families:

The Jewish family was clearly distinguished from non-Jewish ones not just by the degree of their urbanization, their tendency to have fewer children, or the particular position of the main provider, but also by the role of the wife and mother. The Jewish mother had fewer children, went out to work less often than other women, and had had the benefit of a superior education. A simple comparison of the differences in education among men and women in Prussia shows that the gulf between them in the non-Jewish population was twice as large as in the Jewish sector.[72]

This development culminated in the choice of an educated woman whose non-Jewish background ceased to be an impediment to marriage.

A new mother became the center of the modern Jewish household in which a secularized culture had taken the place of the Jewish tradition. There seems to have been a particular emphasis on language acquisition. This made it possible to assess the degree of integration. The concept of acculturation does not suffice here, since the traditional language of the upper class by no means embodied the ideal of a cultured mastery of the language. In the Spier family, for example, where the entire process of sec-ularization appears in accelerated form, more concentrated than in the case of the Wiesengrunds, Spier's mother had the task of finding a German housemaid whose outstanding quality had to be "her pure German." This lofty linguistic ideal was intensified further by such masters of the German language as Hugo von Hofmannsthal and Karl Kraus, but it did not qualify the people who strove to achieve it to become the assimilated members of high society, or even of an established middle class. A clear High German spoken by a young boy in Frankfurt around 1910 might easily stamp him as an outsider. Adorno would recall such a situation from his childhood in his later essay "Words from Abroad": "As I was conversing harmlessly with a comrade in the streetcar on my way to school, old Dreibus, a neighbour who lived on my street, attacked me in a rage: 'You goddamned little devil! Shut up with your High German and learn to speak German right.' I had scarcely recovered from the fright Herr Dreibus gave me when he was brought home in a pushcart not long afterwards, completely intoxicated, and it was probably not much later that he died."[73] Adorno referred to this incident as his first experience of *Ranküne* (rancor or spite), "a word that has no proper native equivalent in German, unless one were to confuse it with the word 'Ressentiment' [resentment], a word currently enjoying an unfortunate popularity in Germany."[74] Two or three generations previously the word used would have been *rishess* (Yiddish for "slander," especially anti-Semitic slander).

Jews who tried an artistic route to emancipation wanted to escape from this *rishess*. Giacomo Meyerbeer escaped from Biedermeier Berlin to Paris; but as early as 1818 he warned his brother Michael Beer, who had belonged to the enlightened circle around Heinrich Heine and Eduard Gans, the disciple of Hegel: "Take care not to forget the iron word *rishess,* something I forgot when choosing my profession. Individuals may forget this word for a while (but not forever), but not in a larger *assembly* of people, since only *one* person need remember in order to recall the natural condition of the entire mass."[75] Meyerbeer was on the same wavelength as Heine when it came to grasping the transformation of the traditional hatred of Jews into a hatred of artists of Jewish origin. "Ninety-nine percent of the readers are *reshoyim* [slanderers]; that is why they will always enjoy *rishess* if it is not too blatant," he wrote in 1839, although he personally had enjoyed considerable success as a composer in Paris.[76] Neither culture nor refinement spells the end of the dislike of outsiders. We can explain Heine's passing flirtation with revolutionary movements in the pre-1848 period as the wish to escape from a society which otherwise offered no way out. The feeling that society outside the family is hostile is one that reaches back into childhood. Even the fantasy of aristocratic origins is influenced by the power of a prejudice that is felt to be ineluctable. Such feelings can even be discerned in Adorno's reflections on Hofmannsthal: "Hofmannsthal also claimed to transcend society, and the thought of the outsider is never foreign to one who must simulate his own society."[77]

To discover oneself in a terrestrial realm beyond money and work is what distinguishes the particular atmosphere that can in fact only be experienced "in immediate, nourishing, warm relations."[78] The less the family can make these a reality, the more this absence of experience turns into a source of rancor that no "child prodigy" can escape.[79] But precisely because the family cannot be the extraterritorial idyll that it ought to be according to the indestructible ideology of the family, the cosseted child ends up with characteristics that inevitably attract hostility, and not just from adults. The prodigy's precociousness provokes external pressure. "If the early maturer is more than a possessor of dexterities, he is obliged to catch himself up, a compulsion which normal people are fond of dressing up as a moral imperative."[80] The prodigy's narcissism, which makes autarchy seem possible in a world of dependencies, invites aggression. We can hear aggressive overtones even in the later reminiscences of Adorno's schoolmates, fellow students, and contemporaries, overtones that condemn the genius to the condition of outsider. The disharmonious experience of his own individuality is implicit in the language that Adorno gave as the crucial explanation for his return to Germany. In Germany, however, resistance to his ideas focused repeatedly on his use of language, above all on his insistence on using words of foreign origin and his savage criticism of the "jargon of authenticity," that trend toward linguistic chauvinism characteristic of post-Nazi Germany. Adorno's plea on behalf of foreign words contains "something of the utopia of language, a language without earth, without subjection to the spell of historical existence, a utopia that lives on unawares in the childlike use of language."[81]

Even these words of Adorno's, which are perhaps not easily comprehensible on first hearing, were broadcast over the radio as part of a service that had been entrusted with a role in public education in the Germany of the post-Hitler period. It was above all pedagogic subjects that introduced Adorno's voice to a public that would have been most unlikely to come into contact with his texts or his music. His pointed criticisms of the normal practices of the Culture Industry and the daily grind in the universities provoked the ambivalent attitude toward any intellectual views advanced with authority that derived from the arsenal of the "Taboos on the Teaching Profession."[82] Adorno's return to Frankfurt University in the 1950s forced him to face up to the constraints of teacher training. His conclusions are scathing:

> The language in the examination papers is outdone by what is heard in the oral part of the exam. Often it is a stammering interspersed with vague, qualifying phrases, such as "to a certain extent," that in the same instant that they are uttered try to evade responsibility for what is said. Words of foreign derivation, even names of foreigners, constitute hurdles that are seldom surmounted without some damage either to hurdle or candidate; for instance, most of the candidates who have chosen for their exam a philosopher who is apparently as easy as Hobbes, speak of him as Hob*bes*, as though the *bes* belonged to the dialect in which *ebbes* means "etwas." The very idea of dialect. One may rightly expect from culture that it accustom a regional language's coarseness to more polished manners.[83]

This comment in a radio talk in 1961 unleashed a flood of listeners' responses that induced Adorno to add a footnote to the text he had revised for publication: "I do not mean that culture signifies that every trace of dialect within a pitiless standard language has been eradicated. It merely suffices, for example, to hear the Viennese intonation in order to learn just how deeply linguistic humanitarianism is realized in such tonalities."[84] This vocal coloring had reached Adorno's ears early on in his parents' house. He several times spoke of Vienna as his "second home."[85] "The human is indissolubly linked with imitation: a human being only becomes human at all by imitating other human beings. In such behaviour, the primal form of love, the priests of authenticity scent traces of the utopia which could shake the structure of domination."[86] We hear echoes of the motif of the homeland not as a bond with the soil but as a social relationship. A sensitive passage in *Minima Moralia* reports on a dream Adorno had in his period of emigration:

> One evening, in a mood of helpless sadness, I caught myself using a ridiculously wrong subjunctive form of a verb that was itself not entirely correct German, being part of the dialect of my native town. I had not heard, let alone used, the endearing misconstruction since my first years at school. Melancholy, drawing me irresistibly into the abyss of childhood, awakened this old, impotently yearning sound in its depths. Language sent back to me like an echo the humiliation which unhappiness had inflicted on me in forgetting what I am.[87]

A powerful emotion is stirred up by a weak verb. Nor does Adorno look to complex verbal constructions to convey the movement of thought from which the emotional traces of love and desire can be gleaned. Not far from the fragment of *Minima Moralia* just quoted we can find the remark, "To happiness the same applies as to truth: one does not have it, but is in it."[88] The weak verb joins together things that are normally not connected: happiness and knowledge. As an adult intellectual, Adorno attempts to hold fast to the things that the social reality of life threatens to destroy—"the advantage of the infinitesimal freedom that lies in knowledge as such."[89] The notion of happiness that Adorno owes to his childhood remains visible in even the most highly rarified extremes of his thought. In his use of language, in the particular cadence of the words, we experience the history of exteriorization that, following the idealistic image projected by Goethe and Hegel, will shape the educational history of a humanity made happy. The idea of happiness continues to live off the ahistorical moment of the absence of contradiction. "Indeed, happiness is nothing other than being encompassed, an after-image of the original shelter within the mother. But for this reason no-one who is happy can know that he is so. To see happiness, he would have to pass out of it: to be as if already born."[90] The émigré's memory is ignited by a word in the dialect of his "hometown," where Adorno experienced being weaned from the security given by his mother. But the returning exile did not at all see himself as a mama's boy and instead recalls playing in the cellars of the house in Schöne Aussicht with boys from the rougher Sachsenhausen district, with its pubs and street brawls. The Frankfurt dialect did not have only hostile connotations: the family of the local dialect poet, Friedrich Stoltze, belonged to the Wiesengrund circle, and Adorno began to learn the piano with Sanna Stoltze, the poet's granddaughter. He heard Frankfurt dialect away from home, too—in its higher forms together with middle- and lower-class variants—as exemplified by his angry neighbor Herr Dreibus. Adorno himself spoke the dialect like a native.

His parents did not spare their only son, Theodor Ludwig, the experience of primary school. In those days, many affluent families still preferred to employ private tutors to prepare their children at home for the *Gymnasium*. The Wiesengrunds were not among them. But even in Oberrad the Wiesengrunds did not really belong to the upper crust who could afford such a luxury. They were well aware that they did not live far from the Gerber Mill, where Goethe had once spent happy hours, both aesthetic and erotic, with Marianne Willemer. But the Wiesengrunds' narrow row house between Gruneliusstrasse and Offenbacher Landstrasse had been chosen from the point of view of practical convenience. Seeheimerstrasse could not be compared with the childhood villas of Benjamin's Berlin or Horkheimer's Stuttgart. The tension between High German and the class-specific Frankfurt dialect lived on in Adorno's mind in emigration. It must undoubtedly have been a factor in his brief three-years' schooling in the Deutschherren Middle School, for even the *Dream Notes*, where a number of schoolboy memories are recorded, contain references to the *Kinner* (children). Conditions in primary schools toward the end of the Second Empire have become embedded in turn-of-the-century German literature. The image of the teacher as a potential child beater forms an extreme contrast with the childhood world as personified by the loving mother. "The child," the adult Adorno writes, conscious of a somewhat bold generalization, "experiences alienation for the first time with a brutal shock; in the development of the individual the school is virtually the prototype of societal alienation per se."[91] But Teddie may well have found the reality of the

Deutschherren Middle School less of a test than his time at the head of all his classes in the Kaiser-Wilhelm Gymnasium, which was also in Sachsenhausen. The school had adopted modern teaching methods and even accepted new technology, as we can see from his mother's contribution toward the purchase of a new slide projector.

Among Adorno's juvenilia there is an essay that appeared in the Frankfurt school newspaper in 1919. Its tone is remarkably similar to that of his lectures on schooling in the 1960s. In contrast to the literary attacks on teachers from Wedekind to Hesse, he leaps to their defense: "He too [i.e., the teacher] is subject to a purpose that lies beyond himself; for them [the pupils] he is not a human being first of all but a teacher, i.e., the mediator of abstract, coercive information that is indescribable in its origins and who now has demands to make in the service of this purpose that lies initially beyond the horizon of the pupils."[92] This is the start of Adorno's identification with those who have knowledge from beyond the family circle.

What began as a sheltered childhood has now taken cognizance of something else. Adorno attempted to grasp the essence of this development in the image of the heliotrope. The world of his mothers is transformed by the arrival of a much-traveled lady: "The cases with the labels from the Suvretta Hotel and Madonna di Campiglio, are chests in which the jewels of Aladdin and Ali Baba wrapped in special tissues—the guest's kimonos—are borne hither from the caravanserais of Switzerland and the South Tyrol in sleeping-car sedan chairs for his glutted contemplation. And just as fairies talk to children in fairy-tales, the visitor talks seriously without condescension, to the child of the house."[93] Adorno has not yet embarked on travels of his own to the worldly holiday destinations of the upper middle class. But ideal images that bring far and near together appear before his eyes and take a form that might have flowed from the pen of Bloch or Benjamin: "Among those nearest him, as their friend, appears the figure of all that is different. The soothsaying gypsy, let in by the front door, is absolved in the lady visitor and transfigured into a rescuing angel. From the joy of greatest proximity she removes the curse by wedding it to utmost distance."[94] The forty-plus-year-old Adorno writes of "what is best in childhood" with an intensity and sadness which equal that of the most impressive pages of Benjamin's *Berlin Childhood,* in which we discern the threat of annihilation that hangs over Jewish family life while remaining invisible to a solitary child: "For the guest comes from afar. Her appearance promises the child a world beyond the family, reminding him that it is not the ultimate."[95]

These recollections of the past were written in full awareness of the horrors of the mass destruction of the European Jews. The lost time, the experience of "that's not what was meant at all," has gained a further dimension, one that makes even one's own childhood appear in a different light. The utopia of the parental generation, one in which origins should cease to be a crucial factor, can no longer be recreated. What has now become the certainty of "that's not what was meant at all" provides an interpretation of one's own past. Adorno's reflections on the George-Hofmannsthal correspondence, about which he and Benjamin were still exchanging letters as late as 1940, refer to a bygone age, to things past. Hofmannsthal and George began their correspondence on artistic matters at a time when children such as Walter Benjamin and Theodor Wiesengrund were trying to shed light on the secrets of their parents' lives. Walter, who was eleven years older, succeeded in doing so sooner than his younger Frankfurt friend. With clinical incisiveness, Benjamin identified George with the Jugendstil:

> In other words the style in which the old bourgeoisie disguises the premonition of its own impotence by indulging in poetic flights of fancy on a cosmic scale and abusing the word "youth" as a magic incantation with which to conjure up intoxicated visions of the future. . . . What is expressed in its formal idiom is the will to evade imminent developments and the presentiments that rise up to confront it. The same may be said of that "spiritual movement" that aspired to the renewal of human existence without paying heed to politics. It, too, amounted to a retrospective transformation of societal contradictions into those hopeless, tragic tensions and convulsions that are so typical of the life of small conventicles.[96]

The blind alley of bourgeois aestheticism is discussed also in Adorno's retrospective essay of 1940. But it is impossible not to see the fascination he felt for George's dictatorial gestures. George himself had originated from a background in vine cultivation and the wine trade quite close to Frankfurt, but it was a lower-middle-class Catholic milieu that George abandoned as quickly as he could. What Adorno defends in his somewhat affected aestheticism is "the utopia of not being oneself."[97] This was a common reaction to the bourgeois realism of his father's generation, in which the children failed to realize that, as Scholem later acknowledged, this realism itself contained a utopian aspect. The memory of this secret of secularized Jewish families was one that Benjamin was able to evoke in his writings better than anyone else. Such secrets live on enigmatically in life forms that are paradoxically Jewish and non-Jewish at the same time. The sadness that Adorno perceived in Benjamin as "a Jewish awareness of the permanence of threat and catastrophe as such"[98] was experienced by Benjamin's younger friend with the admixture of a feeling that can only be described as a kind of autobiographical exhibitionism: "To be near him was like being a child at the moment when the door to the room where the Christmas presents lie waiting opens a crack and the abundance of light overwhelms the eye to the point of tears, more moving and more assured than any brightness that greets the child when he is invited to enter."[99] Benjamin's last letter from Paris to Adorno in New York refers to the joy felt at the sight of the table piled high with birthday presents, and Adorno too has memories of a child's eyes shining with the reflected light from a room full of Christmas decorations. The Adorno who wrote this passage had already read his Proust:

> At half-past twelve I would finally make up my mind to enter that house which, like an immense Christmas stocking, seemed ready to bestow on me supernatural delights. (The French name "Noël" was, by the way, unknown to Mme Swann and Gilberte, who had substituted for it the English "Christmas," and would speak of nothing but "Christmas pudding," what people had given them as "Christmas presents" and of going away—the thought of which maddened me with grief—"for Christmas." At home even I should have thought it degrading to use the word "Noël," and always said "Christmas," which my father considered extremely silly.)[100]

In *Minima Moralia*, whenever childhood is recollected, it is always associated with traveling; the suitcases of the aphorism titled "Heliotrope" had something of the radiance of Adorno's presentiments of a happy adult world. We know today that it was Else Herzberger, through whom Adorno was distantly related to Benjamin, who brought these alluring treasures from abroad. Adorno also encounters her at the deathbed of his aunt Agathe, and it was she who gave Adorno the courage to ask for money on behalf of Benjamin, who was destitute in exile in Paris. Few sociologists suspect that a paper Adorno wrote in 1955 about the family was so close to his own personal experience: "The family has demonstrated its strength under extreme conditions and their extended consequences, their effect on refugees, for example, despite everything, and has in many respects proved to be the engine of life itself."[101] The friendship between Teddie and Else Herzberger came to grief during the emigration, probably because of disagreements about money. Notwithstanding a highly personal attempt at reconciliation on Adorno's part ("My dear Else, you old rogue"), on 12 July 1948,[102] she failed to respond. It seems clear that her lifestyle brought a hint of the luxury of the *haute volée* into Seeheimerstrasse. Nevertheless, Adorno's first experiences of travel had nothing of the Grand Tour about them. The Wiesengrunds began by looking for places in the neighborhood of Frankfurt. For a while, Neuweilnau in the Taunus competed for their attention with their later favorite, Amorbach.[103] But with the stabilization of the German economy after the First World War and the inflation, Amorbach gained the upper hand. Here, with south German baroque, they found the direct counterpart to the English modernity which had held sway over the household in Seeheimerstrasse. Teddie was envied for his electric train set; his father knew his way around England, and in comparison with Teddie's English cousins, the Wingfields, he knew all about the latest toys that a modern child ought to have.

Teddie evidently came into his own in the holidays, in which even his own home appeared in a new light:

> To a child returning from a holiday, home seems new, fresh, festive. Yet nothing has changed there since he left. Only because duty has now been forgotten, of which each piece of furniture, window, lamp, was otherwise a reminder, is the house given back the sabbath peace, and for minutes one is at home in a never returning world of rooms, nooks and corridors, in a way that makes the rest of life there a lie. No differently will the world one day appear, almost unchanged, in its constant feast-day light, when it stands no longer under the law of labour, and when for homecomers duty has the lightness of holiday play.[104]

This fragmentary reflection dating from 1945 affords the reader a glimpse of life in Seeheimerstrasse as if seen through a telescope from California, where this passage was written. What the Adorno legends describe simply as a sheltered childhood is what he thinks of as one dominated by the bourgeois compulsion to work. But the shift that takes place on Fridays or during the holidays arouses notions of setting things to rights, of the reality of a utopia that is different and more than mere wish fulfillment. When Adorno published his sketches about Amorbach and Sils Maria at a time when he was already famous, the German press responded with a shoulder-shrugging indifference to such seeming lack of discipline—the philosopher as travel writer. Fifty years later these fragments emerge as an individual construct that encompasses an entire social experience, a broken promise of happiness that was evoked in the bourgeois century and then disavowed in the short twentieth century of Adorno's lifetime.

This experience is woven artfully into the localities of Amorbach and Sils: "Wolkmann: a mountain that is the very image of its name,[105] a friendly giant. Now he has long since lain at rest, stretched out broadly over the town that he greets from out of the clouds.—Gotthard: the lowest peak in the region, though it bears the name of the mightiest massif of the Central Alps, as if it desired to introduce me gently to mountains while I was still a child."[106] As if in anticipation of his death in Switzerland in 1966, Adorno reminds his readers of his nostalgia for the Alps. In the same year, on what was to be his last visit to the Alps, Monika Plessner recalls her husband, Helmuth, warning his old friend Teddie not to walk too far and to take things slowly. "Don't worry, I am a mountain person. See you later," she remembers him calling to the circle of prominent philosophers in front of the Fischerstube as he set out on the climb up to the Waldhaus Hotel.[107] But his diary entries from Sils Maria in the same year open up a view of death:

Anyone who has ever heard the sound made by marmots is unlikely to forget it. To say it is a whistle is to say too little: it sounds mechanical, as if steam driven. And alarming for that reason. The fear that these little animals must have felt since time immemorial has frozen in their throats into a sort of warning sound; the sound that should act as a protection has lost its lifelike expressiveness. Stricken by panic, they have mimicked death itself. If I am not mistaken, they have receded further and further into the mountains over the last twelve years, as camping has made ever deeper inroads. Even the whistling sounds with which they uncomplainingly accuse the friends of nature are heard more rarely.

Their lack of expression is matched by that of the landscape. That confers on it the pathos of distance that Nietzsche, who took refuge there, talked about. At the same time, the murrains that are typical of the landscape resemble industrial tips, mining slagheaps. Both, the scars of civilization and the untouched regions beyond the tree line, give the lie to the idea of nature as solace, something that gives man a warm feeling. They reveal what the cosmos is really like. The conventional imago of nature is limited, of a bourgeois narrowness, confined to the tiny zone in which the life familiar to us from history thrives; the path is the philosophy of culture. Where the domination of nature destroys that animated but deceptive imago, it seems to approach the transcendent sadness of space. The unvarnished truth of the landscape of the Engadine is superior to that of the petty bourgeoisie, but this is more than made up for by its imperialism, its complicity with death.[108]

It is as if the lifelong themes of Critical Theory all come together once again at this point. The use of political and sociological terms to describe the landscape may seem inappropriate, but Adorno wished to achieve precisely this effect. It touches on idiosyncrasies that can be achieved with a minimal change of focus. "Imperialism" here turns into the experience of boundless expansion, which, however, contains a utopian aspect that is at odds with the death threat represented by the social system as a whole. His reflections on the marmots' whistling evokes the childhood feeling of a nonviolent boundlessness, the no-man's-land close to Amorbach:

> The frontier between Baden and Bavaria ran between Ottorfszell and Ernsthal. It was marked by posts on the highway with imposing coats of arms in the provincial colors spiraling round the posts, blue and white on the one side, if I remember right, and red and yellow on the other. There was a generous space between the two. That was where I liked to walk on the pretext, which I did not actually believe, that this empty space belonged to neither of the two states, that it was free, and that I could hold sway there as I wished. I did not mean this seriously, but that did not diminish my pleasure. In reality, what I probably liked were the state colors whose limits I felt I had escaped. I had a similar feeling in exhibitions like the ILA [the International Aerospace Exhibition] at the sight of the countless flags that fluttered in harmony next to one another. The feeling of the International was familiar to me from home and also from my parents' guests, from whom I heard names like Firino and Sidney Clifton Hall. That International was no centralized state. The peace it promised was brought about by the festive assemblage of different things, the colorfulness of the flags and the innocent frontier markings which, as I was not a little astonished to discover, brought about no change in the landscape. The land they enclosed, however, and which I myself occupied, was a no-man's-land. Later, during the war, this word came to be used for the devastated space between the two fronts. But it is the faithful translation of the Greek—Aristophanic—word that I understood at the time all the better, the less I knew of it: utopia.[109]

Adorno's parents' house in Seeheimerstrasse in Oberrad implanted this promise of happiness in Theodor, their only child. But not just in him. The memory of this particular place recurs also in a letter of 28 March 1941 written by Adorno's oldest friend, Siegfried Kracauer, in the face of the historic catastrophe and after violent personal disagreements: "I am so delighted to see you. The more time passes, the closer I feel to Seeheimerstrasse—nothing can change that anymore."[110] As Adorno recollected in 1964, "for years, Kracauer," who was fourteen years the elder, "read the *Critique of Pure Reason* with me regularly on Saturday afternoons."[111] In later years the name of Kant always acts as a reminder of what German history has failed to make good: "His thought is centered upon the concept of autonomy, the self-responsibility of the reasoning individual instead of upon those blind dependencies, which include the unreflected supremacy of the national. According to Kant, the universal of reason realizes itself only in the individual."[112] Adorno's relationship with his parents' house almost always embodies his relation to tradition, but in the German Jewish history of the twentieth century, this always refers to the rift, or rather the rifts, whose presence in that history cannot be denied. The relationship between tradition and experience is described as precarious in Adorno's essay "Piano Duets, Once Again." The same may be said of "Words without Songs" ("Worte ohne Lieder"), which were written not long before, in 1931, and which have appeared in the *Collected Works* under the heading "Miscellaneous." They too reveal something specific about Adorno's experience in childhood. In fact, Adorno actually said as much to Kracauer, the literary editor of the *Frankfurter Zeitung,* to whom he had submitted them for publication.

The expectation of a trusted friend, the secret of this paradox, is not simply an individual matter. This pattern of experience reminds us, right down to the choice of individual words, of Georg Simmel, whom Kracauer knew well personally. Simmel's sociology of the stranger, which had a seminal influence posthumously on the Chicago School of sociology, generalizes the secular experience of the Jews of central Europe to the point of unrecognizability. They are converted into guests who, in accordance with a succinct formula of Simmel's, come today and stay tomorrow. Simmel's theory is expressed in universal terms, but it is easy to identify the specific experience underlying it. The vague universality of Simmel's ideas on strangers makes it a simple matter to transfer them to the relations between natives and immigrants, but his ideas can also be thought of as bearing the marks of the end of the long bourgeois century. The guest disrupts the unity of domestic existence; he reminds people of their own nomadic past. The orientalism fad of the late nineteenth century transformed this memory into a phantasmagoria. The child ceases to experience his house as a "mighty fortress"; it now comes to feel like an oasis or a caravanserai. With the guest, strangeness can be perceived in oneself: according to Hegel, this is the beginning of history. The bourgeois lifestyle of the end of the nineteenth century denies tradition by inventing it. The discovery of Jugendstil, which Benjamin so accurately described, led with a certain time lag to that of baroque, the misuse of which Adorno never ceased to castigate. The confusion of baroque and neo-baroque elements was part of the cityscape of Frankfurt that Adorno had before his eyes from childhood on. This included the famous Old Bridge, which had stood in front of the house in Schöne Aussicht before it was torn down to make way for a more modern one when Teddie was still a child. It also included the neo-baroque style of the university, which was built in 1914 but whose neo-baroque ornamentations were removed by the architect Ferdinand Kramer on the instructions of rector Max Horkheimer during renovations after 1950.

From the very opening of his novel *Ginster*, Siegfried Kracauer flirts with linguistic tropes which Simmel also reveled in. The relationship of the chief character, Ginster, to his hometown is summed up in the lapidary formulation, "Since, moreover, he grew up in F., he knew less about it than about other towns he had never visited."[113] The yearning for a "second home"[114] must have been great for both Wiesengrund-Adorno and Kracauer. Kracauer felt drawn to Paris, Adorno to Vienna. Adorno remembers the beginning of their friendship as the result of a family arrangement: "I was a student at the Gymnasium when I met him near the end of the First World War. A friend of my parents, Rosie Stern, had invited the two of us to their house. She was a tutor at the Philanthropinum, where Kracauer's uncle, the historiographer of the Frankfurt Jews, was a member of the faculty. As was probably our hostess' intention, an intensive contact sprang up between us."[115] The guest who now became a frequent visitor in Seeheimerstrasse was both like Adorno and somehow different: "To me Kracauer seemed, although not at all sentimental, a man with no skin, as though everything external attacked his defenseless interior; as though he could defend himself only by giving voice to his vulnerability. He had had a difficult time in his childhood, in more than one regard; as a pupil in the Klinger Upper School he had also suffered anti-Semitism, something quite unusual in the commercial city of Frankfurt, and a sort of joylessness hovered over his own milieu, despite its humane scholarly tradition."[116] Kracauer's lower-middle-class background contrasted sharply with the parvenu cultivation of the Wiesengrund-Adorno family in Oberrad, a background which threatened, however, to isolate Teddie, its infant prodigy.

It is obvious that Adorno's childhood was marked by a deep need for friendship. Kracauer, fourteen years older, opened up new vistas for him. The first phase of their friendship coincided with one of Kracauer's first publications; it appeared in the journal *Logos* in 1917–18. The reader can clearly see the influence of the last years of the German Empire as well as echoes of neo-Kantianism and pre-psychoanalytical psychology. In addition, one can discern the witty and elegant style of Georg Simmel, a thinker whom Kracauer greatly admired but against whom he rebelled intellectually in the 1920s: "People truly bound together in friendship are united by an original bond of affection that is not founded on intellectual agreement but is seldom without an element of sensual pleasure which is stimulated by the mere fact of being together. Where this is absent, no friendship will arise, however many emotional points of contact may be present."[117] Beneath the artificially smooth phrases entirely in the spirit of the fin de siècle, Kracauer's text reveals the feelings that periodically provoked profound irritation in his friendship with Adorno. Unlike Adorno, Kracauer had remained behind in America. But even Adorno's late writings, from the 1960s on, are unable to conceal his idiosyncratic reactions to their disagreements. It was simply "a troubled friendship," as Martin Jay succinctly summed it up in a little-known but informative study.[118] As early as Kracauer's essay on friendship of 1917–18, we can see how resemblances and differences prove to be the source of disagreement: "Even friends develop in different directions; the only condition of their friendship is that they should come together in all their essential principles and ideals, and that they should go forward together in enhancing their potential."[119]

The end of Kracauer's essay contains a utopian vision of friendship that reminds us of the essay Adorno would write some forty years later, with its idea of "a family born of freedom."[120] Kracauer sums up the essence of his view of friendship as follows: "It is an ideal, principled community of free, independent individuals, founded on the joint development of their typical potential. To develop together without losing one another, to give oneself so as to possess a larger version of oneself, to merge into oneness and yet to continue to exist separately for oneself: that is the secret of friendship."[121] Adorno's friendship with Kracauer frequently suffered blows to the stability that Kracauer saw as the essential condition of a successful friendship:

> If, however, one friend, unlike the other, has reached a certain stage in the development of his potential, he must unconsciously make use of the energy

released by his newly gained self-confidence, while the friend who has lagged behind succumbs to an influence, having nothing comparable to act as a counterweight. As he gropes his way, he feels humiliated, violated, and hampered at every step. Resentment takes possession of him. Against his will, his friend's actions, thoughts, and value judgments invade his mind and thrust aside his own fumbling initiatives. His instincts waver, his soul becomes dependent, feelings of impotence and weakness ensue. For his part, the friend has no choice but to continue to follow his own nature. Every attempt to mend the situation artificially would merely distort it the more. Only a resolute, temporary breach can bring redemption.[122]

With this word "redemption," Adorno concludes his essay "The Curious Realist" of 1964, his now famous reintroduction of Kracauer to the German public.[123] This memoir of Kracauer also sheds light on childhood, Adorno's as well as Kracauer's: "Freud's idea that the decisive points in the genesis of the individual occur during childhood is certainly true of the intelligible character. The childhood imago survives in the futile and compensatory determination to be a real adult."[124] The intellectual difference between Adorno and Kracauer can be pinpointed by looking at their childhoods. "Kracauer's experiential stance remained that of the foreigner, transposed into the realm of spirit. He thinks as though he had transformed the childhood trauma of problematic belongingness into a mode of vision for which everything appears as it would on a journey, and even what is gray and familiar becomes a colorful object of amazement."[125] Nevertheless, Kracauer's entrance into the apparently secure family environment of the Adorno-Wiesengrunds brought a destabilizing factor with it: that of a "problematic sense of belongingness."[126] For Kracauer, a yearning for friendship meant the hope for a home that could not be put in question: "We wish to have a home and to be a home for others. These needs complement each other like breathing in and out."[127] Kracauer's own character, which Adorno associates with his childhood trauma, coincides with the experience of "a newly emerged type of intellectual,"[128] one for which Scheler and Simmel, for example, had formulated the modes of a new way of living and thinking in advance. The Jewish origin of these intellectuals acquires a determining role by its very absence. The Jewish tradition no longer seemed viable to them, but it left unmistakable traces in the way they experienced life.

The fourteen-year age difference between Kracauer and Adorno marks a threshold. An only child, Kracauer had been born in Frankfurt in 1889. In his generation the break with the Jewish tradition of the large family was abrupt. His grandparents on his mother's side were already living in Frankfurt and had five daughters and two sons. The eldest daughter, Hedwig Oppenheim, married Isidor Kracauer in the 1880s; her younger sister Rosette married his brother Adolf, who was three years his senior. Adolf had entered the practical profession of textile salesman so as to enable his younger brother to become a rabbi. The Kracauers came originally from Silesia, a center of the textile industry in central Europe. As a traveling salesman, Siegfried's father commuted between Paris and Krakow; Isidor, the younger brother, studied first at the Theological Seminary in Breslau (now Wrocław), and subsequently he took classics, philology, history, geography, and German at the university. After graduating, he obtained a position as history teacher at the Philanthropinum in Frankfurt, a Jewish *Realschule* with a reputation for liberalism. It belonged to the Jewish community but was also attended by non-Jews. In 1885 Siegfried's aunt and uncle took over the running of the "Julius und Amalie Flersheim'sche Stiftung," a boarding school for poor, orphaned, or semi-orphaned Jewish children at Pfingstweidstrasse 14. As an only child, Siegfried liked spending time in the Ostend district of Frankfurt, as can be seen from the diaries that he began writing during his childhood. From 1898 to 1904 he attended the Philanthropinum and from 1904 to 1907 the Klinger Oberrealschule in Hermesweg. His father and his uncle died in 1918 and 1923, respectively. Kracauer lived with his mother and his aunt in the Nordend district. His career as correspondent for the *Frankfurter Zeitung* led him into exile in Paris via Berlin. His sisters, with whom he had shared the apartment at Sternstrasse 29, remained behind and were deported to Theresienstadt in 1942.

"In retrospect, it seems to me that, for all the friendliness I was shown, the catastrophe that befell his mother and her sister, who seemed to have an influence over him, in extreme old age had long been anticipated in the atmosphere of Kracauer's home."[129] A sentence like this, of which there are a number in Adorno's writings on Kracauer from the 1960s, relives differences that were the cause of painful irritations. The lower-middle-class Jewish atmosphere must have disconcerted the self-assured and good-looking youth, who seems to have attracted Kracauer for more reasons than one. Siegfried Kracauer wrote in a finely chiseled style, but he had suffered from a speech defect from childhood, and his schoolmates teased him on account of his appearance. Kracauer defended himself after his own fashion. Like the teachers, he kept a little red notebook in which he recorded his treatment at the hands of his fellows. "With him, many things were reactive; philosophy was in no small measure a medium of self-assertion."[130] Adorno seems to have wanted to show in retrospect that he, who had been the significantly younger man, had now left his friend behind. By repeated reference to Kracauer's closeness to Simmel and Scheler, Adorno highlights the generation gap to which Kracauer would never admit throughout his life. In the late texts on Kracauer—not just in "The Curious Realist" but also in his obituary for Kracauer three years later—he stresses just how much further he had advanced. There was no common source shared by the two of them. In retrospect, their former closeness is depicted with a gesture of superiority. Adorno's view distorts the reality, but posterity will thank him for providing a more perceptive insight into the feelings of authors who were so resistant to biographical probings. He would certainly have had to concede that his older friend had been the first to recognize "the sinister implications of the fad for biography."[131]

The difference in their ages conceals other differences that are even more significant and indeed could scarcely be greater between two young friends. On the one hand, the adored prodigy from a good middle-class family, on the other, a solitary, ugly boy born into straitened family circumstances and unable to find suitable companions. The persistence of visible Jewish traits in the Kracauers, even though they had cast off the religious tradition, must have perplexed the young Wiesengrund, who had grown up with the conviction that one's origins were a matter of chance. The strange title of his later appreciation of Kracauer, "The Curious Realist," points to this. We can still sense his mood in the perceptive remark about the way in which "Kracauer's adaptive strategy," which always had "cunning in it, a will to be done with what was inimical and powerful," had been "smuggled" into his theory of film.[132] Adorno quotes Kracauer's own words: "All these characters seem to yield to the powers that be and yet manage to outlast them."[133] Much earlier, in his "Travel Pictures," Heinrich Heine had already commented on this art of "outlasting" as a Jewish survival technique in a modern but only imperfectly secularized world. Much in the essay on Kracauer reminds us of Adorno's "Travel Pictures," above all "the primacy of the optical," which Adorno identifies in Kracauer's thought,[134] and also the idea of traveling as a way of distancing oneself from everyday experience. Adorno is still close enough to get under the skin of an intellectual non-Jewish Jew; but he is also too close not to react with unusual strength of feeling to the pressure of a trauma to which he had not been exposed in his own childhood.

Episodes from school are an integral part of the repertoire of memoirs, especially of Jewish German memoirs. Heinrich Heine's *Memoirs,* for example, play ironically with the new genre of autobiographies of famous people. They contain a passage that parodies the relationship between origins and childhood experience. Goethe's idealizing depiction of his ancestors in *Poetry and Truth* supplies the foil to Heine's text:

> My father was monosyllabic by nature, spoke rarely, and once, when I was still small, at a time when I spent my weekdays in the dreary Franciscan school and my Sundays at home, I took the opportunity to ask my father who my grandfather had been. He replied to my question half laughing, half crossly: "Your grandfather was a little Jew with a big beard." The next day, when I arrived at school, where I found my little classmates already assembled, I hastened to tell the important news that my grandfather was a little Jew who had a long beard. Scarcely had I finished telling them than this news flew from one pair of lips to the next and was repeated in every key, accompanied by a variety of animal imitations. The children leaped over tables and benches, tore the maths tables from the walls so that they flew to the floor alongside the inkwells, and all the while the children laughed, bleated, grunted, barked, and crowed—creating an unholy din whose constant refrain was my grandfather, who was a little Jew with a long beard. The teacher responsible for the class heard the noise and entered the room red in the face with fury and demanded to know who had started this riot. As always in such cases, everyone went quiet and tried to shift the blame, with the result that poor little me was convicted of having started the entire rumpus, and I atoned for my guilt with a severe thrashing.[135]

Erich Pfeiffer-Belli, a boy from an upper-middle-class family in Frankfurt, reports a similarly credible incident from Adorno's schooldays. In the playground of the Kaiser Wilhelm Gymnasium (now the Freiherr vom Stein School), he remembers Adorno as the "much admired but also rather envied" top boy:

> At home he was called Teddy, and this nickname had somehow become known in the *Gymnasium.* The playground, lined with young trees, was dusty and without shade. In the breaks the older boys used to promenade around in a circle while we younger ones rampaged around playing our games. Teddy had a few regular friends who, like him, had not noticed that some enemy or other had pinned a notice to his back with the word "Teddy" in large letters on it. In a

trice a howling mob started to chase him. At the time, Teddy was a rather slender, shy boy who did not actually understand what was going on.[136]

Rather casually written memoirs like these need to be taken with a grain of salt. Even the age difference between the two is not accurate: born in 1901, Pfeiffer-Belli was two years older than Adorno. But the atmosphere described seems to fit the precocious Adorno well enough and to capture the ambivalence with which he was regarded. In 1987 Pfeiffer-Belli seems unable to tell the story without commentary: "We all knew that Teddy was Jewish. The scene in the playground was no anti-Semitic demonstration; it arose from his singularity, the fact that in every class he put everyone else in the shade; it was a stupid schoolboy prank, nothing more."[137]

That sounds a bit too good to be true. Freud's warning about the lack of truth in autobiographies may be extended to the feelings of many Jewish high school pupils in what was still the imperial city of Frankfurt for whom the tensions that might be associated with anti-Semitism were more or less undetectable.[138] Even with hindsight, however, and in full knowledge of the genocide of the European Jews at the hands of German National Socialists, we see that statements about anti-Semitism in the Weimar Republic are often highly contradictory. Adorno repeatedly returned to this topic after 1938, ending up by developing a theory that what made Auschwitz possible was not hatred but *coldness*.[139] References to bullying in the school playground as a form of socialization turn up too frequently in Adorno's writings to allow us to describe his experiences there and on the way to school in all too innocuous terms. Pfeiffer-Belli included himself, as Reinhart Pabst's researches have shown, in what was called the "Harmless Club," consisting of five insolent boys who proudly posed for photographs. Some of them thought it a good joke to waylay "Tedchen Wiesengrund" on his way to school and shout, "Greetings to Father Abraham!" from some hiding place or other. These boys were indifferent to the fact that Teddie's mother was a Catholic and that he himself had been confirmed as a Protestant, thanks to a parson he had found intellectually stimulating. It did not stop them from bequeathing to him "the nightmare of childhood."[140] Peter von Haselberg's amusing account of Teddie's two mothers may have overlooked the fact that it was not simply because of Teddie's defective sense of "sportsmanship" that two adults accompanied him on his daily journey from Oberrad to Hedderichstrasse, where the Kaiser Wilhelm Gymnasium was located: "I remember hearing how upset the two ladies were about some harsh treatment the sensitive boy had received at the hands of his father, and on top of that there was the mockery of acquaintances from Offenbach who thought it was highly amusing to see the two women board the number 16 tram with Teddie and to stay on the lookout to make sure that nothing untoward happened to him."[141]

In *Minima Moralia*, Adorno included a section titled "The Bad Comrade," which he dated 1935, ten years earlier than the other reflections. He tells there of "the five patriots who set upon a single schoolfellow, thrashed him and, when he complained to the teacher, defamed him as a traitor to the class."[142] With hindsight, Adorno sees in these boys the precursors of the Third Reich, the outbreak of which did indeed take his "political judgement"[143] by surprise, but not his "unconscious fear."[144] An event like this brings his experience much closer to Kracauer's than the Adorno of the 1960s would like to think: "So closely had all the motifs of permanent catastrophe brushed me, so deeply were the warning signs of the German awakening burned into me, that I recognized them all in the features of Hitler's dictatorship: and it often seemed to my foolish terror as if the total State had been invented expressly against me, to inflict on me after all those things from which, in my childhood, its primeval form, I had been temporarily dispensed."[145] Adorno's recollection from the year 1935 is enacted in an intermediate space between dream and reality, and this is reflected by the large number of subjunctives in this text. Despite these, the reader does gain a sense of the bad comrades of his schooldays, of those "whose hallooing knew no bounds when the top boy blundered . . . who could not put together a correct sentence but found all of mine too long."[146]

Even after Adorno had established himself as a professor, the memory of his school experiences continued to rankle. His interpretation of the "taboos on the teaching profession" focuses on attitudes toward intellectual labor: "The ambivalence towards the knowledgeable person is archaic."[147] It is remarkable how often the word "resentment" recurs, which we have already encountered in his story about Herr Dreibus, his neighbor: "Out of resentment illiterates consider educated people to be insignificant as soon as the latter confront them with any kind of authority but without, like the higher clergy, assuming an elevated social status and exercising social power. The teacher is heir to the monk: the odium or the ambiguity associated with the monk's vocation was transferred to the teacher after monks had largely lost their function."[148] This ambivalent attitude toward teachers is compounded by their disciplinary powers. It is no doubt the case that the school tyrant with his cane at the ready had already become something of a rarity even in Adorno's own childhood, but as a "last memory trace,"[149] it had still not been finally eradicated from West German schools in the mid-1960s. "The reverse image of this ambivalence is the magical veneration in which teachers are held in many countries, as once in China, and in many groups, for example, among devout Jews. The magical aspect of this attitude towards teachers seems to be stronger wherever the vocation of teacher is bound up with religious authority whereas the negative association grows with the decline of such authority."[150]

The emphatic concept of German idealism continued to feed off this spirit. Helmuth Plessner, who had been born in Wiesbaden in 1892, was a philosopher of sociology whose path frequently crossed that of the Frankfurt critical theorists. It was he who coined the fitting expression "world piety" to sum up the idealized form of life of the educated German middle classes.[151]

The literature of protest against the authoritarian school to which the young Wiesengrund did not wish simply to subscribe throve on the contradiction between the ideals of humanist education and the everyday reality of school. The celebrated Goethe Gymnasium, like the Kaiser Wilhelm Gymnasium, which was more easily accessible from Oberrad and which only opened in 1914, were both considered to be reformed schools to which Jewish parents preferred to send their children instead of to the strongholds of traditional education. But because of the rapid developments in technology and industry, the humanist education of the *Gymnasium* already seemed more than a little stale. The goals of education based on classical German literature[152] seemed to have been undermined even though the cultured middle classes were still deeply attached to them. By around 1910 a clichéd notion of personality had already taken the place of the theory of the education of mankind, of which Adorno reminded his readers in his "Gloss on Personality" of 1966 with a quotation from Wilhelm von Humboldt: "Merely because both his thought and his action are possible only by virtue of a third thing, only by virtue of the representation and elaboration of something, of which the authentic distinguishing trait is that it is not-man, i.e. is world, man tries to grasp as much world as possible and to join it with himself as closely as he can."[153] In Adorno's childhood the validity of the traditional educational values of the German middle classes appeared to be self-evident in both the family and school.[154] In his juvenilia and also in Kracauer's essays in the early 1920s, we still encounter the cult of personality of the late bourgeoisie which Adorno subsequently wanted to see banished to "speeches around 1910."[155] Nevertheless, in his matriculation essay of Easter 1921 we still find him concluding: "To shape the world within the self is the meaning of life. Only by giving shape to the world does the self become a personality."[156]

As we can see from Kracauer's writings, the old powers of the educated middle class had not yet been overthrown by 1920, although they had been gravely undermined. In the essay Adorno wrote in 1958 describing his memories of his schoolteacher Reinhold Zickel, he dates the downfall of the "liberal assumptions about culture under which I had grown up" to the period just before he left school.[157] At any rate, it is abundantly clear that Kracauer's writings around this time revolve frequently around this question of lost meaning. As late as 1915, Kracauer's essay "The Experience of War" is contrasted with everyday middle-class life. As with his famous models Scheler and Simmel, the war represented a challenge to reformulate his criticism of the loss of meaning arising from the process of secularization:

> The life of the majority was enacted in a world of stale social conventions and professions. As the only supra-individual institutions, they made certain goals and possibilities for development available. If one were to leave this realm, one would find oneself in a vacuum; there was little otherwise to bind men together, and not only to bind them together but also to stimulate their loftiest ideals. Politics frequently repelled people as being too petty and was pursued only by a minority. Art likewise satisfied only individual, self-contained parts of the soul. Above all, the most important needs of the soul, its religious needs, lay fallow; there was no active, universally binding faith that was appropriate to our natures and that might have purified and sanctified them.[158]

At the time Kracauer was an enthusiastic supporter of the war, but he nevertheless separated the needs of "aesthetic human beings" from this general experience. These needs were defined for him by what Thomas Mann called "the feeling of isolation." Such a person finds "redemption" in the war: "By sinking into the mass and the renunciation of individuality, the soul receives the gift of immediate life."[159]

Against this background, Kracauer's essays on friendship of 1920 and 1921 can be read in a different light. The unequal friendship with Adorno was preceded by a yearning for friendship that survived the disappointments of the war. According to Kracauer, friendship was supposed to compensate for the inadequacies of bourgeois life: relationships "above all between men whose actions aspire to fulfill their typical dispositions in realms in which they can strive unceasingly for universal goals and in which one can feel at home only if one commits oneself with one's entire being. Artists and complete human beings of every kind are the relevant people here."[160] Here, too, we can feel almost physically the unresolved attitudes of the fin de siècle that underpin Kracauer's feelings of friendship for the schoolboy Wiesengrund-Adorno, "people of very unequal ages":

> Their relationship has a very different meaning for the feelings of each of the participants, but it is at least based on common experience and the blissful sense of equal aspirations. A young man just developing looks to his friend for confirmation of his plans, his spiritual nature. He relies on his older friend, even when he contradicts him; since his inner desire to expand has as yet gone unchecked, he likes the feeling that he is encountering definite limits. Still more or less inhibited, he does not really judge the relationship. He speaks his mind freely, expresses his views in lengthy monologues without being able to ask the older man for true reciprocity. He demands to be the center of attention and often takes just when he thinks he is giving, and gives generously just when he is most demanding. A sense of shame forbids him from becoming overconscious of the older man.[161]

In his friendships Kracauer appears to have been attracted by people different from himself—artists, "complete human beings," and people of a very different age group. Thomas Mann's *Tonio Kröger* was much in the minds of all young people around 1910. Kracauer's later novels *Ginster* and *Georg* are virtuoso variations on the way friends see things differently. His own real-life friendships with Max Flesch, Julius Hentzschel, and Otto Hainebach, the top boy in the Goethe Gymnasium who fell in the trenches in 1916, are transformed by Kracauer into literary constellations. These friendships contain a utopian dimension that is not immune to disappointments. They open up the possibility of life beyond the family, something we can find echoed in Adorno's memory of his school friend Erich: "When my friend Erich and I took some delight in using foreign words at the Gymnasium, we were acting as though we were already the bees' knees. It would be difficult to determine now whether this behaviour preceded the *rancune* or not; certainly the two went together very well."[162] Just as with the beginnings of the friendship with Kracauer, however, Adorno was able to indulge in provocative behavior as a schoolboy because he enjoyed the security of the Wiesengrund family tradition: "I will not deny that I sometimes followed the bad example of an elderly great-aunt. As a child, according to the family history, she had looked up the French word for 'kneading trough' in her French dictionary and then asked her poor tutor for it; when he had no answer she responded scornfully, Tsk! tsk! *La huche.*"[163]

Leo Löwenthal, who had got to know Adorno at the age of eighteen through Kracauer, also refers to Adorno's home background: "It was an existence you just had to love—if you were not dying of jealousy of this protected beautiful life—and in it Adorno had gained the confidence that never left him his entire life."[164] The comparison makes it quite clear: the atmosphere of the parental home distinguishes the Seeheimerstrasse from Kracauer's life at home but also from Benjamin's or Horkheimer's family backgrounds. Adorno himself kept thinking up new epithets from the plant world, such as "heliotrope" and "hothouse plant," to describe his childhood and the particular legacy of his home background. Mysteriously, work and economics somehow lay out of sight, beyond the child's horizon, not unlike the situation with Benjamin, the son of a *rentier:* "In early childhood I saw the first snow-shovellers in thin shabby clothes. Asking about them, I was told they were men without work who were given this job so that they could earn their bread. Then they get what they deserve, having to shovel snow, I cried out in rage, bursting uncontrollably into tears."[165] The contradictions of bourgeois existence are experienced from outside. Right down to his very last lectures, Adorno sustained the theme that alongside the legitimate criticism of the illusory nature of culture, we should not forget its civilizing influence: "[Culture] not only represses nature but conserves it through its repression; this resonates in the concept of culture, which originates in agriculture. Life has been perpetuated through culture, along with the idea of a decent life."[166] In the market-gardening environment of Oberrad, where both Kracauer and Löwenthal visited their younger friend, a secularized cultural utopia seemed to be a genuine possibility.

"Tradition in a strict sense is incompatible with bourgeois society."[167] Oscar Wiesengrund had established a bourgeois family and, apart from what was required professionally, had turned his back on the Jewish tradition. In this respect he was not unlike Leo Löwenthal's father, although, as a doctor in Bockenheim, the latter found it much harder to make ends meet. For Leo Löwenthal, despite his parents' strictly secular lifestyle, Jewishness remained a living reality, and the difference between his father's enlightened liberalism and his siblings' religiosity appears to have been simply a matter of choice. Kracauer has described Löwenthal and himself as "hybrids," caught between traditional Jewishness and a secularized present. Unlike Buber and Scholem, they were unable to find their way back to the Jewish religion, however constituted. Thanks to his youth, Wiesengrund-Adorno appeared to his older friends to have been exempted from the need to face up to this conflict. On 4 December 1921 Kracauer wrote to Löwenthal: "Something incomparable puts him in a position over both of us . . . , an admirable material existence . . . and a wonderfully self-confident character. . . . He truly is a beautiful specimen of a human being; even if I am not without some scepticism concerning his future, I am surely delighted by him in the present."[168]

3. | From Teddie Wiesengrund to Dr. Wiesengrund-Adorno

Experience is the union of tradition with an open yearning for what is foreign.

THEODOR W. ADORNO, "IN MEMORY OF EICHENDORFF"

Anyone who goes in search of Adorno in the 1920s will find no more than a few published documents and autobiographical statements tracing his personal development from the Wilhelminian age to the Weimar era. Nevertheless, he made an enduring impression on almost everyone he met. It is possible to glean some insight from accounts of these early friendships. Adorno, however, stands apart from the generation that in hindsight defines the intellectual picture of the age: Kracauer, Lukács, Benjamin, Bloch, and Horkheimer. All of them were old enough to have had to make a conscious decision whether or not to perform military service. The same may be said of those who later on were to become core members of the Institute for Social Research, such as Löwenthal and Marcuse, among whom the aftereffects of the enthusiasm for the war—disillusionment with it, involvement in revolutionary activity, and the subsequent disappointment—continued to reverberate. Teddie Wiesengrund was only a little younger than these men, but the difference was crucial; this dramatic turn of historical events, one that had been unimaginable even at the beginning of the decade, was something he experienced as a schoolboy. During these years the seemingly secure liberal cosmos was shaken to its foundations. The beautiful prospect [this is the meaning of *Schöne Aussicht*—Trans.] had clouded over, while "the open yearning for what is foreign"[1] had now been aroused. The new made its appearance in the shape of upheaval, the avant-garde, and revolution.

Early on, the young Wiesengrund had had more than his fill of the patriotism that had become rampant everywhere, even in the schools. We need not idealize the past to comprehend the distaste he and his boyhood friend Erich felt for the war propaganda surrounding them. He later recollected his childish resistance to it in "Words from Abroad:" "Foreign words constituted little cells of resistance to the nationalism of the First

World War. The pressure to think along prescribed lines forced resistance into devious and harmless paths, but in times of crisis gestures that are in themselves irrelevant acquire disproportionate significance."[2] After the initial national euphoria, liberal Jewish families like those of both Adorno and Löwenthal soon distanced themselves from the excesses of patriotism. There is evidence to back up claims of violent disagreements between Adorno and his teacher Reinhold Zickel, who went from teaching to the front and ended up back at the school as a war invalid. The fall of the imperial authorities coincided with the collapse of the traditional way of life. Decades later Adorno frequently referred to Paul Federn's pioneering essay in which Federn had coined the term "fatherless society." In his own essay, subsequently repudiated, on Zickel, who had in later years been more closely associated with National Socialism than Adorno realized when he was writing in 1958, Adorno addresses the question of the conflict over authority. "As Freud had already explained, I turned the autonomy I had learned from [Zickel] against him; I soon learned to defend myself, and we frequently quarreled about politics and also about modern art."[3] The "ill-starred"[4] Zickel, an extraordinary teacher, whom Adorno subsequently rediscovered in the ranks of his persecutors, returned to haunt him, confronting him in 1958 with the paradox of his own existence in post-1945 Germany: "reconciliation with the irrevocable."[5] By reflecting on the paradoxes of individual responsibility and social destiny, Adorno came up with the concept of "social biography"[6] in an attempt to make life narratives comprehensible for himself and later generations as a palimpsest of chance and conscious decisions.

In the second decade of the twentieth century we see a coming together of art and life, war and revolution, luxury and poverty. The boundaries between them become blurred. Frankfurt led a curious life behind the front, an uncanny atmosphere that was well captured by Kracauer in his novel *Ginster*. The celebrations on the outbreak of war that took hold of the public assembled on the square in front of the Opera House in August 1914 were combined with the ceremony for the opening of Frankfurt University in time for the winter semester. The Prussian minister of education Trott zu Solz compared the occasion with the glorious founding of Berlin University in 1810. The university's statutes are dated 1 August 1914. True enough, there were no special solemnities, but the shrill pathos of the "ideas of 1914" was unmistakable. Scholarship placed itself in the service of war, and not just in Frankfurt am Main. Kracauer's mentors, Simmel and

Scheler, did not scruple to give their unequivocal support to imperial Germany. Just as the Social Democrats' approval of war credits destroyed their reputation forever in the eyes of a generation of antiwar youth, so too were the intellectual and spiritual leaders of Germany discredited owing to their support for the war in 1914. This profound disillusionment has been largely ignored in the majority of institutional and intellectual histories. But it alone can explain the lifelong mistrust for traditional knowledge in the up-and-coming generation. In 1919 Max Horkheimer heard Max Weber lecture at Munich University. He never forgot how little the theorist of ideal types had to say about the concrete historical situation. In 1965, after hearing a lecture given by Talcott Parsons, the most famous American exponent of Weber's ideas at the time, Horkheimer recalled the "crass disappointment" he and his friends had felt on listening to Weber's discussion of the workers' councils: "It was all so precise, so strictly scientific, so value-free, that we all went home full of gloom."[7]

Kracauer's *Ginster,* too, records the uncanny feeling of alienation triggered in Kracauer by the public and the semiprivate behavior of great scholars—uncanny if only because many of their public statements must have seemed already familiar to him. He had confidently sent a copy of his essay "On the Experience of War," which he had written in 1915, to Max Scheler. Selmar Spier, Kracauer's friend and later his lawyer, remembered this essay in the *Preussische Jahrbücher* as a "skeptical first work."[8] This early piece of "patriotic" philosophy will come as a shock to anyone who has read *Ginster,* which appeared in 1928. But it is all the more valuable as a document of its times. Precisely because Kracauer is keen to introduce what he regards as indispensable elements of consciousness into patriotism, his text differs from the chauvinism of the age. But the naïve interweaving of freedom and service, ideal and reality, will seem startling to anyone familiar with the ironic thrust of Kracauer's later writings. Perhaps a man like Kracauer had first to experience the enthusiasm and the disillusionment himself before he could develop into a radical skeptic during the Weimar Republic. However that may be, it took him a decade to digest the experience: *Ginster* did not appear until 1928, when it was printed prior to publication in the *Frankfurter Zeitung.* This was one year after Arnold Zweig's pioneering war novel *The Case of Sergeant Grischa,* which likewise appeared before publication in the *Frankfurter Zeitung* in 1927. In his review "Who Is Ginster?" Joseph Roth focused on this transition: "It was the war, the completion of the normality in which the world had found itself for decades, that completed Ginster's development or enabled us to recognize that completed development." Roth, who felt an affinity with Kracauer as a writer, summed up the book in these words: "This is a book for simple people, quite simple people, in other words, human beings— none of whom who are 'normal' but are like Ginster: little, fearful, and abandoned. And who are being threatened by something more than human: by war, by 'education,' by culture, by 'reconstruction.' This is a book for quite simple people."[9]

If we glance back at the youthful intelligentsia of 1914, we do not find a uniform picture. The collections of letters that have come to light since the 1960s are full of gaps as far as this particular period is concerned. Not only did letters from abroad have to reckon with censorship, but in addition there were quarrels and silences even between close friends who were far from sympathizing with the war. Lukács, who at the time still called himself Georg von Lukács, became estranged from Ernst Bloch during this period. Both, however, sat in judgment on the older generation of intellectuals and scholars whose acquaintance they had cultivated before the war. There was a story going around that after 1 August, Max Weber dressed up in his uniform in order to receive visits from academic colleagues. Georg Simmel, like Max Scheler, gave patriotic lectures for the general public. Bloch is said to have snubbed him in a chance meeting in the tram in Heidelberg, for after sending him a letter highly critical of his support for the war, Bloch was surprised to have been greeted by his former mentor. In general, such letters were highly problematic. Walter Benjamin wrote a letter in March 1915 to his revered hero Gustav Wyneken announcing the end of their friendship. This was in reaction to a public talk by Wyneken, the inspiration behind the Youth Movement, with the title "War and Youth." In it he celebrated the war as an "ethical experience."[10] As late as the beginning of 1914 Benjamin had been president of the Berlin Freie Studentenschaft (Free Students Association), but the group around him became completely cut off on the outbreak of war, as his contemporary Bernhard Reichenbach recalled in 1962: "The worst experience at the time was this sudden realization that we were isolated from the great majority— yes, that's how it was—even from the people who had voted Benjamin in as president."[11] Benjamin's much-admired friend Christoph Friedrich Heinle, a poet who had just turned twenty, committed suicide on 8 August 1914 together with his girlfriend, Rita Seligson.

In his letter to Friedrich Podszus, who had written a biographical note for the 1961 German edition of *Illuminations,* Reichenbach gave a belated explanation of these events. He attempted, above all, to explain why, shortly after this shattering death of his friends, Benjamin had volunteered for the armed forces: "What had actually happened? We were all at an age when it was our turn, that is, to be called up. By volunteering, we at least had some chance of choosing where our training would take place so as not to be sent to some dreadful place on Lüneburg Heath or Pomerania. This was a way of ensuring that you could at least stay in Berlin for as long as possible in contact with people you liked."[12] The power of conformism is expressed in the wish to stay together and, with luck, to survive in a group of like-minded nonconformists. In these circumstances of being subject to an un-yielding majority, even friendships acquire a special flavor. The unique friendship between Walter Benjamin and Gershom Scholem dates from this moment, a relationship that looked forward from the outset to trans-forming the Wilhelminian normality that had prevailed hitherto. This led in Benjamin's case to the paradox of a solitary communism, while for Scholem the outcome was an almost equally unusual form of Zionism. To-ward the end of the war, both Benjamin and Scholem succeeded in reach-ing the haven of Switzerland, where they would be safe from being called up for military service. This was their first taste of exile, during which they made the acquaintance of Ernst Bloch.

The World War brought a similar experience of the conflict between individual and group to Max Horkheimer, who was somewhat younger. His early literary efforts testify to his rejection of war. It is easy to see how the fierce tensions between him and his parents had led him to reject the conformist values of imperial Germany. In contrast, his friend Friedrich Pollock, who, like Horkheimer, was a manufacturer's son from near Stutt-gart, was no less nonconformist but was still caught up in the war fever. Both had traveled abroad before the war, and for his part Horkheimer claimed it was this experience that prevented him from identifying with the arrogance of the Reich. It would be a mistake to assume that the future founders of the Institute for Social Research all shared the same attitudes. A number of similarities had to come together in order for the desire to bring about social change to assume the concrete shape of an organization. These included a protected childhood in the period of Wilhelminian nor-mality; the experience of war, both at the front and on the home front; an enthusiastic welcome to the fall of the monarchy; and disappointment over the failed attempts at revolution. It was Felix Weil who finally succeeded in persuading his father to set up the Institute for Social Research. It sounds completely plausible when, fifty years later, he mentions these factors as having been crucial in influencing this decision. His father had put the Weil villa at Zeppelinallee 77 at the disposal of the army, to be used as an officers' convalescent home. His son, who as an Argentine citizen was not liable for conscription, volunteered and was at least able to serve behind the lines. The Weil family history has proved fruitful as a source of myths. After Hanns Eisler learned about the financial origins of the institute during a luncheon with Horkheimer, he told Bertolt Brecht about it, and the latter maliciously used the story as the basis for his own *TUI Novel.* On 25 May 1942 he noted in his *Journals:*

> At horkheimer's with eisler for lunch. afterwards eisler suggests a plot for the *tui novel:* the story of the frankfurt sociological institute. a rich old man (weil, the speculator in wheat) dies, disturbed at the poverty in the world. In his will he leaves a large sum to set up an institute which will do research on the source of this poverty, which is, of course, himself. the activities of the institute take place at a time when the emperor too would like to see a name given to the source of the evil, since popular indignation is rising. the institute participates in the deliberations.[13]

This passage shows Brecht as a fertile creator of myth. The Weil story provided him with the material from which rumors are made. The story of the origins of the institute enabled him to launch his own project, the *TUI Novel.* In his conversations with Hans Bunge that were recorded in the German Democratic Republic in 1958 and 1962, Hanns Eisler showed that he was well aware of the way in which Brecht had modified the story to suit his own purposes. In response to Bunge's asking whether there really was a firm named Weil, Eisler replied: "Yes, with head offices in Argentina and Frankfurt. They're the big wheat traders. And it is really true that toward the end of his life, the father made a huge donation: a stunning building with a large number of rooms in it. It simply cries out for scholarship, and for forty years now people have been thinking hard about how all of that came about. It goes without saying that my way of putting it is plebeian. The ideas that are being produced there are quite different—but I think they are accurately explained in this way."[14]

Eisler and Brecht thought of the material as having the potential for a didactic piece about intellectuals, about the curious ramifications of the links between economics and ideas, but the particular features of the Weil story eluded their simplifying gaze. Only if one is fully aware of the circumstances is it possible to follow the tortuous path leading from the wholesale grain trade to the establishment of the institute. Hermann Weil had a breathtaking career in Wilhelminian Germany thanks to the success of the company he had founded in Buenos Aires. On 24 August 1917 this success even gained him access to the general headquarters of the armed forces. Together with his son Felix, he was received there by the Kaiser and invited to a working luncheon. Among the army's leaders Weil was considered to be a specialist in the world grain market whose expertise was in demand among some of the advocates of unlimited submarine warfare. They reformulated his reports for their own purposes, rewrote them in an old-fashioned German style, and published them in professional journals. These publications brought Weil the reputation of being a typical expatriate German ultranationalist. In his unfinished memoirs from the early 1970s, which regrettably have not found a publisher, Felix Weil disputes this portrait vigorously. He claims that Hermann Weil's reports were misused by the German navy for its own purposes and without his father's knowledge. Kurt Riezler, who at the time was the spokesman for the Reich chancellery, referred to Hermann Weil as a "swindler" in a diary entry for 9 June 1917. We must add that the chancellery was opposed to the strategy of unrestricted submarine warfare. Riezler's comment is particularly ironic since ten years later, when the Weils appeared at Frankfurt University as munificent patrons, Riezler had been appointed university registrar, and it was he who contributed in a major way to integrating the institute even though it was regarded with suspicion by many members of the faculty. The fact was that the Weimar Republic had turned many things upside down.

Hermann Weil's rise in society gives us something like a snapshot of the history of German Jews as a whole. He was born in 1868, the tenth child of a Jewish family who lived in rural Steinsfurt, close to Sinsheim on the river Elsenz. His father, Joseph Weil, as a village Jew, was barely able to eke out an existence. According to his grandson Felix, he "was a not exactly affluent farmer and cattle trader."[15] His three oldest sons had emigrated to Montgomery, Alabama, where they opened a general store. Hermann Weil never knew his eldest brother, Gustav. Their father took Hermann out of high school prematurely, and in 1883 he had him indentured for an apprenticeship in the grain trade with the Mannheim firm of Isidor Weismann & Co. Here he quickly rose to become the youngest chief clerk in the grain trade in Germany. At that time Mannheim was a center of the European grain trade: its inland port facilities and its grain exchange mediated between the great European cereal-growing areas and overseas markets. An unsatisfied hunger for education and a need for recognition filled Hermann Weil with a huge ambition to make use of his brains to advance himself socially. Although, or perhaps because, he had fallen in love with one of the daughters of the owner of the company, the talented businessman felt the need to abandon the narrow world of German business and seek his fortune on a larger stage. He studied Spanish in evening classes and then found a job with Mosco Z. Danon in Antwerp. A year and a half later he opened a branch for Danon in the Argentine, in which he himself owned a 20 percent share. In 1896 Hermann Weil was able to return to Mannheim, where he celebrated his wedding to his beloved Rosa according to the Orthodox rite—this on the insistence of his parents-in-law. But it was Argentina that he thought of as the grain-exporting country of the future. He therefore left Danon, and together with his two older brothers from Alabama, Samuel and Ferdinand, he established Weil Hermanos & Cia, the company whose name was known to Hanns Eisler. Danon was in fact ruined as the result of a speculation when he attempted to corner the grain market in order to drive up world market prices. Weil worked more cautiously, capitalized shrewdly on the growth of exports from the Argentine, and did achieve something like control of the Argentine grain market together with two even larger international firms—a position that Weil Hermanos maintained until around 1930.

Felix Weil was born in 1898, at the same time the firm was established. His personal life story reflects the world before 1914 and the transition to the Weimar Republic. His Argentine childhood lasted only until 1907, since his father wanted him to have the benefits of a humanist education. English and French families in Argentina likewise remained committed to their own educational systems. The humanist education that his father had been forced to give up in Sinsheim was something that Felix would now have the opportunity to acquire at the well-known Goethe Gymnasium in Frankfurt am Main. His grandmother on his mother's side and his aunt were already living in Frankfurt. His parents, who were soon to fall ill, returned a little later. From 1910 to 1914 they lived in luxury in the Hotel Imperial on Opernplatz while a suitably ostentatious villa was being built in Zeppelinallee. Even today the large gray building gives one an idea of the wealth of the man who had it built, and who at the time was still only forty-two. It was large enough to serve well into the 1960s and 1970s as the headquarters of the largest sporting association in the Western world: the German football league.

A comparison between the cramped house on Seeheimerstrasse, which seemed to Kracauer to be a bourgeois oasis, and the palatial villa in Frankfurt's diplomatic quarter illustrates the social divide between Wiesengrund the wine merchant and the upper-middle-class magnificence of the Weils—a distinction that can all too easily be obscured by such clichés as "he came from a well-to-do family." Historians and biographers commonly add the attribute "Jewish" to these descriptions, though this epithet too stands in need of further explanation. Throughout his life Felix insisted on being taken for an atheist, or to use his own term, an agnostic. He seems in this respect to have been of one mind with his father; it was solely to please his in-laws that Hermann's wedding in Mannheim had been conducted in accordance with Orthodox ritual. On his birth in Buenos Aires, Felix was given a saint's name, Lucio, because Catholicism in Argentina was regarded as natural unless one wished to make an explicit protest. But when, at a later date, in 1917 Royal Marshal von Reischach offered to have Hermann Weil elevated to the nobility on condition that he agreed to be baptized as a Protestant, he brusquely declined. He did not wish to follow the example of the Weinberg family, the owners of the Casella Works, who used this route to gain entry into Frankfurt's high society.[16] Hermann Weil attempted to establish himself as an affluent philanthropist in Frankfurt. His chosen sphere was medicine, since he suffered from syphilis and hoped to benefit from the advances brought about by Paul Ehrlich, the developer of salvarsan as a treatment for the disease. For Weil, however, Ehrlich's discovery came too late. Then, the Argentine location of Weil Hermanos turned out to have its attractions for the German war economy. On the outbreak of the war, the empire advanced Hermann 20 million gold pesos with which to lay in stocks of grain in Argentina. Felix describes how, after the war, when he wished to lend this money to the republic at a 10 percent profit, he ran into great difficulties because the new finance minister knew nothing about Hermann's secret dealings with the previous government.

Loyalty was the keyword—an obligation that was taken particularly seriously by Jewish citizens who wished to shed their outsider status. This description fit a nouveau riche parvenu like Hermann Weil like a glove. Looking back on the age, Selmar Spier notes: "Young Jewish men poured into the barracks, just like their Christian contemporaries; they too were driven by an old thought pattern, albeit one valid only for Jews: blood sacrifices guarantee equal rights."[17] In 1914 the overseas world changed for German expatriates as well. In the United States you had to decide quite promptly whether you wished to be an expatriate German or an American patriot. In neutral Argentina the country was divided up according to national allegiances which had been preserved among the upper classes by the education system. Felix Weil, whose class in the Goethe Gymnasium qualified for its graduation certificate in 1916, did not rest until he had been called up, notwithstanding his Argentine citizenship. Whereas members of the older generation wished to demonstrate their loyalty to the state and the society that had enabled them to prosper, in the case of the younger people there was a general loyalty to their own generation which even earlier had induced young Jews such as Walter Benjamin to join the Youth Movement. This loyalty concealed feelings and attachments that were of crucial importance for their subsequent development; its more abstract dimension persisted in the need for solidarity, while the more concrete aspect throve in friendships that survived even extreme disagreements over politics and the realm of ideas. As late as 1969 Adorno attempted to clarify this longing with reference to Benjamin: "Over and above this, an influential factor may have been the loneliness from which Benjamin suffered and to which he had been condemned by an exceptional disposition which aroused feelings of rancor in others. Great was his yearning to be able to fit into communities, and to serve new orders, in practical ways too. This impulse formally prepared the way in his youth for a tendency that subsequently took a political direction."[18]

Felix Weil's activities cannot be understood in isolation from his frantic search for love, friendship, and solidarity. Georg Grosz, who received assistance from him during the Weimar period and also later on in New York, regarded "Lix," as he called his generous benefactor, as a "natural Maecenas." Our understanding of Weil's motives is not improved by resorting to the cliché of a father-son conflict, even in the variation involving the father's financial career and the son's academic pursuits. Felix wished to dedicate his unpublished memoirs to "the memory of my father."[19] Almost half a century after his father's death, Felix was concerned to dispel the odium of a reputation based on "speculating" that had attached itself to the name of Weil. Instead of dividing them, his father's philanthropic activities brought them closer together. Having suffered from their separation during his childhood, Felix sought greater closeness to his father throughout his adult life. He had also suffered from his mother's remoteness, a consequence of the family's grand bourgeois lifestyle. Felix and his sister were merely paraded before her in the afternoons in their best clothes. The well-protected but lonely child found a sense of closeness and warmth only with his Indian nurse and cook. His parents returned to Germany simply because they had fallen ill; his mother, who had remained as remote as ever, died of cancer even before they moved into their new villa in Frankfurt. His father's mysterious sickness filled the son with a horror of physical love, since he had been left in the dark about the causes and consequences of syphilis. Felix wanted to be like his contemporaries, but he found it hard. Eventually he took a half-day job in the Frankfurt War Office, while studying economics the rest of the day and keeping open the option of a business career. While studying, he tried to form contacts with other students, chiefly by joining Cimbria, a somewhat old-fashioned student organization that attempted to maintain the liberal traditions of Saint Paul's Church in the 1848 revolution. Originally Cimbria had been called Francofurtia, but the name had been changed because of the ridicule it provoked.[20]

On 10 November 1918 the revolutionary Workers' and Soldiers' Council occupied the luxury hotel the Frankfurter Hof and turned it into its headquarters. The young liberal student Felix Weil, wearing full corporation colors—that is, with sash, cap, and watch-chain ribbon—hurried downtown together with a fellow student, his "fag," and they placed themselves at the disposition of the revolution. They were at once given the task of "seizing" a machine gun depot in the Festival Hall. Minimally armed and basically clueless about weapons, they set out bravely and were able to storm the enemy position without difficulty, since the defenders had already taken to their heels, abandoning the machine guns (which had no ammunition anyway). Amidst great jubilation, the ten machine guns were brought back to the Frankfurter Hof. The following day, the requisite munitions were received from the neighboring Soldiers' Council in Mainz. The day after that, the well-known Social Democrat lawyer and professor Hugo Sinsheimer took control of police headquarters and set up patrols composed of members of the workers' militia. The aim was to establish an alternative to the professional police, who were now widely mistrusted, as well as to the sailors under the command of the legendary swashbuckler Stickelmann, who were felt to be unreliable. Having come to know Felix Weil through his activities in the student union, Sinsheimer included him in this organization, which consisted otherwise of trusted workers. The following night, when there was little opportunity for sleep, Weil borrowed a copy of a Social Democratic Party (SPD) training manual from a worker in which he came across the text of the 1891 "Erfurt Program." It seems very plausible that the young economics student and heir to millions may have concluded that the ideas this contained about the transformation of private ownership of the means of production into social property offered a clear way out of the chaos of the collapse of the nation. At any rate, in the following years "socialization" was to become his chief theme.

Once the situation in Frankfurt had calmed down, Hugo Sinsheimer and Felix Weil, the policemen created by the revolution, returned to the university. Sinsheimer was harassed by nationalist students who disrupted his lectures with anti-Semitic demonstrations against the "Jew and Soviet chief of police." Lix joined a socialist group in Frankfurt. The only other member of what was to become the Institute for Social Research to have joined the same group was the young Leo Löwenthal. Pollock and Horkheimer were in Munich at the time. Thanks to the encounter with socialist workers and the disappointing outcome of the revolution—a set of events which credible witnesses believed to be unworthy of the name—people's attitudes had undergone a change. "Careerism" now became a term of abuse among the socialist students, one they used to distance themselves from the bourgeois wish to better oneself that was typical of their parents' generation. These students now wanted to prepare for the authentic revolution which they felt was imminent. But they could find no teachers at the university who could give them any help. Felix Weil left Frankfurt, and for a brief, turbulent period he studied in Tübingen until he was thrown out of Württemberg as an undesirable alien. The million gold pesos he inherited directly from his mother enabled him to behave like a generous benefactor, but his Argentine passport kept forcing him back into the role of an outsider—sometimes, indeed, for his own good. In Tübingen he quickly became further radicalized. In the course of his activities he met Clara Zetkin, the internationally famous veteran of the workers' movement, who lived not far from Stuttgart. Now in her sixties, she had abandoned the Social Democrats and turned toward the newly founded Communist Party. Even in his later memoirs from the early 1970s Weil still speaks affectionately of this political mother figure, who soon introduced him to people such as Karl Radek, one of the most iridescent figures and outstanding emissaries of the Communist International, mediating between Germany and the Soviet Union. For all Weil's enthusiasm for his new comrades, his Argentine passport prevented him from joining any parties, since any partisan political activity would leave him, as a foreigner, in an untenable legal position. But by the same token, he also remained the master of his own private assets and was well placed to bring people together who would probably have remained unknown to one another without his intervention. The independence from all political parties that would later characterize the Institute for Social Research, and hence ensure that the Critical Theorists would have a unique position in the German political landscape, was in effect preordained by the foreign status of its benefactor.

This unique institute, one that would preserve Adorno from isolation in his exile in the United States and become in effect a home away from home, was the product of the spirit of practical socialism,[21] surprising though this may seem when one considers the legends that have grown up about its origins. Its beginnings can be traced back to the First Marxist Work Week, which took place in May 1923 in Ilmenau in Thuringia and was attended by around twenty-five people. In Felix Weil's memoirs, people and dates all merge together around 1922. What is certain is that the Second Marxist Work Week never took place even though one had been planned. With his father's assistance, Felix Weil succeeded in founding the Institute for Social Research at Frankfurt University. On 22 June 1924 it was officially inaugurated with a formal ceremony as an institute "at" (*an*, i.e., not "of") the university—the "at" is itself programmatic. The Weils wanted to secure the survival of the institute both against changes in political majorities and also against any interference by the Faculty of Economics and Social Science, which was far from being well disposed toward the new foundation. Although the innocent-sounding name Institute for Social Research had been chosen, it was widely suspected that Marxism was to be officially introduced into the university. The setting up of sociology institutes was very much in fashion; the Social Democrats, who were in power in Prussia, were promoting sociology as the spearhead of modernization in such bastions of conservatism as the German universities. The Frankfurt institute became the focal point of an independent intelligentsia that wished to break with its bourgeois origins but whose members were reluctant, apart from a few exceptions, to submit to the discipline of a political party.

Felix Weil had originally envisaged that Kurt Gerlach would be the first director, but in 1922 Gerlach unexpectedly died of diabetes. Gerlach's background, like Weil's, had been in economics. Before the war he had spent time in England, where he had come into contact with the Fabian Society, whose pragmatic socialism had also appealed to Karl Korsch, a later friend of Weil's. The project of founding the institute brought father and son close together again, once Lix had demonstrated to his father with a year-long interlude in the Argentine that he had no talent for the wheat trade. He was not even able to turn his contacts with the Soviet Union to his commercial advantage, for even though the young revolutionary state was threatened with famine and was in urgent need of wheat, Felix showed himself to be more interested in the survival of the revolution than in any increase in his own private wealth. Social Democracy's dangerous loss of authority after 1920 had also made his father mistrustful of the prospects of the Weimar Republic. His pessimism is very evident in a letter he wrote to Georg Voigt, the mayor of Frankfurt, in 1923: "I have been engaged in philanthropic works for a long time now, and would have done even more had I not been so disgusted by the activities of the anti-Semites and the murders of Rathenau and Erzberger."[22] For Hermann Weil, the political re-actionaries were not an option. Like the upwardly mobile members of the middle class in the nineteenth century, he believed in scientific progress—an attitude that had animated the many Jewish co-founders of the university, with Wilhelm Merton first and foremost among them. But war and inflation had consumed the wealth of the founders and hence of the young university as well. Up to 1918 the Social Democrats had regarded the university simply as a reservoir of potential middle-class recruits. Now, however, political support was needed if the young institution was to survive. Reform projects such as the Frankfurt Academy of Labor, in which once again we find Hugo Sinsheimer playing an active role, made the university acceptable to the mainstream Social Democrats, with their respect for culture. Only in this way can we explain the fact that upper-middle-class families like the Weils could find common ground with a Prussian bureaucracy under the leadership of Social Democrats.

The war and the revolution had radicalized everyone who was of importance to the institute that was yet to be established. Kurt Albert Gerlach, the son of a Hanoverian manufacturer, had written a doctoral thesis under the supervision of Ferdinand Tönnies, the pioneer of sociology and author of *Community and Association*. From 1913 he had worked in the Kiel Institute for International Economy and Maritime Trade. Periods of research in England and contradictory experiences with the war economy aroused his interest in the situation of the workers, Marxism, and a planned economy. Gerlach's energetic assistant, Richard Sorge, had joined the Communist Party (KPD) shortly after its foundation. His appointment to a post at the institute encouraged the rumor that he was there as the Trojan horse of the KPD. The two Weils, father and son, were attempting to square the circle: they wanted to establish an academically respectable institution, but one that would be controlled by an independent Society for Social Research. Karl Korsch had become a prominent member of the newly founded United Communist Party in 1920, but his prominence as a card-carrying commu- nist ruled him out for the directorship of an academic institute. After Gustav Meyer, the Social Democrat and well-known biographer of Engels, also declined, the old Austro-Marxist Carl Grünberg turned out to be the ideal choice. The first director of the institute was internationally recog- nized as a scholar, but he left the young people chosen by Weil and his friends free to design their own teaching programs and to run a left-wing publishing house from within the institute building. This publishing house collaborated with the Moscow Marx-Engels Archives to produce the great edition of the works of Marx and Engels, the MEGA. All these activities were coordinated primarily by Friedrich Pollock, Max Horkheimer's clos- est friend. Like Felix Weil, Pollock had studied economics, and he was connected with Weil both professionally and personally through his mar- riage to Weil's cousin Carlotta. From the outset, Pollock acted as a kind of institute manager. Between 1928 and 1930, following Grünberg's retirement he was the caretaker director until Max Horkheimer could formally take over the reins.

Pollock was the man who was closest to Horkheimer throughout his life. Even the young Teddie Wiesengrund thought of the two as an indissol- uble unit, living together as they did in a house in Kronberg that was far superior to normal student living quarters. They lived there "in some se- clusion but with an evident dislike of furnished rooms."[23] Adorno's de- scription in 1965 of Horkheimer, who was eight years older than he, as "a young gentleman from a well-to-do family who displayed a certain de- tached interest in scholarship"[24] could be applied with equal justice to Pollock. The appearance of this pair of friends must also have impressed Felix Weil, a man who was accustomed to arriving at the university in a chauffeur-driven car. Lix had renounced this convenience only in his most radical days in Tübingen. In a conversation in 1965 in which he recalled those times, Friedrich Pollock also commented on the sociological similarities between the somewhat older Pollock and Horkheimer as a factor that must have favorably impressed Felix Weil: "For the most part students lived in more or less precarious circumstances at the time, and here were two people who were financially independent, since each had a wealthy father. Well, he made friends with the two of them and sought their advice. The upshot was that the Institute for Social Research was founded by Horkheimer, Felix Weil, and me in the castle garden in Kronberg; initially it was just an idea. . . . We had a house in Kronberg in the Taunus, and Weil often came out to see us."[25]

Both Horkheimer and Pollock were the sons of factory owners and had experienced real conflicts with their fathers. In the early 1920s Horkheimer was unsure whether he should make an academic career for himself or go back after all to his father's firm. In the Pollock family, the estrangement between father and son was likewise far advanced. The resourceful Pollock was on the lookout for alternatives, and he soon realized that Hermann Weil, who was seriously ill at the time, was an "ingenious man" from whom more was to be expected than from Horkheimer's father or his own: "Although he was a multimillionaire, he understood that such phenomena as Russian Bolshevism, German Marxism, German Social Democracy, anti-Semitism, and the trade unions were all matters that merited *scientific* study, as opposed to research carried out by political parties."[26] The problematic development of Weimar democracy seems to have unsettled Weil senior, and he evidently thought of anti-Semitism as a genuine but unexplored issue. At almost exactly the same time, Max Weber had remarked that in practice it was impossible for young Jews to contemplate an academic career. The older generation of Jewish intellectuals under the empire—Simmel, Scheler, and Husserl, for example—had experienced immensely tortuous careers and religious dislocations, including baptism, which was not an option in the Weils' case for either father or son. Another factor may have been involved here, too. Felix had been repelled by the immoral practice of grain speculation, but his hostility toward his father's conduct of the business was less extreme than in Horkheimer's case. In the course of his training as a manager, Max had witnessed the extent of the physical and moral degradation of the women textile workers in his father's factory. Overwhelmed by indignation at the social injustice of it all, he fled the shop floor at the textile factory and, while working in the office, fell in love with a secretary, a relationship that his parents regarded as a *mésalliance*. The daughter of a bankrupt Christian innkeeper, she did not fit the family tradition of the Bavarian commercial counsellor in whose household the Jewish dietary laws were still maintained. Pollock, by contrast, grew up in a secularized household. His relations with his father were very fraught, whereas Felix Weil always sought closeness with his own father. As a commercial trader, Hermann Weil was highly critical of the exploitative practices of industrial capitalism, regarding them as a source of justified indignation on the part of the exploited workers. Hermann Weil's interest in the development of labor law, a subject to which Hugo Sinsheimer had devoted his efforts, emerged quite logically from his reflections on the aimless unrest that characterized the early Weimar years.

The tendency of young Jewish intellectuals to form a peer group may be linked to the loneliness of this first generation of only children, in contrast to both traditional Jewish families and non-Jewish middle-class ones. Teddie Wiesengrund was a late-maturing prodigy, and his relations with people his own age were not exactly straightforward; this tendency may help to explain why it was he who took the initiative in introducing himself to the older student Max Horkheimer right after a seminar with the psychologist Adhémar Gelb and made special efforts to associate with him. This was in 1921. Adorno's early friendships, both with Kracauer and from around 1923 with Benjamin, have something of the quality of brotherly love about them, and this may have helped to compensate for his breach with a Jewish tradition that had ceased to be viable at the same time that it exposed him to social rejection. Among middle-class Jews of the turn of the century, the transition to the small family was effected even more rapidly than in the rest of society. A generation previously, four to five children had been the norm. The clash between tradition and the new lifeworld was even more dramatic in the case of the Horkheimer family in Stuttgart. The title Horkheimer gave to the institute's first major joint study, "Authority and the Family," seems like a commentary on his own experience of the altered circumstances that determine the individual, right down to his personal feelings. The war had made Jewish participants aware of their special situation. Bitter feelings of disillusionment about German society had been aroused by the populist agitation against Jewish "draft dodgers," and this had been exacerbated by the discriminatory nature of the official "Jew census" of 1916, which counted the Jews serving in the German army. In his character Werner Bertin, Arnold Zweig has captured in exemplary fashion the experience of a Jewish intellectual who goes through the war among ordinary soldiers in a labor battalion. Leo Löwenthal was by no means unique in returning to his secular middle-class home an enthusiastic Zionist. Felix Weil's determination to launch the First Marxist Work Week would not really be comprehensible unless we postulated something like a longing for a peer group appropriate to the new situation.

By 1923 the first flush of enthusiasm for revolution had faded. Relatively little was known about the Russian Revolution; the German Revolution had left widespread disillusionment behind in everyone who had looked to it for fundamental change. The German soviet republics had been put down with much bloodshed in Bremen and especially in Munich and were now no more than brief, soon-to-be-forgotten episodes, although for Horkheimer and Pollock they had been drastic lessons in politics of decisive importance for their entire lives. Even more shattering was the impact on young, politically inexperienced contemporaries of the bloody end of the Hungarian soviet republic. One of the most important participants in the First Marxist Work Week had been a member of its government as People's Commissar for Culture. This was Georg Lukács. His life history sounded adventurous enough even in 1923, when he was in his late thirties. His father, Josef Löwinger, had risen from being a small businessman in Szeged to become a director of the leading Hungarian bank, the Budapester Kreditanstalt, which had brought him the rank of consul in Budapest. In recognition of his services, he had been elevated to the nobility and had taken the name von Lukács. Little Georg, or György, already had the demeanor of a young master. His having remarked as a child, "I never say hello to strange visitors. I didn't invite them,"[27] was one of the stories reported by his mother. Shortly before his death in 1971, Lukács declared to the amazement of his audience, "I always realized that I was a Jew, but it never had a significant influence on my development."[28] His first book, *Soul and Form,* published in both German and Hungarian, opens with a letter to his friend Leo Popper, "On the Nature and Form of the Essay." The first essay in Adorno's *Notes to Literature* bears the title "The Essay as Form." Although the texts are separated by forty years, Adorno's reflections follow from those of Lukács. Teddie's readings with Kracauer in Seeheimerstrasse had not been confined to Kant. They also read Lukács's *Theory of the Novel,* which had been creating a furor at the time. A motif common to both men was their criticism of the excessive influence of science on thought. Adorno's extreme response to the later Lukács can be explained as a reaction to his closeness to ideas developed by the early

Lukács. After his first successes as a writer, Lukács left Budapest and went to Berlin and Heidelberg, where he came into contact with Simmel and Max Weber among others. Together with Ernst Bloch, who was his exact contemporary, he formed a feared duo of intellectual friends who created widespread panic in salons and seminars in Heidelberg before the outbreak of the First World War.

Early in the war Lukács wrote his *Theory of the Novel*, in which he described the world as being in a condition of "absolute sinfulness." His reflections on the state of the novel from the standpoint of the philosophy of history led him to a social prognosis: "It will then be the task of historico-philosophical interpretation to decide whether we are really about to leave the age of absolute sinfulness or whether the new has no other herald but our hopes; those hopes which are signs of a world to come, still so weak that it can easily be crushed by the sterile power of the merely existent."[29] Seldom has the end of the bourgeois age been encapsulated so aptly in the mirror of the pre-bourgeois world as in the writings of the early Lukács. Because of the war, this book could not appear before 1920, and by 1923 his next book, *History and Class Consciousness,* had been published, partly with the assistance of Felix Weil. In this book his aesthetic critique of the bourgeois age was transformed into an idealizing version of communism. Lenin, who came across some of the political articles of the young communist, completely rejected Lukács's idealistic communism: "Their Marxism is a Marxism of mere words."[30] Nevertheless, the intelligentsia in the young Weimar Republic, who were interested in theory, took a different view. In the chaos of the new age, Lukács's road from that of a literary scholar with purely aesthetic interests to that of a radical social critic appeared as a genuine *via regia* to many people in search of new ways of thinking. No wonder Lukács's ideas as they were expressed in *History and Class Consciousness* were the center of attention at the First Marxist Work Week in Thuringia. The only person there competent to debate with Lukács was Karl Korsch, who had the manuscript of his book *Marxism and Philosophy* in his pocket, a book that was likewise destined to be published by Malik Verlag with the financial support of Felix Weil. In this revolutionary text Korsch attempted "an application of the materialist conception of history . . . to the materialist conception of history itself."[31]

In 1923 the little Thuringian town of Ilmenau witnessed what can only be thought of as the most advanced intellectual debate about Marxism and revolution conceivable at the time. On the one hand, the distance from the

Russian Revolution made possible a theoretical discussion that would have been inconceivable in Russia itself, given the conditions obtaining under wartime communism, including widespread famine. On the other hand, the radical nature of the theoretical positions assumed was frighteningly abstract. The identity of politics and theory was achieved by cleansing ideas of almost all empirical content. This applies in particular to the Lukács of *History and Class Consciousness* and his eagerness to salvage German idealism by inserting it into the framework of an idealized party communism. His theory opened up a new role for intellectuals of the kind that had once placed philosophers at the side of kings. By denying the bourgeois individuality which had stamped him with the mark of impotence, the new intellectual moves into the center of world history. In exchange for submitting to a superior discipline, he becomes part of an idealized global party that must be viewed as the spearhead of a revolutionary turn of events. We may be at a loss nowadays to explain why an abstract theory such as this was able to exert such an irresistible fascination, even on the young Wiesengrund in Seeheimerstrasse. The attractions of this political idealism dressed up in its left-wing clothing can be understood only in the light of the deep traumas experienced by bourgeois liberalism and its concomitant notions of progress and education.

The rapid succession of publications between 1920 and 1924, from *The Theory of the Novel* and *History and Class Consciousness* on, documents the leave-taking from the old Europe. The end of the First World War witnessed the overthrow in central and eastern Europe not of modern republics but of ancient dynasties. It would not occur to anyone who reads *History and Class Consciousness,* knowing nothing of Georg Lukács, that ten years previously the same author had been reflecting on the nature of the bourgeois and *l'art pour l'art.* But the blunt juxtaposition of art and politics is precisely what was so fascinating about the young Lukács. Opportunities seem to have opened up for youthful intellectuals who wished to cease being bourgeois; for a brief moment in Europe around 1920, political radicalism and avant-garde artistic consciousness converged. The moment quickly passed, and Lukács was soon forced to submit to the discipline of the Comintern. He then developed into the advocate of a literary realism that tended to condemn the new revolutionary narrative techniques. Kafka, whose writings overwhelmed aesthetic radicals such as Benjamin and Adorno, was for a long time simply rejected out of hand. As early as the Expressionism debate of the early 1930s, Lukács found himself at loggerheads with his former friend Ernst Bloch, who was indifferent to party discipline on matters relating to art. For his part, Lukács always turned up his nose at the idea of free-floating intellectuals. Even after his own terrible experiences in Moscow during the Stalin era and in Hungary in 1956, when he escaped persecution by the skin of his teeth, he still felt he could accuse Adorno of living, like Schopenhauer, in the "Grand Hotel Abyss," "a modern luxury hotel, furnished with every comfort, on the brink of the abyss, nothingness and futility. And the daily sight of the abyss, between the leisurely enjoyment of meals or works of art, can only enhance one's pleasure in this elegant comfort."[32] Lukács thus appears to wish to denounce the alternative possibility of an intellectual life far from political power. For his part, in the 1960s Adorno did not hesitate to unleash a vitriolic critique of Lukács for his "Extorted Reconciliation [with Stalinism],"[33] a critique that can be explained only by his disillusionment with an intellectual he had once admired. Here too we are dealing with "minima moralia." In Adorno's view, it is true that there can be "no good life within the bad one,"[34] but this statement is not intended to exonerate intellectual capitulation.

Adorno's early intellectual closeness to Lukács's work can also be seen in his second doctoral thesis, *Kierkegaard: Construction of the Aesthetic,* which "appeared the day Hitler seized the dictatorship."[35] Although his citation of secondary literature is quite short, Adorno includes no fewer than three references to Lukács—to *Soul and Form, The Theory of the Novel,* and *History and Class Consciousness*—apparently without noticing the fundamental contradictions among these books. The interweaving of art and politics even in an academic study seems to have presented no difficulties for Adorno at the time. In the Kierkegaard book a theme that preoccupied him throughout his life reaches a provisional conclusion: his critique of idealism as the bourgeois ideology par excellence. This critique, however, comes not from outside but from the interior of bourgeois life. Adorno repeatedly returned to this theme, evidently in the belief that Lukács had not dealt with it satisfactorily. What he reproached Kierkegaard with in 1933 is what he would later accuse Lukács of, namely, subscribing to a "reactionary classicism."[36] This inability to take his leave of the bourgeois world even though the critic is able to see through its falseness remained the theme of the Weimar intellectuals long after Weimar itself had ceased to exist. War, revolution, and inflation had undermined the bourgeois way of life, but in the sphere of culture, the world before 1914 seemed to live on. A new generation of cultural critics continued to pick holes in the façade of a bourgeois culture that had existed throughout the long nineteenth century. The failure of bourgeois promises of emancipation exerted a pressure that turned this new generation into social critics. This was as true of Bloch and Lukács as of Kracauer and Benjamin. The young Wiesengrund-Adorno turned them all into key witnesses in his Kierkegaard critique, as we can see from the sparse quotations in his book. The book itself is dedicated to his "friend Siegfried Kracauer."[37]

Despite the personal dedication, Kracauer went ahead with a review of the book for the *Frankfurter Zeitung*. But the proofs were left lying around in the cellar and did not see the light of day until 1990, when the review appeared as part of the posthumous publication of his *Schriften*. The article apparently fell victim to the paper's attempt to adjust to the new National Socialist regime early in 1933. "Kierkegaard Revealed" in fact contains the central ideas that had been discussed by Kracauer and Adorno in the first decade of their friendship. Kracauer's intention in writing the review was evidently to demonstrate "the solidarity of people who have identical or similar views."[38] Even today one cannot but admire Kracauer's ability to unlock a text that is opaque and extremely hard to read. At its center Kracauer discerned "a very incisive critique of *late idealist thinking*."[39] This motif was one that had emerged in the discussions between Kracauer and Teddie in the course of their readings of Kant in Seeheimerstrasse. Amidst the ruins of academic neo-Kantianism, Kracauer had succeeded in bringing Kant back to life. In 1964, in a radio talk which provided the basis for his essay "The Curious Realist," an essay which had both delighted Kracauer and disconcerted him, Adorno confessed: "As he presented it to me, Kant's critical philosophy was not simply a system of transcendental idealism. Rather, he showed me how the objective-ontological and subjective-idealist moments warred within it, how the more eloquent passages within the work are the wounds this conflict has left in the theory.[40] It was not simply "the anti-systematic tendency in Kracauer's thought" that he remembered; he also emphasized "Kracauer's [and his own] aversion to idealism."[41] But the rejection of a neo-Kantianism that relegated philosophy to an academic backwater far from any kind of material concerns could not exactly amount to a promising career move.

The first philosopher at the newly established University of Frankfurt, Hans Cornelius, does not appear to have been a colorless academic by today's standards, but all his students were forced to pass through the eye of the needle of neo-Kantianism. We can see this from the doctoral and *Ha-*

bilitation theses of Max Horkheimer, and also of Adorno's doctoral dissertation. In 1923 Horkheimer wrote an appreciation of Cornelius in honor of the latter's sixtieth birthday. It appeared in the *Frankfurter Zeitung,* where Kracauer was already the literary editor. In this article Horkheimer depicted his university patron as a man of the nineteenth century who stood squarely in the cultured middle-class tradition:

> From Cornelius we possess fundamental works not just on the subject of epistemology, but also and especially in the realms of *aesthetics* and *art education.* . . . Born into the same family as the painter and the composer,[42] Hans Cornelius is an artist and practical art teacher of the rarest kind. He obtained his doctorate in chemistry. . . . His most recent publication, *The Value of Life,* is an outline of ethics in the easily accessible form of a sermon on liberty. It might well serve as a guide to young people, and not only to them, to ease their passage from ethical confusion to the clarity of free action.[43]

Horkheimer elegantly accomplished the task of producing a public essay of congratulations. This businesslike attitude toward academic philosophy must have impressed the young Adorno. His own first works, *Die Transzendenz des Dinglichen und Noetischen in Husserls Phänomenologie* (The Transcendence of the Thinglike and the Noetic in Husserl's Phenomenology) and *Der Begriff des Unbewußten in der transzendentalen Seelenlehre* (The Concept of the Unconscious in the Transcendental Doctrine of the Soul), the dissertation of 1924 and the *Habilitation* dissertation of 1927, exhibit few signs of Adorno's own handwriting but rather more of the philosophical approach of Hans Cornelius. Nor is it very different in the case of Horkheimer, even though he was eight years older. Horkheimer had tried at first to work in the field of Gestalt psychology, which Cornelius was keen on. He then succeeded in obtaining his doctorate in 1922 with a seventy-eight-page thesis on the "Antinomy of Teleological Judgement." This was followed in 1925 with the *Habilitation* thesis, "On Kant's *Critique of Judgment,*" as a connecting link between theoretical and practical philosophy.

Obligatory academic writings like these may have reinforced Kracauer's aversion to idealism. For his part, Horkheimer, who was already committed to the founding of an institute to investigate the causes of socialism and revolution, can scarcely have identified with them wholeheartedly. In the same way, as a man who had welcomed the philosophical reflections of a Lukács in a newspaper as early as 1921, Adorno too could surely have relished the academic products of Hans Cornelius only from a distance.

Kracauer's masterly review of Lukács's *Theory of the Novel* undoubtedly voices the shared views of Teddie and his extramural teacher:

> The powerful need for religion at the present time, for a faith that encompasses the soul, is conditioned by the entire philosophical situation of our age. The process of decomposition in which Western man finds himself, now that the all-embracing edifice of the church has crumbled away piece by piece, is approaching its end, if we are not deceived, because there is nothing left to be undermined. The philosophy of recent centuries is a sustained experiment that travels through the entire world following the disappearance of meaning that could encompass the whole of reality and that irrevocably separates the amorphous manifold of existing things from the spirit that gives them shape, the chaos from the rational subject; it is an experiment that was necessarily doomed to failure because it was undertaken with the inadequate resources of pure thought.[44]

The young Wiesengrund likewise found himself in search of a different kind of thought. His openness to the ideas of Walter Benjamin, whom he first met in 1923, proves it, but their philosophical affinity does not yet become evident in his early academic writings.[45]

Siegfried Kracauer also welcomed Benjamin's writings with unqualified enthusiasm. That was by no means to be taken for granted at the time, since the history of reviewing in the Weimar period is highly complex and difficult to decipher from our vantage point today. The cliquishness that Kracauer complained about in the field of intellectual reviews forced writers into a complicated process of self-advertisement in which they strove to enlist the active support of their friends and acquaintances.[46] This opened the gates to jealousy, resentment, and suspicions of every kind. The letters of Benjamin, Kracauer, and Bloch as well as Adorno testify to the vexations caused by their mutual reviews or failures to review. An additional irritation was what must look nowadays like an exaggerated fear of plagiarism, although in reality it reflects the proximity of the writers to one another and their competitive situation in the Weimar period and in exile. Kracauer was unable to keep his review of 15 July 1928, "On Walter Benjamin's Writings," entirely free of ambivalence. He did not shy away from the almost impossible task of comparing Benjamin's immensely learned book on tragedy, which had been rejected as a *Habilitation* thesis in German literature by Frankfurt University in 1925, with the collection of aphorisms titled *One-Way Street*. As with his review of Lukács, he succeeds in pinpointing the nature of Benjamin's work: "Even if he does not care to dwell 'in the land of the living,' he is able to raid the storehouses of a lived life and to take possession of the meanings that have been deposited there and that are awaiting a recipient."[47] Benjamin's work on the material of baroque tragedies is decoded by Kracauer as the glimpse of a distorted universe that becomes transparent only at the moment of its collapse. It is less systematic than *Theory of the Novel*, but as mirrored in the past and the prehistoric, the present becomes manifest to a far greater extent in all its material richness. In light of the subtlety with which Benjamin changed our view of the baroque, the breakthrough to materialism that becomes visible for the first time in *One-Way Street* necessarily comes as an anticlimax: "This can be explained by his firm belief in the emptiness of immediate existence, which he thinks confused."[48]

When we read these reviews today, we are amazed at the intellectual similarities between these writers and how this gives rise to all sorts of sensitivities and aversions and to the narcissism of minor differences. Kracauer's situation among the intellectuals of the Weimar period underwent a change after he obtained the post at the *Frankfurter Zeitung* in the autumn of 1921. He succeeded in holding on to and even consolidating his position under the aegis of Benno Reifenberg until he was transferred to Berlin in 1928. He became the man people wanted to talk to if they had become stuck in an academic one-way street or wished to make a career as a writer. Kracauer himself had abandoned his own academic aspirations as well as his prospective career as an architect, the career which was supposed to enable him to earn his living but which would not really have succeeded in doing so under the conditions that obtained after 1918. Furthermore, the newspaper consumed five or six hours of his time every day, since he had to concern himself with local Frankfurt news as well as reports on congresses and lectures before getting down to his own articles and theoretical writings. To other writers Kracauer appeared to be in a position of power; he himself, however, could not free himself of feelings of envy for their relative independence, which meant in his view that they could devote themselves wholeheartedly to writing. It has not been possible to this day to explain why Horkheimer and Kracauer never really hit it off, but there must have been a rift quite early on, perhaps because Kracauer's reviewing style was not to Horkheimer's taste.

The posthumous collections of letters read like the stock market reports of the ups and downs of an intelligentsia whose relations ranged from amicable to hostile. We are not concerned here with *the* Weimar intelligentsia, but at most with a specific group whose members cannot easily be reduced to a common denominator. It would also be simplistic to lump them together as left-wing intellectuals. What unites them is their belief that bourgeois society, with all its hopes of emancipation, had come to an end. The Jewish origins of most of these intellectuals may have sharpened their awareness of the new social situation, but not everything can be explained by pointing to their origins. Their individualities are revealed by the blunt divergences separating them. Kracauer's scathing review on 27 April 1926 of "the Bible in German," the translation by Martin Buber and Franz Rosenzweig, broke through all the barriers erected by the proprieties of friendly relations, casting doubt on loyalties of every kind. We cannot say with certainty whether Kracauer simply felt more secure in his new post or whether his more intensive study of materialist theory and the contemporary social phenomena had given him a new confidence. Whatever the case may have been, he now spoke in a different tone, one of extreme hostility to all religious reformers. The process of secularization associated with bourgeois society now seemed to him to be irreversible, one not to be altered by arbitrary subjective decisions. Bloch, who had been offended by Kracauer's earlier review of his book on Thomas Münzer, used this review to effect a rapprochement. Adorno's caustic description of Buber as a "religious Tirolean"[49] fits in with this general rejection of modern religious trends, which were regarded as an unenlightened reaction to the crisis of bourgeois society.

The acerbity of Kracauer's rejection of the new religiosity in the mid-1920s reflects the deep sense of loss unleashed by the process of secularization. Even in his early critique of Bloch in August 1922 titled "Prophetentum" (Prophet Cult), he was not sparing with his gibes: "This gospel has no authority. To unmask its vacuity is a duty if only because it is to be feared that the hypocritical gloss on its surface might prove dangerously seductive to susceptible souls."[50] Could Kracauer have been thinking here of his youthful friends Teddie Wiesengrund and Leo Löwenthal? Bloch felt he had been misunderstood and badly treated. He hit back hard. In "Durch die Wüste" (Through the Wilderness) in 1923, he included a passage that was erased from the 1964 edition:

In this instance we see a little man who is too limited for what he intends and does not even notice how inappropriate his views are; having calibrated his swimming pool thermometer in the philosophy seminar, he now hangs it up in a hot spring and then wonders why the glass shows nothing; a man who has never felt the slightest breath of the passion and metaphysics of someone attempting to understand existence, but who now would like for once to be a little Kierkegaard in search of his Hegel, and who imagines he has found him in *Thomas Münzer* and *The Spirit of Utopia*.[51]

On 16 October 1923 Kracauer recorded his amusement in a letter to Löwenthal: "His polemic against me, 'systematically infamous' as it is, betrays all too clearly his fury at his inability to wound me. . . . We had a good laugh to see Bloch baring his soul in this way."[52] Bloch knew from previous letters just how to get under Kracauer's skin, for in 1921, when Kracauer was still looking for a position, he had applied to Bloch for help. Bloch was familiar with Kracauer's sociological studies as well as his manuscript "Nietzsche and Dostoyevsky." In his anti-critique Bloch now lumped Kracauer together with the general existentialist fashion, which had turned Kierkegaard into a popular writer once again in the 1920s.

For Kracauer and his younger friend Wiesengrund, religion was by no means to be disposed of simply with a critique of the new religiosity, a cause in which someone like Bloch likewise had no stake. This explains why Bloch could take the criticism of the Buber-Rosenzweig Bible translation as the pretext for a reconciliation with Kracauer without loss of face. With the reconciliation complete, Bloch could not resist reverting to earlier debates:

> . . . and I welcome the fact that you are able to make use of a grand-bourgeois newspaper to give the lifeless and contemplative chatter about culture a bad conscience. And not just a moral bad conscience *à la* Kierkegaard, whom the bourgeoisie has been discussing for many years without coming to any harm, but an utter demolition of the foundations supporting the phrases that no longer have relevance and that simply postpone the impact of reality. . . . Like the sociology that is both in decline and that transcends the real world, the bourgeois ideology that behaves in the same fashion contributes dialectically to the building of a new world.[53]

The correspondence then passes on to a discussion of Lukács's *History and Class Consciousness*, which Kracauer regarded with extreme skepticism. We learn incidentally that Teddie, who had meanwhile spent some time in Vienna, had met Lukács in person and on 17 June 1925 had sent Kracauer, who was on tenterhooks, an excited report from which people are barred by law from quoting to this very day. Communism, as Lukács discussed it, was seen as an intellectual option; party membership seemed to almost everyone to be something like an existential myth—except, paradoxically, for the highly exposed Lukács himself, who had already found himself the target of the most violent attacks of the Comintern. This appeared even to magnify his fame among intellectuals with no experience of the party and for whom the everyday struggle between rival cliques and the exhausting trade union activity was unknown territory.

The passion with which these letters are written allows us to glimpse something of the intensity of Adorno's discussions with Kracauer, Benjamin, or Bloch. In these relationships, theory acquires an existential significance. It is perhaps with Kracauer that we can most easily perceive how theory had come to take the place of a defunct religion. In the letter to Bloch already cited, he made a proposal for the "realization of the theory of revolution."[54] "Theology would have to be encountered in the profane whose gaps and rifts, in which the truth lies concealed, would have to be exposed. Religion would have to be plundered and then abandoned to its fate."[55] The contrast with the ordinary person's way of thinking is palpable: These intellectuals take the death of religion seriously as the manifestation of a permanent crisis. They can no longer believe in the replacement of religion by a rational world order. The rationalism of the Enlightenment has lost its credibility, as has the spirituality of German idealism. But this has not meant the end of theology, as is made plain by Kracauer's critical essays on sociology in the early 1920s. In 1922, in the preface to his essay "Sociology as Science," he writes of his intentions in that brief work:

> The example of sociology may show how ill equipped formal philosophy is, given that it remains within the sphere of immanence, to illuminate the sphere of a reality that has been fully embraced by a "meaning" in all its concreteness. . . . In so far as it is based on the assumption of a reality that is dependent on a highly transcendent condition and that gives shape to both the world and the self in equal measure, it should provide a critique of every immanent philosophy, and especially of idealist thought, and should help to prepare within narrow limits the transformation, glimmers of which can now be seen here and there, that will lead an exiled mankind back into the new-old regions of a God-filled reality.[56]

The unease occasioned by the notion of transforming social experience into a new science called sociology is very evident even in words like these that pay their respects to the language of science. The same may be said of the founders of the Institute for Social Research, who found nothing attractive about the way in which this new science went about establishing itself. Criticism of academic sociology accompanies the entire history of Critical Theory from the outset. The young Wiesengrund likewise failed to be attracted by sociology as a student but preferred a variant of non-academic philosophy as practiced by academic outsiders like Walter Benjamin and Ernst Bloch. A "so-called child prodigy" in search of knowledge could not be satisfied in the long run by the "attitude of waiting" adopted by Kracauer in 1922, which he himself described as "a tentative openness in a sense that was hard to explain further."[57] When the Kierkegaard book was reissued in 1962, Adorno wrote this self-characterization which he sent to Bloch on 26 July. He still thought of the book as a piece of juvenilia, while at the same time he conceded that it had the "character of a dream-like anticipation."[58] Above all, however, Adorno believed that he and Benjamin were largely in agreement in their views of Kierkegaard, although he was forced to overlook a number of significant differences. In particular, he and Benjamin agreed about "the coded character of our theology," which Adorno somewhat obscurely called "inverse," "a position directed against natural and supernatural interpretation alike."[59] Ten years older than Adorno, Benjamin held back from Adorno's claim that they were close to each other "with regard to theology."[60] But he signaled an unusual commonality once he had studied the Kierkegaard book, seeing it as an "exploration of that land of inwardness from whose bourn its hero never returned."[61] Thus, he continued, "it is true that there is something like a shared work after all; that there are still sentences which allow one individual to stand in for and represent another."[62] The solidarity of common understanding became the lived utopia of these intellectuals who arose out of the German, and in most instances the German Jewish, middle classes. The inflation—and this is the special feature of the situation in Germany—had destroyed the foundations of an explicitly bourgeois existence. In the Weimar period only a few intellectuals were still able to live off the wealth accumulated by their families. Walter Benjamin's permanent state of economic deprivation is exemplary of the new situation of the independent writer. The Kierkegaard book too contains unequivocal signs of the social situation of the bourgeois *rentier*:

> By denying the social question, Kierkegaard succumbs to his own historical situation, that of the *rentier* in the first half of the nineteenth century. Within commodious limits the *rentier* is economically independent. . . . Yet the limits

of this economic position are evident: excluded from economic production, the *rentier* does not accumulate capital, or in any case incomparably less than an industrialist with a similar estate; nor is he able to exploit economically the intellectual labour of isolated "literary work." . . . He stands in opposition to the progress of economic competition that made his type almost extinct.[63]

Among friends at the time, the term "Marxism" meant precisely this: the exhaustion of the bourgeois way of life. Both idealism and the protest against idealism were identified with this. Benjamin's review of *Kierkegaard*, which was still able to appear in the *Vossische Zeitung* on 2 April 1933, fastens on this particular angle of Adorno's book right at the start:

> The last attempt to take over Kierkegaard's philosophy in toto was inspired by Karl Barth's "dialectical theology." At their outer limits, the waves of this theological movement make contact with the concentric circles set in motion by Heidegger's existentialist philosophy. The present work—Theodor Wiesengrund-Adorno, *Kierkegaard*—approaches the subject from quite a different angle. Here Kierkegaard is taken not forward but back—back into the inner core of philosophical idealism, within whose enchanted circle the ultimately theological nature of his thought remained doomed to impotence.[64]

For this generation of intellectuals the long bourgeois century had already become historical reality, but the social situation of a monadic individual imprisoned in the collapsing social formations of the bourgeoisie appeared oppressively real. Nothing that was old gave any support, since the critics perceived in it no more than the prototype of a catastrophe. The historical interval between the short and the long century was particularly acute in Germany, in contrast to the Anglo-American world, and it enables us to comprehend the radicality of this generation of intellectuals who had only the quality of their own mental faculties to rely on. At the same time, the clash with such an unprogressive institution as the university was predestined from the outset. It was not just the fact that the established academics were extremely disinclined to identify with the republic. The majority of students, too, were dominated by Nazi groups, long before society as a whole was overwhelmed by National Socialism. Max Weber's pessimistic prognosis of 1919 with regard to the careers of Jewish scholars turned out to be the bitter truth of the Weimar Republic.[65] One of its most prominent victims was Walter Benjamin.

The failure of Walter Benjamin to become an academic must have seemed like a dire threat to his young friend Teddie Wiesengrund. Even today it seems barely comprehensible that in 1925 the University of Frankfurt could contrive to turn away a genius like Benjamin. It would, however, be too easy to ascribe the sole responsibility for Benjamin's plight to the anti-Semitism which was endemic in German universities between the wars. After all, when he had previously attempted to establish himself in Heidelberg, he found he had been forestalled by "a Jew called Mannheim . . . who is going to study with Alfred Weber for his *Habilitation*. He is a friend of Bloch and Lukács, an agreeable young man whom I have also met."[66] He was talking about Karl Mannheim, who was to become the object of Adorno's first great piece of sociological criticism. At that time it was not difficult to find oneself caught between a number of different stools. Benjamin's refusal to compromise amounted more or less to a challenge to the German university system, which had become more than conservative during the Weimar period. Benjamin had obtained his doctorate in Berne with the highest distinction, summa cum laude, for "The Concept of Criticism in German Romanticism." In a letter to his friend Ernst Schoen, he talked about the guile he had used in writing it: "It has become what it ought to have become: a pointer to the true nature of Romanticism, something unknown in the critical literature—but only indirectly, because I could no more approach the heart of Romanticism, its messianism, than anything else, that is very obvious to me, without cutting myself off from the possibility of the requisite complicated and conventional scientific approach, which I distinguish from the true one."[67] Benjamin's self-confident claims to have overthrown the entire critical tradition was camouflaged at the time. The inflation put an end to his *Habilitation* project on a linguistic topic in Switzerland. The country had simply become too expensive for a scholar dependent on limited financial transfers from Germany.

Benjamin now found himself under the necessity of moving back into his parents' home together with his first wife, Dora, and it was this enforced return to Berlin that radicalized him. A return to a bourgeois life was not open to him, since he had no profession. As a book collector, he thought he would try to make his way in the antiquarian book market. His chronic lack of money was further aggravated by the birth of his son in 1918. An academic career appeared to be the solution, although he wanted to obtain the *Habilitation* only in order to have a legitimate claim on a private income from his parents which would enable him to survive as a *Privatdozent*. In other words, he had not yet abandoned hope of living the life of a cultivated *rentier*. This entire period was marked by quarrels about his parents' money, which in any case had melted away in the inflation, and the impossibility of surviving financially sharpened his awareness of society's defects. He observed "insecurity, indeed, the perversion of the instincts vital for life, together with the impotence and degeneracy of the intellect. This is the state of mind of the totality of German citizens,"[68] he noted in his "Ideas for an Analysis of the Condition of Central Europe." Benjamin believed that the "decay of the universities" accompanying this general decline was "unmistakable." He thought that the occupants of the new university chairs were either "brilliant, fanatical orators or else urbane, no less brilliant swindlers." He had no faith in the future of a "democratic organization of the sciences in which even in the best case the only deciding factor was competition between talented candidates."[69] All the more challenging was the project for his *Habilitation;* he himself described the introduction as an example of "incredible chutzpah."[70] The project was *The Origin of the German Tragic Drama,* which he proposed to present to the faculty in Frankfurt at the instigation of his friend, the sociologist Salomon-Delatour. But he previously had felt almost caught out by his friend Gershom Scholem, as he admitted in a letter dated 19 February 1925: "Dear Gerhard, you wrote to me in a letter to where I was in Capri and that I have often thought about and have even quoted, that you were following my course of action with great concern and had the impression that now that external circumstances were becoming smoother, my internal resistance to the *Habilitation* would gain the upper hand. Your diagnosis is correct, but the prognosis mistaken, or so I hope."[71]

After the failure of his *Habilitation,* Benjamin described the printed text as a long-overdue "box on the ears that will ring out through the halls of science."[72] In his book on tragedy, Benjamin took few pains to conceal his views, and his very attitude represented a challenge to academic conventions. The consequence was that even Hans Cornelius rejected the text on the grounds that it was incomprehensible. Nor did he change his mind after discussing the matter with his assistant, Max Horkheimer. Horkheimer, who was dependent on the goodwill of the faculty to obtain his own *Habilitation,* evidently did not wish to jeopardize his chances for the sake of what must have seemed to him a lost cause. Horkheimer needed a professorial post in order to be able to succeed Grünberg at the institute. His and Pollock's situation was different from Benjamin's at the time. We can only guess the effect that Benjamin's failure may have had on the much younger

Wiesengrund, who at the time, that is, in 1924, had only just acquired his doctorate with his orthodox study of Husserl under Cornelius's supervision. Adorno did not stumble into the same university trap; fearing rejection, he withdrew his first dissertation for the *Habilitation,* "The Concept of the Unconscious," even though it was far less provocative than Benjamin's. They had met in 1923 in a seminar of Salomon-Delatour's on Ernst Troeltsch's book on historicism[73]—or had it been in the Café Westend, which Kracauer also frequented? In 1964 Adorno could no longer recollect precisely. But he did produce a detailed account of the impression Benjamin had made on him at the time, when he was still only twenty: "It was as if this philosophy had revealed to me for the first time what philosophy would have to be if it were to fulfill its own promise; and at the same time, it showed me where philosophy has failed ever since the Kantian separation of what remains within our experience and what transcends the frontiers of possible experience."[74] But in the very next sentence Adorno goes on to describe the ambivalent impression that Benjamin produced, provoking anxieties and resistance in ordinary academics: "I once expressed this by saying that whatever Benjamin said sounded as if it emerged from a mystery. Not that he was an esoteric thinker in a catastrophic sense, but it was as if insights that fly in the face of ordinary common sense have some particular evidence in their favor that completely dissipates the suspicion of arcane knowledge, let alone bluff, even though some of the qualities of a poker player were not wholly alien to Benjamin's manner of speaking and thinking."[75]

Writing of this sort did not fit the two dominant trends at Frankfurt University in the 1920s. Benjamin must have seemed obscure to neo-Kantians and a rival to the supporters of Stefan George. Only exceptional intellectual outsiders noticed that there might be something unusual about Benjamin. Hugo von Hofmannsthal was one of the first newly successful writers to note the extraordinary qualities of Benjamin's type of criticism. At around the time Adorno met Benjamin, Hofmannsthal accepted Benjamin's essay on Goethe's *Elective Affinities* for the *Deutsche Beiträge,* the journal he had just established. Hofmannsthal wished to continue the tradition of criticism which is itself art. Before discovering Benjamin's essay, he had believed that his task was to remind the public of a forgotten German tradition. Benjamin's essay seemed to him to have maintained the very kind of writing that he had thought extinct. What was distinctive about it was his attempt to rescue tradition by abandoning formalistic philosophy and reinstating the relationship between art and truth. Paradoxically, Benjamin believed that Romantic criticism embodied the situation of a chaotic age in which a tradition had reached its endpoint, namely, that of Goethe as the essence of classicism. From his immersion in Romantic criticism, itself a reaction to the fundamental changes wrought by the French Revolution, Benjamin came to believe that he had grasped the situation of the intellectual who could no longer live either as a citizen or as a traditional artist. Questions of theology, metaphysics, and even esoteric thought remained unresolved in 1919. Hofmannsthal, whose social exclusivity as a nobleman of Jewish origin seemed to guarantee a still viable relationship between aesthetics and truth, appeared to Benjamin to be one of the few people who were in a position to understand his intentions. He seemed to have survived the long intellectual dominance of neo-Kantianism and "Life Philosophy" unscathed. Hofmannsthal appeared acceptable even to Benjamin's parvenu parents; he was not ashamed to show Hofmannsthal's praise of the essay to his father in order to persuade the latter to grant him "a very limited annuity."[76]

The basic feeling of a failed secularization also entered the great book on tragedy. Benjamin does not simply leave the tradition untouched; he reconfigures it anew. Initially he had assembled a vast collection of quotations from literary material with which he had previously been unfamiliar—"a heap of brushwood which I can set alight only with the spark of inspiration that I shall probably have to transport laboriously from somewhere else."[77] The idea of being able to rescue something that bourgeois traditionalism can no longer sustain imparted an audacious, even revolutionary quality to Benjamin's approach to criticism. His planned journal, *Angelus Novus,* was designed to "restore criticism to its former strength"— and this was to be achieved "without any concessions to its public, if necessary."[78] The exclusive and radical nature of these texts cannot fail to have had their effect on Adorno, who was able to read them "very soon afterward,"[79] that is, shortly after they had first met, and even before publication. At the time, intellectual and material revolution coincided in Benjamin's way of thinking, as can be seen in his early "Critique of Violence." The fact that in 1924 Benjamin should have fallen in love with a book such as *History and Class Consciousness* comes as no surprise. The book on tragedy that he was writing at just that period, during a sojourn in southern Italy, conveyed the revolutionary aspirations of an academic discipline that cast doubt on all established knowledge. Benjamin was able to rediscover the basic idea of his *Origin of German Tragic Drama* in Adorno's inaugural lecture. Adorno had said: "The task of systematic inquiry is not to explore the concealed or manifest intentional structures of reality but to interpret the intentionless character of reality, insofar as, by constructing figures and images out of the isolated elements of reality, it extracts the questions which it is the further task of inquiry to formulate in the most pregnant fashion possible."[80] On 7 July 1931, Benjamin, who had been irritated by Adorno's failure to acknowledge his debt to him explicitly, nevertheless wrote, "I can subscribe to this proposition," and indicated his desire "to maintain our philosophical friendship in the same alert and pristine form as before."[81]

Earlier, in 1925, Benjamin had anticipated the failure of his academic career in a letter to Gershom Scholem: "For me, everything depends on how matters shape up with the publishers. If I have no success there, I shall probably speed up my study of Marxist politics, and—with the prospect of traveling to Moscow in the foreseeable future at least for a time—shall join the Party. Whatever happens, I shall take this step sooner or later."[82] He regarded himself as an independent writer—anticipating one of his later titles, we might speak of "the author as producer"—who joins the Communist Party as a consequence of his insight into his own social position. In this letter the words "Moscow" and "the Party" acquire mythic significance. This was no inevitable fate.[83] His brother Georg, who was three years his junior, had taken quite a different path. Through Walter, he too had made contact with the Youth Movement but had then volunteered for service in the First World War, had been wounded, and had returned to Berlin from the battlefield highly decorated and disillusioned. Georg, who was of a practical bent, decided to study medicine and then moved via an intellectual circle of religious socialists to membership in the Independent Social Democratic Party (USPD). As a young doctor, Georg had developed social commitments and gained his doctorate in 1922 with a study titled "Homes for Unmarried Mothers"; he ended up joining the Communist Party (KPD). He then worked in the communist-inspired "Proletarian Health Service" in the Wedding district of Berlin. He also wanted to involve his brother Walter in his new political interests. On 27 July 1925 Walter wrote to Gershom Scholem, "My brother gave me the first selection of Lenin's writings in German as a present."[84] And he made it clear that he was waiting "very impatiently" for the "second volume, the one with his philosophical writings."[85] Scholem too had a brother who had chosen to join the Communist Party and who, like Georg, was later arrested by the Nazis and died in a camp after a long, bitter period of detention. For children of respectable Jewish families, Zionism and communism were both viable options. And while Benjamin was still preoccupied with the *Habilitation,* he wrote to his Zionist friend Gershom, who at the time was still called Gerhard, to tell him that "an intense conflict was in progress between the forces (my own individual ones) in favor of my joining the Party and alternatively my learning Hebrew," adding, "And no fundamental decision is as yet in sight so that I must make the experiment of beginning with one or the other."[86]

Sympathy for the revolution—or, later on, for communism, the party, or historical materialism—by no means precluded other options which appeared incompatible with it from the standpoint of Communist Party ideologues. We have to speak of a paradoxical communism, and not just in connection with Benjamin. In other words, the closer he came to orthodox communism, the more he felt repelled by what it meant in practice. The contradictions involved here were experienced by Lukács, Brecht, and Bloch to the point of denial, whereas Adorno reacted with horror to such commitments entered into against one's better judgment or as a pure act of will. With the later Bloch he succeeded in achieving a reconciliation after Bloch had moved from the GDR to Tübingen. In the case of Brecht, Adorno had kept his distance ever since the Weimar days, and he wasted no time in striving to neutralize the attraction of Brecht's personality for Benjamin. The need for theoretical "comradeship," as Benjamin called it in a letter to Florens Christian Rang in 1923, was greater in this generation than ever before or since in German history. Thanks to the radical social conditions of the Weimar Republic, men who might have been educated members of the middle class developed into intellectuals who were able to believe in a radically transformed society as of 1918 in which the intellect would play a very different role. Their disillusionment with the course of revolution in Germany went hand in hand with a profound sense of their own powerlessness. In retrospect, the attempts by intellectuals to organize themselves in 1918–19 appear both pompous and ludicrous.

It was the traditional educational institutions, and especially the German universities, that shut their doors to cultural innovations—aside from a few exceptions such as the Institute for Social Research in Frankfurt am Main. The Germany of the Weimar Republic can be characterized by the contradiction between a reactionary traditionalism intent on conserving its institutional roots and a radically changing cultural public sphere in which the new intellectuals strove to gain acceptance. We may think of the desire for new intellectual and political groupings as a response to the isolating mechanisms of competition whose very existence had been denied in the traditional world of culture. At the same time, the feeling that intellect was powerless in the face of the war and a failed revolution led to more radical claims for the role of the intellectual: social impotence was to be made good by intellectual radicality. Benjamin was the exemplary personification of this new type of intellectual in the Weimar Republic. Like others, he was unable to discover the sources of his criticism in his social situation, which by the end of the republic had left him almost entirely devoid of any way out, either psychologically or economically. Benjamin's criticism derived its strength from a changed view of the past, one that did not shy away from theological consequences. Paul Klee's *Angel,* which he bought in 1921, stimulated him to ever newer interpretations and self-interpretations. In a material sense, this picture of an angel bound him to two intellectual opposites—to Gerhard Scholem, who for a long time looked after the *Angel* for the homeless Benjamin, and Theodor W. Adorno, who was sent the picture in New York after it had been cut from its frame following Benjamin's death.

When Scholem visited New York and met Adorno, who was staying there in 1937 for a probationary spell at the Institute for Social Research, he realized that Adorno perceived the theological implications of Benjamin's philosophy "on a wholly secularized plane."[87] This observation tells us as much about Benjamin as about Adorno. The theological aspect of Benjamin's thinking cannot be captured positively, and an exact and jealous observer like Scholem not only noticed but also ventured to assert how audaciously and freely Benjamin used to deal with the Jewish tradition, above all, when he was at his most authoritative. As part of an interpretation of Klee's *Angel* in his note "Agesilaus Santander," Benjamin came up with what he regarded as a definitive theory of Jewish name-giving. Scholem rightly declared this to be "a highly imprecise, exaggerated account of the actual situation among Jews."[88] By way of summary, Scholem declared that "Benjamin was not very well informed about matters concerning the Jews."[89] Scholem, however, also regarded Benjamin as a very Jewish writer. In an exchange with Peter von Haselberg in 1978, Scholem pointed out that "it never, ever occurred to Benjamin to describe himself as a German. In this respect he was closest to Kafka. Both men knew that they were German writers, but not Germans."[90] This view of themselves as Jews has nothing in common with everyday classifications of this sort, but opens the door to an understanding of the theological implications of Benjamin's thought which the secularized Adorno understood perfectly. In Kafka, all three men converged while rejecting prevailing existentialist and positive theological interpretations.

The young Dr. Wiesengrund-Adorno came even closer to Kafka both physically and spiritually when he arrived in Vienna in 1925 to study musical composition with Alban Berg. In the circles he now moved in, Kafka had long been a familiar name. The slightly provincial nature of Frankfurt life that the Frankfurters had maintained like a *haut goût* following their absorption into Prussia in 1866 made him receptive toward the Viennese. During the short twentieth century, the latter had developed one talent to perfection, and this was, as the exiled Alfred Polgar put it, the ability to gaze with confidence into the past. He arrived in the early summer of 1925, a child prodigy with a doctorate—and not yet twenty-two. He introduced himself to Berg in a letter of application on 5 February 1925 as "Dr. Th. Wiesengrund-Adorno,"[91] announcing that "I can tell you quite precisely what help I require from you."[92] As a precocious hothouse plant, Teddie had left Frankfurt am Main and his music teacher, Bernard Sekles, in favour of the capital city of modern music. Sekles, the director of the conservatory in Frankfurt, had been teaching him since 1919; his message was to warn him against a modernity that had now ceased to be modern. In distant California, beyond the reach of European rivalries between tradition and modernity, Adorno devoted a "short essay" titled *Consecutio temporum* (Sequence of Tenses) to his former teacher's warning, an essay which he strongly commended to his old mentor Kracauer.[93] Frankfurt was attempting at the time to keep pace with fashion, while Vienna, which had previously been in the vanguard aesthetically, was now, after its huge loss of imperial status, flirting with what it was to be démodé. Such a leaning toward the unfashionable that actually provides proof of one's modernity was something Adorno could appreciate in Benjamin.

The mature Adorno never tired of attempting to correct the false picture of the 1920s—but in vain. In comparison to Frankfurt, Vienna was still a major city, but unlike Paris or London in the 1800s, it could not be described as the capital of the century, as Benjamin was wont to say of Paris. In the bourgeois century, Vienna had become the metropolis of a grandiose, truly European multinational empire in which, remarkably, tradition still maintained its power. This predominance of tradition, a kind of aesthetic ancien régime, provoked a rebellion on the part of the avant-garde—most strikingly by Arnold Schoenberg and his friends. By the time Adorno arrived in Vienna in 1925, the revolution was long since over—not just the aesthetic revolution of 1910 but also the political one of 1918, which had overthrown the monarchy. While Vienna already had the future behind it in the mid-1920s, Berlin was fast becoming the principal European magnet for Vienna's greatest productive talents. Berliners such as Benjamin, though, were already about to take the leap out of the narrow confines of the German-speaking world. By the mid-1920s it was easier for Kracauer, Bloch, and Benjamin to meet in the Place de l'Odéon than anywhere in Germany. Here, they experienced the surrealist shock of the aging of modernity that Adorno has defined more precisely than anyone else—the aging of the new, the palimpsest effect, in other words, the way in which the Culture Industry has led to the constant overwriting of ancient texts that have then to be decoded. The origin is the goal, as Karl Kraus put it—a goal that remains inaccessible—and if the goal were to be attained, it would turn out to be not primary but socially and historically mediated.

In 1925 the young Teddie Wiesengrund, this physically frail intellectual with the vast appetite for books and ideas, had not yet experienced what Kracauer in his last essay tried to comprehend as the palimpsest of life. Teddie Wiesengrund arrived in Vienna as a callow youth. He has given a self-critical account of his impact upon others, particularly on those he revered and loved: "At the time, I undoubtedly displayed a deadly seriousness that could all too easily get on the nerves of a mature artist."[94] And not only a mature artist. To be told today that Adorno studied composition with Alban Berg in 1925 is to be given a false impression. Our modern social memory as conditioned by the marketing processes of the Culture Industry turns this information into the encounter of two "modern classics."[95] But the reality of 1925 was that an overenthusiastic prodigy from the German provinces sought out as a teacher one of his idols, whose own fame fed on the myth of an even greater name, that of Arnold Schoenberg. Berg himself was a name only to people in the know. Schoenberg loved him and was starting also to envy him as Berg began to have successes of his own. The atmosphere of secrecy, in which mistrust, treachery, and hatred were lurking in even the most intimate relationships, was utterly new and menacing to the young hothouse plant from Oberrad who had recently dedicated his first composition to his most important high school teacher.

The catastrophic outcome of the events of 1925 can be explained by the enthusiasm, the willingness on the part of a hyperintellectual Frankfurt youth to identify with an outstanding artist in an urbane social context in which Teddie was entirely out of his depth emotionally. If one reads the original letters, now preserved in the Deutsches Literaturarchiv in Marbach, which Adorno wrote home to Frankfurt in his barely legible scrawl, one gains a sense of what it meant for Alban Berg, who was laboring under an immense pressure of work, to have taken time out for his adolescent pupil and to have "spent an entire afternoon in the Café Imperial giving me a lesson in legible score writing."[96] The correspondence with Kracauer might have enabled a psychoanalyst like Kurt Eissler to do for Adorno what he did for Goethe and reconstruct the traumatic process whereby Adorno developed from a child prodigy into the genius that he had not been from the outset. The way in which Adorno severed his emotional bonds with Frankfurt can best be seen in the reflected images of his paradoxical study sojourn in Vienna. The old idols proved a disappointment. He made the acquaintance of Soma Morgenstern, a young man from Galicia a few years older than himself, who was on familiar terms with Berg and who would later on accompany Joseph Roth on his trawl through the Paris bars of his exile. Through Morgenstern he met Georg Lukács, who had been living in Vienna since the collapse of the soviet republic in Hungary, before moving on to Berlin along with the other members of the Viennese avant-garde. With the exception of Berg, all the great names he encountered in Vienna in the flesh were Jews. In a letter to Kracauer, Teddie talked of his astonishment at Lukács's Jewish and even East European appearance, and was no less surprised by Lukács's elegant clothes, which seemed at odds with the image of a semi-clandestine professional revolutionary. In interwar Vienna he met for the first time an extremely diverse Jewish population that displayed the entire gamut of Jewish experience, ranging from the Hakoah football club, which was in the running for the championship, to Karl Kraus, whose public performances subverted religious concepts of every kind.

Soma Morgenstern subsequently published his recollections of his former friends in a number of books. He had little good to say about Adorno, even though the latter had introduced him to Kracauer, an introduction that seemed to hold out the prospect of lucrative employment. Even their meetings in Paris in the 1930s, at which Benjamin was often present, appear not to have been very enjoyable. Adorno felt himself to have been slandered by Morgenstern, possibly because of gossip from their time in Vienna. Morgenstern wrote a highly readable memoir of his years as a refugee in Paris with Joseph Roth, but when he comes to recollecting the days in Vienna in 1925 in *Alban Berg und seine Idole* (Alban Berg and His Idols), he speaks with some envy of the reversal of fortune that had occurred in the meantime, as can be seen from the way in which he pigeonholes Adorno as "a Jewboy [*Judenjunge*] from Frankfurt am Main."[97] These memoirs did not appear in book form for seventy years, and we have to bear in mind the subsequent record of German-Jewish relations in order to form a judgment of their value. Morgenstern's insight into East European Jewish conditions derived from his life in his hometown of Tarnopol, and he was second only to Joseph Roth from Brody, whose study *The Wandering Jews* is the finest account we have of East European Jews. But when he comes to Adorno, we can see that these posthumous recollections aim mainly to present him as a child prodigy from Frankfurt am Main who fits neatly into the Jewish tradition, and that Morgenstern's task was to protect the casual, nonchalant Berg from him. The unending stream of stories that Teddie Wiesengrund is said to have told in order to impress Morgenstern, the frequent references to significantly older men such as Kracauer, Benjamin, and Bloch, all seem faintly comic in Morgenstern's account, and they all prepare the way for his climactic point that this youth who is consumed by ambition will in later years "shave off his father's name, the Jewish 'Wiesengrund,'" to advance his career.[98] Soma Morgenstern undoubtedly knew Teddie Wiesengrund, but he did not understand the later Adorno.

Vienna in 1925 proved to be a turning point in Adorno's life. The child prodigy developed into a young man. This can be seen from the letters he wrote to Siegfried Kracauer, which nowadays make painful reading. He starts by reporting his involvement in a secret love affair between his "master and teacher" and Franz Werfel's married sister in Prague.[99] He was, however, unable to give Kracauer a frank account of the matter since Berg had sworn him to silence. Despite all that, Teddie Wiesengrund soon found himself moving in social circles, a combination of artists and industrialists, which made his family circumstances in Seeheimerstrasse seem petty and narrow in contrast. This must have affected him all the more powerfully, as he thought of Helene and Alban Berg as the closest thing imaginable to Bloch's idea of "the ideal couple." His own mothers, Maria and Agathe, together with his imaginary origins in the Genoan nobility, suddenly appear remarkably insignificant in comparison with Helene Berg, a great beauty who was able to discuss questions of composition on an equal footing with Alban. The impression of grandeur was further enhanced by the proximity of Berg's house in Trautmannsdorfgasse to the Schönbrunn Palace: Helene, whose beauty was praised by such a connoisseur as Peter Altenberg, a man revered by Karl Kraus and later on by Adorno as well, was the emperor's illegitimate daughter. Adorno's admiration for the couple was made enormously more difficult by the silence imposed on him with regard to his new "master's" infidelity, and it is this that makes his letters to Kracauer both enthusiastic and eloquent, while at the same time sealing his lips. The fact that when Adorno took his leave of him, Berg's last words were the injunction "Be true," with its Wagnerian echoes, has more than one meaning.[100] Adorno felt that he had found the ideal of loyalty embodied in Berg's loyalty to Schoenberg. In a moving letter to Berg's widow, he attempted to explain his own disloyalty to her by his loyalty to Berg.

His readiness to identify with others was subjected to daunting tests in Vienna. In Frankfurt he had been the prodigy from a Jewish business family with unusual domestic arrangements, the rule of two artistic mothers. It was not just this fact that provoked a smile in Vienna. The emphasis with which a twenty-year-old from Frankfurt sought to formulate the essence of a revolution in art that already lay in the past disconcerted the Viennese intellectual aristocracy. Schoenberg's awe-inspiring authority, which the young Teddie found altogether mysterious, must have seemed uncanny to him at the time. Adorno later confessed to Thomas Mann that what upset him about Schoenberg's death was that "what had gone wrong with a fundamentally doomed relationship could never be made good."[101] In letters written in 1925, Schoenberg, like Lukács, appears as an imposing Jewish figure, not as a person to whom the boy from a respectable middle-class family could feel superior, but as an intimidating authority figure who at the same time was something of an actor and a clown. Schoenberg's rejection of the overenthusiastic Teddie was transformed into a boundless admiration for Schoenberg's pupil Berg, who in consequence assumed gigantic stature in Teddie's eyes. In 1968, a year before his death, he tried once again to formulate what he had felt in the 1920s, but this time from the vantage point of the 1960s:

> Rarely have I met anyone who so resembled his name. Alban: that has the Catholic-traditional element—his parents owned a religious supplies shop—as well as something refined, exquisite, something which, despite all constructive discipline and rigour, he never altogether renounced. Berg: his face was a mountain-face [*Berg-Gesicht*], mountainous in the twofold sense that his features were those of someone who is at home in the Alps, and that he himself, with the nobly arched nose, the soft, finely chiselled mouth, and the abyss-like, enigmatically empty eyes like lakes, had something of a mountain landscape. Of an extraordinarily large physique, yet at the same time delicate, as if not quite equal to his own size, his bearing was hunched. His hands, and in particular his feet were amazingly small. Appearance, bearing, and countenance were those of a groping, dreaming giant. It would have been easy to imagine that all objects seemed frighteningly enlarged to him, as is said to be true for horses.[102]

His older mentor, Kracauer, on receiving Adorno's letters, noticed the changes, the dissembling on Adorno's part, but was unable to explain them. The letters were full of emotions that cannot be protected from misinterpretation by banishing them to obscure archives. The supposed secrets have all long since been revealed; they are open to inspection in the published works. Just as Berg encodes the name of his lover in his work, but in a way that enables it to be deciphered, so Kracauer, consumed by jealousy, created a mystery of his own. Many of the most intimate postcards that Teddie wrote him were sent, incredibly from a modern point of view, to Kracauer's work address at the *Frankfurter Zeitung*. Kracauer had earlier spoken candidly in his essay on friendship about the shattering effects of sexual affairs that completely transform relations between friends with a significant age gap, particularly when the younger of the two is about to embark on his first sexual adventures. In addition, following *Ginster* and his going into exile, he even incorporated the emotions he had felt in the second novel he wrote, *Georg*, a novel that found no publisher at the time. At a crucial point in *Georg*, we meet Fred, whom, with the aid of a small change of consonants, we can perhaps identify as a grown-up version of Teddie. The categories of male and female must have undergone yet another change for Teddie in Vienna. In Seeheimerstrasse he had been able to indulge an unfortunate inclination to be overwhelmed by feelings of bliss at the piano, where he was as one with his two mothers. The paradoxical nature of this childhood, which in fact did have an unhappy side, is denied with the projection of a perfectly happy boyhood that was maintained well into old age by both Kracauer and his younger friend Leo Löwenthal. They were unable to understand the change that took place in him around 1925 because they were unwilling to acknowledge the sadness in the gaze of a man who had appeared to them to be so privileged. Both saw themselves as being permanently handicapped in comparison to Teddie. Understandably enough, Kracauer was reluctant to have Teddie as a colleague at the *Frankfurter Zeitung* and preferred to employ the less complicated Soma Morgenstern as its Vienna correspondent.

In Berg, Teddie encountered a masculine role model who revalorized his own father, whom he had otherwise dismissed as someone who practiced a Goethe-like renunciation and who had no more than a layman's interest in the arts. In June 1925, in reply to Morgenstern's question about his religious beliefs, Teddie answered that his father was a socialist. In Vienna he lapsed into a chaos that highlighted the provincial nature of life in Frankfurt. It affected not just his love life but also his religious, ethnic, and political attitudes. He did not really hit it off with Schoenberg because among the latter's pupils the role of radical had already been taken by Hanns Eisler, who was scarcely older than Teddie but who was given preferential treatment by the master despite his rowdy characteristics. Throughout his life Adorno was tormented by Eisler's relative success in his relationships with people; it was as if he had been an elder brother. In the mid-1960s Adorno made notes for an essay on Eisler that he planned to include in volume three of his *Musikalische Schriften:* "Deeply ambivalent attitude toward teacher. Something like a failed identification. A[rnold] S[choenberg] no less ambivalent toward him."[103] Teddie Wiesengrund reported to Kracauer about Eisler, who was the brother of Ruth Fischer, the radical left-wing communist leader in Germany. The language he uses reflects, in a way we can still feel today, his incredulity at being so close physically to a legendary revolutionary organization that was under constant threat of being outlawed. In Vienna, Teddie came into contact with many revolutionaries from Eastern Europe who were there either in exile or else engaged in semi-conspiratorial activities. He felt both attracted and excluded by this "melange" of professional revolutionaries and coffeehouse radicals. In contrast, he found genuine friends among professional musicians. The piano teacher Eduard Steuermann, who became a lifelong friend, was for him the very model of a practicing musician and an uncompromising composer. He was a man who made music professionally in order to earn his living and who remained true to his own compositions despite the fact that they were hardly ever performed and not a single note ever went into print. In Rudi Kolisch he met a pioneer of the new music who succeeded in creating a public for music from which the members of the Schoenberg circle could barely make a living, and he did so at the highest level, first in the Old World and then in the New. In Prague, to which he journeyed in his role as go-between, he became close friends with Hermann Grab, yet another man from a wealthy family with outstanding gifts as a writer and musician. Like almost all those mentioned, Grab too was able to escape from the Nazis to America, where he earned his living with a music school he established. His writing took the form of a few slim volumes whose sensitive melancholy reminds us of Proust and Kafka. Origins and income seem to have played no part in this Bohemia-like Bohemia, this diverse imagined community of Adorno's; it was a counter-image to Frankfurt am Main, where the established families and the industrial nouveaux riches soon let you know if you belonged or not. The Anglophilia and socialist sympathies of an Oscar Wiesengrund speak volumes about the political instability of a German middle class which never succeeded in creating a self-confident national base.

All these novel experiences came together in the person of Alban Berg, who seemed to solve conflicts differently from Oscar Wiesengrund. The biographies of the Wiesengrunds and Bergs overlap regionally. Both families had left Franconia. Berg's father traveled south toward Vienna, while the Wiesengrunds went via Frankfurt to England. For Adorno this was to be of decisive importance. His inclination was to leave Frankfurt for Vienna to qualify for the *Habilitation,* but he did not fit in with the neo-positivist trend which was on the rise there and which subsequently throve under the aegis of Austro-Marxism. His father's contacts extended as far as Oxford, where his uncle Bernard Wingfield, who was a successful manufacturer, had a son studying philosophy.[104] Teddie was able to find a place there as an "advanced student"—not the equivalent of a German *Privatdozent,* but with the prospect of being allowed to study for a Ph.D. at an elite institution. Nonetheless, he only managed to gain permission to embark on this hard slog once he had left Vienna. This must have been a bitter disappointment to him, but no one could earn a living from radical compositions. His activities in writing for musical journals followed a radical critical logic that uncompromisingly and systematically reduced the size of his reading public, to the annoyance of even his most benevolent patrons such as Berg. In consequence, the posts that fell vacant went to more accommodating writers such as Hans Heinz Stuckenschmidt, who seems more like an amiable conversationalist from a provincial culture when compared to Adorno, with his more concentrated analytical incisiveness.

His return to his parents' home, even though made palatable by an Italian tour first with Kracauer and then with his two mothers, must have appeared to him a life-threatening narrowing of his opportunities. By the end of the 1920s we find him back in Frankfurt, leading a dandified life and going to Carnival parties costumed as Napoleon alongside employees from I. G. Farben, who had dressed up as Nazis as a joke before becoming Nazis in earnest after 1933. Together with Carl Dreyfuss, a high-society playboy, Adorno wrote surrealist sketches for the *Frankfurter Zeitung* under the pseudonym "Castor Zwieback." But in general, Kracauer, having advanced to the position of editor, made sure that he wrote as little as possible for the paper. Love affairs were common enough in the theatrical milieu at the time, and the university likewise developed the custom of what were known as crêpe-de-chine lectures. Dr. Wiesengrund's inaugural lecture is supposed to have been one such occasion. It is said that the crème de la crème turned out to hear him, but this is probably not much more than gossip. Despite his marriage, Carl Dreyfuss had an unhappy relationship with the actress Marianne Hoppe, subsequently the wife of the actor Gustav Gründgens. After Adorno's return from exile, she worked with him on Hesse radio, reading passages from Proust while Adorno provided commentary. Adorno helped her in her search for a psychoanalyst, a method of treatment that he himself always felt threatened his productive powers.

At the low point of his exile in America, with poverty staring him in the face, he suggested to Horkheimer that he should undergo training as a nonmedical psychoanalyst. Horkheimer, however, made one final effort to obtain money from Jewish institutions to research the future of the fascist character type. It is a point in favor of Adorno's instinct for self-preservation that even in this time of deep depression, he could see how to make use of psychoanalysis as a tool for investigating the current state of society without undergoing psychoanalysis himself. His studies on anti-Semitism and the impact of fascist propaganda are still regarded as among the shrewdest examples of a psychoanalytically inspired social psychology, compared to which whole mountains of sociology seem insipid. "Out of the firing line,"[105] and still smarting from the threats aimed at him as an outsider, it was not until after a considerable time in California that he succeeded in formulating the idea that fanatical anti-Semites act out their anti-Semitism and their fanaticism only in order to qualify for membership in an overwhelming mass. They consciously dispense with knowledge, but not because they are too stupid. Rather they consciously act as if they were stupid so as to be able to indulge their desire for violence. The music critic who returned from Vienna with the knowledge that radical music was doomed to silence because there was no transformed mankind capable of responding to it found it necessary to explore the society that had also turned him into an outsider if he was to escape the fate of being reduced to silence in his turn.

Adorno later remarked that his failure to produce the musical compositions of which he was capable was the traumatic event of his life. When this danger surfaced during his stay in Vienna, he sought to exorcise it through his proximity to his teacher, Berg, "this object of my highest admiration."[106] But as in one of those nightmares that anticipates the future, it was in Vienna that the nearness of death and the danger of falling silent made itself felt. As late as 1968, a year before his own death, his memories of Berg became problematic for him in a way he could himself scarcely comprehend: "Trying to find words of remembrance for Berg is paralysed by the fact that he himself had anticipated the exercise with macabre irony. When I was studying with him he occasionally amused himself during walks we took together around Schönbrunn by imagining the obituaries Viennese newspapers would one day have in store for him."[107]

Berg attempted to keep at bay the paralyzing effect of the anxiety that Adorno would come to call "eminently Austrian" in later years.[108] Vienna allows us to experience the stratified layers of memory like no other city—except perhaps for Rome, which Freud, living in Vienna, took as the model of a psychoanalytically enlightened theory of memory. "The identity of the city, its simultaneously blessed and cursed incorrigibility, may have been of greater significance for the destiny of those two musicians than the hundred years separating them; one of the paradoxical conditions of Berg's modernity is that not so very much had changed."[109] The comparison between Schubert and Berg suggests itself since the last days of both composers seemed to be characterized by the repetition of "bleak senselessness, the combination of sublime acquiescence and irresponsible indolence"[110] that fits in with "a national tradition" in which he shared. This both identical and nonidentical element of Austrian and German is what enabled Adorno to establish a distance from his social background in Frankfurt in which he would be gripped by the open "yearning for what is foreign"[111] that he had already found in Eichendorff's poems. In Vienna Adorno discovered his "second home,"[112] as he never tired of repeating, but this home too was one he was compelled to leave.

On two other occasions, at decisive moments in his life, he would turn to playing duets. His happiest moments must have included the hours he spent making music or hearing it with Alban Berg. On several occasions they were on the verge of being ejected from Viennese concert halls because they became too boisterous in their response to "beautiful passages."[113] "We once heard [Mahler's] Eighth conducted by Anton von Webern and were so excited that we spoke out loud and were almost thrown out. His favorite piece was the second *Nachtmusik* from the Seventh Symphony, and we often played it in a four-handed arrangement, like much else by Mahler. In fact, he cultivated this by now probably extinct art; he had practiced it since childhood with his sister Smaragda."[114] This picture of Adorno from 1968 captures the open yearning as in a photograph. There is only one other, equally touching passage about four-handed playing among his writings, a kind of returning home. In Auerbach in the Bergstrasse, he had visited his relatives Franz and Agathchen Calvelli-Adorno, who had in part returned to a pious Catholicism and who suffered terrible privations under the Nazis, but who survived. His lapidary account of a visit, dated 12 November 1949, to "Mama my Pet" nevertheless conveys his emotion. "It was an utterly delightful day; we played a lot of music four-handed, Mahler."[115]

Again, after a hardworking year he describes returning to Amorbach, his beloved holiday venue, to which he invited the likes of Hermann Grab, "one of my closest friends . . . a surviving vestige of my youth."[116] On this occasion, too, he was scarcely able to master his feelings in his letters to New York. On 24 September 1950, his mother's eighty-fifth birthday, Adorno was staying in the Hotel Post in Amorbach, and wrote to her about "the only remnant of home still left to me."[117] In Amorbach he met Berthold Bührer, a childhood friend who had become the organist of the Abbey Church. His mother had doubted the wisdom of his returning to Amorbach, and now Adorno found himself reporting to her about who had been a Nazi and who still was one. Adorno attempted to explain to Bührer who he now was after having been forced to leave Frankfurt and Amorbach: "You will be well aware how much my own work is tied up with music. Although, professionally, I am a philosopher and sociologist, I have never stopped thinking of myself as a musician."[118] Amorbach lies on the road to Vienna; it was here that as a child he had discovered "the profound melancholy of the South German–Austrian tone"[119] that had accompanied him into exile. But Adorno also rediscovered America in Amorbach, an America that went with Berg's Americophilia:

> In Berg, for the first time, there was a musical interpenetration of Austro-German and French elements of the sort that became common in music after 1945. Politically Berg was not really committed, but he felt himself to be a socialist, as behooved an orthodox reader of [Karl Kraus's] *Fackel* in the twenties. His emphatic Americophilia was perhaps nurtured by the fact that one of his brothers lived there for many years. More than once I heard him say: if there *has* to be a technological civilization, then at least let it be radical and complete; his predilection, even aptitude for what in America one calls gadgets, may have been a factor here. Unquestionably, he gave some thought to the idea that in America he might extricate himself from the confining circumstances of even his best years and live more comfortably.[120]

Adorno succeeded in combining all these endearing and much-loved things in his life. In this sense he surpassed his beloved master and teacher, who remained in Vienna and did not survive his own "concentration camp"[121] to which he had condemned himself in full awareness of what National Socialism meant. Falling silent was something they all experienced in 1933, even those who had earlier fled from Vienna to Berlin:

> Schoenberg interrupted his work on *Moses* when the fascist dictatorship was established in Germany. He lost his position for which life-long tenure had been contractually guaranteed. He accepted the collective situation without complaining about his own individual fate, indeed, without even wasting time pondering it; at that time, early in 1933, he said that there were more important things than composing music. This statement by this man confirms the seriousness of music better than any pathos-filled declaration about the dignity of art. After brief months of wandering, he emigrated to America; there he was afflicted by the first serious illness of his life. In 1934 he moved to Los Angeles; in 1936 he was made professor at the University of California. He lived in his house in Brentwood Park until his death.[122]

Vienna had prepared Adorno for this experience. He spent the rest of his life trying to come to terms with it. After 1949 the dictum "To write poetry after Auschwitz is barbaric"[123] brought Adorno fame and a somewhat dubious notoriety. We should note that it applies not just to poetry but also to music and theory. For him to have been able to formulate this insight, it was necessary to have passed through the hard school of Vienna.

4. | Adorno as "Non-identical" Man

*Because genius has become a mask, genius has to disguise itself.
The last thing the artist can do is to play himself up as a genius and
act as though he, the master, were in possession of the metaphysical
meaning that the substance of his age lacks.*

T. W. ADORNO, "TOWARD A PORTRAIT OF THOMAS MANN"

When *Doctor Faustus* appeared in 1947, Thomas Mann gave a copy to Adorno with the personal dedication "For the Real Privy Councillor." For his next novel, the "novel about a novel," to which Mann would give the title *Die Entstehung des Doktor Faustus* (The Story of a Novel: The Genesis of *Doctor Faustus*), he needed the personal details of his most important informant. He was sent these on 5 July 1948: "I was born in Frankfurt in 1903. My father was a German Jew, while my mother, herself a singer, was born to a French officer of Corsican, originally Genoese, origin and a German singer. I grew up in a family atmosphere shaped by highly theoretical (also political) and artistic, above all musical, interests."[1]

Mann adapted this information to suit his own purposes. In a prominent position, as an affirmation of Adorno's role as his "assistant, adviser, and sympathetic instructor,"[2] he added, almost too informally, "He's my man."[3] This was then followed by the notice he had incorporated:

Theodor Wiesengrund-Adorno was born in 1903 in Frankfurt am Main. His father was a German Jew, his mother, herself a singer, is the daughter of a French officer of Corsican—originally Genoese—origin and of a German singer. He is a cousin of the Walter Benjamin who, driven to his death by the Nazis, wrote the astonishingly perceptive and profound book on "German Tragic Drama," which is actually a philosophy of the history of allegory. Adorno, as he calls himself, using his mother's maiden name, is a man of similar, aloof, tragically clever and exclusive spirit. Having grown up in an atmosphere entirely dominated by theoretical (including political) and artistic, especially musical, interests, he studied philosophy and music and qualified in 1931 as a *Privatdozent* at the University of Frankfurt until he was driven out by the Nazis. Since 1941 he has been living close to us in Los Angeles, almost a neighbor.[4]

The man thus portrayed is an unfamiliar, scarcely recognizable Adorno, namely, the Adorno who did not live as a public intellectual, an Adorno with an almost private existence on the margins of the émigré community in what Mann called "German California." *Dialectic of Enlightenment,* which he had written with Max Horkheimer in Los Angeles up to 1944, was known to only a very small circle of people. Not until after the liberation from National Socialism could the first tiny edition be published by Querido in Amsterdam. Thomas Mann met Adorno while the latter was working on *Minima Moralia,* which he really thought of as an almost private piece of writing (the dedication reads, "For Max in gratitude and promise"),[5] and which was conceived as a celebration of Horkheimer's fiftieth birthday. Between 1946 and 1947 Adorno added a further section, thus completing the book edition which appeared in 1951. After reading it, Mann confessed to Adorno: "I hung magnetically upon the book for days, and every day I took it up it proved the most fascinating reading."[6] Anyone who knows Mann's attitude toward compliments will be aware that this was overwhelming praise and that Adorno might well have been proud of it. Might have . . . since the entire episode left a bitter aftertaste. Adorno's relations with the close-knit production unit consisting of Thomas, Katia, and Erika Mann ended with deep damage to Adorno, all the more so for their having been made public—to the extent that he lapsed into silence after a quarrel with Erika, Mann's daughter. Apart from a speech in Darmstadt in 1962, which was later included in the *Notes to Literature,* and which Erika also attacked, Adorno published nothing further on Thomas Mann.

We might almost speak of an unrequited love when we consider the documents. Adorno turned out to be an indispensable help to Mann after the author of *Doctor Faustus* had enlisted his assistance in a lengthy letter dated 30 December 1945: "But to write a novel about a musician which may even aspire to becoming *the* novel about music, among other things, simultaneously with other things, calls for more than 'mere initiation,' it requires a 'scholarship that I simply do not possess.'"[7] Mann knew precisely what he wanted from Adorno. Even at this stage, he realized clearly that he could not draw the reader's attention to his assistant's contribution: "without ruining the artistic illusion (a footnote like 'This derives from Adorno-Wiesengrund'? That surely won't do."[8] Mann's *Faustus* project pushed up against the boundaries of what an individual writer could achieve, and yet he did not wish to abandon the illusion of sole authorship. Ultimately, after the work had been completed, he wrote: "This time it has not been a saga of the generations, but a fictional biography in which the measured nature of the writing has entered into a curious amalgam with the demonic nature of the subject, and which, situated in the years between 1894 and 1945, attempts to comprehend the age in which I have lived."[9] Mann's interest in his own autobiography had to jostle for room with the fictional life of the composer Adrian Leverkühn: "It is a life's work of almost criminal ruthlessness, a strange kind of transferred autobiography, a work that has cost me more and has gnawed away at me more deeply than any previous one."[10] The clash resulting from Adorno's contribution emerged soon after the book's publication. The diaries contain the entry, "Adorno in whose bosom the consciousness of his musical part-ownership is seething."[11]

Once the book was finished, Thomas Mann the artist was transformed into Thomas Mann the bourgeois, who sought to clarify the ownership issue right down to the very turns of phrase he had used. "Consider steps to reassure him,"[12] he writes as early as 8 February 1948, and on 13 February he tells Adorno over dinner "of his intention of one day writing something autobiographical about *Faustus*—to reassure him."[13] In the letters, which were published in 1965, we find Mann explaining in the language of the film industry to Jonas Lesser, the literary scholar, on 15 October 1951, that the main reason why he wrote *The Story of a Novel: The Genesis of Doctor Faustus* "was to make sure Adorno was credited."[14] He goes on: "With *The Story of a Novel*, I have put a very bright spotlight on him, and in its glare he swells up in a not very pleasant way so that it sounds just a little bit as if it was actually he who wrote *Faustus*. But that's just between ourselves."[15] The publication of this letter by Erika put an end to any pseudo-discreet remarks *entre nous*. Adorno inevitably felt that he had been publicly cast out. In 1968 he wrote bitterly that "it was as if T. M. had slandered him from beyond the grave."[16] But his familiar use of the initials T. M. still reveals his disappointed affection. The appearance of Thomas Mann's diaries in 1989 makes quite clear the extent to which both Erika and Katia Mann were concerned to minimize Adorno's contribution to the writing of *Faustus*. The "Magician," as he liked to be known, indicates in his diaries that he was only partly willing to be pressured in this way: "The dubiousness of the Faust memoirs, the problem of what the women find unbearable about Adorno declarations are affecting my work mood and are interfering with the progress of the Legend."[17]

Thomas Mann creates the impression that he needed to restore his ability to work, and so he crossed out some of the passages which Adorno had contributed and which were made public only in an appendix to the diaries in 1989. The omissions reduce only the weight, the magnitude, of the "credits." It is impossible to overlook the extent to which Mann stood in need of Adorno's assistance, particularly when a quarrel broke out with yet another Californian neighbor, Arnold Schoenberg, who was beside himself with fury about the treatment of twelve-tone music in the novel: "The adviser and instructor [in the English version he had simply written "informer"] was an earlier student of my since-deceased friend Alban Berg, namely Herr Wiesengrund-Adorno. He is thoroughly familiar with the actual details of this technique and was therefore quite capable of providing Herr Mann with a reasonably precise description of everything which one layman—the writer—requires in order to convince another layman—the reader—that he really understands what is at issue here."[18] This was how he reacted in the *Saturday Review of Literature* on 13 November 1948, thus forcing Mann to "grant him," Schoenberg, "the credit he owed" in his turn.[19] In Mann's diary the quarrel now expanded to become the "Schoenberg Case."[20] Mann prudently did not mention Adorno in his public reply to Schoenberg, since even the mere name was like a red flag, something that drove the composer to make puns. He invented the verb "to adorno" (*adornen*) to describe Adorno's musical counseling. In Schoenberg's eyes, Adorno had become an "informer," and this was at a time when the fear of persecution was spreading among the émigrés of "German California" because of the campaigns against "un-American activities." This general sense of persecution was linked in Schoenberg's case with his own individual feelings of paranoia, feelings that were noted independently by loyal admirers such as Rudolf Kolisch and Hanns Eisler. Adorno became persona non grata in Schoenberg's universe. Mann attempted to communicate at a higher level with Schoenberg—the "authentic" master, as he had called him in the handwritten dedication that Schoenberg had spurned.

The term "the authentic master" may perhaps reveal something of Mann's original intention of inviting Schoenberg to advise him. But Schoenberg was hard to approach, and so Mann seems to have decided in 1943 that Adorno would suit him much better. Despite the omitted passages, *The Story of a Novel* shows clearly how Adorno, who starts off as a somewhat hazy figure in the diaries, fit in almost uncannily with Mann's intentions.

Adorno's first little present, a copy of Julius Bahle's book *Inspiration in Musical Composition,* seemed itself to be a pointer to their future collaboration. Soon after, Adorno presented him with the manuscript of *The Philosophy of Modern Music,* and Mann found himself "peculiarly in tune" *(vertraut)* with Adorno's ideas.[21] In any event, this feeling led him to develop a theory of intellectual property:

> After long intellectual effort, it frequently occurs that things that one has sown in the wind come back to one, changed by another hand and placed in different contexts, reminding one of oneself and one's own ideas. Ideas about death and form, the self and the objects may well appear to the author of a thirty-five-year-old story about Venice as memories of himself. They may claim their place in the philosophical writings of a younger man and at the same time play their functional part in my depiction of people and epochs. An idea as such will never possess much proprietary worth in the eyes of the artist. What matters to him is its ability to function in the spiritual machinery of the work.[22]

In these passages Mann is fixated on his need to salvage his claim to his own individual achievement and at the same time to honor Adorno's contribution. He seems unaware that his own work had long since become an integral part of the younger man's life. On Mann's seventieth birthday Adorno admitted in a letter of 3 June 1945:

> I know that I can only give full expression to my personal gratitude by confessing that the resonance of your words and the character of your imaginative creations impressed themselves so strongly upon me during the years in which I ceased to be a child that I could no longer begin to separate these impressions from the loves and friendships belonging to those years. You have addressed the
> · life which precedes all art, and thereby vouchsafed the fundamental experience of art itself. This spiritual and biological proximity itself complements something else that has also touched me very closely.[23]

Buddenbrooks, Tonio Kröger, and *Death in Venice* were among the most powerful influences of Adorno's youth; it was this experience that Thomas Mann encountered in the writings of the forty-year-old Adorno. The interweaving of biography and autobiography—a form that both Mann and Adorno shied away from—makes for the overlapping of individual lives and historical events that are refracted in the image of the age that we see in *Doctor Faustus.* Much of what Adorno was to write subsequently can be better understood in the light of these overlapping experiences in Californian exile.

Even the seemingly straightforward sentences that Mann reformulated for *The Story of a Novel* can really be understood only when we take into account the biographical and intellectual relationship between the maturing Theodor Wiesengrund and the revered writer of his early years. Adorno left an eloquent reminiscence in the birthday letter: "There was one occasion—it was in Kampen in the summer of 1921—when I followed on behind you for a good way, unnoticed, as you walked, and imagined what it would be like if you were to turn and speak to me. That you have indeed truly spoken to me now, after twenty years, is a moment of realized utopia that is rarely vouchsafed to any human being."[24] The doppelgänger motif comes to mind. Both men were familiar with Freud, for whom the uncanny had ceased to be an insoluble riddle. They seem to have grown very close to each other during the work on *Faustus*. This becomes particularly clear at one point in *The Story of a Novel*. Immediately after Mann confesses how "as a gesture of gratitude he had inscribed the name 'Wiesengrund,' Adorno's paternal name, in the text,"[25] he goes on to talk about the impact of a very private reading of the chapter he had just written. Max Horkheimer was the only other person present: "The effect was extraordinary and, as it appeared, was deepened by the comparison between the so very German foundation and coloration of the book—and my very different private attitude toward the maniacal country of our origins. Adorno, musically attracted and moved by this little reminiscence of his teaching, came up to me and said, 'I could listen to you the whole night long!'"[26] In Mann's text we can see alongside the tribute to Adorno the wish to preserve his distance; the report of Adorno's response in 1944 reveals the same readiness to identify with Mann that we find in the birthday letter of 1945.

"I had the feeling that I was only now, for the first time, actually encountering that German tradition from which I have received everything—including the strength to resist the tradition. This feeling, together with the happiness it grants—a theologian would speak here of a blessing—is something that I shall never forget."[27] The intimacy that Adorno lays claim to may well have felt uncanny to Mann, and his need for distance found expression in the malicious letter to Jonas Lesser in October 1951: "My admiration for his extraordinary intellect is undiminished. There are also brilliant things in the *Minima Moralia*. But I shall certainly leave them all as they stand."[28] There can be no doubt that Mann registered the feelings that Adorno uncharacteristically spoke of, but he relegated them to the place that suited him best. Adorno's suggested biographical notes and Mann's montage of them hint at the two men's different perspectives. Both art and philosophy strive for an understanding of the age. Mann saw in Adorno "an artistic, sociological critique of great progressiveness, subtlety, and depth, with a remarkable affinity for the idea of my work, for the 'composition' in which I lived and had my being."[29] Adorno saw Mann as the living embodiment of the German tradition,[30] from which he had never felt further removed than in the years 1944 and 1945, when news of the mass murder of the European Jews could not be missed by an émigré with his wits about him. The *Minima Moralia* were his reaction to the irreparable damage to life that he was just learning about.

For all that, there are differences of emphasis in the accounts of the two men. Adorno's statement "My father was a German Jew" leads to Mann's repeated insistence on Adorno's paternal name, Wiesengrund.[31] In Los Angeles, in November 1943, Adorno tried to have the name officially reduced to a "W.," but without success. Officially, his name was recorded as Theodore Adorno, both in Los Angeles and subsequently on his birth certificate in Frankfurt. He expressed his regret at the loss of the "W." to his parents, who by this time were living in New York. There has been considerable speculation about this change of name, much of it malicious. The awareness of being an immigrant came together with the wish to become an American for practical reasons. The hope was that naturalization would avert the danger of being classified as an enemy alien and interned. Teddie associated the name Wiesengrund with Germany, with Amorbach, Taunus, and the Odenwald. He was delighted by Thomas Mann's inscribing his name in *Doctor Faustus*. But it was not absolutely necessary to retain such a name in California now that Germany had become the enemy of mankind. A further factor was that many long-established Americans of German origin made no very great effort to conceal their sympathies for Nazi Germany.

Of greater significance, however, than the long-standing and now legalized name was the fact of naturalization. Max Horkheimer had long since recognized this. The Horkheimers had acted as witnesses in 1944 when Katia and Thomas Mann had taken American citizenship. This act of self-adaptation still resonates in the letter Mann wrote to Agnes Meyer immediately after the ceremony: "Afterwards we went to an American restaurant with the witnesses, Professor Horkheimer and his wife, and had a hearty American breakfast, pancakes with maple syrup and coffee. He told me that when he was asked to state on his honor and conscience whether I was a desirable citizen, he had answered: 'You bet!'"[32] Name changes were not on the agenda for people who were already well known. This was not Adorno's case. The Germany of the Weimar Republic, where intellectual insiders might have heard of the name Wiesengrund-Adorno, had vanished into the mists of time. The *Zeitschrift für Sozialforschung,* in which he had made his debut in 1932 under his double-barreled name, was inaccessible to almost everyone in the United States outside a small circle of central European immigrants, for even in emigration the annual issues continued to appear in German until 1939. Adorno's contributions were published over the abbreviated signature "T. W. Adorno," since even in New York, one learned not to draw attention needlessly to German Jews in intellectual professions and so provoke resentment. Paul Lazarsfeld's letters following Adorno's appointment to the Princeton Radio Research Project in 1938 testify to the strength of these prejudices in the academic world.

Escaping from the competitive atmosphere of New York, with its enormous pressure to conform, was undoubtedly one of the motives for moving to distant Hollywood. Thomas Mann, too, was quick to leave the East Coast: "Princeton where we were recently is very pretty. But I am somewhat afraid of the scholarly atmosphere and feel more comfortable with the movie rabble in Hollywood," he wrote to his son Klaus on 12 May 1938.[33] Friedrich Pollock reports that Adorno, of all people, dreamed of a life as a private scholar in California. With America's entry into the war in 1941, the tendency among the émigrés to adopt American citizenship increased. The identification with the America of the New Deal was reflected in the way the immigrants followed the example of President Franklin D. Roosevelt in abbreviating their middle names. Adorno was by no means the first to do so. The example had long since been set on the East Coast by his sociology rival Paul F. Lazarsfeld, who had arrived from Vienna at the start of the New Deal. After America's entry into the war, the productive minds in German California began once again to focus more centrally on their own relationship to Germany—regardless of their political hue.

In the case of the Manns, the Brecht-Eislers, and the Critical Theorists from Frankfurt, Germany was made a focal theme. Reflection on the relation of German culture to National Socialist barbarism touched on a key question of émigré existence, namely, the question of any possible guilt of one's own. In Adorno's letter to Mann in 1945 offering birthday greetings, he said that in his eyes Mann personified the German tradition, from which he, Adorno, in a dialectical turn, derived the strength to resist that tradition. Adorno thought of Mann as the contemporary of his own father, whom he also identified as belonging to the German tradition, referring to him as a "German Jew."[34] Oscar Wiesengrund, however, by no means thought of himself as fully identified with the German tradition. His well-known Anglophilia is an expression of that fact. The equation of Anglophilia with liberalism is one that Mann later made explicit in his Chicago speech of 1950, "My Epoch." It could also be observed in Freud. For the assimilated Jews of central Europe after the failure of the European revolutions of 1848, the identification with English liberalism was a way of participating in the process of bourgeois emancipation without identifying with the radicalism of the French Revolution. The "Epoch" of which Thomas Mann spoke was the tradition-creating bourgeois century, the second half of the 1800s.

Adorno's reference to having grown up in a "family atmosphere shaped by highly theoretical (also political) and artistic, above all, musical interests"[35] was a formulation taken over verbatim by Mann in Story of a Novel. He did not think the somewhat obscure phrase in parentheses, "including political," called for further explanation. Adorno distinguishes the atmosphere of his parents' home in Frankfurt from the climate in which Mann's Reflections of a Nonpolitical Man could be written. The parenthetical phrase is the early sign of the non-identity of German Jewish citizens with German citizens of the empire. The unusual identification of theory, politics, and music in the home has the effect of a signal. In the household of Adorno's parents there was no great gulf between practical life and the artistic life as we find in Mann's experience, caught as it was between the bourgeois atmosphere of Lübeck and the artistic ambience of Munich. In Frankfurt, bourgeois conditions seem to have been turned on their head: a utopian world, free from purposes and an integral part of the bourgeois fantasy of the artist—that is what the young Teddie could experience in his parents' home. It is a utopia Adorno could ascribe to the mature Thomas Mann in the birthday letter of 1945: "Who after all, one might ask, has ever stayed more faithful to the utopia of youth, to the dream of a world unspoilt by ends and purposes, for all your unremitting emphasis upon maturity and responsibility?"[36] Mann had undoubtedly been present in Seeheimerstrasse in the characters of Hanno Buddenbrook and Tonio Kröger. In the same way, to have grown up with Death in Venice must have been one of the "innate merits" of a culturally advantaged middle-class home at the end of the First World War. "Innate merits" is a paradox that Thomas Mann, the extraordinary bourgeois artist, claimed for himself. In this respect Adorno was not a whit his inferior.

Adorno told Mann about his mother, who had contributed the name Adorno, as if to point to his southern origins, something that had endowed Tonio Kröger with the charms of non-identity, the fact that he was not one of the blond, blue-eyed northerners. In Mann's case the idea in the background was that of the "south," symbolized by his mother, Julia, née da Silva-Bruhns, with her "tendencies to the 'south,' to art, to the Bohemian."[37] Mann described his relations with his parents to Agnes Meyer, his German American benefactor, as entirely on the Goethean pattern,[38] divided up between the "serious conduct of life" and "blithe nature," male and female, north and south. He felt himself to be his mother's child, but what he remembers of her is her "sensual, pre-artistic nature" and also the "peculiar *coldness* of her character,"[39] which does not at all harmonize with the image of an idealized south. The *coldness* emphasized by Mann becomes a quintessential quality of the bourgeois subject for Adorno, the social theorist. Adorno's autobiographical sketch for Mann imperceptibly elides his parents' house in Oberrad with a utopian realm in which the catastrophe that befalls Hanno Buddenbrook at the end of the novel is quite unimaginable. "An atmosphere dominated especially by musical interests" does not describe the environment in which Thomas Mann or Tonio Kröger grew up, but it does describe that of Teddie Wiesengrund, who was surrounded by his mother and his Aunt Agathe, both of whom played music to a professional standard. Seeheimerstrasse goes with the double-barreled name Wiesengrund-Adorno; it was neither an upper-middle-class factory owner's home nor the private villa of a captain of industry in which the ladies of the house cultivated middle-class culture as an adornment. Every lapse into the sphere of domestic music making or singing while out hiking produced an irritated reaction in Teddie against his father: "I remember clearly the embarrassment I used to feel when, at my father's request, my mother and her sister—both professional singers—started to sing something like 'O Täler weit, o Höhen.'"[40] In the sketch he wrote for Mann, Adorno quite clearly emphasizes the link between theory, politics, art, and especially music so as to stress his family's distance from the normal educated bourgeois family.

These circumstances are mirrored in a very specific way in the letters Adorno wrote to his parents. Toward the end of 1943 Adorno proudly announced his collaboration with Thomas Mann, and even enclosed the letter he had received from the foremost living representative of German literature. He tells them about the reciprocal invitations and even goes so far as to talk about his contribution to *Doctor Faustus*. One of their replies, however, shows clearly that they did not properly understand the nature of the project and that they thought the Herr Kretzschmar about whom Adorno and Mann were in correspondence was a real person rather than a character in a novel.[41] The son who wanted to make his parents happy by telling them of his success also became anxious that his parents would now start boasting to other émigrés about their son's newfound importance. On 20 October 1943, therefore, he strikes a cautionary note: "But this is strictly confidential, even as far as Julia is concerned, since I would not like this to become known in Jewish circles under any circumstances."[42] Once again, Teddie has idealized his family for external consumption. His own sketch of a social biography for Mann's *Story of a Novel* is itself fitted out with an ideal family which combines all positive values in itself without regard to the actual social structures characteristic of German Jews of the period. This Wiesengrund-Adorno family can be understood only as a compromise between a vanishing bourgeois world and a cultural enthusiasm that attaches itself to everything that the Culture Industry has to offer. While in America, Oscar Wiesengrund himself had developed into the prototypical cultural consumer.

Adorno's description of himself continues with the "young man's utopia" that he had already hinted at in the "birthday" letter.[43] He writes: "I studied philosophy and music. Instead of deciding exclusively for one subject or the other, I have always had the feeling that my real vocation was to pursue one and the same thing in both of these different realms."[44] In *The Story of a Novel*, Mann keeps his distance: "This remarkable mind rejected the professional decision between philosophy and music his entire life. It was all too evident to him that he was actually pursuing the same goal in divergent realms. The dialectical direction of his thoughts and the social and historical philosophical tendency became interwoven with his passion for music in a way that is not entirely unique today, but was in tune with the spirit of the time."[45] Mann remains true to his conception of the artist who is a bourgeois—with "bonds leading back into the past," to the bourgeois age to which he had given his allegiance in "My Epoch" in 1950.[46] Adorno does not fit into the generational pattern with which Mann is preoccupied. His childhood at the end of the bourgeois era is succeeded by early adulthood in *The Magic Mountain*. That novel, however, was the work of a mature, fifty-year-old writer. Mann can also see in Adorno qualities that are more than just individual. At this point it is unclear whether "not entirely unique" applies to the dialectical theory of society or to music. He would obviously have noticed the differences between Adorno and Schoenberg, in whose house he had been introduced to the witty Hanns Eisler, who represented another variation on the theme of the musician with a well-thought-out theory of society. Roles such as these were quite new to Mann's notions of the artistic division of labor. For the author of *Doctor Faustus*, Adorno was a piece of good fortune in that his advice included tendencies of the age that went beyond the merely individual and that provided resistance to the hand of a master in a late work.

Adorno's brief text of 1937, "Late Style in Beethoven," which then found its way into chapter 8 of *Doctor Faustus*, must have touched Mann when he encountered it in the midst of his mighty work—"nothing less than the novel of my epoch."[47] Today the text reads as if, at the end of the 1930s, Adorno was already familiar with the difficult problems that Mann would face a decade later: "In the history of art the late works are the catastrophes."[48] Thomas Mann was able to identify with this sentiment: "Like battles, peril at sea, mortal danger, a difficult work of art brings us closer to God since it produces the pious glance upwards in search of blessing, help, grace—a religious feeling."[49] According to Adorno, the artist's subjectivity lives in a state of tension with the conventions: "Touched by death, the hand of the master sets free the masses of material that he used to form."[50] Mann does not fail to mention Goethe's works, with which he increasingly identified: "Hence the overabundance of material in *Faust II* and in the *Wanderjahre*, hence the conventions that are no longer penetrated and mastered by subjectivity but simply left to stand."[51] "Mortal danger" frequently recurs in *The Story of a Novel*. Adorno's discussion of death in late works must have seemed to Mann to provide a resolution to the difficulties he was encountering with the biography of Adrian Leverkühn, the hero of *Doctor Faustus*: "Death is imposed only on created beings, not on works of art, and thus it has appeared in art only in a refracted mode, as allegory."[52] It comes as no surprise to learn that Adorno gave his neighbor in Los Angeles not only the manuscript of *The Philosophy of Modern Music* but also a copy of Walter Benjamin's book *The Origin of German Tragic Drama*, a present that deeply impressed Mann.

In his autobiographical account of the novel, Mann establishes a close connection between Benjamin and Adorno. At the time when Mann came to know the man who was to become his musical adviser, Adorno's life was still overshadowed by the news of Benjamin's terrible death while fleeing from the National Socialists. Adorno also presented Mann with a copy of his book on Kierkegaard, whose contents closely mirrored Benjamin's ideas in the book on tragedy. Mann believed that he could detect a profoundly German element in that book. He thought he could discern an affinity—a supra-individual quality—between Adorno and Benjamin which manifested itself in "a similarly aloof, tragically clever and exclusive form of spirit."[53] Benjamin had crossed paths with Mann in exile when he published an essay on the Institute for Social Research in *Maß und Wert*, a Swiss journal, with the intention of "rousing the educated bourgeoisie."[54] One passage in this essay might almost seem to have been written personally for Mann, who remained in close contact throughout his life with Ferdinand Lion, the editor of the journal:

> In liberal writing there is currently much talk of the German "cultural heritage." This is understandable, in view of the cynicism with which German history is being written at the present time and German property administered. Yet nothing would be gained if among those who are silent inside Germany or those who are able to speak for them outside, the complacency of would-be inheritors were given free rein, or if the beggarly boast *"omnia mea mecum porto"* were to become the accepted tone. For these days, intellectual possessions are no more secure than material ones.[55]

In the figure of Adrian Leverkühn, Thomas Mann likewise reflected that all too proud claim to German culture. Adrian's "Where I stand is Kaisersaschern" almost sounds like a self-parody of Mann's own "Where I stand is Germany."[56]

Adorno's close ties to Benjamin as well as his friendship with Max Horkheimer, who lived nearby, must have drawn Mann's attention to the group of German Jewish intellectuals who shared common interests under the general rubric of the Institute for Social Research. It is possible that Mann did not perceive his music adviser Adorno as an isolated individual even if he was unaware of the implications of the larger "Critical Theory" that Horkheimer had been promulgating in exile since the early 1930s. Adorno's *Philosophy of Modern Music*, whose first German edition in 1948 contained a blurb by Mann, made no secret of its theoretical links with *Dialectic of Enlightenment*.[57] Adorno wanted his book on music to be thought of as an excursus to *Dialectic of Enlightenment,* which had appeared shortly before, but which was scarcely known. Adorno's role as music adviser to Mann leads us necessarily to the very heart of Adorno's own work. The idea that Adorno was a sociologist of music as well as a philosopher proves to be a paltry classification after the fact. He had found himself forced to resist this pigeonholing in Vienna in the twenties. At that time he found himself in the middle of debates with his friend Ernst Křenek, who lagged behind him in the realm of sociological theory, and also Hanns Eisler, who was his equal on matters of theory. He was repeatedly forced to insist that social categories could not simply be applied to musical material from outside but had to be generated from the material itself. Adorno had not developed into a cultivated music journalist like Hans Heinz Stuckenschmidt. His musicological ideas are not marginal; they are located at the very center of his work. They could not have been articulated, however, without his own experience as an artist. It is this configuration of Adorno's own productive powers that enabled him to imagine what Adrian Leverkühn might well have composed. Mann was inspired to acknowledge the uniqueness of this productive constellation by writing the autobiographical work *The Story of a Novel,* which can actually be thought of as a unique tribute to Adorno. For the family admirers of the "Magician," this meant a sort of act of self-disenchantment on the master's part. Even the term "autobiography," which recurs in Mann's diaries, can only be interpreted ironically, since this autobiography was essentially written to clarify his relationship with another person.

The loneliness of genius in a disenchanted world had inspired Mann to give shape to his own experience as a bourgeois and an artist. He had imposed on his composer Adrian Leverkühn the necessity of a pact with the devil in order to oppose the disenchantment of the world with a new enchantment of art. The quarrels that followed with Schoenberg and also with Adorno enable us to glimpse the extent to which in this novel Mann's own role as a master of his craft was called into question. Adorno's *Philosophy of Modern Music* converts the dilemmas of a lonely mastery into its theme. When we consider that the Schoenberg section of this work dates back to the period 1941–42, the links with Benjamin's theses on the "concept of history" and the *Dialectic of Enlightenment* become immediately clear. In the preface he wrote to the first edition of 1948, at a time when he was still in Los Angeles, Adorno attempted to underline the unity of his own writings.[58] He sustained this notion in almost all his subsequent prefaces and introductions, as if he wished at least to mitigate the damage he had suffered in life, and therefore in his works as well, by pointing to their underlying biographical unity. These attempts at self-interpretation resemble bandages soaked with blood that simply draw attention to an injured man's wounds even though these biographical bandages are intended to help restore the idea of an intact personality. Despite their emphatic dislike of biography and autobiography, both Thomas Mann and Theodor Adorno found themselves obliged to compensate for the damage done to their own lives by paying a tribute in the form of an act of self-disenchantment. Adorno's own compositions date from the period between 1920 and 1945. After 1945 he ceased to appear before the public as a composer.

There can be no doubt that Mann's *Doctor Faustus* bears the wounds of a catastrophe, a late work, in keeping with the meaning Adorno identified in relation to "Late Style in Beethoven."[59] But the catastrophe becomes the subject of the work itself, its content, and as such it threatens to destroy the form. Mann attempts to exorcise the catastrophe, which is the catastrophe of German culture, by containing it within a biographical framework. This compels him to invent Serenus Zeitblom, who is given the task of narrating the life of Adrian Leverkühn. A single individual is unable to bear the weight of this disaster. The biography of Leverkühn, who is credited with the inventions that in reality belong to Schoenberg, contains aspects of the lives of Hugo Wolf and Nietzsche as well. Nietzsche also has a leading role in Horkheimer and Adorno's *Dialectic of Enlightenment.* Confronted by Nazism and the Nazis' attempt to appropriate Nietzsche for themselves, the authors succeeded in liberating the critical potential of Nietzschean philosophy once again. But Hugo Wolf? Given his birth and death dates of 1860 to 1903, he surely belongs to the core period of the bourgeois era. In February 1945 Adorno notes: "Very German: a better model for Thomas Mann's novel than the latter can imagine. And that in its turn is a point in Thomas Mann's favor."[60] In Adorno's eyes a particular national feature of the Germans is "their uncertainty of taste. If a German manages to achieve something great, rich, and yet coherent, as in the *Genesender an die Hoffnung*, he finishes it with a great Wilhelminian fanfare that knocks everything flat. And in general, there is something of the Nazi about him; the popularity of *In der Fremde* is no accident."[61] German bourgeois culture had long since lost its idealized image for Adorno. Mann wanted to endow the character of Leverkühn with a hidden autobiographical strand, but his ironical distancing from Adrian still lay in the future.

Adorno came to the rescue with a bold device, one that may possibly have irritated Mann. For Mann's eightieth birthday in 1955, Adorno dedicated the essay "Fantasia sopra *Carmen*" to him "in warmest admiration," a text which Mann, normally an attentive recipient, never commented on.[62] Adorno mentions *en passant* that Nietzsche, "if anything, understated the subtlety of Bizet's masterpiece, *Carmen*":

> For where *Carmen* becomes entangled in the world of operetta, without ever, be it noted, forgetting the need for a certain compositional selectivity, its act of condescension takes place in the name of style, as the foil to a gravity that has no need of exaggeration because the slightest change of tone towards the frivolous alters the horizon of the music. It is presumably this procedure and not the influence of more modern composers that inspired Adrian Leverkühn in his belief that dissonance should express the exalted and the spiritual, while hell is reserved for the banal and commonplace world of harmony and tonality.[63]

Thomas Mann, who did not long survive his eightieth birthday, can scarcely have overlooked Adorno's own "subtlety," since Adorno is intimating between the lines that it was he who inspired Leverkühn's method of composition without identifying with it. In the "Fantasia sopra *Carmen*," Adorno comments on *Carmen* as it may have appeared to Nietzsche. He thus provides his own solution to what Nietzsche called "The Case of Wagner" by contrasting Wagner with his musical "antipode," Bizet.[64] Adorno reminds his readers that in Leverkühn's music he had anticipated what the bourgeois novelist Mann had not yet achieved—namely, the ironic transcendence of bourgeois form. Adorno sketched the philosophical and historical significance of this in his essay "The Position of the Narrator in the Contemporary Novel," writing: "Only now can . . . Thomas Mann's medium, the enigmatic irony that cannot be reduced to any mockery in the content, be fully understood: with an ironic gesture that undoes his own delivery, the author casts aside the claim that he is creating something real, a claim which, however, no word, not even his words, can escape."[65] As we know, Thomas Mann felt genuinely flattered by this 1954 comment.

By a sleight of hand, Adorno had placed Thomas Mann in an even larger interpretative framework than Mann had done himself. The latter's ambivalent attitude toward his "Real Privy Councillor"[66] may be explained by his feeling that in the younger man he had indeed discovered an objective authority, but one who could not be reduced once and for all to his role in the success of Mann's own artistic project. The attempt to confine him to a more limited role, in this instance to "credit" him for his contribution to the musical special effects in *Doctor Faustus,* was threatened by every public pronouncement by Adorno on the production of the novel. Nor can Adorno be entirely exonerated from the charge of flirting with this role. His sketch "Toward a Portrait of Thomas Mann," which he first gave as a talk in Darmstadt in 1962, provoked an instant protest from Erika Mann. Even in his exchange of letters with Mann's representative, Adorno dwelt on the particular intimacy that bound him to Mann at the time of their collaboration:

> Lastly, on Leverkühn's compositions. The way this worked was that T. M. mainly had the titles all ready and told me what they were. Then, exactly as I said in my talk, I thought up the works. I believe that it was only the Brentano songs that were not done in that way. . . . I considered the same factors as those I would have considered as a composer if I had been faced with the task of composing those works myself; it was exactly the same as when a composer, like Berg, for example, makes a plan before going to work. I have noted down those considerations, and in fact all sorts of notes are still in existence and they were worked on as if they were not preliminary ideas but descriptions of actual compositions. At the same time, T. M. intervened. Many things were changed in the course of discussion; sometimes he worked the intention of the novel as a whole more tangibly into the description of musical details; sometimes he changed the emphases, as he did in the "devil" chapter; lastly, and that was probably the most important thing of all, he cut a lot out, since what we were discussing was after all a novel and not a music guide. I do not believe that his view of these afternoons which I have to say are still vivid in my memory down to their last details would have deviated from my own.[67]

From the point of view of substance, there can be no doubt that Adorno's account is accurate, even if, and in fact precisely when, it is compared with accounts given by Mann. But the relationship also betrays something of the hidden Adorno; as "the psychoanalysts say, he reveals a certain degree of justified narcissism"[68]—something entirely unaccustomed for a writer who was usually parsimonious with his use of the word "I." All the more grievous must have been his sense of hurt when Mann's letter to Jonas Lesser appeared posthumously in 1965. The letter was published by Erika Mann, who had tried to put Adorno in his place as early as 1962. Adorno was of course fully aware that what he was working on in his Californian exile was a work of crucial importance, the last bourgeois novel in the German tradition, which is also how it appeared to Thomas Mann. Mann's diaries leave us in no doubt that he saw himself as the "last representative of the German tradition."[69] The identification of bourgeoisie and national tradition appeared possible only in that particular man and his work, which bridged the gap between Wilhelminian Germany and exile in German California via the intermediate space of the Weimar Republic. Thus Adorno identified himself here as non-identical, as a younger and different man. The intensified attribute "very German" was one he ascribed to Thomas Mann not only in letters but also in the "Portrait."[70] In the slightly provincial climate of postwar West Germany, it comes as a surprise to find Adorno criticizing Mann from a more worldly perspective. Thomas Mann, he writes, "was not a storyteller with a wide bourgeois experience of the world . . . ; he was little concerned with what is called, in the Anglo-Saxon term, the 'ways of the world.'"[71] But Adorno was more generous with his praise when it came to the subject of the "masks of genius"[72] in connection with the idea of the portrait. Adorno emphasized the difference between Mann and Wagner, with his affectations of genius "at the high point of the nineteenth century." For Adorno it was a difference of substance. "The worst thing an artist can do is to play himself up as a genius and act as though he, the master, were in possession of the metaphysical meaning that the substance of his age lacks."[73]

Adorno's comment on Mann reads like a coded commentary on his own experience. The loss of that "metaphysical meaning" is a recurrent motif in his entire life's work. The fascination exerted by the young Georg Lukács and *The Theory of the Novel* coincided with his first sight of Thomas Mann in Kampen shortly after the First World War. But Lukács's philosophy of history is the formulation of a prewar experience, an implicit consequence of the authentic bourgeois epoch of the nineteenth century, as whose representative German storyteller we must regard Thomas Mann. After the end of the First World War, we see the decaying spirit of that epoch reflected in the theoretical essays of Benjamin and Adorno, who hope to find the new by breaking with that tradition. Rather than idealizing it, they observe how, by virtue of its own logic, it lives on deformed by the Culture Industry. In his Weimar publications, Adorno was preoccupied with the changes wrought in the works of the nineteenth century by the impact of the twentieth. Smaller publications, such as the 1931 essay on

Dickens's *The Old Curiosity Shop*, go hand in hand with the larger study of Kierkegaard, who had experienced a revival in Germany after 1918. Considered in its context, that revival reflected the history of German inwardness. This is how Mann appropriated the book for his characterization of Leverkühn. Adorno had to pay for his expulsion from Germany with a profound crisis of production, one that led ultimately to his falling silent as a composer. In a letter to the conductor René Leibowitz, Adorno described as a "trauma" the fact "that because of my biographical destiny and assuredly also because of certain psychological mechanisms I have not achieved nearly as much as a composer as I believe I could have achieved."[74] Leverkühn's fictional compositions arise from the collaboration with Mann at a point in time when Adorno's desire to compose music was in retreat in favor of an enormous productivity in the field of theory. This period was inaugurated by the writing of *Philosophy of Modern Music*. Thus his *Dialectic of Enlightenment* reflects not just a change in the state of the world but one that Adorno experienced at a personal level.

The experience of change led to the formulation of the key concept of the "Culture Industry," which would become the focus of theory in the work produced by Adorno and Horkheimer in California. It would be misleading, however, to conflate the biographical fact that they lived in Los Angeles with their proximity to the Culture Industry as it actually existed in Hollywood. The notion of the cultured middle-class German who develops into the anti-American critic of an all-powerful film industry fits in all too neatly with the arrogant prejudices of the European middle classes of the second half of the twentieth century. This stereotype can be applied neither to Adorno nor to Thomas Mann. The commodification of culture has been a feature of the bourgeois epoch from the very outset. The fact that nothing we encounter in our experience nowadays is unmediated brings about a fundamental change in both philosophical and artistic consciousness. This is the message that Adorno's *Philosophy of Modern Music* conveyed to Mann at the beginning of the 1940s. "Since the heroic decade—the years surrounding the First World War—the history of modern music" is interpreted by Adorno as

an antithesis to the extension of the Culture Industry into its own domain. To be sure, the transition to the calculated manufacture of music as a mass-produced article has taken longer than has the analogous process in literature or the fine arts. The non-conceptual and non-objective element in music which, since Schopenhauer, has accounted for music's appeal to irrational philosophy, has served only to harden it against the market-place mentality. Not until the era of the sound film, the radio, and the singing commercial began was its very irrationality expropriated by the logic of the business world.[75]

This insight reflects a lengthy historical process: "The system of the Culture Industry," according to Horkheimer and Adorno, "originated in the liberal industrial countries." The England of the nineteenth century stands in the background here. By contrast, "in Germany the incomplete permeation of life by democratic control had a paradoxical effect."[76] The fact that Germany lagged behind did not prevent the cultural change; it only retarded it. The identification of music and the belated nation as the stigma of German backwardness predestined Mann's "novel of music" to be the novel of Germany in the era of its downfall.

The tendency of material to become problematic and hence to permit no naïveté belongs among the fundamental experiences of the bourgeois artist. It was a factor that led Mann to write his great letter to Adorno appealing for his assistance: "Perhaps it springs from an inclination as one becomes *older* to regard life as a cultural product, preferring in one's petrified dignity to interpret it through mythic clichés rather than 'independent' invention. But I am only too aware that I have long practised this kind of higher transcription."[77] Adorno's application of Hegel's *Phenomenology* to art must have removed a weight from Mann's mind with its insight that "all immediacy already represents a mediation in itself. In other words, it is only a product of domination."[78] "Late Style in Beethoven" and *Philosophy of Modern Music* become sources not just for "the higher copying" but also of knowledge and self-knowledge. Mann's idea of the "inclination of old age" is still essentially biographical, and this turns out to be too narrow when confronted by the "demise of art which appears imminent today."[79] Simply in order to maintain his own productivity, Mann was forced to defend himself against Adorno's concept-based writing. We see this from the diaries, but not from them alone. Thomas Mann could produce only in the realm of illusion, but this realm was being called into question, according to Adorno, by virtue of developments that were internal to art. In a reflection on Schoenberg's *Glückliche Hand*, Adorno notes that "the work of art that has only art as its object" becomes ensnared in the division of labor.[80] The stylization of loneliness that so deeply characterizes the figure of Adrian Leverkühn might also be understood as the "return to illusion" that Adorno had already objected to in Expressionism.[81] Irony alone enabled Mann to undo the element of illusion in the traditional novel that was to be compared in Adorno's view with the "three-walled stage of bourgeois theater."[82]

According to Adorno, bourgeois opera represented the climactic point of illusion on the stage: "In the nineteenth century, the bourgeois yearning for freedom had successfully escaped into the representative spectacle of opera, just as it had escaped into the great novel, whose complexion opera so frequently recalls."[83] Only with Wagner, who together with Schopenhauer and Nietzsche goes to make up the three-star constellation in Mann's firmament, is the element of illusion sacrificed to a myth that triumphs over freedom. It is the way in which myth and enlightenment become interlocked that defines the bourgeois nature of opera. The opera already foreshadowed "some of the worst abominations" that are singled out for reproach in the context of "today's Culture Industry."[84] *Minima Moralia*, which was written at around the same time as *Doctor Faustus*, reflects from start to finish the continuity of a system that no creative intellectual can resist. Life in Hollywood as it is reflected in Adorno's text is characterized by the all-pervasive machinations of the Culture Industry, of which the cinema is merely the most progressive branch economically. "There is no way out of entanglement."[85] This holds true for producers, distributors, and consumers alike. Adorno's starting point is "the narrowest private sphere, that of the intellectual in emigration."[86] The collaboration between Mann and Adorno took place in precisely this narrowly circumscribed realm. But it was not acted out on any isle of the blessed. Art and scholarship are experienced as aspects of a changing culture that can no longer be linked effectively to national characteristics, unless one can think of oneself in America as being part of a "radically bourgeois country,"[87] as Adorno wrote retrospectively in 1966. In contrast, he thought of Germany as a country in which "for long periods of time in early bourgeois history the meshes of civilization's net—of bourgeoisification—were not so tightly woven . . . as in the Western countries."[88] *Doctor Faustus* depended for its vitality on the existence of this social and philosophical distinction, and Adorno's answer to the question "What is German?"—namely, "The absolute underwent reversal into absolute horror"[89]—was a fitting reflection of this.

In the now celebrated chapter on the Culture Industry in *Dialectic of Enlightenment*, the difference between the pervasive nature of the media and the totalitarian organization of society under the National Socialists threatened to disappear. Despite this, the author of *Minima Moralia* was fully aware that he owed the ability to formulate his ideas to the privilege of a life "out of the firing-line."[90] Even later on, in 1968, he considered it to be an "American experience"[91] that "within the overall development of the bourgeois world, . . . the country displays capitalism, as it were, in its complete purity, without any precapitalist remnants."[92] In America he could adopt "the most advanced observation post."[93] Even as an intellectual émigré, he still positioned himself in the contradictory tradition of European views of America that ranged from the clairvoyant critique of an aristocrat such as Tocqueville to Ferdinand Kürnberger, a liberal who had taken part in the failed 1848 revolution and whose opinions were by no means free of resentment. But after his return to Europe, Adorno was quite clear in his own mind that "unless one withdraws behind a barricade of elitism one cannot avoid in America the question of whether the concept of culture in which one has grown up has not itself become obsolete."[94] In California he encountered the embodiment of this aging culture in Thomas Mann, a man who was well aware of Adorno's dilemmas. Adorno himself returned to Frankfurt am Main in 1949, while advising Mann to remain in California. Mann wrote to him frankly: "I would not gladly lose you to the Germans, but I very much share the desire that you will actually be able to exercise an active influence there. Accept my best wishes for you when you move into your comfortable new apartment, not to mention the Steinway. But I should also like to know more about the academic prospects where you are. You will surely never become an Ordinarius!"[95] Mann evidently knew his German academics and was aware that they would do everything in their power to resist granting recognition to a Jewish returnee.

Mann did not shy away from embarking on a political debate with Adorno. When he was sent a copy of *In Search of Wagner*, not only did he take up the thread of Californian discussions, but also there was an echo of his reaction to Benjamin's old attack in *Maß und Wert*. As an old bourgeois himself, Mann ironizes the idea of a critical concept of culture, in other words, of the possibility that a future society might emerge from the ruins of bourgeois society: "If there were only a single positive word, my honoured friend, that vouchsafed even the vaguest glimpse of the true society which we are forced to postulate! In this respect, and only this, your own reflections from damaged life say nothing. . . . On one occasion you quote

Lukács with approval, and in general much of what you say suggests a kind of purified communism. But then what is *that?* The Russian despotism is a mistake. But is communism really conceivable without despotism?"[96] In this letter of 30 October 1952, Mann's mockery is quite scathing:

> All that I can see approaching, spreading and irresistibly advancing upon us, is barbarism. Our higher literature strikes me as little but a hasty résumé and *parodic* recapitulation of the western myth before the final onset of the night. How many of us are there now who can still "recognize" the "fundamental experiences of the bourgeois era," can still understand the passage [in *Tristan und Isolde*] where the horn "catches the echo of the shepherd's melancholy song"? We are fast shrinking in number and already find ourselves surrounded by masses who can no longer "recognize" anything. May heaven grant us something of that productive energy which can wrest fresh moments of the new from every moment of decay![97]

Here too behind these harsh words lies a deep disillusionment, the turning away from the America of the post-Roosevelt era. The America of the New Deal, which had once succeeded in politicizing the hitherto apolitical Mann, had ceased to exist. The bourgeois artist had left his own age behind him; he felt the present age to be one in which bourgeois civilization was being dismantled.

Adorno thought that bourgeois society continued to live on in "the minds of intellectuals, who are at one and the same time the last enemies of the bourgeois and the last bourgeois."[98] His reflections "from damaged life" achieve their effect not as an elaborate sociological theory of the intellectual but as snapshots of a particular life, namely, the life of an intellectual in emigration. Even this formulation seems too general. *Minima Moralia* has a self-reflexive aspect that has an almost idiosyncratic connection with its author's life. Highly private concerns seem to have been made public, even though there are no autobiographical revelations that might gratify a voyeuristic curiosity. These reflections live in the moment. Their time span, the years 1944–1947, is part of the definition of each entry. The traces of the early news items about what had taken place in Auschwitz pervade the entire book. Looking back on it now, we are amazed to see how long it took for that knowledge to sink in. It is only the distance, the Californian reality "out of the firing line,"[99] that makes possible a type of thinking that is not simply silenced by the sense of one's own impotence. The writing of *Dialectic of Enlightenment* falls into the same period, as does Adorno's contribution to Mann's *Doctor Faustus*. The unity of all these disparate achievements is what defines the spirit of the age, to use an old-fashioned expression. But these efforts—Horkheimer's and Adorno's theoretical efforts and Thomas Mann's literary ones—no longer sum up the objective world in its totality. Their reflections fall back into their subjects, the literary ones into the characters of Leverkühn and Zeitblom, the theoretical ones into the conscious renunciation of tradition from which the authors derive the strength to relegate it to the past. This act of renunciation, however, creates the illusion of an age without history that actually runs counter to the thinkers' intentions. The fragmentary character of Adorno's reflections denies the totality of the system the right to the legitimating illusion of reconciliation. The idea of a *Negative Dialectics* begins to assume concrete shape in *Minima Moralia.*

The aphorisms of *Minima Moralia* acquire their persuasive force through their immersion in the moment. But this approach also stimulates resistance to them. There is a certain coquettishness in the title of the very first fragment: "For Marcel Proust." It signals that we are dealing with an intellectual, "an artist or scholar"[100] who apparently has no need to earn his living. We perceive an echo here of Adorno's reaction to Horkheimer's attitude after 1933, when he assumed that the young Wiesengrund-Adorno, unlike many others, was in a financially secure position. Except for the relatively brief period when he was employed as a *Privatdozent* in Frankfurt, before the Nazis drove him out, Adorno did not earn his living professionally as a scholar until after his arrival in the United States. After his unhappy intermezzo working for Paul Lazarsfeld's Princeton Radio Research Project, at the time when he was engaged in writing *Minima Moralia,* Adorno had just started to undertake some empirical social studies on behalf of the American Jewish Committee (AJC). After some unfortunate financial transactions on the part of Friedrich Pollock, Horkheimer's financial manager, the institute's assets had been considerably eroded. Adorno's dream of living a *rentier*'s life in California, which Pollock had previously mocked, now no longer seemed attainable. His work on *Dialectic of Enlightenment* had to be interrupted and was then broken off. Horkheimer returned to the East Coast for the time being; Pollock established contacts right up to the White House in an attempt to discover new sources of finance. Many of the workers in the institute had found sanctuary in government bodies in Washington. In particular, the Office of Strategic Services (OSS) assembled a distinguished cast of researchers who labored to supply the political and military leadership of the United States with information about the enemy. In ordinary life in America fascist agitation was on the rise, and anti-Semitism would become an object of research of some political relevance. In addition to the AJC, the Jewish Labor Committee was becoming seriously concerned about anti-Semitism, particularly among workers.

At this juncture Horkheimer proposed that the institute should offer assistance, and Adorno became one of the key figures on the West Coast to begin studying anti-Semitism. At the end of his efforts we find the book that made Adorno's reputation among American sociologists even though he was only one of four active directors of the project. But the name change in 1942 that reduced Wiesengrund to W. was decisive. *The Authoritarian Personality,* always cited as the work of "Adorno et al.," achieved worldwide renown. It appeared in 1950, shortly after Adorno had left California en route for Frankfurt am Main. In Germany, in particular, the prejudice that the authoritarian personality was a specifically German phenomenon seemed to be ineradicable. A glance at the origins of the book should correct that impression. Horkheimer had come into contact with a group of researchers around Nevitt Sanford who had worked on pessimism at the University of California in Berkeley. This group then constituted itself as the Berkeley Opinion Study Group. Supported by grants from the AJC, a study was begun that, as Adorno admitted in 1968, could not actually lay claim to having achieved a "representative sample."[101] In addition to students, particularly women students, since male subjects were not readily available in wartime, there were key groups such as "prisoners in San Quentin" and "inmates of a psychiatric clinic" because, as Adorno put it, "we hoped from familiarity with pathological structures to gain information about 'normal' structures."[102] Horkheimer's original plan was an extensive survey combining studies in different American cities, but it turned out to be far more difficult and time-consuming to organize the appropriate test groups than was justified for practical purposes. The entire project benefited from Adorno's own huge productivity, but everything that was achieved at the time was still fragmentary, a work in progress. Neither *Dialectic of Enlightenment* nor *The Authoritarian Personality* was intended to be the final word. Nevertheless that is precisely how they were understood later on because the context in which they had come into existence remained unknown.

Adorno strove to preserve the unity of his work with a constant flow of new texts and revised versions of older ones, whereas Horkheimer, who was some years his senior, did not welcome new editions of what had appeared before 1949. As late as 1968, Adorno was still struggling to give his American writings the shape of a coherent scholarly biography. The contradictions appear to have been ironed out in his retrospective account. But what makes Adorno's productivity in the 1940s so clearly manifest is the juxtaposition, the simultaneity, of diverging interests imposed on him by circumstances at the time. On the one side, it was in his interest to take a close look at the new country he found himself in—simply so as to be able to survive. The opportunity to gain in experience depended in good part on his adjusting uncritically to his new surroundings while retaining his critical faculties. The key theoretical category of non-identity, which would come to occupy a place at the heart of his work, had its roots in the day-to-day émigré experience in California. *Minima Moralia* should be seen as the reflection of the way in which that life was experienced—or else it runs the risk of not being properly understood. Adorno arrived at his celebrated idea of the F scale from "certain tests in American magazines" but also from the "unsystematic observations of several acquaintances."[103] He discovered certain authoritarian reactions in a democratic society in which a conformist self-censorship on the part of his interviewees made it impossible to elicit their undemocratic attitudes simply by putting direct questions to them. The authors were interested in measuring the fascist "potential, in order to be able to work against it. . . . We all considered the work, despite its great size, a pilot study, more an exploration of possibilities than a collection of irrefutable results."[104] Unusually for him, in producing this text Adorno makes use of the first-person plural when reporting on his work with the Berkeley Opinion Study Group. The fact that *The Authoritarian Personality* came to be regarded as a successful piece of American sociology evidently provided him with a sense of relief. This points to a degree of integration in American society that should not be underestimated.

Adorno steadily advanced in the alphabetically arranged list of contributors in the *Zeitschrift für Sozialforschung*. In 1932, while he was still in Germany, he had made his debut with "On the Social Situation of Music" under the name Wiesengrund-Adorno. In 1936, for his first essay on jazz, he had used the grim pseudonym "Hektor Rottweiler"—this at a time when he wished to preserve the possibility of traveling back to Germany from his exile in Britain. After his arrival in the United States, he used the name Adorno for his publications. The switch to English did not come about until the double volume of 1939–40, with "On Kierkegaard's Doctrine of Love," while in the same issue the "Fragments on Wagner" appeared in German. Volume 9 of what had hitherto been the *Zeitschrift für Sozialforschung* appeared in 1941 under the title *Studies in Philosophy and Social Science,* and for the first time all the contributions were in English. The table of contents included three articles by T. W. Adorno. At the very moment when Horkheimer began to withdraw to California, the Institute for Social Research consciously started to address the American public. Adorno not only wrote "On Popular Music" but also took issue with one of the controversial heroes of American sociology, namely, Thorstein Veblen. Adorno had now arrived intellectually in America. He took pragmatism seriously. It culminated for him in the question: "How is anything novel possible at all?"[105] In 1967 this appeared retranslated into German in *Prisms,* his first publication success in Germany. It is as if the different accentuation of his own name acted as a signal. In the consciously changed old environment, to which he did not automatically adjust, the name Adorno appeared as a foreign word that broke with the naturalness of what had been handed down. Adorno had described foreign words as "the points at which a knowing consciousness breaks in."[106] In *Dialectic of Enlightenment* the authors note that names were undergoing a "chemical change."[107] The first names customary in America, which functioned like "the replaceable members of teams,"[108] called for new surnames, too: "The bourgeois, family name which, instead of being a trademark, individualized its bearers by relating them to their own prehistory, sounds oldfashioned."[109] The authorial name Adorno becomes the signifier of non-identity. It functions like a trademark, but also like a foreign word—one, however, that on closer inspection hints at the history of individualization.

In a new language it was of course necessary to find terms that corresponded to the concepts of a critical social theory. Adorno needed a translator for his texts, and it was to him that he explained his key concept: "Freedom postulates the existence of something non-identical."[110] But what did that mean? "The non-identical element must not be nature alone, it also can be man."[111] The critique of identity philosophy meant more than a theoretical program that Marx had left uncompleted when he turned to the critique of English economics. Idealism grasped the *spirit* of the bourgeois era better than any other philosophy. In the form it took in Germany, it revealed the social dynamic of the development by which the domination of nature became an independent process that ended up damaging spirit itself. The self-destructive forces at work in bourgeois society can be read off from their genesis. As Hegel had already perceived in the *Phenomenology,* total identity simply means death. Reflections such as these, derived from the philosophy of history, bore fruit in *Philosophy of Modern Music,* but Adorno resisted the temptation to "deduce all of this directly out of the decline of the bourgeoisie, whose most unique artistic medium has always been music."[112] The critique of the spirit that dominates nature is undertaken in *Dialectic of Enlightenment;* but it assumes concrete shape only in the excursuses. Its lack of historicity, itself a consequence of the autonomy of the bourgeois domination of nature, scars the critique of that domination. The chapter on the Culture Industry, though it concludes with the note "to be continued,"[113] ends up with its own misinterpretation—entirely against the intentions of Max Horkheimer: "It is nonsense to imagine that I could give the work the necessary precision and concreteness, even if I did it together with Teddie. It has to be filled to the bursting point with historical and economic material, otherwise it feels just like spinning out an argument [*Raisonnement*]."[114]

Nowhere could the harsh contradiction between individual productivity and the modern organization of culture be seen more clearly than in Hollywood. Intellectuals in emigration experienced this very personally; this is articulated in the aphorisms of *Minima Moralia,* whose artful character reveals itself only on a second reading. Adorno began by presenting his friend with "Fifty Aphorisms for His Fiftieth Birthday. Max Horkheimer Los Angeles/New York, 14 February 1945."[115] This was followed by another fifty, with the dedication "For Max. On his Return," for the New Year, on his return to Pacific Palisades. We may smile at these numbers games, but they point beyond the concrete text. From his teacher Alban Berg, Adorno had learned about the transparent second meaning of a composition, a technique of encoding that conveys an additional meaning to the connoisseur. In their work on *Doctor Faustus,* he and Mann had played with this technique. The possibility of combining biographical and autobiographical material is linked to this ludic element of the nonidentical. The wish, for example, to identify Adorno with the devil in *Doctor Faustus* reduces artistic freedom to the mere reproduction of the real which even so cannot be captured in that way. The effort required to transcend the bounds of an identical self, the withered legacy of the bourgeois personality, was something Adorno particularly admired in Proust. The ambiguous forms of the literary fragments in *Minima Moralia* cannot simply be called aphorisms in the traditional sense. As Mann remarked, they range from the "long aphorism" to the "short essay." Admittedly, the thinking subject plays a crucial role, but again and again it steps out of its monadic existence, either reflectively or playfully, and loses itself in the mediated world of objects. In length the pieces exceed the traditional aphorism, but they are held in check by their contents.

History, society, and biography are artfully woven together. The compulsion as an adult to become integrated into the system of the social division of labor can find unmistakable expression simply because the reflecting subject is in fact more than an identical career person. The history of Adorno's life cannot be reduced to his individual history. "The son of well-to-do parents":[116] on second reading that might apply with greater justice to Max Horkheimer, Felix Weil, and Walter Benjamin than to Adorno himself. His two mothers came from rather modest circumstances. The family background can only fitfully be referred to as the "agency of the bourgeoisie."[117] That description tells us more about Horkheimer's and Pollock's parents than about Adorno's. But the idea does not assert the identity of history and life history. It attempts rather to articulate the experience of a painful process of social adaptation. Adorno does not advocate a self-chosen isolation as a tried and tested antidote. His talents as a writer are employed to distinguish his social critique from "reactionary cultural criticism."[118]

> Socially, the absolute status granted to the individual marks the transition from the universal mediation of social relation—a mediation which, as exchange, always also requires curtailment of the particular interests realized through it—to direct domination, where power is seized by the strongest. Through this dissolution of all the mediating elements within the individual himself by virtue of which he was, in spite of everything, also a part of a social subject, he regresses, impoverished and coarsened, to the state of a mere social object.[119]

The elimination of the bourgeois within a bourgeois society transforms the weakened individuals into atoms "who capitulate the moment organization and terror overtake them."[120] It is this isolation that Adorno perceives in American society precisely because it is the radical bourgeois society. "Monad," Aphorism 97, is followed immediately by his reminiscence of the late Walter Benjamin, whose "Bequest," according to Adorno, lay in "the obligation to think, at the same time, dialectically and undialectically."[121]

The idea of the non-identical plays a central role that affects everything right down to the most intimate personal relationships. No general theory of friendship is developed such as the theory Kracauer envisaged in the early 1920s. Part Two of *Minima Moralia* ends with "Gold Assay," in which "the identity of each individual with himself" is deemed to be the most wretched consequence of the process of de-bourgeoisification.[122] As a writer Adorno draws closer here to his older friend Max Horkheimer. The same motives that led him to write the birthday letter to Thomas Mann in the same year come to the surface once again: "The human is indissolubly linked with imitation: a human being only becomes human at all by imitating other human beings. In such behaviour, the primal form of love, the priests of authenticity scent traces of the utopia which could shake the structure of domination."[123]

Schöne Aussicht, 1901 (Institut für Stadtgeschichte, Frankfurt am Main)

Adorno's parents on their honey-
moon (Privatarchiv Dipl.-Ing.
Bernhard Villinger, Weissach)

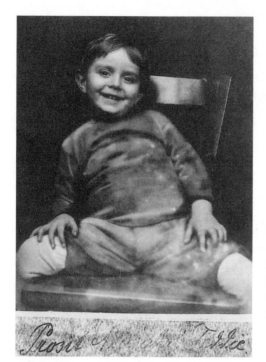

Teddie as a child, used as a post-card by the Wiesengrund family, New Year's 1909 (Universitätsbibliothek Johann Christian Senckenberg, Frankfurt am Main, call number Ms.Ff.A.Stolte 6.1)

At home during the war with Aunt Agathe and his mother, Maria (Institut für Stadtgeschichte, Frankfurt am Main)

Dr. Wiesengrund-Adorno,
second half of the 1920s
(Privatarchiv Elisabeth
Reinhuber, Oberursel)

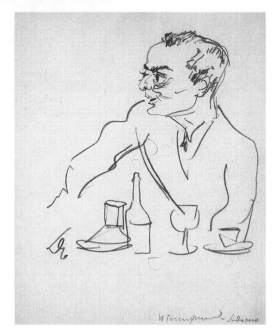

B. F. Dolbin, cartoon, 1931
(Institut für Zeitungsfor-
schung der Stadt
Dortmund)

In Los Angeles in the 1940s (Akademie der Künste, Berlin, Theodor W. Adorno Archiv, photo: Franz Roehn, 1949)

En route to establishing industrial sociology in the German Federal Republic, 1954. Second and third from left: Theodor Adorno with Gretel Adorno (Akademie der Künste, Berlin, Theodor W. Adorno Archiv, photographer unknown)

The reestablished Institute for Social Research in Frankfurt. Max Horkheimer and Adorno surrounded by their associates (Copyright: Archive Centre, University Library Frankfurt a.M., Germany)

With Eduard Steuermann in Kranichstein, circa 1960 (Akademie der Künste, Berlin, Theodor W. Adorno Archiv, photo: Susanna Schapowalow)

At the piano, 1967 (Ilse Meyer Gehrken)

With Gretel Adorno in Sils Maria, 1964 (© Professor Lotte Tobisch-Labotyn)

Sils Maria, summer 1963 (© Professor Lotte Tobisch-Labotyn)

With Max Horkheimer and the Frankfurt SDS, 1967 (Barbara Klemm)

With Hans-Jürgen Krahl in September 1968. To the right, Frank Benseler of Luchterhand Verlag and K. D. Wolff, chairman of the Federal SDS (Barbara Klemm)

In the Institute for Social Research occupied by the SDS, 1969 (Barbara Klemm)

Revising a manuscript at Kettenhofweg 123 (Ilse Meyer Gehrken)

Lecture Hall 6 at Johann Wolfgang Goethe University, Frankfurt (Bildarchiv Preußischer Kulturbesitz/Art Resource, NY)

T. W. Adorno, 1962 (© Archiv S. Fischer Verlag GmbH, Frankfurt am Main; all rights reserved)

5. | Transitions

Bertolt Brecht

"To Those Who Come after Us"

I
Truly I live in dark times!
The guileless word is folly. A smooth forehead
Suggests insensitivity. The man who laughs
Has simply not yet had
The terrible news.

What kind of times are they, when
A talk about trees is almost a crime
Because it implies silence about so many horrors?
That man there calmly crossing the street
Is already perhaps beyond the reach of his friends
Who are in need?

It is true I still earn my keep
But, believe me, that is only an accident. Nothing
I do gives me the right to eat my fill.
By chance, I've been spared. (If my luck breaks, I am lost.)

They say to me: Eat and drink! Be glad you have it!
But how can I eat and drink if I snatch what I eat
From the starving, and
My glass of water belongs to one dying of thirst?
And yet I eat and drink?

I would also like to be wise.
In the old books it says what wisdom is:
To shun the strife of the world and to live out
Your brief time without fear
Also to get along without violence
To return good for evil
Not to fulfil your desires but to forget them
Is accounted wise.
All this I cannot do:
Truly, I live in dark times.

II

I came to the cities in a time of disorder
When hunger reigned there.
I came among men in a time of revolt
And I rebelled with them.
So passed my time
Which had been given to me on earth.

My food I ate between battles
To sleep I lay down among murderers
Love I practised carelessly
And nature I looked at without patience.
So passed my time
Which had been given to me on earth.

All roads led into the mire in my time.
My tongue betrayed me to the butchers.
There was little I could do. But those in power
Sat safer without me: that was my hope.
So passed my time
Which had been given to me on earth.

Our forces were slight. Our goal
Lay far in the distance
It was clearly visible, though I myself
Was unlikely to reach it.
So passed my time
Which had been given to me on earth.

III

You who will emerge from the flood
In which we have gone under
Remember
When you speak of our failings
The dark time too
Which you have escaped.
For we went, changing countries oftener than our shoes
Through the wars of the classes, despairing
When there was injustice only, and no rebellion.
And yet we know:
Hatred, even of meanness
Contorts the features.

Anger, even against injustice
Makes the voice hoarse. Oh, we
Who wanted to prepare the ground for friendliness
Could not ourselves be friendly.

But you, when the time comes at last
And man is a helper to man
Think of us
With forbearance.[1]

Theodor W. Adorno

"Out of the Firing-Line"

Reports of air-attacks are seldom without the names of the firms which produced the planes: Focke-Wulf, Heinkel, Lancaster feature where once the talk
was of cuirassiers, lancers and hussars. The mechanism for reproducing life, for
dominating and destroying it, is exactly the same, and accordingly industry,
State and advertising are amalgamated. The old exaggeration of sceptical Liberals, that war was a business, has come true: state power has shed even the appearance of independence from particular interests in profit; always in their
service really, it now also places itself there ideologically. Every laudatory mention of the chief contractor in the destruction of cities helps to earn it the good
name that will secure the best commissions in their rebuilding.

Like the Thirty Years' War, this too—a war whose beginning no-one will remember when it comes to an end—falls into discontinuous campaigns, separated by empty pauses, the Polish campaign, the Norwegian, the Russian, the
Tunisian, the Invasion. Its rhythm, the alternation of jerky action and total
standstill for lack of geographically attainable enemies, has the same mechanical quality which characterizes individual military instruments and which too
is doubtless what has resurrected the pre-Liberal form of the campaign. But
this mechanical rhythm completely determines the human relation to the war,
not only in the disproportion between individual bodily strength and the energy of machines, but in the most hidden cells of experience. Even in the previous conflict the body's incongruity with mechanical warfare made real experience impossible. No-one could have recounted it as even the Artillery-General
Napoleon's battles could be recalled. The long interval between the war memoirs and the conclusion of peace is not fortuitous: it testifies to the painful reconstruction of memory, which in all the books conveys a sense of impotence
and even falseness, no matter what terrors the writers have passed through. But
the Second War is as totally divorced from experience as is the functioning of a

machine from the movements of the body, which only begins to resemble it in pathological states. Just as the war lacks continuity, history, the "epic" element, but seems rather to start anew from the beginning in each phase, so it will leave behind no permanent, unconsciously preserved image in the memory. Everywhere, with each explosion, it has breached the barrier against stimuli beneath which experience, the lag between healing oblivion and healing recollection, forms. Life has changed into a timeless succession of shocks, interspaced with empty, paralysed intervals. But nothing, perhaps, is more ominous for the future than the fact that, quite literally, these things will soon be past thinking on, for each trauma of the returning combatants, each shock not inwardly absorbed, is a ferment of future destruction. Karl Kraus was right to call his play *The Last Days of Mankind*. What is being enacted now ought to bear the title: "After Doomsday."

The total obliteration of the war by information, propaganda, commentaries, with cameramen in the first tanks and war reporters dying heroic deaths, the mishmash of enlightened manipulation of public opinion and oblivious activity: all this is another expression for the withering of experience, the vacuum between men and their fate, in which their real fate lies. It is as if the reified, hardened plaster-cast of events takes the place of events themselves. Men are reduced to walk-on parts in a monster documentary film which has no spectators, since the least of them has his bit to do on the screen. It is just this aspect that underlies the much-maligned designation "phoney war." Certainly, the term has its origin in the fascist inclination to dismiss the reality of horror as "mere propaganda" in order to perpetrate it unopposed. But like all fascist tendencies, this too has its source in elements of reality, which assert themselves only by virtue of the fascist attitude malignantly insinuating them. The war is really phoney, but with a phoniness more horrifying than all the horrors, and those who mock at it are principal contributors to disaster.

Had Hegel's philosophy of history embraced this age, Hitler's robot-bombs would have found their place beside the early death of Alexander and similar images, as one of the selected empirical facts by which the state of the world spirit manifests itself directly in symbols. Like fascism itself, the robots career without a subject. Like it they combine utmost technical perfection with total blindness. And like it, they arouse mortal terror and are wholly futile. "I have seen the world spirit," not on horseback, but on wings and without a head, and that refutes at the same stroke, Hegel's philosophy of history.

The idea that after this war life will continue "normally" or even that culture might be "rebuilt"—as if the rebuilding of culture were not already its negation—is idiotic. Millions of Jews have been murdered, and this is to be seen as an interlude and not the catastrophe itself. What more is this culture waiting for? And even if countless people still have time to wait, is it conceivable that what happened in Europe will have no consequences, that the quantity of victims will not be transformed into a new quality of society at large, barbarism? As long as blow is followed by counter-blow, catastrophe is perpetuated. One need only think of revenge for the murdered. If as many of the others are killed, horror will be institutionalized and the pre-capitalist pattern of vendettas, confined from time immemorial to remote mountain regions, will be reintroduced in extended form, with whole nations as the subjectless subjects. If, however, the dead are not avenged and mercy is exercised, fascism will despite everything get away with its victory scot-free, and having once been shown as easy, will be continued elsewhere. The logic of history is as destructive as the people that it brings to prominence: wherever its momentum carries it, it reproduces equivalents of past calamity. Normality is death.

To the question what is to be done with defeated Germany, I could say only two things in reply. Firstly: at no price, on no conditions, would I wish to be an executioner or to supply legitimations for executioners. Secondly: I should not wish, least of all with legal machinery, to stay the hand of anyone who was avenging past misdeeds. This is a thoroughly unsatisfactory, contradictory answer, one that makes a mockery of both principle and practice. But perhaps the fault lies in the question and not only in me.

Cinema newsreel: the invasion of the Marianas, including Guam. The impression is not of battles, but of civil engineering and blasting operations undertaken with immeasurably intensified vehemence, also of "fumigation," insect-extermination on a terrestrial scale. Works are put in hand, until no grass grows. The enemy acts as patient and corpse. Like the Jews under fascism, he features now as merely the object of technical and administrative measures, and should he defend himself, his own action immediately takes on the same character. Satanically, indeed, more initiative is in a sense demanded here than in old-style war: it seems to cost the subject his whole energy to achieve subjectlessness. Consummate inhumanity is the realization of Sir Edward Grey's humane dream, war without hatred.

Autumn 1944[2]

Hanns Eisler, the Non-identical Brother

The cold war not only separated many things that belonged together; it also froze our capacity for remembering. Since the end of the short twentieth century, with the demise of the Soviet empire, much has changed. Many a story that had remained hidden has come to light; but equally, many stories succumbed to the general social amnesia and were denied the prospect of a new, unprejudiced scrutiny. Disagreements about the past were the elixir of life to the cold war, and they did not end with it. During the heyday of the cold war, people in the West showed little interest in the past since the East had its own official version, one that changed with the twists and turns of official communist ideology. With the emergence of détente, fissures appeared in the carapace of memory. In 1969, the year of Adorno's death, the original version of Adorno and Hanns Eisler's *Composing for the Films* emerged from such a rent in the façade of the East-West conflict "exactly as its two authors had jointly and definitively completed it in 1944."[3] What was sensational about it was the combination of two names that had been separated by the cold war—at least in Germany. The one author belonged to the history of the Federal Republic, the other to the German Democratic Republic, where he had even composed the national anthem. The public had been in ignorance of their shared past. As émigrés they had tried for years to earn their livelihood in Hollywood. *Composing for the Films* was published by Oxford University Press in 1947 under Eisler's name alone. In 1969 Adorno explained why: "At that time, Gerhart Eisler, the composer's brother, was under attack in the United States because of his political activities, and Hanns Eisler was dragged into the affair. I had nothing to do with their activities and knew nothing of them."[4]

Even thirty years ago only the initiated would have been able to say what was going on in the United States at the time. And Adorno, even at a moment when détente policies were just starting to take effect, had no interest in dredging up the entire story. At the time, Eisler was known in West Germany as the composer of the GDR's national anthem, whereas the "work that obviously lay closest to his heart, his 'Faust' opera,"[5] which was known to only a few connoisseurs, never advanced beyond the project stage. Few people suspected that there had been "an old friendship between Adorno and Eisler dating back to 1925,"[6] although of course this fact makes it utterly improbable that Adorno was completely unaware of Eisler's activities in the United States. It suggests rather that he knew something and guessed more when he goes on to write: "I had no reason to become a martyr to a cause that neither was nor is my own. In view of the scandal, I withdrew my co-authorship. At that point, I had already resolved to return to Europe and was afraid of everything that might have prevented that. Hanns Eisler understood this completely."[7] Then, in 1949, a German version of the book appeared from the East Berlin Henschel Verlag, which incorporated some changes Eisler had made in the text. He also removed the original preface and replaced it with one that spoke the language of the cold war.

In the 1940s and 1950s Adorno seemed content not to be mentioned in the same breath as Eisler. Nevertheless, both men refrained from attacking each other. In 1969 Adorno mentioned that Eisler, who was living in East Berlin, had visited Frankfurt am Main in the 1950s. After all the malicious gossip about the Frankfurters emanating from the circle around Brecht, gossip that was fully reciprocated, the publicly conciliatory tone comes as a surprise. Adorno even defends Eisler's actions in the GDR: "If he had refused to make concessions in the book it would hardly have been published and have been able to exert any influence at all, however limited; Eisler himself would have been in immediate danger."[8] While he thought it necessary to express his dislike of party communism, Adorno did not shrink from blunt statements. When a preface was to be added to the German edition of Paul Massing's studies of anti-Semitism, Herbert Marcuse objected to what he thought went too far in adopting the language of the cold war, and a quarrel broke out between him and the editors, Horkheimer and Adorno. But in the case of Eisler, the conciliatory tendency gained the upper hand. How is this to be explained? Eisler represents a side of Adorno's life that is frequently overlooked—that of the artist who no longer enjoys the support of the bourgeoisie. The artist as a critic of bourgeois society who nevertheless lives in and from within that society: this theme is also articulated in *Composing for the Films*. Both men were confronted with this existential question in their youth in Vienna, at a time when Adorno was also writing his first reviews of compositions by the somewhat older Eisler.

Both Eisler and Adorno found themselves at a crossroads in the Vienna of the 1920s. After a brief period of study at the New Vienna Conservatory, Hanns Eisler, five years older than Adorno, had studied under Schoenberg from 1919 to 1923. Adorno was attempting to make his way in Vienna and hoped to be able to develop his talent as a composer with the aid of tuition from Alban Berg. He had improved his skills as a pianist by studying with Eduard Steuermann, who was also in the Schoenberg circle. Steuermann's sister Salka went to America quite early on, and together with Berthold Viertel she settled in Malibu, at the gates of Hollywood. There she wrote screenplays and kept an open house in which the newly arrived political refugees met the established denizens of the film industry. But all that still lay in the future when Teddie arrived in Vienna as a recent graduate in his early twenties. He had been able to chalk up some successes in Frankfurt, which was after all one of the leading musical cities in Germany at the time, but there were no visible prospects for an independent existence as an academic or an artist. As editor and author for the *Musikblätter des Anbruch,* he developed his expertise as a music critic who knew something about what he was writing. This brought him some recognition, even from Schoenberg, who was not always well disposed toward him. The young Wiesengrund-Adorno introduced a new element into the Viennese discussions: the link between musical practice and social theory. At the time, Eisler was already starting to look beyond the narrow confines of the Schoenberg circle and had cheekily celebrated the fiftieth birthday of "the Master" in 1924 by greeting him as a "musical reactionary."[9] He would rediscover his own ideas mirrored in Adorno's reviews. In Vienna, Adorno also encountered two people who would become the fixed stars in his political and artistic firmament, Georg Lukács and Arnold Schoenberg. But he was not able to establish genuinely cordial relations with either. Hanns Eisler acted as mediator between these different worlds. Eisler's sister Ruth Fischer subsequently became the leader of the German Communist Party in its most radical left phase together with Arkadij Maslow, who would seek to work for the institute in emigration later on. Hanns's brother Gerhart, to whom he remained close, became a key party official who belonged to the so-called conciliators' faction. When he and Adorno met in 1925, Eisler was already known as "the representative composer of the youngest generation of Schoenberg's pupils."[10] Adorno's estimate of Eisler continued to rise from one review to the next. In 1929 he said of Eisler's opus 11, "Zeitungsausschnitte," that "the central force of the songs is their *tone:* at the same time highly differentiated (for example, in the 'Song of Death,' when he mocks the better world to come with sacred chords) and concentrated in a determination to change the world that breaks through the limits of art."[11]

No more than a few years lie between these two publications. In the meantime, Berlin became the place where they would meet. By the summer of 1925, both Eisler and Adorno realized that Vienna held no further prospects for them. When Adorno arrived in Vienna, the artistic revolution already lay in the past. He never actually experienced the heroic phase of the avant-garde. He quickly perceived that the group around

Schoenberg did not possess the same authority that he had imagined from his knowledge of the George circle. Admittedly, the Master was still revered by his pupils, who had now achieved fame in their own right. But the meetings had become more private in character than they had been immediately after the war. Adorno's own teacher Berg had distanced himself slightly from the immediate circle around Schoenberg. In Adorno's recollection, "no doubt a certain liberality separated him from the other Schoenberg pupils."[12] Berg seemed to avoid a certain "tyranny of the circle,"[13] whereas Eisler went out of his way to challenge it. Otherwise he would not have been so reckless as to gossip in 1925 with Alexander von Zemlinsky, Schoenberg's brother-in-law, on the way back from the annual festival of the International Society for Contemporary Music, which was held that year in Venice, and regale him with stories that he must have known would antagonize the Master. Under these circumstances, we must also think of Adorno's review of 1929 as a kind of declaration of solidarity with Eisler.

Both Eisler and Adorno ran up against the limits of an artist's life in 1925. Eisler struck out in new directions, abandoning both Vienna and Schoenberg. Meanwhile, Schoenberg himself left Vienna for Berlin early in 1926, having been appointed to succeed Ferrucio Busoni at the Prussian Academy of Arts. But the breach between him and Eisler could not really be patched up. If we read the letters between the two men carefully, Eisler does not come out of the comparison very well. Even so, we can feel rather more respect for his frank comments on his own behavior from a distance of over twenty years:

> I was twenty-five years old, and Schoenberg thought highly of me. I was the third pupil from among a hundred talented people whom he acknowledged as masters. He now imagined that since I was sitting firmly in the saddle, I would ride alongside him. My communism, he supposed, was a youthful indiscretion and I would eventually get over it. I then did something no one expected: I broke off relations with him. And I did so in a brutish way, ungrateful, truculent, and bad tempered. Scorning his philistinism, I departed abusing him all the while. He behaved magnanimously. The letters he has written to me in recent weeks are the magnificent documents of a unique man.[14]

Schoenberg remained his musical guide. In 1957 Adorno wrote of Eisler, who had died in 1951: "It can scarcely . . . be estimated what Schoenberg, that unique authority, had to give and what he achieved in music overall; not just through the material changes and innovations to which public consciousness has adjusted in the meantime, but through his own compositions, which he extracted from objective social conditions that would scarcely permit such success nowadays."[15]

In November 1918 Schoenberg had been elected president for life of the Association for Private Musical Performances, which aimed to make his own performance practice independent of the bourgeois public. Admittedly, this "Schoenberg Association," as it became known in Vienna, lasted for only three years, after which it was finished off by inflation. But the rigorous purism that was cultivated in it was the precise indicator of a contradiction that could scarcely be tolerated. In 1929 Eisler delivered a scathing judgment on this period: "[In] 1918–1923, at a time of inflation, the Spartakus uprising, the Soviet Republics in Munich and Budapest, the Red Army before Warsaw—at such a time, the only things musicians could think of to fight about were technical matters. Not a single one had any inkling of the climate of the times. The consequence of this 'timelessness' and this tunnel vision of music is that modern music has no public; no one wants it. . . . Modern music leads an illusory existence that can only be maintained artificially."[16] This was typical of Eisler's new tone. He was now writing in the *Rote Fahne* (Red Flag), no doubt through the mediation of his brother Gerhart. But even in this article he speaks respectfully of Arnold Schoenberg while dismissing his *Jacobsleiter* as a "flight into mysticism" ("Arnold Schoenberg, this genuine genius who is making such bold advances in music . . .").[17] Eisler's style really was very different from what was to be expected in a Communist Party newspaper. Moreover, he sought to escape from the trap represented by the contradiction of advanced music and the absence of a public through a resolute radicalism which made no concessions to prevailing opinion, and in this respect he may well have remained more faithful to Schoenberg's own convictions than either man wished to acknowledge.

Adorno and Eisler continued to be linked by their experience of this contradiction. Despite their divergent political opinions, it enabled them to write a book jointly which helped them to sustain a bond that was threatened by the cold war. In *Composing for the Films,* they state that "the operatic theatre finally became estranged from its audience," a break that is labeled "definitive" and dated to the period 1900–1910.[18] It is identified as "the breach between middle-class audiences and really serious music."[19] Both Adorno and Eisler toiled throughout their entire lives to overcome this predicament. Eisler sought the solution in a changed class constellation, symbolized by Berlin. Between Vienna and Berlin lies Baden-Baden. In the summer of 1927 Eisler was invited to present his composition for the five-minute-long experimental film *Opus III* at the Festival Deutsche Kammermusik. The film was by Werner Ruttmann, who soon afterwards was to make his name with *Berlin: Symphonie einer Großstadt*. Eisler received this commission through the agency of Schoenberg, despite their quarrel. In Baden-Baden he met Bertolt Brecht for the first time. Brecht was producing *Mahagonny*, the so-called *Songspiel* he had written with Kurt Weill. They too were attempting to go beyond the terrain of bourgeois art, and for that reason they staged their play in a boxing ring. A tradition-free, sports-oriented America stood for the rejection of bourgeois Europe—an America, however, that was unable to shake off the contradictions of a developed, commodity-based society. As a critical observer, Adorno noted in 1932 that "it is not Mahagonny that is regarded as an ideal, juxtaposed to the bourgeois world, but that world is itself caught in the dim flare of the city of nets."[20] Adorno thought that "the true Mahagonny" belonged in the "opera house," not the musical revue theater.[21]

Eisler, by contrast, wanted to abandon the opera house for good and all. What he wanted was the street—or, in the language of his article "Die moderne Musik" (Modern Music) of 1927, the community. It is scarcely conceivable that Adorno could have been unfamiliar with this essay by Eisler. His criticism of "Zeitungsausschnitte" reads like a response to it. He leaps to the defense of Eisler's musical practice as opposed to Eisler's polemics:

> In a situation—or so we learn from the logic of the songs—in which social conditions have such power over the individual that his freedom is an illusion and the aesthetic communication of such freedom, his personal lyricism, is an ideology, personal lyricism can lay claim neither to truth nor to the interest of society. But since no collective exists that is capable of delivering lyrical contents that have any greater authority than those private ones, and since Eisler sees through the dubious nature of a community art without a community, he dismisses the idea of a positive, fulfilled lyricism and replaces it in radical fashion with a *negative* one.[22]

Adorno notes that the impulse underlying Eisler's music came from outside. He is aware that the "force" that is expressed "comes from politics and not from aesthetic reflection."[23] And even then, he expresses his reservations:

> There is a danger that for the sake of comprehensibility, the musical means have not been brought fully up to the current state of *musical* modernity. . . . It would be possible, therefore, for a revolutionary political conviction to attract reactionary aesthetic ones, whereas if that revolutionary conviction were to be entirely persuasive, it would have to adopt the technical methods that are in tune with the very latest historical achievements. This then is the problem of Eisler's future development, not simply his internal development as a composer, be it noted, but his sociological and theoretical development, since he cannot remain blind to the difference between music that is appropriate in its own terms to the stage reached by society and music that is actually consumed by present-day society.[24]

The differences between Eisler and Adorno would seem to have been programmed in advance. But if we were to take account only of the positions they had adopted by the end of the 1920s, we would be unable to understand how they could possibly write a book on film music together in the early 1940s. And it would be even harder to explain how they were able to maintain contact during the cold war despite their sharp political differences. As late as 1958 in one of his legendary conversations with Hans Bunge, Eisler spoke about the times they had spent together in Hollywood. He referred not just to Adorno, his former friend, but also to his own recent visit to Frankfurt. "He would not really want to be seen with me in public, let alone allow his name to be used," Eisler claimed.[25] Eisler evidently realized just how reluctant Adorno was at the height of the cold war to be mentioned in the same breath as self-declared members of the Communist Party who had taken up residence in the GDR after their return from exile. This reluctance points not only to his mistrust of the GDR but also to his anxieties about the instability of democracy in the West. After all, both men had experienced the McCarthy period and had seen how people could suddenly fall victim to an inquisitorial campaign. Eisler had experienced this personally, since he had been targeted by the House Committee on Un-American Activities (HUAC); Adorno had witnessed this as an observer who did not feel as free to speak out publicly against the committee as people who were more firmly established. Adorno wanted to be able to decide for himself when to leave the United States for Europe.

Hence his statement of 1969, which becomes comprehensible in that context: "I had no reason to become a martyr to a cause which was not and is not my own."[26]

Eisler's and Adorno's paths had parted ways on the question of the "cause," but not as definitively as it might seem from these events. Both men had gone to Vienna in the mid-1920s to escape an untenable situation. Eisler took the road to Berlin, where his brother's connections brought him into close contact with the German Communist Party. Adorno likewise found himself repeatedly drawn to Berlin. He too had plenty of personal contacts there. Through Walter Benjamin he met Gretel Karplus, and through her he met Ernst Bloch. Benjamin, in the meantime, had become closer to Brecht, while at the same time he found himself forced to reflect seriously on the implications of the foundering of his academic career. To his close friends he often spoke of joining the Communist Party, in which his brother had been active since the end of the First World War. Similarly, their friendship with Adorno seems to have brought Bloch and Eisler closer together. "I probably first got to know him in Berlin, around 1932," recalled Bloch, "in a coffeehouse; there were three of us, together with Adorno. Adorno was quite pro-communist at the time."[27] But this calls for further explanation. People were evidently competitive about what implications to draw from the failed revolution, and also about who was the most radical. Adorno developed the connection between revolution and radicalism from the concept of logical consistency. His own radicalism appears to follow logically from "On the Social Situation of Music,"[28] which was the title he gave to his first contribution to the *Zeitschrift für Sozialforschung*, his entrance ticket to the circle around Horkheimer in 1932. As late as 1934 he wrote to Hans Redlich in Vienna:

> But since I am aware of no revolution that has any form other than logical consistency, that is to say, none that has ever emancipated itself from its basis in history, and since absolutely every other procedure, every other ostensibly more radical venture that starts from scratch, takes the form of a bad utopia and for the most part simply represents a backsliding into conditions of production whose substance cannot be recreated out of pure immediacy, I am compelled to stick with logical consistency until an inconsistency makes its appearance whose own truth content proves to be genuine.[29]

These abstract statements only underscore the true situation: in the second half of the 1920s, Adorno developed an aesthetic left-wing radicalism that allowed him to treat Schoenberg as the beginning of a revolution that needed only logical consistency for it to be carried further. But Adorno was extraordinarily sensitive to the ideological dimensions of his own language, and this protected him against the more eye-catching pathos of aestheticizing slogans. His philosophically based left-wing radicalism enabled him to remain true to the aesthetic revolution that Schoenberg had inaugurated while giving him solid grounds for keeping his distance from the cause espoused by the Communist Party. Adorno's essay "Die stabilisierte Musik" (Stabilized Music) of 1928 gave an account of Soviet music which had developed "curiously enough" into a march into "folkloricism."[30] He also noticed the complementary tendency toward a new classicism in the West, which, paradoxically, also entered Soviet culture in the succeeding phase. Adorno's consistent aesthetic radicalism saved him from idealizing the early Soviet Union. The fact was that this was not *his* cause. Since for Brecht, Eisler, and Bloch the decision in favor of communism was politically motivated, they were often forced to make aesthetic claims that went against their own better judgment. Bloch's radical judgment on the Russian communists that they thought like dogs but acted like philosophers was the product of a heroic phase of Soviet communism. The great aesthetic debates of the thirties and forties found these intellectuals initially hostile to the dominant communist ideologues, but they soon lapsed into silence. All three spent the period of Stalinism at its harshest in the United States; they would probably not have survived in the Soviet Union. Even their aesthetic adversary Georg Lukács admitted that it was only through his incredible good fortune that he had been able to survive the mass purges in Moscow.

Confronted with Eisler's radical left-wing furor, Adorno expressed doubts that were designed to facilitate dialectical reflection. In his brief review of Eisler's *Zeitungsausschnitte* Adorno wrote: "We may well ask whether the right to lyrical utterance really has been so completely extinguished, and has become so hopelessly private as is commonly claimed by the voice that inhabits the songs: and whether a consummate work of art would not rather open the gates dialectically to that region of social commitment which Eisler undertakes to enter without detour."[31] Adorno had already thought through the implications of Eisler's opinions, namely, that the fact that "no true lyric poetry is possible today, and that our lives lie so cruelly in the dark, is something that newspaper texts alone can convey."[32] We can already hear the motif that would lead later on to Adorno's celebrated dictum about poetry after Auschwitz. That dictum was evidently anticipated in the debates with Eisler and Brecht. Brecht's lines from his great poem of exile "To Those Who Come after Us" belong at the heart of this discussion, one that was continued in exile in America:

> What kind of times are they, when
> A talk about trees is almost a crime
> Because it implies silence about so many horrors?

In California, Eisler composed his *Hollywood Songbook.* As he recalled in conversation with Bunge in 1958, "The situation was that my then friend Adorno begged me to let him write a preface to it when it was printed."[33] The possibility that Adorno had envisaged in his review of *Zeitungsausschnitte* was made a reality by Eisler under the conditions of exile. He wrote these songs while earning his living in Hollywood, partly through jobbing commissions for the film industry. Subsequently Eisler tried to minimize the importance of this return to the form of the *Lied,* but even so, he told Bunge that "song cycles have played a huge part in the history of music."[34] Exile forced Eisler to turn away from the straight and narrow path of new social commitment; it threw him back into a monadological private form of production without a market, which he financed by producing "functional music" for film.

The ambivalent nature of the artist's social situation can also be seen from the practical example that Eisler gives in *Composing for the Films,* namely, the *Vierzehn Arten, den Regen zu beschreiben* (Fourteen Ways of Describing the Rain), which was written for a documentary film by Joris Ivens. Once again, Eisler tried to play down its importance in conversation: "So in a sense the *Vierzehn Arten, den Regen zu beschreiben* was also fourteen ways of being sorrowful with dignity. That too belongs to art. I do not wish to say that it is the central theme of the twentieth century, what we might call the anatomy of sorrow—or the anatomy of melancholy. But it too may be included in an oeuvre."[35] Even in this gentle denial we can sense the closeness that had come about in the isolation of emigration. It contrasts with the unbridgeable distance from the site of the catastrophe. Eisler took the bold step of basing this work on a twelve-tone row and then of dedicating it to Arnold Schoenberg, who was also living in Los Angeles, on his seventieth birthday. Eisler recollected that Brecht thought there was "something immoral"[36] about his focusing so intently on the way it rains.

Brecht's *Journals* contain this entry for 24 April 1942: "hear eisler's records with the rain poems at ADORNO's. they are very beautiful, remind you of a chinese ink-drawing. . . . After that i feel i have to attack schoenberg, just to shock them."[37] Brecht must have known that such attacks would provoke Eisler as well as Adorno. He noted on 27 April, "[eisler] recounts beaming that schoenberg received the 14 descriptions of rain with words of praise, and will even show the film in one of his university lectures."[38]

Brecht aimed to challenge both Eisler's and Adorno's respect for their teacher. He also wanted to test whether the basic idea of his poem "To Those Who Come after Us" would hold good for the process of grieving. Adorno says that Schoenberg's idea that there were more important things to do than compose music had come to him as early as 1933. Their "attitude" toward their teacher, which aroused such feelings of ambivalence in Brecht, opened the door to a new relation to tradition, one that Brecht could make productive for himself. For Brecht, too, began to write elegies in Hollywood. He referred to them derisively as "messages in a bottle,"[39] thus marking his own remoteness from the site of horror. In 1958 Eisler noted "a quite extraordinary distance in this cycle of poems."[40] Adorno's aphorism "Out of the Firing-Line" belongs in this context. Brecht's *Journals* maintain the vast distance separating Hollywood from the European battlefields. Eisler and Adorno were closer to each other; but Eisler was also prepared to sacrifice Adorno in order to raise a laugh from Brecht. Hans Mayer, who saw himself as Adorno's rival throughout his life and continued to do so after the latter's death, has reported, credibly enough, how Eisler made him laugh with the story that he had persuaded Adorno to play Brecht the songs he had written set to poems by Stefan George. Brecht is said to have commented, "It reminds me greatly of Chopin."[41] Brecht loved to be provocative.[42] Benjamin had suffered from this when he stayed with him in Denmark in the thirties. Among these émigré intellectuals, faced with a mixture of anxiety, terror, and guilt feelings, the greatest term of abuse was "sentimentality." Adorno tried to find words to express the feeling behind this in an aphorism: "In the recollection of emigration each German venison roast tastes as if it had been felled with the charmed bullets of the *Freischütz*."[43] A remark such as this is inconceivable unless we imagine the link between Wiesengrund and Amorbach—the "only piece of home that remained to me," as he wrote on 24 September 1950 to his mother, who had remained in New York, following his first visit back to Amorbach in the late summer.[44]

The émigré community living in the shadow of Hollywood experienced its deepest gloom in the years 1940–1943, after which optimism returned among those who identified with the workers' movement. This was the precise moment in which Horkheimer and Adorno discussed the idea of critical theory as a message in a bottle. Horkheimer had used the term in a letter from New York in 1940 to Salka Viertel, Eduard Steuermann's sister: "In view of everything that is engulfing Europe and perhaps the whole world, our present work is of course essentially destined to be passed on through the night that is approaching: a kind of message in a bottle."[45] The idea of the message in a bottle belongs to the prehistory of *Dialectic of Enlightenment*. It reflects the loss of the traditional addressees of the critical theory of society. In *Minima Moralia* this damaging loss of the political tradition is summed up in the "grimly comic riddle: where is the proletariat?"[46] But where is the joke? During a beach party where much alcohol had been consumed, so the story goes, Adorno is said to have launched the idea of the message in a bottle. Someone asked, "What's it supposed to say?" Eisler is said to have answered in broad Viennese dialect, "I feel *so* awful! [*Mir iss' soo mies!*]," and everyone burst out laughing. Adorno suppresses this joke in *Minima Moralia* because it would have diverted attention from things that could not be forgotten.

As habitual cinema-goers, Horkheimer and Adorno at the foot of Bel Air had recently noted down for their chapter on the Culture Industry the idea that "to be entertained means to give one's consent."[47] In the preface that Adorno and Eisler wrote jointly for *Composing for the Films*, they explicitly point to the theory underpinning the book.[48] It is not the case that two incompatible worlds confronted each other, as subsequent gibes would have us believe. Never had Eisler and Adorno been so close to each other as they were in their isolation from Hollywood when Eisler dedicated his Chamber Symphony to Adorno, a work that had started life as the film music to *White Flood* (1940). In 1965–1966, Adorno noted that he was well aware that this was a piece of *Gebrauchsmusik*, commercial music. But these notes, which were written after Eisler's death, do not amount to an abstract condemnation of Hollywood productions. *Composing for the Films* sees itself as a practical handbook for writing better film music. Adorno lavishes praise on the opening sequences of Charlie Chaplin's film *The Circus*: "Absolute genius!"[49] Adorno envied Eisler his friendship with Chaplin, and as a man with charm, as well as being a profound Wagner critic, Eisler also got on well with Thomas Mann. But he was a genius who paid a high price, which finally broke him. Eduard Steuermann, a friend of both men, summed up the paradox of Eisler's life when he wrote to Adorno, "Things go wrong when he is inspired."[50] Adorno thought of his fate and Eisler's as that of two brothers who had experienced something of a music of the future only to see it return to its old ways. Adorno titled his first great critical music essay of 1928 "Die stabilisierte Musik" (Stabilized Music), in imitation of Comintern jargon, but a jargon that he, like Eisler, had mastered and could play like a virtuoso, using it for his own purposes: "For the tide of music history had overflowed the dams of society, but then receded from those dams again, leaving its most exposed works high and dry."[51] Curiously, Adorno envisaged that the future of music would be based in an America which he had not yet seen and of which one could only hope that people there knew "that construction alone is able to imbue the formless mass with what is."[52] Ten years later, almost all the people to whom this experience meant something had met up in Pacific Palisades, in an empirical America, at a moment of deep sorrow. Eisler, who was a connoisseur of Goethe, said that it was a time for writing elegies: "One does not live in Hollywood unpunished."[53] The joke that glosses over the sadness was an essential part of Eisler, according to Adorno: he was "a very good comrade who could cheer you up better than anyone, though it would not be hard to imagine him saying that his head was full of ideas, but it still had to come off. At the same time, he was not false, he was good-humoured, shrewd, non-identical."[54] He was unable to share wholeheartedly the optimism that emerged toward the end of the war; one could see that he did not entirely believe that the social changes which came about in the shadow of the advancing Red Army would automatically lead to better times. He refused to compose new fighting songs; he made no attempt to disguise his dislike of march music. Instead, he composed the music for Alan Resnais's project for a film about Auschwitz, *Nuit et Brouillard (Night and Fog)*. His own music fell silent in the GDR: "This was the most powerful proof that he had to pay the price for refusing to live as he would have had to."[55]

Fritz Lang, the American Friend

"To be continued . . ."[56] With this lapidary remark the manuscript of the chapter on the Culture Industry in *Dialectic of Enlightenment* ended in

1944. Hardly anyone who came after would read it in this light, but this is undoubtedly how Adorno thought of it. The 1944 chapter was not supposed to be the end of the matter but rather the beginning of an unending analysis of the ways in which the Culture Industry had brought about changes in consciousness. In the first edition of 1947 this chapter is followed by "Elements of Anti-Semitism," which is thought of as twinned with the Culture Industry in that it is a "psychoanalysis in reverse."[57] As with the volume *Composing for the Films* which he had co-written with Eisler, the image of the educated middle-class Adorno turning up his nose at the Culture Industry out of sheer terror at the idea of coming into contact with it is essentially a projection backwards from the end of the twentieth century, by which time the methods of the Culture Industry had prevailed throughout the world and, as we might say with Adorno, had become second nature in our social existence. This was the idea underlying the quotation from Kürnberger's *Der Amerikamüde* (The Man Tired of America) that Adorno chose as an epigraph for *Minima Moralia:* "Life does not live."[58] Looking back from the sixties, Adorno's critics took far too rosy a view of life on the margins of the Culture Industry in the California of the forties. German reviews of books by the returnees are generally colored by feelings of resentment. In actual fact, however, life in the early forties was hardly to be mastered at all without external assistance. Horkheimer started quite early on to look for friends in the film industry. Teddie too had his contacts, if we think of Salka Viertel, for example. Eisler, and almost all the composers who wrote for the films, were the ones who came out best economically. From Teddie's letters to his parents, who supplied him on the West Coast with film tips from the East Coast, it becomes clear that both Horkheimer and Adorno were regular moviegoers, if only to obtain material for the chapter on the Culture Industry.[59] But the fact that in the forties Adorno acquired an inside view of the problems of film production in Hollywood went unnoticed for a long time. His best informant in Hollywood was Fritz Lang, and the two men remained close friends until Adorno's death.

Their friendship is documented in a correspondence that begins with Adorno's return from exile in 1949. This correspondence, amounting to thirty letters from 1949 to 1967, is very private in nature. The letters are unlikely to prove fertile territory for film historians, but their intimate character makes them stand out in Adorno's life as the precious documents of a friendship. The two men knew each other well, but not from the Weimar period, by which time Lang was already a prominent figure. Twelve years his junior and a passionate moviegoer, Adorno of course knew who Lang was, but they did not meet until Adorno had settled in California.

Their friendship dates back to the early forties, when they met through the Los Angeles scene, which was dominated by artists who had emigrated from Germany as well as by technicians and businessmen from the film industry, in which authors, musicians, scholars, and other intellectuals from Germany also moved freely. Los Angeles offered quite specific advantages for émigrés from Nazi Germany. There already were established German film people in Hollywood; some of them had been recruited as talent there as early as the twenties. They now helped the newcomers obtain residence permits and proof that they had the means to support themselves. They persuaded studio bosses to employ well-known writers to produce film scripts, something that often led to bitter disappointment and humiliation. The bosses regarded themselves as philanthropists; the writers felt that they were not badly paid but that they were superfluous, a defining experience for the immigrant writers' guild in Hollywood.

By the time the world began to open up once again, in the later 1940s, Lang had long since established himself in Hollywood, whereas Adorno faced an uncertain future. His financial resources were waning, and he and the others were living on research projects, which meant that by necessity they were constantly writing proposals to American educational foundations—a laborious business. The pioneering study *The Authoritarian Personality* came into being at Berkeley in the Bay Area, out of the academic mainstream, and almost despite rather than because of the rather difficult funding arrangements. Los Angeles at the time was a center not for American academics and scientists but for émigrés from Nazi Germany—and in that group Adorno was not exactly a VIP.

Lang and Adorno became close friends in Hollywood. With their respective partners, Gretel ("Giraffe") Adorno and Lily ("Micky") Latté, they became integrated into the zoo of "nicknames and noms de guerre," an empire of pseudonyms in the close circle around Horkheimer. In 1946 Horkheimer himself, who at the time lived near Thomas Mann in Pacific Palisades, had, "in the name of the totality of dogs," solemnly presented Lang with "a declaration of independence from a degenerate mankind"[60] after consultation with "Hippopotamus King Archibald"—that is, Adorno. In future letters Lang was affectionately called "Badger." Anyone who is aware of the shyness that characterized both Horkheimer and Adorno will know how to evaluate this employment of animal names for their own private use as a sign of the intimate nature of these relationships. They only became really close to each other, however, in Hollywood in 1941. Adorno was finally able to leave New York, where he had lived since 1938 while working at the Institute for Social Research, which was attached to Columbia University, and for the Princeton Radio Research Project. Now that he would be free from the stress of project-driven empirical research, he wanted to devote himself, together with Horkheimer, to their major joint task, the book on dialectics.

Although there is no documentary evidence on the matter, it is inconceivable that their close friend the "Badger" would not have had access to the Culture Industry chapter as it was being written. It is replete with references to films and well-known actors and directors. The underlying ironic tone that can be understood only as the result of familiarity with the objects of its criticism has mostly passed academic posterity by unnoticed: "For centuries society has prepared for Victor Mature and Mickey Rooney."[61] Unfortunately, we have no letters between Adorno and Lang from this period, simply because they regularly talked on the telephone, visited each other, and arranged for readings together. Parties and receptions shortened the days, a particular form of activity that Adorno commented on in *Minima Moralia*. At a party in Malibu "shortly after the war," Adorno on one occasion found himself satirized by Chaplin:

> Harold Russell, the star of William Wyler's film *The Best Years of Our Lives*, had lost a hand in the war and instead wore an artificial claw made of iron, but very effective. When I shook his right hand and it responded to the pressure, I was very taken aback, but realizing at once that I should not let Russell see my reaction under any circumstances, I instantly transformed the shocked expression on my face into a winning grimace, which must have looked even more shocking. Scarcely had the actor departed than Chaplin was already mimicking the scene. So close to horror is the laughter he provoked that only from close up can it acquire its legitimacy and its salutary aspect.[62]

Lang's works stand in for the central idea of the Culture Industry chapter, in which Hollywood is construed as the most progressive system of standardized cultural production, with outriders in Berlin and Moscow. Film as a genre is not condemned from the standpoint of European bourgeois culture, as alleged by the prejudiced view of *Dialectic of Enlightenment* prevalent among media studies experts. The productive imagination that is unable to bear fruit in the Hollywood system has been overlooked both by subsequent critics of the book and by its supporters. What is criticized is "the fusion of culture and entertainment," not only because it trivializes culture but also because it leads to the compulsory "intellectualization of amusement":

> In some revue films, and especially in grotesque stories and "funnies," the possibility of this negation is momentarily glimpsed. Its realization, of course, cannot be allowed. Pure amusement indulged to the full, relaxed abandon to colourful associations and merry nonsense, is cut short by amusement in its marketable forms: it is disrupted by the surrogate of a coherent meaning with which the culture industry insists on endowing its products while at the same time slyly misusing them as pretexts for bringing on the stars.[63]

In reality, the text came into being at the high point of the studio system as the consequence of Adorno's sympathetic observation of actors, composers, writers, producers, and directors of every kind.

The fact that Horkheimer left New York in order to go to Los Angeles and that consequently Adorno ended up in Los Angeles too was owing to their friendship with William (Wilhelm) Dieterle, who had settled in Hollywood with his wife, Charlotte, in 1930. Dieterle had persuaded Horkheimer to abandon the hectic and expensive life of New York, where there could be no question of acquiring a house and garden of one's own, to say nothing of a retreat from the routine of university life. Dieterle became the only film director to have an article published in *Studies in Philosophy and Social Science*, which was the American version of the renowned academic journal *Zeitschrift für Sozialforschung*. In 1941 he wrote about Hollywood's fears of losing the European market.[64] According to Dieterle, Hollywood's film bosses had no liking for Hitler, but political activities against National Socialism had a damaging effect on business. The political scene changed dramatically, however, with the entry of the United States into the war. Now Hollywood wanted to make its own contribution to the war effort. Actors who had been more or less unemployable because of their accents suddenly obtained roles in anti-Nazi films, from SS officers to concentration camp inmates. Moreover, the émigré scene in general profited from the change, since the émigrés' knowledge of Europe was suddenly at a premium. Many of the social scientists looking for work were now appointed to posts in the Office of War Information (OWI) and later the Office of Strategic Studies (OSS).

Even Bertolt Brecht, who had been somewhat worn down economically, now found an opportunity to collaborate with Lang on *Hangmen Also Die*.[65] Brecht had escaped from Europe at the last moment, having set sail for California from Vladivostok in 1941 on the *Annie Johnson*. He still had memories of his unfortunate experience in 1935, when Eisler, who was teaching at the Institute for Social Research's University in Exile in New York, had helped to arrange for a production of *The Mother*, a production that finally failed. He now chose the West Coast as a base. Dieterle and Lang are said to have financed his voyage, thus preserving Brecht from what might well have become a lethal exile in Moscow. Hanns Eisler, who had had some success in films, was also inclining toward Hollywood. Adorno had already met him in London in 1934 and then again in New York in 1938. From 1941 on, all these acquaintances would meet up frequently in Salka Viertel's house; her husband, Berthold Viertel, was one of the few directors Brecht acknowledged besides himself. Salka had started writing screenplays for MGM.[66] She was also involved in 1934–35 when her boss, Irving Thalberg, was negotiating with Arnold Schoenberg over a $25,000 fee for the film music for *The Good Earth* (directed by Sidney Franklin and Victor Fleming). Schoenberg was trying to keep his and his family's heads above water by teaching composition and with poorly paid university teaching. Nevertheless, he acted the *grand seigneur* and great artist throughout the negotiations, rejected traditional film music as mere accompaniment, demanded control over all the sound effects, and doubled his proposed fee. Thalberg had to content himself with whatever was agreed to by the head of the MGM music department. All of this became part of *Minima Moralia*, a book whose title is intended to reflect the guilt felt by the intellectuals who had survived and been expelled into paradise.

Whereas Brecht liked to pretend that he was the victim of Hollywood, such a thought was far from the minds of Horkheimer and Adorno. The Culture Industry—and this too is often overlooked—can be understood only as an ironic concept that takes its cue from the false consciousness of the bosses and their staff. Adorno could not stand reactionary cultural criticism, but he also questioned the simple solution of class struggle that Brecht and Eisler endorsed and commended to others. During this period Brecht was working on *Arturo Ui*, which was convincingly criticized by Adorno, but his most persuasive works—"To Those Who Come after Us" and the "Hollywood Elegies"—accurately reflected the exile situation. Like Brecht, Adorno saw himself not as an immigrant seeking to settle down permanently but as a refugee who had found asylum in America. Lang saw things differently. Despite great irritations and obstacles in his dealings with the studios, he had been able to gain a foothold at the center of Hollywood production. He even managed to succeed in the most American of all genres, the western, with the film *The Return of Frank James* (1940). Lang took genre production to its limits; Henry Fonda's lonely struggle smashes through the superficial veneer of the western, revealing the social mechanisms lying beneath. Lang had succeeded in achieving that sort of impact before, in German with *M* (1931), with Peter Lorre, and in English with *Fury* (1935–36), with Spencer Tracy. Lang knew his way around the star system and was able to turn it to his own advantage. Adorno's conception of the Culture Industry as making use of "ready-mades," of "instant products," could have been taken straight from this.

Brecht regarded Lang as a principal, comparable in his role as film director to Brecht's idea of leading his theater troupe. He tried to blame Lang for all the changes made to the original script of *Hangmen Also Die*. What annoyed Brecht most of all was the fact that there was no role in it for Helene Weigel. But Weigel, a native of Vienna, spoke with such an incomprehensible accent that Fritz Lang, himself Viennese, thought it impossible to use her. There were far too many "language clowns," as they were known in the argot of the cosmopolitan "movie mob," as Thomas Mann called them. Brecht thought of himself as a purist Marxist, but he had no understanding of the social preconditions of film production, since he thought purely in economic terms and looked only for the cinema's dependence on outside capital. But these were just attitudes he adopted. He was able to change his stance when it suited him—or, as he would have put it, when it appeared useful. He found he had no difficulty in seeing through the pseudo-contradictions of nationalist mockery or patriotic rhetoric. On 11 November 1941 he noted in his *Journals:*

> it is difficult for refugees to avoid either indulging in wild abuse of the "americans," or "talking with their pay-checks in their mouths" as kortner puts it when he is having a go at those who earn well and talk well of the USA. in general, their criticism is directed at certain highly capitalistic features, like the very advanced commercialization of art, the smugness of the middle classes, the treatment of culture as a commodity rather than a utility, the formalistic character of democracy (the economic basis for which—namely competition between independent producers—has got lost somewhere).[67]

Even with Brecht there is no simplistic pattern of anti-Americanism at work. His Epic Theater can be thought of as a riposte to the film industry. Adorno notes in the sequel to the chapter on the Culture Industry: "The montage effects which Brecht introduced into drama imply the almost complete interchangeability of time. . . . Thus in spite of its discontinuous nature this procedure comes to resemble the lack of resistance of cinematographic technique, just as in fact all Brecht's innovations could be read as an attempt to salvage the theatre in an age of film after the disintegration of psychology."[68]

Brecht needed the money from *Hangmen Also Die* to finance his other work. According to the credible testimony of Salka Viertel, he was prepared to go much further in selling his labor power. He asked her whether they could not write a purely commercial film script for the studio together—"writing on spec" was a widespread practice in Hollywood. But even this outstanding combination of an experienced screenwriter with one of the most productive and inventive German authors was unable to produce a dream script that would free them both from financial worries. What remained was frustration, corrosive, malicious gossip, and self-irony. Brecht's *Journals* are full of all these. From January 1942 the *Journals* also give a picture, albeit a distorted one, of Lang and Adorno, on both of whom Brecht casts his sharp, sometimes malicious gaze. On the one side, the enormous respect in which Brecht held Adorno's older friend Walter Benjamin transferred itself to Adorno, although he also saw him as potential satirical material for his "TUI" novel. But on the other, Brecht's deliberately provocative anti-intellectualism discomfited Adorno, though only much later did he realize that it was this anti-intellectualism that he disliked in Brecht. He found it hard to take Brecht's conflation of truth with the pretense of being stupid in order to survive. Precisely because they agreed on many matters, it may have been difficult for the FBI and also the Hollywood Culture Industry to distinguish between what must have seemed like microscopic differences that separated them so absolutely. Arguments derived from Brecht take up crucial positions in Adorno's writings. The otherwise ingenious editors of Adorno's works have been unable to identify "the magnificent passage" in Brecht that Adorno deleted from his lectures on metaphysics and emphasized in *Negative Dialectics* when he drew attention to the "failure of culture" because "its mansion," he says paraphrasing Brecht, "is built of dogshit."[69]

Dialectic of Enlightenment gives us the flavor of the discussions that animated the powerless authors, actors, directors, producers, and intellectuals as they exchanged stories about their encounters with the Culture Industry. Brecht's celebrated radio theory was a response to the development of radio in the Weimar Republic; Adorno was familiar with the workings of radio from the time when it was helping Benjamin to keep his head above water following the world economic crisis. This pattern was not exclusive to America; Horkheimer and Adorno noted the tendency toward authoritarian culture in the transition from the telephone to radio: "The former liberally permitted the participant to play the role of subject. The latter democratically makes everyone equally into listeners, in order to expose them in authoritarian fashion to the same programs put out by different stations. No mechanism of reply has been developed."[70] At this point one of Brecht's central ideas from the "prefascist Europe" that had been left behind is applied to the analysis of modern America, an idea that enables Horkheimer and Adorno to make use of their firsthand knowledge of America to arrive at a breathtaking prognosis for the future of television: "Television points the way to a development which easily enough could push the Warner Brothers into the doubtless unwelcome position of little theatre performers and cultural conservatives."[71] Later on, Brecht used such insights to deduce politically dubious consequences: the independence from market forces of his Theater am Schiffbauerdamm compelled him to rely on the authoritarian state of the GDR. He managed to preserve a certain independence, thanks to his guile (and his retention of his Austrian passport), but that dependence inevitably affected the substance of his theatrical productions. The hymns of praise that he wrote after 1949 to whomever it might be, and that his friend Hanns Eisler set to music, continue to trumpet their political stupidity to the world so loudly that the sound has outlasted the demise of actual existing socialism. In this dispute, Adorno, the much-derided "TUI," has been proved right. The arrogant self-confidence that the two mockers, Eisler and Brecht, displayed in Hollywood concealed the difficulties that they too experienced when faced by a cultural machine that subjected them to the standards of an industrially reproduced consumer culture.

The truth was that not even Brecht stood completely apart from that culture, and Eisler certainly did not. The film music for *Hangmen Also Die* made fun of the stupidity of the system by smuggling parts of his *Cominternlied* (Song of the Comintern) into the *Lidicelied* (Song of Lidice). He was even nominated for an Oscar. In contrast to the image Brecht projected, Lang fought to make sure Brecht's fee was honored, and this ultimately enabled Brecht to live with his entourage relatively free from financial worries and to produce two plays in three years. Brecht was not averse to taking advantage of the system to popularize his own approach to theater. He used a star, Charles Laughton, to make sure the American public heard about *The Life of Galileo*. This, however, was not enough to succeed in a completely commercialized theater culture. In the second half of the 1940s it was in fact the great stars who joined forces with critical intellectuals in Hollywood, for they had personal experience of the devaluation of their talent. A director such as Dieterle, who risked his all as a producer in order to maintain what he regarded as quality, found himself faced by one financial disaster after another in the weakening of the economic climate and the early days of television. The rapid introduction of color TV, which began as early as 1950 in the United States, rendered obsolete all the assumptions on which *Dialectic of Enlightenment* had been based. At the same time, Hollywood's political enemies at long last felt strong enough to put an end to what they saw as its combination of moral degeneracy and political unreliability. The McCarthy era, with the unceasing activities of HUAC, left the immigrants with a choice between character assassination, self-abasement, travel bans, deportation, or prison, and there was scarcely any avenue for escape. This was the fate facing the hard core of the German American colony. Lang continued to believe that his future still lay in America until the mid-fifties, when he gave up the struggle. Adorno saw opportunities opening up for him in the Federal Republic that had been blocked in the United States. He refers to them in letters to America, to Lang and Thomas Mann among others, who doubted the wisdom of returning to a Germany that had barely been cleansed of Nazism.

Adorno, who commuted between Frankfurt and the San Francisco Bay Area from 1949 to 1953, felt particularly attracted by university teaching. He recorded his feeling of incredulity at the situation in Germany in 1950: "The most amazing aspect is that although the destruction of the country has been virtually complete, social and economic damage is almost nowhere to be seen. Instead, despite everything, 'normal life' seems to have reasserted itself, at least on the surface. A certain universal de-politicization, as a reaction against the Nazis, appears to prevent both the resurgence of genuine conflict situations and the general realization that Germany has become a colonized country."[72] After a frustrating research year in California in 1953, he returned to Frankfurt once more, telling Lang about a completely impracticable fantasy: "One ought really to be able to commute between the two places—but this obviously has its difficulties and is not likely to make for a contented life. But what is?"[73]

Meanwhile Lang had been having a hard time in Hollywood. No one wanted to promote his films anymore, and he was grateful to receive offers from Artur Brauner in Berlin. The two-part remake of *The Indian Tomb* for the German market failed to make an impact, however. The choice of title for *Der Tiger von Eschnapur (The Tiger of Eschnapur)* harks back to old debates in California about the representation of animality. In the 1960s Adorno began to assemble his recollections of his time in Hollywood. In a congratulatory telegram to Chaplin on his seventy-fifth birthday, he refers to him as a "Bengal tiger as vegetarian." The German reader of 1964 would have found it almost impossible to grasp the significance of such an allusion in Adorno's works.[74] Adorno believed Chaplin capable of extracting a form of reconciliation from the barbarism of the Culture Industry, symbolized here by the image of the predator. The current belief that Adorno's elitist preference for high culture implied a contempt for the film as an art form is contradicted not only by the value he placed on Chaplin but also by the esteem in which he held Lang. Film had been a prominent feature in the Adorno household from the 1920s on. He went regularly to the cinema with his aunt Agathe and was able to discuss films on equal terms with the much older Siegfried Kracauer. Texts from the sixties such as "Transparencies on Film" attest to this. Adorno also introduced one of his most talented pupils, Alexander Kluge, to Fritz Lang, his old friend from his Hollywood days. Kluge reports some of Adorno's witty paradoxes about film, such as the idea that "what disturbed him about film was really only the picture"; such remarks can hardly have come from a mere layman.[75] Adorno's basic theme in his discussions of film was his criticism of a schematic realism, a theme whose ramifications can be traced back to comments he made in the early 1940s.

In the early 1960s, when there was a lively interest in cinema theory in Europe, Lang's work was eagerly discussed among cineastes in publications ranging from the *Cahiers du cinéma* in Paris to the Frankfurt *Filmstudio*. After his return to Europe he frequently visited Adorno. At around this time there was a discussion with the young film empiricists in which Adorno found himself defending the aesthetic autonomy of Lang's approach to cinema. Lang, who was interested in the young people's opinions, took their side against Adorno. Both men wished to influence the younger generation. Adorno's assistant Regina Becker-Schmidt tells a nice story about these discussions. On one occasion Adorno was arguing with Lang about whether Ingmar Bergman's film *The Silence* was pornographic. When Becker-Schmidt was asked for her opinion, she sided with Adorno. Lang said there was nothing surprising in that since the young lady was Adorno's assistant, whereupon Adorno lost his temper, saying, "Since she is my student, she is capable of thinking for herself and has her own ideas." In a rage, Adorno grabbed his hat and coat, but unfortunately they were Lang's, not his own. "He then presented a comic sight. The hat was much too large and slipped down over his ears; the coat was far too long and Adorno's hands and arms disappeared inside them. Adorno looked at them in bafflement, but then—still furious—he shouted: 'And I suppose you think I have identified with you just because I am wearing your hat!' Everyone collapsed in laughter, and peace was restored."[76]

At that time, in the mid-sixties, Lang was greatly admired as a director in Europe, while he was increasingly ignored in Beverly Hills. Adorno, who was revered by his students, was moving toward the high point of his career. Lang had met Alexander Kluge when Kluge was working as a trainee with Artur Brauner. Kluge probably made an ambiguous impression on Lang, since he would have read the brilliant article in *Die Zeit* by Uwe Nettelbeck in which Kluge is reported to have said that he learned from Lang not how to make films but how one could no longer make films in the traditional way. This effectively turned Lang into a negative model for the auteur filmmakers of the Federal Republic and in this way left his imprint on such films as Kluge's *Abschied von gestern (Yesterday Girl)*. Lang was an interested observer of Adorno's subsequent conflicts with his own students. As he wrote to Eleanor Rosé immediately after Adorno's death, he connected Adorno's heart attack in the Swiss mountains with the circumstance that his students "had put into practice what he had been teaching them for twenty years, namely, to rebel. The fact that they rebelled against him was something he never understood, just as, in my view, he never understood modern youth."[77]

Lang had a further discussion with Adorno as late as April 1969, but we know of it only from Lang's own report. He felt unable to convince Adorno, since "somehow it is not possible to persuade very vain people of anything."[78] Adorno had written about Thomas Mann's alleged vanity, evidently in an attempt to defend "the Magician":

That a man of this kind should be dogged by the myth of vanity is shameful in the eyes of his contemporaries but understandable; it is the reaction of those who want to be nothing but precisely what they are. You may believe me when I say that Mann was lacking in vanity, just as he dispensed with dignity. One might put it most simply by saying that in his dealings with people he never thought about the fact that he was Thomas Mann; what usually makes contact with celebrities difficult is simply that they project their objectified public status back onto their personal selves and their immediate existence.[79]

Both Adorno and Lang were in search of an audience. Adorno found one in Europe and posthumously in America—but while Fritz Lang was still alive, such a development did not seem very likely. What seemed more probable was a new backlash, comparable to the one that had ended their common period in California. The name of Richard Nixon, at the time a young, ambitious member of HUAC, did not augur well: he had now become president of the United States. The friendship between Rosé and Lang was marked by a love of animals and nicknames taken from animals similar to that in the inner circle of Wiesengrund-Adorno and the Critical Theorists. Lang's letters contain references to the cloth monkey Peter, who had a significant role in Lang's own life, and Magali the cat, who figures in their correspondence. Lang informed Eleanor Rosé and her cat that "without him," that is, Adorno, "it has become much lonelier."[80]

The close friendship between Adorno and Lang that becomes evident from the archives comes as something of a surprise, so different do the two men seem, as do their respective positions in the production process of the Culture Industry. But Adorno's diaries reveal that it was Fritz Lang and Lily Latté who had accompanied him to the Los Angeles railroad station at the beginning of his great journey back to Europe. But also, during his first sojourn back in Germany, he had felt a "yearning for the Badger," as he confesses in his diary.[81] Given such intimacy, Lang must have been familiar with Adorno's interest in stuffed animals, Teddies and Peters. His extremely personal "Oxford Supplements" which he sent to Horkheimer in 1937, after completing his essay "On Jazz," contain the following observation:

That title of the Debussy prelude, *Général Lavine, eccentric,* seems to be a programmatic anticipation of the idea of jazz. If you give the word *lavine* its German meaning [*Lawine*], for which of course the only other French equivalent is "avalanche," it designates that which erupts, bursts forth without rhyme or reason, and also the terrifying. But again, the "Lavine" here is identical with the socially destructive principle: a general, a general who is made ridiculous by the fact that he is associated with the idea of an avalanche just as at around the same period, around 1910, the rank of consul was made ridiculous through its association with the first teddy bears and the diabolo, since uniformed monkeys were called "Consul Peter." They were presented riding on bicycles. The paradoxical creature that is mocked when mutilated by society and glorified when declared sovereign is the eccentric. When at the end of the prelude he is presented to the public with the spotlight shining on him and he stands there motionless, this could easily be regarded as the model of the jazz subject that later on, compulsively unchanging, keeps repeating the same tableau.[82]

Fritz Lang was no lover of difficult theoretical treatises, but he must have read *Minima Moralia* and known that Adorno had prefaced part three, the leave-taking section of the book, with an epigraph from Baudelaire, "Avalanche, veux-tu m'emporter dans ta chute?"[83] The utopia described in the hundredth aphorism, "*Rien faire comme une bête,* lying on water and looking peacefully at the sky,"[84] had dissipated by the time he provided part three with this motto. Everything depended now on what would become of the "hothouse plant":

> If the early maturer is more than a possessor of dexterities, he is obliged to catch himself up, a compulsion which normal people are fond of dressing up as a moral imperative. Painfully, he must win for the relation to objects the space that is occupied by his imagination: even suffering he has to learn. Contact with the non-self, which in the alleged late maturer is scarcely ever disturbed from within, becomes for the early maturer an urgent need. The narcissistic direction of his impulses, indicated by the preponderance of imagination in his experience, positively delays his maturing. Only later does he live through, in their crude violence, situations, fears, passions, that had been greatly softened in imagination, and they change, in conflict with his narcissism, into a consuming sickness.[85]

6. | Frankfurt Transfer

Every glass of kirsch in the Schlagbaum has more in common with our philosophy than Riesman's collected works.
ADORNO IN SANTA MONICA TO HORKHEIMER IN FRANKFURT,
12 MARCH 1953

I simply wanted to return to where I had my childhood, ultimately from the feeling that what we achieve in life is little more than the attempt to recapture our childhood while transforming it.
THEODOR W. ADORNO, "AUF DIE FRAGE"

Adorno came late and did not stay for long. In 1945 he did not think of returning to Frankfurt am Main immediately. Not until 1949–50 did he take his first trip back to Germany following the end of the Nazi regime, and he returned to America more or less directly. In 1952–53 he spent almost a year at the Hacker Foundation in California. There were good reasons for this. Gaining U.S. citizenship seems to have been one of the chief motives. The fear of having no passport other than a German one cannot be overestimated. Horkheimer, whose example even in these practical matters was of prime importance for Adorno, moved heaven and earth to be allowed to retain his American citizenship, going right up to the U.S. Senate.[1] As we look back on this period, Adorno's return to Germany seems to follow the logic of his entire life. His high public profile in the 1960s stands in striking contrast to his anonymity during his stay in America between 1938 and 1949. Adorno himself provided both his American and German publics with a number of explanations for his return to Germany. He drew a comparison with the tyrants of antiquity, saying that after the fall of a tyrant, the exiles return. Autobiographical statements like these should be viewed with caution. The fact is that in the early 1950s the wisdom of resettling in Frankfurt was by no means self-evident.

We may doubt whether Adorno would actually have gone back to Frankfurt am Main if Horkheimer had not paved the way. The triumphant reception for the returnees that was talked about later did not in fact happen. If we look through the letters that were exchanged at this period, we gain the impression that in the final analysis it was Horkheimer who made the decision to relocate the Institute for Social Research back to Frankfurt when he saw the possibility of doing so. As late as 1948, after his first visit back to Germany, one that led him to Frankfurt via Switzerland and Paris, he had entertained the idea that he might perhaps establish a branch of the institute in Germany. The headquarters would continue to be based in the United States. Horkheimer's identification with America went beyond the pragmatic decision to retain U.S. citizenship. A letter of 4 July 1948 to Friedrich Pollock, his childhood friend who had stayed on in California, contains this revealing statement: "Our work on behalf of the United States and for peace would be far more effective in Europe than in the USA. For there are people there who need us and whom we therefore need in our turn."[2] Pollock, whom Horkheimer addresses with the words "Mon cher Fred," was Horkheimer's closest intimate. He spoke even more frankly on political and academic matters with Pollock than with his own wife, Maidon. We can see this from certain secret memoranda that have been preserved in the Max Horkheimer Archive. It sometimes seems as if there was a special sense of trust between the two men which extended even to private matters. In this letter Horkheimer tells Pollock of his fantasies of purchasing a house. In 1948 the dream location was still the south of France. At the end of the 1950s, when both men retired from their daily routine, they acquired houses next door to each other in the Ticino, and from there they made sporadic excursions to Frankfurt. The two men neither could nor did wish to make a definitive decision in favor of settling in Germany, and their ambivalence persisted for a variety of reasons.

We have to look quite closely to see why Horkheimer was drawn to Europe. The fact was that he felt needed there. This sheds light on the situation of the institute in America. Although Horkheimer had quickly achieved his aim of becoming an American citizen, he kept his distance from academic life in the United States. Paul F. Lazarsfeld adopted a strategy of integration that was the opposite of Horkheimer's. Once the latter had more or less withdrawn to the West Coast in 1940, Lazarsfeld was able to inherit the institute at Columbia University in New York. Together with Robert Merton he established in uptown Manhattan what would be for a long time the most successful of social sciences organizations, the Bureau of Applied Social Research. The lives of Lazarsfeld and Horkheimer, as well as those of Lazarsfeld and Adorno, are connected by a variety of links. Even when he was still director of the Frankfurt Institute during the final phase of the Weimar Republic, Horkheimer had turned to Lazarsfeld, a Viennese empiricist who had created his own institute for research projects unconnected with the university. This was the Wirtschaftspsychologische Forschungsstelle (Research Center for Economic Psychology). When Horkheimer arrived in the United States, bringing the Institute for Social Research with him, he quickly made contact with Lazarsfeld, who had once again built up his own research institute, this time in Newark. A man of great energy, Lazarsfeld had already succeeded in establishing himself at elite universities. He became director of the Princeton Radio Research Project, and it was here that the post of music director was created for Adorno. This furnished Adorno with the material foundation that enabled him to survive in the United States when he arrived in 1938. Later on, Lazarsfeld gave an ironic account of this episode from the history of the Institute for Social Research. His every prejudice was duly confirmed: Adorno, the speculative theorist, proved unable to fit in with an organization for empirical social research based on the division of labor.

The actual situation was more complex, however. It is not known whether Lazarsfeld and Adorno had met in Vienna during the 1920s. At the time, Adorno was a radical artist in an intellectual and political environment that was beginning to disintegrate. We can regard Schoenberg's and Eisler's move to Berlin as symptomatic. Adorno's return to Frankfurt am Main, and also the increasing attraction for him of Berlin by the end of the Weimar period, point to the shifting focus of politics and culture in the German-speaking world. Lazarsfeld's choices, in contrast, were closely connected to the collapse of the Habsburg Empire. In the Austrian rump republic after the First World War, Austro-Marxist social democracy provided opportunities for middle-class Jewish young people. Austro-Marxism can best be understood as a way of life rather than as a coherent set of political ideas and theories. In the Red Vienna of the interwar period, the Austro-Marxist milieu developed as a kind of parallel society to the clerical conservatism of the rest of Austria. Under the impact of the omnipresent anti-Semitism, even before the war social democracy had offered a refuge to young Jews with intellectual interests who no longer wished to earn their living in business. The Austro-Marxist context was a hothouse not only for social scientists such as Carl Grünberg, who had preceded Horkheimer as the first director of the Institute for Social Research, but also for many natural scientists who suffered in the reactionary prebourgeois structures of public life in Austria.

The term "Austro-Marxism" can be highly misleading. The emphasis should fall more on the "Austro" than the "Marxism." The key to understanding the term does not consist in any special Austrian interpretation of Marxism. Austro-Marxism figured itself as progressive; while the bourgeoisie as a whole no longer quite trusted the idea of progress, that idea was cultivated by the Social Democrats. This bourgeois faith in progress provoked the scathing mockery of Karl Kraus, but it also attracted the children of bourgeois families who were frustrated in their academic ambitions by a university disfigured by reactionary attitudes. Scientific rationalism even created a bond between progressive oppositional academics and politically active Austro-Marxists. The fact that young Jewish students leaned toward the apparently more neutral natural sciences and mathematics favored a tendency in the Austro-Marxist milieu to approach the social sciences with methods derived from mathematics and modeled on the natural sciences. The positivism that Adorno encountered among empiricist social scientists in the United States was by no means simply an American invention. It came from the Austro-Marxist milieu and arrived in the United States with the émigrés, and Paul Lazarsfeld must be regarded as one of its precursors.

Lazarsfeld had come to the United States on a Rockefeller scholarship toward the end of the world economic crisis. He should be thought of more as an immigrant than as the typical émigré. While he was pursuing his research in America, Austro-fascism was on the march at home, leading to the destruction of the Austro-Marxist bastion of Vienna in 1934. This triggered the mass emigration of Austrian academics, a process that reached a second high point following the *Anschluß* in 1938. By then Lazarsfeld was already firmly established. In Vienna he had set up his Wirtschaftspsychologische Forschungsstelle and invented a "radio barometer"; in other words, as early as the 1920s he had attempted to discover niches alongside the forbidden territory of the university in which he might earn money through social research. When he arrived in the United States, he brought with him an entrepreneurial talent that was very rarely encountered among academics. He had learned to operate on the boundary separating private enterprise from the Austro-Marxist bureaucracy of the Socialist Party and Red Vienna. During the economic slump Lazarsfeld and his associates discovered the potential of project-driven research on behalf of capitalist enterprises to finance politically motivated social research. The victory of the New Deal in America created a unique constellation that suited Lazarsfeld's experience and ambitions to a T. A progressively minded state bureaucracy developed a growing interest in knowledge about society so as to underpin its policies. The experienced contract researcher knew how to gain that knowledge. A perfect example of such research is provided by radio. Roosevelt's victories, achieved in the teeth of a hostile press, drew attention to the potential of radio. State bureaucracies and private entrepreneurs alike wanted to know how the medium functioned. Lazarsfeld's research promised to deliver the answers.

Throughout their lives, Horkheimer and Pollock pursued the strategy of avoiding excessively close links with politics and business. In Germany the finances of the Weil Foundation had supported the relative political and economic independence of the institute. The two men sought to maintain this independence even from Columbia University, which had provided them with a refuge. But their protectors in the university administration also had their own agendas. Columbia had not kept pace with developments in sociology in the United States, and in comparison to the achievements of the Chicago School, New York sociology was thought to be too theoretical in an old-fashioned way. The Frankfurt Institute, with a large empirical and theoretical project on "Authority and the Family" in train, was to be used to update Columbia and make it competitive. The Frankfurt Institute's full name, the Institute for Social Research, was taken seriously by the powers that be at Columbia. Horkheimer's task was to undertake "social research," in other words, empirical research. In this situation Horkheimer could see the benefits of further cultivating his relations with Lazarsfeld. He involved him in various studies and later on regularly sought to draw him into collaborating on empirical projects. Nevertheless, while they hoped that Horkheimer and his Frankfurt associates would give New York sociology a fresh look, his new colleagues did not primarily have empirical research in mind. In the 1930s Robert Lynd had come out with a publication titled "Knowledge for What?" which questioned the value of the empirical preoccupation with mere fact-finding. What he expected from the Horkheimer circle was a theorized social research that would outshine the descriptive techniques of the Chicago School. "Authority and the Family" seemed to the author of *Middletown* to promise an intimate insight into historical processes that could not be delivered by a merely descriptive urban sociology.

When Adorno arrived in America he seemed to know nothing of these problems or even to suspect their existence. He had no experience of empirical social research. Even worse, as a professional he was really no more than a beginner who had never worked in a proper organization. As far as the sociologists around Lazarsfeld were concerned, Adorno was an émigré artist and philosopher named Wiesengrund, a man with no professional experience as a sociologist. Lazarsfeld, who thought of the Princeton project as a steppingstone to Columbia, must have believed that Adorno's nonconformist attitudes might easily threaten to undermine such ambitions. The feeling of being let down by an unreconstructed outsider can still be sensed in Lazarsfeld's later reminiscences of this episode, colored as they were by hindsight. Between the lines we can also discern the competitive situation of academics in America in the thirties. Jewish scholars in particular, both native and immigrant, were exposed to enormous pressure to adapt. Adorno's reminiscences, too, "Scientific Experiences of a European Scholar in America," which he published in 1968, initially in English, can only be understood against this background. Looking back on that time, Adorno does not regard the adjustment expected of him in a wholly negative light.[3] His experience with the Princeton Radio Research Project changed Adorno's view of himself. The entire nexus of a progressive capitalist society and individual change is something he subsequently described as his "American experience." The change of name that was made official in 1942 in Los Angeles was the consequence: in his decade of American exile, the artist and philosopher Wiesengrund was transformed into the unmistakable Theodor W. Adorno, who appeared in the firmament of the German Federal Republic of the 1950s like an intellectual meteor. The prehistory of this transformation remained obscure apart from a few, at first sight not instantly decipherable autobiographical statements.

For over a decade Adorno had tied his own destiny to the fortunes of the Institute for Social Research in exile. Ever since 1934 he had aspired to a full-time job at the institute. It was Horkheimer and Pollock, however, who had all the available posts at their disposal, and inevitably they were under compulsion to husband the institute's surviving resources carefully. The affiliation with Columbia University was intended to unlock new sources of revenue, but the institute's finances remained precarious. Even among its members conflicts of interest repeatedly occurred. The internal leadership of Horkheimer and Pollock followed the strategy of cooperating with American institutions while leaving enough free time for independent research and publication. But cooperation implied the integration of individual members into American institutions; they had to take on teaching duties at Columbia University. Until 1938 Adorno had only a part-time post at the institute, while the other half of his living had to be earned through his involvement in Lazarsfeld's project in Newark. What hurt Adorno most of all was that Horkheimer had preferred Herbert Marcuse to him. In a furious and unjust letter written from Oxford on 13 May 1935, he reproached Horkheimer "for collaborating directly with a man who in the final analysis is preserved from fascism only by the fact that he is a Jew."[4] Jealousy is scarcely an adequate excuse for his malice here. In the mid-thirties people were still fairly casual about accusing other people of fascism, even among the émigrés. Adorno here is reproaching Marcuse for his failed attempt to qualify for the *Habilitation* under Heidegger's supervision, even though the latter's Nazi sympathies after 1933 were a matter of public record. But at this point in time Horkheimer had long since gained the support of Marcuse, whose interest in Heidegger had lapsed toward the end of the Weimar Republic.

Adorno also believed that he had been badly treated by Pollock in his attempts to obtain a permanent post at the institute. His letters to Horkheimer often convey the impression that he did not really understand the inner workings of the administration. This can be seen in his complaint about working conditions under Lazarsfeld: "And when Fritz P. recently in response to my complaint that working with L. was repugnant replied in a slightly schoolmasterly way to the effect that that is what life is like, he is of course quite right, but as matters stand this makes no contribution to the growth of dianoetic virtue in me. All of this makes me a little anxious, and I have no one, absolutely no one apart from you, and of course Gretel, to whom I can speak quite freely and without dissimulation."[5] Adorno was hoping to shelter beneath Horkheimer's wing. But Horkheimer also valued good relations with Lazarsfeld. When Adorno was released from his duties to go to the Princeton Radio Research Project in 1940, he found that he too had to support institute policy on this point. The institute had to economize; Horkheimer wanted to withdraw from routine university work with its public commitments in New York. More and more institute members were being urged to submit proposals for research funds to foundations such as Rockefeller and Carnegie. As Horkheimer's longtime colleague on the list of salaried members of the institute, Adorno hoped that he would be chosen to collaborate with Horkheimer in California on the planned book on dialectics. Marcuse, too, was talked about as a candidate for this project. Adorno had to stay in his post in New York until the spring of 1941.

The two most important projects that remained to be completed at that time were those on Germany and on anti-Semitism. Beyond his theoretical work, Adorno also had to try to enlist support for the institute itself. He was highly successful in this respect and had evidently profited from his experience with Lazarsfeld in Newark. On 30 July 1940, on Horkheimer's instructions, he wrote to Charles Merriam in Chicago:

> By social research we envisage a constant interaction of theoretical and empirical work in such a manner that the formulation of the problems and hypotheses are prepared by our theoretical analyses, while on the other hand our empirical findings enter into the substance of our theoretical formulations. Putting this negatively, this means a critical attitude pointing in two directions: on the one hand, a critique of the ideological and speculative character of the German sociological tradition to which we oppose the problems of concrete social reality, while on the other hand, we remain critical of the mere collection and classification of "data."[6]

This sounds like an ideal type, but Adorno's decade in America was marked by the tension between theory and empirical knowledge. His curriculum vitae of 1968 conceals his failures, but it also makes it plain that without his American experience, the critical theory of society would have lacked the specific shape that made it so attractive to the younger academic generation after 1945. This had never really become clear to the German public until that point in time, while the American public had never shown any interest in Horkheimer and Adorno. In 1968 the name of Herbert Marcuse was on everybody's lips, but few people were aware of his connection to the history of the institute. In contrast, Adorno's efforts to finish his essay "Scientific Experiences of a European Scholar in America" in 1968, at a time when he was under great pressure, point to his desire to correct a mistaken impression about the history of social research. The American decade in his life socialized him as a scholar, even though he stubbornly continued to defend his autonomy as an individual. *Minima Moralia* served as an accompaniment to the dilemmas of this process of socialization.

His involvement in Lazarsfeld's radio project had been preceded by a number of theoretical studies that now seemed to be largely incompatible with the Newark approach to research. Adorno had been interested in phenomena of mass culture since the days of the Weimar Republic; in England he had written an interpretation of jazz for the *Zeitschrift für*

Sozialforschung "which although suffering painfully from a lack of knowledge about America, at least worked with material that could be considered characteristically American."[7] Before working with Lazarsfeld he had completed his essay "On the Fetish Character in Music and the Regression of Listening," his reply to Benjamin's essay "The Work of Art in the Age of Its Technological Reproducibility." It was not until he began working on the Princeton Radio Research Project, however, that he gained direct experience of the interconnections between music production, consumer research, academic scholarship, and the interests of capital: restricting knowledge to "usable information," he found, may indeed make life simpler for the "research technician,"[8] but it does place a question mark over intellectual integrity.

The often misquoted comment that "wrong life cannot be lived rightly"[9] reflects Adorno's American experience without attempting to play Europe off against the United States. Generations of German students have always tried to read this statement as if it spoke of "the true life" as opposed to the "correct" or "right" one, as if there were an authentic substance in contrast to the falsifying social manifestation. The opposition of German depth to Anglo-American superficiality was one that Adorno had long since come to detest, even though this alleged contrast was common enough in émigré circles. In order to forestall any misunderstanding that he might be arguing from the standpoint of German nationalism, Adorno retrospectively emphasized the idea of European socialization— which, however, he thought of as being in a state of historical decline. In the United States he notes "the decline of the cultivated person in the European sense, which indeed as a social type never could have become fully established in America."[10] This statement, too, is open to being misunderstood as an expression of European snobbery. But the reality is that Europe figures in the writings of Horkheimer and Adorno as a specific amalgam of feudalism and the bourgeois that could not exist "in a radically bourgeois country,"[11] which was how they thought of America. What the Europeans experienced as the non-simultaneity of Europe and America had to become the source of knowledge. But without actual contact with American society, this source of knowledge would be barren. *Minima Moralia* records the experiences of intellectuals in the so-called distribution sphere once it has been subjected to the processes of rationalization. The renowned chapter on the Culture Industry in *Dialectic of Enlightenment* reflects this experience. Even the radicalism of its initial statements about monopoly is fed by the conflictual relation to the institutions from which the person who is unwilling to adjust can expect nothing but rejection.

Culture in America is understood by Adorno not in the sense of national psychological characteristics or cultural anthropology but as that which has been most thoroughly rationalized by the process of enlightenment. His own experience as a social scientist with Lazarsfeld in Newark confronted him with the most advanced state of enlightenment, one that had subscribed to the proposition that "science is measurement."[12] The East Coast academic milieu during the Roosevelt era found itself at the beginning of a boom in project-driven research. Lazarsfeld may be regarded as a pioneer in this administrative research. Horkheimer believed that his own duties could be lightened if Lazarsfeld were to take over social science research at Columbia University entirely. In order to escape from the rationalization of academic work, Horkheimer fixed on California as a kind of extraterritorial sphere. He left the field at Columbia to Lazarsfeld, who established his own Bureau for Applied Social Research. Lazarsfeld's enlightened Austro-Marxism transformed itself into a social-scientific method without preconceptions, and he possessed the skills needed to succeed in a society thirsty for enlightenment. Lazarsfeld described himself in America as a "Marxist on leave," although it turned out to be a leave from which he never returned. The radical quantification of the social sciences extinguished the historical traces that might have reminded anyone of the critique of domination.

In this way, behind the social researcher whom Adorno would subsequently dismiss as a "research technician,"[13] the life history of the political intellectual disappeared. With Lazarsfeld himself Adorno had none too easy a time, since Lazarsfeld was well aware of the problems involved. All the more do we gain the impression, when we read "Scientific Experiences of a European Scholar in America," that it is as if in 1968 Adorno wished to set up the history of his own return as a counterexample to Lazarsfeld, who had in the meantime acquired an international reputation as the doyen of modern social research. Lazarsfeld too returned to Europe on a number of occasions, but much later than Adorno, and he did not stay for long. With research money from the great American foundations and UNESCO, he was able to establish entire scientific institutions. But America remained his base. Later on he maintained that his favorite work was the study he published on American universities during the McCarthy era, *The Academic Mind*. This study likewise conceals the political interests of its author behind an impregnable scientific neutrality, but in its subject matter it seemed to prove that Lazarsfeld had not entirely shed the impulses that had led to his commitment to Austro-Marxism. In 1953 C. Wright Mills, the most promising talent in American sociology, had noisily turned away from the applied sociology practiced at Columbia—an unambiguous criticism of the path of "adjustment," of adaptation à la Lazarsfeld. By that time Horkheimer and Adorno had reestablished themselves in Frankfurt am Main. But for additional security the astute Horkheimer also accepted a guest professorship in Chicago.

Even after 1941 Horkheimer took care to maintain good relations with Lazarsfeld in New York from his base on the West Coast. The findings of communication research were first published in the most American of the issues of the *Zeitschrift für Sozialforschung*, which appeared for the first time entirely in English in 1941 as *Studies in Philosophy and Social Science*, with the place of publication being given as Morningside Heights, New York. This issue, volume nine, opens with Lazarsfeld's essay "Administrative and Critical Communications Research." The three articles by Adorno, who by then had stopped signing himself Wiesengrund, included the essay "On Popular Music," which arose out of his work on the Princeton Radio Research Project. As late as 1968 Adorno still remained grateful to the assistance he had received from his American assistant George Simpson, who had made it possible for him to publish his research in the United States. In the same year Adorno's *Ideen zur Musiksoziologie* (Introduction to the Sociology of Music) appeared as a cheap paperback in the "Rowohlts Deutsche Enzyklopädie" series, a book that had previously, in 1962, been published by Suhrkamp. The basic argument of "On Popular Music" can be found in a lightly revised version in section two, under the title "Light Music." Adorno had published "Some Ideas on the Sociology of Music" as early as 1958. He evidently wished to bring to completion something that had gone awry under Lazarsfeld's direction: "a systematically executed sociology and social psychology of music on the radio."[14] Adorno made no attempt to deny the difficulties attendant on his "experience in America."[15] On the contrary, after his return to Germany he knew how to make good use of his "scientific experiences in America" as a basis for prognoses about trends in Europe. His disagreement with the type of "administrative research"[16] that he had encountered in Lazarsfeld's project entered into and influenced his analysis of music, which did not stop at a rigid antithesis between Europe and America. In the field of "popular music"[17] we may already presuppose the dominance of the production processes characteristic of the Culture Industry that had begun to influence so-called serious music as early as the thirties, thanks to the emergence of radio and the gramophone record. It was reasonable, therefore, that America should have appeared to him as "the most advanced observation post."[18]

In his published writings Adorno sought to preserve a continuity that seems to contradict his own analysis of a "damaged life." The need for biographical coherence is actually invited by the contradictory experience of America. In comparison with a number of other seemingly more readable texts, "Scientific Experiences of a European Scholar in America" drags along with it the legitimating poison of autobiographical narrative against which Freud so urgently warned and which has been generally accepted among critical theorists ever since Leo Löwenthal's critique of the biographical approach in the *Zeitschrift für Sozialforschung*. Motivated by his fear of this source of distortion, Adorno allows himself to be carried away into making self-critical remarks that do not stand up on their own. His difficulties in the Princeton Radio Research Project are ascribed to the fact "that I approached the specific field of the sociology of music more as a musician than as a sociologist."[19] Lazarsfeld's project in Newark was based in an abandoned brewery. Here Adorno could experience a belated induction into his profession, one that overlapped with the difficulties of immigration. In England between 1934 and 1938 he could still think of himself as an academic with the status of a *Privatdozent* who seemed to be independent of the context of social production. At Merton College, with its rich traditions, Adorno was just one of the many foreign academics who had sought refuge in England. Adorno, who had been introduced to Anglophile sentiments by his father, felt no pressure to become English himself. For a resolute philosopher from Germany, it was quite difficult at the time to gain entry to the academic milieu of Oxbridge. America, however, although it accepted immigrants more readily, confronted a new arrival with quite different challenges. Adorno's attempt to define himself as a European refugee was also an attempt to preserve something of the autonomy of a self-determined life that had been fundamentally put in doubt by the fact of exile. The pain he felt at his loss of autonomy reverberates in this retrospective account of his experience in America long after he had returned to Europe.

The operations of social science research with Lazarsfeld in Newark must have reminded him of the constraints that had made it impossible for him to survive as a musician in Europe. His essay "Some Ideas on the Sociology of Music" (1932) sounds like the exposé for a never-ending analysis. His wish to compose music was a desire that never left him. In a way that is quite different from his other writings about society, his writings on music seem to be reflections about himself. The workaday sociology required by Lazarsfeld was concerned at the outset with a secondary phenomenon—consumer attitudes—which, as a producer, Adorno could not simply accept unquestioned. *Introduction to the Sociology of Music,* as he rather modestly titled the book he published in the sixties, still bears the scars of the child who got his fingers burned, Adorno the musician. But the text is concerned with nothing less than philosophical reflections on the process of musical societalization. Ever since 1937 he had worked in his spare time on his Beethoven book, which, according to Rolf Tiedemann, his first archivist, he wanted to call *The Philosophy of Music.*[20] This fact, too, is evidence in favor of the idea of a lifelong, never-ending analysis of music. As if Adorno somehow suspected that this philosophy would never be completed, he tried after his return from America to render visible the social situation of music as well as its philosophical place in the history of music in almost every one of his theoretical texts on the topic. As a musician Adorno measured himself as a theorist against the profoundest justification of dialectical philosophy; that is to say, he strove to avoid placing himself above the subject matter without at the same time being inside it. But this is the very ambition that is threatened with failure when it ventures to tackle the simplest object of a sociology of music, namely, *popular music:* "The sociological interpretation of music is the better grounded, the higher the quality of the music. It becomes dubious in the case of simpler, more regressive or worthless music."[21]

Popular music represents a challenge to social theory. Even in the twenties this challenge was called jazz. But it would be a mistake to think of jazz as merely the abstract American antithesis of the European musical tradition. Jazz recurs as one of the catchwords in Adorno's critical theory. It stands both for the dissolution of the traditional unity of musical life in its bourgeois form and for the revolutionary overthrow of non-syncopated dance music which it "has swept out of fashion and demoted to the realm of nostalgia,"[22] as Adorno maintained in the early sixties. Ernst Křenek, the composer who had been friendly with Adorno since childhood, had composed *Jonny spielt auf,* a programmatic jazz opera which in Adorno's eyes remained a touchstone for a modernity *after* Schoenberg. If the generation around Schoenberg had continued to appeal "undaunted" to a "tradition that was in pieces when they inherited it,"[23] Křenek's jazz opera treated the tradition as something that had been left behind. The changed relations between Europe and America after 1945 were reflected in the changed relations between tradition and modernity. This experience too is reflected in Adorno's assessment of the sociology of music in the 1960s: "It is no accident that the innovations of truly modern composers like Boulez and Stockhausen are saturated with the European tradition, but that even so they make contact at least at crucial points with American composers who from the outset are positioned at an angle to tradition and who are most unlikely to allow it to confront them head on, as we see from the innovations of John Cage."[24] Unless it aspires to do no more than register current consumption, a sociology of music worthy of the name must in theory be able to articulate the general nexus linking the present with a changed musical practice. The Culture Industry's transformation of music into a consumer good by canceling out all pre-bourgeois reserves of tradition starts with light music—and this goes on to change everything, the totality. The definitive critical statement in *Minima Moralia,* "The whole is the false,"[25] applies not just to the affirmative side of Hegel's philosophy but to bourgeois culture as a whole.

The effect of Adorno's experience in America was to demystify bourgeois culture: the contradictions of empiricism challenge theory to reflect on the totality. The German society that gave birth to National Socialism was a drastic demonstration of the failure of the promises of bourgeois emancipation that had formed the theme of "great music of the period around 1800."[26] Adorno thought of himself as being "completely free of nationalism and cultural arrogance."[27] But in America he realized that "the element of enlightenment even in its relationship to culture" was "a matter of course."[28] From this standpoint the relationship between Europe and its tradition becomes precarious—particularly a Europe consisting of nations with a past in contrast to American society with its orientation to the present. Adorno's reflections on the sociology of music contain biographical elements that can be thought of as autobiographical. Beethoven is referred to as the "native son"[29] of the rising bourgeois class: "How harmony between human productive forces and a historical trend is achieved in detail will be difficult to make out; that is the blind spot of cognition."[30] In Beethoven a true consciousness is articulated, a statement seldom found in Adorno's writings. He burdens the sociology of music with "the obligation to pursue the truth of music. Sociologically, that amounts to the question of music as a socially right or wrong consciousness."[31]

Adorno was never able to think of himself as "the native son" of the bourgeois class. He is marked by an element of extraterritoriality of which Felix Mendelssohn is the outstanding example in the history of German music. Adorno senses the traces of a failed emancipation in Mendelssohn that extends into his analysis of his music: "Nor was the upper middle class apt to supply a great many musicians. Mendelssohn was a banker's son, but at least as a Jew, an outsider in his own stratum; the slickness of his compositions has some of the excessive zeal of someone who is not quite accepted."[32] Moreover, this does not apply just to music; Adorno can detect something comparable in Heine as well. In Mendelssohn's retraction of Beethoven's ambitions, Adorno discerns the renunciation proclaimed by Goethe, the retreat of humanity into the private sphere. In the long nineteenth century this attitude established itself as the ideology of Jews who joined the bourgeoisie, an ideology against which the sons of assimilated Jewish families repeatedly rebelled. At the beginning of *Minima Moralia*, Adorno defines the nature of these conflicts, expressing his doubts about the validity of his own rebellion: "One realizes with horror that earlier, opposing one's parents because they represented the world, one was often secretly the mouthpiece, against a bad world, of one even worse. Unpolitical attempts to break out of the bourgeois family usually lead only to deeper entanglement in it."[33]

In the same way, all exit strategies for artists also appear to be blocked. From his very first large-scale publication in the *Zeitschrift für Sozialforschung* in 1932, Adorno's entire output on music theory is an attempt to explain the social situation of music. He was still quoting from this essay in the 1960s, even though he had come to believe that the "constellation of music and class" had changed.[34] In the 1968 preface to *Introduction to the Sociology of Music* he even speaks of the "error" of his old programmatic essay, which lay "in his flat identification of the concept of music production with the precedence of the economic sphere of production, without considering how far what we call production already presupposes social production and depends on it as much as it is distinguished from it."[35] The essay of 1932 still expresses the old left-wing radicalism that attempts to compete with the writings of Eisler and Benjamin. The American experience that was denied to Benjamin was also to alter Adorno's musical activities, since, in contrast to the case of Eisler, it would shift the emphasis onto theory. The topic of "stupidity"[36] in music, first broached by Eisler in consciously provocative fashion, never ceased to preoccupy Adorno after his first meeting with Eisler in Vienna. It is one of his "ideas on the sociology of music." The critique of stupidity attacks the illusory nature of reconciliation in music, something that deluded the emerging Jewish middle class into believing that its assimilation into bourgeois society was successful. By the 1920s at the latest, the promise of universal bourgeois emancipation had been transformed in the eyes of the children of assimilated parents into an ideology. This was a social conflict for which there could be no purely musical solution, since the inner logic of music implies a reflection on its material which Adorno conceived as social in nature. Without artistic experience of his own, he would scarcely have been able to arrive at such an insight: "The composing subject is no individual thing, but a collective one. All music, however, individual it may be in stylistic terms, possesses an inalienable collective substance: every sound says 'we.'"[37]

Against this background we can better understand his explanation of his difficulties with the Princeton Radio Research Project, to wit, that "I approached the specific field of the sociology of music more as a musician than as a sociologist."[38] Adorno found himself unable to accept that the musical extracts offered to test subjects in the survey were simple stimuli that had not been reflected upon. The use of the questionnaire itself transformed music into a consumer good. The fact that the musical material was a socially produced second nature was not acknowledged. His own experience as an artist called precisely for the social character of the musical material to be deciphered. His recurring preoccupation with jazz is an attempt to make good this omission. For Adorno, jazz can be read as a cipher for the music organized by the Culture Industry. He concludes with the inexorable "sociological prognosis" that "as a branch of leisure-time activity music comes to resemble the very things it opposes, even though it only derives its meaning from that opposition."[39] His speculative ideas on the sociology of music in the 1950s incorporate the results of his experience in America at the end of the 1930s: "The Culture Industry ends up preparing to take over the whole of music."[40] Anyone who reads Adorno's essays on jazz without this context runs the risk of missing this indissoluble connection: "The question of the truth and untruth of music is closely linked with that of the relationship of its two spheres, that of the serious Muse and the lower sphere, unjustly termed the Muse of light entertainment."[41] The division of art into serious and light arose from the division of labor in society;

its unconceptualized reproduction in music underscores the element of domination in "high" culture, the burden of which light music promises to jettison.

Interest in jazz grew in Europe between the wars. As early as 1928, when he wrote for the Viennese music journal *Anbruch*, Adorno criticized the false claims of "serious" music with a sidelong glance at popular music: "But sentimental kitsch is always in the right compared to sentimental art with pretensions. This is true of genuine jazz as opposed to attempts to transplant jazz into art music and to 'refine' it—damaging both it and art music in the process."[42] During the period of the international economic crisis, the aesthetic left-wing radicalism of the late twenties coincided with a new attention to the economics of an artist's life. In May 1929 Adorno noted that a "jazz class had been presented at the Hoch Conservatory,"[43] the prestigious Frankfurt music school. Against the wishes of the establishment, Adorno's composition teacher, Bernhard Sekles, had invited Mátyás Seiber to give some classes as a specialist on jazz. With a highly developed sense of realism, Adorno writes: "We ought not to disagree that since the overwhelming majority of young musicians are compelled to earn their living by writing utility music [*Gebrauchsmusik*], we should give preference to a utility music that is produced cleanly and imaginatively, as opposed to the arrogant dilettantism of those who are unable to satisfy the requirements of utility."[44] In the journal he edited, the *Anbruch*, he planned not merely a special issue in 1929 with the title "Light Music" but also, with the same title, a section in the magazine in which "questions [should be debated] concerning the lower, despised type of music, which, however, can no longer be arrogantly excluded from discussion."[45] In Adorno's mind the debate about jazz was linked with the down-to-earth question of the social position of the musician.

As late as his *Sociology of Music* of the 1960s, Adorno reminds his readers of the concept of "utility music," which in the early 1920s settled into the space between "the two suspiciously tried and tested branches of high art and entertainment."[46] At its extremes there arose the possibility of a "communal music," which Adorno describes in two of its variants: Hindemith's petty-bourgeois version and the more class-conscious, proletarian version of Hanns Eisler's choruses. Adorno's critique is no less pointed because of his and Eisler's shared experience as composers: "The immanent-aesthetic results of bourgeois history, including that of the last fifty years, cannot simply be brushed aside by the proletarian theory and praxis of art, unless the desire is to eternalize a condition in art produced by class domination. The elimination of this condition within society is, after all, the fixed goal of the proletarian class struggle."[47] Proletarian utility music in Adorno's view is a blind alley both politically and aesthetically. He gives preference instead in 1932 to Kurt Weill's music, to which he ascribes "genuine polemical social force as long as it sustains its negative thrust."[48] Later on Adorno told Weill that with *Threepenny Opera,* in which "jazz arrangements were played from start to finish," he had given the year 1930 its defining shape.[49] He and Benjamin had come to know the theater collective around Brecht and Weill in the Schiffbauerdamm Theater toward the end of the Weimar Republic. For Adorno this led to the development in American emigration of the figure of the "composer-manager" whose "showmanship" takes possession of music as well as the theater.[50]

Expulsion and exile left their marks on Adorno's texts on jazz. While still in Britain, where, according to Křenek, he underwent "what was fortunately for him the not very arduous pre-school of exile,"[51] he even toyed with the idea that he might make money by thinking up hit tunes. The "itching in one's finger-tips" that he describes in *Minima Moralia,*[52] for example, was something he had felt himself but had rejected: "I do not know of a single case of a composer making his living with jobs for the market and at the same time fully satisfying his own standards."[53] In 1942 Adorno wrote "Nineteen Articles about New Music" ("Neunzehn Beiträge über neue Musik") for a serious American music lexicon. The only one that was accepted was the one on jazz, while for other articles Křenek, whom he had recommended to the American editors, was evidently preferred to him. This article contains in condensed form the basic ideas of his celebrated— or notorious—essay "Perennial Fashion—Jazz," though in its mercilessness it comes closer to his "Farewell to Jazz" of 1933. The jazz to which Adorno was bidding farewell had been a stimulus for European art music; the jazz he encountered after 1933 was the basis for the popular music that was distributed over the radio and on gramophone records. The American lexicon article takes account of this experience in the New World: "Insofar as genuine developmental trends are to be found in jazz, they are connected with the movement toward concentration and standardization and the will to escape from this. Jazz, originally a marginal social phenomenon arising out of the *Lumpenproletariat,* has more and more been subject to a smoothing process at the hands of the communication industry, deprived of its mildly shocking features, and finally it has been utterly swallowed up."[54]

These lines of 1942 give expression to the author's American experience and come closest to a dialectical appreciation of jazz. Adorno would not return to these ideas until the *Sociology of Music* of the 1960s. "Perennial Fashion—Jazz," from the volume *Prisms,* was the first essay with which Adorno reached a wider, nonspecialist German public after 1945.[55] In it jazz is treated as something that is over and done with and about which there is nothing more to be said. With his return to Germany, Adorno wanted to escape from the clutches of the Culture Industry, which he regarded as the inexorable future of modern society. The "Perennial Fashion" in the title alludes to a fundamental idea, one he had formulated back in the 1920s. At that time jazz had appeared to be a fashionable phenomenon characteristic of America which had inspired Křenek to write the first German jazz opera.[56] In the essay America is "glorified as a country of original vitality and technical mastery, at once undiminished, drastic, vivid, and mysterious."[57] In this radio talk of 1932 on Křenek, Adorno speaks of the Jazz Age as of something already in the past, an ending that had become irrevocable by 1933, when he wrote "Farewell to Jazz." In Adorno's essays on jazz, there are a number of overlapping themes: his own experiences as artist and social theorist, a European without knowledge of America, a European migrant in America, and lastly a returnee from American exile. The temptation to use the idea of jazz as a "perennial fashion"[58] with which to establish an element of continuity in his own life means that Adorno fell short of his own dialectical ambitions. His dogmatic statements condemning jazz have reinforced the prejudice that he was inspired by the arrogance of a cultivated European into passing judgment on a popular American phenomenon which he knew nothing about.

When he first published "Perennial Fashion—Jazz" in *Merkur* in 1953, he attracted an immediate riposte from Joachim E. Berendt, who was to become the leading German authority on jazz. Adorno found himself forced to reply. Berendt presented himself as a connoisseur of music who wished to keep his distance from "philosophical and sociological conclusions," but who let himself be carried away into making a "statement," to the effect that "jazz is the most original and vital musical utterance" produced by our century.[59] Adorno reacted touchily to this anti-intellectual attempt to make a mystery of an alleged "originality," which simply warmed up the jazz myth of the twenties without any concern for its place in history. Adorno believed that his personal experience of America, "his knowledge of the specifically American facets of jazz," had given him a superior insight.[60] But that experience can only be grasped sociologically; his purely musical interpretation makes Adorno's critique resemble the phenomenon he was criticizing. The rigidity he objected to in a fashion that constantly recurs renders him insensitive to its details, its actual concrete manifestations. His defense of his dogmatic condemnation of jazz in the face of Berendt's attack is in striking contrast to his trenchant criticism of the cultural conformism of the ideologues of jazz, with their loud, advertising style. Unperturbed, in fact on the whole confirmed by this controversy, Adorno had the essay reprinted in *Prisms,* his first large collection of essays, which was published by Suhrkamp in 1955. It was with this volume that Adorno became visible to the public in Germany, and by the same token, it was then that he left himself open to attack.

Resistance to Adorno's critical theory of society since the early 1970s has become fixated on his jazz critique. It seems to be a blind spot in his work, though not one that can be explained either by Old European cultural snobbishness or by an inadequate knowledge of the subject. In his disparate notes we find an astonishingly detailed knowledge of American jazz. Ever since his stay in New York, he had not just familiarized himself with Tin Pan Alley hits but had also spent time in Harlem, as we can see from his reference to dancing at the Savoy Ballroom. Nevertheless, he must have been aware of the weakness of his own critique of jazz since otherwise he would not have felt compelled to return to its defense in 1963 in "Culture Industry Reconsidered": "The critic is accused of taking refuge in arrogant esoterica."[61] Adorno's criticism of jazz marked the beginning of a theory-based critique of the Culture Industry which belonged in his view to the era of the Weimar Republic. Jazz stands for the isolated artist's tabooed escape route into utility music. His implacable rejection of jazz is an expression of his feeling that it was impossible for him to have an artistic life of his own. In one of his last publications before emigration, he joins Nietzsche in giving an extra kick to whatever is already falling—an attitude he was to distance himself from later on. Adorno reacted to the Nazi ban on "Negro jazz" in 1933 with his "Farewell to Jazz."[62] "After the numbness . . . caused by fascism,"[63] his first more extended piece in exile in Britain was given the simple title "On Jazz," to which he subsequently attached a postscript, the "Oxforder Nachträge," in 1937. The topic of jazz was the last Adorno was to address in Germany; it was also the first topic he chose when he began writing in exile once again. In 1938 his critique of jazz brought him up against the limits of social theory as he embarked on "administrative research" under the direction of Paul Lazarsfeld. Not until he was in California, writing *Dialectic of Enlightenment* in isolation, was he able to translate his own experience into a theoretical criticism of the Culture Industry.

A glance at the famous chapter on the Culture Industry makes jazz visible as an aspect of the social system of advanced capitalism, not something peculiar to American society: "Society is made up of the desperate and thus falls prey to rackets. In a few of the most significant novels of the pre-fascistic era, such as *Berlin Alexanderplatz* [by Alfred Döblin] and *Kleiner Mann was nun?* [*Little Man, What Now?* by Hans Fallada], this tendency was as vividly evident as in the mediocre film and in the procedures of jazz. Fundamentally they all present the self-mockery of the male."[64] The passage gives us pause, since the abrupt transition from social analysis to social psychology reminds us of similar moves in the "Perennial Fashion" essay, where he modulates from sociological analysis to psychoanalytical interpretation. Again and again Adorno's critique of jazz establishes a far from convincing linkage of jazz and sadomasochism, utility music and castration. Jazz becomes a sore point in his social criticism. The social defeat of the bourgeois subject is experienced literally in one's own body. An undamaged, self-determined life becomes impossible for Adorno under the conditions of pre-fascist society because he experienced his professional socialization as an émigré in the Anglo-Saxon countries where the Culture Industry was far more advanced than in continental Europe. Anyone who depends on his own intellectual endeavors for his livelihood discovers in Britain and America that he is entirely dependent on a monopolistic market. Other musicians—Adorno's piano teacher Eduard Steuermann, for example—were condemned to silence in this system. Eisler wrote utility music for films. He and Adorno had written *Composing for the Films* together. The barbarism of the Culture Industry is not treated as the consequence of a cultural lag between Europe and America. The fact was that "pre-fascist Europe was backward in relation to the monopoly of culture."[65]

Minima Moralia repeatedly inquires into the possibility of the moral life in a world in which the sovereignty of the individual is both an ideology and a utopia whose possibility is denied: "The pressure of conformity weighing on all producers further diminishes their demands on themselves. The center of intellectual self-discipline as such is in the process of decomposition. The taboos that constitute a man's intellectual stature, often sedimented experiences and unarticulated insights, always operate against inner impulses that he has learned to condemn, but which are so strong that only an unquestioning and unquestioned authority can hold them in check."[66] This section is titled "If Knaves Should Tempt You." The tenacity with which Adorno clings to his critique of jazz throws light on the threat to his intellectual productivity deriving from his fear of dependency: "The possibility of becoming an economic subject, an entrepreneur, a proprietor, is entirely liquidated. . . . All have become employees."[67] When writing these sentences he is thinking of the bustle of a modern university such as Columbia in New York and the offices of the screenwriters in Hollywood. "Teddie has only one interest," Fred Pollock wrote to Horkheimer confidentially in 1941, "namely, to become a small *rentier* in California as fast as possible, and whatever happens to everyone else is a matter of complete indifference to him."[68] Receiving financial support from the assets of the institute gave Adorno hope that he would be able to survive, if not as a musician, then at least as a social critic.

Dialectic of Enlightenment possesses remarkable extraterritorial features. Formulated in splendid isolation on the West Coast, it appeared in German after the end of the war in an Amsterdam exile publishing house. The fragmentation of its authors' lives is reflected in the publication history of these "Philosophical Fragments." In West Germany it became inside knowledge among people with political interests, and a pirated edition was on sale in the 1960s. Horkheimer had imposed an embargo on their jointly written key work, which had not succeeded in finding a large public in the 1950s, as well as on his own essays from the *Zeitschrift für Sozialforschung,* and this embargo lasted until 1968. Adorno acquiesced in this policy, but he also circumvented it. For him *Dialectic of Enlightenment* was the beginning of his career as a social theoretician, since it was only after it appeared that he acquired his redoubtable reputation as a public intellectual in Germany. Until the publication of *Negative Dialectics* in 1966, he suffered from the diversity of his writings. Any reference to an underlying background in systematic critique had to be banished to the footnotes. In 1948, when he announced the publication of his *Philosophy of Modern Music* as an "excursus to the *Dialectic of Enlightenment,*" he was still in California, and he reached no more than a small, esoteric circle of readers. But he definitively arrived in Germany with his essays in the *Neue Rundschau,* published by the resuscitated S. Fischer Verlag, and in periodicals such as *Merkur* and also *Der Monat.* In short, he quickly abandoned his extraterritorial vantage point.

Adorno's critique of jazz was one of the intellectual transfer payments of which his volume *Prisms* gives us a first overview. For the reading public, the overall grounding in theory underlying these writings remained invisible. Adorno's essays towered over the intellectual landscape like a mighty iceberg of theory, but only the initiated were able to perceive what lay beneath the surface or even knew that it existed. The life and work of the émigrés in America remained largely unknown to the German public throughout their lives, since until Martin Jay's pioneering book of 1973, *The Dialectical Imagination,* only biographical fragments had become available. After 1949 Adorno tried to find publishers for his writings in Germany, while Horkheimer played more of a waiting game, preferring to keep his options open. Politically they neither sought nor found any points of contact; where they succeeded in gaining entry was in the world of scholarship and the university. In the background, Horkheimer still retained his plan of continuing to work on theory in the absence of any onerous public obligations. The withdrawal from New York to California had already been part of this plan, and *Dialectic of Enlightenment* had been its first product. Horkheimer's almost contemporary *Eclipse of Reason* was designed to secure their continued presence in America. In California, Adorno had become Horkheimer's chief collaborator in the theory project, despite Pollock's reiterated doubts about Adorno's reliability. Adorno wanted at all costs to be involved in the development of the critical social theory that Horkheimer had been working toward since the mid-thirties, but he had been largely excluded from the strategic decisions that were designed to make this project a reality. These decisions were for the most part taken jointly by Horkheimer and Pollock.

After finishing *Dialectic of Enlightenment,* Horkheimer felt the necessity of involving himself once again in the American research routine. Most of the institute members had taken part in the war effort and placed their talents in the service of Washington. Their work on its behalf must also be seen in the context of the growing importance of the social sciences in the United States. The tendency to make use of the findings of the social sciences which had emerged since the first years of the Roosevelt administration increased during the war. Both the political and the military leadership became interested in developments throughout the world but also in changes in America itself. The boom in Japanology and Sinology, which now went far beyond philological studies, went hand in hand with studies in racism that were by no means confined just to the ideologies of the enemy states. The studies in *The Authoritarian Personality* that Horkheimer had initiated must be thought of in this context. At the time, Lazarsfeld was involved in one of the largest empirical studies of the day; it appeared later under the series title "The American Soldier." Although the majority of institute members were employed from time to time in government-sponsored activities, Horkheimer and Pollock did not succeed, unlike Lazarsfeld, in securing a continuous flow of financial support from the large foundations such as Rockefeller and Carnegie. Horkheimer found himself forced to take over the research section of the American Jewish Committee (AJC). This meant that he had to spend increasing amounts of time in New York after 1945, which introduced significant delays into the collaboration with Adorno. This is alluded to in the dedication to *Minima Moralia,* where Adorno writes that "one alone continued to perform the task that can only be accomplished by both."[69]

For Adorno, this meant that he too had to return to empirical social research. The "Scientific Experiences" essay reports on this, admittedly not without pride. When *The Authoritarian Personality* appeared in 1950 in the United States, the critical theorists were already inquiring into the possibility of returning to Germany. Horkheimer felt increasingly ground down by the political and organizational infighting in the AJC, which he ascribed bitterly to a "racial struggle."[70] His choice of words reflects his growing frustration at having to depend on the Jewish ticket for economic survival. What he was referring to were the conflicts in the secular Jewish organizations: the ethnic lobbyists whom Horkheimer felt harassed by were mainly from an earlier generation of immigrants from Eastern Europe, while the scholars they were financing were West European Jews escaping from fascism. The struggle for research money did not take place in a free market; applicants depended on their political and personal connections. Adorno and Horkheimer had acknowledged this in *Dialectic of Enlightenment* with their racket theory and the ticket mentality that went with it. From Horkheimer's standpoint, the opportunities available in America to develop a critical social theory that would do justice to the fundamental changes that the twentieth century had wrought seemed increasingly limited. Despite all their doubts about Germany and the Germans, Germany did seem to offer a more favorable climate for reestablishing the institute. A prime consideration, however, was whether it would be possible to secure Adorno's transfer to Germany as the institute's most important member. Horkheimer evidently impressed his German interlocutors in Frankfurt am Main. What they hoped for from his return was a positive image in the Western world, above all in the United States.

By 1948 Horkheimer had explored the situation. He had also secured financing for the trip to Europe from U.S. institutions. His letters to California make stirring reading even today. Shortly before leaving Zurich for Frankfurt, he wrote to Teddie and Gretel, "In general, the good will come only from us and our work."[71] To Pollock he wrote a little later, evidently more skeptical about the situation in Germany: "You know that I am acting as our advance guard. Germany is once again the country of the future and it is more vigorous and zestful and evil than ever. We shall be more isolated in the future rather than less—likewise the importance of our thinking."[72] He expected no enthusiastic welcome from his German colleagues and observed a willingness to conform to the new power relations. Moreover, he saw evidence of rackets on both sides of the Atlantic: "The professors and other professionals are all highly sought after. The Allies are in need of them all down to every halfway competent secretary. Never before have they all felt so important. . . . Yesterday evening I was invited to a meeting with politicians from the Council of the *Länder* together with some academics. I unintentionally revealed my own feelings. The professionals, the turncoats, the established residents—they all get along just fine together."[73] This comes from a letter he wrote in May to his wife, Maidon, who had stayed behind in Pacific Palisades. On 13 June 1948 came the sequel: "The worst thing about the dominant mentality here is not the anti-Semitism, which is of course flourishing, but the absence of change. The earlier modes of thought are still all there—ossified, mummy-like. As for the people, they are—almost without exception—seemingly unaffected by everything that has happened."[74] De-Nazification seemed farcical to him, purely formal, obeying no logic appropriate to actual individual cases. At the end of his trip to Europe there is a heartfelt groan: "If you work with total commitment and do not let yourself be led astray by grave disappointment, it will be possible to convey to some people in Germany today just what ought to be preserved through the dark night of history. And there is scarcely any place where that would be more vitally necessary than Germany,"[75] he wrote in July 1948 to Marie Jahoda, who was in New York battling with the AJC on Horkheimer's behalf.

While Horkheimer was able to regard his trip to Germany in 1948 as a kind of exploratory visit, when Adorno arrived in Frankfurt am Main on 2 November 1949, he was at once confronted with the realities of professional life. Over the Christmas break, after only two months, he took radical stock of the situation: "As far as I am concerned, the chief difficulty is the incessant communication; I sometimes feel like a gramophone record, as if I am wasting my breath; I more than ever feel that one can defend people's interests only at a distance from where they are."[76] The extraterritorial model already has a name, although during his first trip after his return he did not get beyond Amorbach: "Sils Maria is a genuine *topos noetikos*."[77] The need for extraterritoriality had been supplied in America by Pacific Palisades, to which Horkheimer had returned in the meantime. Now that need found itself confronted with an uncanny German experience. In January 1950 Adorno wrote to Leo Löwenthal, who had just taken a job with "Voice of America": "My seminar is like a Talmud school— I wrote to Los Angeles that it was as if the spirits of the murdered Jewish intellectuals had entered into the German students. Eerily uncanny [*unheimlich*]. But for that very reason, in a genuinely Freudian sense, also infinitely homely [*anheimelnd*]."[78] The debate about whether to be in Europe or America can be seen in the ambivalent tone of a letter to Thomas Mann of 28 December 1949: "My own situation is partly responsible for this difficulty of feeling properly at ease."[79] It is clear from this letter as well as others Adorno wrote at this time that he was deeply moved by the interest expressed in him by "young people," by "academic youth."[80] Adorno had conducted his first and last seminars in Germany in 1932 and since then had not worked as a university teacher. He had spent the summer of 1949 finishing off *The Authoritarian Personality*, a project surrounded by many editorial problems. In that situation he felt, as he wrote to Horkheimer, that there was "something very seductive" about the intellectual climate in Germany.[81]

In Frankfurt am Main, it could appear to Adorno as if an autonomous culture was still possible and not simply a lost idealistic illusion of the German tradition. In exile in America, the intellectuals around Horkheimer had experienced the loss of their cultural independence that had arisen from the structural transformation of society. The idea of the autonomy of the spirit contained within itself the hopes for emancipation of Jews who thought of themselves as neither religious nor Zionist. Hence the sight of a new generation of students who felt a need for purity of spirit was able to remind Adorno of the Jewish intellectuals of the Weimar era. But he could not deny his experience either in America or in Germany if he wanted to remain true to his own *Minima Moralia*. In the same letter to Mann,

Adorno tells him about "an otherwise entirely decent student of mine" who had assured him in all earnestness that "'we Germans have never taken anti-Semitism seriously.' He meant this quite sincerely, but I was forced to remind him of Auschwitz."[82] Adorno had to keep explaining to himself just why, despite such events, he expected better things of Frankfurt am Main. He did not keep his ideas on theory or politics to himself, nor did he confine them to private correspondence. As early as May 1950 he published his essay "Culture Resurrected" ("Die auferstandene Kultur") in the left-wing Catholic periodical *Frankfurter Hefte*. In it he said that his first observations of Germany had left him with "an impression of shadowboxing,"[83] which he interpreted by saying, "Politically and anthropologically, what seems to me to determine the life of the mind is the sense that Germany has ceased to be a political subject as a nation-state in the sense that was decisive for the last 150 years."[84] Germany had lost something of its threatening mien, and Adorno could now see it only as a part of Europe. Hence a return to Frankfurt am Main did not have to signify an identification with Germany.

The concept of culture shimmered with the ambivalence of a society without a concrete social alternative. By the time Adorno revisited Europe in 1949, the cold war had broken out. Adorno recollected in 1950 that the "expressionist phase" after the First World War "was distinguished by the hope that socialism might be brought about immediately."[85] The difference between the situation in the 1920s and in 1950 was obvious: "Society is splitting into rigid blocs. People experience events as something done to them, not as matters that concern their own spontaneous activity."[86] Adorno, however, had also pinpointed the loss of spontaneity as the mark of the current stage that culture had reached; the specious nature of the new seemed to him to be an essential characteristic of the Culture Industry. In Germany, though, a neutralized culture had a different function from its role in America: "As an isolated sphere of existence, devoid of any other relation to social reality than the abstract relation of a general need of the age or of nationalist obstinacy, the task of culture is to conceal the regression to barbarism."[87] In this contradictory relation between an enlightened Culture Industry and a shadowlike revival of the bourgeois religion of culture, it was possible for Adorno to carve out a role as a cultural critic and, indirectly, a social critic, a role not available to him in the United States. In retrospect, Adorno regarded his experiences as an author as among the decisive reasons for his return to Germany. A publisher, "incidentally a European emigrant," had rejected his *Philosophy of Modern Music* on the grounds that it was "badly organized,"[88] and a few years later a specialist journal for psychoanalysis had subjected his essay "Die revidierte Psychoanalyse" (Psychoanalysis Revised) to "editing" in the interests of greater comprehensibility: "I give these examples not to complain about the country where I found refuge but to explain clearly why I did not stay. In comparison with the horror of National Socialism my literary experiences were bagatelles."[89]

These lines appear to be the result of Adorno's self-confident awareness that he had succeeded in preserving his autonomy as a theorist. But even this statement was only written down with hindsight in the 1960s. In the early 1950s Adorno was still undecided. Without Horkheimer he would probably not have chosen to return to Germany. Both men were influenced by the wish to enjoy life in Europe. Both had stopped off in Paris before going on to Frankfurt am Main, Horkheimer in 1948 and Adorno in 1949. Full of excitement at his first sight of Europe after his long absence, Adorno wrote to Horkheimer, who was still in Pacific Palisades, that "in the empty, twilit lobby of the Hotel Lutetia, life was still living."[90] This sentence evokes that other sentence from "Tired of America" by the ambivalent democrat of the 1848 revolution, Ferdinand Kürnberger, who returned to Austria-Hungary after a disappointing stay in America. Adorno quoted Kürnberger's statement "Life does not live" as the epigraph to part one of *Minima Moralia*.[91] The reference to that book was evidently intended to remind Horkheimer of feelings they had shared. Kürnberger's book was basic reading among the émigrés, equalled only by Tocqueville's book on America. The phrase ironically sums up the American experience as the loss of immediacy in a purely bourgeois society which casts doubt on the very possibility of any new spontaneity. Without that spontaneity, Adorno believed that innovation is inconceivable. The pressure to conform, which was seen as an integral part of life in America as early as Tocqueville, was experienced as a threat by both Adorno and Horkheimer. The inescapability of the Culture Industry, which even cast a blight on the escape to California from New York, was suspended over their productivity like the sword of Damocles. The time lag between progressive America and backward Europe was felt by both men to be a fast-vanishing opportunity to salvage their possible intellectual collaboration.

Nevertheless, as we can see from a confidential memorandum between Horkheimer and Pollock, there was a profound uncertainty in 1949 about whether to choose Germany or America—and they were well aware of some ominous signs. On 30 March 1949 Pollock produced a "Proof of the Unreliability of Teddie"[92]—at a time when the preface to The Eclipse of Reason was at pains to assure the American reading public that "our philosophy is one."[93] In the spring Adorno had been in negotiations with the psychoanalyst Frederick J. Hacker about a research project in Beverly Hills. This project became a reality in 1952, and by 1953 it had given Adorno the nudge he needed to relinquish the idea of seeking a future in the American research effort. In 1949, however, everything still seemed open. Horkheimer spoke of California to Felix Weil as the "paradise that we found there."[94] He did not succeed in winning Adorno over to the idea of the journey to Europe until the summer. By the end of 1949 Adorno had finally articulated the decisive argument in a letter to Horkheimer: "It is my profoundest and most responsible conviction that the only motive that seriously justifies the German venture is to obtain the security that is so important for our production."[95] His utopia assumed concrete form in security, the very epitome of a bourgeois category. Both men preferred the security of a life as public servants to the liberty of a market organized along the lines of the Culture Industry. In contrast to Horkheimer, who was already a full professor, for Adorno this decision by no means offered a certain career. He could not yet know that the decision in favor of Frankfurt would involve a humiliatingly protracted journey from supernumerary professor to a full professorship. But he took that in his stride in order to be able to work with Horkheimer. Four days previously, in the expectation of the success of publishing ventures such as the institute's "Studies in Prejudice," he had announced to Horkheimer: "You say that we should just concentrate on our own writings. Yes, indeed. And I should like to say once again, at what is perhaps a decisive turning point: this would be the right and proper thing. If you can make this work (and may our indisputable successes contribute to this)—then we should abandon thoughts of Germany, despite everything and once and for all."[96]

Behind all the doubts, however, lay an *enthusiasm* that had gripped Adorno during his first stay in Germany. He sensed a potential public and a receptiveness that for various reasons he had not found in America. In the United States he was forced to submit to Horkheimer's low-profile strategy, which was adhered to until the publication of The Authoritarian Personality. But when the prominent rebel in the world of sociology, C. Wright Mills, praised the work to the skies in 1954 as "perhaps the most influential book of the last decade," Horkheimer could only manage a slight smile when he added gently "although not well organized."[97] The fact was that the decision in favor of Europe had already been reached even though Horkheimer was able to insure against failure by obtaining a chair at the University of Chicago. Horkheimer justified his trips to Chicago by the need to maintain contacts and to observe social trends. After 1953 Adorno never returned to the United States, although he agreed with Horkheimer that "for the analysis of society the better vantage point is over there rather than here in the colony."[98] Western Europe—on this point Horkheimer, Pollock, and Adorno had been in agreement since the end of the 1940s—could still, with some irony, be compared to Greece at the time of the Roman Empire. This appears to explain the title "Graeculus" which Adorno wished to use for a continuation of *Minima Moralia*. One should pick up the tail end of a vanishing tradition of philosophical education in a corner with a cultured past: "while Rome rules the world and the barbarians are already at the gates" is how Horkheimer formulated it in a status report on 18 February 1950.[99] Looking back on his time in America, Adorno could say that he "was first deprovincialized" there: "In America I was liberated from a naïve belief in culture and acquired the ability to see culture from the outside. . . . I was taught this lesson . . . in America where no reverential silence reigned in the presence of everything intellectual as it does in Central and Western Europe far beyond the so-called cultivated classes; the absence of this respect leads the spirit in the direction of critical self-reflection."[100]

The social difference between Europe and America endowed Adorno's critical analyses with a prognostic power that had been bottled up in his decade of life in the United States. His enthusiasm was now expressed in a breathtaking series of publications in which what amounted to a flood of talks, essays, and books poured forth in rapid succession. *Prisms* provided a sense of the spectrum that Adorno could cover. It opened programmatically with "Cultural Criticism and Society"—although Adorno normally abhorred titles containing the word "and." Moreover, his new publisher, Peter Suhrkamp, disliked them too and persuaded him to adopt the title *Prisms* for the entire collection. Adorno had written the introductory essay in 1949 and then published it in 1951 in a *Festschrift* for the seventy-fifth birthday of Leopold von Wiese, the doyen of German sociology. We can read it as a manifesto announcing the return of the "critical theory" to which Adorno appealed in contrast to the established conservative cultural criticism.[101] As a tribute to Leopold von Wiese, the text seems misplaced, unless we read it as a statement that he wishes to be accepted as an interlocutor among German sociologists. Its language seems remarkably convoluted, as if Adorno had modeled himself on the coded "slave language" favored by Horkheimer in emigration. We might almost interpret "Cultural Criticism and Society" as a sequel to Horkheimer's "Traditional and Critical Theory" of 1937. The argument is not to be found on the surface. Cultural criticism is understood as an integral component of the culture that is to be criticized. Adorno interprets it as the breakaway product of an established bourgeois society which is unaware of is own nature as a totality. In its limited, unreflecting nature Adorno discerns the conservative character of traditional cultural criticism. Critical theory, for its part, is supposed to differ from this, but without becoming identified with traditional Marxism.

On closer examination, the essay seems to rest on large assumptions and to be in need of interpretation. Something of the "shadowboxing" character of the culture that he diagnosed in "Culture Resurrected" seems to have stuck to the essay itself. The cold war had already begun, and the relapse into the "slave language" which Horkheimer favored in emigration appeared appropriate. In its political form, Marxism is linked to the "Russians" and the "Soviet sphere," in which it is presented as a "provocative lie which does not seek acceptance but commands silence."[102] Adorno does not just distance himself from Marxist ideology but develops the idea that "as with many other elements of dialectical materialism, the notion of ideology has changed from an instrument of knowledge into its straitjacket."[103] The fact that traditional Marxism had acquired the character of domination is taken by Adorno to be a social reality, one that ruled out direct intellectual contact. The difference between the political climate after the First and Second World Wars, respectively, which he had focused on in "Culture Resurrected," is now forgotten. The absence of social alternatives, which appears transformed here in the antithesis of life and spirit, anticipates the Ice Age of the cold war: "Life transforms itself into the ideology of reification—a death mask."[104] The text makes no concessions to the uninitiated. Anyone who is ignorant of the categories of dialectical thinking will find himself confronted by mere ciphers for which no key is forthcoming. "Critical theory" is meant to bring to life whatever lies hidden behind the death mask. Behind Adorno's critique of reification lies his experience of the Culture Industry in America, in which ideology had been replaced by "advertisements for the world through its duplication."[105] Nonetheless, the transfer of his American experiences to Europe is effected only at the cost of abstractness. Although he does not represent the continuation of any German tradition, not even that of the Weimar era, his text presupposes an educated reader who reminds us of the "imaginary witness" from the "Notes" and "Sketches" appended to *Dialectic of Enlightenment*, "to whom we bequeath it so that it is not entirely lost with us."[106]

Dialectic of Enlightenment was duplicated as a message in a bottle in California, and five hundred copies were sent off in 1945 to Amsterdam, where it was supplemented by the theses of the chapter "Elements of Anti-Semitism," disguised in the spirit of the "slave language" under the subtitle "Limits of Enlightenment." It was then printed by Querido Verlag and sent out into the newly reborn German market. Copies were still available in the Netherlands and Switzerland as late as the sixties, and after that it circulated in pirated editions among a new generation of younger readers. Adorno himself kept hold of a part of his message in a bottle and tried to market it himself under the title *Prisms*. This unloved title reveals something of the contradictory nature of the project:

> For what it stands for conceptually cannot be separated from something non-conceptual, namely the historical status of the word "prisms" and its relationship to contemporary usage. The word is all too willing to be carried along by the currents of contemporary language, like periodicals with modernistic layouts designed to attract attention in the marketplace. The word is conformist through a distinctiveness that costs it nothing; one hears immediately how quickly it will age. Tags like that are used by people who think of jazz as modern music. The title is a memorial to a defeat in the permanent contest between the work and the author. I express this, hoping thereby to add to the title a little poison that will preserve it, mummy-fashion, so that it will not damage the book all that much.[107]

Even in his own book he was disturbed by something of the kind that he disliked in jazz, something that is made up to look timelessly fashionable. What has disappeared from it is history, which draws attention to itself in the aging process, in the speed with which cultural wares grow stale.

By the mid-1950s Adorno's experience of America, which was evident in a fragmentary way in *Minima Moralia*, started to be taken for granted by his German readers. In the aphorism titled "Contribution to Intellectual History," Adorno subsequently queried the concept of the "message in a bottle"[108] that had played such a significant role in discussions among the émigré members of the institute in the thirties. The idea of linking up with a dying European tradition, of addressing "an imaginary posterity"[109]—an idea cherished at a time when Walter Benjamin was still alive—was now rejected at the point when many émigrés were considering whether to return. This, for example, was the case with part three of *Minima Moralia* itself, which was written between 1946 and 1947. At around the same time, Adorno was working on *The Authoritarian Personality*. His colleagues at the institute were skeptical about his talent for cooperation. In a report in 1946 on conversations with other members of the research group on the West Coast, Leo Löwenthal noted: "The immediate consequence to draw is indeed to bring Teddie in an attitude in which he continues to act as a wise adviser and in which he forgets about all his administrative ambitions. Otherwise he has to wake up and to realize how extremely difficult it would be for him to make one simple step in the world without us."[110] Horkheimer and Pollock were starting to think seriously about a complete withdrawal from the public sphere, a course of action Horkheimer returned to repeatedly after his first stay in Frankfurt in 1948. Marcuse almost always contradicted the idea of the message in a bottle. His visits to Germany after the war tended to encourage him to seek out new avenues for public activity. At the same time, with the advent of the cold war, his work in the OSS became increasingly untenable.

Politically and economically, the situation among the émigrés looked bleak at times. By 1941 Adorno saw himself facing financial ruin. He must have had a clear picture of the financial position of the institute, since otherwise he would not have suggested to Horkheimer "that you, Gretel, and I should undergo training as psychoanalysts in our spare time."[111] *Dialectic of Enlightenment*, with its "message in a bottle," was written in a period of isolation, but it could also be seen as a happy moment in the history of the emigration because for the first time since 1933 it was not necessary to take political sensibilities into account. Similarly, the tone that predominates in *Prisms* gives flesh to "the happiness of the infinitesimal freedom that lies in knowledge as such."[112] Adorno retained this tone without making any pedagogic concessions to his public. With its aid he transferred into theory his artistic ideal of a refusal to compromise that was appropriate to the times. The reader will find it hard to disentangle the process by which a radical social critique became separated from the political movement with which it could be associated. At any rate, in *Dialectic of Enlightenment* the breach with the workers' movement has already taken place, while in *Minima*

Moralia the link still shines through in a few passages. But in the absence of the memory of its origins, the radicality of his cultural critique appears abstract. Horkheimer suppressed almost every attempt at political explication ventured after their return, chiefly by Adorno. Even in the thirties, Horkheimer refused to make political statements, however opportune. His political opinions remained a mystery until his letters were published after his death. Even in his letters, Horkheimer's views are tailored to the individual addressees. He writes to members of his family in different terms from the way he writes to Pollock. He even distinguishes between the closest circle of institute members and the more distant ones, to say nothing of outsiders. We might think of him as a diplomat in his own cause. Adorno lacked this talent; his own direct political statements seem blunt and abrupt for the most part. On a few celebratory occasions Adorno revealed something of what separated him from Horkheimer, who had preserved him from "the life of an aesthete not through your principles but through the power of an expanding consciousness."[113]

Prisms displays this consciousness in its critique of objects that lie beyond the aesthetic realm. Their idiosyncratic charm for the German public had its source in such statements as "To write poetry after Auschwitz is barbaric,"[114] which were effective because they struck at the heart of the religious belief in a restored culture. The point of the following sentence was simply ignored by generations of readers: "And this corrodes even the knowledge of why it has become impossible to write poetry today."[115] In *Prisms* Adorno appears as a critic of ideology who finds it impossible to go beyond it despite his dissatisfaction with that role. This was a dilemma he had first encountered in the Princeton Radio Research Project. He had practiced ideology critique in his music theory in the thirties, taking it as far as the critique of reification. While engaged on administrative research, he found himself forced to acknowledge that reification had taken over the medium of enlightenment, that is, science itself: "All reification is a forgetting."[116] This remark noted down in the *Dialectic of Enlightenment* applied to all the products of the mind that had become commodities, the products of science and theory, as well as nonconceptual ideas such as those of music.

Through *Prisms,* critical theory began to take shape as an independent mode of theorizing thinking about society. At that time Adorno still wrote the term in lower-case letters. But its origins remained obscure to the average German reader of the 1950s. Up to the mid-1960s *Dialectic of Enlighten-*

ment had not really found an audience, apart from a few dedicated readers. In 1949 Max Bense traced the roots of the theory back to "a Californian Left"—by which he meant left-wing intellectuals in emigration. Already deeply shocked by McCarthy, Horkheimer panicked at Bense's suggestion. He wrote to Adorno, who was in Frankfurt at the time, asking him to track these rumors down and scotch them where possible. At around the same time, *Sinn und Form,* a magazine which appeared in the Soviet zone of occupation, printed some chapters from *Dialectic of Enlightenment.* Hans Mayer, who had emigrated to East Germany in the meantime, always denied that it was he who had been responsible for the undesired reprint, and there is no reason to disbelieve him. Politically, Horkheimer had long since broken with all organizations connected with the labor movement. His dealings with the American Jewish Labor Committee to help finance the study on "anti-Semitism among American labor" had been his last attempt at political activity. After 1936—that is, after the beginning of the Moscow show trials—he wanted nothing more to do with communists in the party. He had also washed his hands of the international meetings of the anti-fascist left under the banner of culture that accompanied the internal Russian purges. Adorno's aesthetic left-wing radicalism of the twenties, which ruthlessly criticized the mendacious character of Soviet cultural politics, was able later on, in the early forties, to elaborate the difference between critical theory and traditional Marxism without being forced to comment directly on the confusing political consequences of the Stalin-Hitler Pact.

In the early fifties, Adorno's cultural criticism did not reveal its political character until a second reading. It appears on the surface only when he explicitly addresses Soviet cultural policies. An example is the essay "Die gegängelte Musik" (Music in a Straitjacket), which appeared in *Der Monat* in 1948 and was then included in *Dissonanzen.*[117] He pulled no punches here. Music had been transformed, he argued, from the ambivalent ideology of the bourgeois era into an unambiguous instrument of dictatorship. Adorno was eager to distinguish his own brand of criticism from conservative talk of a "cultural crisis," since the demoralization felt about that was something the communist policy of a broad left-wing alliance wanted to exploit for its own purposes. "Cultural crisis," however, was also the catchphrase associated with Karl Mannheim's sociology of knowledge, a school of thought that had preoccupied Adorno at regular intervals ever since he had been a student in Frankfurt. The group around Horkheimer was locked in a heartfelt rivalry with Mannheim, who was the most prominent sociologist in Frankfurt during the Weimar period. His idea of a "free-floating intelligentsia" was a distinct variation on a theory current at the end of the First World War which envisaged the politicization of intellectuals. Like Georg Lukács, Mannheim came from Budapest, and like him, he commuted between Vienna and Heidelberg. The legendary circles of intellectuals—the Sunday Circle in Budapest and the Wednesday Circle in Heidelberg—overlapped. The abortive revolutions in Germany and Hungary made it necessary for intellectuals to rethink their political ideas. During the Weimar period, Mannheim experimented with a sociology that transcended the traditional classes of bourgeois society. In *History and Class Consciousness* Lukács radicalized his theory, attempting a renewal of the Marxian impulses toward emancipation. The Frankfurt sociologists too worked away at this intellectual left-wing radicalism, from which Lukács soon distanced himself. Behind Mannheim's sociology of knowledge the question of revolution, which had been the original starting point, tended to disappear—part of a cumulative process that was continued in emigration after 1933. In Adorno's eyes, the sociology of knowledge was heir to the bourgeois sociology whose leaders in Germany had been Max Weber and Ernst Troeltsch. For Adorno the sociology of knowledge, along with existentialism, became the guardians of traditional theories of the present. The zest with which Adorno attacks the sociology of knowledge in *Prisms*, with its "gesture of innocuous skepticism,"[118] together with traditional cultural criticism and jazz as a "perennial fashion," can be explained by his aversion to the false return of a culture which reifies itself as something timeless.

Critique of reification was the theoretical catchphrase with which Adorno inaugurated his criticism of the Culture Industry when he began working with Lazarsfeld. Jazz as a kind of musical pseudo-rebellion had attracted his attention earlier on while he was still in Britain. He was never really interested in jazz as a specifically American phenomenon. Just as the sociology of knowledge had repressed a radical critique of society, so too had jazz displaced radical music as the epitome of utility music. *Prisms* appeared in 1955. If we attempt to understand it from its standpoint on the margins of theoretical and cultural criticism, the essay collection reveals itself as the work of an exiled intellectual who has returned and is in search of a place for himself. It is as if Adorno now wished to present his share of the message in a bottle personally to a new public without bothering to make it visible as a historical product, except in the general acknowledgments. The essays in *Prisms* are a continuation of *Minima Moralia,* and at their center lie the reactions of intellectuals to the liquidation of tradition *after its demise*.[119] Adorno inquires into the reasons for the success of the sociology of knowledge and of jazz—a question that had already preoccupied him in Britain. As early as 1937 he confided in Löwenthal, at that time acting editor of the *Zeitschrift für Sozialforschung,* that in his contributions he did not wish to be restricted simply to music criticism. What else did he have to offer? An essay on the "new value-free sociology," by which he meant the Mannheim essay. But the only articles accepted for publication in New York after the one on jazz was "On the Fetish Character in Music and the Regression of Listening." The critique of the sociology of knowledge was one of Adorno's first steps toward becoming a Critical Theorist of society who did not wish to be confined to the role of music specialist any longer. It was only by collecting the essays contained in *Prisms* that he was able to appear before the public in the role that he thought suited him best.

By the mid-fifties Adorno had completed the transfer to Frankfurt am Main. Reflecting on his unhappy experience with Hacker in Beverly Hills, he summed up his time in Santa Monica on 12 March 1953: "My belief that it would be peaceful enough here to enable us to get on with our writing proved illusory."[120] Adorno realized that "in September I too shall turn fifty; and neither of us will have children now. Lastly, and above all, . . . one cannot submit to the principle of survival as the highest value without joining the ranks of the fittest and thereby forfeiting one's life. In view of the fact, however, that we can scarcely hope to become the agents of any practical action that might avert disaster, everything depends upon our establishing a continuity that would give us hope that not everything that has developed in us will go to waste."[121] Adorno wrote this emphatic plea for a future in Frankfurt to Horkheimer, who was on the verge of establishing some measure of security by obtaining the post of rector at the university. It was the need for biographical continuity that was to underpin the change of continents: "Every glass of kirsch in the Schlagbaum"—the Schlagbaum is the old pub at the Bockenheimer Warte in Frankfurt—"has more in common with our philosophy than Riesman's collected works." David Riesman is referred to here as an instance of a best-selling work of sociology, *The Lonely Crowd,* a book whose contents come closest to the ideas of critical theory. All the more incisive was Adorno's polemic, which aimed at drawing a dividing line so as "to gain time to think and to live— and the two things are identical."[122] Built in to this intellectual utopia is the hope that there will be "a few young people . . . who will preserve a little of what we have in mind."[123] It is hard to overlook the emotional force with which Adorno pleads the case for Frankfurt. The academic routine in America is depicted as a Social-Darwinist world that an intellectual who wished to preserve his autonomy would do best to flee.

Adorno is well aware of the paradoxical nature of his arguments. They are meant for Horkheimer's eyes, not for the general public. In America the émigrés had "had the great good fortune . . . to be allowed to survive," but at the cost "of a form of existence that has only the negative side of solitude, namely, isolation."[124] By 1952 the conditions of a prolonged stay in California had changed. Emigration would have had to become immigration. On 27 May 1945, shortly after the end of the war in Europe, Adorno had given a talk at the Jewish Club in Los Angeles in which he formulated "questions to the intellectual emigration."[125] Unusually for him, he spoke in the first-person plural, and in so doing he established a new homogeneous collective: Jewish intellectuals with a German cultural past. At that time he issued a plea for an independent self-awareness that would mediate between American experience and European memory. Adorno was able to say this in full consciousness of the fact that "we have escaped the German gas chambers."[126] After their first visits back to Germany, the critical theorists found themselves forced to defend their actions to other émigrés. Adorno tried to justify their actions by appealing to "the old rule that the refugee goes back to see what he can accomplish,"[127] a message that Adorno and Horkheimer subsequently passed on to the German public. This theme too is treated beneath the surface in *Prisms*. It emerges most clearly in "Aldous Huxley and Utopia," where Adorno speaks of "the intellectual émigré" as "a social type . . . by no means only the Jews,"[128] noting that the émigrés had made their appearance for the first time in America as a new social grouping.[129] Ever since the Enlightenment had emancipated European Jews, they had striven to become citizens. Adorno now reformulated this as the idea of the intellectual who preserves the possibility of social change. With his highly opaque essay "Veblen's Attack on Culture," which, like the Huxley essay he had begun in the early forties, he comes close to pragmatism as an American experience. His critique of adjustment now turns into a program: "Today adjustment to what is possible no longer means adjustment; it means making the possible real."[130]

Ever since he had discussed white-collar workers with Kracauer, Adorno had been asking himself about the historical dynamic of class societies which had begun to lose their identity with the onset of "bourgeois society." Looking at Europe now with the estranged eyes of a returnee who had seen the most advanced country in the world building a tradition for itself without a feudal history, he found that everything seemed to have changed from before his emigration. In the old European bourgeois society, the rule of liberalism and its living antithesis, organized socialism, came together to form the total image of the nineteenth century. The new society, even though it could not deny its roots in the familiar old bourgeois society, seemed to the critical theorists in post–New Deal America to represent the genesis of an affluent society to which there was no alternative. They described this new society as the superseding of class society on the foundations of class society itself. Just as the bourgeois class disappears into the "middle classes," so too does the proletariat evaporate under the pressure of Big Business and Big Labor. Nowadays the idea of the melting pot is dismissed by many sociologists of culture as pure ideology; but at that time it really existed. In it the traditional distinctions disappeared. New imagined communities had first to be invented. The American Jews did not exist as a coherent community before the United States entered the war against Nazi Germany; the contract research projects of the institute on behalf of the AJC belong to the formative phase of new communities among which Jews and blacks were the pioneers.

Right from the start the critical theorists in America had inquired into the nature of the new. Initially, in the 1930s, they concentrated their attention on events in Europe. Up to 1939 they published the major essays of the *Zeitschrift für Sozialforschung* in German. A change of attitude did not come until the outbreak of war. Then Herbert Marcuse's "Some Social Implications of Modern Technology" established a link between American and European experience.[131] This implied a question about the new, not as something that emerged first in America, but as something that had been brought over from Europe by the critical theorists. The tendency for cultural life to develop into the Culture Industry was not just an American phenomenon but was to be found in Europe as well. The UFA film studio and media concentration were part of the Weimar Republic too. The question of the newness of products of the Culture Industry did not arise merely in response to Radio City and Hollywood. Adorno began to ask the relevant questions with reference to music and then picked up the question again in his critique of Veblen. In Veblen's theory Adorno perceived America as "capitalism, as it were, in its complete purity without any precapitalist remnants,"[132] as the new Rome of bourgeois society. Guided by this impression, and in competition with Veblen's pragmatism, he arrived at the question: "How is anything new possible at all?[133] The political response that had seemed appropriate to the aesthetic left-wing radicals of the Weimar era had been the politicization of the intellectuals. In the American context it was evident that this response made no sense. *Minima Moralia* had already established that isolation was the harsh reality of the life of intellectuals. And adopting Horkheimer's doctrine of the authoritarian state, Adorno had also learned to despise the Soviet empire, regarding it as a cannibalistic system. Nevertheless, after 1945 his imagination ran riot in an essay titled "Excess," a text he later withdrew from the book publication of *Minima Moralia.* Perhaps he regretted the explicitness with which he had declared that "a union of the intellectuals who still are intellectuals with the workers who still know that they are workers is even more relevant today than it was thirty years ago."[134] Adorno thought that present-day reality was "veiled by technology so that it is no longer possible to speak of a proletarian class consciousness in the largest industrial nation of today."[135] This veil is woven by the Culture Industry. Criticism of the Culture Industry should be an ideology critique that "removes this technological veil . . . from our eyes."[136] The central idea that is being transferred from America to Europe can be found in the essay "Cultural Criticism and Society" of 1949: "Life transforms itself into the ideology of reification—a death mask. . . . Cultural criticism must become social physiognomy. The more the whole divests itself of all spontaneous elements, is socially mediated and filtered, is 'consciousness,' the more it becomes 'culture.'"[137]

America did not just change Adorno's conception of himself as a cultural producer; it also changed his conception of society. By returning to Germany, Adorno and Horkheimer were attempting to escape from a Culture Industry that was expanding into an all-pervasive system. But what they found in Germany in 1950 was a society that was being simultaneously restored and modernized. The buildings that were being restored in a way that was ostensibly faithful to the originals became for Adorno the emblems of a false resurrection: "No one in whom some sense of historical continuity survives will be able to contemplate without embarrassment the faithful reconstruction of buildings destroyed by bombs, such as the Würzburg inn Zum Falken. It is an injustice to everything that was lovable about the past, that is not interchangeable, that exists in the here and now and is unique."[138] Such a comment could be made only by a returnee such as Adorno whose "childhood memory"[139] was being vandalized by a reproduced culture. He turned increasingly to music as his preferred field of social physiognomy. His theory of music emphasizes its cognitive aspect, something that must be a thorn in the flesh of all "art religion."[140] The critical theory of music continues the Enlightenment criticism of religion in a secularized age. Social conditions have changed, but Adorno still harks back to the young Marx's view that "the people is the opium of the people."[141] The experience of mass culture is linked to that of the music producer's necessary isolation from the public. It was in America that Adorno became aware of the social and historical connections that decisively influenced his own future path.

Life and history part company. Adorno returned from America a different man. In music, he maintained his claim to continuity in the face of the social cataclysms that disrupted life in the twentieth century. The living experience of music belonged for Adorno to his parents' home, to "this beautiful protected life in which Adorno gained the confidence that never left him his entire life," as Leo Löwenthal testified. We can still hear in this posthumous declaration Löwenthal's feeling of "jealousy of an existence you just had to love."[142] Adorno experienced the loss of security as early as the world economic crisis, at a time when Walter Benjamin and Siegfried Kracauer were on the verge of ruin. But he must have given others the impression that he was well provided for. This was the case with Horkheimer, who disapproved of Adorno's trips back to Germany in the thirties, but believed him to be more secure financially than he really was. Even when things were going very badly, Adorno inclined toward an upper-middle-class lifestyle, but it was more of an aspiration than the reality it had still been in the parental homes of both Horkheimer and Pollock. Moreover, he too wished to emancipate himself from his origins. His aesthetic left-wing radicalism was supposed to make people forget his bourgeois roots. For all that, Adorno praised Horkheimer because "you preserved me from the life of an aesthete not through your principles but through the power of an expanding consciousness."[143] This can also be read in Adorno's turning to the ideological criticism of music. His ventures into theory in the early twenties are closely linked to his own musical practice; but with his move to Vienna we see a more broadly based process of reflection on the affirmative nature of music, which confronted him with the alternatives of either conforming to the demands of the marketplace or else seeking a different sort of intellectual existence. The appropriation of a critical theory of society based on a return to an undistorted understanding of Marx belonged to the aesthetic left-wing radicalism of the twenties. In exile, however, it brought him into collision with the reality of a workaday world constructed according to the principles of the Culture Industry. The recurrent memory of his encounter with Lazarsfeld—in other words, with a man who should have known better—is emblematic of the situation of a musician compelled to change by social circumstances.

Adorno returned to Germany as a critical theorist of society. The German university system had not yet broken with the tradition of a philosophical sociology even though the sociologists of this kind who had not emigrated no longer possessed the legitimacy they had previously had. This university system did not find it easy to come to terms with an Adorno. Without the aid of Horkheimer's astuteness in university politics, Adorno would never have been able to succeed him at the University of Frankfurt or at the Institute for Social Research. While Horkheimer soon managed to exchange life in Frankfurt's Westend for Montagnola in the Ticino, Adorno only just succeeded in obtaining a foothold in Frankfurt. The kirsch in the Schlagbaum, mentioned earlier,[144] reminds us of his father's roots in the wine trade, but by taking up residence at Kettenhofweg 123, Adorno had arrived as an intellectual in Frankfurt's Westend. The upper-middle-class lifestyle he aspired to was something he could achieve only during vacations, in Sils Maria with its fashionable Waldhaus Hotel. This place acted as a yardstick about which he had already exchanged views with Thomas Mann, himself an enthusiastic visitor to the Engadine. But in addition, Adorno's idea of artistic fulfillment seems reminiscent of a mountain landscape empty of people: "What a child feels when it leaves a footprint in freshly fallen snow is one of the most powerful aesthetic impulses."[145] He even declared this concrete utopia to be one of the "criteria of New Music" in one of the numerous lectures he gave at the summer school in Kranichstein.[146] From 1946 on, Wolfgang Steinicke had established an annual event in Kranichstein, near Darmstadt, at which Adorno came into contact with young musicians and where "an atmosphere was created in which the sense of a common purpose, of solidarity, flourished even in the midst of violent disagreements."[147]

Music can be regarded as Adorno's *promesse de bonheur*. His musical writings can be read as the repeated attempt "to recuperate his childhood in a changed form."[148] Music makes it possible to experience utopian realms that were previously unknown to anyone. Schoenberg had enabled Adorno to perceive "those extraterritorial chords that have not yet been invested with the intentions of the language of music—a kind of musical freshly fallen snow in which the human subject has as yet left no trace."[149] In the early 1920s Adorno had already politicized the idea of a different music. He had invented a new language for music, and even in his last writings he put the old question in a new way: "How can musical spontaneity be socially possible at all?"[150] This impulse arose out of his own artistic sense, but in its bitter criticism of jazz it came up against the limits imposed by his own life experience, for the knowledge of which he himself produced the requisite intellectual tools when he reflected on his time in America. The unwavering insistence on a unity in one's own life renders inflexible anyone who wishes to remain identical with himself—and who acts as if "this identity was always desirable."[151] Generations of Adorno's enemies have derived sustenance from this weakness but have failed to recognize the strength of Adorno's critique of music as ideology: "The affirmative moment of all art, and that of music in particular, is inherited from the ancient magic; the very tone with which all music begins has a touch of it. It is utopia as well as the lie that utopia is here now."[152]

Adorno had linked the idea of a return to Germany with a further joint study to be undertaken with Horkheimer. Unlike Adorno, Horkheimer was not wedded to settling in Frankfurt. During the 1950s he commuted between Chicago and Montagnola, while after 1953 Adorno established a foothold in the University of Frankfurt and in the public life of the Federal Republic of Germany. His American past in exile began to fade, not just for the West Germans but even in his own eyes. His time in America had given him the ability to contemplate dispassionately the failure to achieve greater social changes after 1945. He did not return to Germany until after the cold war had broken out. Already by 1949 it was clear to him that the world was no longer an open place. But his criticism of the culture that had been "resurrected"[153] revived memories of the revolutionary impulse that had animated Expressionism after the First World War. Adorno found a place for himself in Frankfurt as the critic of a schizoid restoration of culture. It was a vantage point from which his past experience of America enabled him to garner a utopian prospect: "In America, the self-evident reification recoils at times, unforced, into a semblance of humanity and proximity—and not just into a semblance."[154] Adorno turned his back on America, the most advanced social observation post, so as to salvage the contents of his own "message in a bottle." A bottle, however, would have sufficed only to contain a summary of his oeuvre. During the two decades following his return, he brought all his energies to bear on bringing his ideas to fruition. Even so, he became aware of a new danger that threatened. It was not just life that had been damaged; the autonomy of the intellect that sustained his writings had suffered too. This dissonance recurs in almost all his writings after his return.

7. | Adorno as "Identical" Man

The task of philosophy is to dissolve the semblance of the
obvious as well as the semblance of the obscure.
THEODOR W. ADORNO, "WHY STILL PHILOSOPHY"

When did Adorno arrive in Frankfurt? There is undoubtedly some truth in the surmise that he and Horkheimer never completely returned from exile. In the 1950s Horkheimer was in serious doubt for a long time about whether he should settle in the United States in preference to Frankfurt. He finally discovered the right place for himself, in Montagnola, in the Ticino. Adorno emphasized in many letters just how much he missed Horkheimer's presence in Frankfurt. The separation of the two men, however, proved to be of benefit to posterity, since it forced them both to become letter writers. Horkheimer never felt as close to Adorno as he had to Pollock. Adorno courted his favor throughout his life. Even in the letter for Horkheimer's seventieth birthday, which Adorno published in *Die Zeit* on 12 February 1965, his attitude was highly respectful. Despite a friendship reaching back forty years, it was only comparatively recently that they had started to use the intimate *Du* to address each other: "You [*Du*] once told me that I think that animals are like humans, while you think human beings are like animals. There is some truth in this."[1]

These intimate confessions must have seemed strange to the West German educated public who provided *Die Zeit* with its devoted readers at the time. At any rate, Horkheimer felt compelled to reply to some critical letters from readers who had reacted unfavorably to Adorno's unusual birthday greetings: "After the letter appeared, Adorno expressed his regrets that he had talked too much about himself. I replied: If you do not talk about yourself, how is anyone supposed to understand me?"[2] Horkheimer was unwilling to see Adorno's birthday letter as an "appreciation,"[3] like articles in other newspapers and radio broadcasts: his "letter, no less objectively, focuses on our relationship."[4] Notwithstanding Horkheimer's response, aspects of the letter must have seemed obscure and highly subjective to outsiders. At the time, only a small minority of the reading public would have been familiar with *Dialectic of Enlightenment*. Had people read it, they would perhaps have realized that the comment about animals was rather more than a piece of sentimentality or an individual quirk. Anyone who knew anything about Horkheimer would have known that he was capable of howling like a dog; according to witnesses, he was as likely to display this disconcerting talent in the streets of Manhattan as at Frankfurt Central Station. Such behavior was of course inconceivable in Adorno. Their speech also differed significantly. Horkheimer's Swabian accent was very noticeable, while Adorno's public voice emphasized his extreme distance from every form of dialect. Frequent attempts have been made to argue that theoretical differences of opinion can be traced back to individual distinctions between the two—the fact that Horkheimer came from an upper-middle-class factory owner's family while Adorno's background was that of a businessman's home in which an enthusiasm for culture extended to professional aspirations in music. But our view of them changes once we perceive the organic unity of the works they produced together. Any attempt to explain Adorno without his relationship to Horkheimer will miss the essence of Adorno.

While Adorno was still a student in 1921, he found in Horkheimer a man he could look up to as if to a much older brother. This distance persisted for a long time. After the Nazi seizure of power in 1933, they parted ways until 1938, when Adorno followed Horkheimer to New York. By the time they began to write down *Dialectic of Enlightenment* in 1943, they already had behind them their key experience of a shared intellectual community. This was something that Adorno defended with all his might against the other members of the institute. It can almost be regarded as an irony of history that Leo Löwenthal and Herbert Marcuse ended up settling in California while Adorno and Horkheimer, along with Pollock, to whom *Dialectic of Enlightenment* was dedicated, returned to Frankfurt am Main. Marcuse above all made strenuous efforts to keep in touch with Horkheimer, whereas Löwenthal soon fell out with Horkheimer and Pollock on the question of pension rights. Marcuse kept on pressing for the resuscitation of the *Zeitschrift für Sozialforschung,* and this was a question that also preoccupied the institute members in Frankfurt. In 1947 Marcuse visited Europe, and during that time he had a shocking encounter with Heidegger, who had remained politically obdurate even after the demise of National Socialism. Following his meeting with Heidegger, he sent Horkheimer a set of thirty-three theses to which Horkheimer promised to respond with a "kind of philosophical program" that he proposed to draft with Adorno.[5] But time passed without anything making its appearance.

In 1956 a discussion took place between Adorno and Horkheimer of which a record has been found in the Adorno archive. Once again, it envisages a joint project, one that varies between a list of theses and a new *Communist Manifesto* that "does justice to the way things are today."[6] The conscientious editor had trouble dating it exactly, but much in it points to 1956. The collectivization of agriculture that had recently begun in China seems to have reminded Horkheimer of Soviet collectivization in the 1930s. This is what had led him to make a sharp distinction between critical theory and traditional Marxism at the time. Horkheimer watched with extreme suspicion while the Twentieth Congress of the Communist Party of the Soviet Union unfolded, culminating in the speech of General Secretary Nikita Khrushchev. After all, Stalin's successors had been fully implicated in the crimes of the regime. Nevertheless, it was Mao Tse-tung's China that Horkheimer regarded as the scene of the bloodiest terror; he speaks again and again of the 20 million dead Chinese sacrificed to the planned process of industrialization. As an avid newspaper reader, Horkheimer preserved a copy of *Time* magazine of March 1956 with its cover story on the terror in China in which this figure was explicitly mentioned. Adorno often had recourse to Horkheimer's newspaper archive. In this particular discussion Adorno seems to have let his enthusiasm run away with him: "I have the feeling that the oriental world will take over the leadership from Western civilization under the banner of Marxism. This will transform the entire dynamics of history. Marxism will be adopted in Asia just as Mexico was taken over in its day by Christianity. Europe will probably get swallowed up in the process."[7] Shortly before this discussion Adorno had admitted, "We know nothing about Asia," and he included Horkheimer in this statement.[8]

In this discussion Adorno emerges as the more radical, but also as more abstract politically. It is left to Horkheimer to keep on pointing out the failures of Marxist attempts to change the world. As throughout their entire correspondence, it is Horkheimer who appears to be more politically aware while Adorno defers to his judgment. The relations between theory and practice that provoked such spectacular debate in the conflicts with the rebellious students in the sixties were even at that time at the center of the discussions between Adorno and Horkheimer. In the latter half of the fifties, the debate with Herbert Marcuse, who had remained in America, drove them to reconsider their attitude toward traditional Marxism. While they were in emigration, Adorno had done everything in his power to dislodge Marcuse from Horkheimer's side, not even shrinking from intrigue. Right up to and including their individual behavior, the debates among the institute members remind us of the wretched history of radical left-wing organizations. Horkheimer himself had led the institute like a left-wing splinter group after taking over the directorship in 1930, and the same tone was maintained in the radical writings he produced in emigration: "The Jews and Europe," "Egoism and the Freedom Movement," or "The Authoritarian State." The addressees were not so much actual people as an imagined community—that of the fighters of the anti-Stalinist resistance to National Socialism. Even when they were in America, the political frame of reference remained that of West European left-wing radicalism of the interwar years, in which the abortive revolution recurred as a leitmotif. Needless to say, even twenty years later Horkheimer and Adorno still referred to their common experiences: "I have a terrible anxiety that when we talk about political events, the kind of discussion that emerges is like the ones that were normal in the institute in those days."[9] According to the most reliable accounts, in particular those of Herbert Marcuse and Leo Löwenthal, the Moscow trials in 1936 unleashed ferocious political debates among institute members. The result of these debates was Horkheimer's essay "Traditional and Critical Theory," which Adorno mentions in his birthday letter in *Die Zeit*, most of whose readers would not have known the essay. The journal in which the essay had appeared in German when the institute was still in the United States had now, in 1949, been consigned to the cellar of the rebuilt institute. The attempt to revive the journal had failed. The discussion, which was recorded, and which then appeared in the volume of Horkheimer's *Gesammelte Schriften* devoted to his posthumous writings, reveals something of the background debates that were not destined for publication.

By the mid-fifties what was left of the old Frankfurt Institute was no more than the core of the Californian membership who had now returned to Germany, and from the late fifties on, Pollock stayed in the background, having withdrawn to the Ticino. He occasionally accompanied Horkheimer on his trips to Frankfurt to attend Adorno's senior seminar. After 1953 Horkheimer was inclined to place the business side of the institute's affairs in Adorno's hands, but he still had the feeling that without his instructions the organization would not function properly—a kind of paternalist control that he had described as "enlightened despotism" in the Weimar era. However that may be, in the years to come Adorno never exercised his powers as director in a dictatorial fashion. Even in the 1960s, when Horkheimer had retired to Montagnola, Adorno remained in the role of the younger man who continued to look up to his senior. This was also the perspective from which the open birthday letter was written. In the mid-fifties it still looked as if the Californian working relationship within which they had written *Dialectic of Enlightenment* could finally be rebuilt. The institute had been reestablished in Germany, the finances were more or less secure, and the Europäische Verlagsanstalt was able to provide an outlet for the institute's publications. Adorno felt that his own publications were safe in the hands of Peter Suhrkamp, while Horkheimer was in demand as a contributor to radio discussion programs. They both had close contacts with various radio stations, much as they had had with Radio Frankfurt in the Weimar period. They also had access to the Frankfurt newspapers. Even though they did not entirely trust *Der Monat*,[10] it printed a number of esoteric-sounding texts by Adorno, while the *Neue Rundschau*, which was published by S. Fischer Verlag, made public some of Adorno's most complex writings, as well as occasional essays that became known to later generations of readers in such collections as *Prisms* and *Notes to Literature*. The empirical addressees of the critical theorists were not the proletariat, nor were they the political splinter groups or aesthetic circles, but the public sphere of West Germany that had emerged after 1945. In the Weimar period the German media could be divided up according to the class they represented. The destiny of Siegfried Kracauer, who was an editor of the *Frankfurter Zeitung*, depended in the final analysis on the decisions of Big Capital. This was something Adorno and Horkheimer had witnessed from close up. When major representatives of the chemical industry began to place their bets on Hitler, this spelled the end of Kracauer's freedom of action as literary editor. But changes in the media had begun to appear even before the end of the Weimar Republic, while in America the émigrés experienced the advanced process of concentration among privately owned media as the Culture Industry. This metaphor, which Adorno and Horkheimer used ironically, gave rise to the easily misunderstood catchphrase that has stuck to Adorno's reputation ever since.

The newly arisen West German public sphere seemed transparent to Adorno and Horkheimer in comparison to the American media, which they had diagnosed as being in thrall to economic monopoly interests.[11] Their experience of Radio City in New York and of film and television in Hollywood had prepared them for a world of networking. Thus Adorno appeared in person in the office of the novelist Alfred Andersch, who earned his living as the editor of the *Abendstudio*,[12] in order to try and capitalize on the competence he had gained through his American experience of the media. In the mid-fifties Weimar already lay in the remote past, but the return to Germany had also brought about a certain distance from America, more so for Adorno than for Horkheimer. After his work in Frederick Hacker's clinic in Beverly Hills in 1952, Adorno had had enough of a marginalized existence. He now pushed his way into the West German public sphere, while Horkheimer remained suspicious of Germany. In contrast, he felt enthusiastic about Chicago, where he taught periodically, both about working conditions at the university and about his leisure time there: "If I did not have so much to do, I would loaf around the entire time downtown."[13] For this reason, in the discussion with Adorno in 1956, he played the part of devil's advocate in challenging Adorno's radical indictment of the Culture Industry: "We want to preserve for the future all that has been achieved in America, for example, the rule of law, the drugstores."[14] Adorno tried to break in with "That goes along with shutting down the television programs if they are just rubbish."[15] But Horkheimer objected that it was precisely the most progressive workers who were beginning to buy television sets and that the question of the standard of living should not be dismissed as irrelevant since it also reflected the difference between America and Soviet communism.

"If I had told my father that mass culture was untrue, he would have replied that it was all fun [*Spaß*]. Renouncing utopia means that you somehow or other opt for something knowing all the while that it is a swindle."[16] With this argument Adorno returns to the beginning of his *Minima Moralia*, his first publishing success in Germany after the end of National Socialism. His intellectual partnership with Horkheimer had succeeded his difficult relationship with his father, who in the meantime had belatedly also managed, together with Adorno's mother, to reach the East Coast of the United States via Cuba. When Oscar Wiesengrund died unexpectedly, Adorno was at work in California. This meant that Leo Löwenthal, who had remained in New York, had to deliver the funeral eulogy. Horkheimer praised the house in Seeheimerstrasse, which combined the "spirit of the Jewish businessman" with the "aura of the singer" that surrounded

Adorno's mother, Maria, the descendant of ancient Italian nobility.[17] In an article he wrote in 1963 for the *Frankfurter Rundschau* for Adorno's sixtieth birthday, Horkheimer also remembers "the shining eyes of her [Maria's] sister Agathe, who was like a second mother to him."[18] Beyond all the congratulatory flourishes and a slight pang of envy toward the domestic atmosphere surrounding Adorno in his childhood, Horkheimer attempts to isolate a quality of Adorno's thinking that had already found expression in the latter's entry ticket to West German culture, his essay "Cultural Criticism and Society": "Wherever Adorno identifies with theoretical trends against reaction and vested interests, namely, with the unswerving analysis of society, with psychoanalysis, and with radical art, he also articulates their entanglement with injustice, which even the most progressive idea cannot evade in the present phase of history."[19] The possibility that the reader of the *Frankfurter Rundschau* would understand this statement seems somewhat greater than is the case with Adorno's comments on Horkheimer's seventieth birthday in *Die Zeit* two years later: "You preserved me from the life of an aesthete not through your principles, but through the power of an expanding consciousness."[20]

Adorno's dual portrait gives a more than superficial picture of Horkheimer and himself: "Your character is determined by the duality of a theoretical and practical talent as mine is by that of the artistic and reflective."[21] The record of the informal discussion of 1956 sheds light on the obscure passages. In the background we really do find the relations between theory and practice, which in the minds of all educated rebels from a respectable background in the Germany following the First World War had been indissolubly linked with the discovery of the early, pre-1848 Marx as mediated by Lenin. Emblematic of this discovery was the name of Georg Lukács, as well as his path from *Theory of the Novel* to *History and Class Consciousness*. Even Lukács, who had undergone a terrible exile in Moscow, attempted a reappropriation of that tradition in the 1950s. All the harsher, then, was Adorno's and Horkheimer's rejection of his *Young Hegel*. Lukács's act of self-denial, undertaken in order to be able to remain in the Communist Party, reads like the obverse of the dilemma facing Horkheimer: "We must deliver an account of matters about which Picasso is able to remain silent. In actual fact, our position must make clear why it is still possible to be a communist and yet despise the Russians."[22] The Spanish civil war of 1936–1938 had taken this dilemma to an extreme, exercising practical partisanship against European fascism while simultaneously denying the existence of the Soviet Thermidor. This was the option chosen by Lukács and also Ernst Bloch, whom the young Wiesengrund had earlier so much admired. In 1956, after the Twentieth Party Congress, both men were anathematized for having wished to reform communism in Budapest and Leipzig, respectively. Lukács was lucky enough to survive the Russian occupation; Bloch escaped a show trial by a whisker but was exposed to constant attacks and restrictions. His flight into the Federal Republic became as inevitable as that of his Leipzig colleague Hans Mayer. The Grand Hotel Abyss of which Lukács spoke so scathingly in the 1960s gained in attractiveness for all those who had previously repressed their doubts about Communist Party practice.

"We must be opposed to Adenauer," Adorno remarks in the course of the discussion in 1956, for otherwise we shall appear to be advocates of anticommunism.[23] The practical Horkheimer responded, "This is possible only if we also mention the factors that make life possible in the West."[24] Nevertheless, Horkheimer keeps coming back to the changed nature of theory and practice as this manifests itself in the absence of a party. His insistence on this suggests that by "party" he means the Communist Party. The terms in which the relations between theory and practice are discussed derive from "Those Twenties."[25] In the sixties some of the students maintained that there was a secret orthodoxy in the reopened Institute for Social Research in the Senckenberg Anlage. And with good reason. In the thirties Horkheimer had arrived at his critique of the Popular Front policy of the Communist Party from the far left, without allowing himself to be maneuvered into the Trotskyist corner, with its rigidly abstract belief in a permanent revolution. His crucial idea and also his crucial action consisted in separating theory from power without advocating the purely private pursuit of scholarship. The emphasis with which all the members insisted on the supra-individual character of the institute and of critical theory can be understood only in this context. It was also this sense of a joint venture that led to the persistence and intensity of the disagreements with Herbert Marcuse, who had made an intensive study of Soviet Marxism in the early 1950s.

There is no doubting that both Adorno and Horkheimer had received their political education in "Those Twenties," but there is an important difference between them, one that recurs in the debates of the 1950s. Löwenthal kept a record of an internal seminar discussion in the winter semester 1931–32, the period immediately after Horkheimer's appointment as director of the institute. It turned out that the role of practice was an issue that crucially divided the two men. Adorno, who had just been awarded the *Habilitation,* took the lead in the discussion. Although he had only just qualified, he did not shrink from directing harsh criticism at the newly appointed director. It is easy to imagine Horkheimer also having been irritated by the lecture Adorno gave on the occasion of the *Habilitation,* with its challenging title, "The Actuality of Philosophy": "When Marx objected that the philosophers had only interpreted the world in different ways, insisting instead that the point was to change it, his statement acquires its legitimacy not only from political practice, but also from philosophical theory."[26] Adorno took the radical impulses that had mobilized German intellectuals after the collapse of the German Empire and reintegrated them into the realm of theory. Horkheimer, by contrast, constantly drew attention to the nontheoretical side of radical theory—the side that over thirty years later Adorno would refer to as "the aspect of your philosophy that the textbook stereotypes call materialism."[27] Horkheimer, who according to Adorno thought that people were like animals, tends to derive his thinking from the French materialism of the Enlightenment, while Adorno does the reverse: feeling that animals are like humans, he aspires to go beyond German idealism. Nevertheless, the difference between the two friends cannot be explained either psychologically or in terms of intellectual history. The particular nature of their relationship is what brings out the particular nature of each man.

In the discussion of 1956 Horkheimer reminds Adorno of their common starting point in the twenties: the topical relevance of the revolution. His attitude toward Marx, however, was somewhat detached, the experience of a failed revolution. For Adorno, what produced the "Actuality of Philosophy" was the revolutionary mood, the cataclysmic intellectual demise of the bourgeoisie at the end of the First World War. The artist's calling for which he seemed predestined by virtue of his family and education was abandoned in favor of philosophy. The question of the lost meaning of the age which he had discussed as an adolescent with Kracauer led him to the limits of aesthetic practice. Through Horkheimer he obtained an *éducation sentimentale* that was available to him neither at home nor at the university: "I have learned from you that the possibility of wanting change need not be purchased with the renunciation of one's own happiness."[28] This was followed by the cryptic sentence, "It is this idea that has healed the theories about society as a whole of the rancor that otherwise poisons them and draws them back under the spell of eternal sameness.[29]

Encapsulated in this sentence are the different life stories of two Jewish intellectuals in the twentieth century. The lives of both men reached deep into the long bourgeois nineteenth century that ended so abruptly in 1914. In that lengthy process the Jews of Germany had only belatedly become citizens in comparison to those of England and France; that process of acceptance was as belated as Germany's development into nationhood itself. When they looked at their parents, Horkheimer and Adorno could see the impulse toward emancipation drying up. They regarded their fathers as nothing more than bourgeois, whether cultivated bourgeois or just plain businessmen. In Horkheimer's parents' house Adorno could at least recognize the Jewish tradition which seemed to him to be easier to rebel against there than in his own family. He approved of the prohibition on graven images in the parental religion in Horkheimer's case because of its promise to extend the scope for hope. Such words remind us of the names of those other friends from the Weimar era, Benjamin and Bloch. *The Principle of Hope* is an answer to the "hope that we have been given only for the sake of those without hope."[30] The self-awareness of this utterly secularized generation of Jewish middle-class children had been shaped by their reading of Proust, Kraus, and Kafka. In 1965 Adorno addressed the messianic aspects of critical theory without still wishing to name them explicitly.

Adorno's birthday letter must have reawakened long-forgotten discussions in Horkheimer's mind. For generations of young Jews who were turning their backs on commercial life, the name of Marx held a peculiar attraction. Moreover, as a historical figure Marx stood in a tense relation to Heinrich Heine, a somewhat later cultural icon of the middle classes in Germany, especially the Jewish middle class. That generation too had struggled to liberate itself from Jewish family traditions and the bourgeois class reality, both of which conflicted with its emancipated ideas of justice. In the years before 1848, with their expectations of a coming revolution, Heine had introduced hedonism as the component of a new life feeling, one that was scarcely compatible with the gruff demeanor of the petty-bourgeois craft associations which formed the recruiting ground of the first communists. Heine constantly made fun of the sectarian aspects of political radicalism, especially in Germany. He admired the cosmopolitanism of Paris as an ideal that would provide an escape from the narrowness of German life. Horkheimer and Adorno thought of themselves as belonging to this tradition. Well into *Minima Moralia,* French culture remains a memory of the dream of emancipation: "In the nineteenth century the Germans painted their dream and the outcome was invariably vegetable. The French needed only to paint a vegetable and it was already a dream."[31] After the liberation, both men returned to Frankfurt via Paris; regular trips to the Seine gave Adorno the opportunity to experience a continuity in his own life and at the same time to keep up to date. Lukács's attempt to ridicule a life lived in the "Grand Hotel Abyss" bears the features of an asceticism characteristic of the radical left which denounces good living as "bourgeois."

Adorno constantly worried away at the figure of Lukács, more so than at any other intellectual who remained faithful to the Communist Party. Lukács was fully conscious of both the Gulag Archipelago and the mass genocide of the European Jews, but none of this caused him to change his attitude toward the party. The ascetic stance was accompanied in his case by the downplaying of subjective experience. In 1949 Adorno pilloried the stance adopted by Lukács, who had by then returned to Budapest from Moscow: "Interpreted materialistically, such a sentence affirms only that suffering persists undiminished under the new form of domination which Lukács confuses with its abolition."[32] He notes that "in his version of Marxism, which has been perverted into a state philosophy,"[33] Lukács claims the bourgeois tradition for himself without any sense of irony, and this allows him to include himself in the "best traditions of humanism."[34] In Adorno's eyes, Lukács denied not only the central experiences of the twentieth century, which were what caused Horkheimer and his colleagues to distinguish critical theory from traditional Marxism, but even his own life history. After 1945 Lukács enlisted the works of Goethe and Thomas Mann in an attempt to reconcile the classical German tradition with contemporary realism. Within the framework of a communist ideology, he then reverted to the bourgeois German model of the notion of renunciation legitimated by Goethe.[35] In the German Jewish history of emancipation, renunciation had become a keyword, signaling the loss of emancipatory drive. Not only was Lukács the prototype of the intellectual who betrayed his class, but also—and this was difficult to admit publicly after Auschwitz—it was he who regarded his Jewishness as a mere "fact of birth," one to which he was indifferent, observing shortly before his death in 1971 that "that was the end of the matter."[36]

A demonstrative indifference toward origins, even one's own origins, was cultivated in the old workers' movement in the nineteenth century, particularly among members of bourgeois descent. The progressive rationalism of the bourgeoisie, including the stance that religious beliefs were a matter of individual conscience, was taken over by social democracy. Political anti-Semitism was regarded as a dangerous rival that mobilized anti-Jewish feelings, to which one's own supporters were held to be immune thanks to the theory of scientific socialism. In this atmosphere Marx's early pamphlet "On the Jewish Question" was discovered and was read at the same time as the rediscovery of *The German Ideology*, which was published for the first time after World War I. This reading of Marx in the light of the successful Russian Revolution and the abortive revolutions in Germany, Hungary, and Italy exerted a strong influence on the intelligentsia of Western Europe, which was becoming politicized at that time. On joining the Communist Party, Lukács dispensed with the title of nobility, the honorific "von," which his father, Josef Löwinger, had been awarded as banker to the Habsburg court. Up to the revolution, the Bolsheviks too cultivated an ostentatious indifference toward origins, partly to set them apart from their rivals, the powerful Bund and working-class Zionist movements. A demonstrative cosmopolitanism was the fashion in professional revolutionary circles until they discovered that the national question could be used as a powerful lever with which to undermine the multinational European dynasties. For politicized intellectuals from middle-class Jewish families, joining the party meant liberation from the snares of anti-Semitism.

Postwar anti-Semitism followed on the heels of the defeat of the German Empire, the half-hearted revolution, and the devastation caused by inflation. Alongside their sense of a burning social injustice, for Horkheimer, Pollock, and also Felix Weil it was the driving force leading to the establishment of their institute and one with which they could attract support from older members of the liberal Jewish middle and upper-middle classes. In the Weimar Republic, the universities, too, were regarded as bastions of an educated anti-Semitism whose long tradition had been a significant factor in the founding of the University of Frankfurt as a counterweight, and hence also the Institute for Social Research. Horkheimer felt that if he were to obtain a professorial chair in Frankfurt, a precondition for being made director of the Institute for Social Research, care should be taken not to allow too many Jews to be awarded the *Habilitation* or to be given too many professorial appointments. As we have seen, the young Wiesengrund-Adorno was well aware that Walter Benjamin's *Habilitation* had been thwarted in the far from philo-Semitic climate of the Frankfurt professoriate, and that Horkheimer, too, who was at the time simply Cornelius's assistant without the *Habilitation,* was not going to risk his own neck in order to defend Benjamin against the will of the majority and the incomprehension of Cornelius, his academic patron. Once Adorno's ambitions in Vienna had come to naught, he again tried to renew his links with Horkheimer and the institute, a place in which he might conceivably undertake theoretical work without regard to his origins. He must have been all the more disappointed when he discovered, after the Nazis seized power in 1933, that he was not in the first rank of those whom Horkheimer intended to rescue from Germany. In the same way, Wiesengrund-Adorno, the *Privatdozent* and writer who had ironically assumed the fierce-sounding pseudonym of Hektor Rottweiler, underestimated for a very long time the extent to which he himself was in personal danger from the Nazis. During the thirties he traveled to Germany from Paris and Oxford, where he had been staying, so as to visit his parents in Frankfurt and his future wife in Berlin and to provide them with foreign currency. He also returned in order to vacation in the Black Forest. His friend Leo Löwenthal referred to the mentality of the German Jewish citizen in order to explain "why Adorno had such an incredibly hard time leaving Germany (we had to drag him almost physically); he just couldn't believe that to him, the son of Oscar Wiesengrund, nephew of Aunt Agathe, and son of Maria, anything might ever happen, for it was absolutely clear that the bourgeoisie would soon become fed up with Hitler."[37] Both Kracauer and Löwenthal believed that Adorno had remained a privileged person from his childhood on.

The combination of political naïveté and aesthetic left-wing radicalism can be identified in many personal documents of the early thirties. Adorno's underestimation of the Nazi threat can also be seen in his attitude toward publishing his writings. He truly believed that it was safe to scatter subversive comments in the articles he published in Germany after 1933 under the pseudonym Hektor Rottweiler. In the sixties these articles—there were no more than a handful—were excavated and used as arguments against him. This was often done all too transparently, since in the meantime Adorno had become the voice whose analysis of the present had brought Auschwitz back to the attention of the public, thus provoking all sorts of strange responses. It was his collaboration with Horkheimer that enabled him to shed these intellectual infantile disorders. His letters are full of bizarre references to Lenin, as if he wanted to outdo the "orthodox Marxism" advocated in Lukács's *History and Class Consciousness*. Adorno's original politicization took place when he was still very young, evidently in the course of his readings with Kracauer. This supplied him with key terms that expanded his horizon beyond his artistic and aesthetic concerns. This habit of thinking in keywords recurs in the taped records of the 1950s, when he would refer to Lenin, in the middle of the cold war, at a time when the Communist Party was banned and even party members scarcely dared to mention his name. It was at this time that he proposed to Horkheimer that they should produce a reworked *Communist Manifesto* that would be "strictly Leninist."[38] Behind the closed doors of the Institute, Adorno's aim in 1956 was not to go back to Marx, but to go beyond him. He told Horkheimer that "I always wanted to try to produce a theory that would be faithful to Marx, Engels and Lenin, while not lagging behind the achievements of the most advanced culture."[39] Paradoxically, summing up the course of his life to that point in 1956, Adorno mentions his road toward politicization. He had arrived at Lenin, he claimed, via music. Using one of his key ideas, the idea that all knowledge is socially mediated, Adorno once again confirmed the importance of Lenin: "Marx was too harmless; he probably imagined quite naïvely that human beings are basically the same in all essentials and will remain so. It would be a good idea, therefore, to deprive them of their second nature. He was not concerned with their subjectivity; he probably didn't look into that too closely. The idea that human beings are the products of society down to their innermost core is an idea that he would have rejected as a milieu theory. Lenin was the first person to assert this."[40]

In reality it was only Lenin's contemporary Freud who noticed people's subjectivity. Horkheimer and Adorno's original idea of writing something jointly, the original seed of *Dialectic of Enlightenment*, was concerned with a critique of the individual. It was the attitude toward psychoanalysis that revealed the split in the material which produced critical theory, on the one hand, and *revisionist* psychoanalysis, as pioneered by Erich Fromm, on the other. The directness of the political vocabulary that was retained until well into the fifties becomes clear from a letter of Adorno's to Horkheimer dated 21 March 1936. Adorno complains that Fromm has placed him in the "paradoxical situation of having to defend Freud. He is both sentimental and false, a combination of social democracy and anarchism; above all, there is a painful absence of dialectical thinking. He takes far too simple a view of authority, without which, after all, neither Lenin's vanguard nor his dictatorship is conceivable. I would urgently advise him to read Lenin."[41] What is striking is Adorno's left-wing radical demeanor and jargon, which here is transferred to psychoanalysis. The tone of "how we criticize Freud from the left" is designed to achieve a political and theoretical agreement with Horkheimer, who at the time was still unapproachable. Adorno thought that "the official line of the journal" was in danger, much as if it were a party central organ, and as an outsider who had been left in Europe, an editor of the *Zeitschrift für Sozialforschung* who was only loosely connected with the board, he was in need of Horkheimer's authority in order to triumph over Fromm, who was the older, more established, and highly respected institute member in New York. The virulence of the discussions that preceded the publication of the individual contributions reminds us of the ruthless infighting among the left-wing sects. A Bolshevist style was imitated. Horkheimer, who had more experience of both politics and psychoanalysis than Adorno, set the tone for a leftist critique of the rest of the world up to 1940. His own radical left-wing manifesto was titled "The Jews and Europe," which testifies to the neutral attitude toward the Jews characteristic of the group around Horkheimer at the outbreak of the Second World War. As early as 1940, however, under the impact of the invasion of Poland, Adorno confessed to Horkheimer "that I cannot stop thinking about the fate of the Jews. It often seems to me as if what we have been accustomed to seeing in the context of the proletariat had now been transferred with a terrible concentrated force to the Jews. I wonder if we should not say what we want to say by linking it up with the Jews, who represent the opposite pole to the concentration of power."[42]

In the first version of his book on Richard Wagner, his "Fragments on Wagner," which appeared in the same issue of the *Zeitschrift* as "The Jews and Europe," Adorno had formulated his own manifesto of a rationalist critique of fascism. In a letter to Benjamin he speaks almost boastfully of having made a decisive contribution to Horkheimer's essay. His letters and the records of discussions from the period allow us to guess at the change of attitude that took place between 1938 and 1940. Adorno had begun by tending to deny the extent to which he was personally threatened by fascism, but having prolonged his stay in Europe and having remained in close touch with Benjamin (and having in part heard about Benjamin through Gretel), as well as with personal contacts in Austria, he seems to have become more sensitive to the approaching storm than others in the group. From early in 1938, while he was still in London, he apparently prepared Horkheimer in New York for the imminent catastrophe in Europe which Benjamin had been expecting throughout the entire decade: "I regard the position of those who have remained in Germany as dire. In the circumstances, the fact that I am counting the days until we are over on your side needs no further commentary."[43] One aspect of his longing for the crossing to New York was the immediate prospect of a war in Europe that was bound to be conducted with all the latest technical innovations. It is a shock to read statements like the one dated February 1938, when he writes, "unless, unexpectedly, I find myself being gassed."[44] This refers to experiments with gas from the First World War, the anonymous character of which Benjamin had long since connected with the devaluation of individual experience. A week later, on 15 February, Adorno provided a clear-sighted, concrete prognosis: "Austria will fall to Hitler, and he will be able to stabilize his position ad infinitum in a world fascinated by success, and he will do so on the basis of the most horrific reign of terror. There can scarcely be any room for doubt that the remaining Jews in Germany will be wiped out; for as the dispossessed, no country in the world will grant them admission. And once again, nothing will be done."[45] In this climate Adorno announced to Horkheimer the arrival of his manuscript on Wagner, which contains a reference to Wagner's repeated assertions about the possibility of a redemption from the curse of Ahasuerus that comes close to the tenor of Horkheimer's essay "The Jews and Europe": "Without any attempt at differentiation, we find intertwined here the Marxian idea of the social emancipation of the Jews as the emancipation of society from Jewry and the idea of the annihilation of the Jews themselves."[46] For the book publication of *In Search of Wagner,* he cautiously eliminated the word "Jewry" from his interpretation of the promised redemption of Ahasuerus through the destruction of the Jews: "Without any attempt at differentiation we find intertwined here the Marxian idea of the social emancipation of the Jews as the emancipation of society from the profit motive of which they are the symbolic representatives, and the idea of the annihilation of the Jews themselves."[47]

Evidently, Adorno did not wish to place too much trust in the intelligence of the West German reading public. His *In Search of Wagner* was preceded by a self-advertisement in the enlightened tradition of the eighteenth century. In the early 1940s he and Horkheimer had developed the concept of the "message in a bottle" as a communicative model. Now, however, on his return to Germany, Adorno felt the desire to find an appropriate audience of the kind that he had discovered in America only with the publication of *The Authoritarian Personality* in 1950. But the beginning of the cold war was accompanied in Germany by powerful waves of emotion against Americanization and the returnees, and this set narrow limits to the reception of his writings. For his part, Adorno was determined to find an audience. The "Wagner" that he presented to the German reading public in 1952 was different from that of the "Fragments." What separated the two texts was the historical abyss of the Nazi crimes against the Jews—but the author only gradually became conscious of this difference. "Wagner's Relevance for Today" appeared in 1964; it was published in the program notes accompanying a performance of *Tristan* in Bayreuth. This lecture formulated an old idea that had been present in the discussions with Horkheimer around 1938: "Everything in Wagner has its temporal core. Like a spider, his mind sits amidst the powerful web of nineteenth-century exchange relationships."[48] At this juncture, biographical experience becomes the key to knowledge: "Wagner no longer represents, as he did in my youth, the world of one's parents, but that of one's grandparents instead."[49] This explains the remarkable makeup of *Zeitschrift für Sozialforschung*, no. 8, the last issue just before the outbreak of war. The "Fragments on Wagner" are followed by Benjamin's essay "Some Motifs in Baudelaire," which is accompanied by Benjamin's discovery of Carl Gustav Jochmann's "Regression of Poetry," a product of the Biedermeier era. Only then do we come to Horkheimer's political pamphlet "The Jews and Europe." By that time war had in fact broken out; this may explain why it was just provided with the date of completion and then stuffed in at the back.

The biographical element that is present in all three essays is a debate with "the world of one's parents." As the youngest of the three authors, Adorno represents a concentrated version of a specific group who were children of the nineteenth century and of parents who had joined the ranks of the middle classes. Now, as victims of persecution, they were destined to be punished in the twentieth century for their parents' origins. This experience goes beyond the bounds of each individual biography. The ideal of an identical individual conscious of himself or herself is belied by social reality. The nineteenth century had lost its authority—even in the shape of the aging parents whom almost all the members of the institute made desperate efforts to rescue from Europe during the late thirties. The first large-scale collective institute study, *Authority and the Family*, which appeared in 1936 in exile, had worried away at the tradition. What finally was seen to underlie it was what Adorno later, in his self-advertisement, called "the primal landscape of fascism."[50] Paradoxically, the American Way of Life concealed this breach with tradition that was constitutive for the entire oeuvre of the critical theorists. They experienced America as a bourgeois society identical with itself, bourgeois society *sans phrase*. It was in America that critical theory acquired its definitive shape, though while they were in America, they were not of it. What its members had in common, "subjective experience," the experience of "the intellectual in emigration," was not made explicit until Adorno wrote *Minima Moralia*.[51] These subterranean interconnections appear in objectivized form in the *Zeitschrift*, no. 8—least obviously in Benjamin's contributions, since Benjamin was in advance of Adorno and Horkheimer in this formulation of subjective experience.

Not until we glance at their letters do we become aware of these common features. In the course of their discussion of Benjamin's Baudelaire essay, the last he published in the *Zeitschrift*, Adorno tried yet again to explain to him the meaning of commodity fetish. What Benjamin's interpretation of shock has in common with the commodity fetish which ultimately brings about the reification of all human relations is its extinguishing of any specific individual experience: "For all reification is a forgetting."[52] Their discussion of theory is accompanied by news about the cataclysm which for Benjamin is not something about to happen but something that has already taken place. He had anticipated to quite a frightening degree the self-destruction of bourgeois society for which there was no remedy. He was beset by profound doubts about his efforts to obtain entry to a different society with the aid of Brecht. Adorno, who had only recently arrived in New York, reported to Benjamin in May 1938 about his talks with Eisler, who was teaching composition at the New School. The picture he gives of Eisler is very vivid:

> He is extremely friendly and approachable, presumably on account of the Institute or the radio project; his latest pose in relation to me is that of an old weather-beaten materialist politico, whose fatherly function lies in protecting the young and inexperienced idealist like me from the illusions of the age, and all by communicating his newest insights that politics must learn to reckon with human beings as they are, and that the workers too are no angels, etc. I lis-

tened with not a little patience to his feeble defence of the Moscow trials, and with considerable disgust to the joke he cracked about the murder of Bukharin. He claims to have known the latter in Moscow, telling me that Bukharin's conscience was already so bad that he could not even look him, Eisler, honestly in the eyes.[53]

They had earlier reached agreement about Bloch, whose judgment of the Moscow trials marked the unbridgeable gulf between the members of Horkheimer's circle and the members of the Communist Party: "Max was just as furious about his essay on Bukharin as we both were. It is inevitable precisely with people like Bloch that they get into hot water once they start to get clever."[54] Even before the Stalin-Hitler pact, the workers' movement had lost its emancipatory potential in the eyes of Horkheimer and Adorno. The triumphalism with which the subsequent victory over Hitler was celebrated confirmed all their doubts. The acid comment of 1945 says it all: "The decay of the workers' movement is corroborated by the official optimism of its adherents."[55]

The limits reached by émigré intellectuals who "let themselves be stupefied neither by the power of others, nor by their own powerlessness"[56] can be seen as early as the letters of the late 1930s. The correspondence with Benjamin makes us painfully aware of how the time left for him to seek a safe haven was slipping away. Even Scholem's offer of a shelter in Palestine under the British Mandate failed to induce him to make a move. Zionism was not seen as an option by the critical theorists, not even in the individualistic version espoused by Scholem. Fromm and even Löwenthal had been through a Zionist phase in the early 1920s. When visiting New York in 1938, however, Scholem felt a certain wariness, which led him to prefer to meet Horkheimer and Adorno in a bar rather than at the institute building. Adorno felt that Scholem treated him with a certain hauteur, at least to begin with. But Scholem represented an authentic engagement with a lost Jewish tradition that had no nationalist overtones. Whereas Adorno's own family had adopted the mixed style of the Jewish middle class, Adorno himself felt attracted by Benjamin's knowledge of the Jewish tradition because it represented a hidden source of knowledge. Adorno never claimed to be an expert on Jewish matters; he always referred questioners to Scholem as the true authority. From the second half of the thirties, however, Jewishness became an increasingly inescapable fact of life for the group around Horkheimer. Benjamin had early on discovered the difference when dealing with the cleverest of followers of the communist line. Brecht, who thought highly of him and with whom he spent two summers in Denmark, had reacted dismissively to the suggestion that Kafka might have had Zionist leanings. Yet Kafka represented a layer of secular experience that Adorno shared with Benjamin:

> With his transposition into archetypes the bourgeois comes to an end. The loss of his individual features, the disclosure of the horror teeming under the stone of culture, marks the disintegration of individuality itself. The horror, however, consists in the fact that the bourgeois was unable to find a successor: "No one is responsible." . . . History becomes Hell in Kafka because the chance which might have saved is missed. This Hell was inaugurated by the late bourgeoisie itself. In the concentration camps the boundary between life and death was eradicated.[57]

Adorno defined the specific nature of this situation with reference to Benjamin as the impossibility of living as a bourgeois and the inability to become anything else: "Benjamin expressed this situation when he defined himself as a person who had left his class without belonging to another one."[58]

It was this certainty that brought Adorno to New York after a detour in Paris. Whereas previously he had faced the prospect of a Benjamin-like isolation in France and Britain, he now experienced an exiled group existence whose dubious nature was charted in *Minima Moralia*. Notes on his own situation are to be found in the section titled "Protection, Help, and Counsel": "Every intellectual in emigration is, without exception, mutilated, and does well to acknowledge it to himself, if he wishes to avoid being cruelly apprised of it behind the tightly-closed doors of his self-esteem. . . . His language has been expropriated, and the historical dimension that nourished his knowledge, sapped. The isolation is made worse by the formation of closed and politically-controlled groups, mistrustful of their members, hostile to those branded different."[59] A picture of the non-identical individual can be found as early as the first few pages of *Minima Moralia*. Adorno spoke subsequently of a paralysis that gripped him when he learned that Benjamin's death in the attempt to escape to safety. The institute ran out of funds early in the 1940s; the *Zeitschrift* could no longer appear in its original form. Its last issue in 1942 was a mimeographed special number "In Memory of Walter Benjamin," which contained Horkheimer's ideas on state capitalism as well as Adorno's reflections on the failure of a relationship, namely, the relationship between Stefan George and Hugo von Hofmannsthal. That was the last topic about which he had exchanged letters with Benjamin. A highly developed individualism is confronted with the undeniable experience that we live "in a world where there are far worse things to fear than death."[60] This idea, reiterated several times by Horkheimer as well, is concerned with emphasizing the supra-individual nature of historical experience that is to be the starting point of all theoretical reflection. Adorno relates this reflection to a childhood memory, a motif from an imagined meadowland *(Wiesengrund)* between the Taunus and the Odenwald: "As long as I have been able to think, I have derived happiness from the song: 'Between the mountain and the deep, deep vale': about the two rabbits who, regaling themselves on the grass, were shot down by the hunter, and, on realizing that they were still alive, made off in haste."[61]

It is only when we reach this point—the common experience of an all-pervasive heteronomy which allows the individual who is subjected to the laws of self-preservation to survive for the most part only through chance—that we truly begin to understand the relationship between Adorno and Horkheimer, a relationship that must have seemed as opaque to the reading public of the postwar era as the taped records of institute discussions must appear to the modern reader. Again and again, from as early as the end of the Weimar Republic, we hear of their intention to formulate a critique of society appropriate to the present age, a critique that is anchored in supra-individual experience but does not abandon the right to individual happiness. Adorno realized early on the falseness of a purely identificatory left-wing radicalism. "We must remain on the outside, we must not identify with the proletariat," they remark in the minutes of a discussion on 25 October 1939.[62] At that time, too, they hoped to formulate theses or a new manifesto. And in fact almost all the elements of the discussion of 1956 turn up here, although only when it is linked up to the letters does it become possible to establish a new definition of the "relation between experience and theory." The doctrinaire handling of the scheme of theory and practice that played a role in the conflicts with party communists outside the institute as well as with exponents of the student movement was rendered irrelevant by actual events. According to Horkheimer, proletarians had ceased to be a historical subject and had instead become the objects of their own organizations. For the theoreticians who held fast to the emancipatory impulse as opposed to the mere power plays and *Realpolitik* of these organizations, the task was to turn "our actual experiences" into the source of our knowledge.[63] Their common experience was the loss of all bourgeois security.

That experience contained one specific feature that would be further intensified: the Jews as the victims of power. The published texts of the time give us only an inkling of the degree to which the individual lives of the émigrés were taken up with their unceasing efforts to rescue relatives, friends, and acquaintances who had remained in Europe without "protection, help and counsel."[64] Adorno must have feared that he would never see his parents again. The consequences of the so-called Kristallnacht, the pogrom of 9 November 1938, had affected them directly:

> I do not know whether you are aware how closely my parents have become involved in all the turmoil. We did succeed in getting my father out of prison, but he suffered further injury to his already bad eye during the pogrom; his offices were destroyed, and a short time afterwards he was deprived of all legal control over his property. My mother, who is now 73 years old, also found herself in custody for two days. Just as both of them were beginning to recover from their terrible experience, my father was afflicted by serious pulmonary inflammation. He seems to have survived the worst of the illness, but this will now keep him in Germany for weeks, perhaps even months, although we have succeeded in the meantime, with the help of American friends, in securing an entry visa to Cuba for both my parents. But it hardly needs saying that we are still extremely concerned as long as they have to remain in that appalling country, and that our attempts to assist them have absorbed all my attention for several weeks now.[65]

The defenselessness of his own parents, who had once seemed to be all-powerful, reversed the traditional pattern: "One of the Nazis' symbolic outrages is the killing of the very old. Such a climate fosters a late, lucid understanding with our parents, as between the condemned, marred only by the fear that we, powerless ourselves, might now be unable to care for them as well as they cared for us when they possessed something."[66] *Minima Moralia* can be read as a sustained effort to interpret the experience of the human subject as a source of knowledge.

"Our relationship to parents is beginning to undergo a sad, shadowy transformation."[67] This assertion seems to have a universalist thrust, but its implications suggest a specific Jewish dimension that sheds light on life in general. The anti-Hegelian assertion "The whole is the false," which is included in *Minima Moralia* without commentary and which seems so pretentious at first sight, derives its truth from this specific historical experience.[68] Although he drafted the phrase "out of the firing-line" in California, Adorno then presented this insight to a postwar German public. This anti-Hegelian statement is then explicated with reference to Aldous Huxley's *Brave New World*, a novel that enjoyed great popularity in postwar Germany:

> Huxley is well aware that Jews are persecuted because they are not completely assimilated and that precisely for this reason their consciousness occasionally reaches beyond the social system. He does not question the authenticity of Bernard's critical insight. But the insight itself is attributed to a sort of organic inferiority, the inevitable inferiority complex. At the same time, Huxley charges the radical Jewish intellectual with vulgar snobbism and, ultimately, with reprehensible moral cowardice. Ever since . . . Hegel's philosophy of history, bourgeois cultural politics, claiming to survey and speak for the whole, has sought to unmask anyone who seeks to change things as both the genuine child and the perverse product of the whole which he opposes, and has insisted that the truth is always on the side of the whole, be it against him or present in him.[69]

Only when the reader arrives at the references in *Prisms* will he learn something about the context of the discussion. This was a seminar in Los Angeles in 1942 in which "Herbert Marcuse introduced a discussion of Huxley's *Brave New World* while Max Horkheimer and the author presented some theses on needs."[70] Adorno does not mention that Brecht and Eisler also took part in this discussion. In fact, their contribution was not very great: "eisler and i, somewhat tired of the way things are going, lose patience and 'get across everyone' for lack of anywhere else to get."[71] Their provocative statements, which Brecht reports with some pride in his *Journals*, can set us on the right path. The West German reading public that first came across the Huxley essay in 1951 in the *Neue Rundschau* and then again in *Prisms* in 1955 was not in a position even to suspect this background. Adorno insists on the continuity of his arguments; his writings make their appearance in Germany like finished products whose delivery date and method have to be guessed at. In the preparatory studies for his TUI novel, Brecht reproduced his encounters with intellectuals in Hollywood in disguised form, dressed up, as it were, in Chinese garb so as to endow them with a lasting shape. No one will begrudge the émigrés the desire to establish continuity. It is possible that it even led to a renewed closeness in California since, according to Werner Hecht's "Brecht Chronology," Horkheimer even asked Brecht for a contribution to the special commemorative issue of the *Zeitschrift* on Benjamin in February 1942,

Walter Benjamin zum Gedächtnis.[72] Then, in August, they moved on to the seminar on needs, which took place at Adorno's house. Other participants included Hannah Arendt's first husband, Günther Anders (originally Günther Stern), Hans Reichenbach, an old friend of Benjamin's and a Social Democrat, as well as (the unrelated) Herbert and Ludwig Marcuse. The seminar was concerned not with the literary appraisal of Huxley's novel but with the changed or unchanged structure of bourgeois society. Under the impact of fascist successes in Europe, Pollock had predicted that the next century would be fascist, but what really provoked Brecht was Horkheimer's bracketing together of Russia and America. If these societies succeeded in abolishing want, would this not cut the ground out from under culture and social criticism in equal measure? The self-confidence with which Brecht and Eisler simply ignored fundamental changes in social systems stood in inverse relation to their isolation.

Although Eisler and Brecht were well informed about events in the Soviet Union, and both men were determined to maintain their show of solidarity with the Soviet Union and the communist world in general, the United States came as a shock to them. Brecht felt like "a sausage in a greenhouse" in Hollywood.[73] The overtness of business interests in America made Brecht's literary unmasking technique superfluous, which explains his tendency to adopt Chinese disguises. In their minds he and Eisler continued to live in Europe. They wrote their "Hollywood Elegies," and Brecht even considered rewriting the *Communist Manifesto* in hexameters. His stylized attitude of radical intellectual simplification prevented him from grasping the earth-shattering changes in Europe and the social changes in America. What Brecht dismissed in Benjamin's "On the Concept of History" as "its metaphors and its judaisms"[74] was precisely "the temporal nucleus of truth"[75] on which Adorno's writings had provided variations in exile. There could be no meeting of the minds with the rationalist Marxism that Brecht liked to defend in an extreme form. Nor did Brecht understand *The Authoritarian Personality,* since he misunderstood anti-Semitism as the consequence of the economic organization of capitalism, reduced capitalism itself to "commerce," and was unable to distinguish the young Marx from before 1848, who wrote *On the Jewish Question,* from the critic who wrote *Capital.* Styling himself a Chinese sage made it impossible for the argumentative Brecht to formulate these changes at the level of theory. Brecht claims that on 18 December 1944 he instructed Adorno about Marx: "And m[arx] advised him [the Jew] to emancipate himself (and himself demonstrated how). adorno can't make a long face, which is a handy failing for a theoretician."[76] The snobbery of which Adorno speaks in connection with George and Hofmannsthal is something he seems to have discovered unexpectedly in someone of quite another stripe in Hollywood.

For Benjamin the new remained unattainable; yet he had not reasoned "Jewish knowledge" out of existence, but made it productive so as to come to know the present: "Sorrow—not the state of being sad—was the defining character of his nature, in the form of a Jewish awareness of the permanence of threat and catastrophe as much as in the antiquarian inclination that cast a spell even on the contemporary and turned it into something long past."[77] Shortly before his ill-starred flight from France, Benjamin gathered together ideas under the ambiguous title "Central Park" that were brought to Adorno in America in 1941 by a Dr. Dohmke, an émigré. Prominent among them are "motifs of rescue": "To the image of 'rescue' belongs the firm, seemingly brutal grasp."[78] The essays with which Adorno appeared before the West German public in 1949 possess this quality. Even in the introduction to the last great work of his to be published in his lifetime, *Negative Dialectics,* he cites Benjamin's comment after reading Adorno's *Against Epistemology: A Metacritique* that "one had to cross the frozen waste of abstraction to arrive at concise, concrete philosophizing."[79] Abrupt pauses alternate with the need for continuity in Adorno's publications in the Federal Republic, marking his lifelong efforts to glue together in his own life the things that the history of society—or what he calls, using a very old-fashioned term, the "course of the world" *(Weltlauf)*—had torn apart.[80] The term itself is one to conjure with; Nietzsche connoisseurs will think of his condemnation of the "philosophy of desiderata," an idea that is part and parcel of the world of Sils Maria, while Hegel readers, who form a very different group, will be reminded of the section in the *Phenomenology* on "virtue and the way of the world," in which the Pietist force of interiorization finds its counterpart in the absolute terror of the French Revolution. The individual seeks to steer a path between renunciation and the threat of terror, the Scylla and Charybdis of the pressure to conform. Outwardly, nothing negative remains visible in Adorno's theory. Terror, "the expression of fear,"[81] had inscribed itself deeply within him; it is a "Jewish awareness"[82] and life experience that becomes a constitutive part of philosophical experience. The identity principle is questioned not just philosophically but by the experience of "a damaged life."[83]

These excerpts from the open letter congratulating Horkheimer on his birthday can be more easily interpreted when we know more about Adorno's life and have read the minutes of the discussions with greater attentiveness: "I have learned from you that the possibility of wanting change need not be purchased with the renunciation of one's own happiness. It is this idea that has healed theories about society as a whole of the rancor that otherwise poisons them and draws them back under the spell of eternal sameness."[84] This initially incomprehensible sentence can be more easily read after reflection; it resolves itself not simply in pleasure but in social criticism. The critical theory that Horkheimer and Adorno brought back to Germany after 1949 criticizes present-day society in the light of experience as reflected through the philosophy of history. Adorno ascribed to Horkheimer "a greater pedagogical influence . . . than everything I had learned or had instilled in me."[85] He also ascribes to him the paradoxical articulation of a supra-individual experience: "Decades later, in emigration, you said something that I could never forget: it was we who had been spared who really belonged in a concentration camp. This statement is inextricably bound up with your will to survive. It is philosophically related to the paradox that you had renounced metaphysical hope, almost like a man of the eighteenth-century Enlightenment, but you did so not with the triumphal gesture of a man with his feet firmly planted on the ground, but in infinite sorrow."[86] Thus if we interpret these remarks as personal reminiscences, we find that the birthday letter contains Auschwitz and the gulags as the supra-individual events of the epoch.

The epoch itself, however, is difficult to define, and after Adorno's death Horkheimer spoke of him "as one of the greatest minds of this age of transition."[87] This may sound like a conventional remark, but it gains in depth when we realize how crucial the concept of "transition" is in Adorno's works. For example, he gave his monograph on the composer closest to him the title *Alban Berg: Master of the Smallest Link* (in German, *Übergang:* "Master of the Smallest Transition"). The talk he gave on the radio in 1956 which recalled Berg's terrible death at Christmas twenty years previously gives us a concrete idea of Adorno's own experience of the passing of time: "The period since 1935 was not one of continuity and steady growth in experience; it was disrupted by catastrophes. People forced to emigrate cannot escape the feeling that long years have been torn out of their lives and it is easy for them to succumb to the delusion that their present existence is just a continuation of what was destroyed then."[88] "The feeling of guilt," the guilt over having survived which was experienced by Jews who had been rescued, has turned into a supra-individual syndrome which accompanied Adorno in a variety of theoretical ideas and artistic practices ever since he began to have an inkling of "the inadequacy of a naïvely aesthetic stance."[89]

Adorno observes about Schoenberg that "he lost his position which had been contractually guaranteed to him in permanence. He accepted the collective fate without complaining about his individual one, indeed, without even wasting much time thinking about it. At the time, early in 1933, he remarked that there were more important things in life than composing music. Coming from him, these words confirm the seriousness of music more than any high-sounding declaration about the dignity of art."[90] This was an anxious time for Adorno, one in which he was waiting for Benjamin to pass judgment on his Singspiel, The Treasure of Indian Joe, which the trustee of Adorno's and Benjamin's posthumous papers has rescued and dated to late 1932 and early 1933.[91] Adorno had already informed Berg that the National Socialists had withdrawn his license to teach when he also confided in him under the seal of secrecy that he had provided the children's story from the world of Tom Sawyer with what he "hoped was decent and fully matured music."[92] Benjamin was no expert on music, and he kept delaying his response to Adorno on the merits of his Singspiel, which was supposed not to be the sort of Songspiel that was fashionable at the time.[93] He finally replied only when pressed by Gretel Adorno. When his response did come, Adorno must have been deeply wounded by Benjamin's rather laboriously presented accusation of a "reduction to the idyllic" in which childhood appears too "immediately."[94] The apparent closeness in their attitudes at the time of Adorno's completion of the book on Kierkegaard can be explained by his exploration there of a comparable bourgeois origin. It threatens to disintegrate here under the impact of fear. In his reply, Adorno speaks of the "image of childhood" (Kindermodell) rather than the experience of childhood (Kindheitszeugnis) that he feels Benjamin mistakenly expected.[95] The situation of both men early in 1934 when these letters were exchanged suggests that fear was more like the theme of everyday life than a problem of artistic representation.[96] Adorno's late prose piece "Regressions" reads like an answer to Benjamin's failure to understand him some ten years previously: "The capacity for fear and for happiness are the same, the unrestricted openness to experience amounting to self-abandonment in which the vanquished rediscovers himself."[97]

The most individual experience contains a potential for survival and also for thought. Perhaps Benjamin felt reminded on reading Adorno's script of his own most individual project, the "Berlin Childhood." As a man who shied away from physical contact, even with his closest friends, he may have found Adorno's text too close for comfort. His preference for Cocteau's *Les Enfants terribles* must have irked Adorno. Their experience of childhood both brought them together and separated them, but reflection on childhood was a pivot around which their theoretical works revolved, right down to the choice of subject matter for their essays. This is revealed very clearly by the minutes of the discussions between Adorno and Horkheimer in New York in the late 1930s: "Human identity, which analysis asserts is the central principle of the individual, does not exist, above all in the present situation."[98] This much is asserted in 1939 in an as yet undeveloped way. But the path to the key idea in Adorno's fully developed critical theory becomes visible when he explains to his English translator, David, in 1940: "Freedom postulates the existence of something non-identical." Adorno advances from this highly abstract proposition, one that clearly shows its roots in Hegel's philosophy of history, and then takes the decisive step toward concreteness: "The non-identical element must be not nature alone, it can also be man."[99] Key statements of Adorno's will not be found in German in such stark simplicity. In his letter to his translator, the classic middleman, Adorno's wish to be understood finally comes to the fore. Despite the Anglophile traditions in the Wiesengrund household, Adorno had read *The Adventures of Tom Sawyer* in German translation. Barely ten years later he finds himself constrained to formulate core ideas of his theory in a foreign language. Adorno was unable to overcome his resistance to the English language, even though he did not speak it with a Berlin accent like Herbert Marcuse or an unmistakable Frankfurt accent like Leo Löwenthal. As the section of *Minima Moralia* titled "English Spoken" makes clear with its account of his childhood experiences with his English relations, Adorno always identified English with the way in which "culture displays its character as advertising."[100] Of all the institute members it was Adorno who was most powerfully influenced in his decision to return to Frankfurt by the opportunity to return to the German language. He had said to Thomas Mann that the "émigré German" they were forced to speak was "a decayed level of language," which, however, dialectically "disclosed the latent possibility of a truly European language.[101]

Faced with catastrophe, both Adorno and Horkheimer were convinced that their combined experience as individuals would assist them in formulating their theory anew. It is astonishing to see how their discussions arrive at the same starting point in both 1939 and 1956. On both occasions they wanted to attempt a sort of new edition of the *Communist Manifesto,* even though their actual experience was not that of the pre-1848 situation of an imminent emancipation. To have asserted that a revolution was imminent in the developed capitalist countries in 1939 or 1956 would have been close to political insanity: "We do not live in a revolutionary situation, and actually things are worse than ever. What is horrifying is that for the first time we live in a world in which it is not possible to imagine things getting better."[102] So that is the novel aspect of the historical situation, one that differentiated it from all preceding ones. Horkheimer resists this idea of Adorno's here with all his might. In 1956 he even recalls a line from *The Treasure of Indian Joe* to support his case, and, unlike Benjamin, he had understood it: "You beggars, hurry to the gate, this is the culture in which we live."[103] Horkheimer wished to draw Adorno's attention to Adorno's own familiar category of the context of "blindness" or "delusion" (*Verblendungszusammenhang*), but to go beyond it to the actual social cannibalism that is more than a mere fact of consciousness. Thus Horkheimer wished to bring the discussion back to a palpable materialism, and Adorno acknowledges this in his birthday letter of 1965: "Your starting point that the individual is doomed, a thing that twitches impotently, is what has presumably given rise to the aspect of your philosophy that the textbook stereotypes call materialism."[104]

The contrasting characterizations that emerge from the public letters of congratulations do in fact point up real differences. Solidarity with animals expanded to include solidarity with all living creatures reminds us of the suppression of both internal and external nature, of domination—a concept that had tended to fade in traditional Marxism because of the priority given to the critique of the economy. The transformation of traditional Marxism into the fetishism of production characteristic of the Stalin era accompanies the erection of an authoritarian state whose fascist shape increasingly resembles that of communism and vice versa. Horkheimer had predicted this in "Walter Benjamin zum Gedächtnis" (In Memory of Walter Benjamin) in 1942, regarding it as the model for the future, a prognosis that earns nothing but mockery from Brecht, who claims in his *Journals* to have put his objections personally in conversation with Adorno. But the idolization of labor has persisted in the workers' movement like original sin ever since the days of the Gotha Program. In its optimism about the onward march of a society based on advances in production, Soviet communism even outdid social democracy, which Benjamin had criticized so incisively in *On the Concept of History*. Russia was transformed from the Promised Land into an anti-utopian labor camp. As 1945 drew to a close, Adorno wrote Aphorism 100 in *Minima Moralia*, "Sur l'eau," concluding part two of his intellectual birthday present to Horkheimer. "Production as an end in itself"[105]—this link connecting the workers' movement with bourgeois society is presented as the horrifying anti-utopian vision of a civilization freed from all historical constraints. It was horrifying even in the shape of the affluent society which at the time could be imagined only in America, perhaps only in California, while Europe lay prostrated in ashes and rubble. It was the assimilation of this American experience that characterized the unprecedented modernity of a critical theory of society which was able to remind us of the origins from which has sprung the utopian idea of something new that is non-identical with the totality: "A mankind which no longer knows want will begin to have an inkling of the delusory, futile nature of all the arrangements hitherto made to escape want, which used wealth to reproduce want on a larger scale. Enjoyment itself would be affected, just as its present framework is inseparable from operating, planning, having one's way, subjugating. *Rien faire comme une bête*, lying on water and looking peacefully at the sky."[106]

Around 1945 Adorno powered ahead on his own with the questions that he wished to resolve in future projects in cooperation with Horkheimer. The last three aphorisms of part two of *Minima Moralia* bring together in a kind of coda the themes that define Adorno's intellectual makeup. His radical doubts about the concept of identity characteristic of bourgeois subjectivity is given concrete shape as a critique of the identity principle. The dilemmas formulated by Benjamin in *On the Concept of History* are further developed as "the obligation to think at the same time dialectically and undialectically."[107] Adorno explores this "bequest" in the very next aphorism, "Gold Assay," in which he draws attention to the catastrophic identification of genuineness and truth in bourgeois thought. In this the anti-emancipatory impulse that denigrates imitation becomes visible: "It leads to the denunciation of anything that is not of sufficient sterling worth, sound to the core, that is, the Jews."[108] Recourse to a supra-individual subject cannot resolve the ambiguity of the social situation. Benjamin repeatedly considered such steps and had recoiled from their implications. In his collaboration with Horkheimer, which also cast doubt on the principle of single authorship, Adorno believed that he might be able to break with the social compulsion to lead a monadic existence. The decisive driving force with which to break the principle of absolute individualism can be identified as fear, and Adorno had already invoked its power at the conclusion of his "Fragments on Wagner." In 1952, in his book *In Search of Wagner,* which signaled his return to the German reading public, he repeated the finale of the 1939 "Fragments": "By voicing the fears of helpless people, it could signal help for the helpless, however feebly and distortedly. In doing so, it would renew the promise contained in the age-old protest of music: the promise of a life without fear."[109]

Behind this promise the hope for a revolution had once lain. Adorno had expressed such sentiments somewhat magniloquently in a letter from London to Benjamin in Paris, dated 18 March 1936: "The goal of the revolution is the elimination of fear."[110] He had boldly added: "That is why we need not fear the former, and need not ontologize the latter. It is not a case of bourgeois idealism if, in full knowledge and without intellectual inhibitions, we maintain our solidarity with the proletariat, instead of making our necessity into a virtue of the proletariat as we are constantly tempted to do—that proletariat which itself experiences the same necessity, and needs us for knowledge just as much as we need the proletariat for the revolution."[111] Who does he mean when he says "we"? Probably Benjamin and himself, perhaps Horkheimer too, or else Bloch, Brecht, and Eisler, even though he was about to warn Benjamin against the abstract support of the last three for the Communist Party, which they identified with the proletariat. In the first major essay on jazz that he wrote for the *Zeitschrift* at around the same time, he criticized "the latest form of romanticism which, because of its anxiety in the face of the fatal characteristics of capitalism, seeks a despairing way out, in order to affirm the feared thing itself as a sort of ghastly allegory of the coming liberation and to sanctify negativity."[112] By 1956 even this negative possibility had vanished. "A party no longer exists," Horkheimer noted baldly in the discussion with Adorno.[113] A capitalism with no alternative revived an idea from *Minima Moralia* that Adorno had included in the aphorism titled "Regressions." The fragments included there are concerned with the memory of songs—children's songs and Taubert's Lullaby, which had inspired Adorno's variation in *The Treasure of Indian Joe.* It is as if at this point in *Minima Moralia* Adorno had resumed the discussion with the now dead Benjamin about whether the beggar driven away by the barking dog in that lullaby was a poor Jew and about the fact that it is only by forgetting him that the child is able to fall asleep.[114] This feeling of concern never left Adorno, and thanks to Horkheimer's materialism, he found himself constantly confronted with "this premonition of futility" when considering the possibility of changing the world.[115] The lullaby recalled in *Minima Moralia* had led him on to *The Treasure of Indian Joe,* but after 1933 he ceased to compose music altogether. The one exception occurred in exile, at a particular juncture, when he set some Brecht poems to music for an antifascist broadcast on American radio. As a social theorist, Adorno inscribes his motifs as themes common to both Horkheimer and himself in the congratulatory letter of 1965. Once they had completed *Dialectic of Enlightenment,* a book that "has continued to be our philosophical benchmark,"[116] Adorno describes their practice in words that every one of his readers could and should apply individually to him: "You turned your energies as an academic and organizer to the task of teaching students how to grasp the incomprehensible fact that became known to us in its full implications only toward the end of the war. You started from the insight that if a repetition of the horror is to be prevented, an understanding of the mechanisms at work will be of greater benefit than remaining silent or freezing in impotent indignation."[117]

At the start of Adorno's congratulatory letter to Horkheimer, we find what looks like the fanciful use of names and animals, but on closer inspection this turns out to have a deeper meaning. At the time of the Weimar Republic, their use of pseudonyms still had something playful about it. At that time Adorno published some sketches with Carl Dreyfus under the name of Castor Zwieback; this represented the friendly interchange of identities. By the time Benjamin became Detlev Holz and Adorno assumed the name of Hektor Rottweiler, however, matters had become more serious. The disguise was designed to enable them to continue publishing under circumstances in which it was not prudent to declare one's identity. For internal use, at a time when they still used the polite form of address with each other, Horkheimer and Adorno called each other "Soft Pear" and "Great Ox," and spoke of themselves as "Pachyderms." Horkheimer followed Brecht's example in resorting to Chinese personas in exile: he could see the advantages in Lao-tzu's idea of making oneself malleable by experience, right down to the point of surrendering one's identity. Calling himself "Rindviech" (a stupid beast, an ox or an ass) points to the pachyderm qualities of rhinoceroses or hippopotamuses but also to their greediness. Adorno was certainly known for the voraciousness with which he devoured vast quantities of books, as well as for his super-human memory. In the Adorno-Wiesengrund family, giving names taken from the Frankfurt Zoo and the Senckenberg Museum of Natural History had an eloquent prehistory, and it may have inspired Adorno to develop a theory of names. He had in fact worked on such a theory in competition with Benjamin in the early thirties, even before the Nazi persecutions made it clear that a name can become a destiny.

The *Frankfurter Zeitung* of 7 August 1930 contained a "Note on Names" which in many ways reminds us of the names Kracauer uses in his novels *Ginster* and *Georg.* There are also references to Proust. Thomas Mann's cre-ative approach to names is not yet mentioned. Adorno had picked up a passage in Marieluise Fleisser's *Pioneers* in which a servant girl replies, when asked what her name is, "I have become a Berta."[118] Such a way of thinking about oneself is unconscious of the semblance of uniqueness and is acquainted at best with the reality of being the first in a series. It leads Adorno on to the idea that "proletarians were divided up into long straight rows of people called Georg, Willy, Fritz, and Franz who contained within themselves the pattern of future lists of casualties."[119] Both friends seem to have been preoccupied by the difference between this and middle-class experience: "The names of the ruling strata are less random for individuals and hence less necessary for the collective. But they too cannot evade the coercive force of names. For their next of kin have merged with their names to such an extent that no power on earth could tear them apart."[120] In *Georg,* which Kracauer had started to work on again, the author identi-fies with the title figure, who also closely observes another character, "Fred," who bears an unmistakable resemblance to the young Teddie. One need only apply the English diminutive to arrive at Freddie for the similar-ity to become obvious; we see, too, how much the ordinary Georg admires the extraordinary and much younger Fred: "His boyish figure was capti-vating, the mournfulness in his eyes came from a distant place which it had to be possible to reach."[121] His awareness that he belonged to a supra-individual group was visible in his gaze.

The entire generation of Jewish intellectuals who met up in emigration had to bear the German names that corresponded to their parents' ideas of normality—from Siegfried and Gerhard via Theodor right down to Max and Walter. Even the change to "Teddie" was consistent with the traditional

Anglophile attitudes of central European middle-class Jews, which permitted Freud, for example, to name his son Oliver after Cromwell. When Teddie wrote his jazz essay in Britain, he added a curious postscript that reveals something of the strengths and weaknesses of his thoughts on jazz. The shock of social coercion, fear of the loss of an individual life, and the desire to be accepted by a supra-individual authority are not really explained by the preface that he added for the reprint in *Moments Musicaux* in 1963 and that had something of the characteristics of a Lichtenbergian lightning rod. Adorno is thinking aloud about the connections between impressionism, jazz, and naming behind which the identity and non-identity of a liberal society and opposition to it lie concealed. The intellectual pitfalls of avant-gardism and snobbery lie in wait. Adorno alludes to Debussy's title "Général Lavine, Eccentric," which he associates with the word "avalanche"—the avalanche that Baudelaire wished to be swept along by.[122] He dates the naming of this eccentric to the period around 1910, "at the same time as the first teddy bear."[123] How could or should his German readers in the early sixties be expected to comprehend all this? Nevertheless, this passage is of key importance for our understanding of Adorno on his return to Germany. Teddy bears are a German-American crossing of stuffed animals (like the ones made by Steiff) with the popular American president Theodore Roosevelt. They were first made in 1903, the year of Adorno's birth. The pet name somehow became attached to him and among his schoolfellows became a generally known nickname.[124] Adorno associated with them the "rancor"[125] that would dog him throughout his life. The child who comes out at the top of his class but is subjected to mockery and bullying is turned into an inauthentic boy because, like an infant prodigy, he would rather perfect his piano playing than take up sport. These are the terrors of socialization that give the lie to the all too rosy accounts of an idyllic Frankfurt childhood: "If the bourgeois class has from time immemorial nurtured the dream of a brutal national community, of oppression of all by all; children already equipped with Christian-names like Horst and Jürgen and surnames like Bergenroth, Bojunga and Eckhardt enacted the dream before the adults were historically ripe for its realization. I felt with such excessive clarity the force of the horror towards which they were straining that all subsequent happiness seemed revocable, borrowed."[126]

In jazz, whose triumphal march through Germany took place in his youth, around 1920, Adorno felt all the terrors of socialization once again. As he noted in the postscript of 1937 in Oxford, "Mockery and pleasure in the name as in the social names of brands."[127] That applies also to teddy bears, the favorite toys of millions, and to the one and only Teddie, who in the eyes of his Jewish friends in Frankfurt enjoyed the privilege of not looking Jewish at first sight. Only the sadness in his eyes links the individual Teddie with the social fate that seemed predestined by his name: "So the expression called human is precisely that of the eyes closest to that of the animal, the creaturely ones, remote from the reflection of the self. At the last, soul itself is the longing of the soulless for redemption."[128] The memory of our animal origins animates Adorno's interest in what Horkheimer conceived as an "anthropology of the bourgeois age" in his major essays for the *Zeitschrift* in the thirties. Adorno wanted his music essays to be understood in the same context. Only by recognizing sensuous experiences as historically variable would it prove possible to restore the dimension of enlightenment to the study of physiognomy. In 1957 Adorno wrote an enthusiastic review of a psychoanalytically oriented study by Paul Moses, "The Voice of Neurosis," with the subtitle "Physiognomy of the Voice," a title that itself evoked memories of the Enlightenment tradition associated with Georg Christoph Lichtenberg. He conceived of this "physiognomy" as an "expressive science."[129] He writes: "Mankind learned to express itself not just through gestures, imitative sounds, cries of suffering and joy, but also by forming words. At the same time, the scope of the voice began to contract to the point where nowadays the melody of the voice represents nothing more than a musical scale of emotions as an accompaniment to a rational mode of articulation."[130] These ideas entered into his philosophy of music. On 6 August 1962 a variation on this idea was taken up in a notebook published by Rolf Tiedemann:

> Music as doubling. A person who sings is not alone. He hears the voice, an other, which is at the same time himself. To become an other to oneself, to externalize oneself. This contains a wealth of possibilities:
>
> The rejection of fear (a person who is afraid sings because then he is no longer alone).
>
> The immanent relation to the species. The collective as a primal phenomenon. In music the solitary person is defined as subject and at the same time as another subject. The spell that is broken is at the same time that of merely existing for oneself.

Objectification. In doubling, the primal phenomenon of reflection—the echo!—the subject becomes objectivized, universal, and thereby a subject.[131]

Reflection is not external to music; motifs constantly recur. "Philosophy actually exists in order to redeem what is to be found in the gaze of an animal," Adorno remarks in the course of a discussion with Horkheimer in 1956.[132] The shock caused by the experience of social reality is rendered eloquent by reflection. This shock can still be discerned in Hektor Rottweiler's jazz essay, the first essay Adorno wrote following the silence induced by the events of 1933. The wounds of life are precipitated as intellectual scars in the unmediated way in which Adorno transfers inferences from the practice of music to economic critique and analytical social psychology—inferences that in later years Adorno himself thought insufficiently mediated. Adorno's subsequent reflections on jazz in the Federal Republic attracted the rancor of those who wanted to label him a spoilsport in a new age. The weakness of his reflections, provoked by his reluctance to expand his own knowledge of the subject, reproduces itself as the very intellectual rigidity that Adorno diagnoses in the "jazz subject." He succeeds in identifying the damage done to the jazz subject as the object of the entertainment industry: "Anxiety causes the subject to drop out and go into opposition, but opposition by an isolated individual, who represents himself in his isolation as purely socially determined, is an illusion. . . . For the specification of the individual in jazz never was and never will be that of a thriving productive power, but always that of neurotic weakness."[133] The fear of social isolation, of the loss of intellectual productive energy, is what inspired the Oxford postscript: "I remember clearly the shock I felt when I heard the word 'jazz' for the first time. It seemed plausible that it came from the German *Hatz* [hunt] and involves the pursuit of a slower quarry by bloodhounds."[134] These sentences were not intended for the German reader of the 1960s. They were directed at friends rather than at imagined bystanders, at Benjamin in Paris or Horkheimer, who was already in New York. The jazz essays repeat the shock of social isolation that Teddie had already experienced as the top boy in his Frankfurt school and that kept catching up with him on his solitary journey into exile. In a subsequent, much attacked essay published in 1933 over his heroic canine name, we find the lapidary sentence that points to a different experience with jazz from that of the majority of his readers of a later generation, who associate jazz with the

Voice of America: "Jazz was the *Gebrauchsmusik* [utility music] of the *haute bourgeoisie* of the post-war period."[135]

The mask of the animal pseudonym was supposed to protect his own productive energies. If the English jazz essay combined an aesthetic and political left-wing radicalism without any tinge of American experience, Adorno did not properly develop his own intellectual voice until *Minima Moralia*. The sound of the highly promising word *mélange* names a coffee-house experience, an implicit "Thank you to Vienna."[136] He writes: "Politics that are seriously concerned with . . . an emancipated society . . . ought not therefore to propound the abstract equality of men even as an idea. . . . Instead, they should conceive the better state as one in which people could be different without fear."[137] The strength to put up with one's fear, to refuse to conform and merge with a new collective is derived in 1945 from his own experience: "The melting pot was introduced by unbridled industrial capitalism. The thought of being cast into it conjures up martyrdom, not democracy."[138] The sensuousness of difference which is preserved in the concept of *physiognomy,* which goes beyond racism of every kind, is linked with the idea of happiness. All these elements are welded together in Adorno's *Mahler: A Musical Physiognomy,* a book for which marginal notes exist as early as 1936 but for which he only discovered the right tone around 1960: "Mahler's deviations are closely related to gestures of language: his peculiarities are clenched as in jargon. . . . Sometimes—and not merely in the recitative—Mahler's music has so completely mimed the gestures of speech that it sounds as if it were speaking literally, as was once promised, in musical Romanticism, by the title of Mendelssohn's *Songs without Words*."[139] Songs without words—Adorno's "Words without Songs"[140] reminded readers even in 1931 of the old utopia of an emancipated society whose reality was unquestioningly taken for granted by the parental generation, but which had begun to look fragile by the time of the First World War. Many of the tensions that the younger generation of middle-class Jewish children hoped to resolve through a commitment to Zionism or left-wing radicalism continued to fester beneath the liberal culture of the parents, who had turned Heine or Mendelssohn into a cultural tradition that provoked their children to rebel.[141] Adorno never wrote the study of Mendelssohn he had planned, although the idea keeps turning up in his "Notes." A star of his childhood that was increasingly obscured by the general amnesia was rescued not by his various "Essays on Wagner," but by a Mahler who enabled the silenced experience of an abortive emancipation to find its voice once more "in the name of music."[142] Adorno the composer vanishes behind the interpreter of Mahler and then surfaces again as Adorno the writer in the seven hundred pages of *Notes to Literature*. Prominently placed among these is his interpretation of Heine's "Heimkehr" (Homecoming) cycle, which Adorno interprets as a "vision of victimhood." Heine's topical relevance results from the universalizing of "homelessness," which is referred to as a wound that transcends his stereotyping of the theme of unrequited love.[143] No composer of Heine's generation was able to set to music the promise of a happiness that had been experienced in childhood, but had been unredeemed, by endowing it with the discordant shape of the commonplace and derivative: "It was not until Mahler's songs about the soldiers who flew the flag out of homesickness, not until the outbursts of the funeral march in his Fifth Symphony, until the folksongs with their harsh alternation of major and minor, until the convulsive gestures of the Mahlerian orchestra, that the music in Heine's verses was released. In the mouth of a stranger, what is old and familiar takes on an extravagant quality, and precisely that is the truth."[144]

This is Adorno's authentic tone, the voice that presented this text, like many of his smaller pieces, over the radio. Making use of the same medium as the one in which Hitler had unleashed his demagogic power, Adorno once again made a home for the "undiluted concept of enlightenment"[145] that had been so despised in the German nineteenth-century tradition. Adorno's Mahler interpretation brings long-buried memories to the surface: "The first trio of the Funeral March of the Fifth Symphony, which already begins grandly enough, does not respond with a lyrical, subjective complaint to the objective lament of fanfare and march. It gesticulates, raises a shriek of horror at something worse than death. It is not surpassed by the frightful figures in Schoenberg's *Erwartung*."[146]

Through every sentence of this interpretation we glimpse Adorno's awareness of the concentration camps, which, as the dark side of European society, accompany all the diurnal manifestations of culture. Adorno's voice, with a clarity of articulation that borders on the artificial, carried this seriousness into every introductory academic class and every radio talk. It was a tone dictated by a fear of false familiarity that verged on paranoia. But his voice wished also to be understood, not esoteric; it was directed toward a public. But Adorno had to leave America in order to make his voice heard as he wanted. It did not seem possible for him as an émigré in the United States to express ideas that were not comprehensible on first hearing. Germany's backwardness, the provincial nature of its mass media that had been prescribed by the Allies' pedagogic policies, enabled him to express ideas that would have been subject to the rules of mass communication in a more advanced America. Unlike Horkheimer, Adorno left America for good in 1953. He evidently wished to make an impact beyond the limits of an academic career, whereas Horkheimer wanted to leave open the possibility of a return. Both men persevered in their search for happiness although Adorno felt himself to be its martyr.[147]

In their unguarded private discussion of 1956, in which they considered the possibility of a new *Communist Manifesto,* the concept of happiness played a crucial role. Adorno retracted his old idea from *Minima Moralia* of "*rien faire:* the stage reached by animals, one in which one does nothing at all, can no longer be retrieved."[148] Horkheimer spins out the thought, remarking that "happiness would be an animal state as viewed from the perspective of someone who is no longer an animal."[149] Adorno replies, saying, "We could learn from animals what happiness is." Horkheimer concludes: "To reach the animal state at the level of reflection—that is freedom. Freedom means not having to work."[150] The cryptic form of the distinction that Adorno had made in the public letter of congratulations in *Die Zeit* in 1965 now becomes clear: "I think that animals are like human beings, while you think human beings are like animals."[151] Horkheimer's materialism goes back beyond the anthropology of bourgeois man, while Adorno's social criticism goes in search of an extraterritorial, not yet societalized space in which human beings who have been societalized can acquire the strength to experience happiness, which nevertheless is not to be had without fear. Mahler and Kafka, the music of the one and the words of the other, are the guarantors of this: "For him [Mahler], as in Kafka's fables, the animal realm is the human world as it would appear from the standpoint of redemption, which natural history itself precludes. The fairy-tale tone in Mahler is awakened by the resemblance of animal and man, desolate and comforting at once."[152] In the 1956 discussion Horkheimer insists that "there must be clarity about the relation between utopia and present-day reality." Adorno responds, "If I . . . write about music, this is because I have all the relevant mediating categories at my disposal."[153] The element of extraterritoriality allows Adorno to offer a "ruthless critique of this culture"—a verbal radicalism that Horkheimer cuts short. To Adorno's suggested compromise, "We live on the culture we criticize," Horkheimer responds almost bluntly, "I mean society."[154]

The intellectual differences between them can be traced all the way back to their childhood, and Horkheimer was well aware of them. He attributes "the incredible versatility of his [Adorno's] works" to "the intellectual and artistic family atmosphere."[155] But he clung to the differences between them: "Yet despite his taking the dialectic to an extreme, what he says remains untrue. For the truth cannot be expressed."[156] Adorno's idea of happiness insists on the non-identical as something not absolutely other. In "Criteria of New Music" he asserts something that, according to Horkheimer, cannot be said at all: "By negating both the general and the particular, new music presses forward to absolute identity, and in so doing, it aspires to be the voice of the non-identical—of everything that refuses to be submerged."[157] The return to Germany brought the "Gold Assay" aphorism of *Minima Moralia* up to date. Adorno defended the non-identical as the "mask of genius" that he had observed in Thomas Mann. As late as 1968, among the benefits of his time in America he included that of de-provincialization, the abandonment of German inwardness. The alleged superficiality that Europeans criticize in Americans to this day questions the very concept of identity that has in the meantime become the conformist pride of the individual—"as though this identity was always desirable."[158]

It was only in Frankfurt after 1953 that Adorno fully became the genius that he was. He appears to have flown for the first time on the journey back from Los Angeles: "It is possible for some experiences to come too late."[159] Adorno's extraterritorial vantage point imposed on him a perception of time that he did not want to reserve for the private sphere, and in 1954 he wrote about it for the *Frankfurter Rundschau:*

> But in the eyes of the émigré the order of time has turned into disorder. . . . If he returns, he will have aged, while at the same time he remains as young as he was when he was banished, much as the dead always remain the same age as when we last knew them. He imagines that he can take up where he left off; those who are of the same age today as he was in 1933 seem to him to be as old as he is. Nevertheless, he has his own real age which becomes intermeshed with that [imagined] one, breaks through it, gives it a deeper meaning, and gives it the lie. It is as if those whom this has befallen and who have been permitted to survive had been transposed by fate into a time frame that was both multidimensional and riddled with holes.[160]

This non-identical émigré would vanish behind the public Adorno. Only in exceptional situations, such as the occasions of public congratulation, do we obtain a glimpse of the human dimensions that lie behind the public figure and without which the individual cannot be understood. Not until the mid-fifties did Benjamin become visible once more, thanks to Adorno's indefatigable efforts, together with those of Scholem, while simultaneously Horkheimer opted to become increasingly invisible. It is only when we glimpse their profiles that Adorno's physiognomy becomes visible as the unmistakable person he was yet as someone who was unimaginable without their community of spirit. In fact, in the twenties and thirties, a feeling arose among them that Adorno summed up in a letter to Benjamin, saying, "In a word, one is still among one's own friends."[161] But none of the attributes connected with the keyword "identity"—neither "Jewish," "German," nor "Marxist"—would suffice to characterize the unique individual who had given birth to the term "non-identity." In 1953, the year of Stalin's death, the Berlin uprising of 17 June, and the end of the Korean War, Adorno was asked what his abiding impressions were of the year. In reply he listed the first volumes of the new edition of Proust's *À la recherche du temps perdu,* Kafka's letters to Milena Jesenska, and a gramophone recording of Schoenberg's *Kol Nidre,* a work that he had heard while still in Los Angeles and that he reckoned to be "the most perfect thing he has done." In his case, too, it would be desirable for him to be removed from the realm of consciousness and be brought home.[162] Who could achieve that if not Adorno?

8. | The Palimpsest of Life

The modern has really become unmodern.
Modernity is really a qualitative, not a chronological category.
THEODOR W. ADORNO, "CONSECUTIO TEMPORUM"

In 1949, in his essay "Cultural Criticism and Society," his entry ticket to a post-Nazi Germany, Adorno wrote, "To write poetry after Auschwitz is barbaric. And this corrodes even the knowledge of why it has become impossible to write poetry today."[1] We must also remind ourselves of Adorno's lecturing style at that time. He did not enter a lecture hall as a well-dressed gentleman with tie, cashmere pullover, and jacket, but according to Alfred Schmidt, his later assistant, he normally wore a windbreaker. He had given up an insecure life in the United States, but Frankfurt University and the German institutions did not exactly roll out the red carpet in his honor. German academic heads were extremely interested in Horkheimer's contacts in America, but even so he had to use all his influence to ensure that Adorno received a secure income. Nevertheless, his influence and Pollock's did not suffice to obtain a post for Marcuse, to the latter's intense disappointment. Adorno had to wait until the mid-fifties before the Johann Wolfgang Goethe University made him a full professor. On their return to Germany there were also significant economic issues to be resolved. Brecht's insinuations to the effect that the "frankfurtists" were Jewish millionaires with a revolutionary image belong to the sad tradition of anti-intellectual intellectualism.

Adorno was prepared to break taboos publicly in Germany. In a society which was all too eager to return to normality after 1945, he acted the part of the bearer of bad news, thus reawakening archaic reactions—those of killing the messenger, for example. In "The Meaning of Working Through the Past" of 1959, an essay that was later to become famous, Adorno remarked, "I wrote once in a scholarly dispute: in the house of the hangman one should not speak of the noose, otherwise one might seem to be harbouring resentment."[2] In this talk Adorno reminds his readers of the discordant tones in the chorus of public opinion that had been produced in response to the voices of the returnees. In 1957 the social psychologist Peter

R. Hofstätter had produced a harsh critique in the *Kölner Zeitschrift für Soziologie und Sozialpsychologie* of the institute's first major study after its return to Germany. It was to this review that Adorno reacted with the biting comment about the house of the hangman. The *Gruppenexperiment* appeared in 1955, at the same time as *Prisms,* but was based on surveys undertaken from 1950 to 1951. It followed logically from *The Authoritarian Personality* and worked with stimuli and qualitative group analyses. The researchers were concerned not with individual responses but with exploring the process by which opinions were formed by applying empirical methods that had been employed and debated in the United States and had also been accepted there in the scientific community. In 1951 C. Wright Mills had written a strongly positive review of *The Authoritarian Personality.* Hofstätter, by contrast, attempted to represent the stimuli with which the German participants were to be activated into responding to the National Socialist past and the East-West confrontation as "an invitation to genuine remorse," and in his view this asked too much of them since it expected them "to shoulder the burden of the horrors of Auschwitz."[3] Not unreasonably, Adorno pointed out coolly that "it was the victims of Auschwitz who were compelled to shoulder the burden of the horrors of Auschwitz, not those people who do not wish to know about them, to their own detriment and the detriment of their country."[4]

Adorno had arrived in Germany again by the mid-fifties. He did not appear with borrowed authority to avenge the persecuted or as the spokesman for the victims. Others looked on with mistrust and open disapproval when they saw the people whom he and Horkheimer were prepared to sit down with and talk to at the same table. Having remained behind in California, friends and acquaintances such as Thomas Mann and Fritz Lang watched the Frankfurters' return with a mixture of skepticism and disapproval. Adorno neither suppressed nor denied who he was dealing with, as Günther Anders reproached him with doing. If we look inside the *Gruppenexperiment,* we can still feel the authors' emotion and also their fear of the reaction they would provoke by asserting that the Germans were not free of guilt and that they responded truculently when told this to their faces. Horkheimer had asked an established scholar, Franz Böhm, to write a preface to the book, evidently so that he might act as a kind of lightning rod.[5] Böhm summed up what he saw as a principal finding of the research, namely, that "there is such a thing as a *non-public opinion* that can diverge strikingly from the official public opinion, but whose propositions run alongside public opinion like the banknotes of a *second currency.*"[6] Today the study still seems alive, chiefly because its authors had a burning desire to know what sort of country they had returned to. In fact, the book provides, as Horkheimer and Adorno had hoped, primary source material of an entirely new kind.[7] What was new, socially, in their encounter with Germany was the exploration of the old—a motif that the world did not discover until thirty years later, when it perceived the way in which the Holocaust was investigated.

It was above all Adorno's "scientific experiences in America"[8] that came to his aid in this book, in particular his ability to seek out the human forms of organization underlying the superficial self-presentation of the interviewees. The rumor that he was investigating the authoritarian German character has some truth in it, in the sense that his work on *The Authoritarian Personality* had been a good preparation for using the tools of the social sciences to generate empirical information that would be of greater value than a simple collection of opinions. His work on Culture Industry adaptations and finished products for the Princeton Radio Research Project went into the interpretation of competing opinion-forming processes and forms of presentation in the *Gruppenexperiment.* This text, framed by preface, postscript, and foreword, and underpinned by a large methodological apparatus, reflects Horkheimer's own feelings of insecurity on entering post–National Socialist terrain. With hindsight, Adorno's involvement seems disproportionate and can be explained only by Horkheimer's concern to avoid presenting any targets for his competitors among the social scientists. According to the testimony of Monika Plessner, who worked as an assistant at the institute, Horkheimer seems to have been terrified that the work his colleagues had produced might not satisfy current academic criteria. In the lengthy period between collecting the data in the winter of 1950 and publication in 1955, Adorno had been working on a research project with Frederick Hacker in Beverly Hills, an activity that intensified his wish to immerse himself in the *Gruppenexperiment.* On the one hand, it increased his nostalgia for Germany because as a researcher, he was more dependent on financial sponsors in California than was the case with professors at a German university. On the other hand, his point of view as an observer looking at Germany from outside was reinforced by his stay in America. The skeptical questions of a friend such as Fritz Lang preoccupied him when he discussed matters with Germans in Germany. This amalgam of ideas and emotions can still be discerned in his essay

"Scientific Experiences of a European Scholar in America" of 1968, for example, in his definition of himself as a "European" as opposed to a "German" or a "Jew." Imperceptibly a further point of view, a "we," enters into his analysis of group opinions, a point of view to which critics such as Hofstätter reacted negatively without saying explicitly what it was that disturbed them.

Later on, Adorno felt some pride when people began to speak of a "Frankfurt School," a term that was linked with the catchphrase "critical theory." In 1955 these terms did not yet exist, but the processes were already in train that would culminate in a sharp distinction between sociology and philosophy at Frankfurt and other German universities. This difference was symbolized by the newly opened building belonging to the Institute for Social Research. The main building of the Johann Wolfgang Goethe University on the opposite side of the Senckenberg Anlage was neo-baroque in style, and the philosophy seminar was situated above the main entrance. Now, however, the institute was to be housed in a new building that was explicitly designed to signal the final victory of modernism in an otherwise highly traditional Frankfurt. The offices of the institute directors and the philosophy professors, however, could be reached only from the other side of a broad avenue which resembled a city motorway on which the new German passion for cars was given free rein. In fact, there were a number of serious accidents close to the institute on the Senckenberg Anlage, and Adorno called for a set of traffic lights to enable pedestrians to cross in safety. The debates about the so-called Adorno lights were followed with some amusement, first in the local and then in the national press, up to and including *Der Spiegel*. The image of the traditional philosopher seemed incompatible with an interest in traffic problems. As the economic miracle town par excellence, Frankfurt was outstanding proof of the general breakthrough of social modernization, and this created a powerful contrast to a continued German adherence to the world picture of an authentic Germany that had long since ceased to exist, if indeed it ever had existed. The myth of a medieval Frankfurt which the Nazis had elevated in the teeth of all the evidence into the "city of handicrafts" had suffered irreparable damage with the bombing of the Old Town. During the rebuilding of the university, Max Horkheimer, as rector, had paid great attention to the architectural alienation effects that were included, above all by Ferdinand Kramer through his aesthetic sensibility and his clever use of materials. The neo-baroque splendors were not simply restored as if nothing untoward had happened. Instead, certain ornaments were removed; entrances were modernized, as were the interiors of the surviving buildings from the turn of the century, when the university had been established; and they were surrounded by a modern campus. Student residence halls, cafeterias, and the library document the desire to make things new without denying the validity of the old.

The Korean boom had brought about a decisive change. Like Adorno's renewed visit to California, the Korean War, ending in 1953, fell between the collecting of data for the *Gruppenexperiment* and its publication. The discussions that took place initially in 1950 were now already viewed as being merely of historical interest: "It would be highly desirable to repeat this study under present conditions, and indeed, it should be repeated regularly, and an archive of tape recordings and written protocols should be maintained."[9] Unfortunately, this suggestion that a new kind of "museum" should be established was never taken up. With the integration of the two German states into the opposing power blocs, the West German debates about the past fell into a coma, from whence they emerged only sporadically. But whenever they did, Adorno's voice could be heard. As early as 1949 he observed, "Even the most extreme consciousness of doom threatens to degenerate into idle chatter."[10] The group discussions strengthened an experience without which he could not have formulated the dictum that was not intended as a critical *aperçu* but that subsequently became so famous. The certain knowledge that culture was being functionalized in order to cast a veil over reality was something the returned émigrés had found confirmed in Hollywood, but the primary insight was one they had brought over with them to America from Weimar. What was new in what Adorno found after his return to Germany lay in the palimpsest of a "resurrected culture: in 1949 people's interest in politics had waned while the administered Culture Industry had not yet taken them over completely. They were thrown back on themselves and their own devices."[11] This was the moment when Adorno's dictum called the entire panoply of the Culture Industry into question. He could do so because he had been laboring away at this critique since the 1930s.

A little article titled "New Opera and the Public" ("Neue Oper und Publikum") of 1930 reflects upon the opera's loss of social significance. The impossibility of earning his living as a musician compelled Adorno to consider whether the rift that had opened up between the development of music and the audience could ever be glued together again. The metaphor of glue or cement had been used by the sociologists around Horkheimer since the late 1920s to characterize the social function of ideology as a necessarily false consciousness. Adorno's music essays in the *Zeitschrift für Sozialforschung* can be understood as a genuine form of ideology critique that does not rely on analogies but derives from reflection on the matter at hand. The constitutive elements of opera—performance and song—are intertwined with society. We glimpse something of the liberal nature of Weimar culture when we see that Adorno was able to publish his critical ideas on the relation of modern music and Frankfurt society in the official brochure celebrating the fiftieth anniversary of the Frankfurt Opera in 1930: "The repertoire is selected in accordance with the belief that the predominant type among the public is the woman with the broad accent who gives it as her opinion that when all is said and done, *Aida* is a lovely opera, and who is ready to defend this opinion vigorously in her coffee-drinking circle of friends."[12] Evidently, in the period between the wars, "the operatic space had been left in the hands of the numerically diminished and intrinsically weakened remnants of a secure middle class who mourn the past and are the last people to allow an art form that was theirs by privilege to be subjected to the radical changes that would be necessary both for the aesthetic shape of the opera and because of the changes in social stratification."[13] *Wozzeck* and *Mahagonny* were the topical challenges to the opera-going public in the final phase of the Weimar Republic. As a pupil of Berg and a good acquaintance of Weill and Brecht, the young Wiesengrund-Adorno was at the forefront of the artistic debate.

Without a historical consciousness, neither tradition nor modernity can be saved. In 1958 Adorno collected pieces of music criticism from the period before 1933 and published them under the title "The Natural History of the Theatre,"[14] dedicated to the memory of his mother, Maria Calvelli-Adorno: "Applause is the last vestige of objective communication between music and listener."[15] Adorno included this text, which at a second glance seems to be a very private essay, in his collection *Quasi una fantasia.* In that volume it follows his essay "Fantasia sopra Carmen," which contains revelations about the part he played in the writing of Thomas Mann's *Doctor Faustus.* Linguistically these texts suggest to the reader a fantasy Italy that owes something to Mann's *Death in Venice,* as do Adorno's imagined origins in the Genoese nobility. The text dedicated to his mother is framed by a homage to Mahler: "Having salvaged an amalgam of happiness and misery from his childhood, he refused to subscribe to any adult resignation or self-abnegation, the official social contract of music."[16] Adorno interprets Mahler's music "as a criticism of culture,"[17] which in the period after Auschwitz reveals something different about the world before Auschwitz. In the "Afterthoughts" he adds: "Could we not think of the path of disillusionment described by Mahler's as by no other music as an example of the cunning not of reason but of hope? Is it not the case that in the final analysis Mahler has extended the Jewish prohibition on making graven images so as to include hope? The fact that the last two works which he completed have no closure, but remain open, translated the uncertain outcome between destruction and its alternative into music."[18] Adorno owed this idea of extending the ban on making graven images so as to include hope to Max Horkheimer, with whom he had unreservedly identified himself since arriving in America.

The idea of Auschwitz had been present in almost all of Adorno's writings since the mid-forties. The guilt of having survived drives Adorno's social criticism onward with "the unwavering radicalism of spirit"[19] which seems appropriate to an avant-garde artist. Adorno's critical theory is nourished by a feeling of solidarity with suffering that distinguishes it from all forms of academic scholarship. The repeated discussions about the mediating links between theory and practice that took place at intervals in the institute and that Adorno conducted with Horkheimer and his own students until well into the 1950s had taken a decisive turn toward the end of 1939. At a time when they were doing the preparatory work in the run-up to their *Dialectic of Enlightenment,* Adorno had confessed to Horkheimer: "Partly under the impact of the latest news from Germany, I am quite unable to separate myself from the fate of the Jews any longer. It often seems to me as if everything we were accustomed to see in connection with the proletariat has nowadays been transferred to the Jews but in a terrifyingly concentrated form."[20] If we take a slightly closer look at their correspondence, even members of a later generation can see that of course this did not mean that the Jews should take over the world-historical role of the proletariat. Ever since the so-called Kristallnacht of November 1938, the Jews, "who were the very antithesis of the concentration of power,"[21] had appeared as the exemplary victims of National Socialist power. In the light of the evident powerlessness of the émigrés in exile, a powerlessness reinforced daily by the news from Germany, the language of revolutionary theory threatened to degenerate into mere rhetoric. A notebook without a cover dating back to the summer of 1939 contains the statement: "The fact that the power of facts has become so horrifying that all theory, even true theory, seems to be a mere travesty—this has engraved itself like a brand in the very organ of theory, namely, language itself. The practice that renders theory impotent surfaces as a destructive element in the interior of theory without regard to any possible practice. Actually, there is no more to be said. The deed is the only form left to theory."[22]

As early as summer 1939 Adorno had identified the central contradiction of critical theory around which his entire future oeuvre would revolve. At its heart is the destructive experience of violence that leaves its mark on both sides of the revolutionary legacy: the weapons of criticism and the criticism of weapons,[23] which the Marx of the period before 1848 had formulated in a way that was still naïve. Adorno's own radical impulse derives likewise from a "new life's feeling of its own power,"[24] not unlike that of the pre-1848 period. This feeling also inspired Ernst Bloch's *Spirit of Utopia* (*Geist der Utopie*), which he wrote after the First World War and which he took back with him to the German Federal Republic in 1961, unaffected either by his exile in America or by his subsequent stay in the German Democratic Republic after 1949. What Bloch hoped for from resuming contact with Adorno once he had finally settled down in Tübingen was to take up from where they had left off. But in his very first private letter of congratulations to Adorno on his sixtieth birthday, he asks the crucial question, "Now that we have grown older what has actually happened to prevent us from being what we used to be to each other in the old days?"[25] Bloch meant this question not personally but rather with a view to "what the history of philosophy may preserve."[26] He may well have felt resentment at the way Adorno had treated him in the *Notes to Literature*, in which he had simply ignored the persecution to which Bloch had been subjected in the GDR at the end of the thaw. The West German public had been able to read both a new edition of Bloch's *Traces* (*Spuren*) and Adorno's reflections on it. But much that had passed between the two men must have been a closed book to the reading public. The tone of Adorno's essay is disconcerting, particularly since he adopts the same tone as when he speaks of Lukács, Bloch's "friend in his youth,"[27] in the same volume. After all, both men had been like philosophical fixed stars in Adorno's firmament, presiding over the ruins of the attempt to become assimilated via the route of middle-class culture, an assimilation that by celebrating Goethe's concept of resignation had turned sorrow and melancholy into the constant companion of even the most successful Jewish life project.

In the twenties there had been a meeting of minds between Adorno's older friends Walter Benjamin and Siegfried Kracauer in the critique of renunciation "as an expression of bourgeois society's restriction of itself to the reified world it has established, a world that exists for it, the world of commodities."[28] In endless talk in Berlin, during the days and even more during the nights, they had formed an inseparable pair whom Adorno had frequently visited on his trips from Frankfurt—particularly since Gretel Karplus, who was to become his wife, was often to be found in their company. Rivalry and jealousy were the new, invidious companions of such intellectual friendships. Kracauer had become an important editor at the *Frankfurter Zeitung,* a newspaper in which all of them—Benjamin, Bloch, and Wiesengrund-Adorno—wished to have their writings published. The culture section absolutely bubbled and fizzed; it was an inexhaustible source of quarrels, envious attacks, and accusations of plagiarism, all of which continued when they found themselves in exile. After 1933 Adorno had obtained access to the review section of the *Zeitschrift für Sozialforschung,* which had a reputation among the indigent émigrés for being both prestigious and lucrative. The off-putting tone Adorno uses when speaking of Bloch, Lukács, and even Kracauer in the *Notes to Literature* can be traced back to this period. Their differences in matters of substance, however, can be explained "in political terms," something that remains undeclared in the *Notes to Literature:* "About this too he [Bloch] tells stories, as if he were speaking about something predecided, virtually assuming the transformation of the world, unconcerned about what has become of the Revolution in the thirty years since the first edition of the *Spuren* and what has happened to the concept and possibility of revolution under altered social and technological conditions."[29]

What was scarcely comprehensible to the younger reader around 1960, because Adorno's criticism is presented as something self-evident, must have been crystal clear to Bloch, since this pronouncement contains the decisive distinction between the critical theorists around Horkheimer and the political commitments of such diverse thinkers as Bloch, Brecht, and Eisler. Since the end of the Weimar Republic, the last three had declared their commitment to the policies of the Communist Party, although they maintained a certain distance in organizational terms. Of the three it was Bloch who had taken the fewest precautions to cover his back when he moved to the GDR in 1949. Brecht and Eisler had at least taken care to hold on to their Austrian passports. The disagreements with the Frankfurters, toward whom Benjamin tended to gravitate, extended back to the end of the Weimar period, and Bloch makes Teddie—which he spells "Teddy"—feel this: "In short, (if I am right) these things were read differently before 1933. And it was improbable that they could be read in any other way. Improbable, too, was what you—didn't do—in America."[30] From Adorno's standpoint in the sixties, matters look quite different. As a child prodigy who had matured very late, he had explained them to Bloch in a letter from the previous year (printed in the appendix to this book), in response to a letter in which Bloch, who had just moved to Tübingen, asked him for a copy of his book on Kierkegaard, which had just appeared in a new edition.

Bloch reminds Adorno in 1963 of their shared past while at the same time denying it. A naïve aesthetic left-wing radicalism had brought Bloch, Benjamin, and Adorno together at the end of the twenties. Brecht and Eisler held similar views until the mid-thirties. The four of them had come together again in exile in America, with Brecht arriving somewhat later than the other three, while Benjamin remained behind in Europe. In the letter to Bloch in 1962 just referred to, Adorno spoke of his own development, referring to "a certain moment of shock which no doubt coincided with the outbreak of Hitler's Reich."[31] Whereas in a notice dated 1966 in *Negative Dialectics* Adorno emphasizes the continuity of his life, here he refers to 1933 as a key turning point. *After* 1933, he intimates to Bloch, matters were read differently. Bloch denies not only the age difference separating Adorno from him, Lukács, and Kracauer but also the political differences. Bloch assures Adorno in his good wishes on his sixtieth birthday that their personal closeness remains intact, and the fact that it was always being reestablished may have covered over many disagreements. After all the quarrels that accompanied *Erbschaft dieser Zeit* (Heritage of Our Times), Adorno could once again call Bloch his "red brother" in 1937,[32] not, however, because of any allegiance to the Communist Party, but because of their common interest in "redskins" following spoors. Bloch's *Traces*, which had appeared in 1930, could be read as reflections from an undamaged life. After his enforced silence in the GDR, Bloch had republished them without commentary in the West in 1959.

The letters from the 1930s provide evidence of a lively exchange of views with Bloch in which Gretel also took part. At the beginning of their friendship Adorno and Bloch had exchanged "music letters." Bloch used to go to the opera in Berlin with "Fräulein Karplus," whom he compared to Katharine Hepburn. In the thirties Bloch formed a relationship with Karola Piotrowska, who was not accepted by either Adorno or Benjamin. Later she was regarded by the friends simply as a Communist Party activist and was blamed for Bloch's identifying himself with Stalin's general line. But they all fell out with Bloch because of *Erbschaft dieser Zeit,* a book he published roughly coinciding with the emigration. Benjamin felt that he was the victim of "theft." Adorno sprang to his aid and administered a drubbing in a letter whose tone infuriated Bloch. These ups and downs of the 1930s were repeated in the 1960s.[33] The example had been set by the Thomas Mann model of slander from beyond the grave which upset Adorno so much in his quarrel with Erika Mann. After Adorno's death, Bloch disinterred the old fairy tale according to which the institute had coldheartedly let him starve in New York. Posthumously published notes of Adorno's make it clear that the quarrels with Bloch in fact date back to Benjamin's original discoveries. At Christmas 1968 Adorno notes: "He [Bloch] is out for revenge. His archaic features are in league with an interest in the market. Revenge because of Benjamin—but on me."[34] Adorno had taken up a double-edged sword. In 1968 Bloch's *Atheismus im Christentum* (Atheism in Christianity) appeared; in 1966 the two-volume selection of Benjamin's letters had come out, edited by Scholem and Adorno. This selection discreetly spared other people still living, but they did not spare Bloch.

In a letter to Alfred Cohn on 6 February 1935 Benjamin produced a brilliantly written but annihilating judgment of *Erbschaft dieser Zeit:*

> The severe criticism I have to make about this book (although not about this writer) is that it is not at all appropriate to the circumstances in which it appears, but is as out of place as a great lord who arrives to inspect a region devastated by an earthquake and who has no more urgent task than to have his servants spread out the Persian rugs that they have brought with them—and that are already somewhat moth-eaten; display the gold and silver vessels—that are already somewhat tarnished; and clothe himself in brocade and damask garments—that are already somewhat faded. It goes without saying that Bloch has excellent intentions and a considerable number of insights. But he does not know how to set them to work intellectually. His exaggerated claims prevent him from doing so. In such a situation—and in such a devastated territory—a great lord has no choice but to give away his Persian rugs to be used as blankets, cut up his brocades to be used as coats, and melt down his precious vessels.[35]

It is striking to see how Adorno followed the example of this method of damning with faint praise in his later review of the new edition of *Spuren.*

Bloch wasted no time in venting his anger as early as his letter of con-gratulations to Adorno in 1963: "It is true that the utopian conscience (even in the way in which I first defined it in 1918) has remained alive, quite explicitly, in your rich and successful writings. But the snag [is] the aban-donment of the great line, the *unum necessarium,* right down to the mock-ery in your 'Grosse Blochmusik" that is unworthy of you."[36] But at the re-quest of Suhrkamp Verlag, Adorno did not shy away from writing "In Honor of Ernst Bloch." In the third volume of *Notes to Literature,* Adorno unexpectedly pays homage to Bloch's *Spirit of Utopia:* "The book, Bloch's first, bearing all his later work within it, seemed to me to be one prolonged rebellion against the renunciation within thought that extends even into its purely formal character. Prior to any theoretical content, I took this mo-tif so much as my own that I do not believe I have ever written anything without reference to it, either implicit or explicit."[37] But gibes are not ab-sent either. Bloch's philosophy is consigned to Expressionism and repre-sented as a narrative form of knowledge that belongs to the past: "It unam-biguously communicates what it unequivocally refuses to communicate. That is Bloch in a nutshell. The transformation that takes place in remem-brance of what he wrote corroborates his own philosophy. Bloch would be able to invent a Hassidic tale to tell of that transformation."[38]

These double-edged compliments scarcely permit another interpreta-tion: only because Adorno had "reread it after more than forty years" did he find it possible to interpret Bloch's philosophy in such a way as to assign it a place close to the *Blauer Reiter,* "in close proximity to sympathy for the occult."[39] In *Negative Dialectics,* Adorno's first major work, one that can be seen as a pendant to *Spirit of Utopia,* Bloch is not even mentioned. "Spiritual experience," a key to Adorno's interpretation of the present, is determined by the relation of the thinker to tradition. The book is very sparing with quotations, but among those included in the tradition we find Plato, Aristotle, Kant, Hegel, Marx, and Freud; contemporary objects of at-tack include Jaspers and Heidegger, while as sources of intellectual inspira-tion, Max Horkheimer and Walter Benjamin are acknowledged as being of equal value. In addition, as evidence of his own ability to establish a fol-lowing, we find quotations from Karl-Heinz Haag, Hermann Schweppen-häuser, Alfred Schmidt, Oskar Negt, and Werner Bekker. The crowning moment of Adorno's introduction is one in which Bloch is suppressed: "To desire substance in cognition is to desire a utopia. It is this conscious-ness of possibility that sticks to the concrete, the undisfigured. Utopia is blocked off by possibility, never by immediate reality."[40] Bloch, who a year earlier had been treated as a source of inspiration in volume three of *Notes to Literature,* is now nowhere to be seen. On the appearance of *Negative Dialectics* in 1966, Bloch hit back mercilessly:

> [This is a book] in which evil certainly may not be exaggerated or even isolated; as in the fashion for raising despair to the skies or in Adorno's jargon of the inauthenticity of the good. [A book that is concerned with] the aforementioned grumbling in itself, together with the dialectic that is nothing but negative and that is compelled to relativize Marx and even Hegel, to the point where there could no longer be any struggle or "algebra of revolution." And reified despair counts for no more than reified confidence of the kind that has been practiced from time immemorial by the church and the authorities with their highly conformist message "Be consoled."[41]

Following their failed reconciliation in the early sixties after he left the GDR, Bloch was concerned to settle accounts here with Adorno's entire oeuvre from *Jargon of Authenticity* on.

On 15 July 1962 Bloch sent Adorno a postcard from his new home in Tübingen, asking him for a copy of the new edition of his Kierkegaard book that Bloch had noticed listed in a brochure from Suhrkamp, which published the writings of both men. The original manuscript of the book, which Bloch must have read before it appeared on 30 January 1933 [the day Hitler came to power], of all dates, must have gone astray in the course of the numerous moves occasioned by his flight and emigration. In 1961 Bloch arrived in Tübingen as a guest professor, leaving his valuable library and manuscripts of his own behind in the GDR. Once there, he and his wife, Karola, were taken by surprise by the sudden building of the Berlin Wall. He now found himself stranded in the West in his mid-seventies and without a secure source of income. Previously, after a lengthy period of exile in the United States, again without an income, in 1949 he had accepted a chair at Leipzig, where he had been forced into early retirement in 1957 after violent altercations with the ruling Socialist Unity Party (SED). For the first time since leaving America in 1949, he met Adorno again at a Hegel conference in Frankfurt in 1958. Adorno is said to have looked forward with considerable anxiety to the reunion since there had been a good deal of bad blood between the two. Anecdotal accounts suggest that Bloch resolved the tension in his normal jovial way. Having discovered Adorno at the entrance to a lecture hall, he apparently rushed up to him, shouting,

"Well, Teddie, how are things?" Despite the harassment he was subjected to, Bloch was well able to exploit his privileged position. Since he was a member of the East Berlin Academy of Sciences, a construct that embraced the two Germanys, the SED did not venture to prevent Bloch from traveling or publishing abroad. After his books ceased to be published by Aufbau and appeared instead with Suhrkamp, Teddie had no qualms about reviewing the reprint of Bloch's *Traces* in 1960 in an expert but ambivalent fashion. Whoever reads the text closely will be aware of his uncanny closeness to Bloch when speaking of such "experiences as the ringing of Christmas bells that gripped us and can never be completely eradicated: the feeling that what exists here and now cannot be all there is."[42] Adorno pays Bloch the greatest compliment when he refers to him as "musical," and compares his philosophy to Mahler's music, but follows this up with the annihilating judgment on his philosophy, "Hope is not a principle."[43]

In the previously mentioned letter of 26 July 1962, an autobiographical document of rare importance, Adorno attempts to combine the assertion of friendship with his feelings of aggression. In one paragraph after another we encounter the key terms of a vanished friendship. Homage is once again paid to Bloch's exemplary first book, *Spirit of Utopia*, which had so enchanted Adorno at the age of seventeen; in response to Bloch's request for his Kierkegaard study, Adorno refers to its "dreamlike anticipation,"[44] that is, as a youthful piece at best. In conversation in 1928, having encountered Bloch as Benjamin's constant companion in Berlin, he had already assured Bloch of the effect his *Spirit of Utopia* had had on him in his youth. Benjamin, eleven years older than Adorno, had meanwhile replaced Kracauer in Adorno's affections. But even his friendship with Benjamin seemed to lack something that was made good by his association with Bloch: music. As a young editor of the Viennese music journal *Der Anbruch*, Adorno published an article by Bloch in 1929 titled "Rettung Wagners durch Karl May" (The Redemption of Wagner by Karl May). Both Bloch and Adorno made names for themselves in the interwar years as journalists seeking to earn their living in the marketplace. The way of life of the freelance writer who has to sell his wares to media dominated by the bourgeoisie in order to survive went together with a political radicalism that could compete with that of the left-wing radicalism of the German Communist Party. Moscow lay at a mythical distance, and Benjamin had visited it in pursuit of Asja Lacis, a woman who was as disturbingly beautiful as she was radical. He continued to flirt with the Communist Party well into the thirties, despite his horror at the reign of terror that gripped the Soviet Union in those years. In 1962, in his dealings with Bloch, who had only just fled the GDR, Adorno tended to play down his own flirtation with an abstract left-wing radicalism before 1933.

In that connection, Adorno turned to the politically skeptical Kracauer, since it was through him that he had become acquainted with Bloch's work, and Kracauer had his own, somewhat checkered relationship with Bloch, the history of which was known to Adorno. As a freelance writer, Bloch had had some bitter struggles with Kracauer in his capacity as editor of the *Frankfurter Zeitung;* he demanded categorical public corrections, accused others of plagiarism, and in addition to increased payments he constantly called for solidarity when he himself was accused of plagiarism. By the same token, Kracauer was not slow in letting not just Bloch but also Horkheimer, Adorno, and Benjamin feel the force of his own newly acquired power. Moreover, confronted by the *Frankfurter Zeitung*'s political change of course at the end of the 1920s, all of them were reminded of their situation as powerless intellectuals forced to fight for economic survival. Horkheimer now became the most important point of reference for the émigré intellectuals. Together with Pollock and Weill he had started transferring the institute's funds abroad even before 1933. Adorno took over editorial duties for the now exiled *Zeitschrift für Sozialforschung*, which continued to appear in German until 1939. Kracauer and Benjamin now had to deal with their much younger friend if they wished to be published and also paid. Adorno, who was in competition with Leo Löwenthal and Herbert Marcuse for Horkheimer's ear, soon slipped into the attitudes of the responsible editor even when inviting his older friends to contribute work. When Bloch's *Erbschaft dieser Zeit* appeared, he felt that Adorno had lashed out at him as if he had been his "boss."[45] In the correspondence around 1934 we encounter the key phrase "inability to relate" *(Beziehungslosigkeit)*, a term Adorno also resorts to later on in his so-called "mini-morals" *(Rälchen)* or "Graeculus" notes to express his disappointment with Bloch's reaction to *Negative Dialectics*.[46] He recognizes belatedly that there can be no question of a "shared experience."[47]

After Bloch's move to the West in 1962, both men seem to have come to believe that their common interests were more powerful than those separating them. In letters to Bloch, Adorno was prepared to sacrifice Kracauer under the seal of secrecy: "Of course, this is strictly between us." Adorno gives a variety of reasons for the difference, which also surfaces in his characterization of Kracauer as "the curious realist."[48] He writes: "I mean to say that the greater the demands one makes on oneself and the more ambitiously one thinks of oneself in a certain sense in consequence, the less one may transfer such ideas to one's own empirical existence and even to one's actual achievement. In this respect, we probably react very similarly."[49] This comes very close to sleight of hand, since the "actual achievement" that would place Adorno on a par with Bloch, namely, a major philosophical work, did not yet exist. For that very reason, the Beethoven passage in *Spuren* may have spoken to him very personally: "Even the young music-maker Beethoven, who suddenly knew or asserted, that he was a genius like no other, was perpetrating a fraud when he considered himself to be Ludwig van Beethoven, whom he had not yet become. He used this effrontery, for which there was no basis, to become Beethoven, and in the same way nothing great would ever have come into being without the boldness, even the brazenness of this kind of anticipation."[50] Adorno sent Bloch the new reprint of the Kierkegaard book, whose importance he played down, crediting it with no more than "dreamlike anticipation,"[51] while feeling confident that the fulfillment of his own genius still lay before him. This fits with a remark Gretel Adorno is said to have made to the effect that she had had the opportunity of marrying two geniuses and that it "turned out" to be Adorno. On a factual level this means that she had preferred Adorno to Benjamin, but there is also the less obvious meaning that a genius is not a genius from birth on, but that some turn out to be geniuses: without chance and hard work, there are no geniuses.

Throughout Adorno's life the name Kracauer was linked with the question of identity and non-identity. In Adorno's view, following Benjamin's death, Bloch remained one of the few people still alive in 1962 who could misunderstand this question. Beneath the surface their disagreements continued to relate to Benjamin, to whom Adorno remained loyal. The friendship with Benjamin provided Adorno with a successor to Kracauer, a mentor who had remained a seeker. His ingenuity as a sociologist, his search for the new, had brought Kracauer to his pioneering treatment of the white-collar worker. His sociological approach opened up for him perspectives that diverged significantly from the traditional prospect for assimilationist Jews of adjusting to the liberal middle class. After the First World War, the only political options available seemed to be Zionism or else the working class. Lukács and Bloch had chosen the latter path, Scholem the former. Having chosen communism, Lukács found himself exposed to vitriolic attacks from the Comintern and forced into self-criticism. Such a fate seemed to act as a deterrent for Jewish intellectuals in the West, whereas at the time when Adorno first met him in 1923, Bloch was able to act the part of a red Bohemian with anarchist overtones, trawling through Berlin cafés and pubs with Benjamin. Academic philosophy, especially Hans Cornelius's neo-Kantianism, must have seemed shallow to Adorno when measured against Bloch's *tone*. Even Horkheimer, Cornelius's assistant, was unable to compete with Bloch's messianic Marxism. The younger students spoke somewhat contemptuously of Horkheimer's cautiously formulated "Swabian Marxism." Wiesengrund-Adorno must have become attached to Bloch, or so it would seem from the various signals between the two, signals that could not be matched by the mysteriously remote Benjamin. The correspondence is full of allusions to games of cowboys and Indians that functioned as a model in the process of leaving behind a non-bourgeois process of growing up, a process Benjamin had refused to understand in the case of the *Indian Joe Singspiel*. The verve with which Adorno leaps to the defense of Benjamin in the quarrel about *Erbschaft dieser Zeit* can be correlated with the intimacy he sought and also experienced with his *Indian Joe*, and even though he became disillusioned, it was an intimacy that he could not find with Benjamin.

We should remind ourselves: Bloch stands out as the one person among the old friends who was "musical."[52] Adorno had just returned to Germany from Vienna; a career as a professional musician no longer seemed open to him. As he had already told Kracauer, he had come up against a complete rejection by Arnold Schoenberg, "the Master." He was another person whom Adorno attempted to take by storm, but Schoenberg had repulsed his advances. He must have been deeply impressed by the superior manner in which another Schoenberg pupil treated "the Master." Eisler, who was only five years older than Wiesengrund when they met in Vienna, was ahead of him in other ways too. He was accepted by Schoenberg, even though Schoenberg's recognition often took the form of outbursts of rage at his talented but insolent pupil. Moreover, thanks to his well-known brother and sister,[53] he had a direct line to revolutionary practice, something that had remained a closed book to Adorno. In 1925 Eisler left Vienna for the bustle of the metropolis— namely, Berlin—while Adorno continued to commute between the rather provincial towns of Frankfurt and Vienna. From time to time they met up again in Berlin. Two men who until then had been little more than names to each other now became fast friends or jealous rivals, sometimes both at the same time. When they met up once again in Berlin, Bloch found that Adorno had become radicalized, and this lasted until their first meeting with Eisler in a Berlin coffeehouse in 1932. In conversation with Alfred Betz in 1973, Bloch recalled: "There were the three of us with Adorno. Adorno was quite pro-communist at the time."[54] But Adorno's first essay in the *Zeitschrift für Sozialforschung*, "On the Social Situation of Music," anticipates the dialectic of musical analysis and social criticism that he subsequently developed in his oeuvre. His starting point was his emancipation from his "older brother," Hanns. Hanns's self-confidence came close to being that of a confidence trickster, and it had enormously impressed Adorno when he first met him in 1925: "I am myself a genius!"

In 1932 he thinks his way through Eisler's

> proletarian communal music, for example, the choruses. . . . However, as soon as music retreats from the front of direct action, where it grows reflective and establishes itself as an artistic form, it is obvious that the structures produced cannot hold their own against progressive bourgeois production, but rather take the form of a questionable mixture of refuse from inwardly antiquated bourgeois stylistic forms, including even those of music for petit bourgeois male choir and from the remains of progressive "new" music. Through this mixture, the acuteness of the attack and the coherence of every technical formulation is lost.[55]

Adorno's criticism of political music follows its immanent logic: "In place of such intermediate solutions, it is conceivable that melodies of vulgar bourgeois music currently in circulation could be provided with new texts which would in this way bring about a dialectical 'refunctioning.'"[56] In his analysis of "the figure of the proletarian composer of the greatest logical consistency for the present,"[57] Adorno does not yet shrink from citing a remark of Brecht's, whom he does not identify as being wholly in the same camp as Eisler at this time. Following the popular successes of *The Threepenny Opera* and *Mahagonny*, he places Eisler on the same plane as "Kurt Weill as the major representative of musical surrealism."[58] His reflections on the possibilities of an artistic and political avant-garde lead Adorno to a critical theory of his own: "This music should not take instructions from the passive, one-sided position of the consciousness of the consumer—even if it be the consciousness of the proletariat; instead, it must intervene actively in consciousness through its own forms."[59] The rejection of aestheticizing left-wing radicalism had taken place even before Benjamin, who was just becoming politically radicalized, formulated his alternatives of the aestheticizing of politics or the politicizing of aesthetics. Evidently two men understood him right away: Horkheimer—who included Adorno's essay in the first volume of the *Zeitschrift für Sozialforschung* as a kind of programme—and Bloch.

Adorno's letter to Bloch in 1962 evokes the memory of how close they once were and how their paths then separated. This parting of the ways continued to preoccupy Adorno. The quarrel between them in 1933 was at bottom a quarrel about 1933 and what it meant for the future, only of course the participants could not really be aware of this. In connection with the idea of the child prodigy, Adorno mentions the name of Kracauer, who had been his mentor at the time when he first met Bloch. It was Kracauer, however, who had first issued a warning, in 1922, about Bloch as a false "prophet." And after his review of Bloch's *Thomas Münzer,* there was a serious falling out between the two, the first quarrel between one of Adorno's friends and Bloch. Bloch put an end to this feud in the midtwenties at a chance meeting with Kracauer in a café on the Place d'Odéon in Paris, when Bloch surprised him by sitting down with him and launching into a discussion which went on deep into the night, so that they ended up "close friends," as Bloch took pleasure in recalling in 1974.[60] This reconciliation had been facilitated by Kracauer's hostile review in the *Frankfurter Zeitung* of the new Bible translation by Martin Buber and Franz Rosenzweig. This review promoted the new literary editor of the *Frankfurter Zeitung* to the status of hero in the eyes of the radicalized secular Jewish intellectuals, who were in constant search of paid work in the Weimar newspaper landscape. Buber had become synonymous with a new wave of ostentatious Jewish religiosity which in the eyes of secular critics idealized the East European Jewry that Jewish German soldiers had seen for the first time on the eastern front in the First World War. In a trend that went beyond Zionism, a Jewish invention of tradition became conflated with a new existentialist religiosity inspired by Kierkegaard as filtered through Dostoyevsky.

With his Hasidic stories, Buber had enjoyed a resounding success among left-wing liberals with a bad conscience. Among the radical intellectuals, however, the rejection of Buber was general, from Benjamin to Bloch, from Kracauer to Adorno, and from Lukács to Horkheimer. Adorno criticized the new need for religion and its accompanying existentialism as primal forms of the "jargon of authenticity," a phrase he used to nail the Heideggerizing newspeak of post–National Socialist Germany. But before he could arrive at that point, he had to undergo a long educational process, one that filled the entire period of the Weimar era. The Jewish intellectuals just referred to could unite in their criticism of Kierkegaard. As early as his first encounter with Lukács in 1925, Wiesengrund was impressed by the fact that, as a revolutionary communist activist, Lukács had long since left such writings as *Soul and Form* and *The Theory of the Novel* behind him. In Seeheimerstrasse, Adorno had not discovered these books until after the First World War, when he had devoured them. By dedicating his study of Kierkegaard to Kracauer in 1932. Adorno sent a clear signal about how they had jointly worked the intellectual trends of the postwar period out of their system. For it had been Kracauer who had inspired Adorno to read Kierkegaard because he seemed appropriate to the attitude of "waiting." Bloch's derisive comments on Karl Jaspers, about which Adorno claims to have heard quite "early on,"[61] establish a common theme in their *éducation sentimentale,* the process of release from Expressionism and existentialism. But the Adorno of the 1960s seems to have been more ambivalent, since he was evidently willing to banish Bloch to the historical prison of his own educational journey when he assigned Bloch a place within Expressionism, which, unlike the existentialism of the sixties, could only be regarded as a shape of consciousness belonging to the past. What had particularly attracted Adorno to Bloch was the latter's self-confident proclamation of his own emancipatory path, one that felt the need neither to deny nor to invent its Jewishness. There was no sign in Bloch of the agonizing self-doubts and insecurities that were so evident in Kracauer or even Benjamin. Bloch's commitment to communism appeared to spring from the sovereign mastery of a political prophet who did not wear himself out in the trench warfare of the Comintern, unlike Lukács, whose self-criticisms following *History and Class Consciousness* aroused such doubts in Kracauer's mind and such anxieties in Benjamin's.

On the question of the comment on the "child prodigy," Adorno had felt stimulated by the visit of Kracauer,[62] whom Bloch too had met up with once again in Munich in 1962 after a long separation. Adorno was working on a publishing coup. Having reintroduced Benjamin to Germany in 1962, he now attempted to repeat the trick with Kracauer. In 1963 Suhrkamp published Kracauer's collection of essays, *Das Ornament der Masse* (The Mass Ornament). It appeared in the same format as the new edition of

Adorno's *Kierkegaard: Konstruktion des Ästhetischen* (Kierkegaard: Construction of the Aesthetic). As early as 1959, with its publication of Bloch's *Spuren*, Suhrkamp had started to disinter the treasures of the German emigration. Although the publisher sought to make its books available cheaply, these books did not sell well until the protest movement began to get under way starting in 1967. Kracauer's later best-seller *From Caligari to Hitler* appeared with Rowohlt in 1958, minus the antifascist thrust of the first American edition of 1947. Kracauer's splendid study of white-collar workers, *The Salaried Masses*, which had appeared in the *Frankfurter Zeitung* in 1930, was reissued in 1959 by Elisabeth Noelle-Neumann in her Allensbach Verlag für Demoskopie, before the paperback edition in 1971 became one of the representative books to achieve a mass circulation as part of the so-called Suhrkamp culture. The publication history of Kracauer's texts sheds light on the palimpsest-like nature of historical memory after 1945, when memory can be said to have taken on features specific to German history and society. As we can see from his letter to Bloch, Adorno's growing influence in West Germany was accompanied by his desire to show the past in its true light but at the same time to prevent an excess of memory from obscuring people's view of the future: "I mean to say that the greater the demands one makes on oneself and the more ambitiously one thinks of oneself in a certain sense in consequence, the less one may transfer such ideas to one's own empirical existence and even to one's actual achievement. In this respect, we probably react very similarly."[63]

What we can hear speaking here in Adorno in 1962 is the self-confidence of an intellectual who has been deprived too long of recognition, but who now begins to taste success. The difficult financial position of freelance writers, particularly those who had been forced into it by the conditions obtaining for would-be academics toward the end of the Weimar Republic, had prevented Wiesengrund-Adorno from prospering, and his emigration meant that he had been forgotten in Germany. What Adorno himself refers to in his German writings as his "adjustment" or "adaptation" to the American university system was something he had refused to accommodate himself to, although he was not able or willing to keep out of it entirely. With Bloch and Kracauer he had two extreme contrasting models before him whom he was beginning to leave behind. To Kracauer, Adorno emphasized that in Germany he could now say what he wanted to say, and by this he meant that he could speak as artistically as only he knew how. Although his musically trained voice enabled him to speak English fairly idiomatically, he always felt restricted in what he could say in a foreign language. The somewhat backward nature of German seemed to Adorno to reflect "a special elective affinity with philosophy and particularly with its speculative element that in the West is so easily suspected of being dangerously unclear, and by no means completely without justification."[64] Bloch, who had already developed his own language, his own style, in the interwar period, delivered what amount to an apologia in emigration in the shape of his lecture "Destroyed Language, Destroyed Culture" ("Zerstörte Sprache, Zerstörte Kultur"). In this he mounted a defense of his private behavior, including his complete dependence on his wife, Karola, and his friends, which enabled him to devote eleven years of his life to working on his two great books, *The Principle of Hope (Das Prinzip Hoffnung)* and *Natural Law and Human Dignity (Naturrecht und menschliche Würde)*. In contrast, Adorno had spent four years in a vain attempt to wangle his way into obtaining a Ph.D. in the English university system before managing to become at least partly integrated into the American social sciences. He had scarcely any time for his own work alongside *Dialectic of Enlightenment* and *The Authoritarian Personality*. He returned to Europe with *The Philosophy of Modern Music* and *Minima Moralia* in his luggage. His "main task," he confessed to Bloch, while at the same time proudly announcing it, still lay before him in 1962. But, approaching sixty, he felt under increasing pressure to "bring all his sheep into the fold," as he liked to put it, using the robust craftsman's way of talking which he had learned from Berg.

The position with Kracauer was different. Fourteen years older than Adorno, he spoke in the early sixties of a "race against time," an expression that Adorno repeated in a letter to Kracauer's widow in 1967.[65] But as Adorno explained to Ernst Bloch among others, what he expected from himself was different from what he hoped for from Kracauer. Parallel to his strategy of relegating Bloch to Expressionism, he also thought of Kracauer's role as something that belonged to the past. He makes this clear in "The Curious Realist." But the public statement does not reveal the whole story, any more than it does with Bloch. Only by consulting the archive can the true story be reconstructed. Adorno's dealings with Kracauer are evidence of a biographical continuity, more so even than with Bloch, and despite, or rather because of, all their ups and downs. Originally Adorno had written "The Curious Realist" as a radio talk in honor of Kracauer's seventy-fifth birthday. Kracauer panicked at the idea, however, and objected to the revelation of the particulars of his life story. He insisted that the account of his writings should be so utterly timeless that it would not be possible to calculate his true age. A personal foible? The unprepared reader of the essay, which appeared in volume three of *Notes to Literature* in 1965, will be disconcerted by the tone in which Adorno speaks of his older friend. The truth is that it was as writers that Adorno and Kracauer grew apart from each other rather than as individuals. In the "child prodigy" letter to Bloch, Adorno had revealed as early as 1962 that "unfortunately, I can scarcely discuss such matters with Friedel anymore, not only because he has donned armor, as if he were a combination of Narcissus and Young Siegfried, but also because he, mindful of the lime leaf, praises my own stuff to the skies a priori, so that I can no longer trust myself to say anything about his."[66] Adorno had to abandon his reticence in order to give the lecture without hinting at the underlying reason for the occasion. After Kracauer's death in 1966, although it provoked Kracauer's widow into protesting on behalf of her late husband, Adorno explained the situation: "I have never known anyone who was so reluctant to accommodate himself to the fact of aging as Siegfried Kracauer. For someone who had suffered from so many handicaps and who was so defenseless in the face of the brutality of life, his powers of resistance gave him a strength that came close to heroism; his will to live grew with every threat. Ultimately, it assumed almost mythical qualities. These even found expression in his face. Extraterritorial, as if from the Far East, it acquired something of a stony aspect."[67]

Extraterritoriality: a concept, an idea, a wished-for dream. The word cannot disavow its affinity with the concept of utopia, of something that exists but possesses no rightful place. Among those fleeing from Germany, it played a precisely defined role. Walter Benjamin used the term *dépaysé* to Gretel Adorno to describe Ernst Bloch's situation at the end of the thirties. On 14 December 1939 Benjamin wrote to "Felizitas," his pet name for Gretel, who had in the meantime married Adorno in England, about their anxieties over "notre ami Ernst," who seemed to him to be "un peu dépaysé," and "non seulement sur la terre mais aussi dans l'histoire mondiale."[68] Kracauer had himself chosen extraterritoriality as an ideal, and it had already put in an appearance in *Ginster*, which like gorse, the plant from which its hero takes his name, is nowhere at home. If we read the correspondence between Kracauer and Adorno, the concept as applied by Kracauer to himself becomes a lot clearer. Adorno had been rather unnerved by Kracauer's unwillingness to have his age mentioned, but two years later he had found words for the deceased man that the latter would not have liked to hear: "Once he had freed himself from his role models and energetically followed his own experience, everything he wrote revolved around selfhood: the indissoluble, the particular, the blind spot of thought; everything revolved, we might say, around that which thought offends against merely by being thought."[69] This opaque "I," the ultimate ground of self-preservation, of Spinoza's *suum esse conservare*,[70] had asserted itself as an intellectual in a foreign land in defiance of every prognosis, even though he was no longer able to speak German without a stutter. His experience, which Adorno refers to in his obituary, was simply different from Adorno's own. Löwenthal in his memoirs followed the line taken by Adorno in *Notes to Literature* and attempted to deduce the different approach to experience from the different class origins of the two men. From the standpoint of their Jewish backgrounds, Löwenthal was closer to Kracauer than to his friend Teddie. Nevertheless, Löwenthal overemphasized the poverty of Kracauer's origins while magnifying the affluence of Adorno's. Adorno never managed to shake off the image of being free from immediate material needs, partly through his own fault. To his annoyance, Horkheimer gave this reason as the explanation for leaving him behind in Germany in 1933. But after that he freely gave Adorno the assurance in writing that he was to be a member of the institute. Adorno tried without delay to use his influence with the institute for the benefit of his old mentor. But despite being in financial straits, Kracauer persisted in refusing to work for the institute or even for the *Zeitschrift* during his exile in France. The principle of extraterritoriality remained valid even in human relations.

Attempts to reintroduce the name of Kracauer in Germany after 1945 were also fraught with difficulty, and this is easy to understand when we recall their disagreements during the period in exile. He and Adorno had their first experience of politics at a time when Adorno was making frequent visits to Berlin to see Gretel, and Kracauer had finally succeeded after bitter power struggles in obtaining an appointment as a writer for the *Frankfurter Zeitung*. In their later correspondence Kracauer insisted that he had become politically active even earlier, specifically in Frankfurt before the Wall Street crash. Adorno took note of this correction. Adorno does not just look at Kracauer in the light of his own experience, which was also not without its blind spots. Kracauer proclaimed his skepticism about all left-wing radical temptations, which in Adorno's eyes amounted to a form of resignation.[71] Just as Kracauer had rejected what he regarded as Bloch's false prophecy from the outset, so too did he have his doubts about Brecht's communism: "He came into conflict with Brecht and made his joke about the Augsburg confusion and when Brecht followed his *Yea-sayer* with the *Nay-sayer,* he declared that he, Kracauer, was thinking of writing the *Maybe-sayer.*"[72] But then in retrospect, Adorno's argument takes a surprising turn. He discerns in Kracauer a peculiar combination of success and a "head-in-the-sand policy": "There was always an element of cunning in Kracauer's strategy of adjustment, a will to deal with the hostile and the powerful by outdoing it in his own mind and thereby detaching himself from it even while compulsively identifying with it."[73] In emigration the two men had grown apart. There had already been irritations enough. Philosophically, Kracauer had refused to take the step from Kant to Hegel, the step from epistemology to the philosophy of history. He remained a man of the Enlightenment who positioned himself *after* German Idealism, and thus extraterritorially even in philosophical terms. In the "anti-systematic tendency in his thinking" he was of one mind with Bloch, Benjamin, and also Adorno, but they differed individually in their methods of digesting their experience. It is hard to define precisely what they had in common, or to find a name summing up the shadow that lurks behind their writings. Adorno spared no effort to define what he regarded as the central experience of history and of his life: the failure of emancipation. Kracauer responded to this with the subterfuge of adaptation, Adorno with the theoretical concept of non-identity, which in practice meant a life lived in contradiction: "There is no right life in the wrong one."[74]

Only by reflecting on the life significance of this statement can we plumb its meaning. It is more than an individual idiosyncrasy. Indeed, it is one of Adorno's most frequently cited statements, and is comparable to the one about "writing poetry after Auschwitz" in the sense that it is mostly misquoted and seldom understood. The title of the aphorism from which it is taken, "Refuge for the Homeless" in *Minima Moralia,* communicates with Kracauer's diagnosis fifteen years previously of the white-collar worker as "spiritually homeless."[75] It is mainly on second reading that we notice that its true concern is with dwelling; what lay behind it was the furnishing of the Adornos' house in California. Every house move triggers the basic elements of the bourgeois idyll—feeling at home, setting up home, establishing oneself. But amidst all this the émigré is made to feel his extraterritoriality, the powerlessness of the individual when confronted by the overall social process. This general social statement acquires its particular flavor, however, only when it is applied to the social history of the nineteenth and twentieth centuries and the lives of the émigré intellectuals. Looked at in the mirror of Adorno's essay on Kracauer, "The Curious Realist," which takes all its quotations from the study on the white-collar workers *(The Salaried Masses),* above all from the section that Kracauer had also titled "Refuge for the Homeless," the history of dwelling turns out to be a history of social mobility. To be enclosed in one's own private dwelling implies exclusion from society, the failure of emancipation. At first sight, the idea of making the world outside inhabitable through labor seems to be the bourgeois project par excellence. But it is the reflection on the life indoors, the interior, the prison of private life that inspired the social criticism of Benjamin, Kracauer, and Adorno himself, most obviously in the Kierkegaard book.

The concrete difference can be seen in a comparison between the houses in Seeheimerstrasse in Oberrad, in which Teddie studied Kant and Bloch under Kracauer's supervision and to the delight of Oscar Wiesengrund, and Sternstrasse in Frankfurt Nordend, in which Adolf Kracauer, a traveling salesman, returned sporadically to his wife, Rosette, and her sister Hedwig, neither of whom survived Theresienstadt in later years. The half-presentiment, half-certainty that those who remained behind had been murdered determines the dramatic tone of this aphorism from the year 1944; the relation between rationalized architecture and concentration camps appears to be a boundless exaggeration to the reader who takes what he is reading literally. In Los Angeles, Adorno recalls "the traditional residences we grew up in,"[76] the old houses of the Frankfurt burghers, which included on the periphery his parents' house in Seeheimerstrasse as well as Schöne Aussicht, belonging to his paternal grandparents. The exclusion from the bourgeoisie, the extreme petty-bourgeois ambience from which Kracauer had to escape, evidently disconcerted Adorno when he first met Kracauer's mother and aunt—a "childhood trauma of problematic membership" that had been unknown to him hitherto.[77] Unknown? Or did he in fact have a feeling of alienness that he resisted or denied? Adorno's remark of 1965 that anti-Semitism "was quite unusual in the commercial city of Frankfurt"[78] sounds almost apologetic, although apart from that comment the essay on Kracauer contains almost nothing that does not remind us of Auschwitz. It is as if by describing Kracauer's childhood in these terms Adorno regresses to the world of his paternal home, in which anti-Semitism was regarded as an obsolete phenomenon, a matter only of farmers living in the countryside—an anti-Semitism of concern only to old-fashioned Jews, most of whom came from Eastern Europe. But the simplistic equations of the liberal German Jews from the bourgeois nineteenth century can no longer be repeated. Horkheimer's bitter polemic "The Jews and Europe" ("Die Juden und Europa") of 1939 had been aimed at the illusions of liberal Jewry. This was the essay that Adorno's students quarried for trenchant quotations just a few years after the Kracauer essay. But the context from which they were taken remained almost as unknown to the politicized students as they were to the anonymous radio audience of the Kracauer essay, to whom Adorno had drip-fed the memory of inextinguishable mass atrocities. Posthumously the Kracauer essay sheds further light on *Minima Moralia*. We can thus glimpse the hidden side of a permanent dialogue, a subterranean conversation in *Minima Moralia*. On the surface we find fragmentary insights addressed to Horkheimer, to whom the book was dedicated, while beneath them we find the interrupted threads of discussions taking place among a generation of exiled intellectuals to whose plight Adorno devotes a lengthy section of his radio talk on Kracauer. Yet Adorno refuses to stick the label "Jewish" on this experience. At the time the technique of ethnic labeling did not yet exist in Germany as it did in America; the provincial West German public sphere still operated with the far more primitive labels of philo-Semitism and anti-Semitism.

Adorno strove to prevent Kracauer's work from being pigeonholed by anti-Semites by emphasizing the individual aspects of his writing, which nevertheless had something reactive about it. Kracauer himself had tried to use his concept of extraterritoriality to deflect the labels of "Jew," "émigré," and "intellectual." Anyone who consults the folder that Kracauer himself had labeled "Letters on Extraterritoriality" (*Briefe zur Extraterritorialität*) in the Marbach Literaturarchiv will feel overcome by the uncanny feeling of a message from another planet. The motif which Adorno had borrowed from Benjamin that hope has been given to us only for the sake of those without hope seems to be fulfilled when we read these texts. Kracauer had given to his film project the English subtitle "Redemption of Physical Reality"; Adorno noted, "The true translation of that into German would be "Die Rettung der physischen Realität.""[79] His attempts to put this into practice, the enormous efforts involved in self-preservation, did not suffice in the confrontation with world history. His individual technique of preserving himself by taking over anything hostile to him with an exaggerated enthusiasm would not have survived National Socialism. Nevertheless, it earned him a surprising success in the United States. At the last moment he succeeded in escaping to America, with the assistance of the institute, and especially the energetic intervention of Löwenthal and Adorno. Unlike Bloch, he spared no effort to learn English, and despite a speech defect he was able to hold his own in American university life. The place in which the extraterritorial Kracauer was able to establish himself was New York, for which he spoke up against Adorno's decision to return home, just as he defended his switch to the English language. In his final, unfinished story, to which he gave the English title "History: The Last Things before the Last," extraterritoriality is given a prominent place in which it is interpreted as the experience of the stranger. He thereby risks falling into the trap against which Adorno had frequently warned him, namely, that the obstinate pursuit of individual experience would correspond precisely to the conformist attitude of society as a whole. In this instance individual experience is dissipated in the general sociological category of the "stranger."

Both Kracauer and Adorno had observed this process in Simmel, who, together with Scheler, had introduced Kracauer to sociology in the first place. In his "formal *Sociology*," his pioneering work which together with Max Weber's study on Protestantism established the discipline in Germany, Simmel had inserted an "Excursus on the Stranger" that converted the complex history of Jewish emancipation in Germany into the figure of the stranger. This complex then migrated into American sociology with the German-speaking exiles and American students in Europe and became famous under the title "The Stranger." Even Paul Lazarsfeld, Adorno's polar opposite, who in the early fifties gave Kracauer work in his Bureau of Applied Social Sciences, thought of himself as being in this tradition. In America the Stranger turned into the "Marginal Man," a man who lived in two different cultures simultaneously, was not properly integrated into either, and was thus in a privileged position that enabled him to judge impartially the society in which he found himself. This is as far as Kracauer's ideas on extraterritoriality extend in his attempt to convert a highly individual experience into a positive category. Adorno and Kracauer had earlier quarreled about the concluding chapter of *Ginster* on its republication, "a work that occupies the no-man's-land between novel and biography."[80] As he told his reviewer Wolfgang Weyrauch, Kracauer finally agreed "with a heavy heart"[81] to publish the book without the final chapter because Adorno had detected elements of accommodation in it—a flirtation with the positive that no one could see more clearly and criticize more scathingly than he. What is at stake in their correspondence, which regrettably has not been published in full, is a no-man's-land of experience that Kracauer too clings to as a common feature, as opposed to Bloch's utopianism. Adorno emphasizes this affinity as a "predilection for lower-order things, things excluded by higher culture—something on which Kracauer and Ernst Bloch were in agreement."[82] It was in fact this quality in both men that attracted Adorno, since it enabled them to strike narrative sparks from their experience even though, according to *Theory of the Novel,* these were supposed to have been extinguished. What Adorno acquired from Kracauer was an inkling of whatever it was that stubbornly eluded the concept and even the word. Rarely has anyone expressed with such sensitivity what it was that a stammerer like Kracauer was able to communicate: "Later . . . this moment of carefulness protected Kracauer from journalism. It was hard for him to get rid of the circuitousness that always had to find everything for itself, even what was familiar, as though it were freshly discovered."[83]

It was perhaps the very challenge to discover anew what was already known that suggested to Kracauer at the key point of extraterritoriality the image of the palimpsest as the appropriate way of representing life: "Sometimes life itself produces such palimpsests. I have in mind the exile who is driven from his home as an adult or who has left it voluntarily."[84] The transition from experience to representation is fluid, not sharp. Kracauer himself wished to disappear behind his novel *Ginster.* He even succeeded in having the novel published without the author's name, merely with the statement "Written by himself." In contrast, Adorno stepped onto the public stage in the early sixties and would have liked to be able to help his old mentor enjoy some publicity as well. What might seem to be quite natural, that is, the gratification of an author's narcissism after a long drought, touched the decisive motive forces of the productive individual and called them into question. Neither man could conceal this from the other or even from himself. They knew each other too well for that:

> The more I get a taste of so-called success, the more thoroughly I become aware
> of the nullity of one's own existence. For that existence then becomes a func-
> tion of success. I hope that this impulse does not come from me but that it lies
> in the relation to reality, and of course the self is not unaffected by that; unlike
> everything it is involved with, the self is a mere abstraction. "The Adorno" who
> is the object of all that activity is actually already a dead man. What it feels like

during one's lifetime is already a foretaste of the extent to which one is nothing even as a living subject. This is proclaimed by the undiminished feeling of the dubiousness of everything upon which success is built.[85]

Success was also the issue in the hardest-fought conflict between Adorno and Kracauer. This concerned the life of Offenbach which Kracauer wrote in exile in Paris and which both Bloch and Adorno deemed impossible: a "musical biography without music."[86] The book was written in a desperate attempt to keep his head above water at a time when Kracauer was in dire financial straits. His new novel, *Georg,* which followed his much-praised *Ginster,* proved to be completely unsaleable, despite a recommendation from Thomas Mann. Kracauer joined the by no means exclusive ranks of those who had absolutely no financial resources at all. He reported this to Benjamin, who had himself been teetering on the economic brink for some time, even before 1933, and he had just quarreled with Bloch about *Erbschaft dieser Zeit,* reproaching him with having repudiated their common position. Kracauer saw these conflicts as the reflection of individual differences rather than political or theoretical disagreements. In the quarrel about *Erbschaft dieser Zeit,* when the young Wiesengrund-Adorno sprang to Benjamin's defense, Kracauer spoke out on behalf of the "boyish rebellion" against Benjamin's hypersensitivities, which were themselves reinforced by the complete lack of publishing opportunities.[87] In the exile period, journals were turned into political forums. Anyone who declined to support either the Communist Party or the Popular Front found it almost impossible to publish anything. Such left-wing intellectuals did find an outlet in the *Zeitschrift für Sozialforschung,* but there it was necessary to submit to Horkheimer's stringent editorial demands. The simplest solution was to write for the review section, which was managed by Leo Löwenthal, and where contributions were paid for. The first years in particular reflect the part played by the need to assist the refugees in the journal. There was no question of a uniform political line or a common theoretical approach. Adorno wanted to exploit Horkheimer's dissatisfaction with the quality of the contributions to give greater scope for Benjamin, but Benjamin was also expected to provide substantial essays, and all this made excessive demands on his time. There was general agreement on the importance of employing Kracauer. Yet Kracauer not only played hard to get; he also felt that he was not being treated with the respect due to someone who had previously been the editor of the *Frankfurter Zeitung.* With

Jacques Offenbach and the Paris of His Time, he hoped to make himself independent, to write a sort of best-seller, something all the exile writers dreamed of. The book was published in 1937 by Allert de Lange in Amsterdam, and according to their financial statement seventy-five copies were sold in 1938.

Against this material backdrop the quarrel between Adorno and Kracauer seems bizarre, but it caused a breach in their friendship that was destined never to be healed. Without this conflict the strangely tormented tone of "The Curious Realist" of 1964 cannot be understood. This was a palimpsest written by Adorno himself. The different layers of the ultimate text can be revealed by the letters, diaries, and "Rälchen" (mini-morals), as he termed the additional entries to *Minima Moralia* which he wrote after returning to Germany but which were not published in his lifetime. By the beginning of 1937, agreement had been reached with Horkheimer to invite Kracauer to participate in an international study of propaganda, and at the same time Adorno wanted him to contribute a section on architecture for an ambitious joint project, "Art and Consumption in the Monopoly Phase."[88] This was to bring together everyone of note from Benjamin to Bloch. To Adorno's dismay, however, although the project was being financed by the institute, Kracauer entered into negotiations with other institutions about additional publication possibilities. Adorno feared that for Kracauer in his struggle to survive, the institute was just one card in the deck, while Adorno relied on it to the exclusion of all else. He could soon see the makings of a conflict, since he regarded the institute as a site of supra-individual theory production, something to which Kracauer was reluctant to commit himself. When the Offenbach book appeared, Adorno felt offended in his sense of solidarity, since he did not wish to be seen as "belonging objectively in such company."[89] Among the émigrés an uncompromising intellectual stance had the function of compensating for political powerlessness. Adorno felt able to rely on Benjamin even though the latter's economic plight was similar to Kracauer's: "With this book Kracauer has essentially resigned himself. He has composed a text that only a few years ago would have found its most ruthless critic in the author himself. And after a ten-year delay, he has finally joined the hosts of those biographers who once rode out under the banner of the blessed Ludwig and found their valiant champions in Marcuse, E. A. Rheinhardt and Frischauer."[90]

Benjamin here formulates for Adorno what he painfully missed in

Krenek and Bloch and believed he had found in Horkheimer—solidarity: "The position which Kracauer has abandoned was not his alone, but was one which we all shared. That is the important thing here."[91] All these quarrels look to us now like the products of intellectual vanity, but they are all concerned with an imagined "we," an imagined community, without which the critical theory of society would have been inconceivable. Horkheimer spoke of a mode of thought that went beyond the individual.[92] Kracauer rejected this, we might almost say, instinctively. As early as 1929 he had written programmatically at the end of *The Salaried Masses*, "Man, who faces death alone, does not find his place in a collective that would like to transcend itself for some final purpose."[93] Exile brought a confrontation with death much closer. Benjamin feared "something worse than death"[94] and took his own life. Bloch attempted to sustain a fictitious "we"; in his letters he included now Kracauer, now Benjamin, and now Adorno in that category—an intellectual avant-garde alongside the political one. In the famous Expressionism debate, even in his exile in Prague, he did not shy away from conflict with other intellectuals associated with the Communist Party, but wanted on principle to keep his distance from formal and informal groupings alike. Adorno circles around this attitude with Kracauer's ironic description of himself as belonging to the "derrière-garde of the avant-garde,"[95] or Brecht's paradoxical verse, "Here you have someone on whom you can't rely."[96] Bloch regularly overestimated Kracauer's interest in a materialist critique of society. Adorno undoubtedly had a surer grasp of Kracauer's motives when he described Kracauer's "social criticism" as one that had come into being "almost against his will."[97] Bloch's appeals to Kracauer sound abstract. In his letters during the 1930s he provocatively positioned him as being close to the cultural politics of social democracy so as to talk him into conflating materialism, Marxism, communism, and Stalin's Russia, a conflation that, in view of the Moscow trials, he himself was beginning to accept only against his better judgment. As late as 1937 we can see an almost fraternal intimacy in the letters between Adorno and Bloch. Adorno was overcome with astonishment when he read the issue of the *Weltbühne* in which Bloch started to publish his apologia for the Moscow trials. In November 1937 he told Benjamin about Bloch's attack on Leopold Schwarzschild's Paris journal *Das neue Tagebuch*, an attack which initiated a series of articles by Bloch that led Benjamin to define his position as being not just outside Germany but outside world history. Adorno found the situation full of paradoxes. It involved the adaptation to a market that could scarcely be thought lucrative for German-language products, as had been illustrated by the fate of Kracauer's book on Offenbach; or again, it meant the pressure to conform politically to parties one had nothing in common with apart from a hatred of National Socialism. Adorno even found himself recommending America to a man as stubbornly European as Benjamin: "It might be a source of some ironic consolation to us that the post we have to defend will prove a lost one everywhere and under all circumstances."[98] Bloch, in contrast, believed in "the next world of communist atheists."[99] Despite being in dire straits materially, however, he escaped not to Russia but via Prague to the United States. His attitude in the 1930s remained hotly debated well into the 1970s. Quite old by that time, he cut a poor figure in these debates. He could scarcely argue that he was ignorant of conditions in the Soviet Union. As more and more letters have come to light, it becomes ever clearer that his defense of Moscow was the result of political calculation. The legend that after his arrival in the United States, the institute under Horkheimer's leadership would "if need be . . . have looked on with a cold smile if we had starved to death" was one that he served up warmed over after the deaths of Adorno and Horkheimer, just as he revived the pun on Adorno's *Jargon of Authenticity,* the "jargon of inauthenticity," which had so annoyed Adorno in earlier years. By making that pun in 1968, Bloch was as good as dead in Adorno's eyes: "Bloch's suicide: he has appropriated the wisecrack of Ludwig Marcuse. What *fraternité.*"[100]

This "Graeculus" notes of 1968 encapsulate the experience of the entire emigration. Adorno's fury is directed not just at that windbag the loquacious Ludwig Marcuse—a man who was constantly confused with Herbert Marcuse until well into the 1960s. This undiscriminating journalist had had the nerve to turn the specific experiences of the twentieth century into gossipy memoirs, *Mein zwanzigstes Jahrhundert* (My Twentieth Century), consisting chiefly of namedropping. But Adorno did not take this Marcuse seriously; his fury was reserved for his former friend Ernst Bloch, who had once appealed to Adorno's sense of solidarity in order to obtain personal benefits. Adorno's diaries around Christmas 1968 are full of emotional death sentences against Bloch: "Coldness. Inability to relate. Buber without the beard."[101] As far back as 1937 Adorno had told Horkheimer of his ambivalent feelings about Bloch, for instance, in a letter dated 22 September: "I keep changing my mind: on the one hand, I have the very greatest sympathy for Ernst, and believe that everything he writes is worth thinking through; on the other hand, it will always be very difficult for us to agree with him, although what I have in mind is not so much his utopianism or his adherence to the party line, but simply *a certain irresponsibility in his style of philosophical improvisation.*"[102]

On 19 January 1938 these reservations moved Adorno to pass a negative judgment on a lengthy manuscript that Bloch had been asked to submit with Horkheimer's approval. The book, with the title *Das Materialismusproblem, seine Geschichte und Substanz* (The Problem of Materialism, Its History and Substance), did not finally appear until 1972: "I have begun reading Bloch's manuscript and darkness has fallen everywhere around us. I see scarcely any possibility of our publishing it. But since I would not like to take the sole responsibility for rejecting a man of Bloch's calibre, a man moreover who is very close to us, I would like to prepare you gently for my request that you too should look this monster in the eyes."[103]

The word "monster" refers here to the length of the manuscript and also to Bloch's manner of writing—the narrative style of his thought: "It must arouse his enduring resentment whenever he comes across an idea that he cannot dismiss as a scholastic concept."[104] This bitter note from the posthumous papers dated 1968 has a further note appended to it: "Windbag mannerisms. Regression to optimism and pessimism."[105] And in fact the course of world history does not appear to achieve contact with utopia as an objective possibility; before one knows it, it has been transformed into a certainty despite everything, a slogan-like knowledge that has itself assumed an extraterritorial dimension. Benjamin noticed this early on and found fault with it in *Erbschaft dieser Zeit.* Bloch must have been aware of this when he read the edition of Benjamin's letters that Scholem and Adorno published in 1966. Adorno ascribes Bloch's need for revenge to his earlier quarrel with Benjamin: "Revenge because of Benjamin—taken out on me." Adorno imputes to Bloch "a messianic *arrogance:* the voice of the narrator when there is nothing more to be narrated. This is what enables him to fit in: a Buber without a beard. Objective playacting. Bloch is the greatest living Bloch-actor—already dead, but has not yet realized it."[106] What Adorno expresses here is the opposite of utopia, namely, black melancholy. In this respect he is at one with Benjamin and the motif from the latter's essay on Goethe's *Elective Affinities,* "Only for the sake of those without hope have we been given hope," which he made so much his own that he told Horkheimer at the beginning of their friendship that it was the central motif of his thought.

Even though Benjamin had written his annihilating critique of *Erbschaft dieser Zeit* in a letter to Alfred Cohn, he did not feel at all hostile toward Bloch. While Bloch was making his way from Menaggio to Vienna and from there to Prague, Benjamin longed for Bloch to pay him a visit in Paris even though he did not feel comfortable with Bloch's closeness to the Russian Communist Party and Comintern politics. He was accustomed to far worse from Brecht, whom he visited in Denmark for the second time in the summer of 1938. In a letter of 20 July he wrote to Gretel, his Felizitas, that Brecht "naturally" recognized that "the [party's] theoretical line was a catastrophe for everything we have been trying to achieve for the last twenty years."[107] In the same letter he sent greetings to Bloch in New York. Adorno announced these developments to Horkheimer on 8 August with the words: "Ernst Bloch has arrived in America. Benjamin writes that in the meantime Brecht too seems to have discovered a hair in his soup— though not to the point where he pushes the plate away."[108] Benjamin had evidently not lost hope; his reference to "we" suggests he still included Brecht and Bloch. Despite Bloch's apologias for the Moscow trials, Horkheimer still made advances to him to collaborate at the institute and the *Zeitschrift,* something that Bloch, who was still in Prague, took very much as his due. Fully aware that it was something of an imposition, Bloch asked Horkheimer to provide the papers and guarantees that he needed for entry into the United States. Bloch never abandoned the fantasy that what he carelessly called the "Institut für Sozialwissenschaft" (Institute for Social Science) was an organization for him to exploit. He imagined that it was backed by lots of money, much as Eisler did, as he confided to Hans Bunge later on in *Fragen Sie mehr über Brecht.* Just after Adorno arrived in New York in 1938, Bloch began to exert moral pressure on him to help him obtain a position at the institute. When this turned out to be impossible because of the economic climate and also because there were political reservations, he expected help out of the pockets of people such as Horkheimer, Pollock, and Löwenthal, whom he assumed to be affluent.

Adorno concluded from this that he should do something publicly to assist Bloch, and so in 1942 he called for a "broader solidarity" on the part of the German émigrés "in order to help Bloch out of his poverty."[109] Bloch had expected private assistance from his good friend Teddie, whom he referred to in correspondence with his student Joachim Schumacher as "the well-to-do Wiesengrund."[110] He was now furious at being publicly represented as a victim in need of charity. He broke off all contact with Adorno even though he had earlier written to him, "I have been sacked from my job as a dishwasher because I couldn't work fast enough."[111] Now, he went on, he was working as a paper packer. What Adorno made of this was: "He now has no time for writing. His relation to paper has finally become realistic. He packs it in bundles, eight hours a day, standing in a dark hole. He has escaped the concentration camp, but this will knock some sense into him."[112] Adorno dressed up his own anger at being forced to adapt to American circumstances with the words: "Anyone who speaks his own language passionately is unable to speak a foreign one. No one understands him anymore."[113] Bloch turned out to be a suitable candidate for Adorno's empathy; the later accusation of an "inability to form relationships" and "playacting" has its roots here, but more particularly in Bloch's personality. "Bloch really has . . . a poor intelligible character" was Adorno's damning judgment in 1968.[114]

By 1968 the disagreements focused on posterity. Adorno imputed to Bloch the neglect of a minimal morality: "His archaic features [are] in league with his interests in the market."[115] Again and again Adorno tried to come to terms with the fact that, as the older "red brother," Bloch refused to acknowledge that Adorno had forgiven him for his Communist Party apologias. But in 1968 Adorno arrived at a summary of their respective life stories, above all because the confrontation with his own life story had become unavoidable. Interested students had begun to ask questions about the lives of their teachers before 1933 and their writings during the period of emigration. Some of the writings that were still locked up in the poison cupboards of the educational institutions in the fifties, and began to circulate in pirated copies in the sixties, now started to trickle onto the market—mainly with prefaces provided by their authors, who had survived National Socialism and Stalinism and who hoped in vain that these prefaces would serve as lightning rods. The new generation's lack of historical experience could not be made good by these traditional Enlightenment methods, and even less with the aid of the "forbearance" for which Brecht pleaded in one of his most beautiful exile poems, "To Those Who Come after Us."[116] As the publisher of Benjamin's writings since the mid-sixties, Adorno had found himself under attack by young communist sympathizers, often very virulently. That alone can explain the following note: "What is the source of this coldness in Bloch? . . . It is as if he had paid for an actual experience with an incapacity for experience. This links him with the generation he is attempting to ingratiate himself with and which attempts to exploit him with the same incapacity for human relationships."[117] What "actual experience" is referred to here and what "incapacity" for which "experience?" Adorno's review of Bloch's *Traces* contains an obscure passage that looks like a key to interpretation: "Bloch's utopia settles into the empty space between the latter and what merely exists. Perhaps what he aims at, an experience that has not yet been honoured by experience, can be conceived only in an extreme form."[118] By "the latter" he means "the narrator's victorious tone,"[119] which fits in well with the backhanded compliment that Bloch "is the only example of a philosopher worthy of the name who has actually done no *thinking*."[120]

Adorno's essay of 1960 on the reissuing of *Traces* may appear to be of marginal importance for his work as a whole, but there is more at stake than an individual life, more than "the empirical person" of whom he speaks in his "prodigy letter" to Bloch on 27 July 1962. In fact, it is his entire output that is at issue. Even the most unassuming works written after his return to Europe conform to his theoretical ideal as he had formulated it in *Minima Moralia*: "In a philosophical text all the propositions ought to be equally close to the centre,"[121] a statement he reiterated in his "Portrait of Walter Benjamin" and one that caught Thomas Mann's eye. But the work is more than a matter of accumulated experience; it was the burden of Adorno's criticism of Kracauer that he played experience off against theory: "The conflict between experience and theory cannot be conclusively decided in favour of one side or the other but is truly an antinomy and must be played out in such a way that the contrary elements interpenetrate one another."[122] In Adorno's view, Bloch's theory failed to satisfy this requirement. The truth of Bloch's experience, the way in which the utopian idea shines through the disintegrating bourgeois world, is what gave his writings the power with which they gripped the young and did not release them through all their ups and downs.[123] But at the same time, this experience shielded itself from the specific experiences of the short twentieth century—from Auschwitz and the postrevolutionary reign of terror. If only for this reason the Bloch who remained identical with himself despite all the changes that society underwent had necessarily to become the "Bloch-actor"[124] who unswervingly clung to the reality of the utopian. In Adorno's critical view this stance remained constant from 1918 to 1968. Bloch's philosophy floats above the social world, only descending from time to time to obtain some narrative material. This is nothing less than "suicide" for a would-be materialist theory.[125] In his "mini-morals" of 1968, Adorno holds his incapacity for human relationships and his coldness responsible.[126] The term "coldness" cannot be applied to Bloch as a human being; no one who knew him could say that. Moreover, many of Adorno's letters express a personal affection, including the use of the familiar *Du*, a rarity with him, though a practice he maintained with Bloch for forty years, one that he never achieved with Benjamin. One need only open Bloch's political essays from the thirties, however, to feel the icy wind of abstract political judgments with which the Moscow murders are observed through the lens of the penal code. It is like nothing so much as the Jacobin impassivity that Hegel criticized in the section of the *Phenomenology* concerned with "absolute freedom and terror" as a terrorist stance, a passage very familiar to Bloch, in which the taking of human life "has no more significance than cutting off a head of cabbage."[127]

Such passages in Bloch's writings had alarmed Benjamin and caused him to judge that Bloch was "un peu dépaysé," a little disoriented. In *The Principle of Hope*, Bloch observes in a crucial passage dealing with extraterritoriality, "To find it easier to believe in something that has not yet appeared calls for a schooled hope; it is to trust in the day while it is yet night."[128] Bloch did not want his book to appear without any reference to time and place, so the Suhrkamp edition states, "Written 1938–1947, revised in 1953 and 1959." This made possible the erasure of many a quotation from Stalin, but the fact was that Bloch had no wish to eliminate everything. Anything that sounded at all plausible he allowed to stand, merely hinting in almost triumphant tones that "after all" [*immerhin*] Stalin had got some things right. Nevertheless, Stalin's declaration of human rights as quoted by Bloch can be endorsed only by those who abstract it totally from the actual practices of Soviet communism and who accept without demur the party's traditional understanding of the relation between theory and practice. Kracauer, who revived his friendship with Bloch after 1961, had already had this experience at the time of his first encounter with intellectuals who were communist sympathizers, and in "the sharp air of that Berlin" he had responded by reacting against theory—by articulating his "suspicions about theory,"[129] a reaction, however, that subsequently made it possible for him to accept Bloch's communist sympathizing with a friendly tolerance. Kracauer himself had "called *Ginster* an intellectual *Schweyk*."[130]

But in the middle of the century, after Auschwitz and the gulags, it was no longer possible to advocate methods of resistance that had their roots in the disintegrating Habsburg Empire. Adorno felt directly threatened by the Schweykian attitude adopted by Bloch. In his essay on the correspondence between Hofmannsthal and Stefan George, Adorno had linked the notions of "attitude" or "bearing" [*Haltung*] with "coldness."[131] On reading this, Benjamin felt very attracted by it and attempted to distinguish "bearing, as I understand it," from the bearing Adorno criticized in George "as a branded skin differs from a tattooed one."[132]

There is no mention here of Brecht, who is also included, though rather incidentally, when they speak of "bearing" or "attitude." Benjamin relates it to "the essential loneliness of an individual,"[133] an idea which helps him to understand Brecht's assumption of "attitudes," including provocative ones. Benjamin's second sojourn in Denmark with Brecht had become easier for him to bear because he believed that Brecht too was affected by the loneliness that he had suffered from his entire life. This loneliness is connected with the curiosity Benjamin felt when observing the relations of Brecht or Bloch to the Communist Party. As with Adorno, Benjamin's critique of the dominant aesthetic had led him to the conclusion that bourgeois society had had its day and was now inexorably doomed. His philological critique, however, was repeatedly transformed into attempts at partisanship. His Marxism contains something decisionistic and external, and comes close to the concept of bearing or attitude that Adorno had criticized as "a notion that is not to be trusted."[134] The casual ease with which Brecht could assume or change "attitudes" both attracted Benjamin and put him off. Adorno felt only put off by Brecht. Beneath the surface, though, not only do little bows in his direction permeate *Notes to Literature,* but also crucial passages in *Negative Dialectics* respond to points in Bloch or Brecht, neither of whom is explicitly quoted. Adorno's motif of the missed moment defines the impossibility of revolution; it arises from his personal experience of history that cannot fail to impinge on theory.[135] At the same time, the missed *kairos,* what in classical philosophy was called the right moment, reminds us of the critique of bourgeois illusions of culture under whose aegis they had all come together: Benjamin, Bloch, Brecht, Eisler, and Adorno.

Goethe's verse "Beautiful moment, do not pass away" could no longer be uttered without embarrassment by the end of the twentieth century.[136]

In an early review of Eisler's *Zeitungsausschnitte: Für Gesang und Klavier,* opus 11, Adorno had already argued that "no true lyric poetry is possible today."[137] The force of Eisler's attack, he maintains,

> stems from politics, not aesthetic reflection: in a situation—or so we see from the logic of his songs—in which social forces exercise power over the individual to the point where his liberty is illusion and the aesthetic communication of such liberty, namely, personal poetry, is ideology, personal poetry is entitled neither to truth in itself nor to the interest of society. But since there is no collective capable of delivering poetic meanings that might be more authoritative than private ones, and since Eisler sees through the questionable nature of a communal art without a community, he abandons the idea of a positive, fulfilled lyrical poetry altogether and instead gives shape to a radical *negative poetry.*[138]

Writing at the close of the Weimar Republic, Adorno feels an almost fraternal identification with Eisler's problem, even though he ends up asking "whether the right to make a poetic statement really has been so utterly extinguished, really has become so hopelessly private, as is the belief that permeates these songs."[139] This does come very close to Brecht's "dark times" when "A talk about trees is almost a crime / Because it implies silence about so many horrors!"[140] The "almost" could well be Adorno's, although in fact it is Brecht's. Eisler and Brecht together produced a musical version of "To Those Who Come after Us" in 1937. Sharing a common knowledge, all three would meet in Hollywood, in Adorno's house, his "refuge for the homeless." Together there, in 1942, they listened to Eisler's *Vierzehn Arten den Regen zu beschreiben* (Fourteen Ways to Describe Rain).

In 1943, at around the time Brecht was writing *Schweyk im Zweiten Weltkriege* (Schweyk in the Second World War), Brecht, Adorno, and Eisler met frequently in Adorno's house to discuss music, theater, film, and politics. Adorno had the opportunity to gain intimate insights into the way Brecht worked, but also into the provocative conversational techniques that had so greatly disconcerted Benjamin in Denmark. We can read in the "Graeculus" notes of the extent to which Adorno felt assaulted by Brecht's provocative anti-intellectualism. In 1965 he records: "I believe that I can at long last define what I so profoundly dislike about Brecht. He, who after all wrote a Schweyk, practiced the gestures of a man who acts stupid so as to unmask bourgeois ideology—and frequently with evidence on his side. . . . But the more he practiced this, the more he acted as if acting stupid were itself the truth, and this finally became as mendacious as the Communist

Party has become since the early thirties. That is one of the difficulties in writing the truth that he suppressed."[141] At this time the German émigrés were all in California, "out of the firing line,"[142] observing the course of the war in Europe and Asia. Inevitably they all had to face up once again to the question of the legitimacy of art. With the money he had earned in films, Brecht was able to finance work on a number of plays; Eisler kept his head above water with film music, and this enabled him to write his *Hollywood Songbook*. On the reverse side of the original score Eisler noted, "Symphony. Dedicated to Th. W. Adorno. A great scholar and composer."[143] Adorno found himself more attracted to Eisler's contradictory nature than to Brecht's sarcasm, while Brecht in turn had difficulty understanding the esteem in which Eisler held Schoenberg, Proust, and Wagner. According to Adorno's posthumous judgment of Eisler, Eisler sought to resolve the antinomy between extreme intellectuality and the need for effective collective action by striking "an *attitude*. The attitude of a wit."[144]

In the mid-sixties, with Eisler's death, the article on Kracauer's birthday celebration in which Kracauer forbade any mention of his birthday, and the reunion with Bloch, there began for Adorno a period of reflection on his own life's history: Who had survived and how? What he had found fascinating in Kracauer had been his novel *Ginster*,

> a work that . . . occupies the no-man's-land between novel and biography. . . . Kracauer called *Ginster* an intellectual *Schweyk*. The book, which has suffered little from the passage of time, becomes productive by not representing the knot of individuality affirmatively, as something substantial. Through aesthetic reflection, the subject is itself relativized. A refined silliness that poses as non-understanding when in fact it does not understand, is the mirror image of absolute individuation. Ginster cunningly tames the reality he inhabits just as strutting celebrities shrivel up in front of him. A naiveté that understands and describes itself as a technique for living is no longer naïve.[145]

The blurred boundaries between novel and biography that Adorno approved of in *Ginster* is something he could not forgive in Kracauer himself. From his retreat in Montagnola, Horkheimer reminded him that even though Kracauer had a tendency toward conformism, in the final analysis he was not one of the enemies. Nevertheless, the indifference to theory that characterizes Ginster's view of life must fail when confronted by the realities of life in the twentieth century. Kracauer was stuck in the medium of experience that could no longer achieve consciousness of itself. The methods used by Schweyk belong to a different era. They no longer ridicule others effectively; instead they invite ridicule: "Times were still good when Hašek wrote *Schweyk,* with nooks and crannies and sloppiness right in the middle of the system of horror. But comedies about fascism would become accomplices of the silly mode of thinking that considered fascism beaten in advance because the strongest battalions in world history were against it. Least of all should the position of victors be taken by the opponents of fascism, who have a duty not to resemble in any way those who entrench themselves in that position."[146]

Adorno aims this criticism at Brecht, who together with Eisler went to East Germany in order to make a reality of ideas that they could only experiment with in Hollywood. He took both men seriously as artists. The unbridgeable gulf between them lies in the realm of art, not in that of political conviction. Ever since his sojourn in Berlin in the late 1920s, he had felt Brecht to be a threat because the older friends who were closest to him and whom he admired seemed to be irresistibly attracted to Brecht, the Leninist of the theater, as Bloch called him. But Brecht's radical manner never succeeded in impressing Eisler the way it impressed Benjamin. This was because he already had an intimate knowledge of Communist Party politics and its pitfalls through his brother and sister, Gerhart and Ruth. Adorno's notes, unpublished during his lifetime, point clearly to the affection he felt for Eisler, who, despite his exaggerated left-wing radicalism, could count on the fierce support of Schoenberg—a recognition that was denied to Adorno. Adorno could in essence regard Eisler as the elder brother he never had, "a very good comrade who could cheer one up like no one else, but it would not be hard to imagine him saying: his head has a lot in it, but it has to come off nevertheless. At the same time, there is nothing false about him, good-humored, shrewd, but non-identical. Mimetic spite: an expressive character. Brother and beat your brains out."[147] In Hollywood the three men were brought together by the need to earn their living—and by sorrow. Even the lapidary notes in Brecht's *Journals* give us an inkling of this:

winge, who comes up to visit me at least once a week from downtown, where he is working in an underwear factory, reads a few of the HOLLYWOOD ELEGIES which i have written for eisler, and says, "it's as if they had been written from mars." we discover that this "detachment" is not a peculiarity of the writer's, but a product of this town: its inhabitants nearly all have it. these houses don't become somebody's property by being lived in, but by means of a cheque, the owner doesn't so much live in them as have them at his disposal. The houses are extensions of garages.[148]

This note of Brecht's makes a connection between Adorno's idea in "Out of the Firing Line"[149] of the observer as a media consumer and his later reflection in "Refuge for the Homeless": "The house belongs to the past. The bombings of European cities, as well as the labour and concentration camps, merely proceed as executors, with what the immanent development of technology had long decided was to be the fate of houses. These are now good only to be thrown away like old food cans."[150]

To the reader born into a later generation, Adorno's statement that "Wrong life cannot be lived rightly"[151] sounds shrill, but it is not to be understood without an awareness of the horrific crimes that were being committed at that very moment in Europe and Asia, albeit far from California. It is a statement that was answered in a would-be practical way by Brecht and Eisler—by writing plays as it were on credit. While Brecht used his work on one new play after another as a kind of drug, Eisler, by his own admission, took increasingly to Scotch. He too played "Tough Baby."[152] Brecht's love of cigars, and cheap ones at that, was an essential part of the image he created for the benefit of the world. When visiting Chaplin, he and Eisler would act like working-class louts who are the only ones who laugh when a film is shown in which, after the Wall Street crash, bankers are seen throwing themselves out of the window. It was the same kind of joking that so repelled Adorno when Eisler told him about the Moscow trials. Disgusted and scarcely in control of himself, Adorno had given Benjamin this report of a conversation he had had in Princeton on 4 March 1938:

I have seen Eisler quite a lot, and on one occasion we had a lengthy conversation. He is extremely friendly and approachable, presumably on account of the Institute or the radio project; his latest pose in relation to me is that of an old weather-beaten materialist politico, whose fatherly function lies in protecting the young and inexperienced idealist like me from the illusions of the age, and all by communicating his newest insights that politics must also learn to reckon with human beings as they are, that the workers too are no angels, etc. I listened with not a little patience to his feeble defence of the Moscow trials, and with considerable disgust to the joke he cracked about the murder of Bukharin. He claims to have known the latter in Moscow, telling me that Bukharin's conscience was already so bad that he could not even look at him, Eisler, honestly in the eyes. I am not inventing all this.[153]

This observation becomes even more telling when we realize that when Eisler had met Bloch shortly before in Prague, he had been extremely depressed, but that the latter, after landing in New York later in the summer, "possibly aboard a ship with eight sails," was "busy challenging our entire century arm in arm with Eisler."[154] The irony with which Adorno reports to Benjamin about Eisler's attempt to ignore the realities against his own better judgment has a signal-like effect: it reminds us of their shared commitment to theory that separates them from Brecht, Bloch, and Eisler.

On 25 February 1935, still reeling from the shock of a six-month visit to Nazi Germany, Adorno had written to Horkheimer from Oxford, repeating, almost plagiarizing, Benjamin's idea of "the rescue of those without hope as the central motif of all my efforts."[155] But it is not until the "Consecutio temporum"[156] that he turns this "central motif" into the counterpart of the hope that Bloch had erected into a principle at a time of hopelessness and that Brecht and Eisler had turned into a "leitmotif"[157] in *Schweyk*, a play that they embarked upon in 1943 and that was ultimately completed not long before Brecht's death in 1956. The compression of the trends of the age into a secular experience takes place only through this palimpsest of life that Kracauer includes among the ultimate realities. Eisler resumed work on *Schweyk* at Brecht's urging—strangely enough, since it was Brecht himself who had found when struggling with *Das Lied von der Moldau* in 1943 that "oddly enough I can't write it. I have the content and I have the lines, but together they don't work."[158] At that moment Brecht truly experienced the "difficulties of writing the truth," something of which Adorno would be reminded once again in the 1960s. Despite, or because of, the Wall and the barbed wire, Brecht advanced to the status of an all-German classic after 1949. In Adorno's own publishing house, the Suhrkamp Verlag, Brecht was the dynamo who brought in entirely new classes of readers. For Peter Suhrkamp, whose goodwill Adorno valued greatly, Brecht became the publisher's trademark. The Frankfurt Stadttheater, with Harry Buckwitz as its artistic director, had chosen Adorno's hometown as the Brecht capital of West Germany. In the shadow of this Culture Industry success, Adorno found himself once again asking the same questions that had caused the parting of the ways. A note dated 1 October

1960 gives us a glimpse of the climate in Germany at the high point of the cold war:

> The political self-censorship that must be practiced by everyone who wishes not to be destroyed, or at least rendered utterly impotent, has an immanent, probably irresistible tendency to be transformed into an unconscious censorship and thereby into stupidity. Even the focusing of my own interests on aesthetics, which admittedly fits in with my own inclinations, has something evasive about it, something ideological—and that is the case even before we come to questions of content. The paralyzing effect of the constant thinking about the East that indirectly makes our thoughts dependent upon it.[159]

Eisler's political and artistic fate becomes for Adorno the touchstone of the focus on the East. At around the same time, Adorno compared himself to Jean-Paul Sartre in the West: "No great philosopher, to be sure, but no one in Germany, not even I, trusts himself to say as much as he does in Gaullist France."[160] A serious call for radical political commitment arrived only with the growing popularity of Herbert Marcuse. Marcuse ignored Horkheimer's reluctance to become involved in public discourse, and he made use of the increasing popularity of the "edition suhrkamp" to publish all the insights that had been carefully stored up, like messages in bottles, in the *Zeitschrift für Sozialforschung*. In the fifties, Horkheimer had kept Marcuse at a distance at a time when the latter wanted to revive the group collaboration or at least the *Zeitschrift*. Of all the critical theorists it was Marcuse who had engaged most intensively with Soviet communism, and in *Soviet Marxism: A Critical Analysis* he had laid bare its insoluble contradictions as a political system with incorruptible clarity. Nevertheless, or precisely because of this, he found fault with some of the statements in a preface for the German edition of Paul Massing's *Rehearsal for Destruction*, which appeared in the institute's series of monographs published by the Europäische Verlagsanstalt with the title *Vorgeschichte des politischen Antisemitismus* (The Prehistory of Political Anti-Semitism). This was an attack on the "taskmasters in the East" who revered Turnvater Jahn, the early-nineteenth-century German anti-Semite. Adorno responded to Marcuse, speaking both for himself and for Horkheimer and arguing that behind his call for

> a kind of balance between criticism of East and West lies the conviction that dialectical materialism is still somehow connected to our own philosophy. Loyalty, however, can turn into disloyalty when it blinds itself to the fact that the

cause to which one imagines oneself remaining loyal has turned into its opposite. We cannot ignore the fact that we are able to write in the West and are even able to achieve something real, nor that in comparison with the East conditions here are paradisal. The fact that all this has material grounds is no news to us.[161]

Beneath the surface of this political disagreement, however, we can still detect the ferment of the experience of mass murder which had been shunted to one side during the cold war and which figured in Adorno's and Horkheimer's "slave language" around 1960 as "the horror."[162] Marcuse, in the meantime, was waiting for Adorno to send him his essay "The Meaning of Working Through the Past." Once he had received it, he incorporated one comment in a crucial passage of what was to become his bestseller, *One Dimensional Man*: "The spectre of man without memory . . . is more than an aspect of decline . . . it is necessarily linked with the principle of progress in bourgeois society."[163]

"Memory as a moral quality"[164]—this idea which Adorno noted down once more in 1969, the year of his death, again takes up Benjamin's idea about Jewish knowledge and condenses it under the conditions of the waning twentieth century. "Infinite hope," Kafka is supposed to have said, "only not for us." The sharpness of the assertion that it is barbaric to write a poem after Auschwitz cannot be softened without trivializing the idea altogether. Commonplace triviality is counterrevolution: that was the claim of Isaac Babel, a man already overcome by despair, at the Soviet Writers' Congress in 1934. This statement left deep traces in the minds of revolutionaries with aesthetic leanings in the thirties. Eisler combined things: the traditional Jewish experience of being the privileged object of persecution with an aesthetic sense, one that inspired his hostility to march music, for example. Nevertheless, he refused to admit that the contradiction between an advanced consciousness and mass popularity was insoluble. In his notes for a radio talk on Eisler that he was never able to finish, Adorno speaks of a failed "experiment undertaken by E[isler] to subordinate himself to a collective which he resisted with guile but in vain. His objective state of despair became a subjective one."[165] Brecht found his way out of the loss of speech with his *Schweyk im Zweiten Weltkrieg*, despite his difficulties writing it. Eisler's resumption of the project in 1956, about which he spoke once more before his death in 1961, takes the *Lied von der Moldau*—"the night has twelve hours and then comes the day"—as "a 'sung' doctrine of dialectic."[166] Eisler's conversations with Bunge between 1958 and 1962 end with a discussion of the differences between the two World Wars that causes Bunge some embarrassment. Eisler harks back to his military experience in the First World War, a subject that Brecht too had heard about on his visits to Schoenberg in Brentwood in 1942 and 1943. Even if Eisler was wise enough not to overemphasize the "Bohemian" element in his music for *Schweyk,* the entire work is predicated on the possibility of national resistance, and this has the effect of relegating the horror of Auschwitz to the background while the stage is dominated by the logic of force and counterforce. In 1951 Adorno had placed the contemplative consciousness at the forefront of his aphorisms for *Minima Moralia* as the consciousness of intellectuals in emigration: "The violence that expelled me thereby deprived me of full knowledge of it."[167] Brecht and Eisler preferred an activist approach and so attempted to make use of theater to overcome this problem even in exile.

The alleged "attachment to the people" that Brecht succumbs to in his Hollywood *Journals* and to which he has recourse even after 1953 in his attempts to reactivate the depressive Eisler, overlaps with the Soviet ideology and its emphasis on notions of resistance characteristic of the people's democracies. In addition, it provides a false slant on history and society. The "aesthetic seriousness" with which Brecht acts does so with a purpose in mind.[168] It is a failed secularization, the "organization for use of something sacred that, in Hölderlin's words, is no longer capable of being used."[169] It is memory that causes Adorno to concern himself once more with the radicalism of Eisler and Brecht. After his return to the GDR and East Berlin, Eisler proved unable to complete the crucial work that he had envisaged— his *Faust* opera, the great parallel project to the *Doctor Faustus* of Thomas Mann and Adorno, at whose origins in Pacific Palisades he had been present. According to Adorno, Eisler's text is distinguished by "his sensitive flair for language: the high quality of the *Faust* text."[170] But he also calls attention to the disappearance of Eisler's productions from the theater repertoire in the GDR: "I do not think it is purely by accident that certain compositions written more than thirty years ago by the late, highly gifted Hanns Eisler, which served aggressive political propaganda in ways that were extremely intensive and considered, including their tone and character—that these compositions, so far as I know, are no longer performed even in the East."[171] These songs of Eisler's originate in the crisis of music around 1930, paralleling the structural crisis in bourgeois society that had not been overcome. The way in which students in the industrialized countries of the West in 1968 dressed up in proletarian clothes must have seemed to Adorno like a bizarre déjà vu. At the end of the Weimar Republic, he claimed, Eisler and Brecht throve on the "conjunction of the subtle and the vulgar. The vulgar as the product of taste, of disgust."[172]

Adorno planned a radio talk after Eisler's death in 1962 for which he obtained a considerable amount of material from East Berlin. In his notes for it he observed pithily in 1965, "Socially the relation of the intellectual to the proletariat amounts to a failed identification."[173] These notes were not published until 2001, but we can still see the respect Adorno felt for Eisler's

> lack of naïveté which in the light of the cataclysms besetting society prevented him from taking the idea of the integral work of art—and what is known as artistic integrity—quite seriously. From the outside, E[isler] is right about the religion of art, but this being-right turns against his own art, for art is possible only if it is taken absolutely seriously, while he saw through it and derided it. . . . And yet he is quite right to have told us that our criteria were—and this was his favorite phrase—those of Horak's Music School [in Vienna].[174]

The word "we" or "us" occurs even more rarely in Adorno's texts than the word "I." At one time he began to use the first-person plural for himself and Benjamin. Later he added Bloch. When he joined the institute in the thirties, he used it to refer to the core members, while in the forties it meant just Horkheimer and himself. But this note from the year 1966 suggests an association with a group that remains invisible alongside the visible Adorno. A "we" group of composers and musicians around Schoenberg, the Master, including such stars as Berg, Webern, and Eisler, but also Eduard Steuermann and Rudolf Kolisch, all of whom were working with the same material—namely, the music crisis of 1930, which was not just a crisis of music but one embracing the demise of the entire bourgeois world. They all tried to survive with the aid of art but without making concessions. Their efforts were accompanied by bitter poverty and silent despair, while often culminating in a sudden elevation to the status of "modern classics,"[175] posthumously for the most part. It is this specific idiosyncratic situation that supplied the context for Adorno's assertion, one that burst on the scene of a resurrected culture in 1949, that to write poetry after Auschwitz is barbaric. The difficulty of articulating the truth of this statement gives rise to the possibility of falling silent, a silence that applies not just to music and poetry: "What Beckett expresses in his dramas and above all in his novels, which sometimes babble like music, has its truth for music itself. Perhaps only that music is still possible which measures itself against this greatest extreme, its own falling silent."[176]

After his return to Europe, Adorno too had fallen silent as a composer, but he continued to play an eloquent part in the musical life of Germany. In the fifties, that life took the form of reifying the idea of art as religion while simultaneously speaking out in opposition to "America, the land of the Culture Industry par excellence."[177] To this day critics have largely ignored Adorno's remark that not only had the official musical life in the United States been transformed since his time there as an émigré but also that in the second half of the sixties he had observed "a very vigorous and spontaneous" interest from below that had generated an authentic "resistance to the Culture Industry" by such musicians as "John Cage and his school."[178] Adorno's comments on falling silent also reflect the experience of Eduard Steuermann, his piano teacher, who, like Rudolf Kolisch, his closest musical friend, earned his living in America for the most part as a professional musician. The correspondence between Steuermann and Adorno is full of remarks about the lack of time, the absence of money, and the impossibility of bringing one's own compositions to completion, let alone of having them performed.[179] From 1950 Adorno took part in the International Vacation Courses on New Music in Darmstadt on the recommendation of his friend René Leibowitz, the composer, and he himself introduced his friends Steuermann and Kolisch. Schoenberg's *Survivor from Warsaw*, which had been composed in America "out of the firing line," was given its first performance in Germany here. In 1962 Adorno wrote an affectionate obituary for Wolfgang Steinecke, who had founded the Kranichstein Musikinstitut and the vacation school in 1946. In it he praised his "life technique," which had, he said, something of the Far East about it.[180] As a member of an older generation, Adorno might be thought to have been out of place in this circle of younger composers, musicians, and critics. He did not hesitate, however, to provide an uncompromising albeit cautiously formulated statement of his musical utopia, one he dedicated to Wolfgang Steinecke in his *Quasi una fantasia*. Adorno claims to have invented the term *musique informelle* as a mark of his gratitude to the country in which the tradition of the avant-garde was identical with the civic courage to issue manifestos.[181] As a musician the political Adorno could speak of the unity of theory and practice even though in politics this had become the ideology of Communist Party domination. He endorses the old slogan of Alois Hába, "the musical style of freedom," but not as "a repeat of the style of 1910. . . . The impossibility of restoring the revolution is a concrete reality, however."[182]

France was the homeland of liberty for the generation of intellectuals who rejected the nationalism of the Wilhelminian epoch. And this included its aesthetic sublimations. France had been the home of revolution on the European continent throughout the long nineteenth century. Paris had granted asylum to refugees from Germany ever since Napoleonic times, a sanctuary for Heine and Börne and a source of strength for the 1848 revolution and beyond. In his "Reading Balzac," Adorno found a charming formulation with which to sum up the attractiveness of Paris: "At the moment in which Paris becomes the *ville lumière,* the city of light, it is a city on a different star."[183] Declarations of love by German-speaking intellectuals from Heinrich Mann to Joseph Roth would fill volumes, and even for Adorno's own friends in the 1920s, Paris was an ultimate reference point. During the Weimar era Bloch, Kracauer, and Benjamin all enjoyed spending more or less lengthy periods of time in what Benjamin called the "capital of the nineteenth century,"[184] in which he buried himself like an archaeologist of the bourgeois age. With Kracauer we can even discern something like a sentimental idealization of the Second Empire, while for Benjamin, conscious of the gap between France and Germany, Paris was a powerhouse from which he attempted to generate intellectual, aesthetic, and political energy. In Paris in the 1920s surrealism had exposed the aging process of modernity. Looking back on that movement, Adorno noted: "After the European catastrophe the Surrealist shocks lost their force. It is as though they had saved Paris by preparing it for fear: the destruction of the city was their centre."[185]

By the end of the 1940s, the force field had shifted; the gap from which Adorno had derived his energy was now the one that had opened up between Europe and America. Nevertheless, it was Paris rather than London that was the magnet. As early as 1949 he had stopped off in Paris en route to Frankfurt, much as Horkheimer had done the previous year. His diary records the split that went right through him. On 28 October he noted: "Burst into tears on the Place de la Concorde. At the station the feeling of being torn apart: no Benjamin there."[186] He felt "seasick on land," observing:

Poverty becomes a style. Many look as if they had donned an air of *résistance,* worn with a certain pride, and yet only because they have nothing else to show, a little bit as in Germany during the pre-fascist period. Many women without stockings, coats reduced to protection against the cold. Scarcely any sign of elegance, many careworn faces. In the center, clumsy and touching attempts to ingratiate themselves with Americans, butterflies struck by a flyswatter. The feeling of people condemned by history and yet still alive. The typical gesture of Paris—people seek to overcome every inefficiency, every stupidity, through a gesture of intelligence, and even just through language. Very much like myself.[187]

On arriving in Paris in 1949, Adorno soon discovered his model for recording and condensing history, namely, a palimpsest that transmits his version of a critical theory of society to subsequent generations without including the immediate experiences of Weimar, the National Socialist regime, and emigration.

In this process of mediating between generations whose experience put them worlds apart from each other, there was a mutual attraction of an erotic nature. As a teacher, Adorno found women students everywhere who were attracted to him and whose attraction afforded him a narcissistic pleasure. Moreover, during the coming two decades he constantly looked for and discovered a mirror image of himself in the products of his students. Even so, his own theory had its effect owing to the shock of the palimpsest—through the misunderstandings, the blunt disagreements that he had already had to endure in Kranichstein at the hands of the younger generation. In this respect the situation differed from the one that obtained in the small circle around Schoenberg and the even smaller one around Berg, despite the fact that there too he often experienced painful irritations. Adorno resisted every temptation to attempt to curry favor with the young. Converging with his dislike of the "jargon of authenticity," his theoretically grounded critique of a false immediacy was reflected in his ordinary day-to-day manners. Adorno combined a kind of conventional formality with an interest in other people that was not falsified by a spontaneous smile; people he spoke to might easily take away the impression that the success or failure of any encounter depended on his first words. Because of his experience of America, he defended the injunction to "keep smiling" as a practical form of humanity, but at his first place of work, in Princeton, he must have appeared more or less unapproachable. Nevertheless, while in later years he would accuse Bloch in a fit of anger of "an inability to relate to others,"[188] as indeed he accused the entire generation of 1968, it is not possible to turn that accusation against him. As far as students whom he knew and recognized were concerned, even though he did not grant them any special favors if they acted in what he felt to be an inappropriate way, he did take an interest in their lives, something that was not to be expected of an overworked university teacher, an author, and—in the late sixties—a media star. In order to judge the conflicts that took place in connection with the student movement which started up in Frankfurt around 1966, we need to consider the particular relationship Adorno had with his students—who incidentally are by no means identical with those who were subsequently labeled "Sixty-eighters."

The records of Adorno's lectures in the fifties and sixties, his correspondence with students, and those of his own private records that are to be found in the *Frankfurter Adorno Blätter* give an authentic picture of the extent to which Adorno was conscious of the impression he was making. In 1960 he made notes for a "mini-moral" on reified consciousness:

> Concepts like "the ability to make contact" and "poverty of contacts" have arisen from psychology and have now all gone into the general wash. . . . The more easily people establish contact, the more they lack the ability to relate to others, i.e., they exhaust themselves at the thing-like façade and are incapable of love. Above all, loyalty has not been granted to the thing-like consciousness and is instead replaced by what is basically a narcissistic transference to other people. Emotional strength calls for a kind of prickliness. . . . The non-reified consciousness constantly places itself in the wrong, appears cold, hostile, antisocial, inhuman.[189]

And years later, when reflecting on Bloch and his popularity with the younger generation, he comments, "Frequently, those able to make contact are those unable properly to relate to others."[190] Adorno condemns Bloch's undoubted warmth as a "fraud," "his kind of demonism."[191] Adorno generated distance as if he needed the space between himself and others as a protective cloak. He could charm people with his voice and his look, in which melancholy and loneliness could often be read, as well as an interest that suddenly flared up or curiosity, an infinite astonishment as well as a kind of naïveté about which one could never be sure whether it was a hangover from childhood or the "second naïveté"[192] he aspired to that was supposed to become manifest after all reflection had been completed: "A private remark of Benjamin's leads us to the secret of his letters. I am not interested in people, he said; I am interested only in things."[193] The spontaneous reaction of old friends lays bare the extent to which Adorno's identification with Benjamin's unpublished writings became the source of new enmities.

Adolph Lowe, the distinguished economist who had been involved in the early history of the institute in the twenties, knew all the participants together with their quarrels from the Weimar period and was even more intimately acquainted with those of the period of emigration. Having discovered the two volumes of Benjamin's letters belonging to Kracauer's widow that had been left on his bedside table, he stole them. On 20 December 1966 he wrote to Karola Bloch, who feared Ernst's reaction to their publication. Lowe admits that the letters contained no "malicious indiscretions," but he tried to mitigate any offense to Bloch by playing down Benjamin's and hence Adorno's significance: "Let the Scholems and Adornos attempt to turn Benjamin into a genius. He had talent and, as Ernst clearly perceived a long time ago, he was genuinely productive at the miniature surrealist level."[194] Lowe is sure that among friends there will be no need "to say anything further about Teddy."[195] A widespread view of Teddie was summed up in the opinion Maidon Horkheimer had once conveyed to Max and was regarded as common sense among old acquaintances and favored students whose own situation or character inspired them to engage in a painful rivalry, to crack jokes, or to seize any opportunity to ridicule him: "Teddie is the most monstrous narcissist to be found in either the Old World or the New."[196] As proof of this statement one might adduce the "child prodigy" letter of 26 July 1962 to Ernst Bloch that has been quoted several times already and that scarcely leaves any activity of Adorno's unmentioned, even unsuccessful ones.

But looked at from a distance in time, Adorno reveals the anxiety of a former child prodigy that he has not completed the work for which "the homespun Goethean expression 'main task' still seems to be the most humane description."[197] His request that Bloch "keep his fingers crossed" evokes the affectionate relationship with his older "red brother" and so damps down his own effervescent narcissism. We should not overlook the final reference to "my little piece on the dialectics of commitment" at the end of the letter, asking him to send a copy to the Waldhaus Hotel, his favorite place to stay in Sils Maria. At that time Adorno had enabled Bloch to obtain new earning opportunities on the radio, where Adorno was already well established as a lecturer and a member of studio discussion panels. In addition, as he hints at the end of the letter, he successfully put Bloch in touch with various cultural activities in the German-speaking world with a view to helping him add to his earnings. As late as spring 1968 he proposed a discussion with Bloch on the "Studio" program on Südwestfunk. But then came what Adorno thought of as a nasty trick—not just as far as he was concerned personally, but because of their "common experience which I regard as stronger than all the ups and downs."[198]

At the end of the "child prodigy" letter, Adorno refers to his essay on commitment, in which he sets out his version of the difficulties of writing the truth. Almost every one of Adorno's texts from the mid-forties on contains the memory of Auschwitz, covered up by *The Principle of Hope*. What seems at first glance to be no more than malice and jealousy is a concern with *Minima Moralia*, the counterpart to Bloch's magnum opus. His experience of the short twentieth century compelled Adorno to formulate a new categorical imperative, something he achieved in the course of completing his "main task," the writing of *Negative Dialectics:* "to arrange one's thoughts and actions so that Auschwitz will not repeat itself, so that nothing similar will happen."[199] The monstrous reality of Auschwitz required as its essential prerequisite "coldness, the basic principle of bourgeois subjectivity,"[200] but the ability to keep on living after Auschwitz is likewise founded on the principle that avenges itself on the individual who survives: "In retribution, he will be plagued by dreams such as that he is no longer living at all, that he was sent to the ovens in 1944 and his whole existence since then has been imaginary, an emanation of the insane wish of a man killed twenty years earlier."[201] Adorno's theory itself becomes a palimpsest; at a crucial point the individual life story of a survivor living "out of the firing line" and his consciousness interpret the objective state of the social world. The difference of principle between Adorno and Bloch sheds its adventitious nature here. In Bloch's case it expresses itself as the denial of a shared experience as a matter of principle. In Adorno's writings, in contrast, this experience progresses in the direction of theory: "The guilt of a life which purely as a fact will strangle other life, according to statistics that eke out an overwhelming number of killed with a minimum number of rescued, as if this were provided for in the theory of probabilities—this guilt is irreconcilable with living. And the guilt does not cease to reproduce itself because not for an instant can it be made fully, presently conscious."[202]

Adorno gave expression to this situation in his teaching; the distinction he drew between ordinary language and educated language is what defines the unmistakable tone of his speaking voice. The lecture hall and the concert hall, but also the radio studio, were the places in which his unique elo-quence could be heard to the best advantage. After 1949 his life took place in such spaces, apart from when he was writing or playing the piano. The connection between the atrocities of the short twentieth century and the conscious refusal to let one's mind be stultified by them are what created for him an audience he could expect to listen to him without understand-ing everything at first hearing. He found each interruption during a lecture painful, not because it offended his vanity, but because it represented time wasted during which his teachings could not be transmitted. He had al-ready conveyed to Bloch in the "child prodigy" letter of July 1962 the sense that his time was limited while simultaneously having "the feeling that whatever I truly exist for still lies before me."[203] Adorno led an unspectacu-lar life which was completely dominated by his desire to make sure that what he had to say would actually be said, just as he had learned from his teacher Alban Berg what an artist absolutely had to do. He noted in his Notebook H *pro domo* in October 1960:

> Almost everything that is to be read has already been said, commonplace and, by virtue of that fact, untrue. The only things left to say are those that elude say-ing. Only the most extreme statements have any chance of escaping from the mush of established opinion. This stands as a maxim behind every sentence I write. One must *defend* oneself against the suggestion that even the normal, the average, can be true after all. Its place in the universal lie, the perfidious com-plicity which every reasonable view urges upon us taints those views. This must be categorically demonstrated at some point. N.B. but it does itself contain something untrue, negative.[204]

Adorno's teaching after his return to Germany consisted of this attempt to carry out the abovementioned program. His works read like an odyssey through world history, especially the section from the earthquake in Lis-bon in 1755 to the heart of the twentieth century. The life of Georg Lukács, his first intellectual ego ideal, was undoubtedly far more spectacular than Adorno's own, but Lukács's work turned in a circle, and Lukács ended up with the same neoclassicist humanist ideal as his father, who had been ennobled by the emperor. Even when living under the conditions of ac-tually existing socialism, Lukács could gaze out stoically from a beautiful old house onto a view of Budapest's Chain Bridge, at the same time that he was accusing Adorno of living comfortably in the Grand Hotel Abyss "be-tween excellent meals and artistic entertainments"[205]—another palimpsest attempting to overwrite his earlier work which was now starting to shine through. For his part, Adorno too linked his memory of *Theory of the Novel* with a mistaken idea, the "theory" of past, pre-bourgeois "epochs filled with meaning," which Adorno likewise interpreted in 1962 in an aphorism titled "Summing Up" as "the starting point of my metaphysical experience."[206] Here too we are confronted in the last analysis with a theodicy of the sort that the Enlightenment had found untenable in the wake of the Lisbon earthquake. Adorno had decided by this time to devote himself to his "main task." The *Dialectic of Enlightenment* that he had written with Horkheimer had been no more than an interlude—whereas in the short twentieth century the optimism that Voltaire's Candide had spoken of could no longer be mentioned even ironically. Through this palimpsestic procedure, Adorno's teaching transmits a "tradition of anti-traditionalism." In that tradition surrealism has a specific mission as the shape of the avant-garde that has now grown old:

> In fact, it is a paradox that anything at all changes within the sphere of a culture rationalized to suit industrial ideals; the principle of *ratio* itself, to the extent that it calculates cultural effects economically, remains the eternal constant. That is why it is somewhat shocking whenever anything from the sector of the Culture Industry becomes old-fashioned. The shock value of this paradox was already exploited by the Surrealists in the Twenties when they confronted the world of 1880; in England at that time a book like *Our Fathers* by Allan Bott had caused a similar effect. Today the shock effect is produced by the Twenties, similar to the effect the world of images of the 1880s produced around 1920. But the repetition deadens the shock effect. The defamiliarization of the Twenties is the ghost of a ghost.[207]

By way of anticipating *Negative Dialectics, The Jargon of Authenticity* had already skewered this idea of the ghostly nature of the present. Adorno had given it the subtitle *A Contribution to the German Ideology.* All the hot air talked about existentialism in Germany after the Second World War was reminiscent in a frightening way of the first attempt at seizing world power that had been triggered by Germany earlier on. In the nineteenth century the socially prestigious humanities had been cultivated as part of a poorly secularized religion of culture. The conception of a seemingly universalistic Germany had produced in writers a virtually limitless nationalism dressed up as cosmopolitanism as early as the period before 1848. The first verse of the far from antidemocratic national anthem, *Deutschland, Deutschland über alles,* is evidence of this. This new hyperpatriotic ideology then became an essential part of the German tradition after the failure of the revolutions of 1848. It repelled members of the political avant-garde such as Marx and Engels, who reacted with their *Communist Manifesto* of 1848. Their earlier critiques of German ideology did not appear on the market until the second half of the 1920s. Under Pollock's supervision, the old Institute for Social Research in Viktoriaallee had acted as an intermediary between the administrators of the Social Democratic Party, who had control of the literary legacy of Marx and Engels, and David Ryazanov of the Marx-Engels Institute in Moscow. After the First World War the publication of Marx's *German Ideology* led to a rediscovery of the young Marx, a process that seemed to be repeated after the Second World War with the appearance of the *Paris Manuscripts,* which were published separately from the East German edition of the works of Marx and Engels. In the case of Herbert Marcuse, the discovery of Marx's early writings in 1932 coincided with his turning away from a Heideggerian existentialism, whereas in 1957 Jürgen Habermas, who was Adorno's assistant at the time, celebrated his debut as a political theorist in West Germany with a spectacular essay titled "The Philosophical Discussion around Marx and Marxism." He later included it in his volume *Theorie und Praxis* (Theory and Practice),[208] which followed from the breakthrough he achieved with *The Structural Transformation of the Public Sphere.* In the meantime, he had left the institute as the consequence of pressure from Horkheimer and had to move to Marburg to study with Wolfgang Abendroth in order to qualify for the *Habilitation.* The publication of his essay triggered a letter from Horkheimer to "Teddie," who in the meantime had been appointed his successor as institute director in the Senckenberg Anlage.[209]

Horkheimer's sharply worded letter is not without piquancy. When it was published in 1996, the name Horkheimer had been relegated to the Adenauer phase of history, while Adorno was widely regarded as an academically obsolete elitist aesthete from an indeterminate epoch lying in the remote bourgeois past. Habermas was perceived as the current head of a critical Frankfurt School and the heir to Horkheimer and Adorno, its founders. The conflicts with the rebellious students had coalesced into the mythical cipher of "1968," in which the chief actors had faded into a group whose members were no longer clearly distinguishable. This too is a palimpsest that has to be decoded if Adorno's thoughts and actions in the 1960s are to be unraveled. In the 1950s Horkheimer had had bad luck with potential successors. He seemed to encounter only people he, in agreement with Pollock, had no desire to encourage. In the 1930s "careerist" had been a leading word of abuse that tended to preclude assistance and cooperation even more than political differences of opinion. For example, after the very first drafts of Alfred Sohn-Rethel's *Intellectual and Manual Labor* were written, Adorno had had to defend its author against precisely this unwarranted suspicion on Horkheimer's part. Once the institute had been revived, following the establishment of the Federal Republic itself, it quickly came to be regarded among younger scholars as a possible springboard for a future career. A list of the people who worked there includes many scholars who became well-known names in postwar German sociology. Ralf Dahrendorf may be mentioned as a prominent example. It was Dahrendorf who may have provided Horkheimer with a model of what he meant by behavior motivated by vanity. Commitment in so far as it advances one's career implies, even from Dahrendorf's autobiographical writings, indifference toward a cause which was not his own.

Habermas studied in Göttingen, Zurich, and Bonn from 1949 to 1954. He joined the Frankfurt Institute in 1956, at a time when Horkheimer and Adorno had already become established among German sociologists. The media, however, did not start to talk about a "Frankfurt School" in the Federal Republic until after the so-called positivism debate in the early sixties, in which Habermas sprang to Adorno's assistance. According to Habermas, during his brief period at the institute from 1956 to 1959, Horkheimer's earlier writings were left forgotten in the cellar, a coherent corpus of work that might be said to form a critical theory was not to be discerned even by a receptive reader at that time. What is needed to form a school is the kind of pupil-teacher relationship that characterized the Second Viennese School, with Schoenberg at its head and Berg as a teacher. Habermas was never a pupil of Adorno's in that sense: as a young man Habermas did not discuss his own projects with Adorno; what he did discuss was Adorno's current ideas and publications. For example, Habermas has recalled a situation in which Adorno "expressed the opinion that for the first time he had understood the connection between identity thinking and the commodity form"—a connection with regard to which Habermas had his doubts, "though without being able to make any impression on Adorno."[210]

Horkheimer's dislike of Habermas must have been evident to Adorno, but even so he was visibly taken aback by Horkheimer's sweeping condemnation in the letter from Montagnola, as we can see from his spontaneous comments in the margins. Horkheimer picked up differences of opinion with Adorno that could also be gleaned from the records of conversations from the 1950s and that were sometimes aired publicly in the senior philosophy seminars. But in the letter Horkheimer stresses what was important for him in the concept of critical theory and complains about the lack of a school that might transmit their ideas. He expresses his surprise that "one can spend . . . a considerable amount of time with us . . . without doing anything to enlarge one's experience of social reality, indeed without bringing any intelligent thought to bear on the present, and without making any effort other than the efforts that are satisfied by reading, by one's perspicacity, and, if need be, the demands of the philosophy seminar itself."[211] At the time, Horkheimer was preoccupied not only by the setbacks in the communist world following the Twentieth Party Congress in 1956, but also with the bloody overthrow of the monarchy in Iraq in 1958, which in his view was yet one further instance of the accelerating process of industrialization and which, following the experience of the October revolution, had rendered the entire concept of revolution suspect. He insisted on this in his letter to Adorno: "The world is full of revolution, and thanks to it terror is on the increase."[212] Adorno noted in the margin, "Yes." Horkheimer becomes even more explicit: "What concerns H. is Marx's theory and practice. Even in the years when National Socialism was emerging, and during the Third Reich itself, we knew that it was futile to look to revolution for salvation."[213] In the course of the letter Adorno himself comes under pressure: "H. is a particularly energetic, active man, and he may have learned a lot from us, especially from you, though scarcely anything that has to do with the experience of social realities. . . . Even the philosophical ideas he has taken from us only sound similar."[214] Horkheimer contrasts Marx's Feuerbach thesis from the early writings with a sentence of Adorno's from *Against Epistemology: A Metacritique*, which Habermas also quotes: "If the age of interpreting the world is over and the point now is to change it, then philosophy bids farewell. . . . It is time not for first philosophy but last philosophy."[215] For the Horkheimer who wrote this letter, Habermas, a mere assistant, was not so important; what was important was the sharp distinction between critical theory and philosophy, since, after the experience of the short twentieth century, critical theory could no longer be something "pure": "He teaches what he purports to combat, pure philosophy, including a doctrine of science in which sociology is confronted with problems from the situation as it was in 1843."[216]

Horkheimer's letter does not express the anger of the teacher toward a rebellious pupil of the kind Schoenberg may have felt toward Eisler. It expresses the mistrust of the former institute director, who by his own confession was something of an enlightened despot, toward a writer whom he knew only slightly and who was beginning to represent the institute to the outside world. It was not Habermas's duty to defend a doctrine of critical theory that he had inherited. In 1964 he left Heidelberg in favor of Frankfurt in order to take up the offer of a double chair in philosophy and sociology. At that point Horkheimer ceased to raise any objections. Habermas had his own theoretical projects, and he now became a young colleague of Adorno's with his own charisma and his own power to attract. In terms of university politics, his views harmonized with Adorno's, but at the level of theory there was no meeting of minds. In 1991 Habermas stated, "I do not think that Adorno has read any book by me."[217] Anyone who regarded himself as Adorno's pupil would have had a right to hope that Adorno would write a preface for his first publication, or even a review. By the early 1960s, however, the young Habermas had no need of such support. And many sought to avoid any hint of a pupil image, since even though many journalists and colleagues did not trust themselves to take up the cudgels against Adorno personally, there were always plenty of attacks on Adorno's followers and the Frankfurt sociological mumbo-jumbo. Early in 1964 Adorno wrote as a visibly committed teacher to Claus Behncke, a young editor at Westdeutscher Rundfunk:

> With increasing frequency I come across people who think highly of me or at least claim to do so and who wax indignant about my so-called imitators—God knows I do not include you in their ranks.. I know it can be irritating to have one's mannerisms copied, but long experience has taught me that matters are not so straightforward. In the first place, I must say that as long as there are still pockets in which the ideas and speech mannerisms of Heidegger and Jaspers prevail, I would rather have someone who imitates me than someone who speaks the jargon of authenticity. In the second place, if young people choose to attach themselves to a teacher, literally or more generally, that is no bad thing. Goethe was well aware that originality is something that has to develop, it is not there from the very outset; we should not forget this.[218]

By the early 1960s Horkheimer had withdrawn to Montagnola and reappeared only sporadically in Frankfurt. It was at this time that Adorno threw himself wholeheartedly and to the point of utter exhaustion into "his main task," *Negative Dialectics,* as he had announced to Bloch.[219] This book was supposed to be the authoritative statement of his teaching, but not his final word. The central themes of the discussion as they were hammered out with Horkheimer recur in future arguments with his students and with Herbert Marcuse. Even after one has read through his literary papers, it seems as if all his future utterances were variations on the relations between theory and practice. He had after all by way of preparation for his inaugural lecture, "The Actuality of Philosophy" on 7 May 1931, made notes on this very topic in the course of "a dreamlike anticipation" before he felt the actual impact of the "shock" of the "outbreak of Hitler's Reich," as he subsequently reported in the "child prodigy" letter to Bloch.[220] He wrote, "Whoever chooses philosophy as a profession today must first reject the illusion that earlier philosophical enterprises began with: that the power of thought is sufficient to grasp the totality of the real."[221] At that time Adorno was uncertain whether he would decide on a career as an artist. *Negative Dialectics* was followed in 1967 by the last ambitious lecture course, one that was repeatedly interrupted by political events. This was *Aesthetic Theory*, which, needless to say, would have been quite inconceivable, even theoretically, without prior reflection on aesthetic practice. From time to time Adorno toyed with the idea of giving *Negative Dialectics* the title *On the Theory of Intellectual Experience*. He had come to accept that there would be no magnum opus among his works. As his editors Gretel Adorno and Rolf Tiedemann revealed after his death, however, citing an unpublished letter from Adorno, *Aesthetic Theory* together with *Negative Dialectics* "will show what I have to throw into the scale."[222] *Aesthetic Theory* was to have had as an epigraph a quotation from Friedrich Schlegel: "What is called the philosophy of art usually lacks one of two things: either the philosophy or the art."[223] Adorno intended to dedicate the book to Samuel Beckett.

According to his life plan, once he had completed *Aesthetic Theory*, Adorno intended to resume work on *Minima Moralia*. The continuation would focus on "life after my return."[224] His notes contain observations that can be read as recollections of the emergence of central theoretical ideas—"the anamnesis of genesis," a basic idea that was noted by Alfred Sohn-Rethel in a private discussion at Adorno's flat in Kettenhofweg.[225] Having by now become a full professor, he remained deeply suspicious of this newfound status:

Anyone who takes up a position in the so-called humanities—as a university teacher—is inspired by hopes for the intellect, for something different, something unspoiled, ultimately something absolute, in whatever form. He is willing to make great sacrifices for this, principally the years of poverty and waiting characteristic of insecure junior lecturing posts. But his profession will drive out all hope, not simply because of the necessity of submitting to the hierarchy, a necessity that is intensified to the bursting point nowadays when scarcely anyone has independent means, but also because of the nature of scholarship itself, which in the name of scholarship negates the very spirit that it promises. The adept's expectation is thus *necessarily* disappointed, the sacrifice was for naught. Resentment as the basic attitude of the university teacher is therefore objectively determined and almost unavoidable. The sole compensation in Germany is the social prestige of the university professor, which still survives, a factor that may have led to his choice of profession in the first place. Hence the insane arrogance, the overweening pride in being a professor; hence too the fetishism of the concept of scholarship regardless of its content.[226]

No university reform of the last fifty years has rendered these comments superfluous, although the professor's social prestige may have diminished somewhat in the meantime. Resentment toward bureaucratized thinking determined the thinking of the entire circle from Benjamin to Pollock. The question of how to preserve one's independence in a general system of dependency was a focal point of *Minima Moralia*. When he heard of the question put to Bloch in 1949, whether he would rather go to Leipzig or stay in America, he replied "Capri." Around and in Positano, in Capri, in their flight from conditions in Germany in the interwar years, they had met up with Russian intellectuals who had also chosen the Mediterranean life in relative poverty in preference to civil war. Adorno's place of choice outside the system, the place he liked to refer to as the *topos noetikos,* once he had returned to Europe was Sils Maria. In December 1949 he had dreamt of this place as being close to extraterritoriality when he wrote to Horkheimer in Pacific Palisades, telling him how completely exhausted he was with work: "And connected with this is the fact that here too I still have the feeling that what we write is infinitely more important than having an immediate impact, if only for the palpable reason that such impact would itself be condemned to a mere propadeutic and scarcely impinges on our real concerns."[227] He did not wish to be the popular university teacher any more than had another university professor, Friedrich Nietzsche, who had fled the city but not from civilization and whose belief that "the true concerns of human beings can only be defended at a distance from them" was one with which Adorno strongly identified.[228]

If the Grand Hotel Abyss that Lukács scorned had a name, it could only be the Waldhaus Hotel, with its view of the Chasté Peninsula. If you turn your gaze to the other side, you can see the Fex Valley, whose meadows, carpeted with flowers, end at the foot of the glacier. The traveler's gaze can explore "the frozen wastes of abstraction"[229] and experience "the pathos of distance,"[230] the expanse devoid of objects that endures in the memories of the great melancholics of the German language—among whom, apart from Nietzsche, one must also include Karl Kraus. Moreover, the name of yet another fixed star from times past can be found in the guest book of the nearby Alp Grüm: that of Marcel Proust. We should not allow ourselves to be misled. The Upper Engadine did not mean escape into isolation or even to unspoiled nature. The adventurous and far more unfortunate history of the Hotel Maloja, within sight of the Waldhaus, exposes the Upper Engadine as the first and last bolthole to escape from a bourgeois society in which achievement makes everything comparable with everything else and renders every notion of tradition obsolete—an extraterritoriality sui generis. The high society in the Grand Hotel contrasts with the sparse quarters in which Nietzsche was housed, from whose mean windows he counted the coaches passing by on their way to parties: "Nowadays, in similar material circumstances, one would become déclassé, expelled from the bourgeois order of things; surrounded by an ostentatiously high living standard, one would feel humiliated by one's own want. Then, however, for the price of an extremely modest way of life one would purchase intellectual independence. Even the relation between productivity and economic base is subject to history."[231] Adorno emphasizes the unheroic aspect of a life that refuses to allow itself to be deprived of the *promesse de bonheur* in 1969, when he once again takes up Lukács's reproach of living in the Grand Hotel Abyss: "This idiocy is part of the general regression that thinks itself revolutionary: this should be included; Chaplin's *Gold Rush* would not be the worst allegory for my ideas. Lukács has plunged into the abyss, mistaking it for salvation. Even there he isn't really present; instead, he creeps around, a broken man, like one of the figures in Beckett that so infuriate him."[232]

The vain hope of salvation through a collective, this hope that has been converted into a principle, Adorno's lifelong political themes in which the names of Bloch and Lukács are made to stand in for his early intellectual experience—all these ideas are still present in his refuge in the Swiss mountains. In 1954 Lukács had singled out Schopenhauer as representative of the retreat to the Grand Hotel Abyss. Ignoring the persecution Lukács suffered following the collapse of the Hungarian uprising in 1956, Adorno subjected his book to a withering critique:

> It was doubtless his book *The Destruction of Reason* which revealed most clearly the destruction of Lukács's own. In a highly undialectical manner, the officially licensed dialectician sweeps all the irrationalist strands of modern philosophy into the camp of reaction and fascism. He blithely ignores the fact that, unlike academic idealism, these schools were struggling against the very same reification in both thought and life of which Lukács too was a sworn enemy. Nietzsche and Freud are simply labelled fascists, and he could even bring himself to refer to Nietzsche, in the condescending tones of a provincial Wilhelminian school inspector, as a man of "above-average abilities." Under the mantle of an ostensibly radical critique of society he surreptitiously reintroduced the most threadbare clichés of the very conformism which that social criticism had once attacked.[233]

To declare one's partisanship for the revolution in the thirties had meant giving one's support to the Communist Party, a fact that once again confirmed the gulf separating Adorno from Lukács but also from Brecht:

> As for the book . . . *The Meaning of Contemporary Realism,* published in the West by Claassen Verlag in 1958, we can detect in it traces of a change of attitude on the part of the seventy-five-year-old writer. These presumably have to do with the conflict in which he became embroiled through his active role in the Nagy government. Not only does he talk about the crimes of the Stalin era, but he even speaks up on behalf of "a general commitment to the freedom to write," a formulation that would earlier have been unthinkable. Lukács posthumously discovers some merit in Brecht, his adversary of many years' standing, and praises as a work of genius his *Ballad of the Dead Soldier,* a poem which must strike the East German rulers as a cultural Bolshevist atrocity. Like Brecht, he would like to widen the concept of socialist realism, which has been used for decades to stifle any spontaneous impulse, any product incomprehensible or suspect to the apparatchiks, so as to make room for works that rise above the level of despicable trash. He ventures a timid opposition in gestures which show him to be paralysed from the outset by the consciousness of his own impotence. His timidity is no mere tactic. Lukács's personal integrity is above all suspicion.[234]

In both the social systems that were regarded by Horkheimer and Adorno at the time of the cold war as belonging to the "administered world," the debate is concerned superficially with art; but underlying Adorno's arguments we realize that what is driving him into the role of the aesthete is the phenomenon of violence. His own distorted image, encouraged on his own admission by his inclinations and the nature of his talent, turned him into the idiosyncratic figure that provoked Brecht's politically motivated anti-intellectualism. In the essay on commitment which he also referred to in the "child prodigy" letter to Bloch, Adorno criticized Brecht's fetishizing of violence, brilliantly anticipating an undigested component later on of the protest movement of 1968: "Already the exaggerated adolescent virility of the young Brecht betrayed the borrowed courage of the intellectual who, in despair at violence, suddenly adopts a violent practice which he has every reason to fear."[235] Brecht's fetishizing of violence had also fascinated Walter Benjamin, who hoped that it might provide succor from the very thing that threatened him. In contrast, Brecht's instinct for self-preservation prevented him from defending fictitious nostrums in Europe. Instead, he opted for emigration in America in preference to Moscow, where his enemy Lukács survived only by chance, as he himself was well aware. Brecht was a political survival artist, but in Adorno's view he had to pay a political price as well as an aesthetic one for his subterfuges. In *Arturo Ui*, Brecht's attempt to grasp the nature of National Socialism from "out of the firing line," namely, in California, he succeeds in putting fascism on the stage but only by personalizing and trivializing it: "Instead of a conspiracy of the wealthy and powerful, we are given a trivial gangster organization, the cauliflower trust. The true horror of fascism is conjured away; it is no longer a slow end-product of the concentration of social power, but mere hazard, like an accident or a crime. This conclusion is dictated by the exigencies of agitation: adversaries must be diminished. The consequence is bad politics, in literature as in practice before 1933."[236]

In the 1930s Bloch, Brecht, and Eisler had all rejected the aesthetics of the Popular Front and hence also the party line. But in order to do so, they were forced into the wildest political reversals of position. It was in Bloch, who had just arrived in New York, that Adorno first observed "the transformation of the corrupted 'Popular Front' morality into a kind of industrious stupidity."[237] Brecht's *Journals* reveal the clues that led Adorno to reject his anti-intellectualism. Brecht adopts a pretended vulgar materialism in December 1944 to explain the connection between "the frankfurt sociological institute (which inspired my TUI NOVEL)," the "new york jews," and Adorno's incomprehension of Karl Marx's "little piece on the jewish question."[238] The previous day Brecht had noted: "these unfortunate intellectuals! are they dangerous? they are dangerous, like cigars cut up in the soup."[239] Thus by the time this intellectual self-hatred became fashionable among the students in 1968, Adorno was well prepared for it, having seen it in Brecht, dressed up in a proletarian cloth cap and leather jacket. Imperviousness to psychology helped both Brecht and later the student activists to achieve the insight that historical processes do not depend on the individual psyche. But the mere knowledge of social structure does not amount to the concrete understanding of a specific historical situation. Brecht, the Leninist of the theater, as he was called by Bloch in the last of his essays to have gained Benjamin's approval, became an artistic and political myth among the rebellious West German students. The path they took was the reverse of Brecht's own. They moved from the widely accepted plays such as *Mother Courage* and *Saint Joan of the Stockyards,* which could even be produced by established figures such as Gustav Gründgens, back to *The Measures Taken.* As early as *Schweyk,* Brecht himself retreated from the proletarian mythology of his left-wing radical phase to the idea of stupidity as the wisdom of the people:

> All roles may be played, except that of the worker. The gravest charge against commitment is that even right intentions go wrong when they are noticed, and still more so, when they try to conceal themselves. Something of this remains in Brecht's later plays in the linguistic *gestus* of wisdom, the fiction of the old peasant sated with epic experience as the poetic subject. No one in any country of the world is any longer capable of the earthy experience of South German muzhiks: the ponderous delivery has become a propaganda device to make us believe that the good life is where the Red Army is in control.[240]

Actually existing socialism necessarily generates an affirmative aesthetics and as such is unacceptable to Adorno as a "refuge for homeless" intellectuals. Adorno interpreted the figure "68" against the background of the twentieth century: 1968 succeeded the warmed-up existentialism of the fifties, the "jargon of authenticity." It was a conformist fad disguised as left-wing radicalism. Left-wing intellectuals from the Weimar epoch who had now grown old could not escape the sense of something déjà vu with all its ambivalence. This emerges clearly from the correspondence with old friends such as Sohn-Rethel and Horkheimer, but also Marcuse, Kracauer, and Löwenthal. The element of the identical that repelled Adorno was to be found less in the specifically German nature of the protest than in its political conformism, dressed up as the movement of an avant-garde.

In the summer of 1967 Adorno kept working steadily on his *Aesthetic Theory,* a book in which he presented his own version of "To Those Who

Come after Us." In the very first lectures he concedes the justice of the criticism from outside of the "blindness"[241] of the autonomous work of art, a criticism that preoccupied both Brecht and Eisler; but the claim to autonomy can no longer be revoked, even if the emancipation failed. The yearning for the new keeps returning; but it can no longer be brought about in a naïve spirit. Adorno's aesthetic message in Lecture Hall 6, which was always full to bursting, was political, one in which he produced in public all the motifs impregnated by his own life's experience, without, however, making the autobiographical script all too visible:

> The relation to the new is modelled on a child at the piano searching for a chord never previously heard. This chord, however, was always there; the possible combinations are limited and actually everything that can be played on it is implicitly given in the keyboard. The new is the longing for the new, not the new itself: That is what everything new suffers from. What takes itself to be utopia means the negation of what exists and is obedient to it. At the centre of contemporary antinomies is that art must be and wants to be utopia, and the more utopia is blocked by the real functional order, the more this is true; yet at the same time art may not be utopia in order not to betray it by providing semblance and consolation.[242]

Adorno's theory liberates aesthetic experience from the shackles of political and practical utility. By resorting to the helpful detour made possible by the illusory alternative of advancing toward socialism or relapsing into barbarism, Brecht, the rationalist, like Bloch, the dialectician, had reconstructed a meaningful connection between reason and revolution. Such a project, however, was irrevocably doomed after the Stalinist regression and the fact of Auschwitz. It was this experience of supra-individual significance that Horkheimer had reminded Adorno of in his Montagnola letter.[243]

This experience is negated by a conception of the unity of theory and practice that is idealist in reality, even though it purports to be entirely materialist. As early as 1944 Adorno had observed how in Brecht, Auschwitz had disappeared behind a rationalistically constructed Marxism. In his late writings Horkheimer had already considered the issue of why Marx's essay *On The Jewish Question* had been marked by rationalist elements that tended to insulate him from historical realities. In conversation with Pollock, Horkheimer thought that this "might perhaps be" ascribed to Marx's desire to become assimilated. In the 1960s Adorno sought to rehabilitate the so-called *Vormärz* period before 1848, which Marx had dismissed altogether too cursorily on ideological grounds. In his essay "Die grosse Blochmusik" Adorno himself had glossed over the historical wound caused by failed attempts at emancipation.[244] But Adorno discovered a special reader who found his broad-based criticism of unshakeable utopian hopes immediately illuminating, like much of what Adorno had to say. This was Paul Celan. His compliments on Adorno's criticism of Bloch are contained in a letter that Celan sent to Adorno together with a prose text, "Conversation in the Mountains" *(Gespräch im Gebirge)*—"a little prose piece peering up at you from below." Celan sent Adorno a two-edged story of Jew Little and Jew Big, the record of an "encounter in the mountains"[245] that never did take place and never could have done so. This palimpsest is particularly puzzling because as an Adorno reader, Celan consciously constructs a transfer between life and literature while sedulously avoiding an actual meeting in real life. Adorno's dictum about poetry after Auschwitz was one that Celan consistently misread as spelling the condemnation of poetry after Auschwitz. A poet's bird's-eye view that accused Adorno remained Celan's own negative view of the German-speaking public sphere after 1945. Celan necessarily felt threatened in his very existence by Adorno's opinion because his ability to survive after Auschwitz depended on his ability to write poetry.

Celan could not have written his response in prose if he had been forced to discard his mistaken notion of Adorno as "Jew Big." In 1959 Peter Szondi, the literary scholar who was friendly with both Adorno and Celan, had lured Celan into a visit to the Engadine so as to facilitate a meeting with Adorno. Szondi too had been preoccupied by Adorno's dictum throughout his own literary studies. As a discordant note emanating from Frankfurt it never ceased to fascinate him. Adorno accepted invitations to Berlin from Szondi; he recommended pupils such as Elisabeth Lenk and Sam Weber to Szondi, and Szondi was one of the few people Adorno felt sufficiently at ease with to invite him to spend time with him in Sils Maria. On 30 August 1960 they sent a joint postcard to Celan with a picture of the lakes of the Upper Engadine. Celan had just published his "evocative prose piece" in the most traditional German journal, the *Neue Rundschau*.[246] Despite his dislike of the publisher, Gottfried Bermann Fischer, Adorno had published some of his best essays there—chiefly because of his admiration for the editor in chief, the literary *grand seigneur* Rudolf Hirsch. The texts he published there included his essay on Kafka of 1953 and the first major Benjamin essay of 1950, both of which were read by Thomas Mann as well as Celan. After reading these essays Celan must have gained the impression that Adorno himself was a kind of second Benjamin "with the nimbus of a sophisticated 'littérateur,'"[247] who was able to write about Proust and Kafka in a manner that differed sharply from that of the "jargon of authenticity." The latter was just gaining currency, and Celan himself was not entirely immune to its attractions. Celan must have felt drawn to Adorno's talk of the "sorrow, the like of which is as rare in the history of philosophy as the utopia of cloudless days," as if he had been a distant relative. Adorno must also have gained his confidence with his observation that "Kafka's remark that there is infinite hope except for us could have served as the motto of Benjamin's metaphysics, had he ever deigned to write one."[248] Dismayed as he was by Adorno's statement about poetry after Auschwitz, he must have felt challenged by another sentence from the Benjamin essay: "Misunderstandings are the medium in which the non-communicable is communicated."[249]

In the summer of 1959 Celan took a room lower down in Sils Baselgia, in the Pension Chasté—at the foot of the gastronomic palace. Thomas Mann's children used to lodge there in earlier years when they wanted to preserve their distance from the Magician, who normally stayed in either the Waldhaus Hotel or the Suvretta Hotel, if not in the neighboring Margna Hotel. Celan consciously chose the Big/Little polarity as a perspective, and his departure on 23 July, a week before Adorno's arrival at the Waldhaus, maintains intact the possibility of a "communication of the noncommunicable." His text records a "missed encounter in the mountains." The empirical visit took place in the Rhine-Main region in May 1960, and Adorno replied on 13 June, evidently pleased and flattered, when Celan sent him the prose text, adding that he was staying at the Imperial Hotel in Vienna at the invitation of the city of Vienna, where he was going to deliver a speech on the subject of Mahler—"but please do not jump to any conclusions from the category 'Big.'"[250] Adorno refused to accept any of the roles offered to him—whether that of "the Jew" or of "Big." He had promised to write an essay on Celan's collection of poems titled *Sprachgitter* (Language Mesh), but it dragged out for years without ever being completed. In 1967, however, at a highly stressful time after 2 June,[251] he took part in a seminar conducted by Peter Szondi on Celan's poem "Engführung" ("The Straitening," or "Stretto"), during which Szondi had spoken somewhat misleadingly of the "refutation of Adorno's all-too famous assertion."[252] As it happens, his remark has suffered a similar fate to

Adorno's, since it is normally quoted without the following perfectly clear statement: "After Auschwitz no further poems are possible, except on the foundation of Auschwitz itself."[253] Adorno gave this idea an even more complex formulation in *Aesthetic Theory*. The Paralipomena contain the argument that picks up his original dictum and varies it with the aid of Schoenberg and Beckett, culminating in the statement that

> his poetry is permeated by the shame of art in the face of suffering that escapes both experience and sublimation. Celan's poems want to speak of the most extreme horror through silence. Their truth content itself becomes negative. They imitate a language beneath the helpless language of human beings, indeed beneath all organic language: It is that of the dead speaking of stones and stars. . . . The infinite discretion with which his radicalism proceeds compounds its force. The language of the lifeless becomes the last possible comfort for a death that is deprived of all meaning.[254]

This passage cannot be regarded as marginal in Adorno's writing since it encapsulates his closeness to Benjamin, who had earlier anticipated a lyric poetry without aura in Baudelaire. Adorno ascribes to Celan's poetry "an increasing abstraction of landscape" that reflects the visual appearance of mountainous regions.[255] From 1967 until his death, Adorno labored at his *Aesthetic Theory* alongside all his official commitments in a desperate attempt to salvage what could be salvaged from tradition and to clarify the misunderstandings that had arisen, fully aware that they were by no means the product of chance. When he met Szondi in Berlin for discussions in 1967, this coincided with the Berlin visit of Herbert Marcuse, who gave two lectures to a mass audience in the largest lecture hall at the Free University. and who was able to form an impression of students in Germany in the course of a number of panel discussions and numerous individual encounters. Marcuse had already met a number of the protagonists, especially the leaders of the Association of German Socialist Students (in German, SDS),[256] during previous visits. Ever since 1964 he had been touted by insiders as the up-and-coming man among those in the organization who were interested in theory because he had been able to incorporate the latest American developments into the analytical framework of critical theory. In 1967 his major work, *One Dimensional Man*, appeared in German translation, and within a year it had become an international best-seller—yet another misunderstanding. Following the May events in Paris, it promised an answer to the clichéd question: What do the students want? The only problem was that in 1968 hardly anyone in Paris had read the book. In Germany the position was different. There a small group, at least some of whom had studied with Adorno and had learned from him, believed that theory was of crucial importance in the attempt to find explanations for the mildew that covered the German republic under Adenauer. Unlike the situation in France or Italy after 1945, no one could be under the illusion that the German population harbored left-wing sympathies; on his return to Germany, Adorno had soon perceived this after a comparison between Paris and Frankfurt in 1949. From this foundation of a traditionless tradition, which was passed down in the form of the apolitical attitudes of the German bourgeoisie, there arose the impression of a *resurrected culture* that Adorno had observed in "Those Twenties"—an essay that acted like a beacon of light for readers such as Celan. The cold war had seemed to provide a definitive answer once and for all to demands for social change. In ordinary life, would-be reformers had to reckon with the standard riposte, "If you don't like it here, try it over there!"—by which was meant the German Democratic Republic (GDR), an appellation one was not supposed to use in those days. Instead you had to call it the SBZ—the Soviet Zone of Occupation—unless you wanted to be suspected of sympathizing with the German Communist Party, which was banned at the time in West Germany. In 1960, even before the Wall was built, Adorno had noted:

> The political self-censorship that must be practiced by everyone who does not wish to be ruined, or at least completely sidelined, has an immanent and probably irresistible tendency to slip into an unconscious censorship mechanism and from there into stultification. The focusing of my interest in aesthetics, however, which admittedly corresponds to my interests, also has something evasive, ideological about it—even before one considers its content. This is the paralyzing effect of the fixation on the East which indirectly makes our ideas dependent on it.[257]

It may sound paradoxical, but the fact is that in contrast to the perceptions of the protest generation, which believed the exact opposite, a change in the rigidities of the world situation could arise only in the West. Herbert Marcuse's prognosis at the end of *One Dimensional Man* had been anything but optimistic. The American original ended in 1964 with the very quotation from Walter Benjamin that Adorno had envisaged as a possible epigraph for his entire metaphysics.[258] Marcuse also wished to keep faith with the victims of history; he too resisted falling prey to the illusion that the American population leaned to the left. On the contrary, he must rather have doubted whether he would find an audience for his views in the early sixties, and this explains why he kept feeling the urge to return to Europe. But he also lived far from the frontline of the cold war. He did not feel inhibited, as Adorno did, by anxieties that this or that sentence might be misconstrued by the reading public. Such statements as "To write poetry after Auschwitz is barbaric," which created a scandal in the German Federal Republic, would have passed unnoticed in America at the time.[259] The factors that inspired a change in Marcuse's language derived from the comparison between West German society and the greater freedom that obtained in America, where the shock of McCarthyism in the late forties had been overcome by the early sixties, and where the civil rights movement had opened up the possibility of new pathways for social protest which expanded still further—worldwide, in fact—with the universal scandal of the Vietnam War. In May 1967 Max Horkheimer had agreed to give a lecture in the America House in Frankfurt to celebrate German-American Friendship Week. Members of the Association of German Socialist Students had earlier organized a demonstration in front of the Town Hall on the Römerberg to protest against an American military parade in the presence of leading German officers and politicians, with Horkheimer as guest of honor. Horkheimer's lecture in the evening was interrupted by shouts of disapproval and heckling, followed by an emotionally charged discussion between him and the students. Both sides wanted to reach an understanding, but in fact, misunderstandings prevailed here too. This was followed by an exchange of letters and a new meeting, this one with Horkheimer and Adorno together. It took place on 12 June 1967 in the Walter-Kolb Residence Hall, the preferred venue of the Frankfurt SDS. Once again the discussion was lively, but both sides were concerned to make sure that contact was not broken off. In particular, the spokespeople of the antiauthoritarian faction in the Frankfurt SDS thought of themselves as the pupils of Adorno and Horkheimer, particularly their outstanding representative, Hans-Jürgen Krahl—the Frankfurt counterpart to the Berlin leader Rudi Dutschke.

Marcuse heard of these confrontations from a variety of sources. His own pupil Angela Davis spent the summer of 1967 in Frankfurt and attended Adorno's lectures and seminars. Marcuse had had his essays from the *Zeitschrift* republished by Suhrkamp, but always with additions pointing out the differences between the thirties and the sixties. He continued to take sides with Horkheimer and Adorno, as he had assured them by letter at the time of the disagreement about the new preface to the German edition of Paul Massing's *Rehearsal for Destruction*. In May 1967 Adorno perceived correctly that Marcuse's wish to resume contact "was determined by anxiety and so as to make sure that it should not come to a serious breach between him and us."[260] In the 1930s Horkheimer's affection for Marcuse had given Adorno real cause for jealousy, but in the second half of the 1960s things had deteriorated to the point where Horkheimer privately made very derogatory comments about Marcuse to Pollock. These disagreements look very different, however, when viewed with hindsight. One item that was clearly not written for posterity was the New Year's card Horkheimer sent to Inge and Herbert Marcuse three years after Adorno's death: "Let us hope we finally meet up happily together again. I am already quite old and become more stupid every day."[261] In the idiom of the old friends, "happily" *(gut)* meant reconciliation. Herbert and Inge, who had been married to Franz Neumann during the New York phase of the institute, responded from La Jolla, "Yes, *auf Wiedersehen!*"[262] But in 1967 Horkheimer was less keen to meet Marcuse. Indeed, he left all contact in the hands of Adorno, who was overstretched both physically and mentally and felt caught on the horns of a dilemma. In the eyes of the public, he was beginning to lose out to Marcuse. Narcissism played more of a role here than vanity, which his friend Fritz Lang, as well as others, believed him to be guilty of. But this was also the source of his identification with his students, whom he had taught to rebel, as Fritz Lang had also rightly observed. Without the category of ambivalence, the relationship between teachers and pupils can no more be understood than could the fraternal relations between the critical theorists under the aegis of Max Horkheimer's enlightened despotism.

The summers of 1968 and 1969 brought a whole series of missed opportunities to meet in the mountains. Marcuse too had been in the habit of spending his summers in the mountains as soon as he could afford it. Adorno did likewise, even though year after year he became increasingly more drained and exhausted. In 1969 even the Engadine seemed too much for "the badly battered Teddie"[263] when he tried to persuade Marcuse to join him at the Murmeltierbrunnen in Zermatt, where they had met in 1967. Only a few years previously they had gone following in Nietzsche's footsteps in Sils and had tracked down a Herr Zuan, who confessed to having belonged to a gang of children who had regularly tormented the philosopher as he wandered around the village in the rain with a red umbrella: "They amused themselves smuggling stones into the closed umbrella, so that they all fell on his head when he opened it up. He would then chase after them, waving the umbrella and uttering threats, but he never caught them. What a terrible situation for the suffering man, we thought, vainly pursuing his tormentors and perhaps even thinking that they were in the right after all, because they represented life as opposed to mind, unless the experience of a genuine lack of pity caused him to doubt the truth of some of his philosophical claims."[264] In 1967, however, Gretel had persuaded him not to go to the Waldhaus Hotel anymore on the grounds that she found "the food there as unpalatable as the people."[265] Instead, they traveled to Crans sur Sierre in the west of Switzerland. In 1968 and 1969 they went to Zermatt, where they did meet up with Marcuse after all. Both did their best to avoid a breach. Nevertheless, justice bids us admit that Marcuse was far better informed about the positions and statements of Adorno and Horkheimer than they were about his. But from the start of the student movement, both Horkheimer and Adorno did make repeated efforts to resume discussions with the rebellious students. After one such encounter, Horkheimer dictated an account of it to Pollock by the fireside: "The oppositional students are very astute for the most part, and they can also see the distortions of Marxism in the so-called communist states, but they firmly believe that it is possible to change society for the better."[266] Horkheimer thought that this was just as naïve in 1968 as it had been in 1958 in Habermas's case, but he was far from being the typical archconservative, rigidly opposed to the student movement, as was widely believed by a superficially informed general public. He was quick to react to anti-Americanism, and he feared a resurgence of anti-Semitism. This explains why he was so concerned about the possibility of new editions of his writings from the thirties and forties, at a time when they had long since been circulating in pirated editions. In particular, the aphorisms from his volume *Dämmerung* (Dawn and Decline), which had appeared in 1932 under the pseudonym "Heinrich Regius," were enjoying a special popularity as graffiti on the walls of Frankfurt University. Horkheimer feared nothing so much as public misunderstandings, and nothing would have been more likely to occur in a tense political climate in which there was not the slightest sympathy for a critical theory of society.

To this day it is widely rumored that Adorno was destroyed by the conflict with the students. But here too Horkheimer's words are more trustworthy than many a statement by interested parties. No one could have forced him to write a sympathetic letter only a few months after Adorno's death to the parents of Hans-Jürgen Krahl, the student leader who had died in a car accident in January 1970. Horkheimer would never have done that had he held Krahl responsible, if only in part, for Adorno's death. Horkheimer himself had chosen to live in Ticino, "out of the firing line," in order to create a distance between himself and the situation in Germany. In the same way, Thomas Mann, his neighbor in California, opted for the view over Lake Zurich in preference to permanent residence in Germany. By 1960 at the latest, following the appearance of graffiti on some synagogues, Horkheimer feared a resurgence of anti-Semitism. He and Adorno had quickly reached the conclusion that the institute should investigate such phenomena. They were assisted in this by the knowledge and expertise they had accumulated in the forties. That expertise enabled them to arrive at a clear political prognosis on the basis of their empirical findings. Adorno's essay "The Meaning of Working Through the Past" had broken the silence on the events of the German past, in particular with the custom of dismissing as Eastern propaganda any critic who pointed out the continuities in the personnel and structures of the West German state, the political parties, and other organizations. Adorno was on friendly terms with Fritz Bauer, the Frankfurt public prosecutor who had played an important part in the capture of Adolf Eichmann, and Bauer kept him well informed. The mass media, and especially the Springer press, themselves had an authoritarian structural bias. As in the case of the synagogue desecrations and neo-Nazi demonstrations, they attempted to show that the budding student movement was being manipulated by Moscow, as this was put in the propagandistic tones of the time. Through his brilliant lecture in November 1959 to an audience from the Council for Christian and Jewish Cooperation, Adorno had gained in prestige that went far beyond his student listeners when he stated, "I consider the survival of National Socialism *within* democracy to be potentially more of a threat than the survival of fascist tendencies against democracy."[267] Anti-Semitism—and this was the new tone, unprecedented in the house of the hangman—was to be represented not as a regrettable, inexplicable event in the past but as a current social problem. At this point Adorno became the beneficiary of the work he had put into *The Authoritarian Personality* in the United States, since this interpreted anti-Semitism not as the function of an authoritarian national character but as a historically determined manifestation of violence that could not be eliminated simply by an enlightened program of information.

Ultimately, this was the flashpoint of disagreement with Marcuse, something that was not realized by most of the students who had been politicized by the events of 2 June 1967. If certain structures cannot be altered by superior arguments, what legitimate methods of change remain? The politically inexperienced students followed a logic of escalation that, as Adorno recognized, was being consciously encouraged in a provocative manner by Hans-Jürgen Krahl. Yet one factor specific to the student movement in Germany was in danger of getting lost in the worldwide eruptions of 1968. One of the driving forces in Germany was what was felt to be the oppressive burden of the National Socialist past. It was imagined that this burden could be shaken off with simple slogans and guides to action such as "Capitalism leads to fascism; down with capitalism!" But when these slogans are reviewed decades later, it is easy to miss the distinction between their introduction in 1967, when they still possessed a slightly ironical overtone, and the deadly earnestness with which people argued about "correct practice" in 1968. Adorno attempted quite early on to explain to his students the difference between a representation for the purposes of agitation and practical reality. He used Brecht as an example to illustrate the distinction, and was deeply shocked to discover that very confusion in someone such as Krahl, "who has been one of my students for years and who is unquestionably one of the most talented."[268] This explanation is to be found in a letter to Günter Grass, who was opposed to the SDS and who acted as a recruiting agent for the Social Democratic Party. Adorno tried to explain to Grass what was happening and why he did not wish to dissociate himself from Krahl: "If you were to see him in a seminar you would not think it was the same person as the man who shouts through megaphones—there is probably something pathological about this divided identity. Incidentally, he had scarcely finished his speech before turning to me and whispering that he hoped I would not take it amiss since it was purely political and not meant personally."[269] Adorno had long since recognized the ambivalent nature of their motives far more clearly than the majority of the student activists themselves did after the events: "One wants to break free from the past: rightly, because nothing at all can live in its shadow, and because there will be no end to the terror as long as guilt and violence are repaid with guilt and violence; wrongly, because the past that one would like to evade is still very much alive."[270]

Ever since his return to Germany, Adorno had not ceased feeling alien in the society of the Federal Republic. In an aphorism of April 1960 he noted, "It is not possible to take pleasure in any single old nook and cranny without feeling ashamed and without feeling guilty."[271] Adorno did not keep feelings like this to himself but introduced them into his teaching. The extant records of his lectures on "negative dialectics" show how very aware he was even in the early 1960s that no political, aesthetic, or theoretical activity can overcome the feeling of survivor's guilt. Long before the student movement, Adorno invented the concept of "pseudoactivity."[272] In his lecture of 23 November 1965 he commented on the experience of American activists, "for example, as an organizer, as such people are known in America; in other words, someone who brings people together, organizes, agitates, and such like. . . . And the more you suspect that this is not true practice, the more doggedly and passionately you become attached to such activities."[273] In short, Adorno criticized the protest movement before it was born. In the spring of 1969 the conflict with the students reached its decisive phase. A group around Krahl was casting around for activities that became increasingly extreme—"more or less under the pressure of their own publicity," as Adorno described it accurately in a letter to Marcuse.[274] The violent blockades of the Springer press that the SDS had organized after the attempted assassination of Rudi Dutschke at Easter 1968 were followed by the spectacular but unsuccessful mass protests against the Emergency Laws. In the run-up to these protests Adorno had called on Otto Brenner, the head of the metalworkers' union, the IG-Metall, and a workers' leader of many years' standing, to organize a general strike. The Frankfurt branch of the SDS tried to revive the flagging enthusiasm for political activities by bringing the demonstrations back into the universities. The protests against the Emergency Laws had been followed by a spectacular occupation of Frankfurt University by the students, who tried to turn it into a political university. The police intervened to put a stop to this by force. With the occupation of the Institute for Social Research, the SDS wished to provoke a further intervention on the part of the police so as to mobilize the students to resist the university authorities without regard to eventual casualties. The fact that this forced Adorno and his colleagues to defend their authority in the building if they were not to fall foul of the university and the politicians was a matter of indifference to the SDS activists.

Adorno wrote an elegant letter to Samuel Beckett on 4 February 1969, from which it emerges that he understood the situation perfectly: "The feeling of suddenly being attacked as a reactionary comes as something of a surprise. But perhaps you too have had the same experience in the meantime."[275] Beckett's reply reached Adorno in the midst of his reassessment of the global political situation, whose contradictory nature could not have been better expressed: "I have not yet been conspiré, so far as I know and that is not so far, by the Marcusejugend [Marcuse youth]. As you said to me once at the Iles Marquises, all is malentendu. Was ever such rightness joined to such foolishness?"[276] What Adorno said to his favorite contemporary writer in a Paris restaurant in 1968 can be gleaned from the projected preface he wrote for *Dialectic of Enlightenment* in February 1969, after he had finally overcome Horkheimer's doubts about the wisdom of a new edition:

> One experience has not been anticipated in the book although it is hinted at in other texts of ours: young people at least have set out to resist the transition to the totally administered world which is not being accomplished seamlessly, but by means of dictatorships and wars. The protest movement in all the countries of the world, in both blocs as well as the Third World, testifies to the fact that wholesale integration does not necessarily proceed smoothly. If this book assists the cause of resistance to achieve a consciousness that illuminates and that prevents people from submitting to blind practice out of despair and from succumbing to collective narcissism, that would give it a genuine function.[277]

In 1969 Adorno wanted to see *Dialectic of Enlightenment* play a role in the present, "since it has remained valid for us," as he had assured Horkheimer publicly in 1965.[278] Without denying that the historical situation was different from that when the book was first written, we can see from the planned preface how everyone could identify with its point of view—not just Horkheimer and Pollock in Montagnola but also Marcuse and Löwenthal in distant California. *Dialectic of Enlightenment*, too, had formulated the secular experience of the short twentieth century "out of the firing line" rather than in the midst of the fray. It would be hard to summarize more succinctly than Adorno precisely what we are to expect from progress, the indispensable component of Enlightenment toward the end of the short century: "It would be advisable . . . to think of progress in the crudest, most basic terms: that no one should go hungry anymore, that there should be no more torture, no more Auschwitz. Only then will the idea of progress be free from lies. It is not a progress of consciousness."[279]

Like the "Heliotrope" in *Minima Moralia,* the "badly battered Teddie"[280] turned his back on Frankfurt to escape the stifling summer heat. But in August 1969, instead of following the stickers on his aunt's suitcase and making his way to the Suvretta Hotel or Madonna di Campiglio—images that he had recalled with such vivid nostalgia during his years in America[281]—he went to the Hotel Bristol in Zermatt. Nor on this occasion did he meet up with Herbert Marcuse in the mountains. Marcuse was on holiday in the French Alps, and it was here that the news of Adorno's death reached him. We can hear the feeling of regret at the missed opportunity when he gave a television interview two days after Adorno's death in which he said that "there is no one who can represent Adorno and speak for him."[282] Marcuse spoke as an individual, but not simply for himself: "My debt to him is endless, and without his work I cannot imagine going on living. But that means that the debate about his work is still to come and must still come, and that it has not yet begun."[283] This was by no means obvious at the time. Most political activists imagined that they could forget Adorno without further ado; the academic world regarded critical theory as a product of the past which had nothing further to teach them. Only those who had shared a "spiritual experience" with Adorno in the sense suggested in *Negative Dialectics* had an intuition that all that could not have been everything. Those who had heard the lectures on *Aesthetic Theory* had remembered: "Great works wait. While their metaphysical meaning dissolves, something of their truth content, however little it can be pinned down, does not; it is that whereby they remain eloquent. A liberated humanity would be able to inherit its historical legacy free of guilt."[284] If now, decades later, we read in print the words we might have heard in Lecture Hall 6, we cannot escape the feeling that in traveling to Zermatt, Adorno was seeking a closeness with death: "In Zermatt the Matterhorn, the child's image of the absolute mountain, gives the appearance of being the only mountain on earth; from the Gorn Ridge it appears as one link in a colossal chain. But Gorn Ridge can only be approached from Zermatt. The situation is no different with regard to perspectives on works of art."[285]

Appendix: Letters

THEODOR W. ADORNO TO ERNST BLOCH

26 July 1962

Prof. Ernst Bloch,
Tübingen,
Im Schwanzer 35

Dear Ernst,

Just to thank you for your card, it was a pleasure to receive it. I hope that the little book will not come as too much of a disappointment. It cannot compare with the broad sweep of the *Geist der Utopie* [Spirit of Utopia], and while I am not unreceptive to the flattering nature of the comparison, I owe it to you to state this bluntly. A good deal of what I wrote in my youth has the character of a dreamlike anticipation, and only after a certain moment of shock, which no doubt coincided with the outbreak of Hitler's Reich, did I truly believe that I was right to do what I did. Like most so-called child prodigies, I am a very late developer, and I still feel today that whatever I truly exist for still lies before me.

Kracauer's visit may have provoked these thoughts in me. You have by now also seen him in Munich. I mean to say that the greater the demands one makes on oneself and the more ambitiously one thinks of oneself in a certain sense in consequence, the less one may transfer such ideas to one's own empirical existence and even to one's actual achievement. In this respect we probably react very similarly. Unfortunately, I can scarcely discuss such matters with Friedel anymore, not only because he has donned armor, as if he were a combination of Narcissus and young Siegfried, but also because he, mindful of the lime leaf,[1] praises my own stuff to the skies a priori, so that I can no longer trust myself to say anything about his. But this, of course, is strictly between ourselves.

In the meantime, my "Introduction to the Sociology of Music" is finished and will be going to the press in the next few days, an esoteric little book, a didactic book, more spoken than written, but perhaps for that very reason a change from virtuous study. Well, you will see. At any rate, I can now devote myself once more to the task for which the homespun

Goethean expression "main task" [*Hauptgeschäft*] still seems to be the most humane description. Keep your fingers crossed.

Will you be coming to the so-called Philosophy Congress in Münster? I am giving a (scholarly) so-called "plenary paper," "On the Dialectics of Progress" ["Zur Dialektik des Fortschritts"], and if I manage to return properly rested, I hope to deliver a truly heretical sermon—the sermon of a heretic. It would be delightful if you could come, although you will probably feel much as I do about the prospect of a Philosophy Congress.

We shall set off on Saturday for the Engadine, for Sils Maria and the Waldhaus Hotel, like old mountain cattle changing their pasture for the new season. Gretel, whose birthday we celebrated in Vienna, had a very nasty accident during a tour of the Wachau. She had a very [crossed out] bad sprain in both feet and all sorts of unpleasant consequences; she is only gradually getting better. She won't be able to do much walking up in the mountains. Apart from that, Vienna was rich and varied, and in part very different from usual; but I shall have to tell you all about it on another occasion. Incidentally, do you know the director of the Austrian College, Alexander von Auer? He is a really pleasant man. If he ever invites you to do anything in Alpbach, you really should go. There is a very entertaining atmosphere up there, and Austria still always provides the consolation of decay.

Do stay in touch.
Much love to Karola and yourself, also from Gretel,

Your old

By the by, do you happen to have an extra typescript, an author's copy or a proof copy of your work on the "noble couple"?[2] I would be very grateful if you could send it to me at the Waldhaus. You would really be doing me a great favor. You have probably seen my little piece on the dialectics of commitment in the *Neue Rundschau;* if not, I shall of course send it to you.

MAX HORKHEIMER TO THEODOR W. ADORNO,
FRANKFURT AM MAIN

Montagnola, 27 September 1958

Teddie,

Letters between ourselves, in so far as they go even minimally beyond technical details, are lame expedients, but I have already announced several times that I wanted to write about Habermas's article in the *Philosophische Rundschau*,[3] and I have now reached the point where I shall do so, despite gout and imbecility. This essay provides us with such a splendid argument for the changes in the Institute that we have discussed that it would be a pity not to make this explicit as soon as possible. When we last talked about it on the telephone, before your departure for Linz, I had taken only a cursory look at it, but now I have read it properly and feel confirmed in my judgment. A talented person who ceaselessly aspires[4] to intellectual superiority finds his way to the Institute and shows that it is possible to spend a considerable amount of time with us—probably over a year in this instance?—without doing anything to enlarge his experience of social reality, indeed, without bringing any intelligent thought to bear on the present, and without making any effort other than the efforts that are satisfied by reading, by his perspicacity, and, if need be, the demands of the philosophy seminar itself. H. takes whatever he deems to be the most advanced ideas of the moment as his model, above all Marx's early writings together with presumably a distorted image of Teddie's and our joint thoughts, and spurs himself on to enormous perspicacity.[5] The document that he has produced on this occasion is a diligent, intelligent, carefully planned, and of course vacuous [*eitel*] work[6] that assesses the philosophical writings which have appeared about Marx in recent years by reference to norms that are constantly repeated and have by now become frozen into clichés. The norms that have been gleaned from "the young Marx" are set in opposition to the older Marx, who in his opinion had been ruined by Engels. These norms are necessarily very threadbare, partly because the *Vormärz*, the period before 1848, was a time of slogans and programs, and in particular because Marx did not infuse his writings with substance before his years in London,[7] and partly because the dialectical Herr H., under the mantle of practicing immanent critique, commits himself on all crucial matters to the norms of the *Vormärz* era and must therefore ignore everything that ties those writings to the first half of the last century, in other words, everything that constitutes their actual life. The constantly reiterated commitment to revolution[8]—I feel the word recurs a hundred times in the article—as the inherent meaning of philosophy sounds historically clueless in H., however frequently he may use the words "strict" or "rigorous." What we learn of the content of philosophy is above all that "the theory of revolution" constitutes the "theory of categories"[9] of ideology critique or critique as such. And this theory is supposed—and this is his "key thesis"[10]—to be transformed into critical-practical activity in order to realize itself; it is not contemplative but interested in a "practical manner" in the transformation [*Aufhebung*] of existing conditions.[11] Thus far philosophy. Sociology, however, may in given circumstances demonstrate "what qualifies the proletariat to become the agent of revolution," since "how otherwise is it to take place[?]"[12] If the workers, however, improperly incline toward the older Marx in preference to the younger one, or even to Engels—there is no mention of other conceivable attitudes that might be adopted by workers—it would be desirable to "present the problematic nature of proletarian class consciousness" in a "sociological manner, that is, logically and concretely."[13]

As for H's curious immanent critique, its immanence does not represent an immersion in the authors under review but is supposed to refer exclusively to Marx, and it even reproaches the Polish opposition for its failure to "develop the partisanship essential to a materialist philosophy of whatever stripe."[14] What he in fact objects to in Marx is that "his scientific prognoses" (his philosophical prognoses with their practical political implications are not considered here) "do not sufficiently take into account the consequences of their being expressed; in short, he has not adequately considered the implications of his own doctrine."[15] In other words, Marx let out the secret that capitalism will be destroyed by its own contradictions, and this has enabled the diabolically cunning capitalists to do away with it to a considerable degree, much as they have eliminated pauperism as a mass phenomenon. Now capitalism still survives even if "class distinctions have not completely fallen by the wayside."[16] As for the proletariat, Marx should have reflected that labor conditions train human beings to think in mechanistic, determinist terms, that is, in terms of cause and effect. This simple fact which, as I have said, drives the workers into the arms of Engels, instead of the pre-1848 Marx, is explained with reference to Sartre's psychological observations that H. probably regards as "practical politics" in contrast to Marx's false prognoses.[17] He does this no doubt because they relate to "a proletarian class consciousness in its function and dialectics"[18] and follow on from Hegel's *Phenomenology*. The author arrives at this conclusion: "A materialist criticism must prove its worth anew by testing itself out in concrete analyses on every historical condition."[19] Apart from the quote from Marcuse,[20] no examples of such analyses are given, but his certainty about their conclusions is powerful. Following on from his earlier essay,[21] H. maintains that the "false" affluent society will be more likely to lead "the self-knowledge of the species" to "reflect upon irrational domination,"[22] in other words, in the direction of the proletarian revolution,[23] than did the poverty-stricken economy of a century ago. H. really does believe that today it is possible "to move the mass of the population to measure itself against the limits of the possible."[24] What expert knowledge of the present; what impressive self-confidence! Marx did not interrogate sociology or realize "that a decision was possible only on the basis of empirical evidence."[25] Now there is an end to mistaken prognoses! Well, we shall not have long to wait. In France, where there is undoubtedly more "poverty in the midst of affluence"[26] than, say, in Germany, the masses are preparing at this very moment to elect de Gaulle and hence to provide empirical evidence that will supplement H.'s immanent criticism of Marx by a practical political critique of H. Of course, this evidence will be unscientific and will hence be rejected a priori as inadequate by H. (The French elections evidently form part of the "theoretical" necessities rather than the "practical" ones. For the former can be calculated with "scientific precision," while the latter, by contrast, cannot be made to prevail "'objectively' with the willpower and consciousness of human beings."[27] At the point of practical necessity, therefore, the old *liberum arbitrium indifferentiae,* the free will of the idealist philosophers, makes its entrance as an incalculable factor, except that for H., freedom makes its appearance exclusively in revolution. How much more profound, then, is the relation of theory and practice in Kant's critique.)

H. does as much violence to philosophy as to sociology. Marx becomes a shibboleth in his essay, because he is meant to be more than "just one humanities problem among others,"[28] since he is somehow to be treated much more respectfully than Montaigne, Spinoza, Voltaire, and Kant, to whom H. impudently delivers a slap on the wrist in passing.[29] Marx is not supposed to be allowed to sink like them to the level of a "classic."[30] This explains why the norms that H. derives from him are given the status of gospel "in interaction with empirical research."[31] As if philosophy had "always deluded itself" into believing that "it could realize itself,"[32] just as if Leibniz and Wolfgang Cramer were one and the same. After all, hadn't the worthy Christian Thomasius proved through his life and his teaching that without "practice . . . all speculation is no more than a body without a soul"?[33] For all his sagacity, anyone who writes like H. writes with blinkers on; he lacks *bon sens* and intellectual tact. He teaches the very thing he purports to combat, pure philosophy, including a doctrine of science in which sociology is confronted with problems from the situation as it was in 1843. You cannot make the leap out of philosophy with the aid of phrases such as "the self-transcendence of philosophy and its realization through practice"[34] or the statement that "philosophy is not capable of being what it claims: the emancipation of mankind."[35] Such reservations are rather inherent components of H's. worldview, comparable to the phrase "only in interaction with empirical research."[36] He reproaches the writers under review with having "narrowed down the genuine philosophical understanding . . . of Marxism in a peculiar way and to have suppressed precisely those aspects of Marx that go beyond 'pure philosophy.'"[37] But what does his non-pure "practical political" philosophy amount to? It thrives, as he says, "from the uncertainty that constantly renews itself from the unresolved tension between theory and practice and can be made to disappear only through the transcendence of philosophy as philosophy."[38] Either he does not mean this uncertainty seriously because in reality he knows how to eliminate the tension, namely, through something that is more than pure philosophy, viz., the "self-awareness of the species," the "practical politics," in short, the revolution—where the only things that remain to be clarified are the accompanying circumstances. Or else the decisive factor really is uncertain. In that event, the definition of what is required really does depend on "concrete analyses," and his philosophy, robbed of its "concrete" content, is even purer, more formalist, than any of the despised philosophies he discusses. All the talk of the "transcending of philosophy" is anyway no more than an intensified idealism.[39] Indeed, if absolute utopia has become the truth, if indeed there is nothing further beyond it, then all speculation ceases, since, as Herr Heidegger is wont to say, "God and the Blessed do not philosophize."[40] As a materialist who refuses to abandon the hopes of the *Vormärz*, however, H. is in a poor position to dismiss as "false"[41] any theory that retains ideas which practice does not help to realize, and to dismiss such ideas as stand on their own. The fact that he does not reflect on the pigheaded nature of his "doctrine of revolution," that he does not recognize how derelict all that seems today, proves, more even than the lack of sociological understanding, the vacuity[42] of his thought, the inability to achieve reconciliation with himself. His ideological materialism itself resembles "the philosophical scheme of a muddled dialectic of the forces and the relations of production"[43] that he criticizes as the state ideology of the Soviet Union. Only in his case it is the muddled dialectic of theory and practice, of philosophy and reality. (What he grandly describes as "the correct evaluation of Marxist critique" turns out to be nothing but a straightforward piece of purpose-directed research. Criticism must "anticipate the investigations of the individual disciplines and allow empirical analysis to supply the conditions governing the possible fulfillment of its aims and to prove their validity."[44] A chemist does precisely that, only he does not dress it up in such vacuous language.) True immanent critique would have to have addressed Marx's ideas themselves, such as the identification of society with a number of European countries—just about comprehensible in the light of conditions before 1848; the concept of a postbourgeois mass uprising in precisely these countries, the most progressive ones, an uprising that is supposed to result in the liberation, once and for all, that philosophy "claims to be";[45] furthermore, the inflated idealist conception of freedom itself that plays the principal role in this materialism; and last but not least, the idea that philosophy will become superfluous once the social relations of human society have been put in order. There is such a thing as nature and the principle ascribed to the "young Marx" that "it must be possible . . . to confront critically every object in the framework of the theory of revolution of historical materialism, nature included,"[46] is either empty of meaning or else it is simply the obverse of the inflated concept of freedom that ultimately excludes nature from reconciliation, treating it as the mere object of domination, an element of chemical metabolism, or, as H. says, of productive labor—H. of course says "concrete" labor—as an element of "the process of the exchange between man and nature."[47] According to H., it is only domination among human beings that counts as "untruth," and not the despoliation of all living creatures that is reproduced in individuals.[48] All these ideas, all these concepts with their internal contradictions, would merit an immanent critique. Herbert Marcuse, who has "rigorously"—things rarely happen without rigor in H.[49]—

"discussed these matters in the spirit of a materialist philosophy" and who "has subjected individual doctrines of Marxism to a necessary revision without reservation(!)"[50] has in fact made a contribution to this topic.

H. has proclaimed a philosophy that at one point he describes as a "preface"[51] and at another refers to, with Merleau-Ponty, as a "critical prologue"[52] to the "experiment"[53] of revolution, over a century after Marx had expected this "contingent"[54] event in Germany as the "immediate"[55] and inevitable postlude to the bourgeois revolution, of the kind that was never able to occur in any bourgeois state, but only in retrograde Russia, and even there in a completely different way from what had been envisaged. H. speaks a lot about the empirical, but today he endorses writings that are built on the conviction that the bourgeoisie is "unfit any longer to be the ruling class in society"[56] and is forced to drive pauperism to an extreme. H. believes that the revolution is more likely to occur in the industrialized nations of 1957 than in 1847, no doubt because he believes—to quote the actual words of the pre-1848 Marx—that "Germany, which is renowned for its thoroughness, cannot make a revolution unless it is a thorough one," and "the day of the German resurrection will be heralded by the crowing of the Gallic cock."[57] All these ideas with their combination of intelligence and blindness I would find quite acceptable in a candidate for the *Habilitation* who is growing up in a university seminar somewhere or other. I would even take pleasure in the fact that the young philosophers in our country do not just consist of Heidegger disciples and existentialists and positivists, but that in contrast to the East, where nonconformist ideas are extirpated, there are still youthful dissenters and people who go their own way.[58] But at present H. is with us in the Institute for Social Research, and I cherish the unusual expectation that the assistants there should be capable of a minimum of responsibility, even when they make their voices heard in journals over which we have no influence. What concerns H. is Marx's theory and practice. Even in the years when National Socialism was emerging, and during the Third Reich itself, we knew that it was futile to look to revolution for salvation. To proclaim revolution here as timely without reflecting on the consequences of "expressing that idea," whose absence in Marx's writings draws H.'s critical fire, can only serve the interests of the masters in the East. Even though H. attacks the latter, those who proclaim revolution would be at their mercy in reality, or else their actions would play into the hands of potential fascists in our own society. There is anyway a deep affinity between "Socialism in One Country" and National Socialism, the two decisive historical phenomena of the first half of this century. It would be far easier to derive the "theory of categories" with which to decipher the contemporary situation from them and from the national uprisings of Mr. Nasser,[59] Abdul Qassim,[60] and the rest of them than from the expectations aroused by Marx's youthful writings. The theory of revolution, interpreted sensibly, can be applied today to backward societies that want to accelerate the process of industrialization by means of a kind of national socialism or state capitalism, a result that is not so easily attained with liberal economic methods. The world is full of revolution, and *thanks to it terror is on the increase.*[61] The essay is teeming with exhortations to be empirical, to the implications of philosophy for practical politics, to the realization that it should "start by reflecting upon the situation in which it finds itself,"[62] but in reality H. does not give a fig about whether his central concept is affected by history and whether it has not long since turned into its opposite.[63] Revolution becomes for him a sort of affirmative idea, a finalized absolute, an idol that utterly falsifies criticism and critical theory as we understand it. One can indeed say, "Society is always a society that must be changed," but in the first place, this may be said of everything *içi bas,* and in the second place, the drastic changes H. expects threaten not so much to establish H.'s idea of the end of history as to reintroduce the ancient doctrine of the cyclical nature of forms of domination. The last constitutional safeguards would disappear and authoritarian rule would become even more quickly established, since it already stands on the horizon.[64] For overwhelming technological, economic, and psychological reasons, revolution in the present means transition to terror of whatever hue.[65] To grasp this does not call for any elaborate "concrete analysis." Anyone who makes the term "revolution" the center of his theory, especially while adopting the pose of the "practical political" philosopher, praises dictatorship, even if unintentionally. There are epochs in which it is more important to prevent change than to make history. Whether Europe still possesses the strength needed for such an act of resistance is very doubtful, particularly since it was in Europe that the process of irresistible change originated. If H. wishes to become a modest part of this process, he must learn to experience things for himself and to articulate them, instead of taking over other people's formulations.

What has to be defended today seems to me not the transformation [*Aufhebung*] of philosophy into revolution but the vestiges of bourgeois civilization,[66] in which the idea of individual freedom and a just society still has a place, as well as natural law as it has been understood during the last few centuries, rather than H.'s free-floating dialectics. We can try to impart to some people energies that have developed here so that they are not simply engulfed in darkness by the catastrophes that threaten us. Now, when continental Europe, with its constantly interrupted and constantly denied civil society, finds itself immediately confronted by a doubly totalitarian society, we see how right Hegel was when he agreed with antiquity that a life governed by good laws should be regarded as the best inheritance that we can be given.[67] In so far as such laws exist, our duty is to preserve them; they are under threat. To employ the general wealth and increase it so that no one need go hungry, to defend the safety and freedom of the individual, to reduce the endless pressure that bears down on everyone, to bring help to those who suffer from unseen poverty—we can do a small, barely perceptible amount to alleviate all these things by sensitizing people to the presence, incursion, and return of barbarism within and without. That is the "practice" of what you write and what we teach. The infinite that necessarily inhabits the finite idea that knows itself to be finite cannot be turned into the existing state of affairs, "society." For all my criticism of the finite, I prefer to stick to Kant and believe in the infinite task. People like H., particularly when they are close to us, inevitably distort our efforts and help to frustrate them. Not so much because he probably employs the Institute's time, money, and personnel for purposes alien to ours, but because his conceptual fetishisms pervert the principles and the sociological understanding of our students.[68] This is intolerable, all the more so as his language and some of the topics he discusses, and not least his tireless activity, attract the young. At select moments there is the risk that he is setting the tone in the Institute.[69] In saying this, I am not thinking so much of the antinuclear campaign when H. intervened as a propagandist on the side of the students[70] as of the reaction of our staff to our invitation to representatives from industry last year.[71] The criticism of some students that we had made too many concessions to industry, their demand for class struggle in a teacup, while all the time we were trying to help our future graduates gain a steppingstone to a decent career was a warning sign. It showed us how narrow and simplistic some of them have already become. If there is to be an esprit de corps in the sense intended by H.'s article, we shall be producing not free spirits, people capable of independent judgment, but followers who swear by particular books, today this one and tomorrow that. H.'s talk of "individuals,"[72] a term which he has borrowed from us, and which Marx, the young one as much as the old one, to say nothing of Engels, would probably have dismissed with a biting comment, is merely a *façon de parler*. The proletariat, the "mass of the people," are crucial for this affirmative philosophy. Its structure remains quite untouched by the conceptual identity—I say the conceptual identity, and not merely the factual one—of mass movement, manipulation, and resentment; its unapproachable center is violent change. In other words, fanaticism. With all our criticism of conditions that cause suffering and that could be ameliorated by methods available to society, with all our sympathy, however ambiguous, for André Gide's "Tout cela sera balayé,"[73] we have always hated the practice of eliminating, liquidating, and repressing, regardless of whether it was carried out by Cromwell, Robespierre, Stalin, or Hitler. I still remember the shock I felt as a student in 1919 when Lenin proclaimed that the workers should act ruthlessly toward those who could not make up their minds. "Shooting," he said, was the proper fate of "the coward in the face of the enemy." The recent bloodbath in the palace in Baghdad,[74] which world opinion accepted as readily as it had the liquidation of millions of ordinary people on every side, recalled the ghastly murder of the czar's family with their children, which acted as the trigger to an endless terror. In the case of our university assistant, however, "the sight of the elimination always acts as a guide to the perception of what is to be eliminated."[75] Needless to say, this statement, which was intended to be purely logical, slipped out in the course of his discussion of "alienation." The alienation between him and us, however, should not be eliminated but should make its entrance as speedily as possible, since otherwise the Institute will be turned into a caricature of what we want it to be. H. is a particularly energetic, active man, and he may have learned a lot from us, especially from you, though scarcely anything that has to do with the experience of social realities. *Even the philosophical ideas he has taken from us only sound similar.* It is worth comparing the "key thesis" from Marx that he uses as a foundation stone with the cautiously phrased, reflective conditional clause that he quotes from *Against Epistemology*.[76] The difference in tone really makes for a completely different statement. As far as I am concerned, you know how much I dislike him and how hard I find it to overcome the feeling. For this reason I have seldom spoken to him and, if I am not mistaken, never alone.[77] This publication does not help to moderate my feelings. As a writer, he probably has a good, even a brilliant career before him; but he can only damage the Institute. Let us put an end to the present situation and induce him amicably to preserve his philosophy in another place where he can turn it into reality.

Forgive this long letter with its many quotations and repetitions. I had to shorten it greatly. But I am still very tired. Please give my best wishes to Gretel and don't be cross with me for not liking H. See you soon. Kindest regards from

Max

(Maidon sends her best wishes and fond regards.

P.S. When this letter was finished, I wanted to give it to you once I had arrived in Frankfurt, as a basis for us to discuss. After I read the first part of the study on students,[78] however, it seemed preferable for you to have had time to digest it before I arrive. Up to now I am familiar only with the introduction. The ideas it contains are broadly similar to those in the essay in the *Philosophische Rundschau*. The word "revolution" has been replaced, presumably under your influence, by "development from formal democracy to material democracy, from liberal to social."[79] But in the minds of the average readers, the "potential" that is supposed to become politically efficacious as a consequence of this development is unlikely to be realized by democratic methods. How should the people that is supposed to be "imprisoned in the shackles of a . . . bourgeois society, in a liberal constitution under the rule of law" make the transition to the so-called political society for which, according to H., it has "long since become ready,"[80] if not through violence? Such declarations are impossible in the research reports of an institute that depends on public funding from this shackling society. If, then, seventy pages of comprehensive categorical statements are followed by the announcement that "more precise information . . . can only be given after the actual study" that will be based on "intensive interviews of 171 representative students of the Johann Wolfgang Goethe University,"[81] that is *tout même* ridiculous.

I know full well how much energy and how much love you have expended on ensuring that this study will become something of which the Institute can be proud, and I can already see, even though I have read only a small part of it, that it leaves even respectable sociological work far behind. But we cannot allow the Institute to be ruined by the truly insouciant attitude of this assistant. What social research means to him is something he has expressed in the *Rundschau* with remarkable frankness for anyone who wishes to hear: it is to secure his "revolutionary philosophy of history intent on establishing an empirical foundation."[82]

Yours,
M)

Theodor W. Adorno to Max Horkheimer

[Frankfurt am Main, for 14 February 1965]

Max,

Even if we did not both detest the official *gestus* that is encapsulated in the word "appreciation" [*Würdigung*], I would not find it possible to write an essay for your birthday that had pretensions to being objective. In a friendship of over forty years, our lives have become so entwined that any ambition one of us might have to say something about the other outside that relationship would deny what really has to be expressed, namely, our common life. Nothing could ever undermine that, whether it be psychological factors, competing interests, or differences in disposition. From you I have learned solidarity, a concept that has seeped from politics into private life, and I confide my gratitude to your sober nature so that it might seek protection there. What gave the concept of solidarity its power over us has faded in politics along with the possibility of spontaneity. In you the memory of this lives on. We are utterly free, you and I, from the illusion that the private person might achieve in isolation what has failed in the public realm, particularly in an era that has set out to liquidate the private sphere. But if the private, obdurately fixed in the particular, has merited this fate, it is to be hoped that it may yet, as it vanishes, gain a right to effect conciliation. Having lagged behind the onward march of history, it nevertheless embodies in its impotence the resistance to it, to the total power of existing circumstances. This is something that our friendship has meant from the first moment on, without our having been aware of it. This is why we are unable to make a neat separation between our objective work and our private lives.

The fact that you are to turn seventy has something incredible about it. Not that we have not aged. But the impulse that brought us together rebels against adulthood. We are tied to two different phases of childhood development; I incline to that of the good, obedient child who purchases through his obedience the freedom to exercise independent thought and opposition. You have retained something of the rebellious youth who is averse to every regulated conduct of life and who sublimates his refractoriness into thinking. This flies in the face of any image of venerable old age that the date suggests. In fact, it seems to me to be only yesterday that we met up once again, in December 1935, in Paris, at the end of the only period in which we had not seen each other for a few years. You described the Institute for Social Research which you had rescued with prudent foresight, by transferring it via Switzerland to America, to Columbia University, as a group of young scholars, although you were already forty years old at the time. Today, like then, you refuse to identify yourself as part of the gerontocracy that calls itself the republic of scholars. Like myself, you probably never felt attracted to the so-called youth movement; but by the same token, you have never denied the element of frailty in life, the natural history of suffering that the individual becomes aware of as he grows older. In contrast, as I now reconstruct it, you have always had something ageless about you that is as incompatible with the idea of inexperienced youth as with the serene maturity that it is supposed to lead up to. When I first saw you in the psychology seminar of Adhémar Gelb, as someone eight years older than I, you scarcely seemed like a student; more like a young gentleman from a well-to-do family who displayed a certain detached interest in scholarship. You were untouched by the professional deformation of the academic who all too easily confuses devotion to learning with reality. Only, everything you said was so acute, so perspicacious, and above all so independent that I quickly came to feel that you were superior to the sphere which you kept imperceptibly at a distance. In another class you read a truly brilliant seminar paper—I think it was on Husserl, with whom you had studied for a few semesters. I went up to you spontaneously and introduced myself. We have been together ever since. Among my early impressions what stands out is that of a slightly daring elegance that was as alien to bourgeois respectability as to the appearance of the other students. Your features, however, were passionate and ascetically narrow. You looked like a gentleman and like a born refugee. Your way of life fitted in with this impression. You had quickly acquired a house in Kronberg, together with Fred Pollock, in which you lived in some seclusion but with an evident distaste for furnished rooms.

You understood not just life's difficulties but also its entanglements. As a man who could see into the heart of the machinery and wanted to change it, you were resolute and also capable of asserting yourself without making concessions. The ability to examine critically the principle of self-preservation and at the same time to use it to secure your own self-preservation—this was a living paradox embodied in you. Decades later, in emigration, you said something that I could never forget: it was we who had been spared who really belonged in a concentration camp. This statement is inextricably bound up with your will to survive. It is philosophically related to the paradox that you had renounced metaphysical hope, almost like a man of the eighteenth-century Enlightenment, but you did so not with the triumphal gesture of a man with his feet firmly planted on the ground, but in infinite sorrow. For whatever made you rebel against positive metaphysics was itself metaphysical, inspired by that possible rejection of actual reality that you expected and still expect at any moment. At the same time, a strict taboo prevented you from confusing the real and the possible; to that extent, despite our commitment to Hegel, you remained a true Kantian. Your parents still adhered to the Jewish law; as their child, you respected the prohibition against graven images and even extended it to the promise their religion held out, namely, of hope. The skeptically reflective aspect of your fundamentally enthusiastic disposition is difficult to grasp in words, but it is something that you must have acquired in your pre-academic life. For seven years you were active as a businessman; originally you were meant to take over your father's factories. It is of equal importance for you that in your rebellion against the commercial world you should have rejected that inheritance entirely as that you should have preserved the concrete awareness of the supremacy of the economy in present-day society and reflected on it in your scholarly work. Your cosmopolitan attitudes, too, averse to German provincialism, are a legacy of those apprenticeship years in Western countries.

It has often been remarked that people whose relation to hope has been broken—and hope is able to function only as a broken, a secret energy source of thought, not directly—gain an emphatic relation to happiness, to that which never recurs. What I found fascinating about you was that from the very first day you made a connection between the idea of a just state of affairs of mankind as a whole and respect for the happiness of every individual, without any hint of that renunciation which has stained the concept of philosophical profundity throughout its history. Two memories of our early time together have remained with me and had a greater pedagogical influence on me than everything else I had learned or had had instilled into me. On one occasion we spoke of a philosopher who had been afflicted by progressive paralysis, but who continued to work until the end with admirable energy, dictating by making signs with one finger, the last limb that the illness had left him. Under the influence of bourgeois preconceptions, I stressed that his illness was not syphilitic in origin. You replied vehemently that that was irrelevant. Even if the man had infected himself, this diminished neither his value nor that of his work. Your reaction gave me a sudden insight into the old untruth implicit in the denigration of pleasure, an idea that would later become one of our theoretical themes. On another occasion we were discussing questions of socialism. As yet ignorant of socialist theory, I maintained that if the others, those disadvantaged hitherto, had their turn in power, that would suffice for the cause of justice. You contradicted this by arguing that only if the entire system were to change could change be approved of; it was not enough for the injustice that had been created to be perpetuated in a new form. The course of events has proved you right. I have learned from you that the possibility of wanting change need not be purchased with the renunciation of one's own happiness. It is this idea that has healed theories about society as a whole of the rancor that otherwise poisons them and draws them back under the spell of eternal sameness.

The two of us were brought to philosophy neither by education nor by scientific method. We gave a philosophical slant to matters that really formed part of sociology or social psychology according to the rules governing the division of labor. We never believed that the theory of society was the totality; but in exchange the totality that comes to form society is all too evidently the untruth. But our experiences did not run in parallel. Instead they converged. Your primary experience was your indignation about injustice. To transform this into a knowledge of social antagonisms, and in particular your reflections on a practice that was explicitly intended to coincide with theory, forced you in the direction of philosophy as the unremitting rejection of ideology. In contrast, I was an artist, a musician, by both origin and early training, but I was inspired by a desire to give an account of art and its possibilities today that should include objective factors, a sense of the inadequacy of a naïvely aesthetic stance in the face of social tendencies. In a short space of time, your political disgust with the course of the world came together with my own, which in my case led me toward music that repudiated complicity of every kind. The tension of the opposite poles from which we came has not diminished and has proved fertile for us both. I have turned you into a conscience that prevented me from ever forgetting practice, the realization of what has been thought, as an aspect of philosophy. Aestheticism is not external to art, it is not its fall from grace; it is regarded as such only by the ethical philistine. It accompanies art, especially where art keeps most strictly to its task, that of the pure critique of the world spirit. You preserved me from the life of an aesthete not through your principles but through the power of an expanding consciousness. My influence on you was perhaps to have reinforced your anti-positivist, speculative streak, and also your reservations about a practice which, by realizing itself in the world, must keep on conceding to the world more than it ought: and perhaps I have convinced you of the relevance of a narrative, a specific form and shape. You too set out to criticize the bad universal and to immerse yourself in the particular. But you run the opposite risk to that of the aesthete, namely, that you do not always pay heed to qualitative distinctions in the drive to achieve a universally human form of action. Through you I have learned to appreciate the gravity of negativity in an undiluted form, which art is constantly tempted to trivialize because of its formal nature, as the postulating of existing images; without a nihilistic component, utopia is a harmless joke. In exchange, or so I conjecture, you have learned from me that without the transcendent element of utopia, utopia or even the truth of the slightest sentence would not exist. To put it boldly, the tension we have been working away at throughout our lives is inexhaustible because it is itself the elusive and fragile truth that we have vainly sought to formulate.

Your character is similarly determined by the duality of a theoretical and practical talent, as mine is by that of the artistic and reflective. In no one else have I found those two aspects, which psychologically tend to preclude each other, so evenly developed as in you. Your ego ideal is their reconciliation: as a living human subject you refuse to let yourself be fragmented by the division of labor, to be crippled by the one-sided development of certain qualities at the expense of others that do not normally go with them. What is most specific to you is surely the unity of these dual qualities. I should like to call it the strength to achieve identification. This is the opposite of the type of thinking that relies on identifying, subsuming, and hence reducing everything to the same plane. Instead, it involves the ability to make oneself identical with others, with those who suffer. Hence your liking for Schopenhauer. But your talent is not a gift for what is known as empathy. It is located somewhere below the ego, with its fixed crystallization; it is a mimetic faculty, so genuine that it makes you feel a slight aversion from every apparent mimesis, every species of playacting, an aversion, incidentally, related to the dislike you feel for any form of intellect that lends itself to a mere means of circulation. You are capable of actually transforming yourself into a different, living being, just as you sometimes howl like a dog with a slow decrescendo. The tenderness that enables you to master such tricks is metapsychological, similar to the tenderness that the intellect sloughed off in order to achieve its own autonomy and that belongs only to physical organs in human beings, as indeed in animals. Your unconditionality is of a comparable tenderness. In your measured, Swabian way, you take things to their limits, persisting in determinate negation, expressing a solidarity with whatever has life, aspires to life. You did not allow your upbringing to deprive you of the habit of perceiving the world like the living creature that vents its fury on it. You have even shown yourself the equal of your enemies by becoming like them, reacting like them in certain situations; this enabled you to outmaneuver them. This calls for an ego that is both very strong and very malleable, resistant and yielding at the same time. By exteriorizing yourself, you preserved yourself. I sometimes think that the strength of your ego consists in your resistance to attempts to destroy your penchant for the diffuse, unrationalized aspects of culture.

You once told me that I think that animals are like humans, while you think human beings are like animals. There is some truth in this. The countermovement away from those extremes may have been productive in our ongoing dialogue. Your starting point, that the individual is doomed, a thing that twitches impotently, is what has presumably given rise to the aspect of your philosophy that the textbook stereotypes call materialism. It differs from the current and vulgar variants in the sense that it does not possess a trace of the malice associated with that concept. You are fully aware that hope attaches itself to the concrete, the individuated, or what our own Karl Heinz Haag calls the "unrepeatable." In your case this knowledge is the basis for your premonition of futility; that the very thing from which all happiness and all truth feeds does not exist. You have absorbed the utopian impulse uncompromisingly in the spirit of criticism, without any affirmative consolation, and even without trusting in a future which in any case could not make reparation for past suffering. I have never been able to oppose this conviction with anything beyond the question whether the inexorable logic that drives you in that direction does not derive its substance from the very thing that it excludes. We have no more been able to answer that question than anyone else.

The materialism that you developed in the great essays in the *Zeitschrift für Sozialforschung* is not positive; it embodies no established scientific method, scarcely even philosophy—if it had been positive, it would succumb to the negative judgment on totalizing, self-gratifying thought that is not the least of the motive forces behind materialism itself. This explains why the work in which you presented something like a program bears the title "Traditional and Critical Theory." You have emancipated materialism from the realm of the apocryphal, the inferior, which it kept lapsing into, by reflecting on it philosophically, in the context of a critique of philosophy. This merged for you with a critique of the objective structure of society. Your idea of theory was from the outset aimed at attacking idealist and positivist tendencies, as well as materialist dogmatism. It is for this reason that quite early on you unleashed the dispute about irrationalism instead of blindly worshiping, like Lukács, at the altar of rationalism, which, given your own Enlightenment sympathies, might have been thought close to your own heart. Your polemical attack on positivism as a prohibition on thinking and a fetishization of scientific method is still unmatched.

The open-mindedness of your thought, your refusal to sign up to fixed principles while at the same time never committing yourself to pluralism, proved its worth in your attitude toward psychoanalysis. The latter had its place in the realm of social knowledge; that of the social cement of psychological moments which turned out, decades later, to play such an overwhelming role in the process of social integration. You read Freud without taking any of the precautionary measures customary in Germany, but remained conscious of the priority of society over the individual caught up in the compulsive mechanisms of psychoanalysis. For that reason you denied it the status of a basic social science. You were disinclined to dilute the force of psychoanalysis in favor of prevailing sexual taboos; but by the same token, however, you perceived early on that, functioning as it did within existing society, it adjusted to that society because of its own postulate of doing justice to reality. In consequence, it constantly teeters on the brink of abandoning its own portion of the critical theory that it originally was. In the world that society has become, all spirit is a form of neurosis; it is better, then, to turn it to good use than to extirpate it so that the machinery runs more smoothly.

Once we had finished the *Dialectic of Enlightenment*, a book that has continued to be our philosophical benchmark, you turned your energies as an academic and organizer to the task of teaching students how to grasp the incomprehensible fact that became known to us in its full implications only toward the end of the war. You started from the insight that if a repetition of the horror is to be prevented, an understanding of the mechanisms at work will be of greater benefit than remaining silent or freezing in impotent indignation. The same motives persuaded you to return to Germany and rebuild the Institute for Social Research, whose director you had been before the Hitler dictatorship. At that time, your doubts about the power of the word were intensified. What might be called your materialist metaphysics, an Old Testament–like awareness of the vanity of living, transferred itself to your attitude toward thought. Even the deepest and truest thoughts, you felt, are scattered by the winds; the persistence of objective ideas is an illusion in the face of the darkness of forgetting. You ascribe no substantial reality to spirit; you seek its essence, truth and freedom, in its self-denial. Your basic feeling is that the adventitiousness of the world is definitive. That feeling, however, confers on what is, whatever emerges from the darkness, the right, despite all its guilt, that you turn to with a love that is not smaller than the shudder you feel at the nature of the existing reality that you nevertheless love.

At its deepest level, the overall system repels you because, in accordance with its own principle, it is heading for its own destruction. In a just society exchange would be not just abolished but also fulfilled; everyone would receive his due that exchange promises him, only to withhold it. You have never denied having patriarchal features, but they were sublimated into an extraordinary flair for power relations, and hence for the ability to ensure that you and yours are in a position to assert their rights by resisting. Your talent in countless situations derives from the constellation of worldly knowledge, the power of resistance, and a quality of always remaining a little detached from reality. You have always been somewhat more successful in getting the better of the natural crudeness of reality than it has been in thwarting you.

The freedom I associate with you can be measured by the resistance it offers; it is identical with firmness, inalienable loyalty without oath. Only people with a strong ego, you once said, by which is meant only free people, are capable of loyalty. Kant attempted to capture the essence of the freedom of the living in his doctrine of the intelligible character. For him, that freedom is a disposition that "one gives oneself." It forms part of life and yet is anything but mere existence. This concept, which in its pure form is impossible to conceive of, is one I find exemplified in you; it is no illusion. People are more in their potential than they are in fact. This "more" is no abstraction. It appears sporadically again and again, even in what we actually are. We are not entirely the products of that mastery of nature that we have invented, that we have inflicted on the world and ultimately on ourselves. This surplus becomes manifest in you, constantly renewing itself. It may be said of you, if indeed it can be said at all of an individual, that you have an intelligible character, and this says much more about your own nature than anything psychological.[83]

21 February 1964

Professor Dr. Theodor W. Adorno
6 Frankfurt am Main
Kettenhofweg 123

Mr. Claus Behncke
Westdeutscher Rundfunk
Abteilung: Kulturelles Wort
5 Köln 1
Postfach 1850

Dear Mr. Behncke,

Please accept my best thanks for your letter. And please believe me when I say that having read the correspondence, I feel that the matter is now closed. I had in any case found it difficult to believe that you would adopt a hostile attitude toward me for no reason discernible to me and was convinced that if such feelings had crossed your mind, you would have told me about them first. I should, however, also like to say that Herr Glaser, for whose Ph.D. thesis I acted as second examiner, is someone of whom I think extremely highly.

That gives me the opportunity to make a comment on a matter of principle. With increasing frequency I come across people who think highly of me or at least claim to do so and who then wax indignant about my so-called imitators—God knows I do not include you in their ranks. I know it can be irritating to have one's mannerisms copied, but long experience has taught me that matters are not so straightforward. In the first place, I must say that as long as there are still pockets in which the ideas and speech mannerisms of Heidegger and Jaspers prevail, I would rather have someone who imitates me than someone who speaks the jargon of authenticity. In the second place, if young people choose to attach themselves to a teacher, literally or more generally, that is no bad thing. Goethe was well aware that originality is something that has to develop, it is not there from the very outset; we should not forget this. Schoenberg, who was undoubtedly one of the most original people I have ever met, was liberal in the extreme in this respect. He never disowned the works he had composed in his youth, which reactionaries of all people criticized for being too Wagnerian. The tendency to make a hard and fast distinction between the so-called fellow travelers or imitators and their supposed leader simply means using the former to beat the latter. You neutralize awkward thinkers by classifying them as unique phenomena and afterwards slip into describing their achievements as exceptional cases which therefore do not count. Above all, it then becomes possible to prevent a tradition from being built up around them. In other words, you can cut them down to size just when they are starting to have an impact. Much of that happens unconsciously, but we ought to reflect on it nevertheless. The indignation about my imitators has gradually become so widely accepted that I am starting to mistrust those who are even more like me than I am myself and who want to turn my ideas into something they are least suited to: property.

I repeat that none of this is aimed at you, but perhaps you could consider whether by insisting on this point one doesn't enter into a social context that signifies the very opposite of what one wanted in the first place.

With best regards
Your old [Adorno]

[Montagnola], 1 September 1969

Dear Mr. Herz,

The fact that I am only now replying to your kind letter of 15 August[84] is to be explained not only by the deep sadness I have been overcome by following the death of Adorno and a number of others to whom I feel attached, but also by the obligations that have arisen in that connection and that I am scarcely in a position to honor. I would ask, therefore, for your understanding if I answer only briefly. I hope that there will be an opportunity in Vienna, Frankfurt, or Switzerland for us to speak to each other.[85]

Your regret that at the funeral of my friend Adorno there was no expression of Jewishness is one for which I have great understanding. The external reasons for this are obvious. His father was of Jewish origin; his mother, who was born Calvelli-Adorno della Piana, was, like her sister, an artist. Both of them were of crucial importance for his education. They represented the Catholic tradition. Teddie Adorno was baptized a Catholic, and because of the influence of a Protestant religious teacher, he was confirmed in the Protestant Church.

I tell you this in order to make Adorno's complicated relationship to religion, to religious allegiance, comprehensible. On the other hand, may I say that the critical theory that we both had a hand in developing has its roots in Judaism. It arises from the idea: Thou shalt not make any graven image of God.

That Adorno identified with the persecuted is proved by his statement that after what has happened at Auschwitz, no more poetry should be written.[86] If he had lived longer, and if we had discussed the funeral beforehand, it is not impossible that the ceremony might have been conducted along the lines you mention in your letter.

I would like to thank you once again and remain, with best wishes,

Yours sincerely

Notes

References to the German editions of Adorno and Horkheimer are as follows:

AGS   Theodor W. Adorno, *Gesammelte Schriften in 20 Bänden*, ed. Rolf Tiedemann, with the assistance of Gretel Adorno, Susan Buck-Morss, and Klaus Schultz (Frankfurt am Main: Suhrkamp, 1986).

HGS   Max Horkheimer, *Gesammelte Schriften*, ed. Alfred Schmidt and Gunzelin Schmid Noerr (Frankfurt am Main: Suhrkamp, 1985–).

1. Instead of an Overture

1. Theodor W. Adorno to Ernst Bloch, 26 July 1962, printed in full in the appendix to this book.

2. Herbert Marcuse, "Reflexionen zu Theodor W. Adorno—aus einem Gespräch mit Michaela Seiffe," in Hermann Schweppenhäuser, ed., *Theodor W. Adorno zum Gedächtnis* (Frankfurt am Main, 1971), p. 51. [All translations are my own unless a published English translation is cited.—Trans.]

3. "Whether or not Adorno's creative energies went beyond the branches of knowledge in which he was an expert—aesthetics, above all musicology, sociology, psychology, and intellectual history—it remains true that he had mastered all these subjects to an almost unparalleled degree. If the term genius can be appropriately applied to any intellectually productive human being alive today, then Theodor W. Adorno must be that person." "Gedenkworte," *Frankfurter Allgemeine Zeitung*, 8 August 1969, HGS, 7:289.

4. *Aesthetic Theory*, trans. Robert Hullot-Kentor (London, 1997), p. 170.

5. Ibid., p. 171.

6. Ibid. [Translation modified—Trans.]

7. "In an obituary for Adorno I have said something I should like to repeat here. If any intellectual in our own age of transition merits the title of genius, Adorno must be that person." Horkheimer in conversation with Bernhard Landau (1969), HGS, 7:288.

8. "Afterword" to *Porträts deutsch-jüdischer Geistesgeschichte* (1961), HGS, 8:191.

9. J. W. von Goethe, *From My Life: Poetry and Truth*, in *Goethe: The Collected Works*, ed. Thomas P. Saine and Jeffrey L. Sammons, trans. Robert R. Heitner, vol. 4 (1987; reprint, Princeton, 1994), p. 17.

10. Siegfried Kracauer, "Die Biographie als neubürgerliche Kunstform" (1930), in *Schriften*, vol. 5.2 (Frankfurt am Main, 1990), p. 19.

11. Siegfried Kracauer, *Marbacher Magazin,* ed. Ingrid Belke and Irina Renz, no. 47 (1988): 110.

12. Sigmund Freud/Arnold Zweig, *Briefwechsel,* ed. Ernst L. Freud (Frankfurt am Main, 1984), p. 137.

13. Sigmund Freud, preface to Marie Bonaparte, *Edgar Poe: Eine psychoanalytische Studie* (Frankfurt am Main, 1981), p. 5.

14. K. R. Eissler, preface to *Goethe: Eine psychoanalytische Studie, 1775–1786* (1982; reprint, Munich, 1987), pp. 11 and 1486.

15. Adorno to Löwenthal, 24 November 1942, in Löwenthal, *Schriften,* vol. 4 (Frankfurt am Main, 1984), pp. 158f.

16. "All the Little Flowers," in *Minima Moralia,* trans. Edmund Jephcott (London, 1974), p. 167.

17. *Prisms,* trans. Samuel and Shierry Weber (Cambridge, Mass., 1983), p. 260. Adorno is referring to Kafka's story "The Hunter Gracchus."

18. Ibid.

19. Adorno to Max Horkheimer, 15 December 1966, published in part in Rolf Wiggershaus, *The Frankfurt School,* trans. Michael Robertson (Cambridge, 1994; 2007), p. 597.

20. *Negative Dialectics,* trans. E. B. Ashton (1973; reprint, London, 1996), p. 363.

21. Walter Benjamin, "The Storyteller," trans. Harry Zohn, in *Selected Writings,* vol. 2 (Cambridge, Mass., 2002), p. 144.

22. "Out of the Firing Line," in *Minima Moralia,* p. 54.

23. Eric Hobsbawm's reflections on long and short centuries can be found in *Age of Extremes: The Short Twentieth Century, 1914–1991* (London, 1995).

24. "Offener Brief an Max Horkheimer" (1965), AGS, vol. 20.1, p. 162. See the appendix to this volume.

25. Walter Benjamin/Theodor W. Adorno, *The Complete Correspondence, 1928–1940,* trans. Nicholas Walker (Cambridge and Oxford, 1999), p. 230.

26. *Prisms,* p. 260.

27. Adorno to Löwenthal, 3 January 1949, in Löwenthal, *Schriften,* 4:174. [The German word for "uncanny" *(unheimlich)* contains the word "homely" *(heimlich).* Freud puns on this in his famous essay "On the Uncanny."—Trans.]

28. "Offener Brief an Max Horkheimer," p. 162. See also appendix.

29. Wolfgang Kraushaar, *Frankfurter Schule und Studentenbewegung: Von der Flaschenpost zum Molotowcocktail, 1946–1995,* vol. 2 (Hamburg, 1998), p. 602.

30. Ibid., p. 671.

31. "Interview zum Tode Adornos" (1969), HGS, 7:292.

32. "Offener Brief an Max Horkheimer," p. 155. See also the appendix to this volume.

33. *Zum Problem der Familie* (1955), AGS, vol. 20.1, p. 309.

34. "Proprietary Rights," *Minima Moralia,* p. 38.

35. *Wird Spengler recht behalten?* (1955), AGS, vol. 20.1, p. 141.
36. "Notes on Kafka," in *Prisms*, p. 263.
37. "All the Little Flowers," p. 167.

2. The House in Schöne Aussicht

1. Walter Benjamin/Theodor W. Adorno, *The Complete Correspondence, 1928–1940*, trans. Nicholas Walker (Cambridge, 1999), p. 159.
2. Walter Benjamin, *A Berlin Chronicle*, in *One-Way Street and Other Writings*, trans. Edmund Jephcott and Kingsley Shorter, (London, 1979), p. 304.
3. Ernst Bloch, *Das Prinzip Hoffnung*, vol. 3 (Frankfurt am Main, 1959), p. 1628.
4. *Auf die Frage: Warum sind Sie zurückgekehrt* (1962), AGS, vol. 20.1, p. 395. Adorno's essay on Heine of 1956 varies the theme of homelessness: "Heine's stereotypical theme, unrequited love, is an image for homelessness, and the poetry devoted to it is an attempt to draw estrangement itself into the sphere of intimate experience. Now that the destiny which Heine sensed has been fulfilled literally, however, the homelessness has also become everyone's homelessness; all human beings have been as badly injured in their beings and their language as Heine the outcast was. His words stand in for their words: there is no longer any homeland other than a world in which no one would be cast out anymore, the world of a genuinely emancipated humanity. The wound that is Heine will heal only in a society that has achieved reconciliation." "Heine the Wound," in *Notes to Literature*, ed. Rolf Tiedemann, trans. Shierry Weber Nicholsen, vol. 1 (New York, 1991), p. 85.
5. *On the Question: "What Is German?"* in *Critical Models*, trans. Henry W. Pickford (New York, 1983), p. 210. [Alternative translation—Trans.]
6. Adorno had planned a sequel to *Minima Moralia* after his return to Germany. It was to be called *Graeculus*. Rolf Tiedemann published a selection in the *Frankfurter Adorno Blätter*, no. 8 (2003): 13f.
7. Siegfried Kracauer, *Ginster: Von ihm selbst geschrieben* (Frankfurt am Main, 1973), p. 20.
8. "Almost Too Earnest" was the title of his response; see "Fast zu ernst" (1951), AGS, vol. 20.2, pp. 569f.
9. Ibid., p. 570.
10. Gershom Scholem, *Zur Sozialpsychologie der Juden in Deutschland 1900 bis 1930* (1978), in *Judaica*, vol. 4 (Frankfurt am Main, 1984), p. 253.
11. Paul Arnsberg, *Die Geschichte der Frankfurter Juden seit der Französischen Revolution*, 3 vols. (Darmstadt, 1983), a continuation of Isidor Kracauer, *Die Geschichte der Frankfurter Juden* (Frankfurt am Main, 1925).
12. *Toward a Reappraisal of Heine*, AGS, vol. 20.2, p. 442.
13. Ibid., pp. 441f.
14. Heinrich von Treitschke (1834–1896) was a renowned German historian. He

was professor of history at the university in Berlin and succeeded Leopold von Ranke as the historiographer of the Prussian state in 1886. He was responsible for launching the notorious anti-Semitism debate of 1879 which helped to infect an entire generation of the professional and academic middle class with anti-Semitic prejudices [Trans.].

15. *Frankfurter Adorno Blätter,* no. 8 (2003): 26f.
16. *Die Fackel,* no. 283/284 (26 June 1909): 19f. ("Die Welt der Plakate"). "In contrast, I was always attracted by the life of the street, and to listen to the sounds of the day as if they were the chords of eternity was an occupation in which one's wish for enjoyment and the pleasure of learning could both be satisfied."
17. "Grassy Seat," in *Minima Moralia,* trans. Edmund Jephcott (London, 1974), p. 22.
18. Ibid.
19. "For Marcel Proust," in *Minima Moralia,* p. 21.
20. "Antithesis," ibid., pp. 26f.
21. "Toward a Reappraisal of Heine," p. 452.
22. "Short Commentaries on Proust," in *Notes to Literature,* 1:179.
23. Ibid., p. 180.
24. "The George-Hofmannsthal Correspondence, 1891–1906" (1939–40), in *Prisms,* trans. Samuel and Shierry Weber (Cambridge, Mass., 1983), pp. 196f.
25. Adorno to Benjamin, 7 November 1936, in *The Complete Correspondence,* p. 158.
26. "Short Commentaries on Proust," in *Notes to Literature,* 1:180f.
27. "Toward a Portrait of Thomas Mann," ibid., 2:14.
28. "Bourgeois Opera," in *Sound Figures,* trans. Rodney Livingstone (Stanford, 1999), pp. 15f.
29. "Short Commentaries on Proust," p. 179.
30. Ibid., p. 178.
31. Ibid., p. 179.
32. Selmar Spier, *Vor 1914: Erinnerungen an Frankfurt geschrieben in Israel* (Frankfurt am Main, 1961), p. 27. Selmar Spier was friendly with Kracauer and they continued to meet into the 1960s.
33. "Über Tradition" (1966), in *Ohne Leitbild,* AGS, vol. 10.1, p. 310.
34. "The George-Hofmannsthal Correspondence, 1891–1906," p. 197.
35. Ibid., p. 199.
36. "Dedication," in *Minima Moralia,* p. 15.
37. "Grassy Seat," p. 22.
38. Ibid.
39. See Reinhard Pabst, *Kindheit in Amorbach: Bilder und Erinnerungen* (Frankfurt am Main, 2003). The birthday article by Andreas Razumovsky appeared on 11 September 1968 in the *Frankfurter Allgemeine Zeitung.*

40. In *Vierhändig, noch einmal, Vossische Zeitung,* 19 December 1933, AGS, 17:303.

41. "I enjoyed reading *Vierhändig.* Strange as it may seem, I ought likewise to start thinking about recording my memories at some point." Walter Benjamin to Gretel Karplus, Paris, 30 December 1933, in Benjamin, *Gesammelte Briefe,* vol. 4 (Frankfurt am Main, 1998), p. 325. Benjamin signs the letter "Detlef," an allusion to his pseudonym, "Detlef Holz," while Gretel is addressed as "Felizitas."

42. *Vierhändig, noch einmal,* p. 303.

43. *Worte ohne Lieder,* originally in the *Frankfurter Zeitung,* 14 July 1931, AGS, vol. 20.2, pp. 537–543.

44. *Vierhändig, noch einmal,* p. 303.

45. Ibid., p. 304.

46. *Zum Problem der Familie* (1955), AGS, vol. 20.1, p. 307.

47. *Vierhändig, noch einmal,* p. 305.

48. Ibid., p. 303.

49. The description of Aunt Agathe as Adorno's "second mother" occurs in Horkheimer's speech congratulating Adorno on his sixtieth birthday. See "Jenseits der Fachwissenschaft: Adorno zum 60. Geburtstag," originally in the *Frankfurter Rundschau* of 11 September 1963, HGS, 7:263. In this essay Horkheimer, who came from a manufacturing background, gives a somewhat idealized picture of life in Seeheimerstrasse.

50. Adorno to Horkheimer, 21 October 1935, following his return to Oxford from Germany: "I have no need to tell you what the loss of Agathe means to me. I am not exaggerating when I say that my entire private existence has fundamentally changed." Theodor W. Adorno/Max Horkheimer, *Briefwechsel,* vol. 1, *1927–1937* (Frankfurt am Main, 2003), p. 82.

51. Adorno to Křenek, 29 July 1935, in Theodor W. Adorno/Ernst Křenek, *Briefwechsel* (Frankfurt am Main, 1974), p. 91.

52. Ibid.

53. "Refuge for the Homeless," in *Minima Moralia,* p. 39.

54. "Grassy Seat," p. 23.

55. "Toward a Portrait of Thomas Mann," 2:18.

56. "The George-Hofmannsthal Correspondence, 1891–1906," pp. 203f.

57. Ibid.

58. Postscript to *Berliner Kindheit um Neunzehnhundert* (1950), AGS, vol. 20.1, p. 171.

59. *Zum Problem der Familie,* pp. 302f.

60. Walter Benjamin, *A Berlin Chronicle,* in *Selected Writings,* vol. 2 (Cambridge, Mass., 2002), 603.

61. *Zum Problem der Familie,* p. 304.

62. "Toward a Portrait of Thomas Mann," 2:14.

63. "Winfried Zillig: Möglichkeit und Wirklichkeit" (1964), AGS, 17:326.

64. *Minima Moralia*, p. 18.

65. Benjamin/Adorno, *The Complete Correspondence*, pp. 329f.

66. Gershom Scholem, "Zur Sozialpsychologie der Juden in Deutschland, 1900–1930" (1978), in *Judaica*, 4:242.

67. Ibid., p. 246.

68. The figures come from Shulamit Volkov, "Jüdische Assimilation und jüdische Eigenart im Deutschen Kaiserreich: Ein Versuch," in *Geschichte und Gesellschaft* (Göttingen, 1983), pp. 336f.

69. Leo Lowenthal, *An Unmastered Past*, ed. Martin Jay (Berkeley, 1987), pp. 17f.

70. Spier, *Vor 1914*, p. 61.

71. Ibid., pp. 63 and 90.

72. Ibid., p. 61. The figures are given in Volkov, "Jüdische Assimilation und jüdische Eigenart im Deutschen Kaiserreich," p. 346.

73. "Words from Abroad," in *Notes to Literature*, 1:185f.

74. Ibid.

75. Quoted from Heinz Becker, *Giacomo Meyerbeer* (Reinbek bei Hamburg, 1980), p. 15.

76. Ibid.

77. "The George-Hofmannsthal Correspondence, 1891–1906," p. 202.

78. "Taboos on the Teaching Vocation," in *Critical Models*, p. 186.

79. Adorno to Ernst Bloch, 26 July 1962, AGS, 1:384 (see also the letter to Bloch of 26 July 1962 in the appendix to this volume).

80. "Hothouse Plant," in *Minima Moralia*, p. 161.

81. "Words from Abroad," p. 192. [Translation adapted—Trans.]

82. "Taboos on the Teaching Vocation," pp. 177–190.

83. "Philosophy and Teachers," in *Critical Models*, pp. 29f. [*Ebbes* is Hesse dialect for High German *etwas*, meaning "something." In other words, the candidates pronounced "Hobbes" as though it had two syllables.—Trans.]

84. Ibid., p. 30, footnote.

85. Adorno to Benjamin, 2 November 1936, in Benjamin/Adorno, *Complete Correspondence*, p. 159.

86. "Gold Assay," in *Minima Moralia*, p. 154.

87. "Second Harvest," ibid., pp. 110f.

88. Ibid., p. 112.

89. "Antithesis," in *Minima Moralia*, p. 26.

90. "Second Harvest," p. 112.

91. "Taboos on the Teaching Vocation," p. 186. [Translation modified—Trans.]

92. *Zur Psychologie des Verhältnisses von Lehrer und Schüler* (1919), AGS, vol. 20.2, p. 719.

93. "Heliotrope," in *Minima Moralia*, p. 177.

94. Ibid.

95. Ibid., p. 178.

96. Walter Benjamin, "Stefan George in Retrospect," in *Selected Writings*, 2:708f. "Here the imperial pretensions are exposed, vulnerable and unprotected, as the pale daydreams of a person suffering from *Weltschmerz:* this permits a reconciliation with them. Benjamin was probably the first to class George's work with the Jugendstil that is so evident in Melchior Lechter's book design." "Stefan George," in *Notes to Literature*, 2:188f.

97. "The George-Hofmannsthal Correspondence, 1891–1906," p. 225.

98. "Introduction to Benjamin's Writings," in *Notes to Literature*, 2:231.

99. Ibid., p. 232.

100. Marcel Proust, *Within a Budding Grove*, pt. 1, trans. C. K. Scott Montcrieff (London, 1970), pp. 129f.

101. *Zum Problem der Familie*, p. 307.

102. *Briefe an die Eltern* (Frankfurt am Main, 2003), p. 467.

103. We have learned about the favorite bolt-holes of the Adorno-Wiesengrunds only recently through the researches of Reinhard Pabst, *Kindheit in Amorbach.*

104. "Second Harvest," p. 112.

105. *Wolkmann* means "cloud man," here the name of a mountain in the Odenwald. [Trans.]

106. *Amorbach* (1966), originally published in *Süddeutsche Zeitung* (5–6 November 1966), in *Ohne Leitbild*, AGS, vol. 10.1, p. 302.

107. Monika Plessner, *Die Argonauten auf Long Island: Begegnungen mit Hannah Arendt, Theodor W. Adorno, Gershom Scholem* (Berlin, 1995), p. 141. [The words "See you later" are in English.—Trans.]

108. "Aus Sils Maria," originally published in the *Süddeutsche Zeitung* (1–2 October 1966), in *Ohne Leitbild*, pp. 326f.

109. "Amorbach," p. 305.

110. Kracauer to Adorno, 28 March 1941. "Siegfried Kracauer, 1889–1966," ed. Ingrid Belke and Irina Renz, *Marbacher Magazin* 47 (1988): 101.

111. "The Curious Realist," in *Notes to Literature*, 2:58.

112. "On the Question: 'What Is German?'" in *Critical Models*, p. 206.

113. Kracauer, *Ginster*, p. 20.

114. Adorno to Benjamin, 7 November 1936, in *The Complete Correspondence*, p. 159.

115. "The Curious Realist," p. 58.

116. Ibid., pp. 59f.

117. Siegfried Kracauer, "Über die Freundschaft," in *Schriften*, vol. 5.1 (Frankfurt am Main, 1990), p. 47.

118. Martin Jay, "Adorno and Kracauer: Notes on a Troubled Friendship," in *Permanent Exiles: Essays on the Intellectual Migration from Germany to America* (New York, 1994), pp. 217ff.

119. Kracauer, "Über die Freundschaft," pp. 49f.

120. *Zum Problem der Familie,* p. 309.

121. Kracauer, "Über die Freundschaft," pp. 49f.

122. Ibid., p. 54.

123. "The Curious Realist," p. 75.

124. Ibid.

125. Ibid., p. 67.

126. Ibid.

127. Kracauer, "Über die Freundschaft," p. 51.

128. "The Curious Realist," p. 62.

129. Ibid., p. 60.

130. Ibid.

131. Ibid., p. 69.

132. Ibid., p. 71. [Translation slightly modified—Trans.]

133. Ibid.

134. Ibid., p. 75.

135. Heinrich Heine, *Werke und Briefe,* vol. 7 (Berlin, 1980), p. 206.

136. Erich Pfeifer-Belli, *Junge Jahre im alten Frankfurt* (Wiesbaden, 1987), p. 51.

137. Ibid.

138. See, inter alia, Spier, *Vor 1914,* p. 83; and Lowenthal, *An Unmastered Past,* pp. 29f.

139. "Coldness," Adorno writes in a note of January 1967, published in the *Frankfurter Adorno Blätter,* no. 8 (2003), "is the historical and psychological failure of the subject."

140. "The Bad Comrade," in *Minima Moralia,* p. 193.

141. Peter von Haselberg, "Wiesengrund-Adorno," in *Theodor W. Adorno,* 2nd enlarged ed. (Munich, 1983), p. 16.

142. "The Bad Comrade," pp. 192f.

143. Ibid., p. 192.

144. Ibid.

145. Ibid.

146. Ibid., p. 193.

147. "Taboos on the Teaching Vocation," p. 180.

148. Ibid.

149. Ibid., p. 183.

150. Ibid., p. 181.

151. Helmuth Plessner stood in for Adorno in the Frankfurt Institute when the latter had to return temporarily to the United States in 1952 and was always more or less in competition with him in the German Sociology Association. While in emigration in Holland, he had written a wonderful essay for his Dutch students in 1935 with the title "The Destiny of the German Spirit at the End of the Bourgeois Age." This was then published in 1958 with a preface. It

appeared in Germany under the title *Die verspätete Nation* [The Belated Nation] (Frankfurt am Main, 1974), pp. 71f.

152. See Spier, *Vor 1914*, p. 80.

153. "Gloss on Personality," in *Critical Models*, p. 164.

154. After his return to Frankfurt, Adorno had the following dream on 10 October 1960: "Kracauer appeared to me. My dear chap, it is a matter of indifference whether we write books and whether they are good or bad. They will be read for a year. Then they will be put in the library. Then the headmaster will come along and distribute them among the kids." *Dream Notes*, trans. Rodney Livingstone (Cambridge, 2007), p. 65.

155. "Gloss on Personality," p. 163.

156. "Die Natur, eine Quelle der Erhebung, Belehrung und Erholung" [Nature, a Source of Edification, Instruction, and Recreation] (matriculation essay, 1921), AGS, vol. 20.2, p. 733.

157. "Reinhold Zickel" (1958–1960, AGS, vol. 20.2, p. 759).

158. Siegfried Kracauer, "Vom Erleben des Krieges, 1915," in *Schriften*, vol. 5.1, p. 15.

159. Ibid., p. 21.

160. Siegfried Kracauer, "Gedanken über Freundschaft," in *Schriften*, vol. 5.1, pp. 141f.

161. Ibid., pp. 142f.

162. "Words from Abroad," p. 186.

163. Ibid.

164. Lowenthal, *An Unmastered Past*, p. 203.

165. "Monograms," in *Minima Moralia*, p. 190.

166. *Aesthetic Theory*, p. 252.

167. "Thesen über Tradition" (1966), in *Ohne Leitbild*, p. 310.

168. Lowenthal, *An Unmastered Past*, p. 203.

3. From Teddie Wiesengrund to Dr. Wiesengrund-Adorno

1. "In Memory of Eichendorff," in *Notes to Literature*, ed. Rolf Tiedemann, trans. Shierry Weber Nicholsen, vol. 1 (New York, 1991), p. 55.

2. "Words from Abroad," ibid., pp. 186f.

3. *Reinhold Zickel* (1958–1960), included in the "Repudiated Writings," AGS, vol. 20.2, p. 760.

4. Ibid., p. 764.

5. Ibid.

6. Ibid.

7. "Wertfreiheit und Objektivität" (1965), HGS, 8:258f.

8. Selmar Spier, *Vor 1914: Erinnerungen an Frankfurt geschrieben in Israel* (Frankfurt am Main, 1961), p. 111.

9. Joseph Roth, "Wer ist Ginster?" *Frankfurter Zeitung,* 25 November 1928, in *Werke,* vol. 2 (Cologne, 1990), p. 999.

10. Walter Benjamin's criticism of Wyneken is to be found in *Gesammelte Briefe,* vol. 1, *1910–1918* (Frankfurt am Main, 1995), p. 263.

11. Bernhard Reichenbach to Friedrich Podszus, 14 August 1962, in *Walter Benjamin, 1892–1940,* ed. Rolf Tiedemann, Christoph Gödde, and Henri Lonitz, *Marbacher Magazin* 55 (1990): 47.

12. Ibid.

13. Bertolt Brecht, *Journals, 1934–1955,* ed. John Willett and Ralph Manheim, trans. Hugh Rorrison (London, 1993), pp. 230f. [TUI, from "*Tellekt-Uell-In,*" is Brecht's pseudo-Chinese pig latin for "intellectual." The point is that in his view, intellectuals get everything backwards.—Trans.]

14. Hanns Eisler, *Fragen Sie mehr über Brecht: Gespräche mit Hans Bunge* (Darmstadt, 1986), p. 27.

15. This quotation is taken from Felix Weil's unpublished memoirs, which are to be found in the Frankfurt City Archives but whose pagination is unclear.

16. The Casella Works were a noted chemical factory based in Frankfurt. They were absorbed into I. G. Farben in 1925. [Trans.]

17. Spier, *Vor 1914,* p. 112.

18. *À l'écart de tous les courants* (1969), AGS, vol. 20.1, p. 188.

19. Dedication from Felix Weil's unpublished memoirs in the Frankfurt City Archives.

20. When spoken, the name "Francofurtia" sounds like the German word for "fart" *(Furz).* [Trans.]

21. For the history of the foundation of the institute, see Michael Buckmiller, "Die 'Marxistische Arbeitswoche' 1923 und die 'Gründung des Instituts für Sozialforschung,'" in *Grand Hotel Abgrund,* ed. Willem van Reijen and G. Schmid Noerr (Hamburg, 1988), pp. 141ff. A very informative account of the life of Felix Weil can be found in Helmut R. Eisenbach, *Millionär, Agitator und Doktorand: Die Tübinger Studienzeit des Felix Weil* (1919), special issue of *Bausteine zur Tübinger Universitätsgeschichte* (n.d.).

22. Eisenbach, *Millionär.*

23. "Offener Brief an Max Horkheimer" (14 February 1965), AGS, vol. 20.1, p. 156. Also see the appendix.

24. Ibid.

25. Ernst Herhaus, *Notizen während der Abschaffung des Denkens* (Frankfurt am Main, 1970), p. 42.

26. Ibid.

27. Georg Lukács, *Record of a Life,* ed. István Eörsi, trans. Rodney Livingstone (London, 1983), p. 27.

28. Ibid., p. 29.

29. Georg Lukács, *The Theory of the Novel*, trans. Anna Bostock (London, 1971), p. 153.

30. Vladimir I. Lenin, *Werke*, vol. 31 (Berlin, 1966), p. 153.

31. Karl Korsch, *Marxism and Philosophy*, trans. Fred Halliday (London, 1970), p. 92.

32. Georg Lukács, *The Destruction of Reason*, trans. Peter Palmer (London, 1980), p. 243.

33. "Extorted Reconciliation," in *Notes to Literature*, 1:216–240.

34. "Refuge for the Homeless, in *Minima Moralia*, trans. Edmund Jephcott (London, 1974), p. 39.

35. Note on *Kierkegaard: Konstruktion des Ästhetischen* (1966), AGS, 2:261.

36. *Kierkegaard: Construction of the Aesthetic*, trans. Robert Hullot-Kentor (Minneapolis, 1989), p. 6.

37. Ibid., p. v.

38. Siegfried Kracauer, "Der enthüllte Kierkegaard" (1933), in *Schriften*, vol. 5.3 (Frankfurt am Main, 1990), p. 263.

39. Ibid.

40. "The Curious Realist," in *Notes to Literature*, 2:59.

41. Ibid., p. 60.

42. Peter von Cornelius (1783–1867) was the painter and Peter Cornelius (1824–1874) was the composer. [Trans.]

43. "Hans Cornelius" (1923), HGS, 2:153.

44. Siegfried Kracauer, "Georg von Lukács' Romantheorie" (1921), in *Schriften*, vol. 5.1, p. 117.

45. See Rolf Tiedemann, "Editor's Note," AGS, 1:382.

46. Siegfried Kracauer, "Der enthüllte Kierkegaard" (1933), in *Schriften*, vol. 5.3, p. 263.

47. Siegfried Kracauer, "Zu den Schriften Walter Benjamins" (1928), in *Schriften*, vol. 5.2, p. 124.

48. Ibid., p. 123.

49. "Tirolean" here suggests a provincial, a backwoodsman. [Trans.]

50. Siegfried Kracauer, "Prophetentum" (1922), in *Schriften*, vol. 5.1, p. 203.

51. Ernst Bloch, *Durch die Wüste* (Berlin, 1923), p. 61.

52. Siegfried Kracauer to Leo Löwenthal, 16 October 1923, in Leo Löwenthal/Siegfried Kracauer, *In steter Freundschaft: Briefwechsel* (Lüneburg, 2003), p. 48.

53. Ernst Bloch to Siegfried Kracauer, 20 May 1926, in Ernst Bloch, *Briefe*, vol. 1 (Frankfurt am Main, 1985), p. 270.

54. Kracauer to Bloch, 27 May 1926, ibid., p. 272.

55. Ibid., p. 274.

56. Siegfried Kracauer, "Soziologie als Wissenschaft" (1922), in *Schriften*, vol. 1 (Frankfurt am Main, 1971), p. 11.

57. Siegfried Kracauer, "Die Wartenden" (1922), in *Schriften,* vol. 5.1, p. 168.
58. Theodor W. Adorno to Ernst Bloch, 26 July 1962, printed in full in the appendix.
59. Adorno to Benjamin, 17 December 1934, in Walter Benjamin/Theodor W. Adorno, *The Complete Correspondence, 1928–1940* (Cambridge and Oxford, 1999), p. 67.
60. Ibid., p. 66.
61. Benjamin to Adorno, 1 December 1932, ibid., p. 20.
62. Ibid., p. 20f.
63. *Kierkegaard,* pp. 47f.
64. Walter Benjamin, *Selected Writings,* vol. 2 (Cambridge, Mass, 2002), p. 703.
65. "When young students come to me to seek advice about qualifying as a lecturer, the responsibility of giving it is scarcely to be borne. Of course, if the student is a Jew, you can only say *lasciate ogni speranza* [abandon all hope]." Max Weber, *Science as a Vocation,* in *The Vocation Lectures,* ed. Tracy Strong and David Owen, trans. Rodney Livingstone (Indianapolis, 2004), p. 7. [Trans.]
66. Walter Benjamin to Gerhard Scholem, 30 December 1922, in Benjamin, *Gesammelte Briefe,* vol. 1 (Frankfurt am Main, 1978), p. 295.
67. Walter Benjamin to Ernst Schoen, 7 April 1919, ibid., p. 208.
68. Walter Benjamin "Gedanken zu Analyse des Zustauds von Mitteleuropa" (1923), in *Gesammelte Schriften,* vol. 4 (Frankfurt am Main, 1972), p. 929.
69. Ibid., pp. 925f.
70. Walter Benjamin to Gerhard Scholem, 19 February 1925, in Benjamin, *Gesammelte Briefe,* 1:372.
71. Ibid., pp. 371f.
72. Rolf Tiedemann, Christoph Gödde, and Henri Lonitz, eds., "Walter Benjamin, 1892–1940," *Marbacher Magazin* 55 (1990): 75.
73. *Erinnerung* [Recollections of Walter Benjamin] (1964), AGS, vol. 20.1, p. 173.
74. Ibid., p. 175.
75. Ibid.
76. Walter Benjamin to Gerhard Scholem, 5 March 1924, in Benjamin, *Gesammelte Briefe,* 1:341.
77. Walter Benjamin to Florens Christian Rang, 10 January 1924, ibid., p. 326.
78. Walter Benjamin, "Announcement of the Journal *Angelus Novus,*" in *Selected Writings,* 1:293.
79. *Erinnerung* p. 174.
80. *Die Aktualität der Philosophie,* AGS, 1:335. [This translation is taken from Adorno/Benjamin, *The Complete Correspondence, 1928–1940,* p. 9.—Trans.]
81. Adorno/Benjamin, *The Complete Correspondence, 1928–1940,* pp. 9f. In the same letter Benjamin told Adorno that he had read the latter's *Words without Songs* "with great pleasure."

82. Walter Benjamin to Gershom Scholem, 20–25 May 1925, in Benjamin, *Gesammelte Briefe*, 3:39.

83. Hilde Benjamin, *Georg Benjamin: Eine Biographie* (Leipzig, 1987), p. 45.

84. Walter Benjamin to Gershom Scholem, 21 July 1925, in Benjamin, *Gesammelte Briefe*, 3:64.

85. Ibid.

86. Walter Benjamin to Gershom Scholem, 20–25 May 1925, ibid., p. 39.

87. Gershom Scholem, *Walter Benjamin: The Story of a Friendship* (London, 1982), p. 206.

88. Gershom Scholem, *Walter Benjamin und sein Engel* (Frankfurt am Main, 1983), p. 75.

89. Ibid., p. 74.

90. Ibid., p. 81.

91. Adorno to Berg, 5 February 1925, in Theodor Adorno/Alban Berg, *Correspondence, 1925–1935,* ed. Henri Lonitz, trans. Wieland Hoban (Cambridge, 2005), p. 4.

92. Ibid., p. 3.

93. "Consecutio temporum," in *Minima Moralia*. p. 217.

94. *Im Gedächtnis an Alban Berg* (1955), AGS, 18:505.

95. Adorno has varied this idea. Cf., e.g.: "It is hard to avoid the conclusion that this twofold aspect—on the one hand, a world that could have taken a turn for the better and, on the other, the extinguishing of that hope by the establishment of powers that later revealed themselves fully in fascism—also expressed itself in an ambivalence in art, which in fact is quite specific to the twenties and has nothing to do with the vague and self-contradictory idea of the modern classics." "Those Twenties," in *Critical Models*, trans. Henry W. Pickford (New York, 1998), p. 43.

96. *Alban Berg: Master of the Smallest Link*, trans. Juliane Brand and Christopher Hailey (Cambridge, 1991), p. 14.

97. Soma Morgenstern, *Alban Berg und seine Idole: Erinnerungen und Briefe* (Lüneburg, 1995), pp. 117ff.

98. Ibid.

99. "The time I was with him coincided with his involvement with Hanna, Werfel's sister. He made use of me as a *postillon d'amour,* for which my frequent visits to Prague to visit my friend Hermann Grab had to provide the pretext. I was a clumsy intermediary and was never able to speak with Hanna on her own. At the same time, the whole business was arranged so incautiously that her husband got wind of it. The affair was doomed from the outset since extreme passions were at stake, but at the same time, Berg was as unwilling to leave his wife as Hanna was to leave her husband and her two children." *Im Gedächtnis an Alban Berg*, AGS, 18:490f.

100. "On the occasion of a longer separation Alban Berg wrote the author a post-card quoting the exchange between Alberich and Hagen from *Götterdämmerung*: 'Sei treu [Be true].' It is the author's dearest wish not to have fallen short of that—without, however, allowing his passionate gratitude to encroach upon the autonomy his teacher and friend developed musically within him." *Alban Berg: Master of the Smallest Link*, p. xviii. Adorno wrote this in September 1968, at the time of his last birthday before his own death.

101. Theodor W. Adorno/Thomas Mann, *Briefwechsel, 1943–1955* (Frankfurt am Main, 2002), p. 87.

102. *Berg: Master of the Smallest Link*, p. 15.

103. *Frankfurter Adorno Blätter*, no. 7 (2001): 123.

104. Evelyn Wilcock has done most to advance our knowledge of Adorno's exile in England in a number of small, scattered publications.

105. "Out of the Firing-Line," in *Minima Moralia*, p. 53.

106. *Berg: Master of the Smallest Link*, p. 13.

107. Ibid., p. 9.

108. Ibid., p. 10.

109. Ibid.

110. Ibid., pp. 10f.

111. "In Memory of Eichendorff," p. 55.

112. Adorno to Benjamin, 7 November 1936, in *The Complete Correspondence, 1928–1940*, p. 159.

113. "Schöne Stellen" (1965), one of Adorno's finest radio talks. See AGS, 18:695ff.

114. *Im Gedächtnis an Alban Berg*, p. 494. See also *Berg: Master of the Smallest Link*, p. 28.

115. To his mother, 12 November 1949 and 24 September 1950, in *Briefe an die Eltern* (Frankfurt am Main, 2003), p. 529.

116. To his mother, 9 August 1949, ibid., p. 520.

117. Ibid., pp. 535f.

118. To Berthold Bührer, ibid., p. 539.

119. *Berg: Master of the Smallest Link*, p. 85.

120. Ibid., p. 12.

121. Adorno records that at the time of the Third Reich, "when he [Berg] buried himself in his house on the Wörthersee so as to be able to work undisturbed on *Lulu*, he called the place where he wanted to concentrate his 'concentration camp.' This remark was not cynical, it was morbid." Ibid., p. 9.

122. *Arnold Schönberg: 1874–1951* (1957), AGS, 18:320f.

123. "Cultural Criticism and Society," in *Prisms*, trans. Samuel and Shierry Weber (Cambridge, Mass., 1983), p. 34.

4. Adorno as "Non-identical" Man

1. Adorno to Mann, 5 July 1948, in Theodor W. Adorno/Thomas Mann, *Correspondence, 1943–1955,* ed. Christophe Gödde and Thomas Sprecher, trans. Nicholas Walker (Cambridge, 2006), p. 24.

2. Thomas Mann, *Die Entstehung des Doktor Faustus: Roman eines Romans* (Amsterdam, 1949), p. 41.

3. Ibid., p. 42.

4. Ibid., pp. 42f.

5. Epigraph to *Minima Moralia,* trans. Edmund Jephcott (London, 1974), p. 5.

6. Mann to Adorno, 9 January 1952, in *Correspondence, 1943–1955,* p. 73.

7. Mann to Adorno, 30 December 1945, ibid., p. 12.

8. Ibid.

9. Thomas Mann to Emil Preetorius, 12 December 1947, in Mann, *Briefe,* vol. 2 (Frankfurt am Main, 1979), p. 576.

10. Ibid., p. 575.

11. Thomas Mann, *Tagebücher, 1946–1948* (Frankfurt am Main, 1989), p. 221.

12. Ibid.

13. Ibid., p. 223.

14. Thomas Mann to Jonas Lesser, 15 October 1951, in Mann, *Briefe,* vol. 3 (Frankfurt am Main, 1979), p. 223.

15. Ibid., p. 226.

16. Adorno to B. Bräutigam, 18 March 1968, *Frankfurter Adorno Blätter,* no. 1 (1992): 31.

17. Thomas Mann, 30 October 1948, in *Tagebücher, 1946–1948,* p. 322. The "Legend" is presumably his novel *The Holy Sinner.* [Trans.]

18. .Ibid., p. 30.

19. Thomas Mann, *Essays, 1945–1955* (Frankfurt am Main, 1997), pp. 98 and 102.

20. Mann, 30 October 1948, in *Tagebücher, 1946–1948,* p. 320.

21. Mann, *Die Entstehung des Doktor Faustus,* p. 45.

22. Ibid.

23. Adorno to Mann, 3 June 1945, in *Correspondence, 1943–1955,* p. 10.

24. Ibid.

25. Mann, *Die Entstehung des Doktor Faustus,* p. 46.

26. Ibid. p. 47. [Adorno's name features in the course of Wendell Kretzschmar's lecture on the arietta theme in the second movement of Beethoven's last piano sonata, op. 111 in C. In the English translation it occurs as "meadowland" (Wie-sengrund), on p. 55.—Trans.]

27. Adorno to Mann, 3 June 1945, in *Correspondence, 1943–1955,* p. 10.

28. Mann to Jonas Lesser, 15 October 1951, in Mann, *Briefe,* 3:226.

29. Mann, *Die Entstehung des Doktor Faustus,* p. 42.

30. Adorno to Mann, 3 June 1945, in *Correspondence, 1943–1955*, p. 10.

31. Adorno to Mann, 5 July 1948, ibid., pp. 24f.

32. Mann to Agnes Meyer, 7 January 1944, in *Briefe*, 2:346. See also *The Letters of Thomas Mann, 1989–1955*, trans. Richard and Clara Winston, vol. 2 (London, 1970), p. 433.

33. Thomas Mann to Klaus Mann, 12 May 1938, in *Briefe*, 3:474.

34. Adorno to Mann, 3 June 1945 and 5 July 1948, in *Correspondence, 1943–1955*, pp. 10 and 24.

35. Adorno to Mann, 5 July 1948, ibid., p. 24.

36. Adorno to Mann, 3 June 1945, ibid., pp. 9f.

37. Mann to Agnes Meyer, 29 June 1939, in Mann, *Briefe*, 2:100f.; cf. Hermann Kurzke, *Thomas Mann* (Munich, 1999), p. 28.

38. "From my father I get my stature and serious conduct of life; from mother dear my blithe nature and my penchant for telling stories." Goethe, "Den Originalen," in Goethe: *Selected Verse*, trans. David Luke (Harmondsworth, 1964), p. 292. [Trans.]

39. Mann to Agnes Meyer, 29 June 1939, pp. 100f.

40. "Kritik des Musikanten" (1956), AGS, 14:81. ["O Täler weit, o Höhen" is a popular folksong based on a poem by Joseph von Eichendorff.—Trans.]

41. Adorno, 20 October 1943, in *Briefe an die Eltern* (Frankfurt am Main, 2003), pp. 222f.

42. Ibid.

43. Adorno to Mann, 3 June 1945, in *Correspondence, 1943–1955*, pp. 9f.

44. Adorno to Mann, 5 July 1948, ibid., p. 24.

45. Mann, *Die Entstehung des Doktor Faustus*, p. 43.

46. Thomas Mann, "Meine Zeit," in *Essays, 1945–1955*, p. 170.

47. Mann, *Die Entstehung des Doktor Faustus*, p. 38.

48. "Late Style in Beethoven," in *Essays on Music*, ed. Richard Leppart, trans. Susan H. Gillespie (Berkeley, 2002), p. 567.

49. Mann, *Die Entstehung des Doktor Faustus*, p. 60.

50. "Late Style in Beethoven," p. 566.

51. Ibid. [Part 2 of *Faust* was published posthumously in 1832, the year of Goethe's death. *Wilhelm Meisters Wanderjahre* (Wilhelm Meister's Journeyman Years) was begun in 1821 and completed in 1829.—Trans.]

52. Ibid., p. 566.

53. Mann, *Die Entstehung des Doktor Faustus*, p. 42.

54. Benjamin to Max Horkheimer, 6 December 1937, in Walter Benjamin, *Gesammelte Briefe*, vol. 5 (Frankfurt am Main, 1999), p. 618.

55. Walter Benjamin, "A German Institute for Independent Research," in *Selected Writings*, vol. 3 (Cambridge, Mass., 2002), p. 312.

56. Quoted in Kurzke, *Thomas Mann*, p. 503. [Kaisersaschern is the—fictitious—birthplace of Adrian Leverkühn in *Doctor Faustus*.—Trans.]

57. Preface to *Philosophy of Modern Music,* trans. Anne G. Mitchell and Wesley V. Bloomster (New York, 1973), pp. xviif.

58. Ibid.

59. "Late Style in Beethoven," p. 567.

60. *Notiz* (February 1945), in *Graeculus* (I), "Musikalische Notizen," in *Frankfurter Adorno Blätter,* no. 7 (2001): 16.

61. Ibid. ["Der Genesende an die Hoffnung" and "In der Fremde" are both from Hugo Wolf's *Mörike Lieder.*—Trans.]

62. "Fantasia sopra *Carmen,*" in *Quasi una fantasia,* trans. Rodney Livingstone (London, 1992), p. 53.

63. Ibid., pp. 55f.

64. Ibid., p. 54.

65. "The Position of the Narrator in the Contemporary Novel," in *Notes to Literature,* ed. Rolf Tiedemann, trans. Shierry Weber Nicholsen, vol. 1 (New York, 1991), p. 34.

66. Thomas Mann, 22 October 1954, in *Tagebücher, 1953–1955* (Frankfurt am Main, 1995), p. 287.

67. Adorno to Erika Mann, 19 April 1962, in *Frankfurter Adorno Blätter,* no. 1 (1992): 14.

68. Ibid.

69. Quoted by Inge Jens, preface to Thomas Mann, *Tagebücher, 1953–1955,* p. xx.

70. "Toward a Portrait of Thomas Mann," in *Notes to Literature,* vol. 2 (New York, 1992), p. 16. [The translation gives "very Germanic."—Trans.]

71. Ibid.

72. Ibid., p. 14.

73. Ibid.

74. Adorno to René Leibowitz, 3 October 1963, in *Frankfurter Adorno Blätter,* no. 7 (2001): 61.

75. *Philosophy of Modern Music,* p. 5.

76. Max Horkheimer and Theodor Adorno, *Dialectic of Enlightenment,* ed. Gunzelin Schmid Noerr, trans. Edmund Jephcott (Stanford, 2002), pp. 104f.

77. Mann to Adorno, 30 December 1945, in *Correspondence, 1943–1955,* p. 12.

78. *Philosophy of Modern Music,* p. 15.

79. Ibid. [Translation modified.—Trans.]

80. Ibid., p. 46.

81. Ibid.

82. "The Position of the Narrator in the Contemporary Novel," in *Notes to Literature,* 1:33.

83. "Bourgeois Opera," in *Sound Figures,* trans. Rodney Livingstone (Stanford, 1999), p. 23.

84. Ibid., p. 20.

85. "Antithesis," in *Minima Moralia,* p. 27.

86. "Dedication," ibid., p. 18.

87. "Über Tradition" (1966), in *Ohne Leitbild: Parva Aesthetica*, AGS, vol. 10.1, p. 310.

88. "On the Question: 'What Is German!'" in *Critical Models*, AGS, vol. 10.2, p. 208.

89. Ibid.

90. "Out of the Firing-Line," in *Minima Moralia*, p. 53.

91. "Scientific Experiences of a European Scholar in America," in *Critical Models*, p. 241.

92. Ibid.

93. Ibid.

94. Ibid.

95. Mann to Adorno, 11 July 1950, in *Correspondence, 1943–1955*, p. 57.

96. Mann to Adorno, 30 October 1952, ibid., p. 93.

97. Ibid. [The phrases quoted by Mann are taken from Adorno's *In Search of Wagner* (trans. Rodney Livingstone, London, 1981, p. 151).—Trans.]

98. "Antithesis," p. 27.

99. "Out of the Firing-Line," p. 53.

100. "For Marcel Proust," in *Minima Moralia*, p. 21.

101. "Scientific Experiences of a European Scholar in America," p. 235.

102. Ibid., p. 236.

103. Ibid., p. 233.

104. Ibid. p. 235.

105. "Veblen's Attack on Culture," *Studies in Philosophy and Social Science* 9 (1941): 411. See also *Prisms*, p. 93, where it is translated as "How is anything new possible at all?

106. "On the Use of Foreign Words," in *Notes to Literature*, 2:289.

107. *Dialectic of Enlightenment*, p. 134.

108. Ibid.

109. Ibid.

110. Adorno to David, 3 July 1941, in Rolf Wiggershaus, *The Frankfurt School*, trans. Michael Robertson (Cambridge, 1994; reprint, 2007), p. 312.

111. Ibid.

112. *Philosophy of Modern Music*, p. 24.

113. *Dialectic of Enlightenment*, p. 272.

114. Max Horkheimer to Felix Weil, 10 March 1942, HGS, 17:275.

115. Wiggershaus, *The Frankfurt School*, p. 371.

116. "For Marcel Proust," p. 21.

117. "Grassy Seat," in *Minima Moralia*, p. 23.

118. "Monad," ibid., p. 148.

119. Ibid., p. 150.

120. Ibid.

121. "Bequest," in *Minima Moralia*, p. 152.

122. "Gold Assay," ibid., p. 152.

123. Ibid., p. 154.

5. TRANSITIONS

1. Bertolt Brecht, *Poems, 1913–1956*, ed. John Willett and Ralph Manheim, with the cooperation of Erich Fried (1976; reprint, London, 1979), pp. 318–320.

2. "Out of the Firing-Line," in *Minima Moralia*, trans. Edmund Jephcott (London, 1974), pp. 53–56.

3. *Zum Erstdruck der Originalfassung* (1969), in *Komposition für den Film* (with Hanns Eisler), AGS, 15:144.

4. Ibid.

5. Ibid., p. 145.

6. Ibid., p. 144.

7. Ibid., p. 145.

8. Ibid.

9. Hanns Eisler, "Arnold Schönberg, der musikalische Reaktionär" (1924), in *Schriften*, vol. 1, *Musik und Politik, 1924–1948* (Munich, 1973), pp. 13ff.

10. "Hanns Eisler, *Duo für Violine und Violoncello, op. 7, Nr. 1*" (1925), AGS, 18:519.

11. "Eisler, *Zeitungsausschnitte: Für Gesang und Klavier, op. 11*" (1929), AGS, 18:527.

12. "Im Gedächtnis an Alban Berg" (1955), AGS, 18:504.

13. Ibid.

14. Note dated around 1950 in Jürgen Schebera, *Eisler* (Mainz, 1998), p. 42.

15. "Arnold Schönberg (I)" (1957), AGS, 18:323.

16. Hanns Eisler, "Über moderne Musik," 15 October 1927, in *Schriften*, 1:32f.

17. Ibid., p. 32.

18. *Komposition für den Film*, 15:60. [See also *Composing for the Films* (London, 1951), p. 57.—Trans.]

19. Ibid., p. 59 [*Composing for the Films*, p. 57.—Trans.].

20. *Mahagonny* (1932), AGS, 19:276.

21. Ibid.

22. "Eisler, *Zeitungsausschnitte*," 18:524.

23. Ibid.

24. Ibid., p. 527.

25. Hanns Eisler, *Fragen Sie mehr über Brecht: Gespräche mit Hans Bunge* (Darmstadt, 1986), p. 43.

26. "Zum Erstdruck der Originalfassung" (1969), in *Komposition für den Film*, 15:144.

27. Bloch in conversation with Albert Betz in 1973, in Hanns Eisler, *Musik einer Zeit, die sich eben bildet* (Munich, 1976), p. 228.

28. See "On the Social Situation of Music" (1932), in *Essays on Music*, ed. Richard Leppart, trans. Susan H. Gillespie (Berkeley, 2002), pp. 391–437.

29. "Antwort eines Adepten: An Hans F. Redlich" (1934), AGS, 18:401f.
30. "Die stabilisierte Musik" (1928), AGS, 18:725.
31. "Eisler, *Zeitungsausschnitte*," 18:527.
32. Ibid., p. 525.
33. Eisler, *Fragen Sie mehr über Brecht*, p. 43.
34. Ibid.
35. Ibid., p. 13.
36. Ibid.
37. Bertolt Brecht, *Journals, 1934–1955*, ed. John Willett and Ralph Manheim, trans. Hugh Rorrison (London, 1993), p. 224.
38. Ibid.
39. Ibid., p. 218. Beneath this entry of 5 April 1942 there is a photograph of the bombardment of Singapore.
40. Eisler, *Fragen Sie mehr über Brecht*, p. 42.
41. Hans Mayer, "Der Zeitgenosse Hanns Eisler" (1994), in *Zeitgenossen* (Frankfurt am Main, 1998), p. 178.
42. Eisler, *Fragen Sie mehr über Brecht*, p. 12.
43. "Dwarf Fruit," in *Minima Moralia*, p. 49. [The title of an opera by Carl-Maria von Weber. A *Freischütz* is a marksman who hits everything he aims at.— Trans.]
44. Adorno to his mother, 24 September 1950, in *Briefe an die Eltern* (Frankfurt am Main, 2003), pp. 535f.
45. Horkheimer to Salka Viertel, 29 June 1940, HGS, 16:726.
46. "Puzzle-Picture," in *Minima Moralia*, p. 194.
47. Max Horkheimer and Theodor Adorno, *Dialectic of Enlightenment*, ed. Gunzelin Schmid Noerr, trans. Edmund Jephcott (Stanford, 2002), p. 115. [Translation slightly modified—Trans.]
48. Adorno and Eisler, "Vorrede" (1944), in *Komposition für den Film*, 15:10.
49. "Notizen über Eisler" (1965–66), *Frankfurter Adorno Blätter* 7 (2001): 123.
50. Ibid., p. 126.
51. "Die stabilisierte Musik," 18:725.
52. Ibid., p. 722.
53. Eisler, *Fragen Sie mehr über Brecht*, p. 42.
54. "Notizen über Eisler," p. 122
55. Ibid., p. 124.
56. AGS, vol. 3, no longer contains the note "to be continued," but the actual continuation is included in the appendix as "Das Schema der Massenkultur. Kulturindustrie. (Fortsetzung)." This was undoubtedly written by Adorno alone, whereas the chapter first published in 1944 was a joint effort, one referred to in the preface Adorno and Eisler wrote jointly for *Composing for the Films*, also in 1944. "Das Schema der Massenkultur" has been translated into

English, under the title "The Schema of Mass Culture," by Nicholas Walker for J. M. Bernstein's volume *Theodor W. Adorno: The Culture Industry* (London, 1991), pp. 53–84.

57. Adorno would make use of this expression after his return from America to characterize calculated media effects, such as in the music business, in *Einleitung in die Musiksociologie* (AGS, 14:110), or in television in, "Television as Ideology," in *Critical Models,* trans. Henry W. Pickford (New York, 1998), p. 67.

58. *Minima Moralia,* p. 19.

59. "Sometimes we go to the movies for the sake of the joint project with Max. On Sunday, we saw *Sweet Rosie O'Grady.* You should really go and see this completely harmless and meaningless film, above all, because of its magical colors. (It is incredible to see the progress made by Technicolor and to realize how much can be done with it nowadays.)" Adorno to his parents, 11 November 1943, in *Briefe an die Eltern,* p. 226.

60. HGS, 12:342–345.

61. *Dialectic of Enlightenment,* p. 126.

62. "Zweimal Chaplin," in *Ohne Leitbild: Parva Aesthetica,* AGS, vol. 10.1, pp. 365f.

63. *Dialectic of Enlightenment,* p. 114. Even earlier, in his pioneering essay of 1938 "On the Fetish Character in Music and the Regression of Listening," he had praised the Marx Brothers for "the great force" with which they conveyed "the insight of the philosophy of history into the decay of the operatic form." (See Bernstein, *Theodor W. Adorno: The Culture Industry,* p. 51). What has been overlooked by recent critics is almost always the irony implicit in the concept of the Culture Industry, which would like to think of itself as a normal industry like the steel or automobile industries but fails to match up to them despite the vigor with which it flaunts its commercialism.

64. William Dieterle, "Hollywood and the European Crisis," in *Studies in Philosophy and Social Science* (1941): 101, published by the Institute of Social Research, New York City. Dieterle produces facts and figures in an attempt to demonstrate the "industrial" character of Hollywood.

65. The episode is described in James K. Lyon, *Bertolt Brecht in America* (Princeton, 1980), pp. 58f.

66. Salka Viertel, *Das unbelehrbare Herz: Ein Leben in der Welt des Theaters, der Literatur und des Films,* with a preface by Carl Zuckmayer (Reinbek bei Hamburg, 1979), pp. 218–221. A trace of the scurrilous dialogue between Schoenberg and Irving Thalberg can still be seen in a later Adorno essay, "Art and the Arts" (1966): "'My music is not lovely,' grumbled Schoenberg in Hollywood when a film mogul unfamiliar with his work tried to pay him a compliment." "Art and the Arts," in *Can One Live after Auschwitz?* ed. Rolf Tiedemann, trans. Rodney Livingstone et al. (Stanford, 2003), p. 371. In "Ger-

man California" people gossiped not only about how much money people earned and how much they could collect in charitable donations: in a letter dated 29 June 1940, Salka Viertel was one of the first people to whom Max Horkheimer confided his new theory of politics: "In view of what is threatening to engulf Europe and perhaps the whole world at the present time, our present work is essentially destined to be delivered through the night that is about to fall; it is a kind of message in a bottle" (HGS, 16:726).

67. Brecht, *Journals, 1934–1955*, p. 170.

68. "The Schema of Mass Culture, in *The Culture Industry*, p. 63.

69. *Negative Dialectics*, trans. E. A. Ashton (1973; reprint, London, 1996), p. 366; *Lectures on Metaphysics*, trans. Edmund Jephcott (Stanford, 2000), p. 118. Adorno's point was that "culture banishes stench because it itself stinks" (*Lectures on Metaphysics*, p. 118). [Trans.]

70. *Dialectic of Enlightenment*, p. 96. Cf. Bertolt Brecht, *Radiotheorie 1927 bis 1932*, in *Gesammelte Werke*, vol. 18 (Frankfurt am Main, 1967).

71. *Dialectic of Enlightenment*, pp. 130f.

72. Adorno to Lang, 29 November 1950, quoted from Rolf Aurich, Wolfgang Jacobsen, and Cornelius Schnauber, eds., *Fritz Lang: Leben und Werk, Bilder und Dokumente / His Life and Work*, Photographs and Documents / *Sa vie et son œuvre, photos et documents* (Berlin, 2001), p. 405.

73. Ibid., pp. 405f.

74. "Zweimal Chaplin" (1964), in *Ohne Leitbild: Parva Aesthetica*, AGS, vol. 10.1, p. 364.

75. Alexander Kluge, "Worauf es mir ankam," *Die Zeit*, 2 September 1966.

76. Regina Becker-Schmidt, "Wenn die Frauen erst einmal Frauen sein könnten," in *Geist gegen den Zeitgeist*, ed. Josef Früchtl und Maria Calloni (Frankfurt am Main, 1991), pp. 233f.

77. Fritz Lang to Eleanor Rosé, 5 September 1969, quoted from Aurich, Jacobsen, and Schnauber, *Fritz Lang: Leben und Werk*, p. 450.

78. Ibid.

79. "Toward a Portrait of Thomas Mann," in *Notes to Literature*, ed. Rolf Tiedemann, trans. Shierry Weber Nicholsen, vol. 2 (New York, 1991), p. 16.

80. Fritz Lang to Eleanor Rosé, 5 September 1969, quoted from Aurich, Jacobsen, and Schnauber, *Fritz Lang: Leben und Werk*, p. 450.

81. *Tagebuch der großen Reise, Oktober 1949. Aufzeichnungen bei der Rückkehr aus dem Exil, Frankfurter Adorno Blätter* (2003): 107.

82. "Über Jazz: Oxforder Nachträge" (1937), in *Moments Musicaux*, AGS, 17:100f.

83. *Minima Moralia*, p. 159. "O avalanche, will you take me with you when you fall?" Charles Baudelaire, "Le Goût du néant," in *Oeuvres Complètes* (Paris, 1975), p. 76.

84. "To do nothing like an animal . . . ": "Sur l'eau," in *Minima Moralia*, p. 157.

85. "Hothouse Plant," in *Minima Moralia*, p. 161.

1. Horkheimer had become a naturalized American citizen in 1940. He returned to Frankfurt in 1950 to reestablish the Institute for Social Research. Mistrustful of the stability and long-term prospects for democracy in Germany, he was extremely unwilling to renounce his American citizenship. At his urging, John J. McCloy, the U.S. High Commissioner for Germany, asked President Truman and Congress to pass a bill granting Horkheimer dual citizenship. For a brief period, it is claimed, he was the only person in the world to hold both German and U.S. citizenship. [Trans.]

2. Horkheimer to Pollock, 4 July 1948, HGS, 17:1003 (in French in the original).

3. "Scientific Experiences of a European Scholar in America," in *Critical Models*, trans. Henry W. Pickford (New York, 1983), p. 215.

4. Adorno to Horkheimer, 13 May 1935, HGS, 15:347.

5. Adorno to Horkheimer, 6 January 1939, HGS, 16:535.

6. Adorno to Charles E. Merriam, 30 July 1940, HGS, 16:744.

7. "Scientific Experiences of a European Scholar in America," p. 216.

8. Ibid., pp. 220 and 225.

9. "Refuge for the Homeless," in *Minima Moralia*, trans. Edmund Jephcott (London, 1974), p. 39. [Literally: "There is no correct life in the false one."—Trans.]

10. "Scientific Experiences of a European Scholar in America," p. 225.

11. "Über Tradition" (1966), in *Ohne Leitbild*, AGS, vol. 10.1, p. 310.

12. "Scientific Experiences of a European Scholar in America," p. 223.

13. Ibid., p. 225.

14. Ibid., p. 227.

15. Ibid., p. 241.

16. Ibid., p. 219.

17. *Introduction to the Sociology of Music*, pp. 21ff.

18. "Scientific Experiences of a European Scholar in America," p. 241.

19. Ibid., p. 220.

20. Editor's postscript in AGS, 16:674.

21. "Some Ideas on the Sociology of Music," in *Sound Figures*, trans. Rodney Livingstone (Stanford, 1999), p. 13.

22. *Introduction to the Sociology of Music*, p. 220.

23. "Tradition," in *Dissonanzen: Musik in der verwalteten Welt* (1956), AGS, 14:128.

24. Ibid.

25. "Dwarf Fruit," in *Minima Moralia*, p. 50.

26. *Introduction to the Sociology of Music*, p. 220.

27. "Scientific Experiences of a European Scholar in America," p. 216.

28. Ibid.

29. *Introduction to the Sociology of Music*, p. 212. [Translation modified—Trans.]

30. Ibid.
31. Ibid., p. 224.
32. Ibid., p. 57.
33. "Grassy Seat," in Minima Moralia, p. 22.
34. Introduction to the Sociology of Music, p. 70.
35. Ibid., p. 233.
36. "Some Ideas on the Sociology of Music," p. 6.
37. Ibid., p. 9.
38. "Scientific Experiences of a European Scholar in America," p. 220.
39. "Some Ideas on the Sociology of Music," pp. 13f.
40. Ibid., p. 13.
41. Introduction to the Sociology of Music, p. 224. [Translation modified—Trans.]
42. "Zum 'Anbruch'" (1928), AGS, 19:602.
43. "Mai 1929," in Frankfurter Opern- und Konzertkritiken, AGS, 19:156.
44. Ibid.
45. Zum Jahrgang 1929 des "Anbruch" (1929), AGS, 19:608.
46. Introduction to the Sociology of Music, p. 191.
47. "On the Social Situation of Music, in Essays on Music, ed. Richard Leppart, trans. Susan H. Gillespie (Berkeley, 2002), pp. 410f.
48. "Neunzehn Beiträge über die neue Musik" (1942), in Theorie der neuen Musik, AGS, 18:750.
49. Ibid., pp. 72f.
50. Introduction to the Sociology of Music, p. 193.
51. Ernst Křenek, preface to Theodor W. Adorno and Ernst Křenek, Briefwechsel (Frankfurt am Main, 1970), p. 8.
52. "If Knaves Should Tempt You," p. 29.
53. Introduction to the Sociology of Music, p. 189. [Translation modified—Trans.]
54. "Neunzehn Beiträge über die neue Musik" (1942), in Theorie der neuen Musik, 18:72.
55. "Perennial Fashion—Jazz," in Prisms, trans. Samuel and Shierry Weber (Cambridge, Mass., 1983), pp. 119–132.
56. "Zur Deutung Křeneks: Aus einer Rundfunkrede" (1932), in Adorno/Křenek, Briefwechsel, 18:571.
57. Ibid.
58. "Replik zu einer Kritik der 'Zeitlosen Mode'" (1953), AGS, vol. 10.2, p. 808.
59. Ibid.
60. Preface to Moments musicaux: Neu gedruckte Aufsätze, 1928–1962 (1963), AGS, 17:11.
61. "Culture Industry Reconsidered," in The Culture Industry, ed. J. M. Bernstein (London, 1991), p. 88.
62. "Farewell to Jazz," in Essays on Music, p. 496.
63. Preface to Moments musicaux, 17:10.

64. Max Horkheimer and Theodor Adorno, *Dialectic of Enlightenment*, ed. Gunzelin Schmid Noerr, trans. Edmund Jephcott (Stanford, 2002), p. 123.

65. Ibid., p. 105.

66. "If Knaves Should Tempt You," p. 29.

67. *Dialectic of Enlightenment*, p. 123.

68. Pollock to Horkheimer, 10 January 1941, HGS, 17:182.

69. *Minima Moralia*, p. 18.

70. Horkheimer to Pollock, 10 July 1948, HGS, 17:1015.

71. Horkheimer to Theodor W. and Margarethe Adorno, 21 May 1948, HGS, 17:974.

72. Horkheimer to Pollock, 12 June 1948, HGS, 17:982f.

73. Horkheimer to Maidon Horkheimer, 26 May 1948, HGS, 17:976.

74. Horkheimer to Maidon Horkheimer, 13 June 1948, HGS, 17:984.

75. Horkheimer to Marie Jahoda, 5 July 1948, HGS, 17:1008.

76. Adorno to Horkheimer, 27 December 1949, HGS, 18:80.

77. Ibid. [a "clever place"—Trans.].

78. Adorno to Löwenthal, 3 January 1949, in Leo Löwenthal, *Schriften*, vol. 4 (Frankfurt am Main, 1984), p. 174.

79. Adorno to Mann, 28 December 1949, in Theodor W. Adorno/Thomas Mann, *Correspondence, 1943–1955*, ed. Christoph Gödde and Thomas Sprecher, trans. Nicholas Walker (Cambridge, 2007), p. 34.

80. Ibid.

81. Adorno to Horkheimer, 27 December 1949, HGS, 18:80.

82. Adorno to Mann, 28 December 1949, in *Correspondence, 1943–1955*, p. 33.

83. "Die auferstandene Kultur" (1949), AGS, vol. 20.2, p. 457.

84. Ibid., p. 463.

85. Ibid., p. 460.

86. Ibid., p. 461.

87. Ibid., p. 460.

88. "On the Question: 'What Is German?'" in *Critical Models*, p. 210.

89. Ibid., p. 211.

90. Adorno to Horkheimer, 28 October 1949, HGS, 18:68.

91. *Minima Moralia*, p. 19.

92. Memorandum from Friedrich Pollock to Max Horkheimer, 30 March 1949, HGS, 18:18.

93. Max Horkheimer, preface (March 1946) to *Eclipse of Reason* (New York, 1947), p. vii.

94. Horkheimer to Felix Weil, 30 May 1949, HGS, 18:39.

95. Adorno to Horkheimer, 27 December 1949, HGS, 18:79.

96. Ibid., p. 85.

97. C. Wright Mills, "IBM Plus Reality Plus Humanism = Sociology," *Saturday Review*, 1 May 1954, quoted here from HGS, 18:276.

98. Adorno to Horkheimer, 27 December 1949, HGS, 18:79.
99. Horkheimer to Pollock, 18 February 1950, HGS, 18:115.
100. "Scientific Experiences of a European Scholar in America," p. 239.
101. "Cultural Criticism and Society," in *Prisms*, p. 31.
102. Ibid., pp. 34 and 31.
103. Ibid., p. 30.
104. Ibid.
105. Ibid., p. 34.
106. *Dialectic of Enlightenment*, p. 213.
107. "Titles," in *Notes to Literature*, ed. Rolf Tiedemann, trans. Shierry Weber Nicholsen, vol. 2 (New York, 1991), p. 6.
108. *Philosophy of Modern Music*, p. 133. [The translation given there is: "It is the surviving message of despair from the shipwrecked."—Trans.]
109. "Contribution to Intellectual History," in *Minima Moralia*, p. 209.
110. Report by Löwenthal (1946), HGS, 17:761.
111. Adorno to Horkheimer, 17 August 1941, HGS, 17:152.
112. "Antithesis," in *Minima Moralia*, p. 26.
113. "Max Horkheimer," AGS, vol. 20.1, p. 159.
114. "Cultural Criticism and Society," p. 34.
115. Ibid.
116. *Dialectic of Enlightenment*, p. 191. Adorno had already formulated this idea earlier in a letter to Walter Benjamin on 29 February 1940; see Walter Benjamin/Theodor W. Adorno, *The Complete Correspondence, 1928–1940*, trans. Nicholas Walker (Cambridge, 1999), p. 321.
117. "Die gegängelte Musik," in *Dissonanzen*, 14:53.
118. "The Sociology of Knowledge and Its Consciousness," in *Prisms*, p. 37.
119. Cf. "Out of the Firing-Line," in *Minima Moralia*, p. 54: "Karl Kraus was right to call his play *The Last Days of Mankind*. What is being enacted now ought to bear the title: 'After Doomsday.'"
120. Adorno to Horkheimer, 12 March 1953, HGS, 18:247f.
121. Ibid.
122. Ibid., 18:248.
123. Ibid.
124. Ibid. pp. 248f.
125. "Fragen an die intellektuelle Emigration," talk given at the Jewish Club, Los Angeles, 27 May 1949, AGS, vol. 20.1, pp. 352f.
126. Ibid., p. 353.
127. Adorno to Horkheimer, 12 March 1953, HGS, 18:248.
128. "Aldous Huxley and Utopia," in *Prisms*, p. 97.
129. Ibid.
130. "Veblen's Attack on Culture," in *Prisms*, p. 94.

131. Herbert Marcuse, "Some Social Implications of Modern Technology," *Studies in Philosophy and Social Science* 9 (1941): 414ff.
132. "Scientific Experiences of a European Scholar in America," p. 241.
133. "Veblen's Attack on Culture," p. 93.
134. "Ausschweifung," appendix to *Minima Moralia*, AGS, 4:301.
135. Ibid.
136. Ibid., pp. 301f.
137. "Cultural Criticism and Society," p. 30.
138. "Tradition," in *Dissonanzen*, 14:142.
139. Ibid.
140. For Adorno's critique of "art religion," see *Aesthetic Theory*, p. 98 and passim.
141. "Die gegängelte Musik" (1948), in *Dissonanzen*, 14:66.
142. Leo Löwenthal, *An Unmastered Past*, ed. Martin Jay (Berkeley, 1987), p. 203.
143. *Max Horkheimer* (1965), AGS, vol. 20.1, p. 159.
144. Adorno to Horkheimer, 12 March 1953, HGS, 18:248.
145. "Criteria of New Music, in *Sound Figures*, p. 195.
146. Ibid., pp. 145–196.
147. "Nachruf auf einen Organisator" (1962), in *Ohne Leitbild*, vol. 10.1, p. 347.
148. "Auf die Frage: Warum sind Sie zurückgekehrt" (1962), AGS, vol. 20.1, p. 395.
149. "Musik, Sprache und ihr Verhältnis im gegenwärtigen Komponieren" (1956), AGS, 16:656.
150. *Introduction to the Sociology of Music*, p. 222.
151. "Scientific Experiences of a European Scholar in America," p. 240.
152. *Introduction to the Sociology of Music*, p. 224.
153. "Die auferstandene Kultur" (1949), AGS, vol. 20.2, pp. 453–465.
154. *Introduction to the Sociology of Music*, p. 36.

7. Adorno as "Identical" Man

1. Adorno to Horkheimer, 14 February 1965, HGS, 18:596. See also the appendix to this volume.
2. Horkheimer to the editor of *Die Zeit* (Hamburg), 25 March 1965, HGS, 18:602.
3. Horkheimer and Adorno, "Diskussion über Theorie und Praxis" (1956), HGS, 19:65.
4. Ibid., p. 46.
5. Horkheimer to Marcuse, 29 December 1948, HGS, 17:1050.
6. Horkheimer and Adorno, "Diskussion über Theorie und Praxis," 19:45.
7. Ibid., p. 46.
8. Ibid.
9. Ibid.

10. Like *Encounter* in Britain, *Der Monat* was edited by Melvin Lasky. In 1967 it was revealed that both journals were financed by the CIA. [Trans.]

11. See Horkheimer and Adorno, *Dialectic of Enlightenment,* ed. Gunzelin Schmid Noerr, trans. Edmund Jephcott (Stanford, 2002), passim, for references to the "Culture Industry" and "monopoly."

12. The *Abendstudio* was a regular cultural program on Radio Frankfurt (subsequently Hessischer Rundfunk) founded by the writer Alfred Andersch in 1948 and directed by him until 1954. It was finally axed in 2003. [Trans.]

13. Horkheimer to Paul W. Freedman, 25 February 1957, HGS, 18:384.

14. Horkheimer and Adorno, "Diskussion über Theorie und Praxis," 19:56.

15. Ibid.

16. Ibid., p. 53.

17. "Jenseits der Fachwissenschaft: Adorno zum 60. Geburtstag" (1963), HGS, 7:272.

18. Ibid.

19. Ibid., p. 263.

20. Adorno to Horkheimer, 14 February 1965, HGS, 18:595; also *Max Horkheimer* (1965), AGS, vol. 20.1, p. 159. See the appendix to this volume.

21. Ibid.

22. Horkheimer and Adorno, "Diskussion über Theorie und Praxis," 19:66.

23. Ibid.

24. Ibid.

25. See "Those Twenties," in *Critical Models,* trans. Henry W. Pickford (New York, 1983), pp. 41–48.

26. "The Actuality of Philosophy," in *The Adorno Reader,* ed. Brian O'Connor (Oxford, 2000), p. 34. [Translation modified—Trans.]

27. Adorno to Horkheimer, 14 February 1965, HGS, 18:596; also "Offener Brief an Max Horkheimer," AGS, vol. 20.1, p. 161. See the appendix to this volume.

28. Adorno to Horkheimer, 14 February 1965, HGS, 18:594; "Offener Brief an Max Horkheimer," vol. 20.1, p. 158. See the appendix to this volume.

29. Adorno to Horkheimer, 14 February 1965, HGS, 18:593; "Offener Brief an Max Horkheimer," vol. 20.1, p. 158. See the appendix to this volume.

30. A reference to the final sentence in Benjamin's essay on Goethe's *Elective Affinities,* "Only for the sake of those without hope have we been given hope." Walter Benjamin, *Selected Writings,* vol. 1 (Cambridge, Mass., 2002), p. 356. [Translation modified—Trans.]

31. "Dwarf Fruit," in *Minima Moralia,* trans. Edmund Jephcott (London, 1974), p. 49.

32. "Ad Lukács" (1949), AGS, vol. 20.1, p. 255.

33. Ibid., p. 256.

34. Georg Lukács, "Heidegger redivivus," in *Sinn und Form* 3 (1949): 38.

35. "The postulate of a reality that must be represented without a breach be-

tween subject and object and which must be 'reflected'—the term Lukács stubbornly adheres to—for the sake of that lack of a breach: that postulate, which is the supreme criterion of his aesthetics, implies that that reconciliation has been achieved, that society has been set right, that the subject has come into its own and is at home in the world. This much Lukács admits in an anti-ascetic digression. Only then would there disappear from art the moment of resignation that Lukács perceives in Hegel and that he would have to acknowledge in Goethe, the prototype of his concept of realism, who preached renunciation." "Extorted Reconciliation: On Georg Lukács's *Realism in our Time*," in *Notes to Literature,* ed. Rolf Tiedemann, trans. Shierry Weber Nicholsen, vol. 2 (New York, 1991), p. 240.

36. Georg Lukács, *Record of a Life,* ed. Istvan Eörsi, trans. Rodney Livingstone (London, 1983), p. 30.
37. Leo Löwenthal, *An Unmastered Past,* ed. Martin Jay (Berkeley, 1987), p. 204.
38. Horkheimer and Adorno, "Diskussion über Theorie und Praxis," 19:66.
39. Ibid., p. 69.
40. Ibid., p. 71.
41. Adorno to Horkheimer, 21 March 1936, in Adorno/Horkheimer, *Briefwechsel, 1927–1937* (Frankfurt am Main, 2003), pp. 129f.
42. Adorno to Horkheimer, 5 August 1940, HGS, 16:764, note 5.
43. Adorno to Horkheimer, 8 February 1938, HGS, 16:385.
44. Ibid., p. 384.
45. Adorno to Horkheimer, 15 February 1938, HGS, 16:392.
46. "Fragmente über Wagner," in *Studies in Philosophy and Science,* vol. 8 (, 1939), p. 14.
47. *In Search of Wagner,* trans. Rodney Livingstone (London, 1981), p. 27.
48. "Wagner's Relevance for Today," in *Essays on Music,* ed. Richard Leppart, trans. Susan H. Gillespie (Berkeley, 2002), p. 599.
49. Ibid., p. 584.
50. "Selbstanzeige des Essaybuches *Versuch über Wagner*" (1952), AGS, 13:504.
51. "Dedication," in *Minima Moralia,* p. 18.
52. Adorno to Benjamin, 29 February 1940, in *The Complete Correspondence, 1928–1940,* trans. Nicholas Walker (Cambridge, 1990), p. 321.
53. Adorno to Benjamin, 4 March 1938, ibid., p. 252.
54. Adorno to Benjamin, 2 August 1938, p. 267. [Translation modified—Trans.]
55. "Deviation," in *Minima Moralia,* p. 113.
56. "Johnny-Head-in-Air," ibid., p. 57.
57. "Notes on Kafka," in *Prisms,* trans. Samuel and Shierry Weber (Cambridge, Mass., 1983), p. 260. [Translation slightly modified—Trans.]
58. "Introduction to Benjamin's *Schriften,*" in *Notes to Literature,* 2:230.
59. "Protection, Help, and Counsel," in *Minima Moralia,* p. 33.
60. "Proprietary Rights," ibid., p. 38.

61. "Regressions," ibid., p. 200.
62. Horkheimer and Adorno, "Diskussionsprotokolle" (1939), HGS, 12:514.
63. Ibid., p. 501.
64. Ibid.
65. Adorno to Benjamin, 1 February 1939, in *The Complete Correspondence, 1928–1940*, pp. 298f.
66. "Grassy Seat," in *Minima Moralia*, p. 22.
67. Ibid.
68. "Dwarf Fruit," in *Minima Moralia*, p. 50.
69. "Aldous Huxley and Utopia," in *Prisms*, pp. 106f.
70. Editor's Afterword, AGS, vol. 10.2, p. 839.
71. Bertolt Brecht, 13 August 1942, in *Journals, 1934–1955*, ed. John Willett and Ralph Manheim, trans. Hugh Rorrison (London, 1993), p. 252.
72. Werner Hecht, *Brecht Chronik, 1898–1956* (Frankfurt am Main, 1997), p. 669.
73. Bertolt Brecht, 23 March 1942, in *Journals, 1934–1955*, p. 210.
74. Bertolt Brecht, August 1941, ibid., p. 159.
75. "Why Still Philosophy," in *Critical Models*, p. 15.
76. Bertolt Brecht, 18 December 1944, *Journals, 1934–1955*, p. 338.
77. "Introduction to Benjamin's *Schriften*," 2:231.
78. Walter Benjamin, "Central Park," in *Selected Writings*, vol. 4 (Cambridge, Mass., 2003), p. 179. Adorno wrote to Scholem on 19 February 1942 about the opportunities Benjamin might have found in California had he been rescued. See *Frankfurter Adorno Blätter* 5 (1998): 154.
79. *Negative Dialectics*, trans. E. B. Ashton (London, 1996), p. xix.
80. From the open letter to Horkheimer on his birthday, 14 February 1965, AGS, vol. 20.1, p. 158. See the appendix to this volume.
81. Adorno to Benjamin, 4 March 1934, in *The Complete Correspondence, 1928–1940*, p. 26.
82. "Introduction to Benjamin's *Schriften*," 2:231.
83. The subtitle of *Minima Moralia*.
84. Adorno to Horkheimer, 14 February 1965, HGS, 18:593; also "Offener Brief an Max Horkheimer," AGS, vol. 20.1, p. 158. See the appendix to this volume.
85. Adorno to Horkheimer, 14 February 1965, HGS, 18:593; also "Offener Brief an Max Horkheimer," AGS, vol. 20.1, p. 158. See the appendix to this volume
86. "Offener Brief an Max Horkheimer," AGS, vol. 20.1, p. 157. See the appendix to this volume.
87. Horkheimer, "Theodor W. Adorno zum Gedächtnis" (1969), HGS, 7:290.
88. "Alban Berg," in *Sound Figures*, trans. Rodney Livingstone (Stanford, 1999), p. 69.
89. Adorno to Horkheimer, 14 February 1965, HGS, 18:594; also AGS, vol. 20.1, p. 159. See the appendix to this volume.
90. "Arnold Schönberg: 1874–1951" (1957), AGS, 18:320f.

91. See Rolf Tiedemann, "Auch Narr! Auch Dichter! Zu einem Singspiellibretto Adornos," *Frankfurter Adorno Blätter 7* (2001): 148.

92. Adorno to Berg, 8 September 1933, in *Briefwechsel Theodor W. Adorno/Alban Berg* (Frankfurt am Main, 1997), p. 276.

93. In the same letter to Berg, Adorno adds, "Moreover, as a *'Singspiel'* [lyrical drama], i.e., not through-composed, but in an intermittent form, alternating dialogue and music; but, for goodness's sake, no 'song' style." Ibid.

94. Benjamin to Adorno, 29 January 1934, in *The Complete Correspondence, 1928–1940*, pp. 23f.

95. Adorno to Benjamin, 4 March 1934, ibid., pp. 25f.

96. Ibid.

97. "Regressions," p. 200.

98. Horkheimer and Adorno, "Diskussionsprotokolle, 1939," 12:440.

99. Adorno to David, 3 July 1941, quoted in Rolf Wiggershaus, *Die Frankfurter Schule: Geschichte, theoretische Entwicklung, politische Bedeutung* (Munich, 1986), p. 350.

100. "English Spoken," in *Minima Moralia*, p. 47.

101. Adorno to Mann, 25 August 1951, in Theodor W. Adorno/Thomas Mann, *Correspondence, 1943–1955*, ed. Christophe Gödde and Thomas Sprecher, trans. Nicholas Walker (Cambridge, 2006), p. 65.

102. Max Horkheimer and Theodor W. Adorno, "Diskussion über Theorie und Praxis" (1956), 19:70.

103. Ibid.

104. Adorno to Horkheimer, 14 February 1965, HGS, 18:596; also AGS, vol. 20.1, p. 161. See the appendix to this volume.

105. "Sur l'eau," in *Minima Moralia*, p. 156.

106. Ibid., pp. 156f.

107. "Bequest," in *Minima Moralia*, p. 152.

108. "Gold Assay," ibid., p. 152.

109. *In Search of Wagner*, p. 156.

110. Adorno to Benjamin, 18 March 1936, in *The Complete Correspondence, 1928–1940*, p. 131.

111. Ibid., pp. 132f.

112. "On Jazz," in *Essays on Music*, p. 473.

113. Horkheimer and Adorno, "Diskussion über Theorie und Praxis," 19:70.

114. "Regressions," pp. 199f. [Taubert's Lullaby includes the words "Doggy bit the beggar-man / tore his coat, away he ran."—Trans.]

115. Adorno to Horkheimer, 14 February 1965, HGS, 18:598; also AGS, vol. 20.1, p. 161. See the appendix, to this volume.

116. AGS, vol. 20.1, p. 162.

117. Ibid.

118. "Notiz über Namen" (1930), AGS, vol. 20.2, p. 533.

119. Ibid.

120. Ibid.

121. Siegfried Kracauer, *Schriften*, vol. 7 (Frankfurt am Main, 1973), p. 256.

122. *Lawine* is the German for "avalanche." The reference is to Baudelaire's poem *Le Goût du Néant*, whose last line reads, "Avalanche veut-tu m'emporter dans ta chute?" Adorno uses this verse as the epigraph to part three of *Minima Moralia*. [Trans.]

123. "Über Jazz," AGS, 17:101.

124. "The Bad Comrade," in *Minima Moralia*, p. 192.

125. This term turns up in a wide variety of contexts after 1945.

126. "The Bad Comrade," p. 192.

127. "Über Jazz" (1937), in *Moments musicaux: Neu gedruckte Aufsätze, 1928–1962*, AGS, 17:104.

128. "Princess Lizard," in *Minima Moralia*, p. 170.

129. "Physiognomik der Stimme" (1957), AGS, vol. 20.2, p. 510.

130. Ibid., p. 511.

131. "Graeculus I: Musikalische Notizen," *Frankfurter Adorno Blätter* 7 (Munich, 2001): 28.

132. Horkheimer and Adorno, "Diskussion über Theorie und Praxis," 1958.

133. "On Jazz," pp. 490f.

134. "Über Jazz," 17:102.

135. "Farewell to Jazz," in *Essays on Music*, p. 497.

136. "Kleiner Dank an Wien," AGS, vol. 20.2, pp. 552ff. ["Melange" is a popular Viennese variety of coffee.—Trans.]

137. "Mélange," in *Minima Moralia*, p. 103.

138. Ibid.

139. *Mahler: A Musical Physiognomy*, trans. Edmund Jephcott (1992; reprint, Chicago, 1996), p. 22.

140. "Worte ohne Lieder" (1931), AGS, vol. 20.2, pp. 537ff.

141. "*Mendelssohn*. Idea: the bourgeois world he projects with its illusion of harmony is so irrevocably lost that it can once again be rescued, for example, in a historical image. What sort of melancholy is the melancholy of the man who is not under threat?" Adorno wonders in March 1960. See "Graeculus I: Musikalische Notizen," p. 24.

142. "Wagner never really belonged among the stars above in my childhood." Adorno to Benjamin, 2 August 1938, in *The Complete Correspondence, 1928–1940*, p. 265.

143. "Heine the Wound," in *Notes to Literature*, 185.

144. Ibid., p. 83.

145. Ibid., p. 81.

146. *Mahler: A Musical Physiognomy*, p. 20.

147. His student Elisabeth Lenk published her extremely illuminating correspon-

dence with Adorno from 1962 to 1969 in Munich in 2001. It contains a sentence from Adorno's records of dreams that he had had and that he had sent her in which he had said of himself, "I am the martyr of happiness." Theodor W. Adoeno and Elisabeth Lenk, *Briefwechsel, 1962–1969,* ed. Elisabeth Lenk (Munich, 2002), p. 135. *"L'Inutile Beauté"* (*Minima Moralia,* p. 171) contains the statement, "The fallen woman like the obsessive one is the martyr of happiness."

148. Horkheimer and Adorno, "Diskussion über Theorie und Praxis," 19:39.
149. Ibid.
150. Ibid.
151. Adorno to Horkheimer, 14 February 1965, HGS, 18:596; also AGS, vol. 20.1, p. 160. See the appendix to this volume.
152. *Mahler: A Musical Physiognomy,* p. 9.
153. Horkheimer and Adorno, "Diskussion über Theorie und Praxis," 19:55.
154. Ibid., p. 69.
155. "Max Horkheimer zum Tode Adornos: Gespräch mit Bernhard Landau" (1969), HGS, 7:87.
156. "Späne: Notizen über Gespräche mit Max Horkheimer," HGS, 14:339.
157. "Criteria of New Music," in *Sound Figures,* p. 156.
158. "Scientific Experiences of a European Scholar in America," in *Critical Models,* p. 240.
159. *Im Flug erhascht* (1954), AGS, vol. 20.2, p. 548.
160. Ibid.
161. Adorno to Benjamin, 4 March 1938, in *The Complete Correspondence, 1928–1940,* p. 250.
162. "Meine stärksten Eindrücke 1953," AGS, vol. 20.2, p. 735.

8. THE PALIMPSEST OF LIFE

1. "Cultural Criticism and Society," in *Prisms,* trans. Samuel and Shierry Weber (Cambridge, Mass., 1983), p. 34.
2. "The Meaning of Working Through the Past," in *Critical Models,* trans. Henry W. Pickford (New York, 1983), p. 89.
3. Peter R. Hofstätter, "Zum Gruppenexperiment von Friedrich Pollock: Eine kritische Würdigung," *Kölner Zeitschrift für Soziologie und Sozialpsychologie* 9 (1957): 97ff.
4. "Replik zu Peter R. Hofstätters Kritik des *Gruppenexperiments*" (1957), AGS, vol. 9.2, p. 392.
5. Franz Böhm (1895–977) was a lawyer and, after the war, a professor at Frankfurt. He played a leading part in the introduction of the social-market economy in Germany as well as in the process of reconciliation with Israel and the payment of reparations to victims of the Holocaust. [Trans.]

6. *Gruppenexperiment: Ein Studienbericht,* ed. Friedrich Pollock (Frankfurt am Main, 1955), p. xi.

7. Ibid., in "Schuld und Abwehr," *Soziologische Schriften,* vol. 2, AGS, vol. 9.2, p. 127.

8. "Scientific Experiences of a European Scholar in America," in *Critical Models,* pp. 215ff.

9. *Gruppenexperiment: Ein Studienbericht,* vol. 9.2, p. 127.

10. "Cultural Criticism and Society, p. 34.

11. "Die auferstandene Kultur" (1949), AGS, vol. 20.2, p. 453.

12. "Neue Oper und Publikum" (1930), AGS, 19:477.

13. Ibid.

14. "The Natural History of the Theatre," in *Quasi una fantasia,* trans. Rodney Livingstone (London, 1992), p. 65.

15. Ibid.

16. "Mahler," ibid., p. 88.

17. Ibid.

18. Ibid., p. 110.

19. "On the Question: 'What Is German?'" in *Critical Models,* p. 208.

20. Adorno to Horkheimer, 5 August 1940, HGS, 16:764.

21. Ibid.

22. "Notiz, Sommer 1939," in *Frankfurter Adorno Blätter* 4 (1995): 7.

23. "The weapon of criticism cannot, of course, replace criticism by weapons." Karl Marx, "Contribution to the Critique of Hegel's Philosophy of Law: Introduction," in Karl Marx and Frederick Engels, *Collected Works,* vol. 3 (London, 1975), p. 182. [Trans.]

24. Karl Marx, "The Philosophical Manifesto of the Historical School of Law," in Karl Marx and Frederick Engels, *Collected Works,* trans. Clemens Dutt, vol. 1 (London, 1975), p. 206.

25. Bloch to Adorno, 14 September 1963, in Ernst Bloch, *Briefe, 1903 bis 1975,* vol. 2 (Frankfurt am Main, 1985), pp. 450f.

26. Ibid.

27. "Ernst Bloch's *Spuren:* On the Revised Edition of 1959," in *Notes to Literature,* ed. Rolf Tiedemann, trans. Shierry Weber Nicholsen, vol. 1 (New York, 1991), p. 210.

28. Ibid., p. 206.

29. Ibid., p. 214.

30. Bloch to Adorno, 14 September 1963, in Bloch, *Briefe, 1903 bis 1975,* 2:451.

31. Adorno to Bloch, 26 July 1962. See the appendix to this volume.

32. Adorno to Bloch, 2 October 1937, in Theodor W. Adorno/Max Horkheimer, *Briefwechsel,* vol. 1, *1927–1937* (Frankfurt am Main, 2003), p. 539.

33. "Graeculus II: Notizen zu Philosophie und Gesellschaft, 1943–1969," in *Frankfurter Adorno Blätter* 8 (2003): 32.

34. Ibid., p. 31.

35. Benjamin to Alfred Cohn, 6 February 1935, in Walter Benjamin, *Briefe*, vol. 2 (Frankfurt am Main, 1968), p. 649.

36. Bloch to Adorno, 14 September 1963, in Bloch, *Briefe, 1903–1975*, 2:451. [Adorno's title "Grosse Blochmusik" is a pun on "Blechmusik," music for brass.— Trans.]

37. "The Handle, the Pot, and Early Experience," in *Notes to Literature*, ed. Rolf Tiedemann, trans. Shierry Weber Nicholson, vol. 2 (New York, 1992), p. 212.

38. Ibid., p. 219.

39. Ibid., pp. 219 and 218.

40. *Negative Dialectics*, trans. E. B. Ashton (London, 1996), pp. 56f.

41. Ernst Bloch, *Atheismus im Christentum* (Frankfurt am Main, 1968), p. 324.

42. "Ernst Bloch's *Spuren:* On the Revised Edition of 1959," 1:201.

43. Ibid., pp. 204 and 213.

44. Adorno to Bloch, 26 July 1962. See the appendix to this volume.

45. Bloch to Adorno, probably in the first half of December 1934, in Bloch, *Briefe, 1903–1975*, 2:423.

46. "Graeculus II: Notizen zu Philosophie und Gesellschaft, 1943–1969," p. 31.

47. Ibid.

48. "The Curious Realist," in *Notes to Literature*, 2:58ff.

49. Adorno to Bloch, 26 July 1962. See the appendix to this volume.

50. "Ernst Bloch's *Spuren:* On the Revised Edition of 1959," 1:204.

51. Adorno to Bloch, 26 July 1962. See the appendix to this volume.

52. "Ernst Bloch's *Spuren:* On the Revised Edition of 1959," 1:201.

53. Gerhart Eisler (1897–1968) was a prominent member of the German Communist Party in the 1920s. Having emigrated to the United States, he later served four years in prison there as a Soviet spy. After the war he was a member of the government of the German Democratic Republic until he fell out with Walther Ulbricht. Ruth Fischer, née Eisler (1895–1961), was a leading member of both the German Communist Party and the Reichstag. Condemned by Stalin for her ultra-left views, she was expelled from the party in 1926. In the thirties her far-left views led her into an association with Trotsky and further anathematization by Moscow. She then turned against communism, denouncing it in articles and in her book *Stalin and German Communism*. She acted as chief witness for the prosecution against her brother Gerhart in the proceedings before the House Un-American Activities Committee. [Trans.]

54. Albrecht Betz, *Hanns Eisler, Musik einer Zeit, die sich eben bildet* (Munich, 1976), p. 228.

55. "On the Social Situation of Music," in *Essays on Music*, ed. Richard Leppart, trans. Susan H. Gillespie (Berkeley, 2002), p. 411.

56. Ibid.

57. Ibid.
58. Ibid., pp. 408f.
59. Ibid., p. 411. [Translation modified—Trans.]
60. Ernst Bloch in *"Tagträume vom aufrechten Gang": Sechs Interviews mit Ernst Bloch,* ed. with intro. by Arno Münster (Frankfurt am Main, 1977), p. 47.
61. "The Handle, the Pot, and Early Experience," 2:212.
62. Adorno to Bloch, 26 July 1962. See the appendix to this volume.
63. Ibid.
64. "On the Question: 'What Is German?'" p. 212.
65. Adorno in a letter to Lili Kracauer, 20 June 1967.
66. Adorno to Bloch, 26 July 1962. See the appendix to this volume and note 1 on p. 410.
67. "Nach Kracauers Tod" (1966–67), AGS, vol. 20.1, p. 194.
68. Benjamin to Gretel Adorno, 14 December 1939, in Walter Benjamin, *Gesammelte Briefe,* vol. 6 (Frankfurt am Main, 2000), p. 368.
69. "Nach Kracauers Tod," vol. 20.1, p. 196.
70. "Reason . . . demands that everyone should strive to preserve his own being as far as he can." Spinoza, *Ethics* (Harmondsworth, 1996), p. 125. [Trans.]
71. "Resignation" was a key term for Adorno and one that recurs constantly in his essays in the sixties.
72. "The Curious Realist," 2:70. ["The Augsburg confusion" is an allusion to Brecht's birthplace, Augsburg, in south Germany and a pun on the Augsburg Confession, the primary statement of faith among Lutherans, drafted by Philip Melancthon in 1530.—Trans.]
73. Ibid., p. 71. [Translation modified—Trans.]
74. "Refuge for the Homeless," in *Minima Moralia,* trans. Edmund Jephcott (London, 1974), p. 39.
75. Siegfried Kracauer, *Die Angestellten,* in *Schriften,* vol. 1 (Frankfurt am Main, 1971), p. 282.
76. "Refuge for the Homeless," p. 38.
77. "The Curious Realist," 2:67.
78. Ibid., p. 60.
79. Ibid., p. 75.
80. Ibid., p. 69.
81. *Siegfried Kracauer: 1889–1966,* ed. Ingrid Belke and Irina Renz, *Marbacher Magazin* 47 (1988): 121.
82. "The Curious Realist," 2:66.
83. Ibid., p. 61.
84. Siegfried Kracauer, "Geschichte—Vor den letzten Dingen," in *Schriften,* vol. 4 (Frankfurt am Main, 1971), p. 84.
85. "Graeculus II: Notizen zu Philosophie und Gesellschaft, 1943–1969," p. 15.

86. This was the title Ernst Krenek gave to his review in the *Wiener Zeitung*, 18 May 1937. See also Krenek to Adorno, 2 September 1937, in Ernst Krenek, *Briefwechsel* (Frankfurt am Main, 1974), p. 124.

87. Kracauer to Benjamin, 24 February 1935, in Walter Benjamin, *Briefe an Siegfried Kracauer* (Marbach am Neckar, 1987), p. 82.

88. Its first working title was "The Art of Mass Consumption," as Adorno reported to Horkheimer in a letter dated 15 May 1937. See Adorno/Horkheimer, *Briefwechsel*, 1:362ff.

89. Adorno's annihilating letter of criticism of 13 May 1935 to Kracauer has not yet been published in full.

90. Benjamin to Adorno, 9 May 1937, in Walter Benjamin and Theodor Adorno, *The Complete Correspondence 1928–1940*, trans. Nicholas Walker (Cambridge, 1999), p. 186. [Emil Ludwig wrote popular biographies of Goethe, Napoleon, and Bismarck, as well as *The Son of Man;* Ludwig Marcuse published biographies of Heine, Strindberg, and Wagner; E. A. Rheinhardt (who was murdered at the Dachau concentration camp) wrote lives of Eleonora Duse, Napoleon III, and Henri IV; Paul Frischauer was known for his lives of Prince Eugene, Garibaldi, and Beaumarchais.—Trans.]

91. Ibid., p. 185.

92. Max Horkheimer's programmatic essay "Traditional and Critical Theory" (1937) was written at the time of the Moscow trials; see HGS, 4:214: "The search for a condition without exploitation and oppression, in which an inclusive subject exists, in other words, a self-aware mankind, a condition with a unified theory formation, a mode of thought that encompasses all individuals, does not yet amount to its realization. The transmission of critical theory in as rigorous a way as possible is of course the precondition of its historical success."

93. Siegfried Kracauer, *Die Angestellten*, in *Schriften*, 1:304.

94. In "Walter Benjamin zum Gedächtnis," Max Horkheimer had published "Reason and Self-Preservation" ("Vernunft und Selbsterhaltung"), which had been written in 1941–1942: "For the individual life was infinitely important because death was the absolute catastrophe. Fascism touches on this basic fact of bourgeois anthropology. It pushes what is anyway falling, namely, the individual, because it teaches him to fear that there are worse things than death." HGS, 5:345. See also Adorno's comment that "what in the days of *art nouveau* was known as a beautiful death has shrunk to the wish to curtail the infinite abasement of living and the infinite torment of dying, in a world where there are far worse things to fear than death." "Proprietary Rights, in *Minima Moralia*, p. 38.

95. "The Curious Realist," 2:62.

96. Ibid., p. 63. ["In mir habt ihr einen, auf den könnt ihr nicht bauen." Bertolt

Brecht, "Vom armen B.B. Of Poor B.B.," in *Poems, 1913–1956* (London, 1976; reprint, 1979), p. 107.—Trans.]

97. Ibid., p. 62

98. Adorno to Benjamin, 27 November 1937, in *The Complete Correspondence, 1928–1940,* p. 229.

99. Ernst Bloch, "Bucharins Schlu¼wort," 5 May 1938, in *Vom Hasard zur Katastrophe: Politische Aufsätze aus den Jahren 1934–1939.* with a postscript by Oskar Negt (Frankfurt am Main, 1972), p. 355.

100. "Graeculus II: Notizen zu Philosophie und Gesellschaft, 1943–1969," p. 31.

101. Ibid., pp. 31f.

102. Adorno to Horkheimer, 22 September 1937, in Theodor W. Adorno and Max Horkheimer, *Briefwechsel,* vol. 1 (Frankfurt am Main, 2003, pp. 412f.

103. Adorno to Horkheimer, 19 January 1938, in Theodor W. Adorno and Max Horkheimer, *Briefwechsel,* vol. 2 (Frankfurt am Main, 2004), p. 15.

104. "Graeculus II: Notizen zu Philosophie und Gesellschaft, 1943–1969," p. 32.

105. Ibid.

106. Ibid.

107. Benjamin to Gretel Adorno, 20 July 1938, in Benjamin, *Gesammelte Briefe,* 6:139.

108. Adorno to Horkheimer, 8 August 1938, in *Briefwechsel,* 2:41.

109. "Für Ernst Bloch" (1942), AGS, vol. 20.1, p. 193.

110. Bloch to Joachim Schumacher, 14 October 1942, in Bloch, *Briefe,* 2:530.

111. Bloch to Adorno, 18 September 1942, ibid., p. 443.

112. "Für Ernst Bloch" (1942), AGS, vol. 20.1, p. 190.

113. Ibid., p. 191.

114. "Graeculus II: Notizen zu Philosophie und Gesellschaft, 1943–1969," pp. 31f.

115. Ibid.

116. See Chapter 5.

117. "Graeculus II: Notizen zu Philosophie und Gesellschaft, 1943–1969," p. 31.

118. "Ernst Bloch's *Spuren:* On the Revised Edition of 1959," 1:204.

119. Ibid.

120. "Graeculus II: Notizen zu Philosophie und Gesellschaft, 1943–1969," p. 31.

121. "For Post-Socratics," in *Minima Moralia,* p. 71.

122. "The Curious Realist," in *Notes to Literature,* 264.

123. "The Handle, the Pot, and Early Experience," 2:13.

124. "Graeculus II: Notizen zu Philosophie und Gesellschaft, 1943–1969," p. 31.

125. Ibid.

126. Ibid.

127. G. W. F. Hegel, *Phenomenology of the Spirit,* trans. A. V. Miller (Oxford, 1977), p. 360.

128. Ernst Bloch, *Das Prinzip Hoffnung* (Frankfurt am Main, 1967), p. 637.

129. "The Curious Realist," 2:70 and 2:64.

130. Ibid., p. 69.

131. "The George-Hofmannsthal Correspondence, 1891–1906," in *Prisms*, p. 193.

132. Benjamin to Adorno, 7 May 1940, in *The Complete Correspondence, 1928–1940*, p. 331.

133. Ibid.

134. "The George-Hofmannsthal Correspondence, 1891–1906," p. 193.

135. *Negative Dialectics*, p. 3. *Negative Dialectics* (1966) opens with this aphorism: "Philosophy, which once seemed obsolete, lives on because the moment to realize it was missed." Ibid.

136. This refers to the scene in which Faust concludes his pact with Mephistopheles: "If ever to the moment I shall say: / Beautiful moment do not pass away! / Then you may forge your chains to bind me, / Then I shall put my life behind me." *Faust*, pt. 1, trans. David Luke (Oxford, 1987), p. 52. [Trans.]

137. *"Eisler: Zeitungsausschnitte,"* AGS, 18:525.

138. Ibid., p. 524.

139. Ibid., p. 527.

140. Bertolt Brecht, "To Those Who Come after Us," in *Poems, 1913–1956*, ed. John Willett and Ralph Manheim, with the cooperation of Erich Fried (1976; reprint, London, 1979), p. 318.

141. "Graeculus II: Notizen zu Philosophie und Gesellschaft, 1943–1969," p. 28.

142. "Out of the Firing-Line," in *Minima Moralia*, p. 53.

143. Albrecht Dümling, *Laßt Euch nicht verführen: Brecht und die Musik* (Munich, 1985), p. 488.

144. "Notizen über Eisler," *Frankfurter Adorno Blätter* 7 (2001): 122.

145. "The Curious Realist," 2:69f.

146. "Is Art Lighthearted?" in *Notes to Literature*, p. 252.

147. "Notizen über Eisler," p. 122. The last phrase refers to the jingle "Und willst du nicht mein Bruder sein / So schlag ich dir den Schädel ein" (If you won't be my brother, I'll beat your brains out). This was a German version of the Jacobin slogan "La fraternité ou la mort" (Brotherhood or death). [Trans.]

148. Bertolt Brecht, *Journals, 1934–1955*, ed. John Willett and Ralph Manheim, trans. Hugh Rorrison (London, 1993), p. 257.

149. "Out of the Firing-Line," p. 53.

150. "Refuge for the Homeless,"p. 39.

151. Ibid.

152. "Tough Baby," in *Minima Moralia*, p. 45.

153. Adorno to Benjamin, 4 March 1938, in *The Complete Correspondence, 1928–1940*, p. 252.

154. Adorno to Benjamin, 2 August 1938, ibid., p. 267.

155. Adorno to Horkheimer, 25 February 1935, in Adorno/Horkheimer, *Briefwechsel*, 1:53

156. "Consecutio temporum," in *Minima Moralia*, pp. 217ff.

157. Hanns Eisler, *Materialien zu einer Dialektik der Musik* (Leipzig, 1973), p. 296.
158. Brecht, 4 September 1943, in *Journal, 1934–1955*, p. 296.
159. "Graeculus II: Notizen zu Philosophie und Gesellschaft, 1943–1969," p. 18.
160. Ibid.
161. Horkheimer and Adorno to Herbert Marcuse, 12 February 1960, in Wolfgang Kraushaar, *Frankfurter Schule und Studentenbewegung* (Hamburg, 1998), p. 127.
162. For example, in an essay written in 1962, "The authentic artists of the present are those in whose works the uttermost horror still quivers." "Those Twenties," in *Critical Models*, p. 48.
163. Herbert Marcuse, *One Dimensional Man* (London, 1964), p. 87n.
164. "Graeculus II: Notizen zu Philosophie und Gesellschaft, 1943–1969," p. 33.
165. "Notizen über Eisler," pp. 124 and 128.
166. Eisler, *Materialien zu einer Dialektik der Musik*, p. 296.
167. "Dedication," in *Minima Moralia*, p. 18.
168. "Anmerkungen zum deutschen Musikleben" (1967), AGS, 17:179.
169. Ibid.
170. "Notizen über Eisler," p. 125.
171. "Difficulties," in *Essays on Music*, p. 646.
172. "Notizen über Eisler," p. 125.
173. Ibid.
174. Ibid., p. 128.
175. "Difficulties," p. 649.
176. Ibid., p. 660.
177. "Anmerkungen zum deutschen Musikleben," 17:168.
178. Ibid.
179. Rolf Tiedemann, *Adorno-Noten* (Berlin, 1984); of particular interest is the correspondence with Eduard Steuermann, who also reports the failure of his proposed plan to provide Ingeborg Bachmann with a libretto.
180. "Nachruf auf einen Organisator" (1962), AGS, vol. 10.1, p. 348.
181. "Vers une musique informelle," in *Quasi una fantasia*, pp. 269–322.
182. Ibid., pp. 274f.
183. "Reading Balzac," in *Notes to Literature*, 1:136.
184. See his essay "Paris, the Capital of the Nineteenth Century," in *Selected Writings*, ed. Michael W. Jennings et al., trans. Rodney Livingstone, Edmund Jephcott, Harry Zohn et al. (Cambridge, Mass., 1996–2003), 3:32. [Trans.]
185. "Looking Back on Surrealism," in *Notes to Literature*, 1:87.
186. "Tagebuch der großen Reise, Oktober 1949: Aufzeichnungen der Rückkehr aus dem Exil," *Frankfurter Adorno Blätter* 8 (2003): 102.
187. Ibid.
188. "Graeculus II: Notizen zu Philosophie und Gesellschaft, 1943–1969," p. 31.
189. Ibid., p. 18.

190. Ibid., p. 31.

191. Ibid.

192. "Richard Strauss," AGS, 16:577.

193. "Benjamin the Letter Writer," in *Notes to Literature*, p. 222.

194. Adolph Lowe to Karola Bloch, 10 December 1966, in Bloch, *Briefe*, 2:801.

195. Ibid.

196. Maidon Horkheimer to Max Horkheimer, 25–26 May 1949, HGS, 18:37.

197. See Adorno to Bloch, 26 July 1962, in the appendix to this volume. [Goethe used this term to refer to *Faust*, a work that preoccupied him for around sixty years.—Trans.]

198. "Graeculus II: Notizen zu Philosophie und Gesellschaft, 1943–1969," p. 31.

199. *Negative Dialectics*, p. 365.

200. Ibid., p. 363.

201. Ibid. [Translation modified—Trans.]

202. Ibid., p. 364.

203. Adorno to Bloch, 26 July 1962. See the appendix to this volume.

204. "Graeculus II: Notizen zu Philosophie und Gesellschaft 1943–1969," p. 19.

205. Georg Lukács, *The Theory of the Novel*, trans. Anna Bostock (London, 1971), p. 22.

206. "Graeculus II: Notizen zu Philosophie und Gesellschaft, 1943–1969," p. 22.

207. "Those Twenties," pp. 42, 45.

208. The essay referred to here was not included in the English edition. [Trans.]

209. For the letter from Horkheimer, see the appendix to this volume. [Trans.]

210. Jürgen Habermas, "Eine Generation von Adorno getrennt," in *Geist gegen den Zeitgeist: Erinnern an Adorno*, ed. Josef Früchtl and Maria Calloni (Frankfurt am Main, 1991), p. 50.

211. Horkheimer to Adorno, 27 September 1958, HGS, 18:437. See also the appendix to this volume.

212. Ibid., p. 444; see the appendix to this volume.

213. Ibid., p. 443; see the appendix to this volume.

214. Ibid., p. 447; see the appendix to this volume.

215. *Against Epistemology: A Metacritique*, trans. Willis Domingo (Oxford, 1982), pp. 39f.

216. Horkheimer to Adorno, 27 September 1958, HGS, 18:440; see the appendix to this volume.

217. Habermas, "Eine Generation von Adorno getrennt," p. 50.

218. Adorno to Claus Behncke, 21 February 1964; see the appendix to this volume.

219. Adorno to Bloch, 26 July 1962, see the appendix to this volume.

220. Ibid. See also the editor's postscript to *Philosophische Frühschriften*, AGS, 1:384.

221. "The Actuality of Philosophy," in *The Adorno Reader*, ed. Brian O'Connor (Oxford, 2000), p. 24.

222. Editors' Afterword, in *Aesthetic Theory,* trans. Robert Hullot-Kentor (London, 1997), p. 361.

223. Ibid., p. 366.

224. On 31 May 1961 Adorno noted: "Title for a future book of aphorisms: "Graeculus: experiences after my return [Graeculus. Erfahrungen nach der Rückkunft]." See "Graeculus II: Notizen zu Philosophie und Gesellschaft, 1943–1969," p. 21.

225. Alfred Sohn-Rethel, "Notizen von einem Gespräch zwischen Th.W. Adorno und A. Sohn-Rethel am 16.4.1965," in *Geistige und körperliche Arbeit,* rev. and expanded ed. (Weinheim, 1989), p. 223.

226. "Graeculus II: Notizen zu Philosophie und Gesellschaft, 1943–1969," p. 20.

227. Adorno to Horkheimer, 27 December 1949, HGS, 18:80.

228. Ibid.

229. *Negative Dialectics,* p. xix.

230. "Aus Sils Maria" (1966), in *Ohne Leitbild: Parva Aesthetica,* AGS, vol. 10.1, p. 327.

231. Ibid., p. 328.

232. "Graeculus II: Notizen zu Philosophie und Gesellschaft, 1943–1969," p. 36.

233. "Reconciliation under Duress," trans. Rodney Livingstone, in Ernst Bloch et al., *Aesthetics and Politics,* ed. Ronald Taylor (London, 1977), p. 152.

234. Ibid.

235. "Commitment," trans. Francis McDonagh, in Ernst Bloch et al., *Aesthetics and Politics,* p. 187.

236. Ibid., p. 184.

237. Adorno to Benjamin, 10 November 1938, in *The Complete Correspondence, 1928–1940,* p. 286.

238. Brecht, *Journals, 1934–1955,* pp. 337f.

239. Ibid., p. 337.

240. "Commitment," in Ernst Bloch et al., *Aesthetics and Politics,* p. 188.

241. *Aesthetic Theory,* p. 27.

242. Ibid., p. 32.

243. See the appendix to this volume.

244. Theodor W. Adorno and Paul Celan, *Briefwechsel, 1960–1968,* ed. Joachim Seng, *Frankfurter Adorno Blätter* 8 (2003): 177–202. In its first version, which appeared in the *Neue Deutsche Hefte* in 1960, Adorno's essay on Bloch's *Traces* bore the title "Great Bloch Music" [*Große Blochmusik:* Adorno puns here on *Blechmusik* = brass band music, a reference to the somewhat ebullient nature of Bloch's rhetoric—Trans.]; a copy of the essay was found in Paul Celan's library, as we learn from Joachim Seng, who has researched the history of Adorno's relationship with Celan. See Joachim Seng, "'Die wahre Flaschenpost': Zur Beziehung zwischen Theodor W. Adorno und Paul Celan," *Frankfurter Adorno Blätter* 8 (2003): 151ff.

245. Celan to Adorno, 23 May 1960, in *Briefwechsel, 1960–1968*, p. 179.

246. On 30 August, Theodor and Gretel Adorno together with Peter Szondi and Wibke von Bonin sent Celan a postcard depicting the lakes of the Upper Engadine; the main part of the text was signed "Yours, Adorno." Ibid., p. 183.

247. "A Portrait of Walter Benjamin," in *Prisms*, pp. 231f.

248. Ibid., pp. 230f.

249. Ibid., p. 232.

250. Adorno to Paul Celan, 13 June 1960, in *Briefwechsel, 1960–1968*, p. 181.

251. The date 2 June 1967 is often regarded as the start of the student protests in Germany. During a demonstration against a visit by the shah of what was then called Persia, a student, Benno Ohnesorg, was shot dead by a policeman [Trans.].

252. Peter Szondi, *Schriften*, vol. 2 (Frankfurt am Main, 1978), pp. 383f. [For Celan's poem "Engführung," see Paul Celan, *Selected Poems*, trans. Michael Hamburger (Harmondsworth, 1990; reprint, 1996), pp. 140ff.—Trans.]

253. Ibid.

254. *Aesthetic Theory*, p. 322.

255. Ibid.

256. Although the German SDS shares the same initials with the Students for a Democratic Society in the United States, the two organizations are otherwise unconnected. The German SDS started life close to the Social Democratic Party, but its members were excluded from the SPD in 1961 because of their rejection of German rearmament. The SDS subsequently provided the breeding ground for the German New Left, including ultimately its anarchist and terrorist tendencies. [Trans.]

257. "Graeculus II: Notizen zu Philosophie und Gesellschaft, 1943–1969," p. 18.

258. "It was only for the sake of those without hope, that hope is given to us." Marcuse, *One Dimensional Man*, p. 201 [Trans.].

259. "Cultural Criticism and Society," p. 34.

260. Adorno to Horkheimer, 31 May 1967, in Kraushaar, *Frankfurter Schule und Studentenbewegung*, p. 233.

261. Horkheimer to Herbert and Inge Marcuse, 17 December 1972, HGS, 18:806.

262. Herbert and Inge Marcuse to Horkheimer, January 1973, HGS, 18:807.

263. Adorno in his last express letter to Herbert Marcuse, 6 August 1969, in Kraushaar, *Frankfurter Schule und Studentenbewegung*, p. 671.

264. "Aus Sils Maria" (1966), in *Ohne Leitbild: Parva Aesthetica*, AGS, vol. 10.1, pp. 328f.

265. Adorno to Herbert Marcuse, 30 June 1967, *Frankfurter Adorno Blätter* 6 (2000): 52.

266. *Späne: Notizen über Gespräche mit Max Horkheimer*, recorded by Friedrich Pollock, HGS, 14:472.

267. "The Meaning of Working Through the Past," p. 90.

268. Adorno to Günter Grass, 4 November 1968, in Kraushaar, *Frankfurter Schule und Studentenbewegung*, p. 473.

269. Ibid.

270. "The Meaning of Working Through the Past," p. 89.

271. "Graeculus II: Notizen zu Philosophie und Gesellschaft, 1943–1969," p. 13.

272. *Vorlesung über Negative Dialektik: Fragmente zur Vorlesung 1965/66*, ed. Rolf Tiedemann, in *Nachgelassene Schriften*, pt. 4 vol. 16 (Frankfurt am Main, 2003), p. 83.

273. Ibid., pp. 83f.

274. Adorno to Herbert Marcuse, 25 March 1969, in Kraushaar, *Frankfurter Schule und Studentenbewegung*, p. 579.

275. Adorno to Samuel Beckett, 4 February 1969, *Frankfurter Adorno Blätter* 3 (1994): 25f.

276. Samuel Beckett to Adorno, ibid., p. 26.

277. From a draft preface, "Zur Neuausgabe der *Dialektik der Aufklärung*" (February 1969), in "Graeculus II: Notizen zu Philosophie und Gesellschaft, 1943–1969," p. 8.

278. Ibid.

279. Ibid., p. 15.

280. Adorno to Herbert Marcuse, 6 August 1969, in Kraushaar, *Frankfurter Schule und Studentenbewegung*, p. 671.

281. See "Heliotrope," in *Minima Moralia*, pp. 177f. [Trans.]

282. Herbert Marcuse, "Reflexion zu Theodor W. Adorno: Aus einem Gespräch mit Michaela Seiffe," in *Theodor W. Adorno zum Gedächtnis*, ed. Hermann Schweppenhäuser (Frankfurt am Main, 1971), p. 51.

283. Ibid.

284. *Aesthetic Theory*, p. 40.

285. Ibid., p. 194.

Appendix

1. The lime leaf is an allusion to the story of Siegfried (in Wagner and before him the *Nibelungenlied*). When Siegfried slew the dragon Fafnir, he was engulfed by the blood of the dying monster, and this rendered him invincible—or would have done had he been entirely covered. But a leaf from a lime tree settled on his back, creating a vulnerable spot, one used later by Hagen to kill him. [Trans.]

2. An essay by Bloch titled "Das Hohe Paar ein altes Ehesymbol" (The Noble Couple, an Ancient Marriage Symbol), now in Ernst Bloch, *Gesamtausgabe*, vol. 14 (Frankfurt am Main, 1961–1978), pp. 267–278.

3. Jürgen Habermas, "Zur philosophischen Diskussion um Marx und den Marxismus," *Philosophische Rundschau* 5, no. 3/4 (1957): 165ff.; all subsequent

Habermas citations refer to this source. See also Habermas, *Theorie und Praxis: Sozialphilosophische Studien,* 2nd ed. (Neuwied, 1967), pp. 261ff. Jürgen Habermas (b. 1929), philosopher and sociologist. Professor at Heidelberg, 1961; at Frankfurt am Main, 1964–1971 and 1983–1994; director of the Max Planck Institute in Starnberg, 1971–1983. In 1956–1959 he was an assistant at the Institute for Social Research in Frankfurt.

4. In this instance Adorno commented in the margins of his copy of the letter, "?." The comments on this and the following notes are taken from the typescript of the letter now in the Adorno Archive.
5. Marginal note of Adorno's: "Surely that's a good thing."
6. Marginal note of Adorno's: "?."
7. Marginal note of Adorno's: "Our thinking isn't actually as simple as that."
8. Marginal note of Adorno's: "?."
9. See Habermas, "Zur philosophischen Diskussion um Marx und den Marxismus," pp. 192 and 217.
10. Ibid., p. 183.
11. Ibid., p. 192: "On the one hand, criticism is 'practical,' interested in the transformation [*Aufhebung*] of existing conditions, and its movement can be determined only by this interest; to this extent the theory of revolution is the doctrine of the categories of criticism. On the other hand, that interest unlocks a point of view, and not a realm that can be developed with the methods of transcendental analysis; to this extent, criticism must look exclusively to science to provide whatever knowledge it desires."
12. Ibid., p. 206: "Nowhere does Merleau-Ponty demonstrate the qualification of the proletariat to become the agent of the revolution in sociological terms—and how otherwise is it to take place[?]"
13. Ibid., p. 232: "Where, however, the necessity of the naturalistic distortion that historical materialism assumes in the minds of the class that is supposed to turn it into reality can be identified sociologically, in other words, logically and concretely, the problem of proletarian class consciousness, the problem of its function and dialectics, becomes visible."
14. Ibid., p. 227: "Even though the opposition [in Poland] could appeal to the origins of historical materialism, its methodological critique of dogmatism brought them close to a positivistic historicism that is incompatible with the partisanship of a materialist philosophy of whatever stripe."
15. Ibid., p. 230.
16. Ibid., p. 231.
17. Marginal note of Adorno's: "I agree with Max here."
18. See Habermas, "Zur philosophischen Diskussion um Marx und den Marxismus," p. 232..
19. Ibid., p. 233.
20. Ibid., p. 234f.

21. "Dialektik der Rationalisierung," *Merkur*, no. 78 (1954).

22. Habermas, "Zur philosophischen Diskussion," p. 233: "Is it not more likely that the self-knowledge of the species will arise as a reaction to the untruth of wealth within a society that already tends toward a higher consciousness than as a reaction against the untruth of poverty within a class whose physical exploitation condemns all efforts on the part of consciousness to the status of social fortuitousness from the outset? Is it not the case that poverty in the midst of affluence is more likely than poverty amidst destitution to provide the conditions that may move the mass of the population to measure that which exists against that which is possible? Ought not a dialectic of false superabundance be more conducive to reflections on irrational domination than a dialectic of true poverty? The degree of generalization at which this question is posed with a view to an immanent critique should not make us forget that a decision is possible only on the basis of empirical evidence."

23. Marginal note of Adorno's: "Probably *not* what he means."

24. See note 21.

25. Ibid.

26. Ibid.

27. Habermas, "Zur philosophischen Diskussion um Marx und den Marxismus," p. 193: "Marx distinguishes between practical and theoretical necessity. The latter characterizes the categories of the social changes that come to prevail 'objectively' over men's heads, and hence can be calculated with scientific precision and predicted in advance; the former, in contrast, belong to an entirely different category of social changes, once that cannot be made to prevail 'objectively' with the will and knowledge of human beings, and which consequently can only be calculated and predicted in advance in the objective conditions of their possibility."

28. Ibid., p. 167.

29. Ibid., p. 209.

30. Ibid.

31. Ibid., p. 234.

32. Ibid., p. 192: "It [philosophy as materialist dialectic] has seen through the illusion of autonomy that has constantly led us to believe that it could both ground itself and make a reality of itself."

33. Horkheimer had quoted from Anni Carlsson, "Christian Thomasius, ein Wortführer der Vernunft," in *Neue Zürcher Zeitung*, 23 September 1958, p. 1. [Christian Thomasius (1655–1728) was a lawyer and philosopher. Appointed professor in Halle in 1694, he was a leading figure of the Enlightenment.— Trans.]

34. Habermas, "Zur philosophischen Diskussion um Marx und den Marxismus," p. 201.

35. Ibid., p. 184, where Habermas summarizes Ludwig Landgrebe's account of

Marx's critique of Hegel: "Not only Hegel's philosophy is false, but philosophy in general: in principle, it liberates humanity only in an abstract form, not in reality. As philosophy, it is not capable of being what it claims to be: the emancipation of mankind." Adorno has noted in the margin: "No indeed."

36. Ibid., p. 234.

37. Ibid., p. 177.

38. Ibid., p. 223: "Science lives on the certainty of its practicability, philosophy on the uncertainty that constantly renews itself from the unresolved tension between theory and practice and can be made to disappear only through the transcendence of philosophy as philosophy."

39. Marginal note of Adorno's: "Perfectly true."

40. As does Plato in the *Symposium:* "None of the gods loves wisdom or desires to become wise—because they are wise already." *Symposium*, §204a, trans. Christopher Gill (Harmondsworth, 1996), p. 40.

41. Habermas, "Zur philosophischen Diskussion um Marx und den Marxismus," p. 184.

42. Marginal note of Adorno's: "This is a repressive category."

43. Habermas, "Zur philosophischen Diskussion um Marx und den Marxismus," p. 170.

44. Ibid., p. 195.

45. Ibid., p. 184.

46. Ibid., p. 175: "For the young Marx dialectics was essentially historical, and a dialectics of nature, independent of social movements, absolutely inconceivable. Nature had a history only in connection with human beings, human beings only in connection with nature. Criticism remains related to revolution in every respect; there is no object, therefore, that cannot be confronted in the framework of the theory of revolution of historical materialism, nature included."

47. Ibid., p. 219: "Labor is the process of exchange between man and nature."

48. Ibid.: "Labor becomes domination, not simply in respect of the commerce between human beings involved in labor. This domination contains, like all violence, an element of the memory that it is an untruth, albeit an existing one."

49. Marginal note of Adorno's: "?"

50. Habermas, "Zur philosophischen Diskussion um Marx und den Marxismus," p. 234.

51. Ibid., p. 174.

52. Ibid., p. 205.

53. Ibid.

54. Ibid.

55. Karl Marx and Frederick Engels, *The Communist Manifesto,* in Karl Marx,

The Revolutions of 1848, vol. 1 of *Political Writings*, ed. David Fernbach (Harmondsworth, 1973), p. 98.

56. Habermas, "Zur philosophischen Diskussion um Marx und den Marxismus," p. 78.

57. Karl Marx, "Critique of Hegel's Philosophy of Right: Introduction," in *Early Writings*, ed. Lucio Colletti (Harmondsworth, 1975), p. 257.

58. Marginal note of Adorno's: "Nota Bene."

59. Gamal Abdel Nasser (1918–1970), Egyptian politician. President of the United Arab Republic, 1958–1961.

60. Abdul Karim Qassim (1914 or 1917–1963), Iraqi general; in 1958 he led a military coup against King Faisal II, after which he became prime minister and effectively sole leader. In 1963 he too was overthrown by a military coup.

61. Marginal note of Adorno's: "Yes."

62. Habermas, "Zur philosophischen Diskussion," p. 192.

63. Ibid., p. 182.

64. Marginal note of Adorno's: "Yes."

65. Marginal note of Adorno's: "Too hasty!"

66. Marginal note of Adorno's: "Well, . . ."

67. Marginal note of Adorno's: "Take care."

68. Marginal note of Adorno's: "*No*, unjust!"

69. Marginal note of Adorno's: "No."

70. In May students and lecturers in the Federal Republic had protested against nuclear rearmament. On this occasion Habermas wrote an article with the title "Unruhe erste Bürgerpflicht" (Unrest Is the Citizen's First Duty). It appeared in *Diskus: Frankfurter Studentenzeitung* 8, no. 5 (June 1958): 2.

71. Horkheimer is referring to the conference "Society, Practice, and Science: What Can Sociology Today Do for the Economy and the Administration?" This took place on 25 April 1958 at the Institute for Social Research. There is a note in the margin by Adorno, "But this is [illegible word]" [Trans.].

72. Perhaps a reference to Habermas, "Unruhe erste Bürgerpflicht," p. 2: "A whole host of motifs enter into that protest. An individual is neither called upon nor in a position to interpret them. For here it is individuals who protest, not organizations."

73. "All that will be swept away." Horkheimer had originally intended this as an epigraph for his essay "Egoism and the Freedom Movement." Cf. Horkheimer to Adorno, 15 May 1936, in Theodor W. Adorno and Max Horkheimer, *Briefwechsel*, vol. 1, *1927–1937* (Frankfurt am Main, 2003), p. 142 and note.

74. In July 1958 the pro-Western king of Iraq, Faisal II, was killed in a military coup. Ideologically, the insurgents were sympathetic to Nasser's pan-Arab movement.

75. Habermas, "Zur philosophischen Diskussion," p. 181: "The analysis of alienation remains therefore step by step the analysis of its abolition. But not as if

the statement of the one leads to the consideration of the other. Rather, the sight of the elimination always acts as a guide to the perception of what is to be eliminated."

76. "If the age of interpreting the world is over and the point now is to change it, then philosophy bids farewell. . . . It is time not for first philosophy but last philosophy." *Against Epistemology*, trans. Willis Domingo (Oxford, 1982), pp. 39f.

77. Marginal note of Adorno's: "Make up for this."

78. Jürgen Habermas, Ludwig von Friedeburg, Christoph Oehler, and Friedrich Weltz, *Student und Politik* (Neuwied, 1961). Habermas was responsible for the first part inter alia, "Reflexionen über den Begriff der politischen Beteiligung."

79. Ibid., p. 55.

80. Ibid.

81. Quoted according to the manuscript; this statement was evidently changed for the printed version.

82. Habermas, "Zur philosophischen Diskussion," p. 182: "The fact that Marx had only an inadequate understanding of Hegel, and that Hegel had already thought in advance of the ideas that Marx subsequently believed he had discovered through his criticisms of him, is the taboo formula that keeps us from the specific problems of a revolutionary philosophy of history intent on establishing an empirical foundation."

83. Published as an open letter in *Die Zeit*, no. 7, 12 February 1965, p. 32, AGS, vol. 20.1, pp. 155ff. A reply appeared in *Die Zeit*, 25 March 1965.

84. Herz had written to Horkheimer following Adorno's funeral, saying that "the funeral of this great man disappointed me and hurt me deeply" because it was not conducted according to Jewish funeral rites. "In the shadow of Auschwitz, a Jew, regardless of whether he was religious or not, should have had the obligation of making a declaration through his death. . . . We Jews and we human beings do not have many Adornos today. That the great man should have failed as a human being fills me with sadness."

85. Herz was a member of the newly established Freud Society in Vienna and was expecting Horkheimer, who belonged to the scientific committee of the society, to go to Vienna to give a lecture.

86. "To write poetry after Auschwitz is barbaric. And this corrodes even the knowledge of why it has become impossible to write poetry today." "Cultural Criticism and Society," in *Prisms*, trans. Samuel and Shierry Weber (Cambridge, Mass., 1983), p. 34. See also "Commitment," in *Notes to Literature*, ed. Rolf Tiedemann, trans. Shierry Weber Nicholsen, vol. 2 (New York, 1992), p. 87; and *Negative Dialectics*, trans. E. B. Ashton (London, 1996), pp. 362f.

Sources

Wherever possible, quotations have been taken from existing English translations of both Adorno and his contemporaries. The principal texts cited are listed here.

Books by Adorno

Adorno, Theodor W., and Walter Benjamin. *The Complete Correspondence, 1928–1940.* Trans. Nicholas Walker. Cambridge: Polity Press, 1999.

———, and Alban Berg. *Correspondence, 1925–1935.* Ed. Henri Lonitz, trans. Wieland Hoban. Cambridge: Polity Press, 2005.

———, and Thomas Mann. *Correspondence, 1943–1955.* Ed. Christoph Gödde and Thomas Sprecher, trans. Nicholas Walker. Cambridge: Polity Press, 2007.

The Adorno Reader. Ed. Brian O'Connor. Oxford: Blackwell, 2000.

Aesthetic Theory. Trans. Robert Hullot-Kentor. London: Continuum, 1997.

Against Epistemology: A Metacritique. Trans. Willis Domingo. Oxford: Basil Blackwell, 1982.

Alban Berg: Master of the Smallest Link. Trans. Juliane Brand and Christopher Hailey. Cambridge: Cambridge University Press, 1991.

Critical Models. Trans. Henry W. Pickford. New York: Columbia University Press, 1998. [A translation of *Eingriffe* (1963) and *Stichworte* (1969), AGS, vol. 10.2, pp. 455–799.]

The Culture Industry. Ed. J. M. Bernstein. London: Routledge, 1991.

Dialectic of Enlightenment. Ed. Gunzelin Schmid Noerr, trans. Edmund Jephcott. Stanford: Stanford University Press, 2002.

Essays on Music. Ed. Richard Leppart, trans. Susan H. Gillespie. Berkeley: University of California Press, 2002.

In Search of Wagner. Trans. Rodney Livingstone. London: NLB, 1981. [New edition with a foreword by Slavoj Žižek, 2005.]

Kierkegaard: Construction of the Aesthetic. Trans. Robert Hullot-Kentor. Minneapolis: University of Minnesota Press, 1989.

Mahler: A Musical Physiognomy. Trans. Edmund Jephcott. Chicago: University of Chicago Press, 1992. [Paperback 1996.]

Minima Moralia. Trans. Edmund Jephcott. London: NLB, 1974.

Negative Dialectics. 1973. Trans. E. B. Ashton. London: Routledge, 1996.

Notes to Literature. Ed. Rolf Tiedemann, trans. Shierry Weber Nicholsen. 2 vols. New York: Columbia University Press, 1991 and 1992.

Philosophy of Modern Music. Trans. Anne G. Mitchell and Wesley V. Bloomster. U.S. edition 1973. London: Sheed & Ward, 1973.

Prisms. Trans. Samuel and Shierry Weber. Cambridge, Mass.: MIT Press, 1983.

Quasi una fantasia. Trans. Rodney Livingstone. London: Verso, 1992.
Sound Figures. Trans. Rodney Livingstone. Stanford: Stanford University Press, 1999.

Books by Adorno's Contemporaries

Benjamin, Walter. *A Berlin Chronicle.* In *One-Way Street* and Other Writings. Trans. Edmund Jephcott and Kingsley Shorter. London NLB, 1979.
————. *Selected Writings.* 4 vols. Ed. Michael W. Jennings et al., trans. Rodney Livingstone, Edmund Jephcott, Harry Zohn et al. Cambridge, Mass.: Belknap Press of Harvard University Press, 1996–2003.
Brecht, Bertolt. *Journals, 1934–1955.* Ed. John Willett and Ralph Manheim, trans. Hugh Rorrison. London: Methuen, 1993.
Korsch, Karl. *Marxism and Philosophy.* Trans. Fred Halliday. London: NLB, 1970.
Lowenthal, Leo. *An Unmastered Past.* Ed. Martin Jay. Berkeley: University of California Press, 1987.
Lukács, Georg. *The Destruction of Reason.* Trans. Peter Palmer. London: Merlin Press, 1980.
————. *Record of a Life.* Ed. István Eörsi, trans. Rodney Livingstone. London: Verso, 1983.
————. *The Theory of the Novel.* Trans. Anna Bostock. London: Merlin, 1971.
Weber, Max. *Science as a Vocation.* In *The Vocation Lectures.* Ed. Tracy Strong and David Owen, trans. Rodney Livingstone. Indianapolis: Hackett Publishing Company, 2004.

Acknowledgments

I can scarcely name all the people to whom I feel a debt of gratitude without being unjust to those from whom I have profited indirectly. Many people have had to be very patient with me in recent years—in both private and public life. My wife, Ewa Claussen, was forced to bear the heaviest burden. Her concern for my well-being has been an indispensable elixir of life. Her advice, even when I did not always follow it, has been likewise indispensable. I was not always able to give her as much help as I wanted; in particular, I would like to have been able to visit my mother-in-law, Erna Leszczyńska, in Warsaw more frequently during her last years. Over the past five years my brother, Hans G. Claussen, has been able to devote himself more than I to our mother, who has needed to be cared for in Bremen. The fact that he shouldered this burden without making any reproaches and our silent understanding in an impossible situation have made it possible for me to write this book. My editor, Peter Sillem, was the person who has best been able to keep his nerve; I am deeply grateful to him for his inexhaustible patience, his sympathetic application of the reality principle, and the confidence he showed in an author who was sometimes reduced to despair by the difficulties of his subject matter. He displayed professional and private qualities that are seldom seen, and not just in the often harsh world of publishing.

Many people who work on Theodor W. Adorno have no special feelings of affection for the Adorno Archive. The fault is to be sought in objective circumstances for which the long-serving editor, Rolf Tiedemann, is often unjustly blamed. He is the most intimate connoisseur of Benjamin and Adorno, and I should like to express my thanks to him as the genuine savior of the flotsam and jetsam that the *Land,* the city, and the university abandoned to private initiative. Personally, I am indebted to him for his sure instinct for the accuracy of my statements about the biographical relations between Adorno and Benjamin. Alongside his extremely valuable editions, the eight issues of the *Frankfurter Adorno Blätter* that he has assembled with such loving attention to detail have been one of my most prized sources. I am extremely grateful to Mr. Tiedemann for his illuminating conversations and skeptical comments; I experienced his abrupt departure as director of the archive as a more painful obstacle to my own research than the archive's somewhat cautious policy toward granting access under his direction. I believe that with him I would have found a more sympathetic reception for my originally more direct account of the relations between Adorno and his older mentor, Siegfried Kracauer. I hope that the strict prohibition on direct quotations from Adorno's side of the correspondence has not deprived my account of its persuasive power. Thanks to Christian Schmidt's self-sacrificing labor of deciphering the handwritten parts of the correspondence, I believe that I have a more exact knowledge of what transpired between the two than has been reported in the secondary literature hitherto. Among the unexpected coincidences I include my belated acquaintance with Reinhard Pabst, who practices the still unrecognized profession of literary detective. He selflessly placed his discoveries at my disposal. He has verified much of what I was unsure about, and he also brought many matters to my attention of which I had hitherto been ignorant. I was able to read the uncorrected manuscript of his book, *Theodor W. Adorno: Kindheit und Erinnerungen* (Theodor W. Adorno: Childhood and Memories), which was due to appear in Suhrkamp for the centenary. That was a pleasure in itself. Thank you. Through the good offices of her daughter Franziska, I was able to meet Elisabeth Reinhuber. She was able to give me authentic details from the family history in the course of an afternoon in England; she read my account critically and provided me with new material about the Calvelli-Adornos. Adorno's cousin Franz Villinger introduced me to the wider ramifications of the Adorno family on a beautiful summer's day in 1999. As a child he had gone with his parents to visit the Wiesengrunds in Schöne Aussicht during the summer holidays and was able to give me a very vivid account of the household.

Institutions such as the Deutsches Literaturarchiv in Marbach, the Stadt- und Universitätsbibliothek Frankfurt am Main, in particular Herr Jochen Stollberg, as well as the archive of the Johann Wolfgang Goethe University in Frankfurt have all gone out of their way to help me. It was a pleasure to work in these places.

I should like to express my particular thanks to my friend and colleague Michael Werz. I owe him a debt that is hard to put into words. Without him I really would have broken down under the burdens of the past five years. In countless situations he not only covered my back but also made use of his various connections and contacts to preserve me from the sterilities of lonely authorship. He was my first reader, and also my Wailing Wall whenever adversity threatened, and he maintained my links with the outside world, in particular with the United States. It is to him that I owe an invitation to the Center for European Studies at Harvard, where I was able to give a talk on my ideas about Adorno's "American experience." On that occasion, in April 2001, my Boston audience included a critical observer named Thomas Wheatland, who, after the discussion, selflessly made available to me his sensational discoveries about the Institute for Social Research during its period of exile in the United States. I hope that his outstanding book, which was as yet unpublished, will soon bring him the international recognition he deserves. Of those who mediated on my behalf between Germany and America, I should like to make particular mention of Eric J. Oberle, my favorite translator, who made it possible for me to obtain an invitation to see Russell Berman in Stanford in the spring of 2000. As early as 1998 I was able to present my ideas on the American experience of the critical theorists in Eric Oberle's translation to a conference on Marcuse in Berkeley that had been convened by Martin Jay, the pioneer of research on critical theory, and organized by John Abromeit. I must also mention the excellent discussions we had after visits to the Hoover Institute in Stanford and in the Adorno Archive in Frankfurt. From this generation of students, whom I met around 1989 in Frankfurt through the mediation of Michael Werz and Helga Flores Trejo, together with the journal *Perspektiven* that they kept going, I should like to make special mention of Rafael Mrowczynski. In addition to his lavish doctoral thesis, Mrowczynski replaced "the staff of assistants" that Adorno reports finding among established American sociologists in *Minima Moralia* and whom he observed with one laughing and one envious eye.

When you write a book about your own philosophy teacher, its contents will inevitably impinge on your own life history and sense of identity. What is called for in such circumstances are friends who can give you the requisite distance, who are not mealy-mouthed, but who understand the difficulties facing a writer who would like to preserve jointly internalized critical aspirations but who does not wish to shut himself off esoterically from readers who never had the opportunity to hear Adorno in person. At the top of this list I must mention David H. Wittenberg. Ever since we both attended Adorno's senior seminar on *Negative Dialectics* in the summer of 1967, he has been the only person to have been present in my life for what is now close to forty years. Angela Davis, who was also there at the time, has long since moved far away. Hans-Jürgen Krahl, who was the first to convey non-autodidactic knowledge of Adorno to me, has been long dead. My first introduction to Adorno took place while I was still at school, when he gave his brilliant lecture on "progress" in Bremen in 1964, the same lecture that he refers to in his "child prodigy" letter to Bloch. I met Ernst and Karola Bloch, and also Hans Mayer, in the intellectually lively and hospitable home of Günther and Irmela Abramzik, which looked out high above the Market Square in Bremen. It was they who gave me moral support in my plans to leave Bremen the day after my *Abitur* exams, since Bremen did not yet have a university at the time. My intention was to go to Frankfurt to study with Adorno in the winter of 1966 in order to prepare for the fantasy profession of sociologist of literature. I have often felt drawn back to Bremen, especially after Bettina Wassmann and Alfred Sohn-Rethel started to invite me. We often sat together in Bettina's shop at Am Wall 164, and less often—unfortunately, though still quite often—we would eat in Jürgen Schmidt's bistro in front of the most wonderful collection of Bordeaux. A photograph of this, in the spirit of the Wiesengrund wine tradition, adorns the little texts of mine that Bettina Wassmann has published: *Abschied von gestern: Kritische Theorie heute* (Farewell to Yesterday: Critical Theory Today), *and Kleine Frankfurter Schule des Essens und Trinkens* (A Little Frankfurt School of Food and Drink).

Among my Frankfurt friends from the 1960s, pride of place must go to the editor Claus Behncke. He was one of the first of Adorno's pupils to be active in the media, and it was through him that I met Herbert Marcuse. Shortly before his death in 2003, Claus's wife, Anica, read him the first chapters of this book. It makes me happy to think that the first pages of this book on Adorno should have given pleasure to such a friend of and expert on Adorno. The last pages of this book were due to be written in the home of Hans-Peter Riese in Washington, D.C. He had been my colleague in the culture section of *Diskus* in the sixties and was then the radio correspondent of the ARD [Germany's primary radio and television network]. That was what was planned with his wife, Michaela, at the beginning of the project back in 1998 in Wiesbaden. Michaela, however, who had conducted the charming interview with Herbert Marcuse on German television immediately after Adorno's death in 1969, herself died suddenly in 2000 while this text was still being written. She had given me her personal copy of "Theodor W. Adorno zum Gedächtnis" (Theodor W. Adorno In Memoriam), with the words, "This will now be safer in your hands."

Ronny Loewy is one of my earliest and best friends in Frankfurt. As a cineaste, it was he who put me on the track of Fritz Lang, and it was this that brought Adorno's love of cinema to light. Ronny's father, Ernst, not only opened my eyes to the world of the German-speaking emigration in Palestine and Israel, but also was the first to give me some idea of the experience of a Jewish returnee in the 1950s. Unfortunately, he too died in 2002. I would have liked to hear his judgment of my work. As far as Jewish questions are concerned, I am greatly indebted to Cilly Kugelmann, a friend of many years' standing and now a leading figure in the Jewish Museum in Berlin. I owe her almost everything in this sphere—factual information, historical knowledge, and a huge number of contacts not just in Frankfurt but throughout the world, contacts that have led to new friendships in their turn. The only comparable friendship as far as both length of time and intensity are concerned is the one with Dan Diner, whose unexpected phone calls from Tel Aviv, Schloss Elmau, or Chicago during these years have always given me moral support. His invitations to Tel Aviv and Leipzig have forced me to concentrate my mind, and at the same time they gave me the feeling that I had something new and interesting to say. Our Walldorf friends, Birgit Schüller and Bruno Schoch, have taken an even closer interest in the writing of this book, through "all its ups and downs." Bruno has had no equal in his ability to encourage my love for the eastern part of Switzerland, and I have learned that theory can thrive only when it has a reliable emotional and culinary foundation.

A doctor's task is to hold together the identity of mind and body. Paul Parin of Zurich is in my view the epitome of medical science, the master of the smallest link between these realms. It was he who wished to send me to Capri in February 2003, when he diagnosed that my stress levels had become intolerably high. My repeated visits to Zurich have been an endlessly valuable source of consultations and acts of friendship. They continued even after the painful death of Goldy Parin-Matthey, and I only wish that Paul had been able to read this text to her beforehand. I have no experience of psychoanalysis and rely entirely on Dr. E.F. for his expertise. Without his help I would never have been able to achieve a proper distance from which to write about someone who was so close to me in real life. Dr. E.F. helped me, too, to "become a person who has matured very late." Among the doctors with hands-on experience I should like to mention Andrzej Borowicz, who in all my illnesses combined diagnostic ability with a friendly manner. I am endlessly grateful to Bernd Hontschik, who treated me in an exemplary fashion for a fracture in my right hand in 2000 and helped to restore my ability to write.

Not least among the features of this book is the fact that it can be read as a declaration of love to the city of Frankfurt am Main, which became my second home following my arrival here on 24 November 1966 in order to study with Theodor W. Adorno. I always return here from different jobs and longer journeys, and I am always delighted to see the familiar skyline from the plane or intercity train. It is this skyline that turns Frankfurt into the most American town in Europe. I like the city best during the Book Fair, when for an entire week its loudmouthed urban normality is matched for once by its metropolitan, cosmopolitan reality. During those October days I can meet my friends in the various publishing houses, small and large, in order to thank them in person. Despite the competitive situation, Suhrkamp has cooperated in a very fair way; I was allowed to read many of the impressive new publications for the Adorno centenary in galley form. I would like to express my special thanks to Matthias Reiner and Bernd Stiegler. I should like to thank the small publishers, too: "text + kritik," with its *Frankfurter Adorno Blätter,* also sent me their proofs, which at the time I needed urgently. Anne Hamilton of Lüneburger Verlag in Klampen helped out with books and tips, as did Dorothea Rein of the Verlag Neue Kritik. As someone with long experience of publishing, Heinrich von Berenberg provided moral support in the form of annual Indian curries and friendly inquiries. One of the most delightful meeting places, one that I shall be able to enjoy again this year without inhibitions, is the Beck reception in the Hessischer Hof, where Herbert Marcuse liked to stay when he came to Frankfurt. Beck Verlag, too, in the person of Ulrike Wegner, has always been very generous with its help.

Nor should I forget to express my thanks to ordinary everyday Frankfurt. Nowadays a text needs more than "a pencil and an eraser." I should like to thank Karsten Fischer, with his Web site, komintern.de, for his prompt rescue of my PC and for making it work again. Culinary matters, too, should not go unmentioned in a book on Adorno. Frankfurt does not indeed have a *ventre de Paris*—but it does have a stomach, situated in the covered stalls of the Kleinmarkthalle. In my own case, the heart of the market is to be found in Müller's asparagus stall, Franck's spices, and Thomas's cheese. Around these shops you can find everything you could conceivably desire, from Turkish lamb to the *bresse-poulardes* in the gallery. Exotic foods are to be found on the corner of the Wolfsgangstrasse and Eschersheimer Landstrasse in the shop belonging to Herr Fehti Azar; in Adorno's day it was run by Herr Pusch. But I find my melange, a Viennese mixture containing 10 percent Guatemalan coffee, in Steinweg, where I can pause for a coffee break and read proofs in a room where one can really "be different without fear." The Steinweg coffee bar is opposite where the former Hotel Schwan used to be, the building where the complex prehistory of the paradoxes of Wilhelminian modernity began with the signing of the Peace of Frankfurt in 1871.

Index

Abendroth, Wolfgang, 317

Abschied von gestern (film), 173

Adenauer, Konrad, 227, 317

Adickes, Franz, 19

Adorno, Gretel Karplus, 1, 12, 157, 164, 182, 200, 208, 246, 269, 270–271, 276, 283, 284, 295, 321, 334

Adorno, Theodor Wiesengrund: and administrative research, 186, 195–196; and aesthetic left-wing radicalism, 157, 192, 210, 215, 216, 217, 232, 270, 275, 279; and aesthetics, 46, 321, 327, 357–358; and America/American experience, 7, 9, 30, 110, 113, 119, 122, 132, 133, 135, 136, 137, 138, 140, 141, 142, 143, 156, 161, 163–164, 165–166, 167–168, 171, 180–181, 183, 184–185, 186, 187, 189, 191, 194–195, 196, 197, 198, 201, 203, 204, 205, 206–207, 212, 213, 215, 216, 218, 223, 224, 225, 236, 237, 239, 241, 249, 257, 259, 263, 265, 270, 281, 296, 301, 302, 303, 309, 311; and American citizenship, 121, 176; and American Jewish Committee, 138; and Amorbach, 48, 49, 50, 112–113, 121, 160, 201; and *Der Anbruch,* 192, 274; and animals, 164–165, 248, 251, 254, 255, 256, 258, 359; and anti-Semitism, 58, 110–111, 139, 202, 234, 286–287, 335–336; and Aristotle, 272; and art, 2, 3, 4, 5, 9, 23, 25, 26, 29, 34, 36, 85, 115, 126, 135, 151, 172, 191–193, 301, 309, 321, 324, 327, 357, 358; and "Art and Consumption in the Monopoly Phase" project, 291; and Asia, 222, 223; and authoritarianism, 139, 140, 215; background of, 143, 221, 284; and baroque, 52; and Beethoven, 188, 189–190; and Berlin, 157; and biography, 2, 5–6, 7, 8, 12, 56, 66, 187, 212–213, 236–237; birth of, 19, 27; and Bizet, 130; and Bloch, 297–298, 299; and Boulez, 189; and bourgeoisie, 2–4, 11, 20, 29, 30, 32–33, 85–86, 124, 129–130, 135, 136, 137, 141–142, 143, 151, 184, 189, 190, 196, 206, 214, 228, 232, 237, 238, 239, 249, 250, 285, 286, 299, 314; and Buber, 279–280, 293, 294; and Cage, 189, 309; and capitalism, 136, 181, 196; as Castor Zwieback, 110, 251; character of, 106–108; and childhood, 7, 11, 14–15, 29, 30, 32, 35, 41–42, 43, 44, 45–46, 47, 48–49, 52–53, 54, 229, 246, 247, 253, 259; and class societies, 213–214; and coldness, 58, 124, 293, 296, 298, 299, 314; and cold war, 156; and Columbia University, 197; and comedy, 302; and commitment, 313, 314; and commodity fetish, 237; and communism, 100, 108, 151, 156, 157–158, 278; and Communist Party, 156, 250, 309, 324; and contemplative consciousness, 307; and critical theory, 7, 50, 141, 161, 183, 205–206, 209–210, 212, 217, 222, 229, 237, 245, 247, 249, 264; and cultural criticism, 206, 218; and culture, 63, 166, 169, 183, 189, 193, 202, 209, 265, 267; and Culture Industry, 42, 103, 132, 134, 135–136, 142, 161, 162–163, 165, 167, 168, 170, 172, 174, 184, 187, 189, 191, 194, 195, 196, 202, 203, 204, 206–207, 211, 214, 215, 217, 224, 225, 263, 265, 309, 387n63; and damaged life, 187; death of, 1–2, 12, 150, 173, 339; and democracy, 140; and Deutschherren Middle School, 44, 45; dissertation of 1924, 87; and domination of nature, 141; and education, 42, 44–45, 57–62; and Eichendorff's poems, 112; and Eisler, 192; and emancipation, 328; emigration of, 25, 43, 232, 235, 237; and empirical research, 180–181, 199, 263; and Engels, 233; in England, 187, 193, 195, 196, 304; and English, 247, 281–282; and Europe, 184–185, 189, 193, 205, 208, 213, 214, 264; and existentialism, 280; and experience, 7, 240; and Expressionism, 135, 218, 280, 282; and extraterritoriality, 41, 190, 197, 201, 217–218, 258, 259, 283, 285, 322; and family, 11, 31–33, 35, 43, 47–48, 53, 54, 55, 62–63, 64, 115, 123, 190, 232, 238; and fascism, 140, 234, 237, 302, 325, 335; and fear, 250; and film, 163, 172, 196; finances of, 36, 138, 208, 216, 302; and Frankfurt, 55, 106, 108, 201, 202, 277; and *Frankfurter Zeitung,* 269; and Frankfurt School, 264; and freedom, 11, 141, 258; and French culture, 230; and Freud, 54, 233, 234, 272; and friendship, 53; and Fromm, 233–234; and genius, 2–3, 36, 42; and George, 25, 29, 153, 244, 299; on George-Hofmannsthal correspondence, 29, 36–37, 46; and German culture, 230, 264; and German language, 247–248; and German public sphere, 224–225; and German society, 30; and German tradition, 120, 121, 122–123; and Germany, 133, 201–202, 215–216; and Goethe, 2–4, 12, 43, 190, 268; and Goethe Gymnasium, 60; and guilt, 314, 337; and Hába, 309; *Habilitation* dissertation of 1927, 87; and Hacker Foundation, 176, 225; and happiness, 43–44, 258, 259; and Hašek, 302; and Hegel, 43, 134, 189, 241–242, 247, 272; and Heidegger, 272, 280; and Heine, 22–25, 26, 28, 190, 230, 369n4; as Hektor Rottweiler, 140, 232, 251, 255; and heliotrope image, 45, 47; and Hindemith, 192; and history, 51, 311; and Hitler, 232, 235, 321; and Hofmannsthal, 29, 34–35, 41, 244, 299; and Holocaust/Auschwitz, 6–7, 7, 12, 25, 46, 58, 121, 137, 148, 209, 232, 245, 246, 257, 261, 267, 285, 286, 287, 306, 308, 314, 327, 328, 329, 330, 332; and homelessness, 25,

Adorno, Theodor Wiesengrund *(continued)*
369n4; and hope, 274, 287, 304, 329; and Huxley, 242; and idealism, 85, 141, 250; and identical element, 326; and identity, 247, 249, 253, 276; and ideology, 266; and individual, 11, 42, 51, 196–197, 239, 240, 250, 255, 259, 288; and individual vs. collective, 191; and Institute for Social Research, 1, 101, 165, 181, 182–183, 199, 208, 217, 284, 291, 308; and Jaspers, 272, 280; and jazz, 183, 188, 191, 192, 193, 194, 195, 196, 198, 207, 211, 212, 218, 250, 253, 255–256; and Jewishness, 15, 58, 63, 64, 81, 238, 241, 244, 254, 264, 267, 268, 280, 287, 365; and Jugendstil, 46; and Kafka, 6, 84, 102, 239, 258; and Kaiser Wilhelm Gymnasium, 45, 57, 58, 60; and Kant, 51, 272, 286; and Kettenhofweg, 217; and Kierkegaard, 93–94, 127; and Klinger Oberrealschule, 55; and knowledge, 43–44, 183, 211, 212, 233; and Kraus, 25; and language, 40, 42–43, 44, 247–248, 281–282, 314–315; and Lenin, 233, 234; and Lisbon earthquake, 315, 316; and lyric poetry, 158–159; and Mahler, 112, 256, 257, 258, 266–267, 274; and Mann, 29; manner of, 311–312; and Mannheim, 95; and Marx, 141, 216–217, 226, 228, 248, 258, 272, 325, 327–328; and Marxism, 109, 206, 210, 222, 223, 230, 233, 234, 235, 248; and masks, 36; and memory, 281, 306, 307; and Mendelssohn, 190, 256; and *Merkur*, 197; and message in a bottle, 161, 207–208, 211, 218, 236; and *Der Monat*, 197, 224; and Moscow trials, 303–304; and music, 9, 31–33, 102, 103–104, 111, 112, 113, 114, 115, 123, 124, 128, 129, 133–134, 140, 142, 151–152, 154–156, 158, 162, 183, 184, 186–196, 197, 198, 207, 209, 210, 211, 212, 214, 216, 217–218, 233, 246, 251, 253, 254–255, 258, 259, 265–267, 274, 277, 278, 279, 308–310, 357; and *Musikblätter des Anbruch*, 152; name of, 121, 122, 139, 141, 181; and names, 164–165, 251–253, 256; and Nazis, 136, 232, 335; and negative dialectics, 337; and *Neue Rundschau*, 197, 224, 328; and the new, 214, 215; and Nietzsche, 49, 129, 130; and non-identical element, 132, 141, 142, 143–144, 162, 239, 259; and non-identity, 140, 260, 276, 285; and Odenwald, 121, 240; and Old Bridge, 52; and origins, 29, 36, 56; and other, 29; and Oxford, 109; and palimpsest, 291, 311, 314, 316; and Paris, 310–311; and Philanthropinum, 55; and physiognomy, 256; and Plato, 272; and poetry after Auschwitz, 7, 209, 261, 285, 306, 308, 328, 329, 330, 332; political statements of, 208–209; and Popular Front, 325; and positivism, 179; and Princeton Radio Research Project, 122, 138, 181, 182, 184, 186, 187, 191, 209, 263; and private life, 286; and progress, 26, 338; and Proust, 26, 29, 37, 142; and psychoanalysis, 5, 110, 163, 196, 233, 234; and radio, 170, 187, 257; and reification, 206, 209, 211, 215, 218, 237, 324; repu-

tation of, 183, 259–260, 317; return to Europe, 136, 309; return to Frankfurt, 171, 172, 178, 186, 204, 212, 220; return to Frankfurt University, 42–43; return to Germany, 10, 14, 42, 139, 171, 176, 186, 188, 194, 199, 200–202, 204, 213–214, 215–216, 217, 218, 221, 225, 236, 253, 257–258, 259, 261, 262, 265, 291; and revolution, 248, 250; and Riesman, 212; and Sartre, 305; and Schoenberg, 257; and Schöne Aussicht, 13, 16, 21, 27, 31, 36, 44, 52, 286; and Schopenhauer, 3, 134; and science, 82; and Seeheimerstrasse, 21, 36, 48, 50–51, 52, 73, 105, 124, 280, 286; and self-censorship, 305, 331; self-description of, 115, 123; and Sils Maria, 48, 49–50, 244, 313, 322, 328, 329; and *Sinn und Form*, 210; and social biography, 66; and socialism, 202, 357; and social research, 185; and society, 29–30, 128; and sociology, 93, 211, 212; and Soviet Union, 210, 215; and spiritual experience, 272; and spontaneity, 202, 203; and Stockhausen, 189; and student protests, 10–11, 332, 334–335, 336, 337; surrealist sketches of, 110; and Taunus, 48, 80, 121, 240; and teaching, 42, 59–60, 311–312, 315, 316, 321–322; and teddy bear, 253, 254; and television, 170, 171; and theory, 198, 203, 240; and theory and experience, 297; and theory vs. knowledge, 183; and theory vs. practice, 228, 267–268, 321, 327; and tradition, 51, 120, 121, 122–123, 138, 161, 189, 208, 272, 331; and University of Frankfurt, 217, 218, 261; and utopia, 20, 43, 46, 249, 272–273, 283; and Veblen, 141, 213, 214–215; and Vienna, 43, 52, 102–103, 105, 106, 108, 109, 111–112, 113, 114, 151, 152, 157, 216, 232, 277; and violence, 268, 324–325; and *Vormärz* period, 327–328; and Wagner, 130, 234, 235, 236; and Webern, 112; and Weill, 193; and whole as false, 189, 241–242; and workers, 215, 238, 249, 250; and World War I, 65, 66, 202; and World War II, 7–8, 10, 11, 235; and wrong life, 34, 184, 285, 303; and *Zeitschrift für Sozialforschung*, 122, 140, 141, 157, 269, 275; and Zermatt, 339

Adorno, Theodor Wiesengrund, correspondence of: Beckett, 337–338; Behncke, 320, 363–364; Benjamin, 9, 34, 36–37, 47, 234, 237, 240, 246, 250, 303–304; Bloch, 270, 271, 272, 274, 275–276, 279, 281, 283, 292, 297, 313–314, 315, 321, 325, 341–342; Celan, 328; Grass, 336; Horkheimer, 34, 182, 200, 203, 204, 233–234, 304, 322, 326, 327, 343–353; Kracauer, 104, 105, 106, 107, 289–290, 326; Křenek, 33; Lang, 171; Leibowitz, 133; Löwenthal, 10, 201, 326; Lukács, 106; Thomas Mann, 116, 119, 120, 122–123, 125, 134, 136–137, 144, 171, 201–202; Marcuse, 10, 326, 337; Merriam, 183; Oppenheim, 34; parents, 112–113, 124–125, 163; Redlich, 157; Sohn-Rethel, 326; Steuermann, 162, 309

Fabian Society, 78
Fallada, Hans: *Kleiner Mann was nun?*, 196
Fascism, 140, 148, 149, 234, 237, 302, 325, 335
Federn, Paul, 66
First Marxist Work Week, 77, 82, 83–84
Fischer, Gottfried Bermann, 328
Fischer, Ruth, 108, 152
Fleisser, Marieluise: *Pioneers*, 252
Fleming, Victor, 167
Flesch, Max, 62
Fonda, Henry, 168
France, 229–230, 310
Frankfurt Academy of Labor, 78
Frankfurt am Main, 15–22; Central Station, 19;
    Frankfurter Hof, 75; Frankfurt Opera House,
    19–20, 30, 66; Jews in, 17–19, 21–22, 28, 38;
    and modernization, 264; Ostend district, 55;
    Palmengarten, 19; and World War I, 66
Frankfurter Zeitung, 18, 38, 51, 67, 86, 87, 107, 108,
    224, 252, 269, 275, 279, 284, 290
Frankfurt Opera, 266
Franklin, Sidney, 167
French Revolution, 26, 98, 123
Freud, Sigmund, 5, 54, 58, 111, 120, 123, 187, 233, 234,
    253, 272, 324, 360
Frischauer, Paul, 291
Fromm, Erich, 233–234, 238
Fury (film), 168

Gans, Eduard, 41
Gelb, Adhémar, 81, 355
George, Stefan, 25, 29, 30, 46, 97, 153, 160, 239–240,
    244, 299
Gerlach, Kurt Albert, 77–79
German Confederation, 18
German Democratic Republic, 307, 331
German Empire, 19, 21, 22, 24, 35, 53, 123
German Revolution, 75, 78, 82, 100, 101, 103, 157,
    211, 231
Germany: Biedermeier period, 22, 26, 41; and
    bourgeoisie, 135; collapse of middle class in, 94;
    and culture, 134; defeated, 149; education in, 42;
    Imperial, 67, 69; post-Nazi, 42; Second Empire,
    28, 44; unification of, 17. *See also* Weimar Re-
    public
Gide, André, 351
Goethe, Johann Wolfgang von, 104, 108, 190, 268,
    299, 363; and Adorno, 43; and biography, 2–4;
    and childhood, 15; and Eisler, 162; *Elective
    Affinities*, 29, 97–98, 294; and family, 32; *Faust
    II*, 126; as genius, 5; and Lukács, 230; and Mann,
    124, 126; *Poetry and Truth*, 3, 11, 57;
    Wanderjahre, 126; *Wilhelm Meister*, 9, 11, 30;
    and Marianne Willemer, 44
Goethe Gymnasium, 60, 62, 72, 74
Gold Rush (film), 323

Good Earth, The (film), 167
Grab, Hermann, 109, 112
Grass, Günter, 336
Grey, Sir Edward, 149
Grosz, Georg, 74
Grünberg, Carl, 79, 96, 178
Gründgens, Gustav, 110, 326

Haag, Karl-Heinz, 272, 359
Hába, Alois, 309
Habermas, Jürgen, 317, 318–320, 334, 343–353;
    *The Structural Transformation of the Public
    Sphere*, 317; *Theorie und Praxis*, 317; "Zur
    philosophischen Diskussion um Marx und den
    Marxismus," 317, 343–353
Hacker, Frederick, 204, 212, 225, 263
Hacker Foundation, 176, 225
Hainebach, Otto, 62
Hangmen Also Die (film), 167, 168, 169, 170–171
Hašek, Jaroslav: *The Good Soldier Schweyk*, 302
Haselberg, Peter von, 27, 58, 101
Hecht, Werner: "Brecht Chronology," 242
Hegel, G. W. F., 43, 51–52, 148, 189, 247, 272, 285,
    350, 356; *Phenomenology*, 134, 142, 244, 298, 345
Heidegger, Martin, 94, 182, 221, 272, 280, 317, 320,
    346, 348, 363
Heine, Heinrich, 22–25, 26, 28, 41, 190, 229–230,
    256, 310, 369n4; "Heimkehr" cycle, 257; "The
    Lorelei," 24; *Memoirs*, 57; "The Return Home,"
    23; "Travel Pictures," 56
Heinle, Christoph Friedrich, 68
Hentzschel, Julius, 62
Herz, Otto O., 365
Herzberger, Else, 47, 48
Hindemith, Paul, 192
Hirsch, Rudolf, 328
Hitler, Adolf, 59, 148, 166, 224, 232, 235, 257, 361
Hobsbawm, Eric, 8
Hofmannsthal, Hugo von, 28, 29, 30, 34–35, 40, 46,
    97, 98, 240, 244, 299
Hofstätter, Peter R., 261–262, 264
Holocaust, 6–7, 12, 25, 46, 58, 121, 137, 148, 209, 232,
    245, 246, 257, 261, 267, 285, 286, 287, 306, 307,
    308, 314, 327, 328, 329, 330, 332. *See also* Jews
Hoppe, Marianne, 110
Horkheimer, Maidon, 177, 200, 313
Horkheimer, Max: Adorno's open birthday letter
    to, 8–9, 10, 220–221, 223, 224, 226, 228–229, 245,
    248, 251, 354–362; and Adorno's parents, 225–
    226; and America, 133, 141, 163–164, 185, 201, 203,
    204, 223, 224, 225; and American citizenship,
    121–122, 176, 177, 389n1; and American Jewish
    Committee, 199, 210; and American research,
    198; and animals, 258, 359; and anti-Semitism,
    231, 334, 335; and authoritarian state, 215; back-
    ground of, 79, 80–81, 143, 216, 221, 356; and